Transformative Property Law
Festschrift in honour of AJ vd Walt

Transformative Property Law

Editors:

Gustav Muller
LLB LLD (Stellenbosch) Diploma (Åbo Akademi)
Senior Lecturer, Department of Private Law, University of Pretoria

Reghard Brits
BCom (Law) LLB LLD (Stellenbosch)
Senior Lecturer, Department of Mercantile Law, University of Pretoria

Bradley Slade
BCom (Law) LLB LLM LLD (Stellenbosch)
Associate Professor, Department of Public Law, Stellenbosch University

Jeannie van Wyk
BBibl (Pretoria) LLB (Unisa) LLM (Witwatersrand) LLD (Unisa)
Emeritus Professor, Department of Private Law, University of South Africa

Series editor: **GJ Pienaar**

B Jur et Comm LLB LLD (Potchefstroom)
Professor of Private Law and Research Fellow, Faculty of Law
North-West University (Potchefstroom)
Fellow of the South African Research Chair in Property Law

JUTA

Transformative Property Law

First published 2018

21 Dreyer Street, Sunclare Building, Claremont, Cape Town, 7708

Typeset in 10.5 pt on 13.5 pt Serifa BT

Production Coordinator: Deoni Conradie
Editor: Ria de Kock
Proofreader: Bronwyn Manuel
Indexer: Daphne Burger
Cover Design: Drag & Drop
Cover Illustrator: Louwra Marais
Typesetter: ANdtp Services, Cape Town

ISBN: 978 1 48512 891 5

About Juta's Property Law Library

The 1996 Constitution states that the Bill of Rights is the cornerstone of democracy in South Africa and that it enshrines the rights of all people in the country and affirms the democratic values of human dignity, equality and freedom (section 7). The Constitution provides that the Bill of Rights applies to all law and that it binds natural and juristic persons to the extent that it is applicable (section 8) and that the courts must promote the spirit, purport and objects of the Bill of Rights when interpreting legislation and when developing the common law and customary law (section 39).

The relationship between the Bill of Rights and the development of private law is complex and contentious; some commentators are sceptical towards what they refer to as the constitutionalisation of private law and would restrict direct influence of the Constitution on private law to the minimum. According to their view, reforms that are required by post-apartheid transformation should be effected by legislation or constitutional remedies (including legislation to abolish apartheid laws), while further amendments to the common law should take place by way of small, incremental developments according to the 'normal' logic of uncodified private law. In effect, case law has shown that this could leave the larger part of the common law unaffected by reforms, unless a particular principle or institution of the common law is directly or indirectly in conflict with the Constitution. Other commentators disagree with this approach, arguing that the large-scale social and political reforms foreseen and required by the constitutional transformation of South African society, combined with the fact that the apartheid regime was totally discredited, indicates that the Constitution intends to bring about and inspire wide-ranging changes in the law and in social arrangements, which must have a fundamental effect on private law. In this perspective, the common law cannot be left entirely or even largely untouched by post-apartheid transformation.

As far as property law is concerned, it is clear that the new constitutional dispensation brought about by the 1993 and 1996 constitutions must have visible and lasting effects on private law because of the effect that apartheid land law had on widespread social and economic marginalisation and poverty. The substantive social and economic reforms foreseen by the new constitutional order can only be realised if reformist goals and norms find expression in the rules and practices of property law. Legislative reforms have to play a large part in this process, but legislation cannot do all the work and therefore judicial and doctrinal development of the common law and customary law is equally important. It is therefore necessary to consider the direct and indirect effect and the implications of the Constitution for the whole of existing property law, including uncodified common law, case law and legislation.

The Property Law Library is aimed at revisiting and reassessing the whole of South African property law, including the uncodified common law that is mostly embodied in case law and academic writing, in order to establish how each aspect of property law was influenced by apartheid law, how it responds to the new constitutional dispensation (including land reform), and whether it could make a contribution towards the transformation of South African law and society.

For this purpose, the Property Law Library will eventually consist of a number of monographs, each of which is focused on one specific aspect of property law. *Transformative Property Law* consists of 20 essays by a combination of senior and young scholars from South Africa, the United States of America, the United Kingdom, Ireland, the Netherlands, Belgium, and Zimbabwe. The essays focus on the themes that Professor Van der Walt developed during the first 10 years of the research chair, namely: (a) the single system of law and subsidiarity principles; (b) the marginality principle; (c) the development of the common law of property; (d) constitutional property law; and (e) property theory. This volume also includes a list of all Professor Van der Walt's research outputs and a list of all the Masters and Doctoral students that he supervised during his career.

Volumes in Juta's Property Law Library:

Recently published titles:

Transformative Property Law Festschrift in Honour of AJ van der Walt (2018) G Muller, R Brits, B Slade & J van Wyk (eds)

Property Remedies (2017) ZT Boggenpoel

The Law of Servitudes (2016) AJ van der Walt

The Law of Landlord and Tenant (2016) S Viljoen

Real Security Law (2016) R Brits

Property in Minerals and Petroleum (2016) E van der Schyff

Law of Property Casebook for Students / Sakereg Vonnisbundel vir Studente 8th ed (2015) AJ van der Walt

Inleiding tot die Sakereg 7de u (2016) AJ van der Walt & GJ Pienaar

Introduction to the Law of Property 7th ed (2016) AJ van der Walt & GJ Pienaar

Land Reform (2014) JM Pienaar

Planning Law 2nd ed (2012) J van Wyk

Constitutional Property Law 3rd ed (2011) AJ van der Walt

Sectional Titles and other Fragmented Property Schemes (2010) GJ Pienaar

The Law of Neighbours (2010) AJ van der Walt

Forthcoming titles:

Planning Law 3rd ed (2019) J van Wyk

Property in Water (2019) M Kidd

Property Aspects of Environmental Law (2019) W Freedman

Property in Housing (2019) G Muller & S Viljoen

Sectional Titles 2nd ed (2019) GJ Pienaar & JG Horn

The Law of Possession (2019) EJ Marais

Intellectual Property (2019) M du Bois & R Shay

Expropriation Law (2020) H Mostert

Property and Insolvency (2020) R Brits

Restrictive Covenants, Restrictive Conditions and Title Conditions (2020) J van Wyk

Constitutional Property Law 4th ed (2020) B Slade

Virtual Property (2020) W Erlank

Property in Customary Law (2020) JM Pienaar & E du Plessis

Neighbour Law 2nd ed (2021) G Muller

Festschrift: Editor's note

Sadly, the decision to produce this *Festschrift* was made a mere two days before the untimely passing of Professor AJ van der Walt. Although it would be impossible to confine a tribute to him and his legacy to a single book, this *Festschrift* represents a sincere attempt of many colleagues, former students and friends to honour this great academic and man in perhaps the most fitting way – by producing research of the highest quality on some of the themes that were closest to his heart.

As the first incumbent of the DST/NRF South African Research Chair in Property Law, which celebrated its decennium in 2017, Prof Van der Walt's primary research goal was to develop the theoretical foundations for the transformation of property law in the new constitutional era. It is with this in mind that this collection of essays aims to honour Prof Van der Walt's legacy. As founding editor of Juta's Property Law Library, it is also apt that this tribute is included in the series that he conceived.

In view of the general line of research done under the auspices of the research chair, it was decided that contributions to this volume should focus on a number of themes that Prof Van der Walt and his students worked on in recent years, namely (a) the single system of law and subsidiarity principles; (b) the marginality principle; (c) the development of the common law; (d) constitutional property law; and (e) property theory. As the titles and content of the contributions indicate, all the authors took up this challenge with great enthusiasm and indeed produced exceptional works under one or more of these themes. Prof Van der Walt would have loved nothing more than to behold other scholars – especially young ones – take up the mantle and pursue these themes to the next frontier.

The scholars who contributed to this volume are a welcome combination of leading international, established and emerging scholars – all of whom have both known and been deeply inspired by Prof Van der Walt's life and work. In fact, several of the essays were co-authored by a senior and a young academic, which is something that prospective contributors were encouraged to do and is a tribute to Prof Van der Walt's unprecedented passion for developing young academics. The list of authors also represents a balance of scholars from South Africa and other countries, like the United States of America, the United Kingdom, Ireland, the Netherlands, Belgium, and Zimbabwe. The contributors to this volume are global leaders in property law scholarship, which is a testament to Prof Van der Walt's global networks and influence.

Ultimately, the volume consists of 20 scholarly essays, which were authored or co-authored by 33 individuals, while an additional 40 specialists kindly acted as anonymous peer reviewers. This volume also includes a list of all Prof Van der Walt's research outputs and a list of all the Masters and Doctoral students that he supervised during his career.

Each contribution in this volume represents original research of a high scholarly standard, which is illustrated by the fact that each essay was put through a rigorous process of double-blind peer review. Although the book contains essays aimed at honouring a particular academic, the content will no doubt be of value for subject specialists, researchers, advanced students, practitioners and the judiciary alike, since most of the topics are on the forefront of global thinking on property law.

A big thank you must go to each contributor for the time spent and effort exerted in contributing essays of such a high quality in honour of Prof Van der Walt. The same gratitude is extended to the persons who acted as peer reviewers so as to ensure that the quality of this volume lives up to a standard fitting for the man it honours. Last but not least it is necessary to thank Marlinee Chetty and her team from Juta, who were onboard with the project right from the start and who have provided tremendous support and assistance in completing it.

The editors
Pretoria and Stellenbosch, South Africa
June 2018

Table of Contents

TRIBUTE BY JOHAN D VAN DER VYVER

During my academic career as lecturer/senior lecturer/professor in the Department/Faculty of Law of the Potchefstroom University for Christian Higher Education (1958–1978), ad hominem professor in the Faculty of Law of the University of the Witwatersrand, Johannesburg (1979–1985), and the I.T. Cohen Professor of International Law and Human Rights in the School of Law of Emory University in Atlanta, Georgia in the United States of America (1995–), I encountered many students, colleagues and friends with scholarly brilliance, superb personalities, and loyal camaraderie. The name of André van der Walt appears in the uppermost segment of the best of the best in this regard. Although his academic assignments and publications cover a wide spectrum of legal disciplines, he was particularly famous for his expertise in the Law of Things or Property Law.

André commenced his studies at the Potchefstroom University in 1975 and completed his B.A. (Law) degree of that University in 1977. During this time he was a student in several of my classes, including – I am extremely proud to say – the course I taught in Property Law. From our very first encounter I could see that this was a person with superb qualities. He was evidently a brilliant and highly dedicated scholar, he had a profoundly humble personality, and he was loyal to and supportive of his fellow students. In all those years I never saw any sign of discontent, arrogance or capriciousness in his communications or conduct. He was always relatively quiet, good tempered and profoundly respectful toward the lecturing and administrative staff and in his relations with fellow students.

When I joined the Faculty of the University of the Witwatersrand, Johannesburg, I introduced an extra-mural course-work LL.M. degree in Property Law. I was responsible for the teaching of a (mandatory) course on the theoretical construct of Property Law, but insisted that the lecturers in a variety of other (selective) courses must be confined to legal practitioners. This was to ensure that students will be exposed to problems emanating from the practical implementation of different components of Property Law. Those legal practitioners included prominent persons such as (later Chief Justice) Ismael Mahomed and (at the time retired) Professor Denis Cowen. André took the course in 1985-1986, and I again had the great privilege of having him as a student in my class on Theoretical Foundations of Property Law. Students were also required to write a dissertation on an approved subject. I supervised his dissertation entitled *The Conservation of the Built-Up Environment*. André was awarded the degree cum laude, and also received the prize awarded to the best student and one for the best LL.M. dissertation.

Our roads again crossed in 1995 when I was invited to participate in a conference on Property Law on the Threshold of the 21st Century, that was held at the University in Maastricht in The Netherlands and which was co-organized by André van der Walt and Professor Gerrit van Maanen of the University of Maastricht. My own contribution was one on Property in International Human Rights Law.

André also had an illustrious academic career. He was appointed in 1981as a lecturer in the Department of Legal Philosophy of Potchefstroom University and promoted to the rank of Senior Lecturer in 1983. In 1987 he moved to Pretoria to become a Professor in the Department of Private Law of the University of South Africa. In 2000 he finally accepted the offer to become a Professor in the Department of Public Law of the University of Stellenbosch. He was to the best of my recollection the very first law professor in South Africa to be awarded an A1 grade by the National Research Foundation, and this supreme rating was based on his academic achievements and publications over a period of seven years, evaluated by five of his peers, two of whom were selected from countries other than South Africa. I followed his career with great interest because we shared so many common academic interests. In 2010 he was appointed Extraordinary Professor in the Faculty of Law of the University of Pretoria charged with the special task of promoting postgraduate study and research outputs, and again André and I had something in common: In the same year I was appointed Extraordinary Professor in the Department of Private Law of the University of Pretoria.

His doctoral thesis on *Die Ontwikkeling van Houerskap (The Development of Holdership)* (November 1985), as well as several of the books he wrote, occupy a special place in my personal law library. Those books include *Constitutional Property Law*; *The Constitutional Property Clause: A Comparative Analysis of Section 25 of the South African Constitution of 1996*; and *Constitutional Property Clauses: A Comparative Analysis*. Mention should of course also be made of outstanding books which he co-authored, such as *Sakereg Studentehandboek (Law of Property Students' Textbook)*. Although I was his mentor in Property Law during his undergraduate studies and for purposes of his Masters' Degree, there emerged over time so much in this field that I could learn from him.

It is a simple fact of life that personal brilliance and superb achievements seldom coincide with personal humility and modesty. André van der Walt was again an exception to this rule. What more can one say? He was in every respect a good man, and his passing leaves an insurmountable gap in the academic community of South Africa – and indeed of the world.

Johan D van der Vyver

TRIBUTE BY PROFESSOR GERRIT PIENAAR

Andre van der Walt was not only a brilliant and versatile academic, but he was also a loyal husband, friend, colleague and tutor to the legal fraternity in South Africa and worldwide. His recent death on 5 November 2016 has left a huge void. As constitutional lawyer with extensive knowledge of the South African property clause and related constitutional matters, as well as property clauses worldwide, he ranked among the top comparative constitutional property lawyers in the world.

Andries Johannes van der Walt was born on 5 March 1956 in Postmasburg and completed his primary education in Johannesburg and his secondary education at the Potchefstroom Gimnasium. He obtained the B Iur et Art degree in 1977; Hons BA (cum laude)(Philosophy) in 1978; LLB (cum laude) in 1980 and LLD in 1985, all from the Potchefstroom University. In 1986 he obtained an LLM (cum laude) from the University of the Witwatersrand. He taught law at the Potchefstroom Law Faculty from 1981 to 1986 and was subsequently appointed as professor of Private Law at UNISA. In 2000 he became professor of Public Law at the University of Stellenbosch. During his brilliant career two exceptional achievements can be highlighted. In 2002 he received an A1 rating as researcher from the National Research Foundation, which rating was repeated in 2008 and 2013. The A1 category is awarded to a researcher who is recognised by all the reviewers (nationally and internationally) as an international leading scholar in his field and for the high quality and wide impact (beyond a narrow field of specialisation) of his resent research outputs. In 2002 Prof van der Walt was one of only 5 South African scholars from the Humanities and Social Sciences and the only lawyer to be awarded an A1 rating. His second outstanding achievement, indicating his international stature, was a Tier 1 South African Research Chair in Property Law (funded by the Department Science and Technology and hosted by the University of Stellenbosch) which was awarded to him in 2008 for a ten year period. Since 2008 17 doctoral and 13 LLM students completed their postgraduate studies at the South African Research Chair in Property Law under his supervision.

Since 2008 Professor André van der Walt had concentrated his research on the SA Research Chair in Property Law. The aims of the Chair were (and still are) to analyse the theoretical foundations of property law in post-apartheid South Africa, to determine the implications of the new Constitution for the development of post-apartheid South African law and to contribute to the development of property law in this new paradigm. His interest in the confluence of these three aspects led to the establishment of the series Juta's Property Law Library, of which he was the editor-in chief. Since 2010

12 volumes by himself and other property lawyers in South Africa have been published in the series, and another 10 volumes are being planned for future publication.

He published widely in South African and international law journals and chapters in collective works and he wrote several monographs and textbooks. The two most comprehensive and comparatively most wide-ranging books published by him in the field of constitutional property law are *Constitutional Property Clauses* (2011), an analyses of legal systems in Europe, the Americas, Southeast Asia, Australia and Africa, and *Constitutional Property Law* (first edition 1997, second edition 2005 and third edition 2011). The latter is the most comprehensive treatise on South African constitutional property law with references to specific topics in foreign systems. Three of his monographs, *Property in the Margins* (2009), *Property and Constitution* (2012) and *The Law of Servitudes* (2016), as well as several journal articles, are based on the idea that the transformation of law eventually works right through to technical detail in legislation and doctrine; transformation cannot be done by the constitution or a constitutional court only, but it also requires serious legislative and doctrinal work to succeed. For these publications he received worldwide recognition from his peers. He received numerous invitations to speak at conferences locally and abroad, to act as examiner for doctoral theses, as well as to write recommendations for appointments, promotions and research awards.

One of Professor van der Walt's main contributions was his tireless effort to establish a unitary or single system of property law by developing statutory and common law principles according to constitutional imperatives. In this regard he stated: 'This single-system-of-law principle also shifted the debate about the effect of constitutional democracy and transformation on established rights, including property rights. Instead of merely regulating conflict between the protection of vested rights and the promotion of constitutional reforms, the Constitution requires that rights be protected even as reforms are implemented, simultaneously and optimally, so as to promote the spirit, purport and objects of the Bill of Rights in line with section 39(2).' (*Property and Constitution* (2012 20-21)).

Professor van der Walt's expertise and doctrinal leadership on constitutional property matters were often used as authority by South African courts, and especially the Constitutional Court, which often quoted directly from his publications. A well-known theory of his regarding the hierarchy of property rights is often applied by the courts. In several Constitutional Court cases, but most predominantly the case of *First National Bank of SA Ltd t/s Wesbank v Commissioner, South African Revenue Services* 2002 (4) SA 768 (CC) the Court endorsed his theory that ownership is not the strongest and most protected real right in a hierarchy of rights (as was the case in terms of Roman-Dutch principles), but that ownership in the new constitutional dispensation is one of many rights which enjoy equal protection under the property clause (section 25 of the Constitution). Furthermore, it is the Court's duty to maintain a delicate balance between a range of diverse property rights without relying on a hierarchy or predominance of specific rights. The Constitutional Court quoted him in this respect: 'The meaning of section 25 has to be determined, in each specific case, within an interpretative framework that has due cognisance of the inevitable tensions which characterise the operation of the property clause. This tension between individual rights and social responsibilities has to be the guiding principle in terms of which this section is analysed, interpreted and applied in every individual case.' (par xx p 794B of the report). This principle was again emphasised in *Port Elizabeth Municipality v Various Occupiers* 2005 (1) SA 217 (CC) and many subsequent cases with reference to the theoretical basis laid by Professor van der Walt.

During his lifetime Professor van der Walt received several honours and awards. Besides several research awards from the Potchefstroom University, UNISA, the University of Stellenbosch, the National Research Foundation and the Oppenheimer Research Foundation he received prizes for the best publication on constitutional law in the *Journal of Contemporary Roman-Dutch Law* in 1986 and 1998. He was also co-recipient of the Top Researcher Award (Humanities) of the Human Sciences Research Council in 1993, was co-recipient of a research award of the Royal Dutch Academy in 1996, was elected as Visiting Fellow Commoner, Trinity College, University of Cambridge in 2004 and 2010, and visited Germany as an Alexander von Humboldt scholar in 1990, 1996, 2003 and 2010. He often acted as external examiner for post-graduate dissertations and theses for most of the law faculties in South Africa as well as for several abroad, more specifically Cambridge, Maastricht, Dublin, Warwick, Leeds, Yale and Duke.

On a personal level André van der Walt was a dignified, yet down-to-earth, colleague and supervisor. He was a dedicated husband, loyal friend, sympathetic (but rather perfectionistic) supervisor, who supported quite a number of financially disadvantaged students with University funding and bursaries. The memory of his academic brilliance, compassion, character and sophisticated sense of humour is shared by his wife Christa, his academic colleagues in South Africa and abroad, the wider legal community in South Africa, as well as his undergraduate and postgraduate students.

Gerrit Pienaar
Professor of Law
Northwest University (Potchefstroom)

TRIBUTE BY PROFESSOR JEANNIE V WYK

RECALLING HIS EARLY CAREER

During the late 1980s the University of the Witwatersrand (Wits) offered a two-year coursework LLM in Property Law. It was really the first such programme offering courses such as Property Law, Expropriation Law, Real Security Law and Environmental Law. In 1986 André Boraine, now University of Pretoria Law Faculty Dean, and I, then senior lecturer in Department of Private Law at University of South Africa (Unisa), registered for the LLM. We drove to Johannesburg every Saturday morning for lectures. André van der Walt, who had obtained a Doctorate in Law from Leiden University the previous year also registered for the LLM and drove from Potchefstroom to attend lectures. Some of our lecturers included (now) Constitutional Court Justice Edwin Cameron, Supreme Court of Appeal Justice Ralph Zulman, Land Claims Court Justice Antonie Gildenhuys and Professor Johan van der Vyver, now at Emory University, Atlanta, United States of America and Visiting Professor, University of Pretoria.

I recall that most of our co-students were pretty impressed that André already had a doctorate and we wondered why he should want to do an LLM afterwards. André was, of course the best student, obtaining the degree cum laude. His dissertation entitled 'The conservation of buildings and townscapes in South African law', led to a number of other publications on the topic and also resulted in him writing a chapter on 'Guidelines for cultural resources management in Pretoria' for a book published by the municipality and the Human Sciences Research Council in 1993.

That is how we met. Immediately after obtaining the LLM at Wits in 1987 André was appointed as a full professor at Unisa, also in the Department of Private Law. So we became colleagues at Unisa. In March 1987 he held his inaugural lecture on 'Die funksies and omskrywing van besit' ('The functions and description of possession'). On welcoming him to Unisa by the Dean, colleagues were reminded of his 'brilliant study career' in which he obtained all 4 of his degrees cum laude. Armed with the LLM, I wanted to do a doctorate and what better supervisor could there be. So in 1987 I became André's first doctoral student and like so many of his later doctoral students, still cringe at the thought that the first draft I gave him to look at was not really up to his standards. I learned quickly and 3 years later the LLD was mine.

We were colleagues in the Property Law group from 1987 to 2000 when André was appointed at Stellenbosch University. In this brief contribution to the Festschrift and tribute to André I would like to highlight that period of his early academic career because we were very close colleagues, few will remember this period of his academic life and it typifies the remainder of his life.

1987–2000 was a turbulent time in South Africa's history. The period 1990–1994 was dominated by two factors. The first was the process of negotiations aimed at a democratic constitutional dispensation. The second was a dramatic escalation in levels of violence in the country, with a consequent increase in the number of gross violations of human rights. Being in Property Law meant that we witnessed all the early pre-1994 land reform initiatives. The first of these included the Conversion of Certain Rights into Leasehold Act 81 of 1988, the Abolition of Racially Based Land Measures Act 108 of 1991, the Upgrading of Land Tenure Rights Act 112 of 1991 and the Less Formal Township Establishment Act 113 of 1991. Already in 1990 André addressed land-reform issues when he spoke at the University of Transkei on 'Land law without the Land Acts' and arranged the conference on Land reform and the future of landownership in South Africa on 2 November 1990. It brought together '... academics, legal practitioners, town planners, people from various branches of the business sector, government departments and others. The keen and widespread interest in the seminar and current social and political topicality of the papers convinced the organisers and sponsors of the seminar, Juta and Co, to publish the proceedings' (Preface vii) in 1991. His words, in his paper entitled 'The future of common law landownership' (21-35) still ring true today:

> ... despite all the major problems facing lawyers in a time of great social flux and uncertainty, original thinking and legal imagination can build upon existing and available values, principles and ideas in order to revive the enormous potential of land ...

In the same year he addressed Lawyers for Human Rights on land rights and gave a guest lecture at University of the North on the repeal of apartheid legislation. In 1993 he made two presentations on the impact of a Bill of Rights on Property Law, one to the Wits Law Students Council and the other at the SA University Law Teachers Congress. All this happened before the acceptance of the Interim Constitution, during the negotiation process.

By his intimate involvement in land reform and constitutional property issues André showed that our lives and work as Property Law academics were radically altered and he embraced the new dispensation with open arms. His publications during that period attest to that, where he dealt with issues such as the transformation of the concept of ownership towards post-apartheid land law, the development of ownership to meet the needs of a non-racial society in South Africa and Constitutional Property Law. André's contribution to transformation was not restricted to his writing. 1994 saw the adoption of the interim Constitution and in that year he served on the Commission for the Allocation of Land, as provided for in the interim Constitution. In 1996 South Africa had a final Constitution and André wasted no time becoming involved. In the following year he advised the Department of Land Affairs on tenure reform and assisted the National Land Committee on drafting the Extension of Security of Tenure Bill. Together with Dawid van Wyk of Unisa's Department of Constitutional Law a certificate course on Constitutional Litigation was initiated in 1995.

Very soon into his appointment at Unisa in 1987 André started a discussion group with the Property-Law colleagues. We read a variety of legal literature including the work of Carol Rose, Joseph Singer, Kevin Gray, Frank Michelman, Gregory Alexander and Jennifer Nedelsky. Many of the bearers of these names were invited by him, Dawid van Wyk and Gretchen Carpenter, Unisa Law Faculty's constitutional lawyers, to present lectures at the universities of South Africa, Stellenbosch, Cape Town and Witwatersrand in 1997. Later they would become associated with the South African Research Chair in Property Law at Stellenbosch University. This was all new and challenging as we were really used to doing things on our own and all the department did together was undertake South African case discussions. While most of these discussions focussed on purely Private-law matters, Property Law created some opportunities to debate the early impact of land reform thinking. One specific and quite heated case-discussion comes to mind. It was on the *Diepsloot Residents' and Landowners' Association v Administrator, Transvaal* decision that commenced in the (then) Transvaal Provincial Division of the High Court in 1993 and ended up in the (then) Appellate Division in 1994 (1994 (3) SA 336 (AD)). We had a hard time convincing our colleagues of the correctness of the decision not to grant a temporary interdict restraining the Administrator from permitting, in terms of the Less Formal Township Establishment Act 113 of 1991, the so-called 'Zevenfontein squatters' to settle on land adjacent to Diepsloot, an area comprising smallholdings. The application was premised on the intended settlement creating a nuisance and causing unlawful interference with the rights of the Diepsloot residents to the enjoyment of their properties. Back then it was almost unthinkable that one could argue against the Diepsloot residents in favour of the large group of homeless people who needed a place where they could settle. To understand his transformational and progressive views in context one needs to go back to the thinking at the time. André wrote on the case and referred to it on numerous occasions in his publications. In a 1994 paper presented at the SAPOA Annual Convention he referred to Diepsloot, concluding that it 'offers an excellent example of exactly the kind of conflict between existing property rights and state promotion of social justice through land reform' (paper published as 'The future of private ownership of land' 1994 *Codicillus* 4-18 17).

The group discussions became conferences that André organised. The first was the 1991 conference on Land reform and the future of landownership in South Africa. In 1994 André and Gerrit van Maanen at Maastricht University, the Netherlands, co-organised a conference Property on the threshold of the 21st century. It was held because, in their words in the Foreword, "we were fascinated by the huge social, economic and political transformations which were taking place in South Africa, Eastern Europe and elsewhere, and by its implications for property regimes". In those days there was no Internet and no email, presenting almost insurmountable problems to contact property lawyers the world over. South Africa was coming out of a period of extreme isolation and sufficient contacts had not really been established with colleagues 'north of the Limpopo'. The conference brought together scholars from all over the world. 26 of the papers were published in the almost 700 page proceedings. 6 of these were contributions by South Africans. This was the beginning of the many opportunities André created for colleagues and students to engage with other scholars in an international context.

The Unisa Law Faculty published a wonderful Faculty journal twice a year *Codicillus*. Part of the contents was always 'From the Dean's desk...' containing reports of activities of the Faculty members. These activities did not include publications, but included details of conference attendance, overseas visits, invitations to address specialist audiences etc. André always featured, to such an extent that his activities were often introduced as 'As usual, Professor van der Walt had a very busy programme...'. Small wonder, in the 13 years he spent at Unisa André published 5 books, approximately 42 journal articles and edited 3 conference proceedings. He spent much time overseas, always pursuing research on a particular Property-law project. In 1990 he received the prestigious Von Humboldt award to work in Cologne for a year. It was on one of his train trips there that he found time to read the final draft of my thesis. He often found himself travelling - in 1995 he visited the USA to discuss the constitutional property clause, in 1997 he visited Yale Law School and Duke University Law School. Maybe an extreme example is 1998 when he visited the London Institute for Advanced Legal Studies and the University of Reading, then John Marshall Law School in Chicago, University of Illinois, Yale Law School, Georgetown University Law Center, Duke University Law School, Harvard Law School and finally Wellington New Zealand where he delivered a conference paper on the constitutionalisation of property in Canadian, Irish, Indian, Australian, Austrian, German and South African law.

André's influence on my early academic career, which was shaped during those 13 years while he was at Unisa, is enormous. As I wrote in the Foreword to my book *Planning Law* (Juta 1999) his inputs into the writing 'guided and assisted me immensely'.

During his first few years at Stellenbosch after 2000 our contact was limited to the annual South African Property Law Teachers gatherings. After 2007 when he was awarded the prestigious Tier 1 South African Research Chair in Property Law and he initiated a series of regular seminars at the Research Chair, we saw more of one another. On one of those occasions he suggested that I write a second edition of *Planning Law*, with him as editor, as part of the Juta's Property Law Library. I was deeply honoured at his suggestion, a feeling that was reiterated when he appointed me to be a Fellow of the Research Chair. On those occasions that I visited Stellenbosch we would always find time to share a glass of (always excellent) wine and a (always stimulating) chat.

I followed his work at the Research Chair with interest, part of which also included the regular examination of the theses of his doctoral students. The standard of those theses was superb and attest to André's academic leadership, scholarship and influence in every perceivable aspect of Property and Constitutional Property Law. How often did I say to so many at the Research Chair how privileged they were to be a part of something so special. André's legacy will remain in countless ways that include not only his students and their contributions, his research and academic excellence, but also his sincerity, humanity, humour and ability to make people feel respected and special.

Jeannie van Wyk
Professor Extraordinarius
University of South Africa

TRIBUTE TO ANDRÉ VAN DER WALT DELIVERED DURING THE STELLENBOSCH UNIVERSITY – FACULTY OF LAW CEREMONY, 11 November 2016

Dear friends and colleagues,

André van der Walt had many talents. He was exceptionally analytical – with a knack for cutting to the bone – something we experienced very often at faculty board meetings: he would listen carefully and start his comments with:

'Three things are important here...' – and he would list them calmly and logically. So, while he was listening to the various colleagues, he would already have abstracted the most pressing matters. He was very committed, loyal and hard-working. He was massively productive. He was brilliant. He was an A-rated researcher. He was a teacher and mentor. He was a friend.

Considering his many talents and contributions, two things I find especially striking: his ability to approach something in an original and unique way and, coupled herewith, the talent to craft the necessary terminology or coin the pertinent phrase to make sense thereof - and not only so that A-rated scholars would understand it. No, so that it would make sense to us all.

In 2001 Andre published an article in the South African Law Journal 'Dancing with codes – protecting, developing, limiting and deconstructing property rights in the constitutional state'.[1] I quote from the publication:

> 'My analysis should be judged on two different levels. On one level I argue that the image of apartheid land law and of transformation land law as two stationary positions is unsuitable and I therefore propose a different metaphor for the two forms of jurisprudence – that of dancing, which allows us to compare apartheid land law and transformation land law as two different dancing codes. However, even when we trade the static imagery of position, standing, for the more complex imagery of dancing, we still have to resist the temptation to see transformation as linear movement or progress – from [sovereignty] to justification, from one dancing code to another, or from volkspele jurisprudence to toyi-toyi-jurisprudence.... On a second level, [however], I suggest that we should not only switch to a more complex metaphorical code such a dancing when discussing transformation, but that we should also deconstruct the codes we dance to, pause to reflect upon the language in terms of which we think and talk and reason about constitutionalism,

[1] AJ van der Walt 'Dancing with codes –protecting, developing, limiting and deconstructing property rights in the constitutional state' (2001) 16 *SALJ* 1-27.

> about rights and about transformation and recognise the liberating and the captivating potential of the codes shaping and shaped by that language.'[2]

Dancing entails purposefully selected sequences of human movement. It has aesthetic or symbolic value and can be categorized and described with reference to its choreography, music or repertoire of movements. It can be meticulously choreographed or it can be wild and untamed.

André van der Walt was a choreographer *per excellence*: by approaching a property issue or a constitutional matter from a very specific – often unique – vantage point, he would proceed to logically unpacking and purposefully selecting relevant and applicable sequences. Refreshing, ground breaking, crystal clear.

A choreographer is usually actively involved behind the scenes. This entails tirelessly working away in devising, planning and arranging necessary and relevant steps and thereafter making sure they work in practice. The end result is often much more than the sum total of workable sequences and movements, but a true work of art. But sometimes it is necessary to join in with the dancing, often to lead or to demonstrate. This André did exceptionally well too. He would indicate the necessary steps to be taken and would demonstrate how it is to be done, exactly - taking one's hand, guiding, pulling and even pushing and letting go, when needed - with the necessary instruction and words of encouragement.

That is also why his influence extends the Research Chair, the Stellenbosch Faculty of Law and South African borders. In this regard I would like to quote from an email received from prof Brendan Edgeworth of the University of New South Wales in Australia.

'No doubt many others have also by now made this point, but I have to say that he has been a giant internationally in his field of research, not simply by virtue of his scholarship which represents an unsurpassed blend of incisive doctrinal analysis, sensitive calibration of policy formulation and philosophical reflection. But equally, his energetic and thoughtful leadership has greatly raised the profile of the discipline. He has brought South African issues and debates to an international audience, while at the same time, introducing so many of us beyond your shores to South African debates and scholarship via the Chair and its many-faceted and prolific, research agenda. An international community of scholars does not simply grow, organically. It needs leaders to nurture it, to make connections and introductions, to

---

[2] AJ van der Walt 'Dancing with codes –protecting, developing, limiting and deconstructing property rights in the constitutional state' (2001) 16 *SALJ* 262-263.

organise meetings, to knit together approaches from diverse national, methodological and philosophical traditions.

Without Andre's planning and organisational efforts, many of the scholars working in the field would never have met one another and would never have engaged with each others' work, at least not to the extent that they currently do. Moreover, because of the international standing of his work, so many of us wished to engage with him personally and were naturally drawn to any symposium and gathering he organised.'

While his massive impact on Property Law and Constitutional Law is - at some level indeed quantifiable as his NRF A-rating indicates international leadership, also reflected in the quote above, it is – to my mind – the other dimension of Andre that is especially powerful – and that is his impact on students and colleagues. He has guided and influenced everyone he has worked with – here and abroad. André challenged his students and demanded commitment and excellence. His guiding hand, his advice and encouragement was ever-present - sometimes subtle and other times quite robust and vocal. But never-failing. It is in this regard that the following quote rings true where André is concerned:[3]

> "The mediocre teacher tells. The good teacher explains. The superior teacher demonstrates. The great teacher inspires."

André was a wise, inspirational teacher and mentor. He was kind and extremely generous in sharing his vast experience and extensive networks. He was instrumental in developing a whole new generation of scholars and in this process founded numerous academic careers, extending South African borders.

I think André would find it very amusing that I compare him to a choreographer and dancer. But I think he was both: He was a choreographer because he was actively involved in the nitty-gritty of research and the academia, often behind the scenes, but he was also a dancer who entered in to the fray: he challenged paradigms, he contested codes of dancing – be it volkspele or toyi-toy-jurisprudence, he constantly questioned the status quo, he asked difficult questions – usually very meticulous and systematic and always, always honest and unafraid.

As a great choreographer, as a great artist his legacy will continue – in his many publications and books, but also in the numerous students and colleagues who joined in the dance with him. We will miss him.

Juanita Pienaar
Stellenbosch

---

[3] William Arthur Ward.

Chapter 1

Move along to where? Property in service of democracy

(A tribute to André van der Walt)

Timothy M. Mulvaney & Joseph William Singer***

*[P]roperty must reflect, and must be accountable to, the fundamental choices we have made in favour of living in a democracy characterised by dignity and equality.****

AJ van der Walt

1 Introduction

When cities prohibit sleeping on sidewalks and in parks, those homeless persons whom the police ask to 'move along' from these public spaces have begun to respond with a simple question: 'Move along *to where?*' If the police do not have a specific answer to this question – if, for example, shelters are full or closed during the daytime, and invitations by private parties are not at hand – those who have been asked to 'move along' are subject to a sovereign

* Professor of Law, Texas A & M University School of Law. Thank you to Ashley Hedrick and Finn, Jack, and Elliott Mulvaney.

** Bussey Professor of Law, Harvard Law School. Thanks and affection go to Martha Minow and Mira Singer. This project was supported in part by funding provided through the research program at Harvard Law School and Texas A&M University School of Law. We would both like to thank the participants in the Progressive Property Conference in April 2017 for their helpful comments and suggestions.

*** AJ van der Walt 'The modest systemic status of property rights' (2014) 1 *J L Prop & Soc'y* 15–106.

command with which they have no capacity to comply.[1] We may think of a homeless person as a person without real property. But, as Jeremy Waldron reminds us, '[e]verything that is done has to be done somewhere.'[2] If one has no place where one can legally move along to, then one has no place where one can legally perform life's most essential functions.[3] The state has condemned this person to die, not because of anything she did, but as a result of her circumstance.

Of course, the command to move along is not literally a death sentence. But if the law instructs that there is no place where a person is entitled to be, what in fact is it? How does it operate as 'law'? It is not an *enforceable* law, at least not all of the time. It seems the command to move along is obscuring what is really going on, and that is lawmakers' attempt to hide from their consciousness the fact that such a command – if consistently made and consistently followed – would turn people into outlaws. Taken to its logical end, this command could only work if the people subject to it ceased to exist.

Certain fundamental values characterise our democracy, among them the values of dignity and equality. The meanings of these values are, of course, contested. Yet it would seem that under *any* reasonable conception, they must include a human being's equal right to exist. And yet the uncomfortable sequence outlined above illustrates an approach by which the state initially defines property rights and rigidly enforces those rights without concern for the consequences of doing so in individual cases. On this approach, it is only after defining and enforcing property rights in this way that the state can move to respect fundamental democratic values in the space that remains.

Drawing inspiration from the work of our friend, André van der Walt, we advocate an alternative course. Property, in our view, is a socially constructed institution that exists *in service of* our fundamental democratic values. Identifying these values, that is, comes first. Conceiving of property as existing in service of democracy suggests that the state bears a primary obligation to define and to enforce property rights in a manner that respects fundamental democratic values.

On this alternative approach, something is amiss when property law casually and mechanically renders a person homeless and, in some instances, even calls into question this person's right to exist. This dilemma has several

[1] John Austin quipped that only a 'stupid or cruel legislator may affect to command that, which the party cannot perform, although he desire to perform it'. See J Austin *Lectures on jurisprudence* 136 (S Austin 2 ed 1861–1863) (emphasis removed), cited in JW Singer 'Legal realism now' (1988) 76 *Cal L Rev* 465–544 497 n105.

[2] J Waldron 'Homelessness and the issue of freedom' (1991) 39 *UCLA L Rev* 295–324.

[3] J Waldron 'Homelessness and the issue of freedom' (1991) 39 *UCLA L Rev* 295–324.

layers. At the outset, it bears noting that the problem of homelessness is not beyond the reach of our material resources in the US.[4] But having chosen not to recognise an affirmative right to housing (as South Africa has done) and provide the resources necessary to realise such a right, it does not seem especially demanding to require the state to avoid affirmatively causing or contributing to homelessness without substantial justification. Therefore, among other measures, the state should deem it relevant in every case that eviction may make the displaced person homeless (as, again, South Africa has done). But given that the state has chosen not to pursue this course either, we suggest in this paper that the state should *at the very least* enforce the limited property rights that it has already explicitly conferred on tenants to protect them from eviction in specific instances. Yet, below, we offer two ongoing stories that indicate the state is not even taking this minimal step.

These stories emphasise that, on the face of its rental housing codes, the state has defined property rights in landlords (as owners of reversions) and tenants (as owners of leaseholds to habitable units) that in some partial way respect dignity and equality. However, its approach to enforcement has created conditions that allow landlords routinely to deprive tenants of their property rights under these laws. As illustrated in some detail below, the legislature has failed to fund enforcement adequately; the executive is not using the funds that have been appropriated to prevent displacement; and the judiciary is acting as a bystander when unrepresented tenants do not raise what would be an effective defence relating to code violations. In this role, as an accomplice of sorts to the landlord's conduct, the state itself is depriving tenants of their property rights, and it is doing so without due process or just compensation.

2 Eviction

> *As a general rule, people who rent residential property will have less power and be more open to arbitrary (or at least non-negotiable) exercise of social and economic power by others, unless the rental market is pointedly and specifically regulated in some way to prevent or restrict those exercises of power.*[5]
>
> AJ van der Walt

---

[4] Indeed, some studies suggest that investing in eliminating homelessness would *save* the state money in the form of avoided emergency health care and related costs.

[5] AJ van der Walt *Property in the margins* 60 (2009); S Maass & AJ van der Walt 'The case in favor of substantive tenure reform in the landlord-tenant framework' (2011) 128 *SALJ* 436–451; AJ van der Walt & S Maass 'The enforceability of tenants' rights (part 2)' 2012 *TSAR* 228–246.

In many tenancy proceedings in South Africa, judges are tasked by statute with considering whether tenants have somewhere else to live before they sign an eviction order.[6] That a tenant does not have somewhere else to live does not mean that a court must or will refrain from evicting that tenant; however, it may lead a court to delay execution of the order or, perhaps, even refuse to issue it at all.[7] In contrast, under prevailing US law, whether or not an evicted tenant might have somewhere else to live is regularly deemed immaterial. The fact that an eviction will result in homelessness does not affect the property rights of the parties. Judges operate under the impression that they can order evictions upon landlords' requests – and call on sheriffs' officers to implement such orders when they are not complied with voluntarily – without concerning themselves with the impossible position in which those orders might place tenants.[8]

In his last lecture, Professor Van der Walt revealed the injustice of the prevailing US approach by explaining that property law is best understood as 'part of a single system of law that is driven and inspired by the Constitution'.[9] There is not one set of laws governing relations among persons (eg landlords and tenants) and an entirely different set of laws governing these persons' relations with the state. If the constitution is premised on certain fundamental values, then the laws governing relations among individual persons cannot violate those values without adequate justification. That is, the values embedded in the constitutional framework are horizontally applied to the common, statutory and administrative law of private property.

[6] See eg Prevention of Illegal Eviction from and Unlawful Occupation of Land Act 19 of 1998 (applicable to unlawful occupiers, including previously lawful tenants who 'hold over' following the termination of their leases, applied in *Ndlovu v Ngcobo; Bekker and Another v Jika* 2003 (1) SA 113 (SCA)). Professor Van der Walt lamented the decision in *Brisely v Drotsky* for holding that, absent explicit statutory direction, courts have no authority to consider the availability of alternative accommodation in common-law eviction proceedings, despite the Constitution's command that they take into account all 'relevant circumstances'. AJ van der Walt *Property in the margins* 120–21 (2009). Section 26(1) and (2) of the South African Constitution places an obligation on the state to abstain from any action that would unnecessarily deprive people who already have housing of their rights to occupy that housing. See eg *Government of the Republic of South Africa and Others v Grootboom and Others* 2001 (1) SA 46 (CC).

[7] AJ van der Walt *Property in the margins* 123 (2009) ('considerations . . . such as the social or economic status and circumstances of the occupier and the availability of alternative accommodation, can influence the decision whether to allow eviction in a specific case').

[8] For a notable exception, see *United States v Duro*, 625 S. Fupp. 2d 938, (C.D.Cal. 2009) (refusing to order eviction of tenants from substandard and dangerous conditions because they had nowhere else to go).

[9] AJ van der Walt 'Property law in the constitutional democracy' (2017) 28 *Stell LR* 8.

It is a contradiction to adopt a fundamental value – one as simple as the equal claim to exist – and then, without justification, to delegate the power of the state to people who are entirely free to ignore that value.[10]

In a democracy characterised by the fundamental values of dignity and equality – a democracy that the property system *was created to serve* – the justification for allowing the state to ignore the possibility that its actions at the hands of landlords might render people homeless and, in some cases, go so far as to call into question these people's very existence, is wanting. Property law cannot treat the concerns of homelessness as irrelevant. A state that evicts a tenant when such an eviction is not justified as consistent with these fundamental values is shaping and enforcing a property law system that is at war with itself, for it undermines one of the key reasons for having property rights in the first place.

3 Two stories in eviction law

> *[A]ny property dispute that also involves a non-property constitutional right such as life and human dignity should, as a first step, start off with ensuring or safeguarding the non-property right...*[11]
>
> AJ van der Walt

None of the foregoing is meant to imply that tenants should not pay their rent when it is due. Rather, we merely seek to emphasise that the state should *take into account* the possibility that an eviction order may consign a tenant to the streets. On this view, the state must take great care not to evict a tenant when doing so would render that person homeless – and this is especially true when the law gives the tenant a substantive defence to an order of eviction despite non-payment of rent. Surprisingly, though, while eviction is the leading cause of homelessness in the US, especially for families with

---

[10] The contradiction is evident in the US Supreme Court's 'state action' jurisprudence, which in many instances denies that the US. Constitution's guarantee of 'equal protection of the laws' applies to relations among human beings. See eg E Chemerinsky 'Rethinking state action' (1985) 80 *Nw U L Rev* 503–557; S Gardbaum 'The "horizontal effect" of constitutional rights' (2003) 102 *Mich L Rev* 387–459; I Saidel-Goley & JW Singer 'Things invisible to see: State action and private property' (2018) 6 *Tex A&M L Rev* (forthcoming). See also ET Freyfogle 'Private ownership and human flourishing: An exploratory overview" (2013) 24 *Stell LR* 430–454 449 (critiquing the 'public-private' distinction for its emphasising that the government acts in the public interest while private owners can act purely in their own interest, when the very purpose of having a private property system is to benefit society as a whole).

[11] AJ van der Walt 'The modest systemic status of property rights' (2014) 1 *J L Prop & Soc'y* 15–106.

children,[12] it is often effected when the rent *is not actually due*. This section highlights two instances in which the state facilitates this injustice.

The first focuses on the legislature's failure sufficiently to fund enforcement of housing codes and the executive's failure, with the enforcement resources that *are* made available to it, to prevent the displacement of tenants in the face of landlord non-compliance. The second concentrates on courts' evicting tenants who lack legal representation, a large percentage of whom may well have a viable defence to their landlord's claim for unpaid rent in light of their landlord's failing to maintain their units in accordance with the applicable housing code. Following these stories, we propose several potential reforms that could improve the current state of affairs.

3.1 Story #1: Eviction through non-enforcement of housing codes

Many US jurisdictions have adopted state or local housing codes. The existence of such codes means that landlords have *obligations* to provide heat, hot water, light, ventilation, door locks, pest control, and other basic services to their residential tenants. It also means that tenants are *entitled* to these services. On the face of it, housing codes' articulation of these obligations and entitlements add specificity to a value proposition that is fundamental to our democracy: that all people, including landlords and tenants alike, have an equal right to live in dignity.

In a system that takes these obligations and entitlements seriously, a tenant alleging that her landlord has failed to fulfil these obligations can call an inspector to visit her home, document the failings, and enforce them against the landlord through a variety of measures. The goal of enforcement in a given case is not solely or even primarily to punish the non-compliant landlord but rather to improve housing conditions by bringing this property up to code and deterring future offences.

What happens if the state *does not* take these obligations and entitlements seriously – if it fails to enforce housing codes, allows rental buildings to become so dilapidated that they pose imminent danger to the public, and pays no mind to tenants who are displaced when the state ultimately must order these dilapidated buildings vacated? In the 1960s and early 1970s,

[12] See United States Conference of Mayors *Hunger and homelessness survey* (Washington, DC: United States Conference of Mayors, 2013).

numerous analysts found these failings quite widespread.[13] One particularly thorough study, which involved personal interviews with over 130 code enforcement officials in myriad US cities, outlined the basic ills: limited funding, limited staffing, a dearth of training requirements for inspectors, a 'complaint inspection' system that focuses only on the specific violation the calling tenant alleges (as opposed to an 'area inspection' system requiring periodic comprehensive inspections of all rental properties),[14] and inattention to the plight of tenants displaced by the state's complicity in their landlords' obstinacy.[15] These failings could prompt one to conclude that, despite the law ostensibly requiring it, property rules surrounding the leasing of residential units in that era were not in actuality designed in a way that respects our most fundamental democratic values.

Despite considerable academic attention in the intervening fifty years, these failings continue apace today. Consider, for instance, the current state of housing code enforcement in what by many metrics is considered one of the country's most progressive states, Vermont.

On the face of it, Vermont's code represents the state's allocative decision to set specific minimum standards for the creation of residential leaseholds.[16] These laws afford all tenants security from their landlords' interfering in numerous ways with their occupancy and use of their rented

---

[13] See eg RE Carlton, R Landfield & JB Loken 'Enforcement of municipal housing codes' (1965) 78 *Harv L Rev* 801–860; J Bribetz & FP Grad 'Housing code enforcement: sanctions and remedies' (1966) 66 *Colum L Rev* 1254–1290; BR Dick & JS Pfarr Jr 'Detroit housing code enforcement and community renewal: A study in futility' (1969) 3 *Prospectus* 61–93; B Ackerman 'Regulating slum housing markets on behalf of the poor: Of housing codes, housing subsidies, and income redistribution policy' (1971) 80 *Yale LJ* 1093–1197.

[14] A complaint inspection approach must be driven exclusively by calls from low-income tenants who often may be unaware of enforcement services or do not avail themselves of those services, either in light of other priorities or in fear of landlord retribution. Among other advantages, area inspections permit landlords to make investment decisions on the assumption that neighbouring properties will be kept to code; while a given landlord still may find it more profitable not to maintain his rental units, compelling him to do so does not put him at a competitive disadvantage with his similarly situated peers.

[15] See RE Carlton, R Landfield & JB Loken 'Enforcement of municipal housing codes' (1965) 78 *Harv L Rev* 801–860, 804–820.

[16] A state statute obliges landlords to provide rental premises that are 'safe, clean, and fit for human habitation, and which comply with the requirements of applicable building, housing, and health regulations' Vt Stat tit 9 §4457. The state's Department of Health promulgated statewide minimum housing code standards. See 'Rental Housing Health Code,' 12–5 Vt Code R §25:1.0 et seq ('The purpose of this code is to protect the health, safety and well-being of the occupants of rental housing. This code establishes minimum health and habitability standards that *all residential rental housing in Vermont must conform to*' (emphasis added)). Local governments are free to establish more stringent standards, and several of Vermont's largest cities have chosen to do so.

units.[17] Landowners obviously maintain the ability to let their properties for residential purposes, though they ostensibly are limited by the code's requiring that they provide a series of basic services and amenities.[18] Yet a landlord's obligation to ensure the habitability of rental units and a tenant's security of having this complied with are meaningful only to the extent that these obligations are reasonably enforced.

Resource constraints often are a primary and understandable reason underlying the reality that not all arguable violations of all laws can possibly be pursued. Housing code violations – like, say, violations of posted speed limits – occur so frequently that avoiding non-enforcement wholesale would be an impractical goal; that the law's expansiveness outpaces its conceivable enforcement does not necessarily raise concerns regarding the state's accountability. However, residential tenants might inquire whether there is *some juncture* at which the state's pointing to a lack of resources loses some of its potency. That is, is there some juncture when an enforcement scheme makes a property right reflective of the values of dignity and equality so empty that one should question whether that property right actually should be deemed an existing right at all?

In Vermont, enforcement of the state's housing code is primarily the province of local governments. According to state statute, every municipality must have a Town Health Officer, whose responsibility it is to enforce the bulk of the housing code and numerous other public health and safety

---

[17] Vt Stat tit 9 §4457 ('In any residential rental agreement, the landlord shall be deemed to covenant and warrant to deliver over and maintain, throughout the period of the tenancy, premises that are safe, clean and fit for human habitation and which comply with the requirements of applicable building, housing, and health regulations.'); 12–5 Vt Code R §25:1.0 et seq (rental housing health code establishing minimum standards for rental housing).

[18] These services and amenities include the provision of adequate and safe boilers, Vt Stat Ann tit 20 § 2881 et seq; 12–5 Vt Code R §25:7.0; fire safety measures, Vt Stat Ann tit 20 § 2681 et seq; electrical installations, Vt Stat Ann tit 15 § 881 et seq; 12–5 Vt Code R §25:9.0; plumbing, Vt Stat Ann tit 26 § 2198 et seq; potable water, Vt Stat Ann tit 10 §1971 et seq; sewage disposal, Vt Stat Ann tit 24 §1971 et seq; bathroom facilities, Vt Stat Ann tit 24 §3501 et seq; and insect- and rodent-free quarters, 12-5 Vt Code R §25:6.0.

protections.[19] Several of the state's largest towns provide a salary for their Town Health Officers, and in some instances, Deputy Town Health Officers, too. In most towns, however, including all of those in the poorest areas of the state, Town Health Officers are compensated, if at all, only for reasonable expenses incurred.[20] In this latter group of towns, the town council – known in many parts of Vermont as the 'select board' – regularly solicits volunteers interested in assuming the position.[21] The state does not require Town Health Officers to have any experience regarding public safety and health hazards or to complete any training. Instead, the state mails each new Town Health Officer a manual that it encourages the appointee to read.[22]

The state does not require Town Health Officers to conduct inspections at any recognised intervals; instead, inspections occur only upon the complaint of a tenant or, in certain instances, a tenant's neighbour. Even these inspections, though, are not certain. According to one prominent attorney who regularly represents tenants, some Town Health Officers are disinclined to perform inspections, including, in one recent instance, an unwillingness due at least in part to the Town Health Officer's asserted fear that he would contract the bed bugs of which the tenants were complaining.

Even where inspections are performed, relief for tenants is not always on the horizon. Consider, for example, the facts presented in *Alger v Department of Labor & Industry*.[23] In response to tenants' repeated calls complaining about serious code violations, the state occasionally issued orders requesting compliance from these tenants' landlords. However, for years, the state failed to utilise the code's enforcement provisions, including its powers to

---

[19] This individual is responsible, according to the state, for 'investigating possible public health hazards and risks within the town or city; taking action to prevent, remove, or destroy any public health hazards; taking action to lessen significant public health risks; and enforcing health laws, rules and permit conditions, and taking the steps necessary to enforce orders' – http://healthvermont.gov/environment/town-health-officer. See also 18 Vt Stat §602a. The Division of Fire Safety, under the auspices of the state's Department of Public Safety, promulgates building code regulations relating to fire hazards. These regulations often overlap with the Department of Health's regulations regarding the habitability of residential units, such that Town Health Officers implicitly are tasked with enforcing them, too. Where they do not overlap, their enforcement presumably is outside the jurisdiction of Town Health Officers.

[20] 18 Vt Stat § 602(b).

[21] By default, the chairperson of the town's select board – akin to the town's mayor – serves as the town's Town Health Officer if the town does not identify a volunteer to recommend to the state's Department of Health, who formally makes the non-paid appointment.

[22] The Vermont League of Cities and Towns conducts an optional annual training program for Town Health Officers.

[23] *Alger v Dep't of Labor & Indus.* 917 A.2d 508 (Vt 2006).

pursue injunctive relief, impose administrative penalties, assess fines, and seek prosecution.[24] The state's course of action effectively allowed these landlords to ignore order after order, for non-compliance brought no injurious consequences, at least in the near or medium term. Only when the violations created such precarious living conditions that the premises could not be safely occupied did the state act. And while it conceivably might have moved to fix the problems, the state instead ordered the units vacated, some upon a week's notice and others with no notice at all.[25]

A tenant's unexpected and unwelcome relocation is economically and psychologically disruptive, especially where alternative accommodations, if available at all, are far from the tenant's current employment and children's school. And state law entitles tenants to habitable housing *in the units they choose to rent*. Where a landlord fails to comply with her obligations to provide such housing, the landlord is depriving the tenant of property rights recognised under state law. But does *the state* bear some responsibility, too, when it *creates the conditions* that allow landlords to do this? Here, the state created these conditions in at least two ways: *first*, by constraining the extent to which meaningful housing code inspections could be conducted through a lack of funding and training, and, *second*, by disregarding the habitability issues revealed by those inspections that did occur until vacation was the state's only rational option.[26] For all practical purposes, the state's reaction to landlords' non-compliance adjusted the state's original allocative decision that provided tenants security from their landlords' interfering with their occupancy and use by denying tenants their security right, or, one might say, redistributing it to their landlords.

Alger presented a bit of a messaging war. The tenants referred to the state's approach to code enforcement as 'a voluntary . . . scheme' that is 'inherently ineffective with respect to ensuring anything but the minimum level of housing code compliance necessary to avoid imminent hazards'.[27]

---

[24] *Alger v Dep't of Labor & Indus.* 917 A.2d 508, 511–513 (Vt 2006).

[25] *Alger v Dep't of Labor & Indus.* 917 A.2d 508, 511 (Vt 2006).

[26] The state has long had the power to order the vacation of a building when serious public health concerns or other pressing public interests demand it. The common law recognised the state's authority to abate nuisances at the owner's expense through orders to vacate, see eg *Egan v Health Dep't,* 20 Misc. 38 (NY Sup. Ct 1897), and currently, summary vacation powers are codified in many housing codes. The question here, though, is whether the state has any obligation to enforce its own laws in a way that reduces the prospects of such displacement from happening.

[27] Fourth Amended Complaint, at ¶ 3, *Alger v Dep't of Labor & Indus.*, 917 A.2d 508 (Vt. 2006) (No s479-02 Fc), 2007 WL 5600833.

Others more benignly described the state's approach as 'comply or close'.[28] Yet, regardless of the label one chooses, the result in the end is the same. Though one would imagine that Vermont's housing code was principally enacted to protect low-income tenants, the state's approach to the code's enforcement seemingly has just the opposite effect: it displaces these tenants from their homes.

Should the persons displaced by the state's approach to code enforcement not have anywhere else to go, the state has made them homeless. It is, of course, unlikely that the state is determinedly trying to deprive people of their homes. But homelessness is the foreseeable result of a policy that enforces a housing code by ordering buildings vacated without ensuring that displaced persons have a place to which they can go. The state is acting in a manner that shows moral indifference to the effects of its law enforcement policy.

The state's approach can even create a windfall for unscrupulous landlords. These landlords can ignore orders to remedy code violations with the confidence that they can continue to collect rent even though they are failing to respect the tenants' property rights to habitable housing. Initially, landlords avoid spending money by failing to pay the costs of repairs. Thereafter, the state steps in to eject the landlords' tenants before the landlords are legally able to do so, saving the landlords the costs and delays of eviction proceedings. With the tenants gone, the landlords can make some repairs, find new tenants (perhaps at a higher monthly rate), and start the whole process over again.

The state appears to be operating under the assumption that non-enforcement of law is not an exercise of state power. The tenants' property rights in their leaseholds include the right to safe housing as defined by the housing code. Landlords have the obligation to comply with the code, and that obligation is only meaningful if the state will enforce it. If the tenants set up tents in the backyard of their landlord's home, the police will protect the landlord's property right to exclude by enforcing state trespass law. Should the state not feel a similar responsibility to protect the property rights of tenants to habitable housing?

Property rights work only because the state protects them through law. Non-enforcement means non-protection. As seminally outlined by Professor Wesley Newcomb Hohfeld, a legal right entails a 'correlative' duty to act or refrain from acting.[29] Professor Hohfeld's analysis pressed us to contemplate

---

[28] *Alger v Dep't of Labor & Indus.* 917 A.2d 508, 524–525 (Vt 2006) (Burgess J. concurring in part and dissenting in part).

[29] See WN Hohfeld 'Some fundamental legal conceptions as applied in judicial reasoning' (1913) 23 *Yale LJ* 16–59 28–32.

the effect upon others when legal rights are acknowledged and exercised.[30] Correspondingly, of course, it also induced us to consider the effect upon others when legal rights are *not* acknowledged. If a 'duty' cannot be enforced, no duty actually exists, and there is, therefore, no corresponding legal right.

In *Alger,* the state explicitly argued that it 'owe[d] *no duty* to tenants'.[31] Yet the state's approach to enforcing its housing code both denies tenants' property rights to habitable housing and, upon the state's issuance of orders to vacate, in some cases renders people homeless.[32] This is especially noteworthy in circumstances, as here, where these people *have done nothing wrong.* Under the system described here, tenants in Vermont can timely pay rent, timeously raise concerns with both their landlords and the state regarding housing code violations, receive no meaningful relief, and, when conditions become bad enough, be expelled by the state at a moment's notice to the streets, where they may or may not be allowed to sleep.[33] To call this 'inaction' seems untoward given that the state is depriving tenants of property rights that existing law says they own. The state has on the face of it conferred property rights, only to step aside and allow non-owners to appropriate those rights for free. To say that the state owes no duty to tenants is to say that it has no duty to protect property rights.

Failings in housing code enforcement theoretically might be alleviated in part by protecting tenants from eviction when landlords violate their duty to provide habitable housing. This threat might prompt landlords to respond more quickly and meaningfully to tenants' housing code concerns than they otherwise would, and thereby reduce the likelihood of orders to vacate akin to that at issue in *Alger.* However, although the law in most states (including Vermont) now implies such a warranty in all residential leases,[34] this

---

[30] WN Hohfeld 'Some fundamental legal conceptions as applied in judicial reasoning' (1913) 23 *Yale LJ* 16–59 28–32.

[31] Brief of Defendants/Appellees at 6, *Alger v Dep't of Labor & Indus.* 917 A.2d 508 (Vt. 2006) (No S479–02 Fc), 2005 WL 1464527 at *6.

[32] Several Vermont legislators recently proposed a bill aimed at improving housing code enforcement statewide. Among other provisions, the law would assure that funding appropriated for housing services is not, as is currently often the case, repurposed; impose fees to generate revenue that would be dedicated to inspections; require landlords to file and post in rented units a notice certifying compliance with the housing code before renting a given unit; and compel area inspections of all rental properties every two years. Vermont House, Bill 181 (introduced February, 2017).

[33] The City of Burlington, Vermont, for example, prohibits 'the use of any public park for sleeping between the hours of 10:00 pm and 7:00 am'. *See* Burlington, VT, Code of Ordinances, Ch 22, art 7.

[34] See eg *Hilder v St. Peter* 478 A.2d 202 (Vt 1984); *Willard v Parsons Hill Partnership,* 882 A.2d 1213 (Vt 2005).

warranty has proven ineffective in most cases involving poor tenants. There are a host of procedural and substantive hurdles that limit the warranty's effectiveness,[35] several of which serve as the centerpiece of our second story below.

3.2 Story #2: Eviction without legal counsel

Consider the situation of tenants in substandard housing evicted because they stopped paying rent. As discussed above, the law in the US requires landlords to comply with the local housing code. If the landlord does not comply, the tenant is protected by a doctrine called the implied warranty of habitability. The doctrine entitles the tenant to stop paying rent until the problem is fixed. And if the tenant has notified the landlord of the habitability issue and the landlord has failed to fix the problem in a reasonable time, the tenant cannot be evicted for non-payment of rent.[36]

Lawyers know about this rule of law. They learn it in the first year of law school. Tenants who are represented by lawyers often get to stay in their homes. The courts will not evict them because their lawyers, often after bringing to light potential violations of the landlord's duty to provide habitable premises, help negotiate a settlement. If you have a lawyer, the law lets you keep your apartment while it pressures your landlord to bring it up to code.

Tenants who do not have lawyers, on the other hand, do not know about this rule of law. The implied warranty of habitability is a defence to an eviction claim, and tenants who do not know about this defence do not raise it. Without offering a defence, they are evicted for non-payment of rent. They are evicted – and potentially rendered homeless – because they are not aware of a rule of law that entitles them to stay in their homes. To be sure, they are the only ones who do not know about this rule of property law. The landlord knows. The landlord's lawyer knows. The judge knows. They know that if the tenant spoke up, at the right moment and in the right way, the tenant would not be forced to leave her home. They know but they do nothing about it. Instead, they operate with the understanding that defences are raised

---

[35] See eg PA Franzese, A Gorin & DJ Guzik 'The implied warranty of habitability lives; making real the promise of landlord-tenant reform' (2016) 69 *Rutgers U L Rev* 1–45; DA Super 'The rise and fall of the implied warranty of habitability' (2011) 99 *Cal L Rev* 389–464.

[36] To raise this defence successfully, some jurisdictions require that the tenant prove she stopped paying rent *because of* the housing code violation. For a critique of this approach, see eg D Kennedy 'The effect of the warranty of habitability on low income housing: "milking" and class violence' (1987) 15 *Fla St U L Rev* 485–519.

exclusively by the defendant. If the defendant does not raise a defence, she loses the case.

But are these eviction cases somehow different? Evictions cause people with homes to become people without homes. Of course, many tenants find someplace else to live. But some do not. And importantly, if the law allows the tenant to stay in her home, the law gives her property rights in her continued tenancy. When the court evicts her, the court deprives her of property rights she has under current law. It does so not because she is not entitled to stay, but simply because she is unaware of the protections that the law provides to her.

The result of this set of circumstances is that the judge is taking a property right away from the tenant that the tenant has a right, under current substantive law, to keep. The only reason she is not able to keep it is because she did not comply with the procedural rules to raise the legal defence at the appropriate time. She did not do so because she is too poor to afford a lawyer and because the US does not adequately fund legal services for the poor, resulting in many poor people going unrepresented when they would be entitled to receive legal services if the government had chosen to fund them adequately to meet the need.

How is the tenant being granted due process of law? She has notice and an opportunity to be heard. But she does not have an *effective* opportunity to be heard because she does not have a lawyer to tell her what she owns. The state has created eviction procedures that routinely deprive tenants of property rights they own under state law. It does so because neither it nor the US Supreme Court views the loss of a home as a deprivation of a fundamental right that should be effected only in full compliance with the procedural rights of the parties. Similarly, the tenant is being deprived of a right to continue occupying her home when the substantive law (properly applied) would allow her to keep her home. She is deprived of this property right without compensation by a court of law, the quintessential state actor.

So we have a person with a home rendered potentially homeless by agents of the state applying the laws of the state in a half-hearted and incomplete way. It is not evident that this result complies with basic constitutional norms. It is not evident that the tenant has been afforded appropriate process. It is not evident that the parties' property rights have been respected.

oOo

The stories outlined in this section depict the state as on the face of it *defining* tenants' property rights in a manner that respects dignity and equality. However, they illustrate that this professed definition is fleeting, for the state is not fulfilling its obligation to *enforce* these property rights in a manner that respects dignity and equality. For all intents and purposes, then, the property law system is operating in these stories much as it operates in the context of the police commanding the homeless to 'move along' so as to comply with a prohibition on sleeping in public spaces: without concern for consequences in individual cases and in disregard of the fundamental values that characterise our democracy.

Consistent with these values, homeless people have a right to be somewhere and tenants have a right to habitable housing. Yet the state at times orders both to 'move along' in violation of these rights. It does so because those enforcing the law conceptualise property rights as divorced from democratic values. But democracies cannot legitimately define property rights in a manner that ignores these values. Property rights do not exist in a vacuum. We recognise them *because* they promote values such as dignity and equality. We cannot shape or enforce them in ways that deny these basic values.

4 Law reform

How might we mend this unjust state of affairs? In this section, we outline several potential legal reforms.

For starters, tenants might seek novel applications of existing liability schemes against the state. For example, perhaps constitutional takings law could be interpreted to recognise that decisions not to enforce existing regulations should be assessed to determine the extent to which deprivations resulting from these decisions are justified without compensation.[37] It is true that no federal or state court has found a taking based on the non-enforcement of an existing regulation, and most courts to have addressed such claims have rejected them summarily.[38] However, it is not clear this categorical approach is consistent with the view that property exists in service of fundamental democratic values. Housing codes do not merely define the obligations of owners who lease property for residential purposes. They also confer rights on owners of leaseholds. Housing codes recognise that tenants have a right

[37] TM Mulvaney 'Non-enforcement takings' (2018) 59 *BC L Rev* 145–215.

[38] The Texas Supreme Court most recently articulated this majority view in *Harris County v Kerr*, 2016 WL 3418246 (Tex 2016) ('the law does not recognize takings liability for failure to complete [a flood control plan]'). The Vermont Supreme Court's decision in *Alger*, *Alger v Dep't of Labor & Indus.* 917 A.2d 508 (Vt 2006), is one of just four cases nationwide to deem a non-enforcement takings claim sufficient to survive summary judgment. See *Jordan et al v St. Johns County*, 63 So. 3d 835 (Fla Dist Ct App. 2011); *Swartz v Beach*, 229 F Supp 2d 1239 (D. Wyo. 2002); *Litz v Maryland*, 131 A.3d 923 (Md 2016).

to live in dignity that is equal to that of landlords. Tenants are *entitled* under these laws to habitable housing. Non-enforcement takes that property right away.

One who adopts a narrow view of the 'state action' doctrine may question whether non-enforcement alone constitutes state action. But even those who harbor such a view would be hard pressed to deny that an order to vacate or an order of eviction that comes on the heels of non-enforcement is state action. Since these actions are occurring because the landlord deprived the tenant of property rights protected by law and because the state failed to protect these property rights, there is a reasonable argument that the state unjustifiably has taken the tenants' property rights without just compensation. The prospect of having to pay takings judgments in this instance might prompt the state to change course on its approach to creating, funding, and implementing enforcement mechanisms.[39]

However, we recognise the gravity of constitutionalising even a narrow interest in enforcement that is protected by a mandatory compensation remedy. Therefore, we concentrate in the remainder of this section on non-constitutional measures that might attend, at least in part, to the harms experienced by those shouldering an unfair brunt of non-enforcement.

First, rather small substantive adjustments to statutes and local ordinances involving habitability protections could have a significant impact. In many US cities – including Vermont's largest city of Burlington – local law states that if an inspector orders premises vacated because they endanger the health and safety of the occupying tenants or the general public, the landlord is responsible to pay the relocation costs of any displaced tenants.[40] Those states that do not currently impose this requirement statewide should

---

[39] In noting this possibility, we do not mean to suggest that monetary costs are always wholly commensurate with political costs. On this issue, see eg LA Fennell 'Taking eminent domain apart' (2004) 2004 *Mich St L Rev* 957–1004 994–95; DJ Levinson 'Making governments pay: markets, politics, and the allocation of constitutional costs' (2000) 67 *U Chi L Rev* 345–420 345; K Wyman 'The measure of just compensation' (2007) 41 *UC Davis L Rev* 239–288 246–48. For the argument that local governments are particularly likely to be risk-averse when it comes to takings liability, *see* C Serkin 'Big differences for small governments: local governments and the takings clause' (2006) 81 *NYU L Rev* 1624–1698, 1665–70.

[40] See Burlington Code of Ordinances, Ch. 18, Art. II. Div. 1, Sec. 28. Mirroring San Francisco and certain other cities, Portland, Oregon adopted an ordinance in February of 2017 that goes beyond Burlington's ordinance in that it requires landlords to pay relocation costs in all cases of no-cause eviction. See http://www.oregonlive.com/politics/index.ssf/2017/02/portland_landlords_must_pay_re.html.

do so.[41] Moreover, state legislatures might consider strengthening such a provision by (i) requiring landlords to demonstrate on a periodic basis that they have sufficient capital on hand to cover temporary relocation costs for their current tenants should the need arise, and/or (ii) drawing on the repair and receivership programs in place in some jurisdictions to task the state with initially funding displaced tenants' relocation, which the state could seek to recoup from the responsible landlords via some type of lien or indemnification suit.[42]

Second, relatively simple procedural reforms could allow tenants, under the implied warranty of habitability, to realise their rights that, as described above, in many instances have proved elusive for low-income tenants lacking legal representation. For one example, consider the canons of judicial ethics. In Massachusetts, these canons were recently changed to allow judges to help unrepresented parties by explaining the rules of procedure.[43] This is a deviation from the basic rule that judges must be neutral between the parties and cannot favor one over the other; it is a deviation from the principle that the parties are in charge of their own lawsuits with the judge simply serving as a referee to enforce existing rules. However, the canons do not allow judges to help unrepresented parties by telling them what their substantive legal rights are. But if the judge knows that the tenant has legal rights,

[41] Statutory law in Vermont is not clear on this point. The owner of a mobile home 'that is condemned by a governmental agency due to the willful failure or refusal of the owner to comply with any obligations imposed by law shall provide for reasonable relocation costs of affected leaseholders and residents, except when the owner can demonstrate that he or she has no financial capacity to comply'. Vt Stat Ann tit 10 § 6265. This provision presents several potentially large holes. First, it implicitly precludes the landlord's paying relocation costs when his failure to comply with the applicable housing codes is not willful, even if it is reckless or negligent. Second, it encourages landlords to organise their finances in such a way that they do not have reserves on hand to pay the relocation costs upon condemnation, at which point they are exempted. Third, it is not evident the provision applies when the state does not condemn a building but rather orders a building vacated until the landlord performs repairs. Fourth, it appears that there is no corollary provision under Vermont statutory law that is applicable to rental properties that are not mobile homes.

[42] In those jurisdictions permitting receivership, courts under certain conditions may appoint a state or private entity as a 'receiver' to operate and fund restoration of an occupied residential building until the landlord demonstrates sufficient reserves to perform the needed repairs. See eg Multifamily Housing Preservation and Receivership Act, NJ Stat §2A:114–42.

[43] Mass Supreme Judicial Court R 3:09: Code of Judicial Conduct, Rule 2.6(A) ('A judge may make reasonable efforts, consistent with law, to facilitate the ability of all litigants, including self-represented litigants, to be fairly heard'); see also Judicial Guidelines for Civil Hearings Involving Self-Represented Litigants, http://www.mass.gov/courts/court-info/trial-court/exec-office/ocm/jud-institute/jg-self-rep.html.

and the landlord knows that the tenant has legal rights, and the landlord's lawyer knows that the tenant has legal rights, why is there a violation of the neutrality principle for the judge to tell the tenant what everyone but the tenant knows?

We could change the rules governing the conduct of judges to require them to explain to tenants being evicted that they have a right to remain in their homes if those homes are in violation of the applicable housing codes. Landlords would not like this direction, of course, but they have no right to violate the housing code in the first place. Therefore, they cannot complain that their property rights are being violated by this change in judicial ethics rules. Indeed, it is the landlord that is violating the rights of the tenant, first by not maintaining the property and second by evicting the tenant when those violations persist.

Similarly, if even less dramatically, we could to begin to protect tenants' property rights in habitable units by altering eviction procedures to ensure that tenants facing eviction are notified of their legal rights and the means to assert them. For example, the summons sent to the tenant could include instructions on what the implied warranty of habitability is and how to assert it.[44]

For another procedural reform, rather than making a violation of the implied warranty of habitability a defence, we could change the burden of proof to make it an element of the landlord's claim for eviction. We could require landlords who want to evict tenants to obtain a certificate from the housing inspector showing that they are in compliance with the housing code before they can obtain possession of the property from the tenant. A more moderate (and admittedly likely less effective) approach might be to require landlords to plead affirmatively that they are in compliance with the implied warranty of habitability, using common terms that are accessible to legally unsophisticated tenants.[45]

Adopting even just one among this small sampling of potential constitutional, statutory, and procedural reforms would lead to the state's more accurately respecting current law, which imposes obligations on landlords to provide basic services to their tenants and which confers property rights on tenants

---

[44] For a time, the City of Detroit included information on the implied warranty of habitability on the form summons used by landlords in eviction proceedings. According to some analysts, this led to a significant increase in tenants' raising the defence in eviction court. *See* JI Rose & MA Scott '"Street talk" summonses in Detroit's landlord-tenant court: a small step forward for urban tenants' (1975) 52 *J Urb L* 969–1034 997–1019.

[45] See eg L Cunningham 'Procedural due process aspects of D.C. eviction procedures' (2005) 7 *Rutgers Race & L Rev* 107–148 113.

to the same in a manner that respects the fundamental democratic values of dignity and equality.[46]

5 Conclusion

The stories of eviction described above paint the following picture: We have granted rights to tenants on the face of rental housing codes, but we have not created, funded, and implemented enforcement mechanisms designed to ensure that those rights are real. We have stood by while courts make tenants homeless even though, under existing law, these tenants may well have the right to remain in their homes. We have operated on the assumption that the state has no responsibility when it forcibly removes a tenant from her home and later asks that person to 'move along' from her makeshift camp in the park. In short, we have pretended that these matters largely involve relations among private parties, relations that the state bears no legal or moral obligation to shape.

André van der Walt knew better.

Free and democratic societies hold that all human beings are created equal and thus are equally entitled to pursue happiness. The property law system in such a society, therefore, must be based on the premise that each person must have a realistic opportunity to live with the material basis needed to allow such equal pursuit. One embodiment of these principles is the law's regulating the conditions under which landlords can rent residential premises to tenants. The law does not assign property rights to landlords and allow them to exercise their rights in any way they please, regardless of how they might affect those over whom they have power. Instead, the law regulates property relationships to ensure that tenants have property rights needed to live safely in dignity, just as landlords do. That is, at a threshold level, property law appropriately recognises that landlords and tenants have equal rights to live in dignity.

The property system requires identifying minimum standards for property relationships that are compatible with democratic values, and thereafter defining and interpreting property rights accordingly. Housing codes reflect

---

[46] We note, though, that these reforms are not offered to detract from or replace efforts – through social demonstration or other more formal means – to stimulate open conversation about the reality that fairly administering a private property system in service of democratic values requires significant public investment. Enforcing housing codes costs money. But enforcing any property laws costs money. We have deemed some property relationships inconsistent with the values that characterise our democracy, including arrangements by which landlords and the state treat tenants as less than human. Tax revenues must be sufficient and sufficiently allocated to make it so on the ground.

one set of such minimum standards. Mirroring debates surrounding most minimum standards 'regulations', there has been considerable academic discussion regarding whether, as a matter of economic theory, housing code enforcement hurts poor people by decreasing the supply of affordable housing.[47] But if the economic argument remains contested, the moral one should not.

Relieving landlords of the obligation to provide safe and habitable housing would treat poor tenants as second-class, i.e., unequal, citizens. If empirical study confirms that both landlords and tenants need subsidies to ensure that housing is safe and habitable, a society that does not provide those subsidies – or otherwise ensure that safe and habitable housing is available to each human being – has created a property law system that treats the poor as if they were not equally entitled to live in dignity. A society that does this protects the property rights of the rich but not the poor. A society that adopts such a stance is not a truly democratic society. The fundamental values of dignity and equality come first, and our property system must be shaped to embody those values. Democracies do not serve property rights; property rights serve democratic values.

.

47 Some scholars suggest that landlords subject to housing code obligations will abandon rental properties they find too expensive to repair to the housing code's liking or recoup the costs of repairs they do perform by raising rents. See eg R Posner *Economic analysis of law* 9 ed (2014); N Komesar 'Return to Slumville: A critique of the Ackerman analysis of housing code enforcement and the poor' (1973) 82 *Yale LJ* 1175, 1188–91. Others, though, contend that code enforcement also *increases* housing supply by eliminating landlords' premature 'milking' of rental properties (ie by eliminating landlords' halting maintenance and collection of as much rent as possible thereafter until a unit is un-rentable at any price, at which point the landlords will abandon the unit), and that therefore such increases must be weighed in context against the potential decreases resulting from abandonment or cost-recoupment. See eg D Kennedy 'The effect of the warranty of habitability on low income housing: "milking" and class violence' (1987) 15 *Fla St U L Rev* 485–519.

Chapter 2

The marginality of property in expropriation law: A comparative assessment

Bradley V. Slade & Rachael Walsh***

1 Introduction

Two related trends in constitutional property law currently appear to be running in opposite directions. On the one hand, particularly with the ongoing development of 'progressive property' theory, theoretical analyses of property law are increasingly focused on property's ends – on the values that property is or should be designed to realise – as well as its means.[1] Expropriation law is one of a number of areas of property law that have been analysed in this way.[2] On the other hand, most courts appear to be increasingly reluctant to engage with the substance of property law, with its values, preferring to focus instead on procedural issues. This is certainly

* Associate Professor, Department of Public Law, Stellenbosch University.

** Assistant Professor, Trinity College Dublin. Aspects of this work were presented at a colloquium on 'The Core Principles of Expropriation Law' in The Hague, 18–20 June 2015, and I am grateful to the participants for their feedback.

[1] On progressive property, see GS Alexander, EM Peñalver, JW Singer, LS Underkuffler 'A statement of progressive property' (2009) 94 *Cornell L Rev* 743. On the prioritisation of the means of property law over its ends, see H Smith 'Mind the gap: The indirect relation between ends and means in American property law' (2009) 94 *Cornell L Rev* 959–989.

[2] See GS Alexander 'The public use requirement and the character of consequentialist reasoning' in B Hoops et al (eds) *Rethinking expropriation law II: The context, criteria and consequences of expropriation* (2015) 113–135.

true of expropriation law, where courts in many jurisdictions have generally been willing to police the *process* through which expropriation decisions are reached, and the procedural fairness of the legislative frameworks for such decision-making, but have not intervened in a significant way in relation to the substantive merits of expropriation decisions.[3] Both courts and academics increasingly emphasise the right to be heard within administrative processes as a key factor that tends to affirm the constitutionality of expropriation as an interference with property rights, and that further justifies a hands-off approach to judicial review of expropriation powers and decisions on constitutional grounds.[4] Provided that the relevant statutory scheme for expropriation includes an opportunity for the adversely affected owner to object, and provided that administrators apply that scheme properly, the outcomes of administrative processes concerning expropriation tend not to be afforded very significant weight by courts.[5] While they are active in supervising the *process* of expropriation, they generally do not concern themselves much with the *merits* of expropriation.

This chapter analyses these trends in light of Professor Van der Walt's magisterial arguments concerning the 'modest systemic status' of property.[6] Through comparative analysis, it argues that perhaps the most significant public law decision that can be taken concerning private property, the decision to expropriate, is made by administrators, meaning that the scope of an owner's security of possession raises significant administrative law questions for property law. It is at the administrative level that the owner's right to object arises, through 'participation rules' that grant an owner the

[3] For discussion of academic responses to this trend, see R Walsh 'Reviewing expropriations: Looking beyond constitutional property clauses' in B Hoops et al (eds) *Rethinking expropriation law I: Public interest in expropriation* (2015) 125–152 128–131.

[4] See T Merrill 'The economics of public use' (1987) 72 *Cornell L Rev* 61–116 64; L Mansnerus 'Public use, private use, and judicial review in eminent domain' (1983) 58 *NYU L Rev* 409–456 409. See also R Walsh 'Reviewing expropriations: Looking beyond constitutional property clauses' in B Hoops et al (eds) *Rethinking expropriation law I: Public interest in expropriation* (2015) 125–152 128–130.

[5] See R Walsh 'Reviewing expropriations: Looking beyond constitutional property clauses' in B Hoops et al (eds) *Rethinking expropriation law I: Public interest in expropriation* (2015) 125–152; R Walsh '"The principles of social justice" and the compulsory acquisition of private property for redevelopment in Ireland and the United States' (2010) 32 *Dublin ULJ* 1–23.

[6] AJ van der Walt 'The modest systemic status of property rights' (2014) 1 *J L Prop & Soc'y* 15–106.

right to be heard and related procedural entitlements.[7] Where expropriation decisions are reviewed by courts, the focus is generally on the process that was followed by administrators, rather than on the merits of the acquisition decision. We argue that this primacy of participation rules in expropriation law marks a further instance of the 'modest systemic status' of property identified by Van der Walt, since in the expropriation context the right to secure possession of property is afforded limited substantive protection. Instead, an owner is guaranteed judicially defended fair process in relation to an expropriation decision, and usually also compensation. The focus of this chapter is, however, on the decision to expropriate private property and an owner's ability to challenge that decision, not on the assessment of compensation. Its aim is to better understand to what extent the protection of fair procedures for owners, as opposed to secure possession of private property, is the primary goal of courts in supervising the administration of statutory expropriation regimes.

The chapter examines this question through comparative analysis of two jurisdictions with innovative (and, in some respects, idiosyncratic) constitutional guarantees for property rights: Ireland and South Africa. As will be seen, these jurisdictions both protect property rights at a constitutional level and at the same time explicitly recognise the power of the state to restrict and take property rights in the public interest. While the history and context of constitutional property law in these two jurisdictions differ significantly,[8] the constitutional guarantees for property rights in both jurisdictions attempt to capture property's dual function as an individual right and a social institution, and as such, were of significance in Van der

[7] For a detailed exploration of 'participation rules' and their relationship to other forms of protection for property rights, including property rules and liability rules, see R Walsh 'The evolving relationship between property and participation in English planning law' in N Hopkins (ed) *Modern studies in property law: Volume* 7 (2013) 263–290, noting for example at 271, '[w]hereas property rules afforded an owner a veto, and liability rules gave her control of value, participation rules simply gave her a voice in the debate over the scope of her rights'.

[8] On the history of the Irish constitutional property clauses, see R Walsh 'Private property rights in the drafting of the Irish Constitution: A communitarian compromise' (2011) 33 *Dublin ULJ* 86–115. For background to the South African constitutional property clauses, see M Chaskalson 'The property clause: Section 28 of the Constitution' (1994) 10 *SAJHR* 131–139; AJ van der Walt 'Notes on the interpretation of the property clause in the new Constitution' (1994) 57 *THRHR* 181–203; AJ van der Walt *The constitutional property clause* (1997) 1–29.

Walt's research.[9] Judged simply by the outcomes in expropriation cases in these jurisdictions, it is clear that an owner's right to fair procedures is afforded a higher level of significance than security of possession of privately owned property. This trend is analysed in the first parts of the paper, which compare the nature and impact of process rights in expropriation law in both jurisdictions. It concludes that in the context of perhaps the most significant public law interference with property rights – the outright taking of property through expropriation – an owner's presumptive entitlement to exclude is replaced by an entitlement to compensation coupled with a right to participate in relevant administrative processes, which courts will police to ensure that fair procedures are applied.[10]

The chapter then proceeds to analyse the content of the participatory rights accruing to an owner in the expropriation context through a comparative analysis of existing Irish and South African law and, where it concerns the latter jurisdiction, the proposed changes to the expropriation procedure outlined in the Expropriation Bill of 2015.[11] A number of key common elements of administrative process in expropriation law are identified: the right to be heard; the right to notice; the right to have representations taken into account; and the right to reasons. The chapter argues that these elements now form important parts of an owner's rights: they are the means through which the right to claim security of possession and/or value are vindicated most commonly for owners potentially adversely affected by expropriation decisions. Accordingly, the strength of those rights, and their impact, are

[9] While Professor Van der Walt was the leading expert on constitutional property law in South Africa (see the authoritative source AJ van der Walt *Constitutional property law* 3 ed (2011), and his yearly updates on constitutional property law in the *Annual Survey of South African Law*), he also wrote insightfully about Irish constitutional property law (see AJ van der Walt 'Property, social justice, and citizenship: Property law in post-apartheid South Africa' (2008) *Stell LR* 325–346; AJ van der Walt 'The protection of private property under the Irish Constitution: A comparative and theoretical perspective' in E Carolan & O Doyle (eds) *The Irish Constitution: Governance and values* (2008) 398–411, and the chapter on Ireland in AJ van der Walt *Constitutional property clauses* (1999) 229–244).

[10] This trend towards participation rule protection of property, and its significance, was identified by Van der Walt already at an early stage. At the dawn of the new constitutional dispensation in South Africa, Van der Walt wrote as follows (discussing developments in 'new property'): 'the focus of property theories is shifting towards participatory rights with regard to common property and away from exclusive rights to individual property. Obviously this development is of the utmost importance for constitutional and human rights theory since it implies a shift away from defensive and performance rights towards participatory rights.': AJ van der Walt 'Property rights, land rights and environmental rights' in D van Wyk et al (eds) *Rights and constitutionalism – The new South African legal order* (1994) 455–501 458.

[11] Expropriation Bill B4-D 2015.

important considerations in any assessment of the protection of property rights in the public law context in a particular jurisdiction.

Finally, returning to Van der Walt's theoretical insights, the chapter argues that the comparative analysis of Irish and South African constitutional property law suggests that property has 'modest systemic status' where expropriation is required for the realisation of constitutionally legitimate democratic objectives, since in those contexts, the law seeks to protect the rights of an owner to a fair and inclusive process (rights that in many legal frameworks exist and are protected outside of any constitutional property clause that might exist), rather than protecting secure possession of property. While property rights may be important factors that are weighed in the mix of a particular administrative decision-making process, such processes are ultimately oriented towards securing the public interest.[12] In such contexts, constitutional property rights provide a further argument for fair and transparent administrative processes involving robust participatory mechanisms. Such participation schemes provide owners with an important opportunity to voice objections to a proposed acquisition, whether on the basis of the nature of the interference with their rights, the nature of the public interest advanced to justify the acquisition, or procedural non-compliance. However, such processes fall far short of providing owners with a 'right to keep' property.[13] Rather, the effect of constitutional property rights protection in the context of expropriation is largely to trigger and shape what Frank Michelman refers to as 'the general right to fair treatment and to equal concern and respect enjoyed by citizens in a democratic state', which he notes is also guaranteed by due process and equality protections.[14]

2 The content and role of fair procedures in expropriation law

2.1 Introduction

This part compares the general legal frameworks for expropriation in Irish and South African law and the role played by participation rules, which confer on an owner a right to be heard within the administrative process of

[12] Indeed, the very fact that such processes are initiated in any given case indicates that some public actors have identified some need for the exercise of expropriation powers, whether by public or private actors, or a combination of both.

[13] On the 'right to keep' private property, see DJ Kochman 'Keepings' (2015) 23 *NYU Envtl LJ* 355–389; FI Michelman 'Good government, core liberties, and constitutional property: An essay for Joe Singer' (2016) 5 *Brigham-Kanner Property Rights Conference Journal* 27–42.

[14] FI Michelman 'Good government, core liberties, and constitutional property: An essay for Joe Singer' (2016) 5 *Brigham-Kanner Property Rights Conference Journal* 27–42 42.

an expropriation. It further analyses the significance of participation rules in *judicial* decision-making concerning the constitutionality of expropriation powers or of particular expropriation decisions, as well as the role of constitutional property rights in shaping the participation rules that are applied in expropriation law.

2.2 The general framework of Irish and South African expropriation law

The Irish constitutional protection of private property is contained in article 40.3.2° and article 43 of the Irish Constitution of 1937.[15] Together, they protect both the institution of private ownership and individual property rights, while also recognising the power of the state to delimit the exercise of property rights to meet 'the exigencies of the common good' and to realise 'the principles of social justice'. Neither article 40.3.2° nor article 43 specifically refers to expropriation or compensation.[16] Nonetheless, expropriation in the public interest has been recognised by the Irish courts as being in principle constitutionally justifiable (subject to a requirement

---

[15] Article 40.3.2° provides:

'The State shall, in particular, by its laws protect as best it may from unjust attack and, in the case of injustice done, vindicate the life, person, good name, and property rights of every citizen.'

Article 43 states:

'1. 1 The State acknowledges that man, in virtue of his rational being, has the natural right, antecedent to positive law, to the private ownership of external goods.

2 The State accordingly guarantees to pass no law attempting to abolish the right of private ownership or the general right to transfer, bequeath, and inherit property.

2. 1 The State recognises, however, that the exercise of the rights mentioned in the foregoing provisions of this Article ought, in civil society, to be regulated by the principles of social justice.

2 The State, accordingly, may as occasion requires delimit by law the exercise of the said rights with a view to reconciling their exercise with the exigencies of the common good.'

[16] The applicable Irish terminology is not consistently used by courts, legislators and administrators – judicial decisions, statutes and administrative decisions variously refer to expropriation, compulsory acquisition and compulsory purchase. For discussion of terminological differences in comparative constitutional property law, see AJ van der Walt & R Walsh 'Comparative constitutional property law' in M Grazidei & L Smith (eds) *Comparative property law: Global perspectives* (2016) 193–215.

to pay full compensation in most circumstances).[17] When interpreting statutes that enable compulsory acquisition, the courts must presume that they are constitutional, and insofar as is possible, adopt an interpretation that is consistent with the Constitution.[18] Where this is not possible, courts can strike down such powers, as well as particular compulsory acquisition decisions, for non-compliance with the Constitution.

Irish expropriation law is not codified in respect of the *reasons* that may justify compulsory acquisition – rather, different statutory powers have been enacted empowering different bodies to compulsory acquire property for specific statutory purposes (which may be broadly expressed).[19] The decision to expropriate is usually taken by independent administrators exercising statutory powers,[20] but in some contexts, a decision to expropriate can be taken through a process that is entirely internal to the acquiring authority.[21] An adversely affected owner may have a specific statutory right to appeal to the High Court on the basis that a confirmed compulsory purchase order is beyond the administrator's prescribed powers, or on the basis that the interests of the applicant have been substantially prejudiced through non-

[17] For example, the ability of the (now disbanded) Land Commission to compulsorily acquire property for land reform pursuant to statute was accepted by the courts as constitutional in a number of cases: see *Fisher v Irish Land Commission* [1948] IR 3; *Foley v Irish Land Commission* [1952] IR 118; *Dreher v Irish Land Commission* [1984] ILRM 94. The Supreme Court's latest pronouncement on compensation in *Rafferty v Minister for Agriculture* [2014] IESC 61 is that full compensation for all consequential losses is presumptively required by the Constitution for deprivations of property by the state, subject to the possibility of proportionate, socially just statutory exceptions.

[18] *East Donegal Co-Operative Livestock Mart Ltd v Attorney General* [1970] IR 317 340–341.

[19] Powers of compulsory acquisition exist, for example, in s 3 of the Derelict Sites Act, 1990, s 28 of the Vocational Education Act, 1930, s 17 of the Air Raid Precautions Act, 1939, s 49 of the Roads Act, 1993, ss 71 and 207 of the Planning and Development Act, 2000, and s 93 of the Water Services Act, 2007, to name but a few. However, there is a significant degree of commonality in the way in which compensation payable to an expropriated owner is assessed, regardless of the particular statutory context. A significant number of different statutes that facilitate compulsory acquisition of property include the same compensation assessment rules, which are set out in the Acquisition of Land (Assessment of Compensation) Act, 1919. However, some statutory expropriation powers are accompanied by discrete compensation rules: see for instance the National Asset Management Agency Act, 2009.

[20] The expertise of these administrators varies depending on the statutory context in which particular expropriation decisions are made: in many cases, An Bord Pleanála (the Irish Planning Board) has ultimate confirming power.

[21] For example, the Industrial Development Agency can decide to acquire property based on its expert judgment as to the need for such acquisition to encourage industrial development, pursuant to s 16 of the Industrial Development Act, 1986. This power is discussed further below.

compliance with a statutory requirement.[22] However, in most statutory contexts, an owner is limited to a High Court judicial review challenge to an expropriation decision.[23] Such a challenge in Irish law (simplifying considerably) can generally only concern the procedure by which an expropriation decision was reached by an administrator (including issues such as whether it was within the scope of an administrator's powers and was a reasonable decision), not the merits of that decision.[24] The Irish courts have repeatedly said that the reasonableness of expropriation decisions will be strictly scrutinised.[25] However, when called upon to determine such judicial review challenges, the Irish courts have generally deferred to the outcomes of administrative decision-making processes, at least where there has been compliance with fair procedures and the administrator has adhered to the limits of its statutorily conferred power.[26]

Section 25(2) of the Constitution of the Republic of South Africa, 1996, states that property may be expropriated in terms of law of general application, for a public purpose or in the public interest, and subject to the payment of just and equitable compensation.[27] The purpose served by the expropriation is said to justify the expropriation[28] and courts generally adopt a deferential

---

[22] This right of appeal arises under s 78(2) of the Housing Act, 1966, and applies to acquisitions pursuant to the Housing Act, 1966 (a very commonly invoked statutory power of compulsory acquisition).

[23] If the expropriation was pursuant to the powers established by the Planning and Development Act, 2000, the circumstances in which a judicial review challenge can be brought are further limited (both as to timing and grounds) by s 50A(2)(d) of the 2000 Act.

[24] For detailed elaboration of the scope of judicial review challenges in Irish law, see DG Morgan *Hogan and Morgan's administrative law* 4 ed (2012).

[25] See *Clinton v An Bord Pleanála* [2007] IESC 19, [2007] 4 IR 701; *Rafferty v Minister for Agriculture* [2014] IESC 61.

[26] For detailed discussion of the deferential approach of the Irish courts in reviewing expropriation laws and decisions, see R Walsh 'Reviewing expropriations: Looking beyond constitutional property clauses' in B Hoops et al (eds) *Rethinking expropriation law I: Public interest in expropriation* (2015) 125–152; R Walsh '"The principles of social justice" and the compulsory acquisition of private property for redevelopment in Ireland and the United States' (2010) 32 *Dublin ULJ* 1–23.

[27] During the constitutional drafting process, there were heated debates on whether a constitutional property clause should be included in the Constitution: see M Chaskalson 'Stumbling towards section 28: Negotiations over the protection of property rights in the interim Constitution' (1995) 11 *SAJHR* 222–240. However, with the ultimate inclusion of s 25 in the Constitution of 1996, the debates on the desirability of the constitutional property clause ceased, and focus shifted to, among other things, the meaning of property, the distinction between deprivation and expropriation, the meaning of public purpose and public interest, and the calculation of compensation: See AJ van der Walt *Constitutional property law* 3 ed (2011).

[28] *Harvey v Umhlatuze Municipality and Others* 2011 (1) SA 601 (KZP) para 82.

approach to where the public interest lies.[29] Similar to Irish expropriation law, various pieces of legislation in South African law award expropriatory powers to different bodies.[30] However, unlike Irish law, South African law has a general over-arching expropriation Act. The Expropriation Act 63 of 1975 was promulgated to address the need for a uniform expropriation Act, applicable throughout the Republic, to streamline both the procedure of expropriation and the calculation of compensation.[31] The 1975 Expropriation Act is therefore regarded as the 'primary statutory instrument for expropriation of property in South Africa'[32] even though it predates the 1996 Constitution by 20 years. The South African Parliament is currently considering the 2015 Expropriation Bill in order to replace the 1975 Expropriation Act with one that fully complies with the Constitution. The 1975 Expropriation Act affords the Minister of Public Works the general authority to expropriate property for public purposes. The Act also sets out an expropriation procedure that must be followed in cases where property is expropriated in terms of the Act or in terms of other enabling legislation.[33] This procedure does not provide for the owner to be heard before a decision to expropriate property is taken. It only provides for the right of the owner to be heard as far as it concerns the amount of compensation that is offered by the expropriating authority in the expropriation notice.[34] However, since the decision to expropriate is regarded as an administrative action,[35] the decision to expropriate is

[29] PJ Badenhorst, JM Pienaar & H Mostert *Silberberg and Schoeman's The Law of Property* 5 ed (2006); A Gildenhuys *Onteieningsreg* 2 ed (2001) 98–99. AJ van der Walt *Constitutional Property Law* 3 ed (2011) 459, 465 argues that although the public purpose requirement has lost much of its original purely defensive flavour, the courts will still strike down an expropriation if 'not properly authorised, frivolous, arbitrary or corrupt'.

[30] For instance, specialised legislation such as the National Roads Agency Limited and National Roads Act 7 of 1998 grants the Minister of Transport the authority to expropriate property for constructing national roads.

[31] M Jacobs *The law of expropriation in South Africa* (1982) 4.

[32] *Du Toit v Minister of Transport* 2006 (1) SA 297 (CC) para 2.

[33] See for instance the applicability of the Expropriation Act 63 of 1975 when an expropriation is carried out in terms of section 41 of the National Roads Agency Limited and National Roads Act 7 of 1998. Furthermore, in terms of section 5 of the Expropriation Act 63 of 1975, local authorities are bound to follow the procedure set out in the Expropriation Act when exercising powers to expropriate in terms of other enabling legislation. See further section 26 of the Extension of Security of Tenure Act 62 of 1997. .

[34] See ss 9–10 of the Expropriation Act.

[35] *Erf 16 Bryntirion (Pty) Ltd v Minister of Public Works* [2011] ZASCA 246, 1 December 2011 para 12; *Offit Enterprises (Pty) Ltd and Another v Coega Development Corporation (Pty) Ltd and Others* 2010 (4) SA 242 (SCA) para 36.

reviewable in terms of the Promotion of Administrative Justice Act (PAJA).[36] Apart therefore from the procedure that must be adopted in terms of the Expropriation Act, and which entitles an owner to object to non-adherence to that procedure, the decision to expropriate must also be procedurally fair in terms of the principles of administrative justice and may be reviewed on that ground.[37] As the cases discussed below indicate, the courts have used the participatory framework in terms of administrative law to determine whether the adopted expropriation procedure in a particular case was procedurally fair.

While in Irish expropriation law, wholly internal expropriation powers that do not provide for any independent oversight have been criticised judicially as outliers,[38] the decision to expropriate in South Africa is always completely internal to the expropriation authority. An expropriating authority may decide to expropriate property and the expropriation is complete once the expropriation notice has been served on the property owner. An expropriating authority is not required to obtain the approval of an external body or a court before it makes the final decision to expropriate. Therefore, even if during the expropriation procedure the property owner argues that the expropriation is unlawful based on substantive grounds, such as not being for a public purpose, the expropriating authority can continue with the expropriation regardless. It would then be up to the owner to institute legal proceedings if she wants to attack the expropriation on substantive grounds.[39]

Accordingly, the general legal approach to expropriation differs somewhat between Ireland and South Africa, since the South African approach focuses on a centralised expropriation Act that governs all expropriations, whereas the Irish approach involves a more disaggregated statutory framework, and

---

[36] 3 of 2000. This Act seeks to give effect to s 33 of the Constitution, which guarantees lawful, reasonable and procedurally fair administrative action.

[37] The decision to expropriate can, however, also be subjected to scrutiny in terms of the administrative law principle of reasonableness. With reference to s 6(2)(h) of PAJA, which states that an administrative action is reviewable if the exercise of the power 'in pursuance of which the administrative action was purportedly taken, is so unreasonable that no reasonable person could have so exercised the power or performed the function'. O'Regan J in *Bato Star Fishing (Pty) Ltd v Minister of Environmental Affairs* 2004 (4) SA 490 (CC) para 44 stated that '[s]ection 6(2)(h) should … be understood to require a simple test, namely that an administrative decision will be reviewable if, in Lord Cooke's words, it is one that a reasonable decision-maker could not reach'. See further C Hoexter *Administrative law in South Africa* 2 ed (2012) 346–350.

[38] *Reid v Industrial Development Agency* [2015] IESC 82 paras 82–84.

[39] However, when the owner and the expropriating authority cannot agree on the amount of compensation, it must be referred to a court for adjudication. See s 25(2)(b) of the Constitution, 1996.

accordingly greater scope for administrative rules to vary depending on the context in which a particular expropriation arises. The more detailed process and participation rules set out in the proposed South African Expropriation Bill, considered further below, demonstrate the extent to which good administrative procedure is increasingly prioritised as an important justificatory aspect of an expropriation power. In both jurisdictions, owners lack any veto rights in respect of a proposed expropriation, and are confined to relying on administrative participation rights and/or limited rights to take legal challenges in respect of expropriation decisions. As such, property rule protection for owners' security of possession has been replaced by a combination of liability rule and participation rule protection in both legal frameworks.[40] However, as will be seen in further detail, the *content* of the participation rules that guarantee an owner a voice in an expropriation procedure differs in some respects.

2.3 Constitutional shaping of administrators' procedural duties

The Irish Constitution imposes procedural duties of fairness on administrators reaching decisions concerning expropriation (and indeed on administrators generally), which the courts have been willing to police. Perhaps the *locus classicus* of this line of authority is *O'Brien v Bord na Mona*.[41] The case concerned compulsory acquisition by the national authority charged with developing and managing the use of turf in Ireland, pursuant to section 29 of the Turf Development Act 1946. The statute enabled the board to acquire land without confirmation by any external body and without any opportunity for an owner to appeal to such a body against an acquisition decision. The plaintiff challenged the decision on the basis of a lack of independence and potential bias on the part of the Board in making an acquisition decision. The High Court held that the procedure in question did not satisfy the constitutional requirements in relation to natural and constitutional justice. Finlay P set out the procedural steps to be followed before making a compulsory purchase order:

> First, before deciding to acquire any particular piece of property, the acquiring authority must give ample and fair notice to the owner of such property of its intention to do so; it must give him an ample opportunity to make representations or objections and then consider such representations or objections in a judicial

[40] See G Calabresi & AD Melamed 'Property rules, liability rules and alienability: One view of the cathedral' (1972) 85 *Harv L Rev* 1089–1128; R Walsh 'The evolving relationship between property and participation in English planning law' in N Hopkins (ed) *Modern studies in property law: Volume* 7 (2013) 263–290.

[41] [1983] 1 IR 255 (HC) (SC).

manner; finally, it must reach a decision whether to acquire or not upon the basis of that consideration.[42]

Given the importance of fair procedures in compulsory acquisition processes, he held that these requirements applied even in circumstances where an owner's objections to a proposed acquisition would have been rejected upon consideration by the acquiring authority.[43]

The Irish courts have identified a spectrum of 'rights to be heard', ranging from opportunities to make informal submissions to trial-like oral hearings with opportunities for cross-examination, and have suggested that in general, the rights of an owner whose property is to be expropriated fall closer to the formal than the informal end of that spectrum, given the seriousness of the interference with constitutionally protected property rights involved in expropriation.[44] *Effective* participation rights have also been held to include a right to prior notice of a decision that may adversely affect property rights (even falling short of outright expropriation), which must clearly communicate the details of the proposed interference.[45] An owner is also entitled to access the materials grounding an adverse decision, in order to enable him or her to determine whether a basis exists for challenge.[46] Administrators must engage effectively with owners and give real meaning to their right to be heard in

[42] *O'Brien v Bord na Mona* [1983] 1 IR 255 (HC) (SC) 286.

[43] *O'Brien v Bord na Mona* [1983] 1 IR 255 (HC) (SC) 287. On appeal, the Supreme Court held that the absence of a right of appeal from the board's decision, and the absence of any external confirmation, did not amount to a breach of natural and constitutional justice, since the function of the board was administrative in nature, not judicial. However, the court did not disagree with Finlay P's general statement of principle concerning the procedure to be followed in compulsorily acquiring property.

[44] *Lord Ballyedmond v Commission for Energy Regulation* [2006] IEHC 206 [3.5]. At para 7.6 of its judgment, the High Court described what was required as follows: '[a]n inquiry into a possible compulsory purchase is not like a criminal trial where the defendant is entitled to require proof of each and every element of the criminal offence charged. It is a general inquiry into the appropriateness of making the compulsory purchase order sought.' However, an oral hearing is not required in all circumstances: See *Egan v An Bord Pleanála* [2011] IEHC 44, upholding the compulsory acquisition of a derelict site without an oral hearing.

[45] For example, in *MacPharthalain v The Commissioners of Public Works* [1994] 3 IR 353, the Supreme Court held that the decision to designate the applicants' lands as sites of international scientific importance, without giving them notice or an opportunity to be heard, adversely affected their property rights, and consequently breached the requirements of natural justice. O'Flaherty J said that the case demonstrated the need to inform landowners about decisions that could affect them and to give them an opportunity to dispute such decisions: *MacPharthalain v The Commissioners of Public Works* [1994] 3 IR 353 359.

[46] *Electricity Supply Board v Cork County Council*, unreported judgment, 28 June 2000 (HC). See also *Wymes v An Bord Pleanála* [2003] 11 JIC 1405 (High Court of Ireland).

matters that affect their property rights by considering their representations 'in a fair and impartial fashion'.[47] In *Clinton v An Bord Pleanála*,[48] the High Court identified a constitutional duty requiring acquiring authorities to give reasons for their expropriation decisions, while in *Hygeia Chemicals Ltd v Irish Medicines Board*,[49] the Supreme Court emphasised the importance of *clear* administrative procedures, as well as the need to afford owners adequate time to prepare a response to a proposed deprivation of property rights. Furthermore, in *Dellway Investments v National Asset Management Agency*[50] (considered further below), the Supreme Court held that circumstances of urgency should not be readily accepted as a justification for denying an owner fair procedures in respect of an administrative decision that seriously interferes with property rights.

Consequently, the Irish courts have held that the Constitution's protections for property rights, coupled with the principles of natural and constitutional justice, impose extensive duties of procedural fairness on administrators who exercise statutory powers that may result in the deprivation of property rights. However, an important unsettled point in Irish law is whether an owner is constitutionally entitled to have an expropriation decision taken by an independent decision-maker, or whether the acquiring authority itself

---

[47] *Dunraven Limerick Estates Co v Commissioners of Public Works* [1974] IR 113 133 & 139.

[48] [2005] IEHC 84. On appeal (*Clinton v An Bord Pleanála* [2007] IESC 19, [2007] 4 IR 701), the Supreme Court appeared to assume that such a duty existed, without addressing it directly.

[49] [2010] IEHC 4. The case concerned the deprivation of a licence to sell pharmaceutical and/or chemical products for veterinary use, which the court held was a restraint of property rights. It held that there had been a failure to provide fair procedures, given that there were no rules or regulations governing the process of internal appeal against licence annulment and the standard adopted by the relevant authority for deciding on revocations was 'wholly opaque.' The appellant could not discover the precise details of the internal appeals process, nor indeed the exact nature of the decision to be appealed, within a reasonable time of the appeal that was held. Furthermore, the licence holder was given insufficient time (9 working days) to prepare for the appeals process. Finally, tight time limits on oral submissions (20–30 minutes), coupled with a refusal of an adjournment, were held to breach the requirements of fair procedures, since there was no full advance exchange of relevant material and arguments to facilitate preparation of a response by the adversely affected owner. On adjournments as an aspect of fair procedures in expropriation, see also *Wymes v An Bord Pleanála* [2003] 11 JIC 1405 (High Court of Ireland).

[50] *Dellway Investments v National Asset Management Agency* [2011] 4 IR 1. For detailed analysis of the fair procedures aspect of this decision, see D Kenny 'Fair procedures in Irish administrative law: Towards a constitutional duty to act fairly in *Dellway Investments v NAMA*' (2011) 34 *Dublin ULJ* 47–73; A O'Neill, 'Fair procedures: An inviolable constitutional requirement?' (2011) 33 *Dublin ULJ* 319–338.

can be the sole arbiter (subject to judicial review) of the appropriateness of expropriation. This issue arose recently in *Reid v The Industrial Development Agency (Ireland)*.[51] Section 16 of the Industrial Development Act, 1986, empowers the Industrial Development Agency (IDA) to compulsorily acquire land to provide or facilitate the provision of sites for the establishment, development or maintenance of an industrial undertaking.[52] The decision-making process is entirely internal to the IDA – it decides to acquire the lands, issues a 'record of decision', and notifies the affected parties. There is no statutory provision for adjudication or confirmation by any external body, or for an appeal (other than through a judicial review challenge). The Supreme Court suggested that such wholly internal statutory processes were rare and somewhat anomalous,[53] and queried their appropriateness in light of the guarantees for fair procedures contained within article 6 of the European Convention on Human Rights.[54]

In South African law, as noted above, the empowering legislation does not detail the administrative process for the exercise of expropriation powers, which may be exercised on a wholly internal basis by acquiring authorities. However, the Expropriation Bill of 2015 seeks to give effect to sections 25, 33 and 34 of the Constitution, and thereby to reshape South African expropriation procedure in light of constitutional requirements.[55] One of the aims of the Bill is to set out 'procedural norms and standards'

---

[51] [2013] IEHC 433 (HC), [2015] IESC 82 (SC).

[52] It must be of the opinion that industrial development will or is likely to occur as a result of the acquisition, and that such development will conform to prescribed statutory criteria, such as providing or maintaining employment, which are set out in s 21 of the Act.

[53] In *Reid v The Industrial Development Agency (Ireland)* [2015] IESC 82 (SC) para 82, McKechnie J stated that '...intervention of an independent third party inspires overall confidence in the process and unless made practically impossible or exceedingly difficult by compelling countervailing circumstances, should be provided for.'

[54] European Convention for the Protection of Human Rights and Fundamental Freedoms 1953, 213 UNTS 222, ETS 5. The relevant part of article 6 of the European Convention provides: 'In the determination of his civil rights and obligations or of any criminal charge against him, everyone is entitled to a fair and public hearing within a reasonable time by an independent and impartial tribunal established by law.'

[55] Section 25(2) specifically provides that property may be expropriated in terms of law of general application, for a public purpose or in the public interest, and is subject to just and equitable compensation. Section 33(1) guarantees the right to administrative action that is lawful reasonable and procedurally fair. Section 34 state that '[e]veryone has the right to have any dispute that can be resolved by application of law decided in a fair public hearing before a court or, where appropriate, another independent and impartial tribunal or forum.'

to guide expropriating authorities.[56] In this regard the Expropriation Bill sets out a detailed expropriation procedure that must be followed when the power of expropriation is exercised. The procedure set out in this Bill will be mandatory throughout the Republic, irrespective of the enabling legislation relied upon to expropriate property. In terms of the notice of expropriation, an expropriating authority must set out the purpose of, and relevant reason for, the intended expropriation, and invite affected property owners to make submissions to the expropriating authority.[57] The owner is therefore notified that she is able to object to the expropriation and make submissions concerning the intended expropriation. Although the project for which expropriation is sought has already been designed, the expropriating authority is nevertheless obliged to consider any objections and/or submissions of the owner before taking a final decision to expropriate the property.[58] However, the lack of independent review, coupled with the sequencing of project planning and consideration of representations, raises the possibility that representations may not always be accorded significant weight by administrators, with a risk of what Sherry Arnstein characterises as 'mere tokenism' in such circumstances.[59] Notwithstanding this concern, in giving effect to section 33 of the Constitution, the Bill goes a long way in setting up a participatory framework for expropriation. If the Bill is promulgated and the expropriation procedure outlined in the Bill gives proper effect to the right to procedurally fair administrative action, procedural fairness in the context of expropriation will be adjudicated in terms of the Expropriation Bill and not PAJA. The procedural fairness requirements outlined in PAJA will only supplement the Expropriation Bill if the latter does not fully address the procedural fairness requirements in PAJA.[60]

However, since the Expropriation Act currently does not provide for an expropriation procedure that complies with the rights and values of the new constitutional dispensation, particularly the notion of procedural fairness, South African courts rely on the principles of administrative justice in determining whether a fair expropriation procedure was adopted in any particular case. Procedural fairness in administrative law is considered on a case to case basis, and is sensitive to the relevant context within which it

---

[56] See Preamble to the Bill.

[57] Clause 7(2) of the Bill.

[58] Clause 7(5) of the Bill.

[59] SR Arnstein 'A ladder of citizen participation' (1969) 35 *J Am Inst Planners* 216, 217.

[60] Section 3(5) of PAJA; C Hoexter *Administrative law in South Africa* 2 ed (2012) 367. See also *Sidumo and Another v Rustenburg Platinum Mines Ltd and Others* 2008 (2) SA 24 (CC) paras 91–104.

is considered.[61] Section 3(2)(b) of PAJA sets out the minimum standard for a procedurally fair administrative action. An expropriating authority must, in terms of this provision, give adequate notice of the proposed expropriation, allow for a 'reasonable opportunity to make representations', and duly inform the owner of her right to request the reason for the expropriation.[62]

South African courts have relied upon the principles of administrative justice to determine whether the owner's right of participation, within the framework of procedural fairness, has been respected. For example, in *Erf 16 Bryntirion (Pty) Ltd v Minister of Public Works*,[63] the Minister of Public Works expropriated the applicant's property for purposes of upgrading and enhancing the Bryntirion estate (the location of the official presidential residence, presidential guest houses and the houses of some cabinet ministers). The Department of Public Works, responsible for the upgrade of the estate, first contacted the owner with an offer to buy the property at market value. It specified its aim as being to upgrade the security of the estate, but the owner rejected the offer. The department requested the owner to reconsider and invited the owner to a meeting so as to explain the reason for wanting to buy the property to the owner in person. This request was also rejected by the owner. The Minister ultimately took the decision to expropriate the property in order to realise the stated purpose. The applicant instituted proceedings requesting the decision to expropriate to be reviewed and set aside. The applicant argued that the expropriation was not for a public purpose, was procedurally unfair, and was not justified by the reasons supplied by the department.[64] The High Court and Supreme Court of Appeal accepted that the expropriation was for a public purpose and that the expropriation was rationally connected to the upgrade of the

---

[61] Section 3(2)(a) of PAJA; C Hoexter *Administrative law in South Africa* 2 ed (2012) 365.

[62] Section 3(2)(b) of PAJA. Section 3(2)(b) also requires that a clear statement must be made of the administrative decision, in this case the decision to expropriate. This implies that a decision has already been taken. This component therefore assists any affected party to enforce his or her right of appeal or review. C Hoexter *Administrative law in South Africa* 2 ed (2012) 376, relying also on L Baxter *Administrative law* (1984) 587, argues that the clear statement of the administrative decision should ideally be made only after representations have been made by the effected party.

[63] *Erf 16 Bryntirion (Pty) Ltd v Minister of Public Works* [2010] ZAGPPHC 154 (12 October 2010) and *Erf 16 Bryntirion (Pty) Ltd v Minister of Public Works* [2011] ZASCA 246 (1 December 2011).

[64] *Erf 16 Bryntirion (Pty) Ltd v Minister of Public Works* [2010] ZAGPPHC 154 (12 October 2010) para 2. The applicant raised 14 grounds of review, which the High Court reduced to three, the first of these being that the expropriation is not for a public purpose as required by the Expropriation Act.

security of the Bryntirion estate to ensure the safety of the President, cabinet Ministers and foreign state guests.

With regard to procedural unfairness, the applicant argued that he was not given adequate notice of the impending expropriation, that he was not given adequate opportunity to make representations, and that he did not receive all the relevant information that he needed to make meaningful representations. Both the High Court and the Supreme Court of Appeal held that the decision to expropriate was procedurally fair. The applicant's right to be heard was held to have been adequately respected, since the applicant was granted four opportunities to make representations to the minister as to why the decision to expropriate should not be taken, even though the applicant only made representations on two of these occasions.[65] Due to the nature of the project, namely the upgrade of the security of the presidential estate, some sensitive information was withheld from the applicant. However, the courts accepted that fairness depends on the context of each specific case.[66] It was held that the applicant received 'sufficient information' to enable him to make proper representations.[67] In that regard, the courts held that the right to be heard had not been violated. On the question of notice, the Supreme Court of Appeal found that the applicant was supplied with essential information setting out the basis upon which the decision was taken. The courts did also not accept the applicant's argument that the decision to expropriate was not justified by the reason for the expropriation. From the start of its dealings with the applicant concerning the property, the department made clear to the applicant that the reason it sought to acquire the property was to upgrade the security of the presidential estate. Having accepted that the expropriation was for a valid public purpose, the courts held that the decision to expropriate was justified in terms of the reason supplied.

Another South African decision that illustrates the courts' emphasis on a fair expropriation procedure is *eThekwini Municipality v Sotirios Spetsiotis*.[68] In this decision the applicant expropriated the respondent's lease for various upgrades and developments to the beachfront area in preparation for the 2010 Soccer World Cup. Having accepted that the expropriation procedure in the Expropriation Act was complied with, the respondent challenged the expropriation on two grounds; procedurally on the ground that the provisions

---

65 Section 3(2)(b) of PAJA.

66 *Erf 16 Bryntirion (Pty) Ltd v Minister of Public Works* [2011] ZASCA 246 (1 December 2011) para 12 and *Erf 16 Bryntirion (Pty) Ltd v Minister of Public Works* [2010] ZAGPPHC 154 (12 October 2010) para 62.

67 *Erf 16 Bryntirion (Pty) Ltd v Minister of Public Works* [2011] ZASCA 246 (1 December 2011) para 12.

68 [2009] ZAKZDHC 51 (6 November 2009).

in PAJA were not complied with, and substantively on the ground that the expropriation was not rationally connected to a public purpose or a public interest.[69]

With regard to PAJA, the respondent argued that the adopted procedure did not afford him a reasonable opportunity to make representations as required in terms of section 3(2)(b)(ii) of PAJA. The applicant sent a notice of expropriation to the respondent that invited the respondent to make a written submission if he had any objections to the intended expropriation. The notice of expropriation also stipulated the amount of compensation that was offered. The respondent responded in writing, rejecting the offer of compensation and stipulating what he regarded as adequate compensation. The respondent rejected an increased compensation offer, and, while reserving his rights, stated that he would be willing to negotiate a consensual cancellation of the lease. The respondent's letters of objection were submitted to the expropriating authority prior to making the final decision to expropriate. Furthermore, there was evidence that the respondent's architects met with the municipality and made several proposals concerning the respondent's argument that the expropriation was unnecessary.[70] The court therefore found that section 3(2)(b)(ii) or PAJA had been complied with since the applicant was given, in the specific context, a reasonable opportunity to make representations.

In summary, in both Irish and South African law, constitutional considerations, including constitutional property rights, have influenced the *content* of the owner's right to be heard at the administrative stage of expropriation proceedings. The courts have been willing to involve themselves in reviewing the detail of expropriation procedure, and have identified at least the following elements of a common core of expropriation procedure as being constitutionally required: a right to notice of a proposed expropriation; a right to be heard (in writing or orally depending on the circumstances of a particular expropriation decision); a right to access material required to mount an objection to a proposed expropriation, including adequate reasons for an administrative expropriation decision; and a right to have representations considered by the relevant administrative body. The Irish courts have further emphasised the need for clear administrative procedures and for adequate time to prepare a response to a proposed adverse decision.

---

[69] The court did not pay much attention to whether the purpose of expropriation was for a public purpose, but nevertheless found that there was a rational connection between the expropriation and the development, which is for a public purpose.

[70] *eThekwini Municipality v Sotirios Spetsiotis* [2009] ZAKZDHC 51 (6 November 2009) para 11.

Judges in both jurisdictions have suggested that the content of participation rules protecting security of possession are context dependent, and may vary in strength. This is significant – the reason for an expropriation may not only justify the expropriation *per se*, but also may justify a particular form of expropriation procedure. However, it appears in particular from the decisions of the Irish courts that the purpose of an expropriation and/or its context cannot generally justify a *total* denial of fair procedures to an adversely affected owner – rather, it may simply influence where on the spectrum of procedural entitlements an owner's rights are situated in a particular case.

Significantly, neither Irish nor South African law guarantees that the administrative procedure leading to an expropriation decision will be independent, in the sense of being led by an administrator that does not have an interest in the acquisition decision being approved. In South African law, this lack of administrative independence is a feature of *all* expropriation decisions, while in Irish law, it arises in the context of a relatively rare number of statutory powers, which have been criticised by the courts as outdated in light of modern understandings of the requirements of fair procedures.[71] We argue that if judges are to continue to defer substantially to administrative expropriation decisions, and to afford weight to administrative procedural compliance when expropriation powers or decisions are challenged, the relevant administrative procedures should be constitutionally required to be independent in nature. Such a requirement of independent and impartial administrative adjudication can be justified normatively as a requirement of the rule of law.[72] Absent such a requirement, there is a real risk that regardless of the *formal* procedure adopted, the interests of adversely affected owners will not be given full consideration or afforded any meaningful weight by the relevant administrative decision-makers.[73] Rather, the process may be systemically weighted in favour of administrative decisions granting expropriation orders, which courts are likely to be reluctant to second-guess both on the grounds of their comparatively limited expertise in relation

---

[71] The Supreme Court in *Reid v Industrial Development Agency* [2015] IESC 82 noted the submission of counsel in that case that only two such statutory powers remained in Irish law.

[72] See KM Stack 'An administrative jurisprudence: The rule of law in the administrative state' (2015) 115 *Colum L Rev* 1985–2018 2015, arguing that '[a]t a most basic level, the rule-of-law value of procedural fairness requires an impartial decider in adjudications.'

[73] For helpful discussion of the possibility of disconnection between formal procedural rights and meaningful participation, see SR Arnstein 'A ladder of citizen participation' (1969) 35 *J Am Inst Planners* 216–224.

to planning decisions and the greater democratic accountability of the politically elected branches of government.[74]

2.4 Process as a factor in determining the constitutionality of expropriation powers and decisions

Where a fair procedure is adopted, including an opportunity for an adversely affected owner to be heard, that fact weighs heavily in favour of the constitutionality of an expropriation scheme or decision in both Irish and South African constitutional property law. Consequently, as this section will demonstrate, the presence of statutory provision for fair procedures in expropriation law, and the observance of such procedures by administrators, are both factors that are weighed by courts in favour of the constitutionality of expropriation powers and decisions.

For example, in *Central Dublin Development Association v Attorney General*, Kenny J upheld the constitutionality of the first Irish planning control regime, the Local Government (Planning and Development) Act, 1963, against a wide-ranging challenge to its provisions on property rights grounds. He invoked the procedural rights afforded to owners under various provisions of the Act in support of his conclusions. In particular, Kenny J held that planning authorities were bound under the Act to consider objections in relation to the boundaries of obsolete areas (which were designated areas that could be compulsorily acquired for redevelopment), and determined that 'any objector is entitled to require that he should be given an opportunity to state his case before a person appointed by the planning authority'.[75]

The constitutional significance of procedural guarantees, in particular a right to be heard, also arose in dramatic circumstances in relation to the Irish legislature's response to chronic instability in the banking sector that resulted from a collapse of the Irish property market. *Dellway Investments v National Asset Management Agency*[76] concerned the exercise of powers conferred on the National Asset Management Agency (NAMA) by the National Asset Management Agency Act, 2009, which aimed to facilitate the restructuring of bank debt. The aim of the scheme was to transfer loans of systemic significance (generally associated with development land) to a state

[74] For discussion of these reasons for judicial deference to expropriation decisions, see NS Garnett 'The neglected political economy of eminent domain' (2006) 105 *Mich L Rev* 101–150; JE Krier & C Serkin 'Public ruses' (2004) *Mich St L Rev* 859–875 864–865; LE Blais 'The public use clause and heightened rational basis review' (2016) 48 *Conn L Rev* 1497–1515.

[75] (1975) 109 ILTR 69 89, hereafter *Central Dublin Development Association*.

[76] [2011] 4 IR 1, [2011] IESC 14.

body, which would work out those loans in an orderly fashion.[77] The hope was that this would remove uncertainty surrounding development loans and thereby restore confidence in the Irish banking sector. Two key issues arose in *Dellway* in relation to the compatibility of this statutory regime with the Constitution's protection of property rights. First, the appellants argued that they had an entitlement to be heard in advance of the acquisition of their loans by NAMA, based on the significant impact that such acquisition would have on their property rights. Second, the appellants argued that the Act was an unjust attack on their property rights, insofar as the breadth of its definition of eligible assets and the vagueness of the criteria for the exercise of the Agency's power of acquisition impeded challenges to acquisition decisions via judicial review.

The Supreme Court decided that the potential adverse impact of the acquisition of the appellants' bank loans by NAMA required that they be afforded fair procedures, including a right to be heard, in advance of the acquisition. The court identified a real risk of adverse effects on property rights, including the loss of the right to deal freely with a commercial property portfolio and the loss of the equity of redemption *qua* mortgagor. Accordingly, the court held that the appellant had a right to be heard, notwithstanding the urgent nature of the economic crisis that the 2009 Act was designed to address.[78] Furthermore, the court upheld the constitutionality of the Act as a proportionate interference with property rights.[79] Notably, Murray CJ stated that the procedural rights of affected property owners that the court held were constitutionally required to be observed prevented in part the possibility of any unjust attack on property rights. He pointed to the fact

[77] The power to prescribe classes of bank assets susceptible to acquisition was conferred on the Minister for Finance by s 69 of the 2009 Act and was exercised by the Minister through the National Asset Management Agency (Designation of Eligible Bank Assets) Regulations, 2009. NAMA in turn is given the power to acquire an eligible bank asset of a participating institution under s 84(1) of the 2009 Act.

[78] At para 88, Fennelly J stated: 'If a decision made concerning me or my property is liable to affect my interests in a material way, it is fair and reasonable that I should be allowed to put forward reasons why it should not be made or that it should take a particular form. It would be unjust to exclude me from being heard.' However, in the subsequent decision of the High Court in *NAMA v McMahon* [2014] IEHC 71 paras 45–46, the High Court emphasised that the agency was only required to adhere to fair procedures where property rights could be adversely affected, and accordingly it recognised that in some circumstances, the balance of rights would augur in favour of the appointment of a receiver to property without notice to the adversely affected owner. In reaching this conclusion, the court emphasised the possibility of judicial review of NAMA's decisions, in addition to the normal private law remedies available in relation to mortgages.

[79] [2011] IESC 13, [2011] 4 IR 1.

that the appellant was entitled to make representations to NAMA, which it had to consider. Furthermore, the appellant could mount a judicial review challenge against NAMA's acquisition decision. The fact that an owner was entitled to such fair procedures prior to a transfer of loans was held in turn to weigh in favour of the constitutionality of the statutory power of compulsory acquisition from a property rights perspective.

In reviewing particular expropriation decisions, the Irish courts apply a heightened standard of review, because of the serious impact of expropriation on property rights.[80] However, notwithstanding this standard of review, Irish courts tend to defer substantially to the legislative and/or administrative determination of the public interest in expropriation, and to afford property rights only marginal practical significance where they are advanced as a substantive, standalone ground for impugning an expropriation decision.[81] While they will interpret the scope of statutory expropriation powers narrowly,[82] they are considerably less willing to engage in searching review of the merits or proportionality of particular expropriation decisions. The courts generally accept broad purposes for expropriations, such as redevelopment or regeneration, and hold that the means adopted to pursue such ends (for instance public or private development) are primarily a matter for the acquiring authority, with which they are reluctant to interfere.[83] They regard the observance of appropriate fair procedures as an important factor weighing in favour of the constitutionality of a particular expropriation decision. For example, in *Egan v An Bord Pleanála*, the High Court emphasised the advance notice afforded to an owner of a potential compulsory acquisition of his derelict property, and the opportunities he had to make submissions concerning the proposed acquisition and/or take steps to improve the property to obviate the need for acquisition, in upholding its constitutionality.[84]

---

[80] See *Clinton v An Bord Pleanála* [2007] IESC 19, [2007] 4 IR 701; *Rafferty v Minister for Agriculture* [2014] IESC 61.

[81] For discussion of this trend, see R Walsh 'Reviewing expropriations: Looking beyond constitutional property clauses' in B Hoops et al (eds) *Rethinking expropriation law I: Public interest in expropriation* (2015) 125–152; R Walsh '"The principles of social justice" and the compulsory acquisition of private property for redevelopment in Ireland and the United States' (2010) 32 *Dublin ULJ* 1–23.

[82] *Rafferty v Minister for Agriculture* [2014] IESC 61.

[83] See *Crosbie v Custom House Docks Development Authority* [1996] 2 IR 531; *Clinton v An Bord Pleanála* [2007] IESC 19, [2007] 4 IR 701. For further analysis of this trend, see R Walsh '"The principles of social justice" and the compulsory acquisition of private property for redevelopment in Ireland and the United States' (2010) 32 *Dublin ULJ* 1–23.

[84] *Egan v An Bord Pleanála* [2011] IEHC 44.

In South African law, courts generally adopt a deferential approach to the question of whether an expropriation is justifiable in terms of the legislative and constitutional requirements.[85] The courts' general view in this regard is summed up best by the Supreme Court of Appeal's decision in *Erf 16 Bryntirion v Minister of Public Works*. Delivering judgment on whether the expropriation of property to upgrade the security of the presidential estate was valid on substantive grounds, the court stated that '[i]t is for the expropriating authority to decide how best to achieve its purposes. The evaluation of whether an expropriation is expedient or necessary lies with the expropriating authority.'[86] In this decision the Supreme Court of Appeal did not regard the availability of less intrusive alternative means of realising the ultimate purpose of the expropriation as a valid objection against an expropriation.[87] In adopting a rationality type review of expropriation decisions, the non-acceptance of the less intrusive means argument is indicative of South African courts' deference towards the administrators' decision to expropriate property.[88]

The High Court and Supreme Court of Appeal's decisions in *Erf 16 Bryntirion* show a deferential judicial approach to the decision to expropriate property in the public interest, with the courts pointing to procedural safeguards for owners at the administrative level as supporting such an approach. As shown above, the courts considered whether the owner's right to participate, judged within the administrative participatory framework, was respected during the expropriation process. The fact that the courts were satisfied that the owner was afforded the right to be heard in a matter that directly affected his rights may explain in part why it adopted a deferential approach towards the ultimate decision to expropriate, on the basis that a proper administrative procedure was understood by the court potentially to

---

[85] See for instance *Fourie v Minister van Lande* 1970 (4) SA 165 (O), a pre-constitutional decision, where the court adopted a deferential approach towards the decision of the administrator to expropriate property for a public purpose. This deferential tendency has continued in the constitutional dispensation. See further BV Slade *The justification of expropriation for economic development* (unpublished LLD dissertation, Stellenbosch University, 2012) chs 2 & 4.

[86] *Erf 16 Bryntirion (Pty) Ltd v Minister of Public Works* [2011] ZASCA 246, 1 December 2011 para 16.

[87] This was also the position adopted by the High Court (*Erf 16 Bryntirion (Pty) Ltd v Minister of Public Works* [2010] ZAGPPHC 154 (12 October 2010)). See further BV Slade 'The less invasive means argument in expropriation law' 2013 *TSAR* 199–216.

[88] See BV Slade 'The less invasive means argument in expropriation law' 2013 *TSAR* 199–216.

strengthen the validity of expropriation decisions.[89] The inclusion of a very detailed expropriation procedure in the new Expropriation Bill seems to support the conclusion that the adoption of a procedurally fair process, which emphasises an owner's right to be heard, may justify the continuation of a deferential approach on the side of the courts towards the ultimate decision to expropriate property for public purposes.[90]

3 Participation rules, expropriation, and the 'modest systemic status' of property

Professor Van der Walt has, through his scholarship, eloquently and convincingly argued that property is of relatively 'modest systemic status' in a democratic society.[91] In Van der Walt's view, the protection of property rights should not be approached from the individual perspective, but from a systemic perspective.[92] In this regard, he argues that the presence of a constitutional property clause (or multiple clauses protecting various aspects of property) does not mean that the protection of individual property rights should feature 'front and centre;'[93] instead, the primary purpose of constitutional provisions dealing with property is to legitimise state action that seeks to promote constitutional goals and objectives and to prevent state action that would have unwanted systemic effects.[94]

---

[89] The traditional deferential approach of the South African courts, which was especially prevalent during apartheid, can also in part be explained on the basis of the English administrative law that forms part of South Africa's colonial history. See, in this regard, C Hoexter *Administrative law in South Africa* (2011) 13–15.

[90] It should, however, be noted that South African courts are increasingly questioning the rationality of a decision, whether administrative or executive, more strictly if that decision was made without having regard to all the relevant information. In this regard, a court may regard the adopted process to be coloured with irrationality, which can render the ultimate decision irrational and invalid. See in this regard *Democratic Alliance v President of the Republic of South Africa* 2013 (1) SA 248 (CC), especially paras 33–37, 95. In the expropriation context specifically, this argument may render the less invasive means argument more viable if the ultimate decision to expropriate was made without having regard to all the possible alternatives. On the less invasive means argument in South African generally, see AJ van der Walt *Constitutional property law* 3 ed (2011) 499–503; BV Slade 'The less invasive means argument in expropriation law' 2013 *TSAR* 199–216.

[91] AJ van der Walt *Property and constitution* (2011) 138; AJ van der Walt 'The modest systemic status of property rights' (2014) 1 *J L Prop & Soc'y* 15–106.

[92] AJ van der Walt *Property and constitution* (2011) 138.

[93] AJ van der Walt 'The modest systemic status of property rights' (2014) 1 *J L Prop & Soc'y* 15–106 103.

[94] AJ van der Walt *Property and constitution* (2011) 138–141.

In this vein, in his seminal article, 'The modest systemic status of property rights', in the *Journal of Law, Property, and Society*, Van der Walt sets out his understanding of the marginal significance of property in a legal system that aims to secure equality and dignity as core fundamental values.[95] As he puts it, '[p]rotecting property rights is a legitimate objective of the legal order, but relative to the primary norms that prescribe how we want to live in society it is a systemically modest one'.[96] He argues that '[t]he protection of property rights only features after the fact, once the primary goals of securing fundamental democratic objectives have been achieved'.[97] In that article, Van der Walt confines his argument to disputes implicating property and constitutionally entrenched rights, such as human dignity, life, and the right to freedom of expression. In those contexts, he argues that the protection of property fulfils a secondary role, only moving in 'after everyone has left, brandishing buckets and mops, cleaning up the property debris once the real work of maintaining the democratic legal system has been completed.'[98]

In substance, this approach means that the core function of constitutional property rights is to ensure that interferences with property rights are consistent with *other* (non-property) rights and values, and with other legal requirements. As Van der Walt argues, 'the protection of property rights assumes the form of ensuring that the inevitable burden that is imposed on existing property rights by the achievement of non-property constitutional goals complies with constitutional requirements and, insofar as that is possible, other statutory and common-law rules and principles'.[99] This reference to 'non-property constitutional goals' confirms that while Van der Walt confined his analysis to disputes between property and non-property *rights*, he envisaged that property could also be of 'modest systemic status' in cases of conflict between property rights and other systemically significant constitutional goals (for example, in the South African context, the constitutionally prescribed goal of land reform).

Van der Walt's approach suggests that the main purpose of property rights in such contexts is to keep legislators and administrators within

[95] AJ van der Walt 'The modest systemic status of property rights' (2014) 1 *J L Prop & Soc'y* 15–106.

[96] AJ van der Walt 'The modest systemic status of property rights' (2014) 1 *J L Prop & Soc'y* 15–106 102.

[97] AJ van der Walt 'The modest systemic status of property rights' (2014) 1 *J L Prop & Soc'y* 15–106 103.

[98] AJ van der Walt 'The modest systemic status of property rights' (2014) 1 *J L Prop & Soc'y* 15–106 105–106.

[99] AJ van der Walt 'The modest systemic status of property rights' (2014) 1 *J L Prop & Soc'y* 15–106 103.

the constitutionally prescribed limits of their powers, with those limits defined primarily by non-property rights and values. Property rights are not insignificant, but they do not necessarily or always win out, since the protection of property rights is not the central goal of the legal system. For example, Van der Walt follows Jennifer Nedelsky in arguing that it is normatively just that property should be subject to the demands of equality because of the relative lack of capacity and legitimacy that courts have for addressing distributive issues as compared to the legislative and the executive branches of government.[100] Van der Walt suggests that where the legislature has determined the appropriate scope of property relative to non-property rights, courts should generally respect that determination.

Against this theoretical backdrop, we argue that the comparative analysis in this chapter of Irish and South African property law demonstrates that Van der Walt's argument that the protection of property plays a relatively modest systemic role is also descriptively true in cases where expropriation occurs through administrative action. As the expropriation case law discussed in this chapter demonstrates, courts tend to prioritise participatory processes within the framework of procedural fairness over the question of whether the right to secure possession of property should be protected. In substance, courts are concerned to protect an owner's right to fair procedures in rights-restrictive decision-making processes, rather than to a 'right to keep' property. This marginality of property reflects the fact that expropriation powers are an important tool for realising public goals as determined by the legislature and the executive. Security of possession is necessarily and systemically limited by expropriation, which is in turn controlled through process constraints.

In such circumstances, property has, as contemplated by Van der Walt, a limited role. It is largely concerned with 'tidying up', through policing the expropriation process and weeding out expropriation decisions that do not reflect other constitutional values or non-property rights. The comparative analysis in this chapter demonstrates that the presence within a constitution of guarantees for property rights may influence the nature and strength of the process constraints that courts impose upon the legislature and executive.

[100] AJ van der Walt 'The modest systemic status of property rights' (2014) 1 *J L Prop & Soc'y* 15–106 95 says that '[t]o the extent that these political issues may not be removed from political deliberation (and state regulation), property cannot be allowed to function as a trump – its protection must always be subject to consideration of the justice of its distributive effects'. Van der Walt was discussing Nedelsky's arguments in J Nedelsky 'Should property be constitutionalized? A relational and comparative approach' in GE van Maanen & AJ van der Walt (eds) *Property on the threshold of the 21st century* (1996) 417–432.

This means that constitutional property rights perform a rights-protective function even where a process focus is adopted by judges.[101] In a jurisdiction such as Ireland, which lacks an express standalone constitutional guarantee of fair procedures/due process in non-criminal law contexts, this represents a potentially important function of property rights.[102] In contrast, in South African law, where such standalone protections are afforded in all contexts, in particular section 33 of the Constitution and the legislation giving effect to that right, the role of constitutionally protected property rights in securing fair procedures might be fulfilled just as successfully by those distinct procedural guarantees.

However, Van der Walt's framework apparently requires more than procedural propriety to justify a restriction on property rights. He argues that in order to justifiably limit property rights, a competing democratic objective must be of greater significance than the protection of property rights, and furthermore, must reflect *constitutional* values or rights. Contextual analysis is required on the part of judges to make this determination, which in the expropriation context must involve some consideration of the *substantive* legitimacy of expropriations, rather than merely their procedural regularity. Accordingly, from Van der Walt's perspective, a general stance of total deference towards the substantive merits of expropriations involves an inappropriate abdication of courts' constitutional responsibilities. While the primacy of participation rules in expropriation law appropriately reflects property's 'modest systemic status' where expropriation is employed to secure important democratic objectives, space must remain for judges to supervise administrative compliance with that latter requirement. Assessed against this standard, the approach of both the Irish and South African courts in reviewing the constitutionality of expropriation decisions (as distinct from expropriation powers) is overly deferential to administrative

---

[101] For examples of academic arguments supporting a process-focused approach to the Takings Clause of the Fifth Amendment of the US Constitution, see WM Treanor 'The original understanding of the Takings Clause and the political process' (1995) 95 *Colum L Rev* 782–887 872; P Boudreaux 'Eminent domain, property rights, and the solution of representation reinforcement' (2005) 83 *Denv L Rev* 1–55.

[102] While the Irish Constitution expressly guarantees the right to a fair criminal trial (article 38), it makes no specific provision in respect of civil procedure. The Supreme Court debated whether the right to fair procedures only arises in the context of breaches of constitutional rights in *Dellway v National Asset Management Agency* [2011] 4 IR 1, without reaching a clear or definitive conclusion: for discussion, see D Kenny 'Fair procedures in Irish administrative law: Towards a constitutional duty to act fairly in *Dellway Investments v NAMA*' (2011) 34 *Dublin ULJ* 47–73; A O'Neill 'Fair procedures: An inviolable constitutional requirement?' (2011) 33 *Dublin ULJ* 319–338.

assessments of the merits of, and need for, such decisions in particular cases. Very limited scrutiny of the merits of expropriation decisions with reference to constitutional values or rights is undertaken, with judges apparently reluctant to engage with the ends of expropriations, or their impact on adversely affected constitutional rights (including property rights).

4 Conclusions

Overall, the comparative analysis of Irish and South African law in this chapter suggests that participation rules play a significant role in justifying a deferential judicial approach to reviewing the constitutionality of expropriation decisions and statutory powers of expropriation. In turn, constitutional protections for property rights influence the nature and content of such participation rules. Accordingly, property rights protections at the constitutional and administrative levels are mutually and dynamically related through the development and application of participation rules.

Participation rules may vary in their strength and significance as vehicles for property rights protection, depending on the purpose for which the property is to be expropriated or the statutory power pursuant to which it is acquired. In most cases, a right to be heard will be afforded to a potentially adversely affected owner, including a right to notice, a right to access necessary information to make meaningful representations, a right to make representations that are considered by the relevant administrative decision-maker, and a right to reasons for an expropriation decision. However, the comparative analysis in this chapter demonstrates that the administrative process through which expropriation decisions are reached and applied is not in all circumstances independent – rather, the body that makes the initial decision to expropriate may in some cases be the final *administrative* voice on the issue, subject to the possibility of a legal challenge by an aggrieved owner. Such a lack of administrative independence has been rightly criticised by the Irish courts as reflecting an outdated understanding of the requirements of fair procedures in the modern regulatory state.[103] The presence or absence of independent administrative decision-making processes should be an important consideration for courts in determining how much weight should be given to a particular administrative procedure in justifying as constitutional either an expropriation power or a particular expropriation decision.

The current trend among judges and academics in many jurisdictions is to give fair, inclusive administrative procedure significant weight as a factor

[103] See *Reid v Industrial Development Agency* [2015] IESC 82 paras 82–84.

that contributes to the constitutional justifiability of expropriation powers and decisions. However, we need a deeper understanding of the content, role, and effectiveness of administrative participation rules in expropriation law if process is to continue to play such an important role in justifying the shift from property to liability rule protection involved in expropriation. This chapter has sought to illustrate the significance and complexity of administrative property law in the context of expropriation, in order to prompt further academic reflection on these relatively under-explored issues. Administrative law and procedure is now an important space within which property rights '….are circumscribed, defined, by the demands of living in a democratic society.'[104] Since courts weigh the procedural fairness of expropriation powers and decisions in the balance in assessing the constitutionality of such powers or decisions, the legitimacy and inclusivity of those procedures is of crucial significance to the constitutional justification of expropriation as a public power. This takes property scholars into complex and contentious public law territory concerning the legitimacy of administrative action and discretion that merits further consideration by property scholars,[105] as well as raising important questions concerning the real-world implementation and impact of participatory procedures.[106] This chapter has not tackled these difficult questions, but rather has merely sought to highlight their significance.

---

[104] AJ van der Walt 'The modest systemic status of property rights' (2014) 1 *J L Prop & Soc'y* 15–106 102.

[105] For detailed exploration of this theme in the context of property law, see E Scotford & R Walsh 'The symbiosis of property and English environmental law: Property rights in a public law context' (2013) 76 *Mod L Rev* 1010–1045, especially 1040–1044. See also KC Davis *Discretionary justice: A preliminary inquiry* (1971); J Mashaw *Bureaucratic justice: Managing social security disability claims* (1983); P Craig 'Theories and values in public law: A response' in P Craig & R Rawlings (eds) *Law and administration in Europe: Essays in honour of Carol Harlow* (2003); M Adler 'Understanding and analysing administrative justice' in M Adler (ed) *Administrative justice in context* (2010); T Prosser 'Regulation and legitimacy' in J Jowell & D Oliver (eds) *The changing constitution* (2011).

[106] On this issue, see R Walsh 'The evolving relationship between property and participation in English planning law' in N Hopkins (ed) *Modern studies in property law: Volume* 7 (2013) 263–290 285-287. For perspectives on the problems of ensuring meaningful participation in regulatory regimes, see also SR Arnstein 'A ladder of citizen participation' (1969) 35 *J Am Inst Planners* 216–224; C Allen *Housing market renewal and social class* (2008); C Allen & L Crookes 'Fables of the reconstruction: A phenomenology of "place shaping" in the North of England' (2009) 80 *Town Planning Review* 455–480; B Nevin 'Housing market renewal in Liverpool: Locating the gentrification debate in history, context and evidence' (2010) 25 *Housing Studies* 715–733; J Rossi 'Participation run amok: The costs of mass participation for deliberative agency decision-making' (1997) 92 *Nw U L Rev* 173–249.

What is clear from the analysis in this chapter is that judicial supervision of process is required, as well as a limited power to review the substantive merits of particular expropriation decisions and powers in order to ensure that the power of expropriation is in fact employed to secure democratic objectives that accord with constitutional values. While property's 'modest systemic status' suggests that judges should not adopt an invasive approach in exercising this power of supervision, but rather should respect the competence and legitimacy of the legislature and the executive, particularly on distributive matters, they have an important role to play in reminding those branches of government about any direction that a constitution may provide concerning the values and objectives that should be realised through the exercise of coercive state powers. Against that backdrop, a process focus is likely to be an appropriate and legitimate approach for judges to take in reviewing expropriation powers and decisions in the vast majority of cases. However, it cannot be relied upon absolutely as a means of ensuring that the administrative sphere's control of property rights coheres with constitutional rights and values. To return to Professor Van der Walt's framework, property may be of 'modest systemic status' in expropriation, but it is not irrelevant, and should not be treated as such by judges charged with upholding the complex balance of rights and values sought to be captured in constitutional property clauses such as those in the Irish and South African Constitutions.

Chapter 3

Race and property

*Gregory S. Alexander**

1 Introduction

Georgetown University is an internationally distinguished university with a sizeable capital endowment.[1] It also used to own African slaves. The university, founded in 1789 by Jesuit priest John Carroll,[2] owned slaves from its beginning. The Jesuits first received them as gifts in 1717, and they used them to work on the several farms and plantations that the Jesuits owned throughout Maryland. In 1838, Thomas Mulledy, SJ, sold 272 enslaved men, women, and children belonging to the Jesuits to two individuals in Louisiana. The Jesuits' plantations had become unprofitable, and burdened with debt, the Jesuits sold the slaves for a sizeable profit.[3] Even after the mass sale

* A Robert Noll Professor of Law, Cornell University, Ithaca, NY, USA. I am greatly indebted to Professors Bernadette Atuahene and Joseph Singer for very helpful comments on an early draft of this paper. This essay is a shortened version of a chapter from my forthcoming book *Ownership and obligations: The human flourishing theory of property*, to be published by Oxford University Press. Some aspects of this essay are more fully explained and worked out in other chapters of that book. In the interest of keeping this essay within manageable length, I have not repeated all the arguments in support of some of the premises stated here. This essay is dedicated to the memory of André. Even before I first met him at a conference in Maastricht, his work both inspired and challenged me. His influence on my writing and on me personally continued as our relationship deepened into a friendship that I shall always cherish.

[1] As of 2016, Georgetown's capital endowment was $1 484 billion. See https://en.wikipedia.org/wiki/Georgetown_University.

[2] *History of Georgetown* https://www.georgetown.edu/about/history.

[3] M Quallen 'Slavery inextricably tied to Georgetown's growth' *The Hoya*, 23 October 2015.

of slaves, Georgetown continued to use hired slaves for labor. Slavery was not abolished in Maryland until 1864, and the last records of Jesuit-owned slaves were an 1867 census of emancipated Maryland slaves.[4]

On 1 September 2016, Georgetown University formally announced plans to atone for its past as a slave-owning institution and participant in the slave trade, the profits from which probably saved it from ruin.[5] The plans include the creation of an Institute on the Study of Slavery and Its Legacies, commissioning a memorial to honor the 272 slaves sold, and renaming two campus buildings from the names of two university officials involved in the slave sale to the names of one of the slaves shipped off to Louisiana and a woman who founded a school for black girls in Washington, DC. The university will also offer to descendants of all the slaves whose labor benefitted the university an admissions preference similar to that offered to children and grandchildren of alumni. Historians who have studied slavery and universities state that they are unaware of any other universities whose pasts have been tied to slave ownership that have offered admissions preference to the descendants of slaves.[6]

Reactions to the Georgetown plans have been mixed. Some critics have argued that the university has not gone far enough to atone for its slave-owning and trading past. Some thought that the university should offer scholarships to descendants.[7] One critic calculated that the $110 000 that the university received in 1838 for the sale of its slave is worth roughly $3.3 million in today's dollars. 'Using that purchase as a baseline, at least $50 billion would be owed to the descendants of the 12 000 to 15 000 enslaved people owned by the university's Jesuit priests,' the critic argued.[8] She suggested that a more genuine step toward atonement would be establishment of a $1,5 billion endowment for guaranteed admission regardless of income together with full scholarships, including housing and monthly stipends, in perpetuity to the descendants of enslaved people who labored for Georgetown. In

[4] http://slavery.georgetown.edu/timeline.

[5] R Swarns 'Georgetown University plans steps to atone for slave past' *NY Times*, 1 September 2016, available at https://www.nytimes.com/2016/09/02/us/slaves-georgetown-university.html.

[6] R Swarns 'Georgetown University plans steps to atone for slave past' *NY Times*, 1 September 2016, available at https://www.nytimes.com/2016/09/02/us/slaves-georgetown-university.html.

[7] R Swarns 'Georgetown University plans steps to atone for slave past' *NY Times*, 1 September 2016, available at https://www.nytimes.com/2016/09/02/us/slaves-georgetown-university.html.

[8] S Master 'Georgetown University's "reparations" plan is worthless white guilt repackaged as justice', available at http://www.theroot.com/georgetown-universitys-reparations-plan-is-worthless-1790856615.

an interview with the *New York Times Magazine*, Georgetown professor Michael Eric Dyson suggested individual reparations in the form of Individual Reparations Accounts (IRA), which they would contribute to groups like the United Negro College Fund.[9]

Dyson's suggestion provides an appropriate departure point for this essay, for what I want to discuss here is what obligations, if any, property owners, both institutional and individual, morally owe to descendants of slaves. This topic is usually framed in terms of reparations, but I wish to reframe it here. I want to consider it from the perspective of human flourishing. Such an approach has several advantages over a reparations frame of reference. For one, it avoids complicated questions growing out of the demands of reciprocity that commonly accompany reparations analysis. Under the human flourishing theory the basis of owner obligations is not reciprocity but interdependence, a condition that is ontologically inherent in every person and at all times. A second advantage of the human flourishing theory is that it shifts our primary attention from resources to capabilities. Resources are certainly relevant to certain capabilities, but their role is secondary. The main concern is to provide those to whom we owe obligations with the basic abilities without which those persons cannot live what any reasonable person would consider a fulfilling life. How those persons choose to exercise the basic abilities, or whether they choose to exercise those abilities at all, is up to them. But they must have the opportunity to flourish through such capabilities.

My aim in this chapter is not to provide a comprehensive review of the developments in redress for slavery or to develop a complete theory of reparations that responds to all of the many issues that others have raised regarding reparations. Rather the goal is more modest: to conjecture how the human flourishing theory of ownership and its approach to owner obligations might influence moral considerations as to whether existing white property owners whose direct ancestors economically profited from chattel slavery morally owe obligations to present-day descendants of now-deceased slaves and, if so, on what theory. I then speculate whether even those whites whose ancestors did not directly profit from slavery or slave trading might owe moral obligations to members of the black community for the myriad injuries that resulted both from chattel slavery and the Jim Crow regime. I emphasise that I have not fully worked out all aspects of the

---

[9] See Interview by A Cox 'Michael Eric Dyson believes in individual reparations' *NY Times Magazine*, available at https://www.nytimes.com/2017/01/04/magazine/michael-eric-dyson-believes-in-individual-reparations.html?rref=collection%2Fsectioncollection%2Fmagazine&action=click&contentCollection=magazine&region=rank&module=package&version=highlights&contentPlacement=7&pgtype=sectionfront.

argument that follows. The discussion is meant to offer some possible ways of thinking and to stimulate discussion. I offer no definitive theory of which whites owe moral obligations to which members of the black community. That is a very large and complex set of issues. Nor do I offer any blueprint for a comprehensive plan of meeting one's moral obligations. The discussion here is tentative and speculative in nature. It is one way, for there certainly are others, of exploring the relationship between ownership of property and race, and looking beyond, between property, race, and citizenship, in modern American society through the lens of a human flourishing theory.

2 What obligations do institutions owe to African-Americans? The case of Georgetown University

Georgetown University is a large and wealthy institution.[10] It is also a member of multiple communities. These include the Roman Catholic Church, the Society of Jesus (the 'Jesuits'), and the District of Columbia. It is furthermore a member of the African-American community. Its membership in the African-American community exists on the basis of several factors, one of which is the sheer fact that it used to own African-American slaves. That fact alone is sufficient to establish an immediate and binding relationship between the university and the African-American community. Whether or not any of the former Georgetown slaves left descendants surviving today (and they did), Georgetown's ownership of black slaves alone connects it with the black community in ways that other universities and institutions whose pasts do not include ownership of black slaves or immediate profit from the slave trade are not so connected. To be sure, the forced nature of the relationship makes it different from paradigmatic consensual relationships. The fact that the connection was not mutually consensual, however, does not bar the creation of a relationship that is characterised by strongly emotive ties and profound memories that have shaped both sides' lives, and have created conditions of ongoing interdependency. The existence of surviving descendants of those slaves only deepens those communitarian conditions further. Less directly but still relevant, Georgetown is tied to the black community by virtue of its black students, faculty, administrators, alumni, and supporters. To be sure, Georgetown historically has been a white institution, and it remains predominantly white. Nevertheless, today its ties to the African-American community are very real. Indeed, particularly because it would have failed had it not been for its ownership of slaves, Georgetown has a relationship

[10] Georgetown's enrolment is 4 793. See https://www.georgetown.edu/about/key-facts.

with the black community that, while not unique, is very special and is not shared by most American universities or other institutions.

From its inception, the university has been dependent upon African-Americans. The university's status as a slave owner can be traced to that of the Jesuits, who first landed in Maryland in 1634.[11] The Jesuits received land grants in Maryland, and they managed farms first using indentured servants, then slaves. The first documentation of Jesuit slave ownership in Maryland dates to a 1717 deed of gift from William Hunter.[12] Pope Clement XIV suppressed the Jesuits in 1773. The Jesuits' land and slaves were incorporated in 1792 into the corporation of the Roman Catholic Clergy, which managed them. The Society of Jesus was not officially restored until 1814.[13] John Carroll, the first Catholic bishop in the United States, founded Georgetown University in 1789.

Slave ownership came early to the fledging university. One of its first directors, Rev John Ashton, was a slave-owner whose slaves sued him for their freedom. Similarly, one of the early Georgetown College presidents, Rev Francis Neale, SJ, owned slaves who sued for their freedom.[14] Georgetown used its slaves for the same purpose as other slave owners did, ie, labour. Records from Georgetown College in the late 18th century indicate that the college's slaves worked as artisans, cooks, and waitresses. The university's Working Group on Slavery, Memory, and Reconciliation reports that 'there was a substantial African-American presence at the school in its early years'.[15] There was also a substantial African-American presence in the Georgetown neighborhood. In 1800, the neighborhood of Georgetown had a population of some 5 100, of whom over 1 400 were slaves and over 270 were freed blacks. Slavery and the slave trade were a reality within Georgetown well into the 19th century.[16]

In 1838, Thomas Mulledy, SJ, then the president of Georgetown College, sold 272 enslaved men, women, and children owned by the Maryland Province of the Society of Jesus to Henry Johnson and Jesse Batey, both of

---

[11] Georgetown University Working Group on Slavery, Memory, and Reconciliation, Historical Timeline 'The African-American Presence at Georgetown', available at http://slavery.georgetown.edu/timeline.

[12] 'First documentation of Jesuit Ownership of Slaves in Maryland', available at http://slavery.georgetown.edu/timeline.

[13] The Jesuit Plantation Complex in Maryland, http://slavery.georgetown.edu/timeline.

[14] W Thomas III 'The Timing of *Queen v Hepburn:* An exploration of African American networks in the early republic' *O Say Can You See: Early Washington, DC, Law & Family*, August 2015, available at http://earlywashingtondc.org/stories/queen_v_hepburn.

[15] ''The African-American presence at Georgetown', available at http://slavery.georgetown.edu/timeline.

[16] K Menzie Lesko, V Babb & C Gibbs *Black Georgetown remembered* (1991).

Louisiana.[17] The actual event was particularly vicious. Mulledy, fearful of slaves trying to escape, arrived secretly on the Jesuits' Maryland plantation, accompanied by sheriffs. Families were split apart, and the slaves were sent to Louisiana, where they lived out their lives. Mulledy used the substantial proceeds for building projects, including a new library, a museum, and improvements, and to increase the number of students who boarded at the college. The overall effect was not only to clear Georgetown's debts but to begin its transformation into the urban, elite center of higher education that it is today.[18]

Georgetown University's membership in the black community has been extraordinarily important to its ability to flourish as an institution. Indeed, Georgetown literally owes its existence to its ties to the black community. Were it not for the facts that Georgetown gratuitously received slaves and later sold them for a substantial profit, it is likely that the young university in 1838 would not have survived financially. In this most immediate way, the African-American community historically has contributed, albeit entirely without its consent, to Georgetown's capability to survive and to flourish. Even beyond this obvious contribution to the university's capability to flourish, the African-American community has continued to contribute to the university in various ways, large and small, that have enabled Georgetown's ability to flourish and to become the elite institution that it is today. Among the more obvious contributions, its faculty, staff, and student body include African Americans who come from extraordinarily diverse backgrounds, measured geographically, socio-economically, politically, and in terms of aspirations. They add a richness to the university community that enhances both the university's reputation and its educational mission.

Georgetown University and the black community are interdependent and have been so at least since the Maryland Jesuits first received slaves in 1717. The substance of the interdependency and the capabilities that each has enabled the other to develop have changed over time as the relationship between the university and the black community has changed. Georgetown broke the relationship that had existed with the ancestors of present-day descendants of its slaves when it sold those slaves in 1838. To restore a relationship with these descendants – one that rested on an entirely different footing from the one it had with its slaves – Georgetown has now taken steps to create scholarships, and other benefits, for the present-day descendants of

---

[17] 'The sale', available at http://slavery.georgetown.edu/timeline.

[18] M Quallen 'Slavery inextricably tied to Georgetown's growth' *The Hoya*, 23 October 2015, available at http://www.thehoya.com/quallen-slavery-inextricably-tied-to-georgetowns-growth.

Georgetown slaves. In doing so, it creates a relationship of interdependency between itself and members of the black community. It is that fact and the university's moral obligation to itself that gives rise to its obligation to support the community that has enabled it to flourish.

It would be a mistake to think of these obligations in terms of reparations, although that is the common way of framing the discussion about what, if anything, present property owners owe to descendants of now-deceased slaves. The reason why the obligation that property owners owe to members of the African-American community under the human flourishing theory should not be conceived in terms of reparations is that reparations are a matter of remedying past harms. Alfred Brophy explains reparations as 'programs that are justified on the basis of past harms and that are designed to assess and correct that harm and/or improve the lives of victims into the future'.[19] As Brophy's explanation makes clear, reparations are primarily backward-looking and aimed at giving redress to past victims or their modern day representatives.

Commentators discussing redress to descendants of slaves often claim or assume that the form of justice that is required in cases such as that of Georgetown is corrective or restorative justice.[20] Corrective justice obviously is a possible basis for redress, and it is particularly appropriate when redress takes the form of some specific restitutionary remedy, such as return of wrongfully appropriated property. The case of Georgetown is not such a case, however. What is required here is not corrective justice but a form of social justice that is based on the facts of belonging and inevitable interdependency among members of communities, the form of social justice that I have been tracing so far.

Bernadette Atuahene has developed the concept of 'dignity restoration.' By that term, she means 'material compensation to dispossessed populations through processes that affirm their humanity and establish their agency'.[21] This is very close to what I am discussing here. I take Atuahene's compensatory measures to be non-restitutionary. It aims at something other than, something more than correcting an economic injury. Atuahene discusses the concept in the context of South Africa, where the government has, as she puts it, 'tried to move from reparations to the larger more robust

[19] A Brophy *Reparations pro and con* (2006) 9.

[20] See eg E Posner & A Vermeule 'Reparations for slavery and other historical injustices' (2003) 103 *Colum L Rev* 689–747 691.

[21] B Atuahene 'Dignity takings and dignity restoration: Creating a new theoretical framework for understanding involuntary property loss and the remedies required' (2016) 41 *Law Soc Inq* 796–1115.

task of dignity restoration'.[22] She emphasises how dignity restoration looks beyond outcomes by emphasising process. Restoration can take many forms, occur over an extended length of time, and involve non-state as well as state actors. It provides not only resources but opportunities. Because it emphasises process, restoration ideally involves claimants in the process, giving them a voice in how restoration proceeds. This process complements the interdependent character of the relationship among the parties. This underscores the difference between dignity restoration and restitution and in that respect is very similar to the sorts of actions that fit best under the human flourishing theory.

Under the human flourishing theory, the basis for the moral obligation is not reciprocity, at least not reciprocity alone. Rather, it lies in the fact of interdependence between the individual and the community to which she belongs. To be sure, there is a sense in which interdependence involves reciprocity. But the obligation is not a matter of *quid pro quo*. The obligation is more deeply rooted than that. It is ontological, not contractual. The obligation to contribute is an aspect of the obligation to belong and the obligations that we owe to ourselves. Our obligations to ourselves give us an obligation to support the communities and the kind of society that support the culture from which we receive the capabilities necessary for us to flourish. Interdependence, not reciprocity, then, is the key to the obligation to make contributions.

This is not to say that slavery and other injuries resulting from various forms of racism practised over many years are irrelevant under the human flourishing theory. That is not and cannot be the case. It is slavery and other forms of racism that binds Georgetown so closely to the African American community. Those injuries connect Georgetown with the black community in a way that, say, the State University of New York (SUNY) at Stony Brook is not. Whatever problems Stony Brook University may have as an institution with the African American community, the fact is that it was not founded on the backs of slaves. Founded in 1957, it came after both the end of chattel slavery and the Jim Crow era. It owes its existence and growth to the coffers of the state of New York and the taxpayers of the Empire State. Georgetown, by contrast, owes its existence to slaves and the slave trade system. These facts, these moral harms, are at the very basis of Georgetown's obligation to contribute to development of the capabilities necessary for members of that community to flourish.

---

[22] B Atuahene 'Dignity takings and dignity restoration: Creating a new theoretical framework for understanding involuntary property loss and the remedies required' (2016) 41 *Law Soc Inq* 796–1115 797.

What, then, are the obligations that Georgetown, as a property owner, owes to the black community? Because Georgetown's contributions should be ones that are appropriate to it, Georgetown University, as an educational institution, is best suited to enable African Americans to acquire educational capabilities. Specifically, the university is well-suited to enable other members of its community to pursue the educational goals that are increasingly important in modern American society. Those goals obviously include degrees at higher educational institutions, including Georgetown. As I indicated earlier, the university has already announced that it will offer to descendants of all the slaves whose labor benefitted the university an admissions preference similar to that offered to children and grandchildren of alumni.

That seems like a good start, but there is no reason to stop there. Some of the descendants of Georgetown slaves criticised the university for failing to take further steps. One critic wrote, 'If Georgetown is authentically interested in reconciliation and atonement for its history, it should appropriate its $1,5 billion endowment to offer guaranteed admission (or a path to admission) regardless of income or felony status, and full scholarships – including housing, computers and books, and monthly stipends – in perpetuity to the descendants of enslaved people whose labor and bodies built the university.'[23] It might be appropriate for the university, as an educational institution, to offer tutoring to black high school students, particularly in the District of Columbia, who hope to attend college. Moreover, some (or perhaps many) of the African American students who are admitted to Georgetown, with or without the benefit of the admissions preference, may not be able bear the freight of the Georgetown tuition plus room and board expenses. Georgetown is an expensive school. A further and important step that the university might take is offering scholarships to black students, especially those who are descendants of Georgetown slaves (difficult as they may be to identify and locate), who attend Georgetown. This would be a direct and meaningful way of contributing to an important capability.

There is no reason why the contributions that Georgetown makes have to be confined to university-level education. Georgetown is an urban school in a city with a large black population, and one form of contribution to education might be through assistance, in cash, kind, or both, to public schools in predominantly black neighborhoods in the District of Columbia. The university might make its students, undergraduate, graduate, or both, available, gratis, as tutors to students in inner-city neighborhood schools at

---

[23] S Master 'Georgetown University's "reparations" plan is worthless white guilt repackaged as justice' *The Root* 5 September 2016, available at http://www.theroot.com/georgetown-university-s-reparations-plan-is-worthless-1790856615.

middle-school or high-school level. It could offer incentives to its students to participate in such a tutoring program through a variety of mechanisms, ranging from course credit to cash compensation.

Other means of enabling members of the African American community to acquire educational skills might be possible. I have sketched only a few obvious candidates. Georgetown perhaps best fulfills its moral obligation if its contributions pertain to the acquisition of education as a capability. To give agency to those who were dispossessed claimants, Georgetown might allow them to determine how Georgetown should fulfill its obligations to them. Giving them voice in this way advances the human flourishing goal of promoting their autonomy capability. The contributions that any property owner makes in fulfilling its moral obligation to members of its communities should only be those that are appropriate to that person or institution. Propriety here depends upon a number of considerations, one of which is expertise or specialisation that the owner may possess. This is why it makes sense to say that the contributions of Georgetown, an educational institution, should have something to do with education, rather than, say, construction of new low-cost housing.

What is important, indeed crucial, however, to fulfilling an owner's moral obligations is that the owner undertake actions that contribute concretely to enable members of the black community to acquire the capabilities without which those persons cannot hope to experience fulfilling lives. This means that such actions, although they may include strictly symbolic gestures, cannot be limited to symbols alone. Apologies, acknowledgments, plaques and other memorials are a good start, but they are only a start. For an institution that has profited from slavery and the slave trade as Georgetown University did, they are inadequate means of enabling members of the black community, to which it has so long belonged, to acquire any of the basic capabilities that are essential to their leading a fulfilling life – good health, decent education, practical reasoning skills, security, and so on. This is why the measures that Georgetown has taken were appropriate, although, as I have indicated, perhaps not completely so, to satisfy its moral obligation to its community.

Georgetown is hardly the only university to have benefitted from slave ownership or slave trading. Brown, Harvard, and Yale, to name only three,[24] all have acknowledged different ties to slavery and taken various steps to atone for these ties. In all three cases, none of the steps approaches what Georgetown has done. The University of Virginia, the College of William and

[24] H Ojalvo 'Beyond Yale: These other university buildings have ties to slavery and white supremacy', *USA Today*, 13 February 2017, available at http://college.usatoday.com/2017/02/13/yale-university-buildings-slavery-white-supremacy.

Mary, Columbia University, the University of North Carolina at Chapel Hill, and several other universities have all undertaken efforts to study their respective past involvements with the slave trade and with slavery generally.[25]

Beyond universities, other institutions have also publicly acknowledged that they or their institutional predecessors profited from slavery. For example, New York Life, the nation's third largest insurance company, disclosed that during the first half of the nineteenth century it sold policies on the lives of slaves. In fact, by 1847, such policies accounted for one-third of all the policies it had sold.[26] Company executives state that slave policies generated only about 5 percent of its total revenues during the three fiscal years in which the policies were sold. They claim that the policies were not profitable and did not drive the company's growth. Historians point out, however, that the slave policies did have an impact on the company's growth. The company had two years of revenue to invest before death claims exceeded annual premium payments.[27] In recent years New York Life has provided philanthropic support to the black community, including a $10 million endowment to the Colin Powell Center for Policy Studies at the City College of New York, sponsorship of the National Museum of African American History & Culture and other initiatives.[28]

The human flourishing theory stresses that contributions owners make should be in a form and to an extent that are appropriate to those owners. For New York Life, its contributions to those members of the African American community who represent the slaves exploited through life insurance policies might take the form of fixed annuities, immediate or deferred. The amount of each annuity should be reasonable to both parties and subject to negotiation. One possible index for the amount, of course, would be the equivalent in today's prices of the insured amount of each slave. That approach seems unduly complex and unfair, however. The insured values of individual slaves would vary greatly according to time, gender, age, health, and other factors.[29]

---

[25] 'Universities studying slavery', available at http://slavery.virginia.edu/universities-studying-slavery.

[26] R. Swarns 'Insurance Policies on Slaves: New York Life's Complicated Past' *NY Times*, 18 December 2016, available at https://www. nytimes.com/2016/12/18/us/insurance-policies-on-slaves-new-york-lifes-complicated-past.html.

[27] R. Swarns 'Insurance Policies on Slaves: New York Life's Complicated Past' *NY Times*, 18 December 2016, available at https://www. nytimes.com/2016/12/18/us/insurance-policies-on-slaves-new-york-lifes-complicated-past.html.

[28] R. Swarns 'Insurance Policies on Slaves: New York Life's Complicated Past' *NY Times*, 18 December 2016, available at https://www. nytimes.com/2016/12/18/us/insurance-policies-on-slaves-new-york-lifes-complicated-past.html.

[29] *Historical Statistics*, Table Bb215–218. Index of slave values, by age, sex, and region: 1850.

Hence, the values in today's prices of the individual policy amount would vary greatly. Whatever the index and whatever the amount, New York Life's contribution – and New York Life was not the only insurance firm whose corporate predecessor insured slaves[30] – should take some form that is relevant to its business.

Is the moral obligation confined solely to organisations which themselves, or whose predecessors, were directly tied to the slave trade? Recall that in the case of Georgetown I suggested that the basis of its moral obligation was the injury, both physical and moral, that it had inflicted on blacks. But in fact the source of that obligation is broader than that. Membership in a community involves obligations. All of us, including institutions, have special responsibilities to ourselves, and those responsibilities include an obligation to belong to communities without which we cannot flourish. It is not enough simply to belong, however, for we owe it to ourselves, if we are to develop the capabilities necessary for us to flourish, that we support those communities. This obligation to support, then, is an interpretation of the interdependence that is inherent in our condition.

Given this source of the obligation to support the communities to which we belong, there is no obvious reason why the moral obligation to contribute to the black community, however that obligation is met, must be limited just to those institutions that historically were immediately or directly tied to slavery or the slave trade. Many, perhaps most, organisations and institutions have ties to the black community. They have these ties, as property owners, by virtue of their dependence upon the black community for development of the capabilities that are necessary for their flourishing. Commercial organisations depend to varying extents upon the black community for their success. The same is true of eleemosynary organisations. The black community has a long history of supporting charitable and religious organisations in small and large ways. A 2012 report by the Kellogg Foundation found that black people are substantially more inclined to make charitable donations than their white counterparts.[31] Nearly two-thirds of African American households donate each year, contributing a total of $11 billion annually.[32] A study in the Chronicle of Philanthropy reported that blacks give 25 per cent more of

[30] Aetna, for example, has acknowledged that it, like New York Life, sold policies on the lives of slaves during the antebellum period. See 'Aetna Apologies for Slave Insurance', available at http://articles.latimes.com/2000/mar/11/business/fi-7637.

[31] 'Cultures of Giving: Energising and Expanding Philanthropy by and for Communities of Color,' *W.K. Kellogg Foundation Report* 2012.

[32] 'Cultures of Giving: Energising and Expanding Philanthropy by and for Communities of Color' *WK Kellogg Foundation Report* 2012.

their discretionary income to charity than whites do.[33] The objects of black charitable giving is not confined to churches. Groups such as the Boys and Girls Clubs of America receive a disproportionate amount of donations from blacks.

My greater concern is with commercial organisations, especially those more recently established. Consider Apple Inc. Apple was founded in 1976, and, given its recent origin, we can safely assume that it has no ties to slavery or the slave trade. Does Apple owe any moral obligations to make contributions to the black community? If the obligation were owed as reparations for historical injustices, a measure a corrective justice, Apple might plausibly be able to respond that it owes no such obligations. It was in no way responsible for slavery, nor did it in any way profit from slavery or commercial trafficking in slaves. The case for Apple's responsibility as a matter of corrective justice could be made, but it would be more attenuated and, to many people, less compelling than that of firms like Aetna.

Suppose we look at the question of Apple's moral obligation from the perspectives of its membership in the black community and flourishing. The first point to consider is Apple's membership in the black community. On what basis might Apple be considered to be a member of this community? Consent is the obvious basis. Apple might well agree that given the support African Americans have given Apple and its products over the years and given the fact that Apple purports to stand for values of great importance to people of colour – inclusivity, non-discrimination, diversity[34] – Apple might well agree that it is a member of the black community. But, as I have already argued, membership in a community is not premised on consent alone. What matters is a sharing of core values, such that, whatever other differences may exist between the two parties, they are bonded in some substantial respect and draw from that bond support that enriches their lives. Taking Apple's mission statement at face value, both Apple and the black community share a deep commitment to values that are essential to both of them and bond them together.

Apple's membership in the black community means that a relationship of interdependence exists between the two. It is that relationship that provides the foundation for Apple's obligation to contribute to the black community, a community which facilitates the development of Apple's necessary

[33] M Anft & H Lipman 'How Americans Give' in *The Chronicle of Philanthropy*, 1 May 2003, available at https://www.philanthropy.com/article/How-Americans-Give/188055.

[34] Apple's mission statement: 'The most innovative company must also be the most diverse.' See https://www.apple.com/diversity.

capabilities, so that members of that community – black Americans – may themselves flourish.

A stark contrast may perhaps help to make the point. Apple is not the Ku Klux Klan. The Klan owes no moral obligation to contribute to the black community. It is in no sense a member of that community. No relationship of dependence exists between the Klan as a property owner and the black community. There is no sharing of value, no support, mutual or otherwise, absolutely nothing connecting the two that might with any plausibility be labelled community. The Klan does not need the black community to make money. Apple does. Apple could not have flourished as it has done without the various forms of support it has received from the black community. Moreover, Apple and the black community share core values that are fundamental to the identities of both. Apple is a member; the Klan is not. Of course, the Klan is dependent on the black community for its existence in a sense. Without blacks (and other hated groups), the Klan would not exist. But, again, the Klan's connection with the property community is not property-based in the way that Georgetown's or even Apple's is. Insofar as we limit the moral obligation to persons and entities who are connected with the black communities through property relations, Apple owes moral obligations to enable flourishing; the Klan does not. In the final section of this chapter I will consider whether the limitation of the property basis for the moral obligation should be removed, in which case, the Klan would indeed owe obligations (which doubtless would remain unmet).

Apple might meet its moral obligation to the black community in different ways. Of course, it might make monetary contributions to charitable organisations that serve the needs of the black community. More creatively, it might make more concerted efforts to make good on its mission statement of inclusiveness and diversity by hiring more African American employees. Apple states that 22 percent of its current employees and 27 percent of its new recruits are "underrepresented minorities."[35] But that broad category lumps together blacks, Hispanics, Native Americans, Native Hawaiians, and other Pacific Islanders. Apple's data do not itemise the percentage or number of African Americans specifically. Within the tech industry black representation has historically been low, and Apple's commitment to diversity creates an especially good opportunity for it to meet its moral obligation to contribute to the capabilities of members of the black community by hiring and training additional black computer scientists and engineers. It might augment its efforts through programs that mentor aspiring black computer scientists and engineers while they are in college. These are only a few possibilities. There

[35] https://www.apple.com/diversity.

may be other ways in which Apple could meet its obligation to the black community.

Apple is hardly the only firm to carry this responsibility. If we think about the reasons why Apple is morally obligated to contribute to the development of the capabilities necessary for African Americans to lead flourishing lives, we will quickly realise that many other firms bear the same responsibility. Indeed, it is hard to think of a large firm that does not have this moral obligation.

The main point to stress here is that under the human flourishing theory the contributions that an institution makes are not, strictly speaking, reparations. The basis for the moral obligation to contribute is not reciprocity or any sort of *quid pro quo*. Rather, it lies in the fact of interdependence between the individual and the community to which she belongs. As I have emphasised, the obligation to contribute to members of a community grows out of the owner's membership of that community and its dependence upon that community for its own ability to flourish.

3 When do individual persons have obligations to African Americans, and what are those obligations?

My family, my direct ancestors on the Alexander side, arrived in this country from Donegal, Ireland (and before that, Kintyre, Scotland), in 1735. The three Alexander brothers (a fourth Alexander brother remained behind in Donegal) arrived in Pennsylvania and resided in Chester County, Pennsylvania, for ten years before moving to Virginia. There, they all took up residence in what is now Rockbridge County, which is located in southwestern Virginia. My direct ancestor bought land and farmed it.

I know all this about my ancestors because my brother has done extensive genealogical work on our family. When he learned that our direct ancestor, Archibald Alexander, had purchased land in Virginia and farmed it, my brother was concerned that Archibald may have owned slaves. After all, Virginia certainly recognised slavery in the mid-18th century, and landowners commonly owned slaves to farm their land. The possibility was there. My brother's research revealed that Archibald did not own slaves. He and his wife farmed the land themselves. The reasons are not entirely clear, but one possible reasons is that Archibald was not wealthy enough to own slaves. Apparently, his farm was relatively small, and he had no other source of income or wealth. He was essentially a subsistence farmer. Eventually, he sold the farm and moved, as so many others from that part of Virginia did, west to Kentucky and eventually to Missouri.

Suppose it had been otherwise. Suppose, that is, my direct ancestor, Archibald, had been a slave owner. Would this mean that I am under a moral obligation of some sort to the present-day descendants of those slaves, or, if they cannot realistically be identified and located, to the black community generally? The more important question comes if we dispense with the thought experiment that my direct ancestors owned slaves. Am I then under no obligation because there is no property nexus for such an obligation? In the thought experiment my ancestors' status as slave owners provides the nexus with property, in the same way as it did for firms like Aetna whose predecessors were engaged in slave-trading. But the facts, at least as far as I know, are otherwise. My ancestors did not own slaves, nor were they engaged in the slave-trading business. Is there, then, no property nexus for my moral obligation to members of the black community? If I am indeed under an obligation to them, is it merely by virtue of my status as a citizen, in which case the obligation is not endogenous to property ownership itself but is externally imposed by the state? That is one possible answer, but I think it is not necessary to rely on citizenship. I think there is a property nexus here. As a property system, slavery affected not only the slaves themselves, but it also affected and corrupted many other forms of property. Profits from slave trading enabled slave owners to purchase land as well as more slaves. They worked their way into the corporate system, corrupting property held by large firms such as Aetna. Even after slavery legally ended, its legacy – and very real injuries – continued in the form of Jim Crow, and in that form, the property nexus expanded. The expansion continued as segregation corrupted the property system both formally and informally. An example of this process is chronicled in the recent book by Richard Brooks and Carol Rose which details how racially restrictive covenants continued to be used, and further entrenched segregation, in Chicago,[36] even after the Supreme Court had declared them legally unenforceable.[37] This racial corruption of property has become so widespread that it is practically impossible to determine whether any single piece of property has or has not been tainted by the vestiges of slavery and Jim Crow. The reality, then, is that at least some property that I own is racially corrupted property.[38]

Past allocations and holdings of property have lasting consequences. People today, like me, who may think of themselves as innocent, are nevertheless

---

[36] R Brooks & C Rose *Saving the neighborhood: Racially restrictive covenants, law, and social norms* (2013).

[37] *Shelley v Kraemer* 338 US 1 (1948).

[38] A comparable argument could be made for Native Americans, much of whose land was taken from them in ways and on terms that were morally, if not legally, corrupt. Their status under the theory I am tentatively offering here, while not identical with that of African Americans, is similar in relevant respects. Because there are differences, however, I confine my discussion only to the case of obligations owed to African Americans.

using property that has been affected by both the conquest of Native nations and slavery and racial discrimination. The obligations that I owe to members of the black community, then, stem from my status as a property owner rather than as a citizen. They are internal to my ownership rather than external from the state.

As a property owner, then, do I owe an obligation to members of the black community?[39] In posing this question, I am not asking whether morally I owe reparations either to the descendants or to the black community. As I have stressed, the moral obligation I have in mind is one that is connected to my membership in the black community, if in fact I am such a member, and the mutual dependency that exists between me and members of that community, if indeed such a relationship of interdependency exists. The immediate question, then, is whether I am a member of the black community. At first blush it might seem strange to ask the question. I am a white person, and as far as my research has disclosed I have no black ancestors or other relatives. The question presents an opportunity to pose a much deeper question, though. What is the basis for membership in a community that is identified by race? What is it that makes a person part of a racial community?

Several observations are in order here. First, community is a concept that is both contested and protean. Its elasticity, however, does not render it meaningless. However difficult it may be to define, we experience community and being members of communities throughout our lives.

Second, communities come in various stripes, including voluntary and involuntary. I am, at least in a certain familiar sense, a member of my family whether I wish to be or not; I was born into it. On the other hand, I am a member of the community of the Cornell Law School by virtue of my choice and that of my colleagues. This distinction, between voluntary and involuntary communities, however, is less binary than it may appear. Some people do not experience themselves as being members of the group that is their family of origin. Conversely, there are members of what are customarily considered voluntary communities who testify that they experienced themselves as compelled to join their respective communities. Perhaps the best we can say in answer to the question of what makes a person a member of a community, particularly a community that is based in something other than contract alone, is that what is important is how one experiences community. Do I experience myself as a member of this community or that? It may not always be necessary that the community accepts me as one of its own. Not

---

[39] I am only discussing the obligations that white property owners may owe. As to the homeless and those who live in desperate poverty such that effectively they own no property, I would make no such claim.

all communities are based on agreement, and, again, it matters what the purpose is of asking about membership in a community. Agreement is more important for some purposes than for others. But the really relevant question is whether I experience myself as a member of the community in question.

Third, and related to the point just made, community has different meanings when used in different contexts. Its colloquial meaning – the meaning it has in ordinary conversation when I say I am a member of the Cornell community or the community where I live – may not be the same when I use the term in a different context and for a different purpose. The suggestion that a white person or a predominately white institution may be a member of the black community may give pause. Other terms might seem more suitable. Better, perhaps, to say that I am an ally or a friend of the black community. Despite these concerns, I wish to use the language of community for a specific reason. The language of community is a conceptual/normative language in which to talk about who is within my circle, rather than always being the lay person's common meaning of community. What I am discussing in this context is not a colloquial expression or even a sociological term but a special signification of particular types of relationships that are based on interdependency such that the persons within those relationships nurture each other's essential capabilities, and so enable each other's flourishing.

Finally, it is important that we not get caught up in binary oppositions in all this. We need to remember what is at stake in asking whether I, or an institution such as Georgetown University, is a member of the black community. In the discussion so far what has been at stake is the determination of whether I owe moral obligations to members of the black community. But perhaps I owe these persons moral obligations of support whether or not I am a member of the black community. For there may still be a relationship of interdependency of such a kind that we nurture each other's essential capabilities and enable each other's flourishing. That is the real question in the human flourishing calculus, i.e., whether a special relationship exists between me and the black community, special in the sense that we each contributes to each other in ways that enable the development of those capabilities that are essential for us to flourish.

Is it possible, then, that I, a white person, may be a member of the black community? Without essentialising the concept of race, it may be useful – and I am offering this distinction tentatively – to distinguish between being a member of the black community, in the particular sense in which I am using the term, and being a member of the black race. For although I am not a member of the black race (at least let us so stipulate, simply to put aside the very complex questions about the nature of race and whether race even exists), I may indeed be a member of the black community. Here membership in a racial community becomes a matter of whether a relationship of interdependency exists between me and the black community, a relationship in which members of that community and I contribute to one another's necessary capabilities.

There is both a positive, or empirical, and a normative dimension to this matter. Positively, have I used or do I use my resources, resources that I own, to contribute in significant ways to the security, autonomy, health, or sociability, for example, of members of the black community? Or do members of the black community use my assets or rely on them in some way that materially contributes to the development of their necessary capabilities? Do I use my resources to contribute to their education, or facilitate development of their ability to engage in practical reasoning? Do members of the black community contribute to the development of those capabilities that are necessary for my flourishing? Do they enable my sociability? Do they educate me, and so on? The normative dimension of this is that how I view myself and how I view the kind of person I strive to become are matters that are intimately involved with investigating the positive questions. The investigation deeply implicates my moral self-portrait and the moral sketch I am drawing of myself. Seeing oneself as a member of a racial community other than one's own (or what is conventionally taken to be one's race) is not a question of having black or Asian friends, although that certainly seems like an obviously good idea for such a person. Nor is it a question of atonement for past and present injustices committed against members of that community, liberal white guilt, as it were. Rather, the perception of oneself as a member of that community grows out of living the experience of being part of rather than separate from. It is a question of having moved beyond otherness and been able to experience connectedness. Community is based on sharing of values, interests, or experiences. No white person can claim to share the racial experiences that a black person has gone through, but that difference, profound as it is, does not itself prohibit sharing in other important respects between a white person and members of the black community. Deep commitments to justice, demands that all human beings be treated with respect and dignity, hope that violence between members of different races will end – all of these values and aspirations are ones that can be and are shared between many black and white persons. These shared values and commitments provide adequate grounds for establishing a sense of community between white and black persons.

Supposing, then, that white people can be members of the black community, what are the implications for the moral obligations that a white property owner owes to members of the black community? If I consider myself a member of the black community, do I owe moral obligations to that community of the sort that I have described up to this point? More precisely, what are the contours of those obligations?

If I experience myself as a member of the black community, then I think I do morally owe obligations to my fellow community members. Membership in that community, like any community, means that its members and I are interdependent upon each other for developing the capabilities that enable us to live flourishing lives.

I am particularly dependent upon the black community for fostering in me sociability. I grew up in an all-white ethnic neighborhood on the North Side of Chicago. I literally did not know a black person until I entered college, and even then, my contact with members of other races was very limited. My race-consciousness and contact with members of the black community were greatly increased in law school and much more so when I took my first tenure-track teaching position, in Georgia. Athens, Georgia, in those days (circa 1975–76), was still very much in the midst of the social and political changes of the Civil Rights movement. Athens society was a palimpsest of the Jim Crow era. Traces of past white- and black-only public drinking fountains, for example, were still visible. The small local Catholic Church that I attended was a locus of civil rights activity and had experienced serious backlash for it. The parish was multi-racial and had been active in the civil rights movement in the town, leading at one point to a burning Cross on its front lawn. I was active in my church, and so became acquainted with a number of African-Americans in my parish. In addition, quite of few of my students were black, and during my time at Georgia, I got to know several of them well. This continued after I moved to Ithaca, New York, and Cornell.

An important aspect of the capability that my membership has enabled me to develop is education about what it means to be white in America. In his recent book *Between the world and me*,[40] Ta-Nehisi Coates suggests that it is not his job to educate white people about racism or how to act. That seems quite right to me, but the development of education as a capability that I am discussing does not result from tutorial sessions with black friends. Rather, it results from openness, willingness, and sensitivity not only in conversations with black friends and colleagues but also in lectures, public debates, news sources, and the like.

Like many other white Americans, I once assumed that racism was confined strictly to overt acts like racial slurs and exclusions of blacks from restaurants, bars, housing, and other public places. I was entirely ignorant of less transparent but more insidious forms of racism, let alone of the inherent advantages of being white. In housing, for example, non-whites are

[40] T Coates *Between the world and me* (2015).

significantly more likely to be evicted than white renters. As the authors of a major recent empirical study state, 'One of the most striking geographic relationships we observed is the close parallel of non-white communities and eviction filings.'[41] It is no secret that people of color face discrimination in the criminal justice realm as well. In *Floyd v City of New York*,[42] for example, federal district judge Shira Scheindlin held that the New York City Police Department's application of its stop-and-frisk program discriminated against people of color. She relied in part on data finding that of police stops conducted between 2004 and 2012, about 83 percent were of blacks and Hispanics while those groups accounted for just half the population.[43] In the workplace, the famous 1991 study by the Urban Institute found that on average white testers were significantly favored over black testers.[44] Subtle racism operates at even more prosaic levels. Eduardo Bonilla-Silva in his widely-discussed book *Racism without Racists*[45] analyses how white people sometimes deploy various rhetorical moves about colour-blindness to mask racist attitudes. For example, using 'I am not a racist' or 'Some of my best friends are black' as discursive buffers to statements that could be taken as racist. Bonilla-Silva also gives examples of common rhetoric that 'otherises' blacks softly, as he puts it: 'these people,' 'those people.'[46] Then there are micro-aggressions such as whitesplaining, such as comments aimed at shutting down conversation about race ('You're being divisive'; 'There's no such thing as race – we're all human') and comments that deny the legitimacy of a black person's feelings about race ('You're being overly sensitive').

I have also learned about the enduring reality of white privilege in modern America. Most white people have a generally positive relationship with law enforcement authorities. They do not experience the everyday fear of the police that blacks, even wealthy blacks, do. White people do not have violent stereotypes associated with their race. White people can live in any neighborhood in which they choose to live and can afford to do so. Moreover, Cheryl Harris explains how the sheer fact of being white is a form of property:

---

[41] J Sims, I Aley, L Dundore, T Laemmli, S Long & R McFerren, 'Evicted in Dane County, Wisconsin: A collaborative examination of the housing landscape' University of Wisconsin Department of Urban and Regional Planning (2016), available at https://gobigread.wisc.edu/wp-content/uploads/sites/3/2015/06/EvictedInDaneCounty_final.pdf.

[42] 959 F. Supp. 2d 540 (S.D.N.Y. 2013).

[43] Ibid 959 F. Supp. 2d 540 (S.D.N.Y. 2013) at 558.

[44] M Favreault, *Discrimination and upward mobility* (Urban Institute, Washington, DC, 1991).

[45] E Bonilla-Silva *Racism without racists: Color-blind racism and the persistence of racial inequality in America* (4 ed 2014).

[46] Ibid at 105.

'The wages of whiteness are available to all whites, regardless of class position – even to those whites who are without power, money, or influence. Whiteness, the characteristic that distinguishes them from blacks, serves as compensation even to those who lack material wealth. It is the relative political advantages extended to whites, rather than actual economic gains that are crucial to white workers.'[47] All this and more I learned through fellow members of the black community.

More has been involved in this experience than education. Through my interactions with black colleagues, students, fellow parishioners, and others, I have gradually gained a greater capacity to see matters from the perspective of others and to empathise with them, and I have greater sympathy for people who come from backgrounds very different from my own and who have experienced the world in a far less benign way than I have been privileged to enjoy. This is what sociability involves. It makes the invisible visible, and it has enabled me to cross boundaries that once seemed impermeable. It would be an expression of hubris for me to say that I now understand what it means to be black, but my perspective has certainly changed. The capacity to see that not everyone is treated the way that I am treated is not one that I could have developed on my own. Nor could I have developed that capability through conversations with white friends and colleagues. The capability developed only through many conversations, some very uncomfortable at times, with friends, colleagues, and other members of the black community.

Being dependent upon the black community for nurturing my capabilities of education and sociability, what moral obligations do I have towards its members? Before venturing some possible answers, let me stress again that whatever obligations I do have are not by way of reciprocity. As in the case of Georgetown University, my obligations result from the interdependence that exists between me and the black community. Recall that our obligations to ourselves to belong to communities mean that we have the obligation to support those communities and the kind of society that supports the culture from which we receive the capabilities necessary for us to flourish. Understanding that this is the basis for my moral obligations helps frame the available options for meeting those obligations.

The spectrum of possible ways in which I might contribute to the black community so that its members can develop the capabilities necessary for their leading flourishing lives is quite broad. I have colleagues who have adopted black children. This action directly connects their status as property owners with their interdependence with the black community. But adoption is much more than a matter of sharing one's home with a child. It involves a

[47] CI Harris 'Whiteness as property' (1993) 106 *Harv L Rev* 1707–1791.

profound commitment to that child as a human being who is worthy of love and dignity. It also represents a connection with the black community and a commitment both to the child and members of that community to nurture the relationships that enable development of one's own capabilities, particularly education and sociability.

At the other end of the spectrum but still connected to property ownership, I might make contributions to the various institutions aimed at improving the lives of African-Americans. These institutions range from the NAACP to the United Negro College Fund to the Black Lives Matter Movement. If I am serious about supporting the communities that nurture the capabilities that enable me to flourish, I need to put my money where my mouth is. Contributions of money seem the minimum way in which I can meet my moral obligation.

Between these two positions range a great variety of possible ways in which I can act upon my moral obligation. Political activism is one such possibility. I might become politically active in causes that disproportionately affect black people. The issues include both national issues such as police violence and more local issues such as lead poisoning in local water supply systems.

Ordinary encounters with others, including friends and family, also may provide me with opportunities to act on my responsibilities. White people sometimes make statements or use language in the presence of an all-white audience that they would not make in the presence of African Americans. Rather than remain silent in the face of racist comments or behavior, my obligation is to speak. Even if doing so creates an uncomfortable situation, I have a moral obligation publicly to reject racist talk. As I know from my own experience, silence in these situations may well be taken as assent or at least tolerance of the intolerable.

The discussion in this essay has been intended as only tentative, simply a beginning of how we might think differently of race, property, and moral obligations to each other. Human flourishing and capabilities as the means to leading a fulfilling life provides, I believe, an illuminating way of approaching very different and controversial questions. I hardly claim to have given the last word. My only hope is that is that it is a word worth considering.

Chapter 4

Section 21 of the Insolvency Act and the final Constitution's property clause: Revisiting *Harksen v Lane NO*

*Reghard Brits**

1 Introduction

The purpose of this contribution is to revisit the Constitutional Court case of *Harksen v Lane NO and Others*,[1] particularly the part of Goldstone J's majority judgment which concerned the constitutional validity of section 21 of the Insolvency Act 24 of 1936 in light of the interim Constitution's property clause. *Harksen* was the Constitutional Court's first opportunity to interpret and apply the property clause, which at that point in time was contained in section 28 of the interim Constitution.[2] It has been twenty years since *Harksen* was handed down on 7 October 1997, and since then we have adopted a new

* Senior Lecturer, Department of Mercantile Law, University of Pretoria. Formerly undergraduate research assistant (2009), doctoral candidate (2010–2012) and postdoctoral fellow (2013–2015) of AJ van der Walt. My gratitude to Hermie Coetzee for reading and commenting on this contribution.

[1] 1998 (1) SA 300 (CC).

[2] Constitution of the Republic of South Africa Act 200 of 1993. The judgment also considered other constitutional provisions, such as the right to equality, but these aspects fall outside the scope of this contribution.

property clause in section 25 of the final Constitution[3] and numerous further cases have been decided.

In *Harksen* the claimant argued that the effect of section 21 of the Insolvency Act (the automatic transfer of a solvent spouse's property to the trustee of the insolvent spouse's estate)[4] amounted to an expropriation of property and that it was therefore invalid because no compensation (as required by the Constitution) was paid. As explained below, this argument failed dismally, one of the reasons being that it should never have been framed as an expropriation case but as a deprivation case.[5] But as I aim to show, even as a deprivation case, it would probably have been unsuccessful.

With the benefit of hindsight, there are several matters one can investigate with reference to *Harksen*, such as the conceptual distinction between deprivation and expropriation as well as the methodology for deciding property challenges. However, my main aim is to consider the substantive justification of section 21 of the Insolvency Act and how a case like *Harksen* would be decided today under the property clause in the final Constitution.[6] Would a different outcome be reached under section 25 – not in terms of the expropriation provisions in section 25(2) and (3), but in terms of the prohibition against arbitrary deprivation of property in section 25(1)?

I will argue that the effect of section 21 entails a deprivation and not an expropriation of property but that, despite the problems surrounding section 21, the deprivation of property contemplated by section 21 is probably not arbitrary as meant in section 25(1) of the final Constitution. During my analysis, I will also draw upon some of the comments that André van der Walt made in response to *Harksen*.

---

[3] Constitution of the Republic of South Africa, 1996. *Harksen* was decided after the final Constitution came into operation on 4 February 1997 but the cause of action arose when the interim Constitution was still in force.

[4] See section 2 below.

[5] AJ van der Walt & H Botha 'Coming to grips with the new constitutional order: critical comments on *Harksen v Lane NO*' (1998) 13 *SAPL* 17–41 23–25; RG Evans 'The constitutionality of section 21 of the Insolvency Act 24 of 1936' (1998) 9 *Stell LR* 359–372 362, 372; RG Evans *A critical analysis of problem areas in respect of assets of insolvent estates of individuals* (2008) unpublished LLD thesis University of Pretoria 407; L Steyn 'Human rights issues in South African insolvency law' (2004) 13 *Int Insolv Rev* 1–25 13.

[6] It may or may not be that s 21 violates one or more of the other rights in the Constitution (such as equality), but my focus is exclusively on the property perspective.

2 Section 21 of the Insolvency Act[7]

The general purpose of section 21 is to prevent or rectify the situation where someone colluded with his spouse to insulate certain assets from his creditors.[8] An example is where the husband transfers assets to his wife without due consideration or where the husband's funds are used to acquire assets in the wife's name – all with the aim of hiding the assets from the husband's creditors. Section 21 seeks to address this kind of underhanded behaviour by providing that, upon the sequestration of the insolvent spouse, all the separate property of the solvent spouse vests in the Master of the High Court and thereafter in the trustee[9] of the insolvent spouse's estate.[10] Therefore, ownership (*dominium*) of the solvent spouse's property passes, by operation of law, from her to the trustee of her spouse's insolvent estate.[11] The solvent spouse's property may from that point on be treated as if it were the property of the insolvent spouse and the trustee is thus empowered to deal with the property.[12]

However, this transfer of ownership is not meant to be permanent, but is only aimed at ensuring that the insolvent estate is not defrauded of any property – that the spouses did not collude or simulate transactions to hide assets from the insolvent spouse's creditors. Property that is shown rightfully

---

[7] For more detail on s 21, see PH Meskin, PAM Magid, JA Kunst, A Boraine & D Burdette *Insolvency law and its operation in winding up* (Service Issue 48, Jul 2017) para 5.30; R Sharrock, K van der Linde & A Smith *Hockly's insolvency law* 9 ed (2012) 79–85; E Bertelsmann, RG Evans, A Harris, M Kelly-Louw, A Loubser, M Roestoff, A Smith, L Stander & L Steyn in C Nagel (ed) *Mars The law of insolvency in South Africa* 9 ed (2008) 207–221; RG Evans *A critical analysis of problem areas in respect of assets of insolvent estates of individuals* (2008) unpublished LLD thesis University of Pretoria ch 10.1.

[8] *De Villiers NO v Delta Cables (Pty) Ltd* 1992 (1) SA 9 (A) 13; *Harksen v Lane NO and Others* 1998 (1) SA 300 (CC) paras 36–37; *Beddy NO v Van der Westhuizen* 1999 (3) SA 913 (SCA) 916; *Janit v Van den Heever and Others NNO (No 1)* 2001 (1) SA 731 (W) para 7.

[9] To simplify the explanation, I will henceforth only refer to transfer to the trustee, but this should each time be understood to include the prior transfer to the Master.

[10] Section 21(1). Section 21 is only relevant when the spouses are married out of community of property and one of them is sequestrated. If they are married in community of property, both will be sequestrated and s 21 will not be relevant. The spouses contemplated in s 21 include persons of any gender, same-sex spouses, persons who are not married but who live together as spouses, and persons who are married according to any law or custom: see s 21(13). For simplicity, I refer to the insolvent spouse as male and the solvent spouse as female.

[11] See section 4.1 below.

[12] Section 21(1). However, it seems that the solvent spouse is not prohibited from dealing with the property. Hence, any alienation of the property will remain valid until the trustee has it set aside: see *Motala and Another NNO v Moller and Others* 2014 (6) SA 223 (GJ) paras 15–17; and also RG Evans 'Sequestration of the estate of a spouse: What happens to the "property" of the solvent "spouse"?' (2014) 77 *THRHR* 632–641.

to belong to the solvent spouse will be released to her. Importantly, though, the burden is on the solvent spouse to prove that the property should be so released.[13] There are a number of grounds[14] which the spouse can rely on to claim her assets, which, if proven, compels the trustee to release the property to her.[15] The main grounds for release are when the spouse can prove that she acquired the property before her marriage to the insolvent;[16] or if she acquired it during the marriage, that this was done by a valid title as against the creditors of the insolvent.[17] A further ground is if she can show that she acquired the property with the income or proceeds of, for instance, the aforementioned categories of property.[18]

If the trustee refuses to release the property,[19] the solvent spouse may apply to a court for an order of release; for an order staying the sale of the property; or for an order entitling her to the undistributed proceeds of the property. The court may then make any order it thinks just.[20] The vesting of the solvent spouse's assets in the estate of the insolvent spouse can also be temporarily postponed by a court if, for example, the solvent spouse carries on business as a trader or if she will suffer serious prejudice due to the immediate transfer of her property.[21]

Regarding the trustee's powers over the solvent spouse's property, it is stipulated that, as long as she is in the country and the trustee is able to ascertain her address, he shall not, except with the court's permission, realise her property until the expiry of six weeks after he notified her in writing of his intention to do so. This notice must also be published in the Government

---

[13] On the onus of proof, see *Beddy NO v Van der Westhuizen* 1999 (3) SA 913 (SCA) 916–917; *Maudsley v Maudsley's Trustees* 1940 WLD 166, 169. See also *Rens v Gutman NO and Others* 2003 (1) SA 93 (C) 96–97; *Snyman v Rheeder NO* 1989 (4) SA 496 (T) 505–506.

[14] Section 21(2).

[15] On the trustee's duty to release the property in view of the dramatic nature of the vesting clause in s 21, see eg *Enyati Resources Ltd and Another v Thorne NO and Another* 1984 (2) SA 551 (C) 557–558.

[16] Section 21(2)(a).

[17] Section 21(2)(c). See further RG Evans 'Release of solvent spouse's property under section 21(2)(c) of the Insolvency Act 24 of 1936' (2004) 15 *Stell LR* 193–200.

[18] Section 21(2)(e).

[19] She can also bypass the trustee and apply directly to a court: see *Hawkins v Cohen NO* 1994 (4) SA 23 (W).

[20] Section 21(4). For cases in which the solvent spouse applied to a court to have her property released, see eg *Banks v Josephs NO & another* [2009] JOL 23929 (C); *Rens v Gutman NO and Others* 2003 (1) SA 93 (C); *Beddy NO v Van der Westhuizen* 1999 (3) SA 913 (SCA); *Jooste v De Witt NO* 1999 (2) SA 355 (T); *Hawkins v Cohen NO* 1994 (4) SA 23 (W); *Snyman v Rheeder NO* 1989 (4) SA 496 (T); *Foot NO v Vorster* 1983 (3) SA 179 (O); *Coetzer v Coetzer* 1975 (3) SA 931 (E).

[21] Section 21(10). See eg *Van Schalkwyk v Die Meester* 1975 (2) SA 508 (N).

Gazette and in a local newspaper, and must invite all separate creditors of that spouse to prove their claims.[22]

As the abovementioned arrangement suggests, the interests of the creditors of the solvent spouse will not be ignored if the assets are realised by the trustee of the insolvent spouse. For instance, they may prove their claims against the solvent spouse and are entitled to share in the proceeds of her property according to their security rights and in priority to the creditors of the insolvent spouse.[23] In other words, although the solvent spouse's assets vest in her insolvent spouse's estate, an attempt is made to balance this by creating the opportunity to have such assets released as well as by protecting the interests of the solvent spouse's creditors.

It can be mentioned that, both before and after *Harksen*, section 21 has been analysed and criticised by several scholars.[24] The South African Law Reform Commission has also suggested that section 21 should be left out of (or replaced in) any new insolvency legislation to be enacted in future.[25] It is therefore not a very popular mechanism amongst commentators, both due to and irrespective of constitutional arguments. It is obviously not possible to consider every nuance and issue surrounding section 21 in this contribution, and hence I limit myself to the constitutional challenge under the property clause. In what follows I summarise the judgment in *Harksen* and then re-evaluate the matter with reference to section 25 of the final Constitution.

---

22 Section 21(3).

23 Section 21(5). See also s 21(6)–(9).

24 See eg NL Joubert 'Artikel 21 van die Insolvensiewet: Tyd vir 'n nuwe benadering? *De Villiers NO v Delta Cables (Pty) Ltd* 1992 (1) SA 9 (A)' 1992 *TSAR* 699–706; RG Evans 'A critical analysis of section 21 of the Insolvency Act 24 of 1936' (1996) 59 *THRHR* 613–625; RG Evans 'A critical analysis of section 21 of the Insolvency Act 24 of 1936' (1997) 60 *THRHR* 71–83; DM Matlala 'Some aspects regarding the vesting of property of the solvent spouse in the trustee of the insolvent spouse's estate' (2002) 43 *Codicillus* 2–13; RG Evans *A critical analysis of problem areas in respect of assets of insolvent estates of individuals* (2008) unpublished LLD thesis University of Pretoria chs 10.1, 11.3; A Boraine & R Evans 'The law of insolvency and the Bill of Rights' in Y Mokgoro & P Tlakula (eds) *Bill of Rights compendium* (Service Issue 34, Oct 2014) ch 4A6.

25 See the discussions by eg L Jansen van Rensburg 'Die weglating van artikel 21 van die Insolvensiewet 24 van 1936 – bied die konsep Insolvensiewet van 1996 voldoende alternatiewe beskerming?' 1997 *TSAR* 674–688; L Stander 'Weer artikel 21 van die Insolvensiewet – het ons iets beter?' (2001) 26 *JJS* 93–103 99–102; L Stander 'Artikel 21 van die Insolvensiewet – reg of weg?' 2005 *TSAR* 316–329 325–328.

3 *Harksen v Lane NO*[26]

In terms of section 21 of the Insolvency Act, when Mr Harken's estate was sequestrated, all Mrs Harksen's property vested in the trustees of her husband's insolvent estate. The trustees also caused her property to be attached in accordance with the Act. Importantly, Mrs Harksen did not apply for the release of the property, which – as explained above – is the prime option to protect her legitimate interests in the property. Instead, she challenged the constitutionality of section 21, and one of her arguments was that section 21(1) constitutes an expropriation of property without compensation – therefore falling foul of the compensation requirement in section 28(3) of the interim Constitution.[27]

It is important to emphasise that Mrs Harksen did not try to argue that there had been a *deprivation* of property for purposes of section 28(2) of the interim Constitution,[28] but insisted on basing her case on the supposed *expropriation* of her property in violation of the compensation requirement in section 28(3).[29] Before going further, it is necessary to summarise briefly the content of section 28.[30] The then property clause consisted of three parts. Subsection (1) included a so-called institutional guarantee ('Every person shall have the right to acquire and hold rights in property and, to the extent that the nature of the rights permits, to dispose of such rights'), while subsection (2) dealt with deprivation ('No deprivation of any rights in property shall be permitted otherwise than in accordance with a law') and subsection (3) with expropriation ('Where any rights in property are expropriated pursuant to a law referred to in subsection (2), such expropriation shall be permissible

[26] For other summaries and discussions of the case, see eg T Roux 'Constitutional protection of property and land reform' 1997 *ASSAL* 332–355 333–334; RH Zulman 'Insolvency law' 1998 *ASSAL* 463–476 465–469; L Jansen van Rensburg & L Stander 'Weeg die belange van die skuldeisers swaarder as die belange van die solvente eggenoot? *Harksen v Lane* 1998 (1) SA 300 (KH); 1997 11 BCLR 1489 (KH)' 1998 *TSAR* 334–343; AJ van der Walt & H Botha 'Coming to grips with the new constitutional order: critical comments on *Harksen v Lane NO*' (1998) 13 *SAPL* 17–41; RG Evans 'The constitutionality of section 21 of the Insolvency Act 24 of 1936' (1998) 9 *Stell LR* 359–372; AJ van der Walt 'Striving for the better interpretation – a critical reflection on the Constitutional Court's *Harksen* and *FNB* decisions on the property clause' (2004) 121 *SALJ* 854–878 861–864.

[27] *Harksen v Lane NO and Others* 1998 (1) SA 300 (CC) para 31.

[28] Paragraph 40.

[29] AJ van der Walt & H Botha 'Coming to grips with the new constitutional order: critical comments on *Harksen v Lane NO*' (1998) 13 *SAPL* 17–41 19.

[30] See further eg M Chaskalson 'The property clause: Section 28 of the Constitution' (1994) 10 *SAJHR* 131–139; AJ van der Walt 'Notes on the interpretation of the property clause in the new Constitution' (1994) 57 *THRHR* 181–203; J Murphy 'Interpreting the property clause in the Constitution Act of 1993' (1995) 10 *SAPL* 107–130; AJ van der Walt *Constitutional property clauses: A comparative analysis* (1999) 320–358.

for public purposes only and shall be subject to the payment of agreed compensation or, failing agreement, to the payment of such compensation and within such period as may be determined by a court of law as just and equitable, taking into account all relevant factors…').

After discussing the distinction between deprivation and expropriation,[31] Goldstone J heeded Mrs Harksen's insistence on making an expropriation argument and therefore decided the case under section 28(3). However, the court ultimately held that section 21 of the Insolvency Act did not involve an expropriation. According to the judge, whether the transfer of ownership effected by section 21(1) qualifies as an expropriation depends on the context and purpose of section 21 as a whole.[32] In this regard the judge explained that the 'purpose and effect is clearly not to divest, save temporarily, the solvent spouse of the ownership of property that is in fact' hers.[33] Instead, the 'purpose is to ensure that the insolvent estate is not deprived of property to which it is entitled'.[34] The court went on to hold that it was understandable and justifiable for the Act to place the onus on the solvent spouse to prove her ownership, essentially because she would have more information regarding her ownership than the trustee.[35]

The court also emphasised that section 21 does not 'contemplate or intend that such transfer should be permanent or for any purpose other than to enable the trustee to establish whether any such property is in fact that of the insolvent estate'.[36] There is no intention to divest her permanently of property that is rightfully hers or to prejudice her interests in her property.[37] This is borne out by the fact that section 21 contains provisions empowering the solvent spouse to approach the court to have her property released and to receive protection against a trustee who wishes to sell her assets prior to their release.[38] Another such provision is the one authorising the court to order that certain of the solvent spouse's property should be temporarily excluded from the operation of section 21(1) if the spouse is a trader or is likely to experience serious prejudice arising from an immediate vesting.[39]

---

31 *Harksen v Lane NO and Others* 1998 (1) SA 300 (CC) paras 32–35.
32 *Harksen* para 36.
33 *Harksen* para 36.
34 *Harksen* para 36, citing *Van Schalkwyk v Die Meester* 1975 (2) SA 508 (N) 510.
35 *Harksen* paras 36, 60.
36 *Harksen* para 37.
37 *Harksen* para 37.
38 *Harksen* para 37.
39 *Harksen* para 37.

The court pointed out that the whole aim of section 21 'is merely to ensure that property which properly belonged to the insolvent ends up in the estate':[40]

> The statutory mechanism employed is temporarily to lay the hand of the law upon the property of both the insolvent spouse and the solvent spouse and to create a procedure for the release by the trustee or the court of that which in fact belongs to the solvent spouse.[41]

In other words, the court concluded that section 21 does not have 'the purpose or effect of a compulsory acquisition or expropriation of the property of the solvent spouse whether by a public authority or at all' and hence 'there is no basis for regarding the effect of [section] 21 as an expropriation of the rights in the property of the solvent spouse'.[42] Consequently, section 21 was found not to violate section 28(3) of the interim Constitution.[43]

While dealing with the question of discrimination (a matter not discussed here), Goldstone J also made some interesting remarks worth noting for purposes of the property issue. In the earlier high court case of *Enyati Resources Ltd and Another v Thorne NO and Another*,[44] in the course of stressing the trustee's duty to release the property without undue delay when the necessary proof of ownership is provided, Berman AJ pointed out that '[t]he divesting of the property of the solvent spouse and the vesting thereof in the hands of the Master (and thereafter in the hands of the trustee) constitute a drastic and arbitrary invasion upon, and inroad into, the proprietary right of citizens'. This statement was relied on in *Harksen* to argue for the constitutional invalidity of section 21. However, Goldstone J rejected this contention in the following terms:

> Whilst in no way wishing to minimise the inconvenience, potential prejudice and embarrassment that the provisions of [section] 21 of the Act may cause to a solvent spouse, and even accepting that those consequences may be described as 'drastic', I cannot agree that they are arbitrary or without rationality. In my opinion, the Legislature acted rationally in taking the view that the common law and the statutory remedies relating to impeachable transactions were insufficient to enable the Master or a trustee to ensure that all the property of the insolvent spouse found its way into the insolvent estate. In particular, it must be

40 *Harksen* para 37.

41 *Harksen* para 37.

42 *Harksen* para 38.

43 *Harksen* para 40. O'Regan and Sachs JJ delivered dissenting judgments regarding the application of the equality clause but agreed with the majority judgment when it came to the property issue.

44 1984 (2) SA 551 (C) 558.

> acknowledged that remedies other than that provided by [section] 21 cast an *onus* on the Master or the trustee to establish ownership of property claimed from the solvent spouse. If a claim were to be contested, inevitable delays inherent in the legal system would result. Those delays, certainly in cases of collusion, could well be fatal to the recovery of property rightfully belonging to the insolvent estate.[45]

This finding was not made in the part of the judgment dealing with the property clause, but it ties in nicely with that aspect too. It is also an instructive comment that could apply to the property clause in the final Constitution and the arbitrariness test contained therein. I return to this point in section 4.2 below.

Although the Constitutional Court therefore held that section 21 does not contemplate an expropriation of property under section 28(3), it made no finding as to whether it involves a deprivation of property under section 28(2) and, if so, whether such a deprivation is justifiable. In the next section I will consider whether section 21 constitutes an arbitrary deprivation of property as contemplated in section 25(1).

4 Section 21 and the property clause in the final Constitution

4.1 Deprivation or expropriation?

Like section 28 of the interim Constitution, section 25 of the final Constitution provides for two categories of property interferences: deprivation and expropriation. Despite different terminology, this is also a common distinction in many other legal systems. *Harksen* is often presented as an example in South African case law of the theory in terms of which deprivation and expropriation are differentiated as two distinct forms of property interference, with no overlap.[46] However, not only was this theory not reflected in the wording of section 28 of the interim Constitution,[47] but it was also subsequently established that, under section 25 of the final Constitution, a categorical distinction is not the correct interpretation of the two concepts. Instead, ever since the judgment in *First National Bank of SA Ltd t/a Wesbank v Commissioner, South African Revenue Service and Another;*

---

[45] *Harksen* para 59 (footnotes omitted).

[46] AJ van der Walt *Constitutional property law* 2 ed (2005) 132; AJ van der Walt 'Striving for the better interpretation – A critical reflection on the Constitutional Court's *Harksen* and *FNB* decisions on the property clause' (2004) 121 *SALJ* 854–878 862.

[47] AJ van der Walt & H Botha 'Coming to grips with the new constitutional order: Critical comments on *Harksen v Lane NO*' (1998) 13 *SAPL* 17–41 25–26; AJ van der Walt 'Striving for the better interpretation – a critical reflection on the Constitutional Court's *Harksen* and *FNB* decisions on the property clause' (2004) 121 *SALJ* 854–878 862–863.

First National Bank of SA Ltd t/a Wesbank v Minister of Finance,[48] deprivation is understood as the broader, all-inclusive category of property interferences, with expropriation being a narrower, more specific category of deprivation. Hence, although all expropriations are deprivations, all deprivations are not expropriations.

A deprivation under section 25(1) is broadly defined as 'any interference with the use, enjoyment or exploitation of private property'.[49] For the interference to qualify as a deprivation, it must be 'significant enough to have a legally relevant impact' on the affected rights.[50] Therefore, the deprivation concept does not have to entail a loss of ownership, since it includes any interference with or regulation of property. There is some uncertainty in South African insolvency law surrounding the precise proprietary consequence of section 21 – whether or not the vesting of property in the trustee literally involves a transfer of ownership from the insolvent (and his spouse) to the trustee. Some have argued that, for the sequestration process to be managed effectively, it is not necessary to regard this vesting as a transfer of ownership in the normal property law sense.[51] The courts have not taken a final position on this

[48] 2002 (4) SA 768 (CC) para 46.

[49] *First National Bank of SA Ltd t/a Wesbank v Commissioner, South African Revenue Service and Another; First National Bank of SA Ltd t/a Wesbank v Minister of Finance* 2002 (4) SA 768 (CC) para 57. See also *Reflect-All 1025 CC and Others v MEC for Public Transport, Roads and Works, Gauteng Provincial Government and Another* 2009 (6) SA 391 (CC) para 36; *Offit Enterprises (Pty) Ltd and Another v Coega Development Corporation (Pty) Ltd and Others* 2011 (1) SA 293 (CC) paras 38–39, 41.

[50] *National Credit Regulator v Opperman and Others* 2013 (2) SA 1 (CC) para 66. See also *Mkontwana v Nelson Mandela Metropolitan Municipality; Bissett and Others v Buffalo City Municipality; Transfer Rights Action Campaign and Others v Member of the Executive Council for Local Government and Housing, Gauteng and Others* 2005 (1) SA 530 (CC) para 32; *Chevron SA (Pty) Ltd v Wilson t/a Wilson's Transport and Others* 2015 (10) BCLR 1158 (CC) paras 17–19. See further AJ van der Walt *Constitutional property law* 3 ed (2011) 206–209.

[51] See eg RG Evans 'Who owns the insolvent estate?' 1996 *TSAR* 719–724; NL Joubert 'Artikel 21 van die Insolvensiewet: Tyd vir 'n nuwe benadering?'; *De Villiers NO v Delta Cables (Pty) Ltd* 1992 (1) SA 9 (A)' 1992 *TSAR* 699–706 704–705; and also L Stander 'Die eienaar van die bates van die insolvente boedel' (1996) 59 *THRHR* 388–398.

question, but some[52] (including the Constitutional Court)[53] have convincingly assumed that there is indeed a transfer of ownership. For present purposes it is not necessary to reflect on this interesting theoretical question. In any event, even if section 21 does not literally involve a transfer of ownership, the interference with her property (the right to dispose of it or otherwise deal with it as owner) is clearly legally significant enough to qualify as a deprivation for section 25 purposes.[54]

It should however be mentioned that, if the solvent spouse cannot prove her title to (or ownership of) the asset in question, then she logically has no constitutional property entitlement with regard to that asset to begin with. In other words, there can only ever be a deprivation of property with reference to those assets that rightfully belong to her, and these assets are those that will, in the normal course, be released to her if she can prove her title. This point emphasises the temporary nature of the deprivation and, by itself, goes a long way to refute the arguments against the validity of section 21.

Although it is quite clear that section 21 involves a deprivation of property, the more controversial question would be whether the deprivation can also amount to an expropriation of the solvent spouse's property, as was contended on behalf of Mrs Harksen. However, it must be considered that, according to the methodology for deciding constitutional property cases, before reaching the expropriation question, it is necessary to first test the deprivation for compliance with the requirements of section 25(1). Is the deprivation authorised by law of general application, and does it permit an arbitrary deprivation of property? Once it is found that section 21 violates these requirements, and if this violation is also not justifiable under section 36 of the Constitution, then the section is invalid and the matter ends there. However, if section 21 does not violate the requirements of section 25(1) or if it does so justifiably (under section 36), then one may go on to determine whether the property interference falls within the definition of an expropriation and whether it then complies with the requirements contained

[52] See especially *De Villiers NO v Delta Cables (Pty) Ltd* 1992 (1) SA 9 (A) 14–16, where the Appellate Division in *obiter dicta* disagreed convincingly with the contrary view expressed in eg *Stand 382 Saxonwold CC and Another v Kruger NO* 1990 (4) SA 317 (T) 323 that ownership (*dominium*) of the solvent spouse's property does not actually transfer to the trustee. See also *Janit v Van den Heever and Others NNO (No 1)* 2001 (1) SA 731 (W) para 7; *Snyman v Rheeder NO* 1989 (4) SA 496 (T) 500; *Van Niekerk v Wolmarans en 'n Ander* 1976 (4) SA 629 (T) 630–631. However, see the apparent misreading of *Harksen* in *Shrosbree and Others NNO v Van Rooyen NO and Others* 2004 (1) SA 226 (SE) 229–230.

[53] *Harksen* para 31.

[54] Paragraph 98 (per O'Regan J).

in section 25(2) and (3) of the Constitution, and if not, whether the violation is justifiable under section 36.[55]

So, assuming for the moment that the deprivation is found to comply with section 25(1), or that it violates the subsection but justifiably so under section 36, then the next question according to the methodology is to determine whether the deprivation also qualifies as an expropriation. This question is tricky in view of the fact that section 21 is commonly understood to involve a transfer of ownership, which is a consequence typically associated with the notion of expropriation. This, in turn, creates the temptation to classify the effect of section 21 as an expropriation, especially if the claimant desires the compensation that would accompany the supposed expropriation. The situation might have been less complex if the effect of section 21 did not involve anything resembling a transfer of ownership, since property interferences that do not involve a transfer of ownership will mostly not be regarded as expropriations. Nevertheless, it is important to consider that the difference between deprivation and expropriation does not depend solely on whether or not ownership is transferred, since this is but one factor. As explained above, the court in *Harksen* rejected the argument that section 21 involved an expropriation even if the section did constitute a transfer of ownership. Therefore, at this juncture it is useful to consider some of the remarks Van der Walt made in response to this finding.

Van der Walt (in an article co-authored with Henk Botha)[56] was critical of *Harksen*, not necessarily of the outcome or of matters pertaining to insolvency law as such, but of the court's treatment of constitutional property law principles.[57] Although the court was correct to not classify the effect of section 21 as an expropriation, Van der Walt was sceptical of the reasoning

[55] This methodology originates from *First National Bank of SA Ltd t/a Wesbank v Commissioner, South African Revenue Service and Another; First National Bank of SA Ltd t/a Wesbank v Minister of Finance* 2002 (4) SA 768 (CC) para 46, and was formulated well by T Roux 'Property' in S Woolman, M Bishop & J Brickhill (eds) *Constitutional law of South Africa* vol 3 2 ed (Original Service, 2003) para 46.1.

[56] AJ van der Walt & H Botha 'Coming to grips with the new constitutional order: Critical comments on *Harksen v Lane NO*' (1998) 13 *SAPL* 17–41. Although co-authored with Botha, it is safe to assume that Van der Walt wrote the part on the property issue, while Botha wrote the part on the equality clause. In the main text I will henceforth only refer expressly to Van der Walt when referring to views expressed on the property clause.

[57] See especially AJ van der Walt & H Botha 'Coming to grips with the new constitutional order: Critical comments on *Harksen v Lane NO*' (1998) 13 *SAPL* 17–41. See also AJ van der Walt 'Striving for the better interpretation – a critical reflection on the Constitutional Court's *Harksen* and *FNB* decisions on the property clause' (2004) 121 *SALJ* 854–878 861–864.

that led to this conclusion.[58] For instance, the distinction between deprivation and expropriation is more complex than *Harksen*'s focus on the question whether there was a permanent physical dispossession or actual acquisition of property by the state. First, it is possible for an expropriation to take place without the physical acquisition of property by the state, as could happen in instances of the complete destruction of property (for example incorporeal assets) by the state.[59] Secondly, the fact that the transfer of ownership was not intended to be permanent is an important consideration, but it cannot be enough reason for not regarding the transfer as an expropriation, since expropriations can indeed be temporary.[60]

In response to *Harksen*, Van der Walt also explained that the fact that ownership is transferred to the trustee does not mean that there is an expropriation. He pointed out that the effect of section 21 is analogous to the forfeiture or confiscation of property where the property was, for example, presumed to have been used in committing a crime. As with such statutory provisions, it seemed to Van der Walt that the key attribute of section 21 is not the fact that ownership is transferred; the focus is rather on placing 'the burden of proof of ownership on the solvent spouse', which indicates that section 21 is a 'regulatory provision' that must be 'treated as a deprivation of property and not as an expropriation'.[61] Hence, the question is not whether the temporary vesting of the solvent spouse's property in the trustee qualifies as an expropriation but whether it is a valid regulation of the rights in that property.[62] In a sense, therefore, it seems to me that, by shifting the onus of proof in this manner, section 21 regulates the ability to vindicate one's property. The transfer of ownership is almost incidental, which is supported by the temporary nature of the transfer.

Accordingly, as Van der Walt explained, if the court in *Harksen* had regarded section 21 as a regulatory (and not expropriatory) provision, it would have had to evaluate the reasonableness and justifiability of section 21 in light of the general limitation provisions in section 33 of the interim

[58] AJ van der Walt & H Botha 'Coming to grips with the new constitutional order: Critical comments on *Harksen v Lane NO*' (1998) 13 *SAPL* 17–41 22.

[59] AJ van der Walt & H Botha 'Coming to grips with the new constitutional order: Critical comments on *Harksen v Lane NO*' (1998) 13 *SAPL* 17–41 21–22.

[60] AJ van der Walt & H Botha 'Coming to grips with the new constitutional order: Critical comments on *Harksen v Lane NO*' (1998) 13 *SAPL* 17–41 22–23; AJ van der Walt 'Striving for the better interpretation – A critical reflection on the Constitutional Court's *Harksen* and *FNB* decisions on the property clause' (2004) 121 *SALJ* 854–878 862.

[61] AJ van der Walt & H Botha 'Coming to grips with the new constitutional order: critical comments on *Harksen v Lane NO*' (1998) 13 *SAPL* 17–41 23–24.

[62] AJ van der Walt & H Botha 'Coming to grips with the new constitutional order: Critical comments on *Harksen v Lane NO*' (1998) 13 *SAPL* 17–41 24.

Constitution.[63] This would have involved a proportionality test that asks whether the effects of section 21 are proportionate to its purpose. Hence, even if the purpose of section 21 is valid and justified, it could be that the effects are 'disproportionately harsh or unfair on the solvent spouse'.[64] Van der Walt argued that there are two benefits to this approach. Firstly, section 21 would have to be tested on a case-by-case basis and not in general. Secondly, the possible discrimination embodied in section 21 might have an impact on whether the deprivation of property is proportionate.[65]

In light of the above, and considering the word limit of this contribution, I take it for granted that the effect of section 21 cannot, either conceptually or logically, be classified as an expropriation of property. Instead, as Van der Walt also emphasised, it is necessary to judge it as a regulation or deprivation of property. His remarks assumed the law as it stood under the interim Constitution, but as explained below, the approach to testing deprivations under the final Constitution differ significantly from that under the interim Constitution. In what follows, I therefore contextualise the justification of section 21 in terms of the deprivation clause in the final Constitution.

4.2 *Arbitrary deprivation of property?*

Section 25(1) provides: 'No one may be deprived of property except in terms of law of general application, and no law may permit arbitrary deprivation of property.' Since one can assume that the Insolvency Act, which authorises the deprivation, readily qualifies as law of general application,[66] the main question for our purposes is whether the deprivation authorised by section 21 is arbitrary as meant in section 25(1).

It is difficult to determine in the abstract exactly whether or not a provision like section 21 authorises an arbitrary deprivation of property. A somewhat easier way to phrase the question is perhaps to ask whether section 21, in view of its purpose, context and general consequences, is designed in a way which ensures that its application does not lead to arbitrary deprivations of property in individual cases. In what follows I briefly set out the general

---

[63] AJ van der Walt & H Botha 'Coming to grips with the new constitutional order: Critical comments on *Harksen v Lane NO*' (1998) 13 *SAPL* 17–41 24.

[64] AJ van der Walt & H Botha 'Coming to grips with the new constitutional order: Critical comments on *Harksen v Lane NO*' (1998) 13 *SAPL* 17–41 24.

[65] AJ van der Walt & H Botha 'Coming to grips with the new constitutional order: Critical comments on *Harksen v Lane NO*' (1998) 13 *SAPL* 17–41 24–25.

[66] For a contrary view that s 21 does not qualify as law of general application, see L Jansen van Rensburg 'Die weglating van artikel 21 van die Insolvensiewet 24 van 1936 – bied die konsep-Insolvensiewet van 1996 voldoende alternatiewe beskerming?' 1997 *TSAR* 674–688 677.

definition of the arbitrariness test and then provide some thoughts regarding the considerations that, in my view, could influence the general validity of section 21.

For a deprivation to pass the arbitrariness test, the deprivation must be procedurally fair (procedural arbitrariness) and there must be a sufficient reason for the deprivation (substantive arbitrariness).[67] Regarding procedural arbitrariness, one could possibly point to procedural fairness issues with the fact that the solvent spouse is burdened with the onus of proof to have her property released. Another problem might be the fact that the transfer of her assets takes place automatically without specific judicial authorisation.[68] However, it is arguable that a procedural challenge against section 21 is not very strong. First, the deprivation under section 21(1) is indirectly authorised by the high court that grants the sequestration order with reference to the insolvent spouse – a power which is discretionary and which could be influenced by the potential effect that the order would have on the solvent spouse. Secondly, the court has a wide discretion (based on what it considers just) to order that the solvent spouse's assets should be released. Thirdly, as the court in *Harksen* indicated, it seems that there are adequate reasons for burdening the solvent spouse with the onus to prove her title to the property. I am open to a more detailed scrutiny of whether the procedure surrounding this deprivation is truly fair, but for now I will assume procedural fairness and instead focus more closely on the substantive side of the test.

The substantive arbitrariness test asks the question whether, under the circumstances of the case, there is a 'sufficient reason' for the deprivation.[69] This entails that one must first determine whether there is a legitimate reason for the law in question and secondly whether there is a sufficient nexus between this reason and the effect of the deprivation on the right-holder. In other words, considering the complexity of relationships involved

---

[67] *First National Bank of SA Ltd t/a Wesbank v Commissioner, South African Revenue Service and Another; First National Bank of SA Ltd t/a Wesbank v Minister of Finance* 2002 (4) SA 768 (CC) para 100.

[68] Although the meaning of procedural fairness is not clear in this context (cf AJ van der Walt 'Procedurally arbitrary deprivation of property' (2012) 23 *Stell LR* 88–94), from cases like *National Credit Regulator v Opperman and Others* 2013 (2) SA 1 (CC) paras 69, 76 and *Chevron SA (Pty) Ltd v Wilson t/a Wilson's Transport and Others* 2015 (10) BCLR 1158 (CC) paras 22–24, it is apparent that the presence or absence of a judicial discretion is an important consideration when evaluating the procedural fairness of a deprivation.

[69] The following summary of the test is based on *First National Bank of SA Ltd t/a Wesbank v Commissioner, South African Revenue Service and Another; First National Bank of SA Ltd t/a Wesbank v Minister of Finance* 2002 (4) SA 768 (CC) para 100, where the test was set out in detail. See further AJ van der Walt *Constitutional property law* 3 ed (2011) 237–270.

(such as between the purpose of the deprivation and the person whose property is affected; between the purpose of the deprivation and the nature of the property; and between the purpose and extent of the deprivation), one must compare the means and ends of section 21(1) and judge whether the reason for the deprivation is adequate in view of its effect.

An important element of the arbitrariness test is determining the level of scrutiny that is to be used when evaluating the abovementioned nexus. As will become clear below, the level of scrutiny is particularly important when evaluating whether section 21 complies with the arbitrariness test. Under the interim Constitution, the deprivation provision in section 28(2) did not contain an internal justification standard such as the arbitrariness test contained in section 25(1) of the final Constitution. One possibility was that a deprivation under section 28(2) did not need much, if any, substantive justification, since all that was required was proper authorisation by a law. The other option was that the substantive test had to be found in the interim Constitution's limitations clause (section 33), which, in similar way to the limitations clause in the final Constitution (section 36), mandated a strict proportionality test for any limitations of rights in the Bill of Rights.[70] Unlike section 28(1) of the interim Constitution, however, section 25(1) of the final Constitution contains an internal substantive justification requirement in the form of the arbitrariness test. Hence, section 36 (the limitations clause) is only relevant, if at all, after it is found that the deprivation is arbitrary.[71]

The Constitutional Court[72] has explained, and it is generally accepted, that the level of scrutiny in the arbitrariness test will fluctuate on a continuum between a mere ('thin') rationality test on the one end of the spectrum and a ('thick') proportionality test on the other end. A mere rationality standard is the lowest level of scrutiny and simply requires a rational connection between the purpose of the deprivation and the means chosen to achieve it (its effect). A proportionality test, on the other hand, is the strictest level of scrutiny and requires that the purpose of the deprivation must be narrowly proportionate to its effects – although this test is probably not as strict as the full proportionality test contained in section 36. A practical way to explain the difference is that, in the case of a proportionality test, the deprivation

[70] See eg *S v Makwanyane and Another* 1995 (3) SA 391 (CC) para 104.

[71] It has become clear that s 36 might never be relevant in property disputes. It contains a stricter test than the arbitrariness test, and hence it is logically unlikely for a deprivation that is arbitrary to be justifiable under s 36. See eg *National Credit Regulator v Opperman and Others* 2013 (2) SA 1 (CC) para 73.

[72] *First National Bank of SA Ltd t/a Wesbank v Commissioner, South African Revenue Service and Another; First National Bank of SA Ltd t/a Wesbank v Minister of Finance* 2002 (4) SA 768 (CC) para 100(g).

in question must be the least invasive way (or the last resort) to achieve the contemplated purposes. If the purpose can be achieved in another way that would be less detrimental to the right-holder, then the deprivation in question will probably fail the test. Conversely, a rationality test does not necessarily require the deprivation in question to be the least invasive way to the achieve the purpose. As long as the deprivation is effected in a way that is a rational choice to achieve the purpose, the test will be satisfied.

Regarding the validity of section 21, much will therefore depend on how strictly the deprivation is scrutinised. In the abstract it is not possible to provide a complete answer, since the divergent facts of different cases may lead to different levels of scrutiny. Notwithstanding, in my view, it is arguable that the level of scrutiny will, in most instances, be nearer to the rationality side of the spectrum. The reasons for this prospect include the following: The purpose of section 21 is legitimate and an important cog in the overall functioning of insolvency law; the deprivation only relates to this narrow purpose and does not contemplate a situation where the solvent spouse necessarily loses any assets that are rightfully hers; there is a close connection between the purpose of the section and the person who is deprived of property, as well as between the purpose and the property subject to deprivation; the deprivation is not meant to be permanent but is intended to be temporary only, in order to establish the true ownership of the property; the section provides reasonable mechanisms through which the spouse can have her property released; and the section provides ample protection for the separate creditors of the solvent spouse.

Interestingly, many of the points made by Goldstone J in *Harksen* in the course of explaining why the disputed effect of the Insolvency Act did not fall within the definition of expropriation would fit more appropriately under the substantive arbitrariness test contemplated in section 25(1). In fact, his reasoning – which includes many of the points made in the paragraph above – points to the overall rationality of section 21.

Commenting on another insolvency case in which constitutional property arguments were unsuccessfully raised,[73] Van der Walt stated that, 'since

[73] *Gainsford and Others NNO v Tiffski Property Investments (Pty) Ltd and Others* 2012 (3) SA 35 (SCA), in which the constitutionality of s 34 of the Insolvency Act was challenged. Without going into detail, the effect of s 34 in this case was that the registration of a mortgage bond was void *ab initio*. The Supreme Court of Appeal rejected the argument that this voiding of the mortgage amounted to an arbitrary deprivation of property. It held that the mortgage did not constitute 'property', as it was void *ab initio* – thus it never existed as a vested property interest. It also found that, even if the mortgage was 'property', the deprivation effected by s 34 was not arbitrary, since there was a rational connection between the purpose and effect of s 34.

the legislation involved [the Insolvency Act] regulates conflicting individual property interests and not public health or public safety in the narrow sense, a thin rationality version of the [arbitrariness] test would probably be applicable rather than something closer to proportionality'.[74] To my mind, this comment applies equally in the present context and thus supports my argument that section 21 – like most other insolvency-related deprivations – should probably be judged according to a standard that is closer to a rationality test and not one closer to a proportionality-type test.

In order to evaluate the justification of section 21, it is useful to compare it with the alternative mechanisms currently available, such as the other provisions in the Insolvency Act that allow for the setting aside of certain pre-sequestration transactions. While section 21 is used to recover property from a spouse, the trustee must resort to more onerous procedures to recover property from other persons. An example is section 26, which is aimed at undoing a pre-sequestration transaction in terms of which the debtor disposed of his assets without value (for instance, donated it or sold it at below market value).[75] Another example is section 31, which provides for the setting aside of any pre-sequestration transaction in terms of the which the debtor colluded with another person to dispose of property in a manner that prejudices existing creditors or prefers one creditor over another.[76] Both sections 26 and 31 could arguably be used by the trustee to achieve the same purpose as section 21.

The main practical difference between arrangements like those in sections 26 and 31 and the rule in section 21 is that, in the former cases, the trustee must institute proceedings for the recovery of the relevant property from the person to whom it has been disposed of,[77] whereas, in the latter case, the property automatically transfers to the trustee upon sequestration and it is the solvent spouse that must institute proceedings to have her assets

---

[74] AJ van der Walt 'Constitutional property law' 2011 *ASSAL* 245–292 249–250.

[75] In simple terms, if the disposition without value occurred more than two years before sequestration, the trustee can have the disposition set aside if he can prove that, immediately after the disposition was made, the debtor was factually insolvent (s 26(1)(a)). If the disposition took place within two years of sequestration, the onus is on the person who received the disposition to prove that, immediately after the disposition was made, the debtor was not insolvent. If the person cannot prove this, the disposition without value can be set aside (s 26(1)(b)).

[76] Other provisions with similar setting aside functions include those for the setting aside of voidable preferences (s 29), undue preferences to creditors (s 30), and the voidable sale of a business (s 34). In addition, the trustee can rely on the common-law *actio Pauliana* to set aside a disposition aimed at defrauding a creditor.

[77] Section 32.

released.[78] Is this differentiation between an insolvent debtor's spouse and other persons (with whom he could have colluded to defraud the estate of assets) justifiable? Is there a sufficient reason for section 21 to have the effect (deprivation) that it has if there are other, less invasive remedies available to achieve the same purpose? Should it be easier for the trustee to get hold of property just because the counterparty is the debtor's solvent spouse? Is it justifiable for section 21 to go so far that the trustee receives ownership of all the solvent spouse's property just so that the estate can eventually keep only those that the solvent spouse is not rightfully entitled to (considering also the risk that some of her property might end up not being released at all)?

If a strict proportionality-type test were to apply, then the abovementioned questions seem to place section 21 in a very bad light and thus might indicate that the deprivation is indeed arbitrary – mostly because the purpose can be achieved in a less invasive way as well as in a manner that treats the persons with whom the debtor could have transacted more equally. Hence, section 21 might more readily be judged as permitting an arbitrary deprivation of property in violation of section 25(1) of the Constitution.

However, if a 'thinner' rationality test is applied to section 21, there is a greater chance that the deprivation will survive the arbitrariness test. The questions posed above will then not reflect negatively on the validity of section 21, since it is not required for section 21 to be the least invasive way to achieve the purpose. It would not matter that there are other provisions available to achieve the same purpose or that section 21 is procedurally more beneficial for the trustee than the other mechanisms. All that matters is whether the effect of section 21 is *a* rational way to achieve the purpose. In view of the importance of the purpose behind section 21, which forms an intricate part of the overall purpose of the Insolvency Act as a whole, I do not believe that the effect of section 21 can readily be classified as an irrational choice to achieve that purpose. It might not be the best choice, it might not be the least invasive choice, and it might not be the most popular choice, but the point is that section 21 is not an irrational choice. Even if section 21 in its present form might not leave one with a sense of satisfaction, one must concede that there is at least a rational connection between the purpose of ensuring that the estate and its creditors are not defrauded of any property, and the temporary transfer of the solvent spouse's property in order to ensure that none of the property that should rightfully go towards the claims of her husband's creditors are lost to the estate. One of the central features of any efficient insolvency system is to ensure that the estate's creditors are not denied any assets that should be available to satisfy their

[78] Section 21(4).

rightful claims against the debtor. For this goal to be a reality, insolvency legislation must unavoidably contain certain mechanisms – sometimes very drastic and unpopular ones – that facilitate the collection of all assets that legitimately belong in the estate. As long as these measures remain rational and procedurally fair, one should generally respect the legislative choice to deal with these matters in this way.[79]

If the test was stricter than a mere rationality test, perhaps a test that moves more towards the proportionality side of the continuum, even then one might argue that there is a good enough reason to distinguish between the debtor's spouse and his other associates. Due to the close relationship between a debtor and his spouse, it would be much easier for them to collude or otherwise transact with one another in such a way that it is rendered close to impossible for the trustee to use one of the other mechanisms in the Act to retrieve the property. Therefore, a more drastic instrument that shifts the burden of proof from the trustee to the spouse seems more justifiable, otherwise the chances might be very good that the estate will lose out on assets that should legitimately go towards paying the creditors. Also, if the property rightfully belongs to the solvent spouse, it will not be unreasonably onerous for her to prove that she, for instance, acquired it with a valid title against her husband's creditors. Under the present structure of section 21, the chances that a spouse would be able to have her assets released if they truly are hers are arguably much higher than the chances that her assets will unjustly be permanently lost to her and her creditors. It is clearly not the intention of section 21 to deprive a solvent spouse or her creditors of assets that legitimately should go to them, and there are enough safeguards in place to prevent the draconian or *mala fide* abuse of section 21 by the trustee.

Consequently, it is my general contention that section 21 does not authorise an arbitrary deprivation of property *per se*. However, it firstly may be that a court is in future presented with a set of facts that indicate an arbitrary deprivation of property, in which event it might be necessary to re-interpret or amend the section in a way that closes the identified gap. Secondly, when interpreting section 21 and applying it to the facts of a case, courts must naturally keep the purpose of the section in mind. Moreover, when deciding whether to release certain assets, courts must always consider that their refusal to do so would have to live up to the constitutional standard that the resultant deprivation of property, if any, may not be arbitrary.[80]

---

[79] See also *Harksen v Lane NO and Others* 1998 (1) SA 300 (CC) para 59.

[80] As s 39(2) of the Constitution provides, all legislation must be interpreted in a manner that promotes the spirit, purport and objects of the Bill of Rights, which includes the protection against arbitrary deprivation of property.

The same holds true if one considers the case from the other side. If an asset is released (or does not vest in the first place), even though it should rightfully be available to the insolvent spouse's creditors, these creditors could experience a deprivation of property that might be judged as arbitrary. One should also consider that, if section 21 is removed without replacing it with something that can efficiently achieve the same purpose, this may mean that the trustee will not be able to collect all the property that should legitimately be included in the estate, which in turn might mean that the creditors do not receive what they are entitled to. In other words, a failure of insolvency legislation reasonably to ensure that the debtor is prevented from defrauding his creditors could mean that the creditors themselves are arbitrarily deprived of property. This is not to say that section 21 in its present form is ideal for all intents and purposes, but that if or when it is replaced, its reason for existing in the first place should not be forgotten, otherwise the efficacy of the sequestration process as a whole might become seriously undermined.

It should be stressed that it is not necessarily my position that section 21 contains the best or most reasonable way to deal with collusion between spouses. I am not even arguing that the section should remain in its exact current form in future insolvency legislation. The section can probably be criticised for being out of touch with modern tendencies and it may even be constitutionally problematic for other reasons, but my contention is that the reason for doing away with section 21 is not found in the property clause of the final Constitution. Overall, therefore, constitutional property law does not, in my view, provide a strong enough argument to challenge the legislative choice to treat the assets of solvent spouses in the way the Insolvency Act does in section 21. The purpose of insolvency law is so important for the functioning of our society and economy that section 21 will be valid as long as there is a rational link between its effect and purpose, and providing that the section includes reasonable safeguards for solvent spouses and their creditors. On a more general level, the same should be true for almost all instances where insolvency-related legislation interferes with vested property interests to achieve an important policy purpose.

5 Conclusion

As important as section 25 of the final Constitution is to ensure that property interferences remain within the bounds of the values of our constitutional democracy, it should never become a tool that is used to hamper the proper balancing of private property interests with the collective public interest. The latter includes the orderly and equitable resolution of insolvent or over-indebted circumstances. When 'the hand of the law is laid upon the estate'[81] of a debtor (and his solvent spouse), the effect is just one of several deprivations of (or interferences with) property authorised by insolvency legislation in South African law. There is, in principle, nothing wrong with this. Deprivations or regulations of property are part and parcel of any free and democratic society. The Constitution permits such regulations, on condition that they must be authorised by law, procedurally fair and substantively not arbitrary.

Importantly, no compensation is payable to the holder of the regulated property, unless the interference in question qualifies as an expropriation of property. However, as a general rule, one should accept that the effects of insolvency legislation will almost never involve expropriations of property. If a claimant alleges that a particular interference goes beyond a normal deprivation of property, the answer is not to claim compensation under the expropriation clause but to argue for the arbitrariness of the deprivation. In insolvency law, as in other fields, the arbitrariness test will then serve as a check on the otherwise legitimate regulation of property interests. However, one should not be too quick to judge the effect of a regulation before its purpose is properly understood and contextualised. With the benefit of hindsight, this is perhaps precisely the mistake Mrs Harksen made.

81 *Walker v Syfret NO* 1911 AD 141 166.

Chapter 5

Tenure security and the reform of servitude law

S Viljoen & J Strydom***

1 Introduction

A number of constitutional provisions[1] are important when considering the development of the common law in line with the Bill of Rights, and the judiciary has a vital role to play in this regard.[2] Arguably, these provisions place a positive obligation on the judiciary to develop the common law 'in each and every case in order to avoid breaching their constitutional mandate, and to further the Constitution's vision of a transformed legal order.'[3] One academic who fiercely argued for the development of the common law was Professor

---

* Associate Professor, Department of Public, Constitutional and International Law, Unisa.

** Senior Associate, Cliffe Dekker Hofmeyr Inc. A final word of thank you to André – you will always have a special place in our hearts. We miss you dearly.

[1] Specifically ss 2, 7(2), 8(3), 39(2) and 173 of the Constitution of the Republic of South Africa, 1996.

[2] LTC Harms 'Ontwikkeling van die gemenereg in die lig van artikels 39(2) en 173 van die Grondwet' (2004) 7 *PER* 1–22 9. See also D Cornell & N Friedman 'The defence of the Constitutional Court: Human rights and the South African common law' (2011) 5 *MLJ* 1–31 15. Nevertheless, the primary drive for large-scale law reform should essentially be undertaken by the legislature and not the courts: *Carmichele v Minister of Safety and Security* 2001 (4) SA 938 (CC) para 36.

[3] D Cornell & N Friedman 'The defence of the Constitutional Court: Human rights and the South African common law' (2011) 5 *MLJ* 1–31 17.

André van der Walt. According to Van der Walt, in contrast to widespread statutory developments that have taken shape in property law, 'precious little has been done about the development of the common law itself'.[4] Van der Walt envisioned a type of development under the Constitution that would promote constitutional goals and, at the same time, reinforce the legitimacy of the common law.[5] Van der Walt also called for a purposive interpretation of legislation to give effect to the Bill of Rights. The Constitutional Court recently confirmed that if a single provision in legislation affects rights in the Bill of Rights, section 39(2) of the Constitution of the Republic of South Africa, 1996 mandates the court to promote the purport, spirit and objects of the Bill of Rights in the process of interpreting the provision in question.[6]

Our aim in this chapter is to determine whether common-law property rights, specifically servitude law, can be interpreted to provide legally secure tenure for unlawful occupiers who reside in informal settlements. From the outset, we accept that a clear connection exists between the section 26(1) right of access to adequate housing and the section 25(6) right of strengthened tenure for all;[7] no form of occupation can be adequate and therefore constitutionally compliant if it is legally recognised as 'unlawful'; and the judiciary must proactively develop the common law and interpret legislation to fulfil its mandate in relation to both strengthened tenure for the previously dispossessed and access to adequate housing for all. Our enquiry is not concerned with the judicial task of curing constitutional rights violations, but rather judicial activism in giving substantive content to these fundamental rights.

---

[4] AJ van der Walt 'Development of the common law of servitude' (2013) 130 *SALJ* 722–756; AJ van der Walt 'Developing the law on unlawful squatting and spoliation' (2008) 125 *SALJ* 24–36 34. He explains that the development of the common law is perhaps also the area of the transformation process that is most controversial.

[5] AJ van der Walt 'Developing the law on unlawful squatting and spoliation' (2008) 125 *SALJ* 24–36 34. Similar to the 'false' distinction between apartheid land law and private property law during the apartheid era, Van der Walt argued that no distinction should be drawn between constitutional commitments, which could be perceived as an area of public law, and private property law. Significant reforms of property law that are directed to correct legacies of apartheid land law must take place as part of private law, rather than in a 'nebulous constitutional sphere which would ostensibly leave private-law tradition untouched': 35. See also D Cornell & N Friedman 'The defence of the Constitutional Court: Human rights and the South African common law' (2011) 5 *MLJ* 1–31 18.

[6] *Makate v Vodacom (Pty) Ltd* 2016 (4) SA 121 (CC) paras 87–90.

[7] AJ van der Walt & S Viljoen 'The constitutional mandate for social welfare – systemic differences and links between property, land rights and housing rights' (2015) 18 *PELJ* 1034–1090 1051, 1070, 1073.

> Every legislative, executive and judicial decision embodies a choice between upholding remnants of the older order and enforcing change brought about by the new; every decision to uphold the existing law implies a sacrifice of constitutional reform, even when it is indubitably correct or unavoidable. Even more importantly, every decision in favour of stability and certainty or vested and acquired rights inevitably comes at the price of suppressing plurality, dissent and change.[8]

We agree. The thrust of our argument is for the judiciary to acknowledge the dire legal position of the most vulnerable in our society who reside in informal settlements; recognise that their insecure tenure is at odds with a range of constitutional provisions; respond to its obligation in rectifying this factual unconstitutionality; and creatively reflect on existing common-law measures to fill the gap between the unlawful occupation of land and home-ownership. In addition, we also suggest that a purposive interpretation of legislation, with a view to enhancing constitutional goals, can result in substantive tenure reform for destitute households. This is not a tall order. We are of the view that a novel constitutionally inspired interpretation of both established common-law doctrine and statute law may result in significant tenure reform. This interpretation does not require either major developments of the common law or extensive revision of our laws and can be brought about if small, incremental changes are introduced in the spirit of constitutional reform.

2 Insecure tenure in informal settlements

At the end of the apartheid era, the dominant theory of land rights, namely that ownership is considered the most important patrimonial right, and to a large extent absolute, had a significant and, we might add, lasting impact on the formulation and implementation of housing policies and laws.[9] During this transitional period, Van der Walt argued that the thrust of reform legislation in the context of land rights was centred on the provision of private landownership, instead of on the creation and development of suitable land-use rights – a notion that arguably diminished the impact of the overall reform process on the development of housing rights.[10] These

---

[8] AJ van der Walt 'Normative pluralism and anarchy: Reflections on the 2007 term' (2008) 1 *CCR* 77–128 84–85.

[9] AJ van der Walt 'Informal housing and the environment: Land rights in transition' (1992) 7 *SAPL* 201–214 201. See also DP Visser 'The "Absoluteness" of ownership: The South African common law in perspective' 1985 *Acta Juridica* 39–52 48; AJ van der Walt 'Personal rights and limited real rights: A historical overview and analysis of contemporary problems related to the registrability of rights' (1992) 55 *THRHR* 170–203.

[10] AJ van der Walt 'Informal housing and the environment: Land rights in transition' (1992) 7 *SAPL* 201–214 205.

remarks remain relevant and arguably call for some reflection. One of the most puzzling aspects of our housing regime is the occupation rights of the most vulnerable – what types of occupation rights have been considered adequate for those who are unable to afford shelter, especially those living in informal settlements?

Initially, a range of developments, both policy-based and in the form of statutory enactments, were introduced. The apartheid-style land laws were repealed,[11] existing rights, such as leasehold, were upgraded into ownership[12] and numerous communities were settled in a speedy and efficient manner.[13] Regardless of these developments, a number of problems remained, including informal rights in land.[14] The land reform programme was subsequently introduced as a three-tiered approach consisting of redistribution,[15] tenure reform[16] and restitution.[17] The tenure reform programme is important for our enquiry, which is mainly concerned with the housing rights of households residing in informal settlements.[18]

In this regard, it seems that the Interim Protection of Informal Land Rights Act 31 of 1996 is the only piece of legislation that applies to vulnerable

---

[11] PJ Badenhorst, JM Pienaar & H Mostert *Silberberg and Schoeman's The law of property* 5 ed (2006) 588.

[12] Upgrading of Land Tenure Rights Act 112 of 1991.

[13] See specifically the Less Formal Township Establishment Act 113 of 1991; J van Wyk *Planning law – principles and procedures of land-use management* (1999) 173–175.

[14] PJ Badenhorst, JM Pienaar & H Mostert *Silberberg and Schoeman's The law of property* 5 ed (2006) 590.

[15] Redistribution is mainly a facilitative programme and its focus is therefore on making available grants and subsidies to enable individuals to gain access to land: PJ Badenhorst, JM Pienaar & H Mostert *Silberberg and Schoeman's The law of property* 5 ed (2006) 594.

[16] Tenure reform aims to rectify and abolish some of the effects of apartheid as it strengthens existing tenure forms weakened by apartheid land law and introduces new forms of tenure that revise the common law.

[17] Section 25(5) of the Constitution makes provision for the redistribution of land, s 25(6) mandates tenure reform and s 25(7) allows for the restitution of land.

[18] Section 25(6) of the Constitution requires tenure that is legally secure, which essentially means that tenure reform embodies a legal or rights-based approach: JM Pienaar *Land reform* (2013) 390. Pienaar further argues that '"legally" may allude to a) the content, definition and delineation of the particular form of tenure; or b) the enforceability thereof'. The former implies legally defined rights, whereas the latter 'is not so focused on the *definition* or *legal basis* of the tenure reform, as long as it can be enforced and it protects against interference and eviction'. We are of the opinion that the latter approach should be avoided for the sake of legal certainty; it also fails to respond to the gradual realisation of the right of access to adequate housing. In our opinion legally secure tenure should be interpreted to provide strengthened tenure rights, either acknowledged in terms of common-law doctrine or statutorily conceptualised.

households who continue to live in informal settlements.[19] The aim of the Act is to protect rights and interests in land which are not formally protected in laws, for the duration of the land reform process.[20] It is therefore structured as an interim solution for vulnerable occupiers during the land reform process. It protects insecure rights, such as unregistered communal rights, 'against deprivation [in a way] similar to that afforded to traditional property rights'.[21]

Section 26 of the Constitution must be read with the tenure reform objective[22] to ensure a nuanced approach to the housing rights of those living in informal settlements. It provides that everyone has a right of access to adequate housing, that the state must take positive legislative measures,[23] within its available resources, to give effect to this right, and that no person may be evicted arbitrarily. Part of the initial housing policy was to introduce and develop a variety of tenure forms that would give effect to both sections

---

[19] The Communal Property Associations Act 28 of 1996; the Communal Land Rights Act 11 of 2004; the Land Reform (Labour Tenants Act) 3 of 1996; and the Extension of Security of Tenure Act 62 of 1997 are not discussed since they apply to rural areas. The Prevention of Illegal Eviction from and Unlawful Occupation of Land Act 19 of 1998 is also irrelevant, because it regulates eviction proceedings. It is not aimed at providing strengthened tenure rights.

[20] The application of the Act has been annually extended since its inception, when it was intended as an interim measure: PJ Badenhorst, JM Pienaar & H Mostert *Silberberg and Schoeman's The law of property* 5 ed (2006) 619.

[21] DL Carey Miller (with A Pope) *Land title in South Africa* (2010) 461–467.

[22] JM Pienaar *Land reform* (2013) 385 explains that tenure reform may be achieved by complex, multi-dimensional and divergent approaches. A concept such as tenure security may be rooted in property law and corresponding concepts and constructions. However, tenure also relates to issues such as how land and property is held, who exercises control over property and when control is exercised. These issues in turn have an impact on other considerations such as the economy, social and power relations, democracy and the exercise of basic human rights such as the right to family, culture and religion. Tenure reform will therefore not only have implications for patterns of land ownership or control, but will also result in the gradual reform on a socio-economic level.

[23] The Housing Act 107 of 1997 reflects the government's aim in promoting 'housing development', which is a key phrase in the Act. Section 1(a) of the Act generally defines 'housing development' as the establishment of residential environments in which citizens will have access to residential structures with secure tenure. *Government of the Republic of South Africa and Others v Grootboom and Others* 2001 (1) SA 46 (CC) para 35 confirmed that section 26(1) recognises that housing requires more than a residential structure. The court does not mention security of tenure, although considering the basis upon which the pre-1994 government, and private landowners, could evict occupiers occupying land without tenure security, one can infer that security of tenure must form part of the provision of adequate housing.

25(6) and 26, but individual ownership has been the main form of tenure delivered.[24]

In light of this brief overview it seems that the focus of the legislative scheme (consisting of the land reform and access to housing provisions) has been to provide occupiers of informal settlements with, firstly, some interim relief against eviction throughout the reform process and, secondly, homeownership, through either a process of upgrading weak existing rights into ownership or the provision of a newly completed RDP house. Even though the protection against eviction objective might initially have been formalised in the Interim Protection of Informal Land Rights Act, it later surfaced in practice by way of judicial developments. In some cases the courts granted suspended eviction orders, coupled with a positive obligation on the state to provide alternative accommodation,[25] whereas in others the courts simply decided not to grant the eviction order.[26] From a constitutional perspective, cases in the latter group are highly problematic, because they fail to ensure legal certainty. The possible common-law development that we propose for this constitutional issue is discussed in the next section,[27] which speaks to the clarification of unlawful occupiers' rights in the event that an eviction order is held to be unjust.

However, the threat of an eviction order should not prevent unlawful occupiers of informal settlements from accessing courts in the hope of strengthening their tenure rights.[28] The provision of ownership by way of

[24] L Royston 'Security of urban tenure in South Africa: Overview of policy and practice' in A Durand-Lasserve & L Royston (eds) *Holding their ground: Secure land tenure for the urban poor in developing countries* (2002) 165–181 176. See also JM Pienaar 'Access to housing in South Africa: An overview of dimensions and mechanisms' (2011) 36 *JJS* 119–140 128 for an explanation of the housing subsidy scheme and its focus on ownership. Conversely, the 1994 White Paper on housing stated that '[o]ne of the most significant and short-term interventions required of the Government will be to provide the widest range of options for the rapid attainment of secure tenure': Republic of South Africa, Department of Housing *White Paper: A new housing policy and strategy for South Africa* (1994) 3 2 2.

[25] See for instance *Sailing Queen Investments v The Occupants La Colleen Court* 2008 6 BCLR 666 (W); *The Occupiers, Shulana Court, 11 Hendon Road, Yeoville, Johannesburg v Steele* 2010 9 BCLR 911 (SCA); *City of Johannesburg Metropolitan Municipality v Blue Moonlight Properties 39 (Pty) Ltd* 2012 (2) SA 104 (CC).

[26] See specifically *Modderfontein Squatters, Greater Benoni City Council v Modderklip Boerdery (Proprietary) Limited (Agri SA and Legal Resources Centre, Amici Curiae)*; *President of the Republic of South Africa and Others v Modderklip Boerdery (Proprietary) Limited (Agri SA and Legal Resources Centre, Amici Curiae)* 2004 (6) SA 40 (SCA) ('*Modderklip*'); *Port Elizabeth Municipality v Various Occupiers* 2005 (1) SA 217 (CC) ('*PE Municipality*').

[27] See section 3 below.

[28] The second part of our argument follows in section 4 below.

RDP houses has proven to be a time-consuming process; while it is unclear to what extent the upgrading process has had any success. What is however clear from the evictions case law is that thousands of poor households continue to occupy rudimentary structures in appalling conditions with legally insecure tenure, often for lengthy periods of time.[29] In the absence of innovative housing policies and laws that aim to address the plight of the poor, the focus shifts to the judiciary and its power to come to these individuals' assistance. Of course, the judiciary is not empowered to craft new laws in the form of statutory provisions that would provide the required tenure security, but it can do a great deal when either interpreting legislation or developing the common law to that effect. In the sections that follow we argue that essential features relating to personal servitudes, including the fact that they are limited real rights, which entitle the holders thereof to use and enjoy the property of the owners,[30] render them favourable for vulnerable groups who occupy informal settlements with insecure tenure.[31]

3 Formalisation of the right not to be evicted

In both *Modderklip* and *PE Municipality*, the respective courts held that eviction orders were unjust and that the occupiers had to remain on privately owned land.[32] While the respective courts' efforts to uphold the occupiers'

---

[29] See for instance *Residents of Joe Slovo Community, Western Cape v Thubelisha Homes and Others* 2010 (3) SA 454 (CC); Housing Development Agency 'South Africa: Informal settlements status' (2013); www.thehda.co.za/uploads/files/HDA_South_Africa_Report_lr.pdf.

[30] PJ Badenhorst, JM Pienaar & H Mostert *Silberberg and Schoeman's The law of property* 5 ed (2006) 321; CG van der Merwe *Sakereg* 2 ed (1989) 458. A praedial servitude is not considered for purposes of this piece since it relates to two pieces of land and the servitude is constituted in favour of one piece of land over the adjacent piece of land. See AJ van der Walt *The law of servitudes* (2016) 71–77, where he argues that a praedial servitude vests over a specific piece of land, regardless of the identity of the owners, whereas a personal servitude benefits a specific individual in her personal capacity. See also *Hotel De Aar v Jonordon Investment (Edms) Bpk* 1972 (2) SA 400 (A) 405–406.

[31] If the settlement is established on agricultural land, the court would have to join the Minister of Agriculture, Forestry and Fisheries, because the Subdivision of Agricultural Land Act 70 of 1970 prohibits the registration of multiple personal servitudes in respect of agricultural land without the consent of the Minister.

[32] In *Modderklip*, an informal settlement consisted of 40 000 persons residing on 50 hectares of private land. The landowner obtained an eviction order, but it was practically unenforceable. The Supreme Court of Appeal granted a constitutional remedy, which took the form of constitutional damages due to the breach of a constitutionally entrenched right and had the advantage that the occupiers could remain *in situ*, until the state could either expropriate the land or remove the occupiers elsewhere. This was confirmed by the Constitutional Court in *President of the Republic of South Africa and another v Modderklip Boerdery (Proprietary) Limited (Agri SA and others, Amici Curiae)* 2005 (5) SA 3 (CC).

section 26 rights are commendable, the results are, in the words of the Constitutional Court, 'manifestly unsatisfactory to all concerned'.[33] These decisions create insoluble questions, including what are the content and parameters of the constitutional relationship between the landowner, the municipality and the unlawful occupier; can this relationship be structured to uphold the landowner's rights while creating a form of tenure security for the occupier; and what are the duties of the municipality in the interim?

With reference to these cases we argue that the law of personal servitudes – developed with a view to strengthening precarious tenure – may facilitate legal certainty in some instances where unlawful occupiers reside on private or state-owned land. The use of servitude language in the social housing context may not be as far-fetched as it initially seems. Section 26(3) of the Constitution states that no person may be evicted from their home, or have their home demolished, without an order of court made after considering all relevant circumstances.[34] This provision, read with the provisions of the Prevention of Illegal Eviction From and Unlawful Occupation of Land Act 19 of 1998 (PIE), restricts the exercise of ownership entitlements insofar as unlawful occupiers can only be evicted if such an order is judicially held to be just. Considered from this perspective, we argue that this limitation could resemble a personal negative servitude that operates in favour of the unlawful occupier.[35]

A personal servitude is a real right and it attaches to a specific individual.[36] Such a servitude is limited in lifespan and terminates on the death of the

See also AJ van der Walt 'The state's duty to protect property owners v the state's duty to provide housing: Thoughts on the *Modderklip* case' (2005) 21 *SAJHR* 144–161 for a detailed discussion of the case. In *PE Municipality* the Constitutional Court also decided against the eviction of 68 people, due to the lengthy period of time that the occupiers had resided on the property, the lack of alternative accommodation and the fact that the municipality and landowner did not present evidence that they required the land for another use: para 59.

[33] Para 61.

[34] PIE gives effect to this negative right.

[35] CG van der Merwe *Sakereg* 2 ed (1989) 463 confirms that personal servitudes can be positive or negative servitudes.

[36] CG van der Merwe *Sakereg* 2 ed (1989) 506; CG Hall & EA Kellaway *Servitudes* 3 ed (1973) 1–5; PJ Badenhorst, JM Pienaar & H Mostert *Silberberg and Schoeman's The law of property* 5 ed (2006) 467–479; AJ van der Walt *The law of servitudes* (2016) 455–456; *Felix en 'n Ander v Nortier NO en Andere* [1996] 3 All SA 143 (SE) 148; *Lorentz v Melle* 1978 (3) SA 1044 (T) 1049; *Barclays Western Bank Ltd v Comfy Hotels Ltd* 1980 (4) SA 174 (E) 178; *Van Rensburg and Another v Koekemoer and Others* 2011 (1) SA 118 (GSJ) paras 14, 15 & 17; *National Stadium South Africa (Pty) Ltd and Others v Firstrand Bank Ltd* 2011 (2) SA 157 (SCA) paras 31–32.

holder.[37] It can therefore not be transferred to another party.[38] It can generally also not pass by succession to another person upon the death of its holder.[39] However, Van der Merwe argues that it might be useful for the courts to develop the law by allowing some personal servitudes to be perpetual, provided that such a development is restricted to cases where it is necessary and justified.[40] Personal servitudes are enforceable against the owner and all third parties, since it is a limited real right.[41] Personal servitudes can be constituted for a fixed period of time, for the lifetime of the beneficiary or for a period of time until the occurrence of a future event.[42] Interestingly, Van der Walt argues that a landowner can create 'several, separate, independent usufructs (*or probably other personal servitudes*) over different, ideally identified (but physically undivided) parts of the servient land'.[43] In such an

[37] Section 66 of the Deeds Registries Act 47 of 1937 states that no personal servitude of usufruct, *usus* or *habitatio* purporting to extend beyond the lifetime of the person in whose favour its created shall be registered, nor may a transfer of cession of such personal servitude to any person other than the owner of the land encumbered thereby, be registered. See also CG Hall & EA Kellaway *Servitudes* 3 ed (1973) 1–5; PJ Badenhorst, JM Pienaar & H Mostert *Silberberg and Schoeman's The law of property* 5 ed (2006) 467–479.

[38] CG van der Merwe *Sakereg* 2 ed (1989) 506; AJ van der Walt *The law of servitudes* (2016) 73. Van der Walt clarifies that the holder is however entitled to transfer some of her use entitlements, while the servitude right itself may not be alienated.

[39] Section 66 of the Deeds Registries Act 47 of 1937. CG van der Merwe *Sakereg* 2 ed (1989) 506; AJ van der Walt *The law of servitudes* (2016) 72. Van der Walt also mentions that one of the most interesting questions in modern servitude law is 'whether personal servitudes should always terminate with the death of the servitude holder': 73.

[40] CG van der Merwe 'Can personal servitudes be worded in such a way that they are perpetual in nature and thus freely transferable and transmissible?' 2013 *TSAR* 340–348 342–343, 347–348.

[41] PJ Badenhorst, JM Pienaar & H Mostert *Silberberg and Schoeman's The law of property* 5 ed (2006) 322; CG van der Merwe *Sakereg* 2 ed (1989) 458; *Ex parte Geldenhuys* 1926 OPD 155 163–164; *Willoughby's Consolidated Co Ltd v Copthall Stores Ltd* 1913 AD 267; *Lorentz v Melle* 1978 (3) SA 1044 (T) 1049C; *Barclays Western Bank Ltd v Comfy Hotels Ltd* 1980 (4) SA 174 (E) 178; *Felix en 'n Ander v Nortier NO en Andere* [1996] 3 All SA 143 (SE) 148.

[42] PJ Badenhorst, JM Pienaar & H Mostert *Silberberg and Schoeman's The law of property* 5 ed (2006) 339.

[43] AJ van der Walt *The law of servitudes* (2016) 121; CG van der Merwe *Sakereg* 2 ed (1989) 516; *Parkin v Parkin* (1869) 2 Buch 136. A number of servitudes can be created on one piece of land and registered as such by means of a diagram: regulation 73(2) of the regulations promulgated in terms of section 10 of the Deeds Registries Act 47 of 1937, as amended by GN 1224 of 2003 as from 26 September 2003. Section 6A of the Subdivision of Agricultural Land Act 70 of 1970 prohibits the establishment of a personal servitude over part of agricultural land.

instance the servient land as a whole is the object of the servitude, not the specific piece that the holder may use and enjoy.[44]

Personal servitudes are usually created by agreement, after which the right is registered.[45] These rights only come into being once they are registered.[46] In contrast, praedial servitudes can be established by way of a court order, usually on the basis of necessity.[47] These rights are established automatically, without registration, although it is generally advised that they should also be registered to fulfil the publicity function.[48] Van der Walt argues that in these instances the imposition of a servitude on the servient land must be justified and it is therefore not surprising that the establishment of these servitudes is usually based on a clear public purpose.[49] The creation of a personal servitude by way of a judicial decision, on the basis of a specific need, does not form part of our law; although that does not mean that the creation of such a right on such grounds should not be introduced or at least explored with reference to constitutional demands.

There is established authority for the acquisition of a right of way of necessity in Roman-Dutch law.[50] This praedial servitude is acquired from a servient tenement, without the co-operation of the servient landowner (and often against her will), when the dominant tenement is completely cut off from access to public roads. There are four principal differences between

---

44 AJ van der Walt *The law of servitudes* (2016) 460. A similar rule applies to the establishment of numerous usufructs over one piece of land – the object of each usufruct remains the whole of the land: 470, referring to JC Sonnekus 'Bewoningsreg (habitatio) – Verval dit weens versteuring (vernietiging) van die bouwerk?' 2009 *TSAR* 450–469 454; JC Sonnekus 'Bewoningsreg (habitatio) – Aard van die regsobjek en die effek daarvan op die registrasie van die reg' (2015) 26 *Stell LR* 63–84 73–80.

45 PJ Badenhorst, JM Pienaar & H Mostert *Silberberg and Schoeman's The law of property* 5 ed (2006) 342. Registration can take place by means of a reservation in a deed of transfer or through registration of a notarial deed against the title deed of the servient tenement. In the case of the latter, the notarial deed must be accompanied by an endorsement against the title deed. See specifically section 67 of the Deeds Registries Act 47 of 1937. See also the Alienation of Land Act 68 of 1981, which requires that an agreement granting a servitude must be in writing and signed by both parties to be valid.

46 AJ van der Walt *The law of servitudes* (2016) 279.

47 AJ van der Walt *The law of servitudes* (2016) 338–339. South African law distinguishes between permanent and temporary rights of way of necessity. In the case of a permanent right of way, compensation is payable by the dominant landowner. A temporary right of way of necessity can only be used in emergencies and compensation of the servient landowner is not required.

48 AJ van der Walt & TN Raphulu 'The right of way of necessity: A constitutional analysis' (2014) 77 *THRHR* 468-484; AJ van der Walt *The law of servitudes* (2016) 279–281.

49 AJ van der Walt *The law of servitudes* (2016) 76–77.

50 See AJ van der Walt *The law of servitudes* (2016) 337.

rights of way of necessity and consensual servitudes of right of way:[51] a right of way of necessity is created by court order and not by contract; a court will only award a right of way of necessity in instances of actual necessity;[52] a court may grant compensation when awarding a permanent right of way of necessity as opposed to consideration payable in terms of contract; and the right of way of necessity can terminate if the necessity element falls away. In respect of the first requirement, Van der Walt argues that necessity creates the servitude as soon as the situation arises and the court confirms the existence of such a limited real right.[53] It seems that the owner of landlocked land has a *de facto* claim of necessity, and the court order 'probably creates a limited real right in the form of a right of way of necessity by operation of law'.[54]

Similar to rights of way of necessity, a court can arguably create a negative personal servitude in favour of unlawful occupiers in the case where an eviction order is found to be unjust. Contributing factors that indicate necessity are for example the sheer number of occupiers, which render an eviction order unenforceable in the near future (*Modderklip*) or the lack of suitable alternative accommodation (*PE Municipality*). Unlike a right of way of necessity, which has its foundations in the common law, the proposed novel negative personal servitude in the social housing context arguably originates in section 26(3) of the Constitution once a court decides against an eviction order. A decision of this kind arguably has the effect of creating a personal negative servitude in favour of the occupiers. Such a servitude restricts the owner's entitlements, albeit temporarily, until either the court grants the eviction order[55] (once the necessity requirement has fallen away) or the local authority resolves the issue by acquiring the property.[56] Given that real rights are created when the court refuses an eviction order, registration is arguably

[51] CG van der Merwe *Sakereg* 2 ed (1989) 485–486.

[52] AJ van der Walt *The law of servitudes* (2016) 349 explains that a right of way of necessity will only be granted if the applicant can prove necessity. The applicant must prove that her land is cut off from public roads or that she has no useful or serviceable access to public roads; that for purposes of using her land beneficially, she requires access to a specific road running over a specific servient tenement and that she is unable to obtain a servitude by way of consensus.

[53] AJ van der Walt *The law of servitudes* (2016) 362.

[54] AJ Van der Walt *The law of servitudes* (2016) 362.

[55] The court's decision not to grant the eviction order is arguably in line with section 26(3) of the Constitution.

[56] See for instance section 9(3) of the Housing Act 107 of 1997; section 2 of the Expropriation Act 63 of 1975.

not necessary.[57] Depending on the circumstances, a court may order a local authority to pay some consideration for the creation of the negative personal servitude, since the local authority is ultimately responsible for giving effect to the housing provision. Importantly, consideration will not follow automatically on the creation of a limited real right, because this servitude is created on a temporary basis.[58] Nevertheless, some consideration may be suitable if it is in the form of constitutional damages to lessen the burden of what might amount to an arbitrary deprivation.[59] Our proposition for the courts to create a personal negative servitude on the basis of necessity may seem odd in light of the fact that the only recognised servitude to be established by way of a court decision, on the basis of necessity, is that of a right of way of necessity, which is of course a preadial servitude. However, this does not mean that personal servitudes, such as the personal negative servitude that we propose, can and should not be able to vest by way of a judicial decision if it is undoubtedly in the public interest and necessary from a constitutional viewpoint. Our point of departure is direction-giving in this analysis, which is to determine ways in which some development of our common law of property (specifically that of servitude) can give effect to the constitutional right of access to adequate housing, read with the right to secure tenure. With reference to the Constitution and the hierarchical position that it fulfils in our legal system, the need to secure marginalised occupiers' rights is a critical obligation for both the legislature and the courts. Moreover, the Constitution dictates that the courts *must* develop the common law to give content to rights in the Bill of Rights. It may therefore be asked why a development similar to what we suggest has not taken shape since the courts are duty-bound to steer our common law along these lines. From this perspective the suggestion that the courts should be able to create personal servitudes on the basis of necessity is not all that far-fetched.

In conclusion, a number of features distinguish a negative personal servitude arising from housing necessity from ordinary personal servitudes, and it is essential for the courts to develop the common law in this regard, while unique characteristics relating to the proposed servitude must also

[57] However, the judgment may on direction of the court be noted as a caveat against the title deed of the property in question in the relevant deeds office as an additional step towards legal certainty.

[58] AJ van der Walt *The law of servitudes* (2016) 338–339.

[59] This was likely the case in *Modderklip*. See specifically J Strydom & S Viljoen 'Unlawful occupation of inner-city buildings: A constitutional analysis of the rights and obligations involved' (2014) 17 *PELJ* 1207–1261.

be highlighted.[60] Firstly, the establishment of a negative personal servitude arising from housing necessity requires some development of the common law in that the judiciary would have to create a *personal* servitude on the basis of necessity. To date, legal precedent exists only for the creation of a praedial servitude. Nevertheless, considering the justification for a praedial servitude of right of way of necessity, the proposed development would be founded on a similar basis, namely necessity and public interest. Furthermore, the termination of a negative personal servitude arising from housing necessity justifies its creation in that it will terminate once the need falls away – it is uniquely limited in time to address the specific need. Thirdly, as clarified by Van der Walt, a court can create several, separate and individual personal servitudes over different parts of the servient land, but the land in its entirety is the object of the servitude.[61] This means that individuals within a community can be awarded personal servitudes in their personal capacity. A specific person (likely the head of the household) can therefore be the holder of the right, while the object of the servitude is the parcel of land in its entirety. Regardless of the fact that communities of this kind may grow or even diminish, individual households that form part of the community will be awarded a negative servitude and therefore provided with legally secure tenure. Essential to this award is the principle (embedded in all personal servitudes) that the right is not transferrable; the award is aimed at ensuring *legally* secure tenure for the individual/household. This characteristic of personal servitudes makes it apt for tenure reform in informal settlements, although the law may have to be developed to allow for the succession of these rights, especially to members of the household. A development of this kind is likely necessary and justified.

Overall, the proposed development will ensure legal certainty amongst the parties involved (including the landowner, occupiers, local authority and third parties), but, more importantly, it will strengthen the occupiers' tenure from 'unlawful' to that of limited real rights. Even though the content of these rights are phrased negatively, in that the occupiers may not be evicted until

[60] Van der Merwe confirms that one of the shared characteristics between personal and praedial servitudes is that both can be negative servitudes. See CG Van der Merwe *Sakereg* 2 ed (1989) 463. Van der Merwe and De Waal define personal servitudes as limited real rights that impose burdens on immovable property, thereby restricting the rights, powers or liberties of the landowner in favour of another person. See CG van der Merwe and MJ de Waal 'Servitudes' in WA Joubert and JA Faris (eds) *The law of South Africa* vol 24 2 ed (2010) 540. A personal negative servitude would typically restrict the owner of the servient tenement from exercising certain entitlements in favour of a person or juristic entity.

[61] AJ van der Walt *The law of servitudes* (2016) 121.

certain measures are in place, the court can structure the right in such a way that it will in effect operate perpetually. This can be done in two ways, by either clarifying that the occupiers may remain on the land as holders of limited real rights, while the state clarifies the legality of their occupation (by either purchasing the land or even leasing it from the owner),[62] or guaranteeing that their rights will 'continue' as limited real rights once they have been relocated to suitable alternative accommodation. In the case of the latter, the court ensures safeguards by guaranteeing that the occupiers will firstly be awarded a negative personal servitude, up until such time as their relocation is the most logical option, whereafter they must be awarded *legally* secure tenure in their new location, which arguably translates into rights of a similar standing. It is of course not possible to transfer their limited real rights to the new location,[63] which is why it is doctrinally sound to argue that their negative personal servitude will cease to exist once the necessity element has fallen away – when they are in fact relocated – after which their new rights in the new location may be established.[64] By way of a structural interdict the court can oversee an order of this kind to ensure governmental compliance with constitutional demands, which in our scenario is tenure reform and the right to housing.[65]

4 Acquisitive prescription in informal settlements

Even though a substantial percentage of households have been awarded private ownership, a mounting number remain destitute, waiting for the state to respond to their plight. In the interim, we propose that the law of servitude can play a significant role in the strengthening of these individuals' tenure rights, absent any state involvement. Our central argument in this section is that any community that either constitutes an informal settlement or forms part of such a settlement is at liberty to approach a court and claim

---

[62] In the alternative the state can expropriate the property or even the use right of the owner. See specifically section 9(3) of the Housing Act 107 of 1997; section 2 of the Expropriation Act 63 of 1975; S Viljoen 'The temporary expropriation of a use right as interim measure in the South African housing context (part 1)' 2014 *TSAR* 359–376 371–374.

[63] CG van der Merwe *Sakereg* 2 ed (1989) 15.

[64] Due to spacing constraints we are unable to elaborate on the practical establishment of such new rights. The underlying objective should however be to ensure that evictees are awarded *legally* secure tenure and the court should oversee governmental compliance in this regard.

[65] These orders, likely granted as structural interdicts, may be noted as a caveat against the title deed of the property in the relevant deeds office. Even though this is not necessary to create the negative personal servitudes, which come into being on the granting of the court order, the noting of the judgment will fulfil the publicity function on a symbolic level.

a personal servitude of *usus* on the basis of acquisitive prescription, provided that the community complies with the statutory requirements.

Servitudes can be acquired by prescription in terms of the requirements set by the Prescription Act 68 of 1969 if the acquiror has exercised the entitlements of a holder of that kind of servitude over the servient land and in line with the requirements for acquisitive prescription.[66] The basic requirement for acquisitive prescription is the actual use of the servitude for an uninterrupted period of 30 years.[67] Section 6 of the Act requires that the acquiror must have 'openly and as though he were entitled to do so, exercised the rights and powers which a person who has a right to such servitude is entitled to exercise, for an uninterrupted period of thirty years.'[68] In *South African National Parks v Weyer-Henderson and Others*[69] the court confirmed that absolute continuity in the exercise of the servitude is not required since the degree of the required exercise is dependent on the nature of the right, the nature of the property as well as the kind of use to which it is put. The same logic was reiterated in *Cillie v Geldenhuys*,[70] where the Supreme Court of Appeal held that the nature and scope of the right acquired will depend on the nature and scope of the right exercised. The distinction drawn by the court in *Swanepoel v Crown Mines Ltd*[71] between unlawful possession and possession that is in itself illegal is also important. The latter precludes prescription, whereas the former is subject to the rules and principles that regulate prescription.

---

[66] AJ van der Walt *The law of servitudes* (2016) 287. Acquisitive prescription is an original method of acquiring property and the servitude right will vest automatically once all the requirements are met: 322.

[67] AJ van der Walt *The law of servitudes* (2016) 289. It is not necessary to register a servitude acquired by way of prescription, although registration is generally required to fulfil the publicity function: 290.

[68] In addition to actual use, the claimant must also prove that her use was open and as if of right. Another related requirement is that use must be exercised without force or violence: AJ van der Walt *The law of servitudes* (2016) 296–297, referring to the *nec vi* requirement in the Prescription Act 18 of 1943. Moreover, it is sufficient if use is exercised openly towards the public – acquisitive prescription is not based on the owner's knowledge and consequent neglect to claim his property: CG van der Merwe *Sakereg* 2 ed (1989) 277; *Buckland v Manga* [2008] 2 All SA 177 (E) 180. AJ van der Walt *The law of servitudes* (2016) 304–307 concludes that the requirement of open possession reflects the common-law requirement of *civilis possessio*, which basically renders the adverse user requirement redundant. At 310 Van der Walt also concludes that the *animo domini* requirement for acquisitive prescription of ownership does not apply in the context of acquisitive prescription of servitudes.

[69] 2007 (3) SA 109 (SE) para 23.

[70] 2009 (2) SA 325 (SCA) para 15.

[71] 1954 (4) SA 596 (A) 604–606.

Prescription provides legal certainty to a long-standing factual situation, which is mainly in the interests of third parties who could be misled by the factual possession of property that is not formally endorsed by law.[72] This function of acquisitive prescription is referred to as the 'quieting of disputed title' and is particularly important where 'the register does not reflect the true state of affairs'.[73] Another interesting argument for recognising acquisitive prescription is that it shifts rights relating to scarce resources, such as land, from lower-valuing owners to higher valuing users when the voluntary exchange of those rights in the private market is associated with high transaction costs.[74] The assumption is that such a shift is both efficient and fair since the owner can interrupt the prescription period by either granting a right or evicting the possessor.[75] In the case where the property is privately owned, acquisitive prescription will constitute a deprivation and must therefore comply with section 25(1) of the Constitution.[76]

The continued unlawful occupation of land for an uninterrupted period of 30 years is arguably subject to prescription and such an occupier should be able to claim a servitude of *usus*,[77] depending on the circumstances. A person who claims such a right in land can 'apply to court by petition for an

---

[72] AJ van der Walt *The law of servitudes* (2016) 324, referring to CG van der Merwe *Sakereg* 2 ed (1989) 269. See also AJ van der Walt *The law of servitudes* (2016) 323–324 for the alternative argument that prescription is justified on the basis of the owner's neglect.

[73] AJ van der Walt *The law of servitudes* (2016) 324. See also *Pienaar v Rabie* 1983 (3) SA 126 (A) 137–138.

[74] AJ van der Walt *The law of servitudes* (2016) 328. This is one of two law-and-economics arguments.

[75] AJ van der Walt *The law of servitudes* (2016) 328.

[76] AJ van der Walt *The law of servitudes* (2016) 331. Acquisitive prescription does not however amount to expropriation: 329–331. In short, Van der Walt concludes that in light of the clear purpose of prescription; the strict possession requirements; the 30-year term; and the ease with which the owner can interrupt the term, there seems to be sufficient reason for the deprivation as required in section 25(1). See also AJ van der Walt & EJ Marais 'The constitutionality of acquisitive prescription: A section 25 analysis' 2012 *TSAR* 714–736.

[77] Usufruct (*ususfructus*), use (*usus*) and habitation (*habitatio*) are the most prominent personal servitudes. Usufruct is mainly utilised in rural areas where the purpose is to entitle the holder to farm. A servitude of this kind is therefore not apt for our argument. The social function of usufruct is to enable the *usufructuary* to generate some income during the lifetime of the usufruct: CG van der Merwe *Sakereg* 2 ed (1989) 508. *Habitatio* is also difficult to prove in the context of informal settlements, because the right attaches to another's dwelling. In the case of informal settlements, the occupiers construct the dwellings themselves on the land of another, which rather resembles a right of *usus*, because they utilise the land of another in such a way as they see fit. Moreover, they use adjacent land to some extent as well, which the right of *habitatio* prohibits: AJ van der Walt *The law of servitudes* (2016) 494.

order authorising the registration of the property in her name'.[78] An unlawful occupier who has resided in an informal settlement for thirty years should fairly easily be able to prove that she exercised the rights and powers of a servitude of *usus* as if she were the holder thereof in an open and transparent manner.[79] The holder of a servitude of *usus* is entitled to possess and use the thing and if it is land, she and her family may occupy the land.[80] The content and extent of the servitude of *usus* is dependent on the nature of the property that the right attaches to.[81] In the case of land, 'the usuary and her household may use the land in the sense of living on it',[82] which is exactly what a household residing in an informal settlement does – they live on the land of another.

In some cases an individual/household would be able to comply with the prescription requirements, whereas in other cases a community would likely be able show that they have resided on a piece of land for thirty years and have exercised their rights, similar to holders of the right of *usus*.[83] Based on the logic that a court can create several, separate and individual personal servitudes over different parts of the servient land, while the land in its

---

[78] AJ van der Walt *The law of servitudes* (2016) 323, referring to section 33 of the Deeds Registries Act 47 of 1937. If the claim is opposed, the acquiror would have to prove, on a preponderance of probabilities, compliance with all the requirements: CG van der Merwe *Sakereg* 2 ed (1989) 288–289; PJ Badenhorst, JM Pienaar & H Mostert *Silberberg and Schoeman's The law of property* 5 ed (2006) 172–173.

[79] Such an occupier would also be able to show that she intends to stay on the property as if she were the holder of the right. See specifically EJ Marais *Acquisitive prescription in view of the property clause* (2011) unpublished LLD thesis University of Stellenbosch 42.

[80] PJ Badenhorst, JM Pienaar & H Mostert *Silberberg and Schoeman's The law of property* 5 ed (2006) 341; CG van der Merwe *Sakereg* 2 ed (1989) 521; AJ van der Walt *The law of servitudes* (2016) 490.

[81] CG van der Merwe *Sakereg* 2 ed (1989) 521.

[82] AJ van der Walt *The law of servitudes* (2016) 490.

[83] See for instance Housing Development Agency 'South Africa: Informal Settlements Status' (2013); www.thehda.co.za/uploads/files/HDA_South_Africa_Report_lr.pdf. Furthermore, it is trite that major informal settlements across South Africa (including Soweto, Tembisa, Kayamandi, Langa, Nyanga and Khayelitsha) were initially established before or during the apartheid era. These settlements have gradually grown in numbers and many occupiers or communities have arguably resided in these townships for thirty years or more. Moreover, as these settlements grew new households settled as unlawful occupiers, often by way of 'clusters' next to the original settlement. It would not be surprising if some of these groups of settlers also took occupation during the 1980s; more than thirty years ago. Joe Slovo for example was established as an informal settlement in Langa during the 1990s, implying that at least some of the communities will be able to argue for prescription in the near future. Furthermore, various smaller communities of informal settlers have mushroomed across South Africa since 1994, and in some instances it should be possible to argue that these smaller communities will acquire a right of *usus* once they have met the requirements for acquisitive prescription.

entirety is the object of the servitude, it follows that one piece of land – occupied by numerous households over different periods of time – can be the object of a personal servitude of *usus*. It would likely be easier to prove that a community has resided on a piece of land for thirty years than that individual households have done so. Moreover, as confirmed in the case law, absolute continuity in the exercise of the servitude is not required, since the degree of the required exercise is dependent on the nature of the right, the nature of the property as well as the kind of use to which it is put. Regardless of these considerations, a community would probably be able to prove that as a whole, it has been in existence for the required thirty years and that its members have exercised their occupation rights in a manner that resembles the servitude of *usus*, which they have done openly for all others to witness. Similar to what was argued in the previous section, individual households who form part of the community will in such an instance be awarded a personal servitude of *usus* and therefore be provided with legally secure tenure. The rights awarded are therefore individualised in the sense that each individual or household would acquire a right of *usus*, while the object of the servitude is the parcel of land in its entirety.[84]

Our proposal, up to this point, is founded on the provisions of the Prescription Act and existing common-law doctrine as it has developed in both the courts and academic literature. A significant qualification is however the fact that the State Land Disposal Act 48 of 1961 prohibits the acquisition of state land through prescription.[85] Even though the Prescription Act binds the state, it goes further to state that the provisions of the Act shall not affect the provisions of any law prohibiting the acquisition of land or any right in land by prescription.[86] The logic and continued relevance of this qualification in the law of servitude is questionable, especially in the social housing framework. In light of sections 25(6) and 26(1) and (2) of the Constitution, it seems peculiar to allow prescription in cases where occupiers reside on private land, but not state land. The state is tasked with the duty to ensure strengthened tenure rights for previously dispossessed persons; provide access to adequate housing; and, above all, proactively utilise scarce resources to give content to fundamental rights. The growing magnitude of

[84] The common-law development relating to succession, as suggested in the previous section, should likely also apply in these cases, whereas a court should generally also be able to prohibit the state (as owner of the land) from requesting security from the community. For more details in this regard, see CG van der Merwe *Sakereg* 2 ed (1989) 524; AJ van der Walt *The law of servitudes* (2016) 497.

[85] Section 3 of the Act simply states that '...State land shall ... not be capable of being acquired by any person by prescription'.

[86] Sections 18 and 19.

our informal settlements clearly shows that the state has not stepped up to this task and in the interim some communities have settled on state land for lengthy periods of time to such an extent that they have established vibrant communities, but from a legal perspective they technically continue to occupy the land as unlawful occupiers. The law is clearly not in sync with the factual reality and our proposal is that these pre-1994 laws should be interpreted by the judiciary to allow prescription to take place. The underlying objective is of course to allow for the gradual strengthening of vulnerable households' rights, and the judicial award of a limited real right could possibly provide an incentive for these occupiers steadily to upgrade their homes, and lead to more dedicated assistance from the local authority in creating vibrant, sustainable communities.

5 Constitutional analysis

As a point of departure, we structure our argument for the development of the law of personal servitude on the obligation of the judiciary both to interpret legislation and to develop the common law in line with the Bill of Rights so as to further the constitutional vision of a transformed legal order.[87] Even though we are of the view that personal servitudes may have a multitude of applications in the informal housing sector, we limit our argument to the judicial recognition of negative personal servitudes, in cases where an eviction order is held to be unjust, and the acquisition of the right of *usus* by way of acquisitive prescription.

Before we align our proposal with Van der Walt's work, an essential distinction must be drawn between our proposal and the starting point of his work.[88] Both the subsidiarity principles (as explained with reference to the Constitutional Court jurisprudence)[89] and constitutional analysis, as suggested when developing the common law,[90] take as a point of departure the infringement of a constitutional right. Our proposal is not centred on the infringement of a constitutional right, but rather on the gradual realisation thereof. This difference should however not stand in the way of a constructive alignment of our proposal with Van der Walt's work.

---

[87] Section 173 read with section 39(2) of the Constitution.

[88] AJ van der Walt 'Normative pluralism and anarchy: Reflections on the 2007 term' (2008) 1 *CCR* 77–128; AJ van der Walt 'Development of the common law of servitude' (2013) 130 *SALJ* 722–756.

[89] AJ van der Walt 'Normative pluralism and anarchy: Reflections on the 2007 term' (2008) 1 *CCR* 77–128.

[90] AJ van der Walt 'Development of the common law of servitude' (2013) 130 *SALJ* 722–756.

Van der Walt argued that in the new constitutional dispensation, constitutional law must be the point of departure for the justification and structuring of the process of developing the common law.[91] However, a preliminary question is *whether* the common law should play a role in a given dispute, since legal analysis of any kind must take both the supremacy clause (section 7 of the Constitution) and the single-system-of-law principle (as it was articulated in *Ex Parte President of the Republic of South Africa: In re Pharmaceutical Manufacturers Association of South Africa*)[92] as its point of departure. Read together, these principles dictate that any area of law is inherently part of the single system of South African law, which is 'shaped by the Constitution as the supreme law, which derives its force from the Constitution, and which is subject to constitutional control'.[93] One must therefore first determine the relationship between the different sources of law, including constitutional provisions, legislation and the common law, and their given authority that might apply to a legal dispute.[94] This approach as suggested by Van der Walt stems from a range of Constitutional Court decisions where a single, integrated process was enunciated on how the single system of law principle should be developed.[95] This process rests on two principles which set out the way in which the correct source of law should be chosen to apply to a legal dispute. In terms of the first principle, a litigant who claims that a constitutional right has been infringed is obliged to rely on legislation that has been enacted to give effect to that right. In such an instance the litigant may not rely on the constitutional provision directly.[96] According to the second principle, a litigant who claims that a constitutional

[91] AJ van der Walt 'Development of the common law of servitude' (2013) 130 *SALJ* 722–756 735. In the rarest cases would historical, comparative or policy analysis assist parties in a given dispute to solve property-related problems in an uncontroversial manner: 736.

[92] 2000 (2) SA 674 (CC) para 44.

[93] AJ van der Walt 'Development of the common law of servitude' (2013) 130 *SALJ* 722–756 738.

[94] AJ van der Walt 'Development of the common law of servitude' (2013) 130 *SALJ* 722–756 738.

[95] AJ van der Walt 'Development of the common law of servitude' (2013) 130 *SALJ* 722–756 739. See specifically AJ van der Walt 'Normative pluralism and anarchy: Reflections on the 2007 term' (2008) 1 *CCR* 77–128; AJ van der Walt *Property and Constitution* (2012) Ch 2.

[96] *South African National Defence Union v Minister of Defence* 2007 (5) SA 400 (CC) paras 51–52; *MEC for Education: KwaZulu-Natal v Pillay* 2008 (1) SA 474 (CC) paras 39–40; *Chirwa v Transnet Ltd* 2008 (2) SA 24 (CC) para 59; *Walele v City of Cape Town and Others* 2008 (6) SA 129 (CC) paras 29–30; *Nokotyana & others v Ekurhuleni Metropolitan Municipality & others* 2010 (4) BCLR 312 (CC) paras 47–49. One should also note that a litigant can rely on a constitutional provision directly if she attacks the legislation for

right has been infringed must rely on legislation enacted to give effect to that right and may not decide to rely on the common law directly when bringing an action to protect that right.[97] In the absence of legislation, a litigant can rely directly either on the common law or on the constitutional provision. However, *a litigant can also rely on the common law instead of legislation to the extent that the legislation was not intended to address a specific aspect of the common law*, provided that the common law is not in conflict with either the constitutional provision or the legislative scheme. In such an instance, the common law might also require some development to give effect to a constitutional right, on the condition that the common law must fit in with the broader legislative scheme.[98]

If a court decides against an eviction order, the courts' application of PIE (read with section 26(3)) results in a legal quagmire where the occupiers continue to reside on the land unlawfully, often for years on end, while the landowner's use of the land is suspended. PIE does not facilitate the upgrading of tenure rights nor does it explain the legal relationship between occupier and landowner. Either the legislative scheme is inadequate, therefore, in that it fails to give content to fundamental rights, or the required statutory measures are simply absent.[99] According to the subsidiarity principles, the avenue for the development of the common law therefore opens up, because the required legislative scheme is not in place and the judiciary is tasked with developing the common law to fulfil fundamental rights.

---

failing to give effect to her right: *South African National Defence Union v Minister of Defence* 2007 (5) SA 400 (CC) para 52; *Minister of Health NO v New Clicks South Africa (Pty) Ltd (Treatment Action Campaign and Another as Amici Curiae)* 2006 (2) SA 311 (CC) para 437; *Sidumo v Rustenburg Platinum Mines Ltd* 2008 (2) SA 24 (CC) para 249; *Engelbrecht v Road Accident Fund* 2007 (6) SA 96 (CC) para 15.

[97] *Bato Star Fishing (Pty) Ltd v Minster of Environmental Affairs* 2004 (4) SA 490 (CC) para 25; *Minister of Health NO v New Clicks South Africa (Pty) Ltd (Treatment Action Campaign and Another as Amici Curiae)* 2006 (2) SA 311 (CC) para 96; *Chirwa v Transnet Ltd* 2008 (2) SA 24 (CC) para 23; *Fuel Retailers Association of Southern Africa v Director-General: Environmental Management, Department of Agriculture, Conservation and Environment, Mpumalanga Province* 2007 (6) SA 4 (CC) para 37; *Walele v City of Cape Town and Others* 2008 (6) SA 129 (CC) para 15. See specifically AJ van der Walt 'Normative pluralism and anarchy: Reflections on the 2007 term' (2008) 1 *CCR* 77–128 103–105; AJ van der Walt *Property and Constitution* (2012) Ch 2.

[98] AJ van der Walt *Property and constitution* (2012) Ch 2 section 3.1; AJ van der Walt 'Normative pluralism and anarchy: Reflections on the 2007 term' (2008) 1 *CCR* 77–128 115–116.

[99] The legislative scheme refers to all the laws that have been enacted to give content to sections 25(6) and 26(1) and (3) of the Constitution. None of these laws have responded to the rights of unlawful occupiers residing in informal settlements.

According to Van der Walt, the decision whether the common law requires development must firstly be rooted in a clear understanding of the common-law position, whereafter proper constitutional analysis must be undertaken to determine whether the law must be developed. If so, the court should engage in further constitutional analysis when deciding the *direction* in which the common law should develop, while policy and other considerations may play a role. Moreover, once the court has developed the common law, the impact on competing interests, such as property rights and the right to housing, has to be determined with reference to the Constitution.[100]

The common-law position in the context of a servitude originating from necessity is to a large extent uncontested. Servitudes of necessity are created in a specific context, namely where a parcel of land is completely landlocked without access to public roads. To date, South African law does not recognise instances where personal negative servitudes are created by court order due to circumstances of necessity. We argue that in the *Modderklip* type of case, where a court decides against an eviction order on the basis of necessity, the court can clarify the rights of the occupiers by awarding them a negative personal servitude – this development of the common law is not directed to cure a constitutional breach, but rather to promote and fulfil a fundamental right. The justification to develop the common law in these cases seems straightforward, although the *direction* in which the developments should take place is more complicated.

Arguably, the weighing of rights as proposed by Van der Walt should take place upon deciding whether the occupiers should be evicted, and once it is held to be unjust, the court should promote legal certainty by clarifying the rights of the occupiers as negative personal servitudes. The direction and way in which the development takes place is accordingly alongside the provisions of PIE, with the final and added advantage of a doctrinal clarification of the effect of section 26(3); towards the 'initial' realisation of section 26(1). As previously mentioned, the required developments call for minor adjustments to some servitude law principles in a very specific scenario. Finally, the question whether the development conflicts with other constitutional rights, especially a private owner's section 25(1) right,

[100] AJ van der Walt 'Development of the common law of servitude' (2013) 130 *SALJ* 722–756.

is somewhat redundant since the judicial decision not to grant the eviction order in fact impacts the owner's rights.[101]

In relation to our second proposal, the Prescription Act does envisage the acquisition of a personal or praedial servitude if the requirements for prescription are met. Even though the Act does not explicitly cater for the possibility that a community (as opposed to an individual) may claim a servitude of *usus*,[102] it is doctrinally possible to create several separate and individual personal servitudes over different parts of the servient land, while the land in its entirety is the object of the servitude. It would arguably be possible for a community to approach a court and claim 'individualised' personal servitudes of *uses*, while the object of the servitude is the land in its entirety. A request of this kind is probably more pragmatic than individual claims for the recognition of prescription.

On the other hand, we also argue that section 18 of the Prescription Act, read with section 3 of the State Land Disposal Act 48 of 1961, must be qualified in cases where prescription would apply to informal settlements to allow for the vesting of personal servitudes of *usus* over state land. In light of section 39(2) of the Constitution, our interpretation of these provisions is that they effectively limit rights in the Bill of Rights by preventing destitute groups from strengthening their housing rights, and the judiciary is therefore obliged to promote the spirit, purport and objects of the Bill of Rights by allowing prescription to apply in these instances. In *Makate v Vodacom (Pty) Ltd*[103] the Constitutional Court confirmed that 'every court that interprets legislation is bound to read a legislative provision through the prism of the Constitution.'[104] Also, in *Fraser v Absa Bank Limited*[105] it was stated that the Constitutional Court 'has made clear that section 39(2) fashions a mandatory constitutional canon of statutory interpretation'.[106] This dictum was further clarified to mean that '[i]f the provision under construction implicates or affects rights in the Bill of Rights, then the obligation in section 39(2) is activated. The court is duty-bound to promote the purport, spirit and objects of the Bill of Rights in the process of interpreting the provision in question.'[107]

---

[101] Even if such a decision is held to be arbitrary, the court can grant constitutional damages to 'cure' the breach: *Modderklip* para 42. See also J Strydom & S Viljoen 'Unlawful occupation of inner-city buildings: A constitutional analysis of the rights and obligations involved' (2014) 17 *PELJ* 1207–1261 1228.

[102] Section 6 states that a 'person' can acquire servitude by way of prescription.

[103] 2016 (4) SA 121 (CC).

[104] *Makate v Vodacom (Pty) Ltd* 2016 (4) SA 121 (CC) paras 87–90.

[105] 2007 (3) SA 484 (CC).

[106] *Fraser v Absa Bank Limited* 2007 (3) SA 484 (CC) para 43.

[107] *Makate v Vodacom (Pty) Ltd* 2016 (4) SA 121 (CC) paras 87–90.

Van der Walt went even further by stating as follows: 'Considering that pre-constitutional law survives only to the extent that it is consistent with the Constitution and that all legislation must be interpreted to promote the spirit, purport and objects of the Bill of Rights, it must now be the case that all legislation, whether specifically intended to codify existing law or not, either gives effect to the rights in the Bill of Rights or is unconstitutional.'[108] '[P]re-constitutional law can only survive in so far as it does not conflict with constitutional provisions and can be interpreted in conformity with constitutional rights and values.'[109] Effectively, these provisions constitute an obstacle in the path of vulnerable occupiers' realisation of their housing rights and the judiciary is therefore duty-bound to declare them unconstitutional, at least in the instances that we have set out.

6 Conclusion

This chapter shows that the common law of servitude can play a vital role in the fulfilment of the constitutional right of access to adequate housing, provided that the area of law is interpreted and developed by the courts to this end. We firstly argue that the courts are empowered to acknowledge a personal negative servitude for vulnerable groups in difficult cases where an eviction order is not prudent. The justification for the creation of such a right is the public interest and legal certainty to all concerned. The necessity for the creation of the right is founded on the constitutional right of housing and security of tenure. Regardless of the fact that the right of way of necessity is the only servitude currently established by way of a court decision, a personal negative servitude can and should also be *acknowledged* by the courts in the instances that we have set out, because judicial decisions against eviction orders effectively create rights akin to what we propose. The difference lies in the acknowledgement and conceptualisation of the right, rather than the actual effect. However, our proposition goes much further than the extant jurisprudence, because it introduces legally secure tenure for the occupiers and legal certainty for all affected parties.

Secondly, we argue that a vast number of communities who reside in a variety of informal settlements should be able to claim a personal servitude of use on the basis of prescription. Even though minor common-law developments would be required to accommodate such a reform, the judiciary would also have to declare section 3 of the State Land Disposal Act

---

108 AJ van der Walt 'Normative pluralism and anarchy: Reflections on the 2007 term' (2008) 1 *CCR* 77–128 107.

109 AJ van der Walt 'Normative pluralism and anarchy: Reflections on the 2007 term' (2008) 1 *CCR* 77–128 110.

48 of 1961 invalid due to its thwarting effect in the context of securing tenure rights for the previously dispossessed. A pre-constitutional law can hardly continue to operate in the constitutional dispensation if its impact is directly at odds with the fulfilment of fundamental rights. Similar to the argument relating to the establishment of a personal negative servitude, the argument to allow prescription in informal settlements to acknowledge a personal servitude of use may seem far-fetched and even radical, mainly because of its potential impact and reach, but it is founded on undisputed common-law principles as well as statutory provisions, read with supreme, direction-giving constitutional mandates. Minor interpretations and developments are suggested alongside these principles, provisions and mandates to result in large-scale tenure reform.

Chapter 6

A constitutional vision for property: *Shoprite Checkers* and beyond

Frank I Michelman & Ernst J Marais***

1 Introduction

1.1 Words recalled from a friend: Property and higher values

Not so long ago – it was July of 2015 – one of us exchanged with André van der Walt some first thoughts about the then-new decision from the Constitutional Court in *Shoprite Checkers v MEC*.[1] We sorted through the various opinions and came to that of Justice Johan Froneman. 'Absolutely fascinating,' André called it. And why? By reason, André said, of that opinion's 'invocation of normative considerations relating to "higher" rights or values when deciding property disputes' – 'albeit,' our dear friend went straight on to add, 'in what might not be the perfect case for it'.[2] Those words from André provide the seed for this chapter. For it happens that each of us co-authors independently has been struck by those same features in that same opinion.

---

* Robert Walmsley University Professor, Emeritus, Harvard University.

** Senior Lecturer, Department of Private Law, Faculty of Law, University of Johannesburg.

[1] *Shoprite Checkers (Pty) Ltd v MEC for Economic Development, Eastern Cape* 2015 (6) SA 125 (CC).

[2] Email message from André van der Walt to Frank I Michelman, July 23, 2015 (in possession of Frank I Michelman).

It may be no accident that we, like André, found our minds engaged by Froneman J's opinion in *Shoprite Checkers*. We are both, after all, learners from Professor van der Walt, Marais as a 2011 alumnus of the South African Research Chair in Property Law and Michelman as a long-time overseas academic *copain* in the study of constitutional protection for property. Together we aim here, largely through the shared lens of André's scholarship, to explore the opinion and the thought behind it, and to weigh its possible bearing on the future of property adjudications both in and beyond South Africa. André's thought about a 'constitutional vision' for property rights[3] is a guiding star in what follows (as it may also have been for Froneman J, judging by his citations of André's work at key points in his *Shoprite Checkers* opinion,[4] and then again in his very recent opinion in *Daniels v Scribante and Another*,[5] about which we also will have something to say).

1.2 The 'not so perfect case'

Shoprite, a juristic person in business for profit, had acquired, in 1989, under national law then in force, a licence without terminal date to sell table wine in its grocery stores throughout the Eastern Cape.[6] In 2003, the provincial government enacted a new law abolishing for the future the type of licence Shoprite held under the old one. Under transitional provisions of the new Act, licences like Shoprite's continued in force for periods of up to 10 additional years, during which time the holders could convert to formal registrations to sell table wine and other forms of alcohol, although this could now only take place on premises separate from grocery stores.[7] Shoprite, preferring to carry on with its established business model, chose not to convert to a formal registration under the new Act.[8] When, by force of the new Act, its old-order license expired in 2014, Shoprite went to court to complain of an arbitrary deprivation of its property, contrary to section 25(1) of the Constitution of the Republic of South Africa, 1996 ('the Constitution').

Given prior decisions and the text of the section, it was common cause among the parties and justices that Shoprite's challenge could succeed only

---

[3] See AJ van der Walt *Property and constitution* (2012) ch 3.3.

[4] *Shoprite Checkers (Pty) Ltd v MEC for Economic Development, Eastern Cape* 2015 (6) SA 125 (CC) paras 37, 46 footnote 75.

[5] 2017 (4) SA 341 (CC).

[6] *Shoprite Checkers (Pty) Ltd v MEC for Economic Development, Eastern Cape* 2015 (6) SA 125 (CC) para 7ff.

[7] Section 71(5) of the Eastern Cape Liquor Act 10 of 2003: See *Shoprite Checkers (Pty) Ltd v MEC for Economic Development, Eastern Cape* 2015 (6) SA 125 (CC) para 7ff.

[8] *Shoprite Checkers (Pty) Ltd v MEC for Economic Development, Environmental Affairs and Tourism: Eastern Cape* 2014 JDR 2451 (ECG) paras 31–33.

by persuading the court on three points: (i) that its old-order wine licence constituted 'property' for purposes of section 25, (ii) that the new law's application 'deprived' Shoprite of all or some part of that property, and (iii) that the deprivation was 'arbitrary' within the section's intendment.[9] In a judgment agreed to by three other justices, Froneman J found in Shoprite's favor on the first two claims but against it on the third. These bottom-line conclusions gained majority support from the court as a whole, so Shoprite lost its case.

1.3 Enter the 'higher values'

This looks like one of a class of cases involving a business-firm claimant coming to court in quest of protection for a commercially valuable regulatory holding of the type classified by property-law theorists as 'new property' (if indeed 'property' at all).[10] Theorists have coined that term to designate advantageous legal positions thrown up by operations of the regulatory state – Shoprite's wine licence, for example – that appear to merit some kind or level of assurance against unfair or arbitrary amendment or withdrawal.

The question in *Shoprite Checkers* was whether and how far the Constitution, and specifically section 25(1), should be deemed a source of such assurance for Shoprite's wine license. Froneman J's response to that question builds out from a central proposition on the ends pursued by the Constitution's choice to include, among the rights to which it extends its special mantle of regard, the right (in the words used by Froneman J) of 'holding property'.[11] The point of that inclusion, as laid down by Froneman J in *Shoprite Checkers* (and this might come as a surprise to many constitutional lawyers around the globe), is *not* 'primarily to advance economic wealth maximisation or the satisfaction of individual preferences,' but rather is – in keeping with the South African Constitution's overall 'framework of values' – to 'secure living a life of dignity in recognition of the dignity of others'.[12]

Thus enter the 'higher values' into the stream of decisions of property disputes. For Froneman J did not just toss that proposition into his opinion as idle theoretical speculation. Directly from it flows an inference of major practical import for South African constitutional litigation beyond the

[9] *First National Bank of SA Ltd t/a Wesbank v Commissioner, South African Revenue Service and Another; First National Bank of SA Ltd t/a Wesbank v Minister of Finance* 2002 (4) SA 768 (CC) para 46.

[10] The term is owing to CA Reich 'The new property' (1964) 73 *Yale LJ* 733–787.

[11] *Shoprite Checkers (Pty) Ltd v MEC for Economic Development, Eastern Cape* 2015 (6) SA 125 (CC) para 50.

[12] *Shoprite Checkers (Pty) Ltd v MEC for Economic Development, Eastern Cape* 2015 (6) SA 125 (CC) paras 4, 36, 50. See the discussion in section 2 below.

Shoprite Checkers case. The level of protection accorded against deprivation of a property interest, reasoned Froneman J, must depend on the 'kind' of interest at stake. Protections should be stronger where interests are 'related to the exercise, protection or advancement of [other] particular individual rights under the Bill of Rights' than where they are not.[13]

We note here that Froneman J's *Shoprite Checkers* opinion, for a minority of four justices, is only one among a set of three opinions by which the case was decided, and the only one to bring up the '"higher" rights or values' as a potentially decisive or even relevant consideration.[14] Still, that opinion now stands poised to exert possible influence on the future direction of South African constitutional-property adjudications.[15]

1.4 Proprietary distinguished from 'higher' interests and values

Section 25(1) of the Constitution forbids laws permitting arbitrary deprivations. Deprivations of what? Well, of *property*. And yet Froneman J's *Shoprite Checkers* judgment would make always potentially decisive, in any judicial appraisal of a challenged law's consistency with section 25(1), that law's impact, if any, on claims to human dignity, equality, and freedom, whose constitutionally protected status is specifically and sufficiently declared by constitutional clauses *outside of* section 25. A claimant suffering substantial loss to some item in its asset portfolio from actions of the state might lose its claim under section 25(1) because, and just because, the asset-type in

---

13 *Shoprite Checkers (Pty) Ltd v MEC for Economic Development, Eastern Cape* 2015 (6) SA 125 (CC) paras 4, 50.

14 Madlanga J, writing also for Tshiki AJ, agreed with Froneman J (but for different reasons making no reference to the 'higher' values) that the old-order license amounted to constitutional property and that there was a deprivation of property. Moseneke DCJ, writing also for four others, disagreed that the license was property. Froneman J's four and Moseneke DCJ's five (but the latter again for different reasons ignoring the 'higher' values) agreed, over dissent from Madlanga J's two, that the new Act's adverse impingements on Shoprite's interests were not arbitrary by applicable constitutional standards. Froneman J's decision is also discussed by EJ Marais 'Expanding the contours of the constitutional property concept' 2016 *TSAR* 576–592; IM Rautenbach 'Dealing with the social dimensions of the right to property in the South African bill of rights' 2015 *TSAR* 822–833; AJ van der Walt 'Section 25 vortices' 2016 *TSAR* 412–427, 597–621.

15 Nor ought one to overlook the potential bearing of Froneman J's *Shoprite Checkers* reasoning in global conversations over constitutional property law in which André van der Walt also had a leading role. For consideration of closely related themes in a comparative-constitutional context, see FI Michelman 'The property clause question' (2012) 19 *Constellations* 152–163. For the same in relation to United States constitutional law, see FI Michelman 'Good government, core liberties, and constitutional property: An essay for Joseph Singer' (2016) 5 *Brigham-Kanner Property Rights Conference Journal* 27–43.

question shows insufficient linkage to enjoyment of *other* constitutional rights deemed more critical to individual dignity and self-fulfillment.[16]

Such a view may seem surprising from a strictly textual standpoint.[17] The Constitution constructs its Bill of Rights around a succession of clauses, each one of which is apparently meant to add its own designated interest or value to the full complement of those for which the Bill of Rights demands a special regard.[18] Presumably, each clause adds something of its own to the full array and does not merely duplicate what the other clauses already contribute. If we ask which interest section 25(1) uniquely injects into the full protected array, it seems the answer can only be: the interest in holding property.

But then what exactly is this interest meriting protection that is not already covered by other clauses on life,[19] dignity,[20] freedom,[21] security,[22] privacy,[23] association,[24] movement,[25] trade,[26] equality,[27] and procedural justice[28] (not to mention housing,[29] sustenance,[30] and health care[31])? Most straightforwardly, it would be the particular concern of a person, natural or juristic, for full retention and command of lawfully obtained asset-holdings together with the assemblage of legal privileges and powers normally attendant upon such holdings. That is the interest which section 25(1) apparently singles out as meriting protection – on its own, so to speak, and apart from any further connection to other interests of the person covered elsewhere in the Bill of Rights.

---

16 *Shoprite Checkers (Pty) Ltd v MEC for Economic Development, Eastern Cape* 2015 (6) SA 125 (CC) para 50. See the discussion in section 4.1 below.

17 Madlanga J goes so far as to say that Froneman J has denied the right to property the status of a 'self-standing' or 'stand-alone' constitutional right: See *Shoprite Checkers (Pty) Ltd v MEC for Economic Development, Eastern Cape* 2015 (6) SA 125 (CC) para 139.

18 Compare *Dawood and Another v Minister of Home Affairs and Others* 2000 (3) SA 936 (CC) para 35: 'Section 10 [of the interim Constitution] . . . makes it plain that dignity is not only a *value* fundamental to our Constitution, it is a justiciable and enforceable *right* that must be respected and protected' (original emphasis).

19 Section 11 of the Constitution.

20 Sections 1(a), 7(1), 10, and 39(1)(a) of the Constitution.

21 Sections 1(a), 7(1), 12, 15, 16, and 39(1)(a) of the Constitution.

22 Section 12 of the Constitution.

23 Section 14 of the Constitution.

24 Section 18 of the Constitution.

25 Section 21 of the Constitution.

26 Section 22 of the Constitution.

27 Section 1(a), 7(1), 9, and 39(1)(*a*) of the Constitution.

28 Sections 34-35 of the Constitution.

29 Section 26 of the Constitution.

30 Section 27 of the Constitution.

31 Section 27 of the Constitution.

Froneman J's *Shoprite Checkers* judgment does not contradict that conclusion but does impose on it a heavy qualification. His judgment would have the courts always, when passing upon the consistency of a law with section 25(1), take into account *not only* that law's imposition of a loss to property entitlements and values *but also* the possible ramifying effects of that loss to other interests named in the Bill of Rights. Taking our cue from André van der Walt's words at the head of this chapter, we use the expression 'higher-values linkage' (or sometimes simply 'linkage') to refer to such effects.[32] By 'higher-values linkage' we mean how the holding of property – in a given case – is able (i) to further the constitutional values of human dignity, equality and freedom (given that the mentioned values underlie all rights in the Constitution), and, related to this matter, (ii) how it is able to promote other fundamental rights in the Bill of Rights (such as the right freely to choose one's vocation).[33] It is, as we explain further below, the view of Froneman J that a linkage assessment must potentially figure in every judicial appraisal, in terms of section 25(1), of the constitutionality of laws that impair in some way the enjoyment of proprietary advantages. From that view, it would appear to follow that section 25(1) does *not*, in the last analysis, place on a level with other constitutional rights the protection of 'property' understood as the interest pure and simple in retaining whatever at the moment one has in the way of economic entitlements.

1.5 Plan of the chapter

In the view of Froneman J, consideration of an asset-holding's higher-values linkage comes at two points in an adjudication under section 25. First, it comes in at what we will sometimes below call the 'gateway' stage of deciding whether 'property' is at stake in the dispute: A 'link' of the matter in question to 'constitutionally sanctioned self-fulfillment' will 'strengthen [and so correspondingly, it would seem, the absence of any such link will

[32] Compare EJ Marais 'Expanding the contours of the constitutional property concept' 2016 *TSAR* 576–592 583, who describes Froneman J's reliance on other fundamental rights to decide the property question as a 'linking approach'. We shall here be reconsidering Marais' worry there (at 583) that the linking approach might 'unnecessarily complicate the property question'. We shall also speak to the potential problems AJ van der Walt 'Section 25 vortices' 2016 *TSAR* 412–427, 597–621 identifies in Froneman J's opinion. See the discussion in section 4.3 below.

[33] *Government of the Republic of South Africa and Others v Grootboom and Others* 2001 (1) SA 46 (CC) paras 23, 83; *Port Elizabeth Municipality v Various Occupiers* 2005 (1) SA 217 (CC) paras 15–23; *Pharmaceutical Manufacturers Association of SA and Another: In re ex parte President of the Republic of South Africa* 2000 (2) SA 674 (CC) para 44.

weaken] the case for recognition of it as property'.[34] Second, linkage or its absence affects the rigor of the test for arbitrariness, once a deprivation of property has been found: 'If the deprivation is of property closely connected to fundamental rights and constitutional values, then sufficient reason for [it] should approximate proportionality. If not, rationality might suffice.'[35]

Our specific concern here will be with cases where linkage factors might possibly be counted decisive at either or both of the is-it-property or is-it-arbitrary questions in a section 25(1) litigation. We will be asking what purpose or value could possibly be served by introducing linkage considerations at the is-it-property stage (as Froneman J would do) that is not at least as fully and aptly met by reserving it for the is-it-arbitrary stage.

Why raise this question? Because, while we think the case for consideration of linkage at the is-it-arbitrary stage is strong and follows smoothly from prior doctrine, introduction of it at the is-it-property stage strikes us as generally more problematic, as certainly more surprising in view of prior doctrine, and so as needing further explanation.[36] Accordingly, our plan for the chapter will be as follows. In section 2, we present the general case for linkage as developed by Froneman J in his *Shoprite Checkers* judgment, also taking guidance from scholarship of AJ van der Walt. In section 3 below, we describe Froneman J's application of linkage at the is-it-arbitrary stage of a section 25(1) adjudication and explain our support for that approach, again drawing for that purpose from works of Van der Walt. In section 4 below, we take up Froneman J's proposal for linkage at the is-it-property stage. We explain why that strikes us as a more problematic step, recounting briefly a list of possible objections to it. We then go on, though, to explain sympathetically what we think must be the motivation for it. In section 5 below, we reflect more broadly on connections between our explorations of the work of Froneman J in *Shoprite Checkers* and Professor van der Walt's legacy.

2 A single system of law: Negative protection for property and the Constitution's 'framework of values'

Especially as viewed against South Africa's history of exclusion of the majority of the population from land-ownership in the greater part of the country, one easily sees why a dedicatedly transformative Constitution, like South

[34] *Shoprite Checkers (Pty) Ltd v MEC for Economic Development, Eastern Cape* 2015 (6) SA 125 (CC) paras 64–68.

[35] *Shoprite Checkers (Pty) Ltd v MEC for Economic Development, Eastern Cape* 2015 (6) SA 125 (CC) para 80.

[36] See the discussion in sections 3 and 4 below.

Africa's, would include positive express supports for the claims of everyone to have access to the material means required for a life lived in dignity.[37] The point or function, in such a Constitution, of a clause giving 'negative' protection to property – protection, that is, against laws stripping away possessory or proprietary advantages that the claimants have previously enjoyed – is not quite so obvious. Of course, some explanations come easily to mind. The clause might have been included for reasons of economic policy (say, a choice for a market economy), or in order to satisfy demands of an international political order, a global investor community, or internal constituencies without whose support the new constitutional project could not go forward.[38]

In the explanation of Froneman J in *Shoprite Checkers*, the Constitution's overall guiding aim for section 25(1) is not, however, to be found in any of those causes. Rather, it lies in 'a close nexus [of property] with . . . personal liberty'.[39] Constitutionally speaking, asset-holding is valued not as an independent end but rather as a means 'to secur[ing] for [the] holder a sphere of liberty in the economic field in which he or she can lead a self-governing life'.[40] Behind and explaining property's inclusion in the array of protected rights thus lies a perception of a vital practical link between an apt measure of respect for security of property and fulfillment of higher – more 'fundamental' – protected rights respecting human dignity, equality, and freedom.[41]

We call that the 'linkage' account of section 25(1). Froneman J draws it out of a reflection on the South African Constitution's overall 'framework of values,' in which a human interest simply in secure retention and enjoyment of what one has lawfully acquired surely gets *some* consideration – nothing in Froneman J's *Shoprite Checkers* judgment would strip that interest of all constitutional regard – but it does not occupy the highest rank. It is only, in the view of Froneman J, within that framework that we can properly decide

---

[37] See sections 25(5)–(7) and 26–28 of the Constitution.

[38] FI Michelman 'Liberal constitutionalism, property rights, and the assault on poverty' (2011) 22 *Stell LR* 706–723 715ff.

[39] BVerfGE 24, 367 (1968) (*Deichordnung*), translated by DP Kommers and RA Miller *The constitutional jurisprudence of the Federal Republic of Germany* 3 ed (2012) 632 and quoted with approval by Froneman J in *Shoprite Checkers (Pty) Ltd v MEC for Economic Development, Eastern Cape* 2015 (6) SA 125 (CC) para 54.

[40] *Deichordnung*, translated by DP Kommers and RA Miller *The constitutional jurisprudence of the Federal Republic of Germany* 3 ed (2012) 632 and quoted with approval by Froneman J in *Shoprite Checkers (Pty) Ltd v MEC for Economic Development, Eastern Cape* 2015 (6) SA 125 (CC) para 54.

[41] *Shoprite Checkers (Pty) Ltd v MEC for Economic Development, Eastern Cape* 2015 (6) SA 125 (CC) paras 50, 60. See, for instance, the rights listed in footnote 76 below.

the 'levels of constitutional protection' appropriate to the types of legal position claimed as property in cases that come before the court.[42]

This position resonates strongly with André van der Walt's work, especially that work's recognition of a 'constitutional vision of property' distinct from that of pre-constitutional private law.[43] Van der Walt describes this vision as a 'wide[,] normative [conception] of what the property system [which includes both constitutional and private property law] should look like and what it should do in view of the spirit, purport and objects of the Bill of Rights.'[44] Using the single-system-of-law principle as a point of departure, and drawing on German constitutional law and the work of Joseph Singer,[45] Van der Walt maintains that systemic objectives – rather than individual subjective concerns – must henceforward be the starting point for all further development of South African property law.[46]

That principle, of course, comes from *Pharmaceutical Manufacturers Association of SA and Another: In Re Ex Parte President of the Republic of South Africa and Others.*[47] The court there confirmed that there is in South Africa only one system of law, which is shaped by the Constitution, and all sources of law derive their force from the Constitution and are subject to constitutional control.[48] The principle not only excludes parallel legal systems, it furthermore steers South African law as a whole toward the systemic objectives which the Constitution envisions for a single legal system.[49] These objectives are geared towards achievement of a society based on the values of human dignity, equality, and freedom.[50] In the property context these objectives translate into preventing arbitrary deprivation of (and eviction from) land, tenure insecurity, homelessness, and lack of access to resources, to name but a few hardships.[51]

As AJ van der Walt teaches (using a term he adopted from Henk Botha), a constitutional vision of property thus requires for section 25 a different

---

42 *Shoprite Checkers (Pty) Ltd v MEC for Economic Development, Eastern Cape* 2015 (6) SA 125 (CC) para 4.

43 AJ van der Walt *Property and constitution* (2012) ch 3. See also AJ van der Walt *Property and constitution* (2012) ch 4; FI Michelman 'Liberal constitutionalism, property rights, and the assault on poverty' (2011) 22 *Stell LR* 706–723 719–720.

44 AJ van der Walt *Property and constitution* (2012) 122 n 44. See further 131–168.

45 AJ van der Walt *Property and constitution* (2012) 130ff.

46 AJ van der Walt *Property and constitution* (2012) 122–131.

47 2000 (2) SA 674 (CC).

48 Paragraph 44.

49 AJ van der Walt *Property and constitution* (2012) 26–27, 40, 81–91, 95–97, 111 and the sources he cites. See also ch 2 generally.

50 AJ van der Walt *Property and constitution* (2012) 26–27, 40, 95–97.

51 AJ van der Walt *Property and constitution* (2012) 143–144, 150–151.

'angle of approach'[52] from that which has prevailed in private law. As Van der Walt explained the difference, section 25 is 'objective- rather than object- or rights-focused'.[53] The focus does not fall on some sweeping class of objects (or rights) abstractly demanding protection as property (and so also on some uniform level of protection that is due to whatever falls in that class). Rather, the focus falls on whether (and, if so, how) protection of the proprietary interest at hand will promote the objectives which the Constitution envisions for the whole legal system.[54] The emphasis goes to whether (and, if so, how) protecting those interests will promote the conditions which the Constitution sets as its objectives for the 'property' component of its single system of law.[55] The approach is thus 'from the perspective of the property system as a whole rather than from the perspective of an individual property entitlement'.[56]

Thus, in sum, on Van der Walt's understanding, the aim for section 25(1) is not protection of current holdings as an independent end but rather protection as a means to the end of a society based on human dignity, equality, and freedom for all.[57] The aim can therefore be described as prevention of deprivations that are arbitrary in the sense of being excessive or extraneous with regard to the systemic goals, as distinct from prevention of all deprivations that may happen to be in some degree painful or unwelcome. This does not make protection of holdings unimportant in constitutional morality or law.[58] Rather, it shifts the 'focus' away from negative avoidance of the pains of state limitation of property to positive realisation of the constitutional objectives.[59] An emphasis on avoidance is deemed too prone to overemphasise the protective element of the property clause at the expense of its reformative aspirations, and so to frustrate rather than promote the

---

[52] AJ van der Walt *Property and constitution* (2012) 105 footnote 259.

[53] AJ van der Walt *Property and constitution* (2012) 141–142.

[54] AJ van der Walt *Property and constitution* (2012) 132–140, with reference to ss 25(7), 26(3), 24(a), 24(b)(iii), 25(5), 25(6), 26(1) of the Constitution. See also 139–147 and 169.

[55] See the sources cited in the previous footnote above.

[56] AJ van der Walt *Property and constitution* (2012) 130, citing JW Singer *Introduction to Property* 2 ed (2005); JW Singer *Entitlement: The paradoxes of property* (2000).

[57] AJ van der Walt *Property and constitution* (2012) 141–142.

[58] AJ van der Walt *Property and constitution* (2012) 142–143; AJ van der Walt 'The modest systemic status of property rights' (2014) 1 *J L Prop & Soc'y* 15–106 27.

[59] AJ van der Walt *Property and constitution* (2012) 141–143ff, ch 4.

transformative goals of the Constitution.[60] In sum, according to Van der Walt, an objective-normative vision of constitutional property –

> allows the property clause to do the special, concrete legal work of ensuring that the property system displays the desired characteristics and avoids the unwanted effects indicated by the Constitution, but does not allow it to do the additional work of providing additional, supreme-law, rule-formalist protection of existing property holdings in a way that could undermine the desired characteristics or have unwanted effects in the property system.[61]

These views of Van der Walt are echoed in Froneman J's *Shoprite Checkers* opinion. What Van der Walt calls 'vision', Froneman calls 'framework':

> There is, as yet, little common ground on how we conceive of property under section 25 of the Constitution, why we should do so, and what purpose the protection of property should serve. . . . This judgment suggests that our evolving conversation on this issue should continue to seek our conception of property within the framework of values and individual rights in the Constitution. It further asserts that the level of constitutional protection should depend on the kind of constitutional interest involved and the core purpose associated with that type of property interest.[62]

3 The constitutional framework of values and a differentiated standard for 'arbitrary'

Section 25(1) stipulates that a property deprivation may permissibly occur only in terms of law of general application, which law may not permit arbitrary deprivation of property. Froneman J confirmed in general the meaning Ackermann J in *First National Bank of SA Ltd t/a Wesbank v Commissioner,*

[60] AJ van der Walt *Property and constitution* (2012) ch 4, especially 181–184. Van der Walt here provides a response to the critique S Sibanda 'Not purpose-made! Transformative constitutionalism, post-independence constitutionalism and the struggle to eradicate poverty' (2011) 22 *Stell LR* 482–500 raises against transformative constitutionalism for being unable to combat poverty effectively. See also the response of FI Michelman 'Liberal Constitutionalism, Property Rights, and the Assault on Poverty' (2011) 22 *Stell LR* 706–723 to Sibanda's critique. See further S Sibanda 'Not quite a rejoinder: Some thoughts and reflections on Michelman's "Liberal constitutionalism, property rights and the assault on poverty"' (2013) 24 *Stell LR* 329–341.

[61] AJ van der Walt *Property and constitution* (2012) 183.

[62] *Shoprite Checkers (Pty) Ltd v MEC for Economic Development, Eastern Cape* 2015 (6) SA 125 (CC) para 4. See also par 36: 'The task of all, but especially the courts, is to seek our own constitutional conception of property within the normative framework of the fundamental values and individual rights in the Constitution. The level of constitutional protection would then depend on the kind of constitutional property interest involved and the core purpose associated with that type of interest.'

South African Revenue Service and Another[63] (*FNB*) attached to 'arbitrary', namely that a depriving law will be arbitrary if it does not provide sufficient reason for the deprivation in question or if it is procedurally unfair.[64] Procedural fairness was not an issue in *Shoprite Checkers* and, accordingly, Froneman J focused his attention on the 'sufficient reason' requirement.[65]

According to prior authority endorsed by Froneman J, sufficiency of reason looks to a 'complexity of relationships'.[66] Required of a property-depriving law is a sufficient *nexus* between the means employed (namely the deprivation in question) and the purpose which the authorising law seeks to achieve, between that purpose and the affected person, and between that purpose and the nature of the property.[67] Also highly relevant, of course, are the extent and severity of the deprivation.[68] Froneman J, holding all these factors in view, makes the test for sufficiency substantive, not formal. He locates it along a continuum moving between thin rationality on the one end and thick proportionality on the other.[69] The substantive non-arbitrariness test

---

[63] 2002 (4) SA 768 (CC).

[64] *Shoprite Checkers (Pty) Ltd v MEC for Economic Development, Eastern Cape and Others* 2015 (6) SA 125 (CC) para 77, citing *First National Bank of SA Ltd t/a Wesbank v Commissioner, South African Revenue Service and Another; First National Bank of SA Ltd t/a Wesbank v Minister of Finance* 2002 (4) SA 768 (CC) para 100.

[65] For discussions of what procedural fairness under section 25(1) might entail, see AJ van der Walt *Constitutional property law* 3 ed (2011) 264–270; E van der Sijde *Reconsidering the relationship between property and regulation: A systemic constitutional approach* (2015) unpublished LLD thesis Stellenbosch University 220–226.

[66] *Shoprite Checkers (Pty) Ltd v MEC for Economic Development, Eastern Cape and Others* 2015 (6) SA 125 (CC) para 77. See also *First National Bank of SA Ltd t/a Wesbank v Commissioner, South African Revenue Service and Another; First National Bank of SA Ltd t/a Wesbank v Minister of Finance* 2002 (4) SA 768 (CC) para 100.

[67] *Shoprite Checkers (Pty) Ltd v MEC for Economic Development, Eastern Cape and Others* 2015 (6) SA 125 (CC) para 79. See also *First National Bank of SA Ltd t/a Wesbank v Commissioner, South African Revenue Service and Another; First National Bank of SA Ltd t/a Wesbank v Minister of Finance* 2002 (4) SA 768 (CC) para 100ff.

[68] *First National Bank of SA Ltd t/a Wesbank v Commissioner, South African Revenue Service and Another; First National Bank of SA Ltd t/a Wesbank v Minister of Finance* 2002 (4) SA 768 (CC) para 100.

[69] *Shoprite Checkers (Pty) Ltd v MEC for Economic Development, Eastern Cape and Others* 2015 (6) SA 125 (CC) para 77, citing *First National Bank of SA Ltd t/a Wesbank v Commissioner, South African Revenue Service and Another; First National Bank of SA Ltd t/a Wesbank v Minister of Finance* 2002 (4) SA 768 (CC) para 100. See also *FNB* para 65.

is thus contextual in nature, depending on the facts and circumstances of each case.[70]

So, for example, Froneman J confirmed that lighter scrutiny will be in order if the affected property is not a real right and if the impact of the deprivation is slight.[71] Of greater interest to us is his addition of 'higher values' considerations to fixation of the severity of the test. While *FNB* did find that the particular use to which an interest is put may be relevant when deciding the non-arbitrariness question,[72] it did not expressly factor into the equation the constitutional values and other fundamental rights.[73] It is therefore significant that Froneman J quite pointedly took these values and rights into account in establishing the level of scrutiny appropriate to Shoprite's wine licence.[74] He held that insofar as the proprietary position in question may be related to other fundamental rights the holder enjoys – in this case Froneman J brought up specifically the right to choose one's vocation freely – the level of protection will be stronger than in cases where no such relation exists.[75]

---

[70] *First National Bank of SA Ltd t/a Wesbank v Commissioner, South African Revenue Service and Another; First National Bank of SA Ltd t/a Wesbank v Minister of Finance* 2002 (4) SA 768 (CC) para 63, confirmed in *Reflect-All 1025 CC and Others v MEC for Public Transport, Roads and Works, Gauteng Provincial Government, and Another* 2009 (6) SA 391 (CC) para 47.

[71] *Shoprite Checkers (Pty) Ltd v MEC for Economic Development, Eastern Cape and Others* 2015 (6) SA 125 (CC) para 77, citing *Mkontwana v Nelson Mandela Metropolitan Municipality and Another; Bissett and Others v Buffalo City Municipality and Others; Transfer Rights Action Campaign and Others v MEC, Local Government and Housing, Gauteng, and Others (Kwazulu-Natal Law Society and Msunduzi Municipality as Amici Curiae)* 2005 (1) SA 530 (CC) paras 34–35. See also *First National Bank of SA Ltd t/a Wesbank v Commissioner, South African Revenue Service and Another; First National Bank of SA Ltd t/a Wesbank v Minister of Finance* 2002 (4) SA 768 (CC) para 100.

[72] *First National Bank of SA Ltd t/a Wesbank v Commissioner, South African Revenue Service and Another; First National Bank of SA Ltd t/a Wesbank v Minister of Finance* 2002 (4) SA 768 (CC) para 54.

[73] These values and rights also did not play a visible role in subsequent cases that applied the substantive non-arbitrariness test in detail: see *Mkontwana v Nelson Mandela Metropolitan Municipality and Another; Bissett and Others v Buffalo City Municipality and Others; Transfer Rights Action Campaign and Others v MEC, Local Government and Housing, Gauteng, and Others (Kwazulu-Natal Law Society and Msunduzi Municipality as Amici Curiae)* 2005 (1) SA 530 (CC); *Reflect-All 1025 CC and Others v MEC for Public Transport, Roads and Works, Gauteng Provincial Government, and Another* 2009 (6) SA 391 (CC); *National Credit Regulator v Opperman and Others* 2013 (2) SA 1 (CC), to name but three. However, a notable exception is the recent decision in *Daniels v Scribante and Another* 2017 (4) SA 341 (CC).

[74] *Shoprite Checkers (Pty) Ltd v MEC for Economic Development, Eastern Cape* 2015 (6) SA 125 (CC) paras 50, 79–80ff.

[75] *Shoprite Checkers (Pty) Ltd v MEC for Economic Development, Eastern Cape* 2015 (6) SA 125 (CC) paras 50, 6–64.

Froneman J's determination that the level of scrutiny depends on the effect(s) the deprivation has on other fundamental rights[76] merits full approval, for reasons we set out above in section 2 largely by reference to AJ van der Walt's scholarship. Indeed, the latter had written, prior to the decision in *Shoprite Checkers*, that the public interest side of the arbitrariness equation must include non-property constitutional values such as the advancement of human dignity and the defeat of discrimination.[77] In play here is a further dimension of the single-system-of-law principle: The same set of leading values must underlie the Constitution's protection of property as also underlie other fundamental rights deemed essential to dignity, to personhood and, in the words of Froneman J, to 'socially-situated individual self-fulfilment'.[78]

Tying the strictness of the test for arbitrariness to linkage considerations finds support in other countries' practice and in other scholarship. It corresponds to the approach followed in German constitutional law, where interests that are located nearer the individual personality and liberty of a property holder – such as having a home – enjoy stronger protection from state limitation than property which serves a purely commercial purpose.[79] It finds a strong echo, also, in Margaret Jane Radin's work on property

[76] Froneman J (at *Shoprite Checkers (Pty) Ltd v MEC for Economic Development, Eastern Cape* 2015 (6) SA 125 (CC) paras 42–46) refers to several fundamental rights against the background of deciding the section 25 dispute. These rights are the following: the right to have access to adequate housing (section 26(1), healthcare services (section 27(1)(a)), sufficient food and water (section 27(1)(b)), social security (section 27(1)(c)), the right to choose one's vocation freely (section 22), the right to freedom and security of the person (section 12) and the right to dignity (section 10). Compare AJ van der Walt *Property and constitution* (2012) ch 3. The right to choose one's vocation freely featured prominently in Froneman J's judgment: see especially *Shoprite Checkers* para 61 and compare BVerfGE 7, 377 (1958) (*Apotheken-Urteil*), translated by DP Kommers and RA Miller *The constitutional jurisprudence of the Federal Republic of Germany* (2012) 666-670, and DP Kommers and RA Miller *The constitutional jurisprudence of the Federal Republic of Germany* 3 ed (2012) 659.

[77] AJ van der Walt *Property and constitution* (2012) 126–129.

[78] *Shoprite Checkers (Pty) Ltd v MEC for Economic Development, Eastern Cape* 2015 (6) SA 125 (CC) para 50. Compare AJ van der Walt *Property and constitution* (2012) 132–147; *Deichordnung*, translated by DP Kommers & RA Miller *The constitutional jurisprudence of the Federal Republic of Germany* 3 ed (2012) 631–633; *Affordable Medicines Trust and Others v Minister of Health and Others* 2006 (3) SA 247 (CC) para 59 (which cites *Apotheken-Urteil*, translated by DP Kommers and RA Miller *The constitutional jurisprudence of the Federal Republic of Germany* 3 ed (2012) 666-670; DP Kommers and RA Miller *The constitutional jurisprudence of the Federal Republic of Germany* 3 ed (2012) 659. See similarly EJ Marais 'Expanding the contours of the constitutional property concept' 2016 *TSAR* 576–592 587–588.

[79] AJ van der Walt *Property and constitution* (2012) 127–128; AJ van der Walt *Constitutional property clauses: A comparative analysis* (1999) 135–141.

and personhood.[80] Radin distinguishes between two types of property relationships, namely personal (or constitutive) property, which is essential for humans to achieve proper self-development, and fungible property, which serves the purposes of generic economic wealth.[81] Given the centrality of personal property to the chances for a dignified life, such property in her view merits stronger protection than fungible property.

From views such as these, which we would endorse, it follows that the stronger the link of the asset concerned to the 'personal' side, the stricter the scrutiny of the depriving law. So where the proprietary interest is essential for someone's right to housing, or the right to choose a vocation freely, proportionally strong reasons will be required to justify the deprivation. Where purely economic concerns are at stake, rationality will suffice.[82]

The latter was of course the case in *Shoprite Checkers*. In Radin's classification, the wine licence in Shoprite's hands was an item of fungible property, which Shoprite valued for the sake of purely economic concerns. In no way could it be said to support Shoprite's dignity, as it might conceivably have done for a natural person. Setting aside a wrinkle soon to be noted in section 4.1 below, these considerations might all have gone toward explaining why Froneman J decided against Shoprite on the question of arbitrariness. Given that wrinkle, it seems other considerations must have been decisive – such as that the wine-license was not a real right but rather a personal incorporeal right and moreover a specimen of 'new property' for which constitutional protection may have been deemed problematic given its public-law origin. The deprivation, furthermore, was not total, as Shoprite still had the ability to sell table wine, although this now had to take place in terms of a different licence and on premises separate from its grocery stores.[83]

[80] AJ van der Walt & EJ Marais 'The constitutionality of acquisitive prescription: A section 25 analysis' 2012 *TSAR* 714–736 728, citing MJ Radin 'Property and personhood' 1982 *Stanford LR* 957 959–960.

[81] MJ Radin 'Property and personhood' 1982 *Stanford LR* 957 959–960; MJ Radin *Reinterpreting property* (1993) 2.

[82] *Shoprite Checkers (Pty) Ltd v MEC for Economic Development, Eastern Cape* 2015 (6) SA 125 (CC) para 80.

[83] A discussion of the requirements for deprivation, and how Madlanga J's view of what constitutes a deprivation potentially differs from the one adopted by Froneman J, is beyond the scope of this chapter. Suffice it to say that a limitation must be 'significant enough to have a legally relevant impact on the rights of the affected party' for it to amount to deprivation of property: See *Shoprite Checkers (Pty) Ltd v MEC for Economic Development, Eastern Cape* 2015 (6) SA 125 (CC) para 73 (citing *Reflect-All 1025 CC and Others v MEC*

4 Linkage at the 'is-it-property' stage of review?

4.1 Froneman J's discussion

Froneman J drew a further derivation from the linkage account, which we now have to deal with. His judgment calls for reviewing courts to take account of the affected holding's linkage to the higher rights and values not only at the bottom-line 'is-it-arbitrary?' stage of a judicial inquiry under section 25(1), but also even at the initial stage of deciding whether the adversely affected *nexus* of extant legal relations in question counts as 'property' coming under the protective umbrella of section 25(1).[84] This move is not to our minds so easy to defend. It calls for further investigation.

It is of course easy to see how the is-it-property question comes up in the *Shoprite Checkers* case. Shoprite's wine license, if property at all, is 'new property', and the extent of section 25(1)'s protection for new property remained unsettled when the case came to court. (In *FNB* the court, having ruled that ownership of land and tangible movables must 'lie at the heart' of the property concept of section 25(1), forbore to attempt a more comprehensive definition.)[85] In this situation, Froneman J, directing himself to the question of whether Shoprite's old-order wine license qualifies as property under section 25(1), wrote as follows:

> There is much to be said for the High Court's finding that once the licence is granted, an enforceable personal incorporeal right is vested in the recipient to trade in accordance with the conditions attached. These rights are transferable, subject to approval by the licensing authority. The right to sell liquor is thus clearly definable and identifiable by persons other than the holder; has value; is capable of being transferred; and is sufficiently permanent, in the sense that the holder is, in terms of administrative law, protected against arbitrary revocation by the issuing authority. This is close to recognition [as property] on conventional private law

for Public Transport, Roads and Works, Gauteng Provincial Government, and Another 2009 (6) SA 391 (CC) paras 35–36); AJ van der Walt *Constitutional property law* 3 ed (2011) 209; AJ van der Walt 'Section 25 vortices' 2016 *TSAR* 412–427, 597–621 606–607. For a recent case that confirms this point, see *South African Diamond Producers Organisation v Minister of Minerals and Energy NO* 2017 JDR 1222 (CC).

[84] A proprietary interest must usually satisfy three requirements to qualify as constitutional property, namely (i) it must be a concrete asset by reason of having vested in terms of established legal principles, (ii) it must have value, and (iii) it must be transferable: See *Shoprite Checkers (Pty) Ltd v MEC for Economic Development, Eastern Cape* 2015 (6) SA 125 (CC) paras 67–68; *National Credit Regulator v Opperman and Others* 2013 (2) SA 1 (CC) paras 57–64. See further AJ van der Walt *Constitutional property law* 3 ed (2011) 111–143 and the sources cited there.

[85] *First National Bank of SA Ltd t/a Wesbank v Commissioner, South African Revenue Service and Another; First National Bank of SA Ltd t/a Wesbank v Minister of Finance* 2002 (4) SA 768 (CC) para 51.

> grounds. The potential objective link to constitutionally sanctioned self-fulfilment only strengthens the case for recognition of it as property.[86]

Really? *What* link? It is, as we have said, hard to see how the holding of a wine license (or any asset) could assist the self-fulfillment of Shoprite, a juristic person. Froneman J also, however, had in view the teaching of *FNB* that the question of a holding's status as protectible property is to be decided 'objectively' and not by 'the subjective interest of [any particular] owner in the thing owned'.[87] Froneman J accordingly found it in order to consider a possible scenario in which a natural person holds a wine license essential to the success of a business which makes up a part of that person's self-fulfillment; and it was *that* conceivable linkage of wine licenses as a class to 'the fundamental right to choose one's trade or vocation' that Froneman J concluded would strengthen the objective case for their recognition as property protected by section 25(1), and so help get Shoprite past that first hurdle in its claim for constitutional relief.[88]

Now if, as Froneman J thus concludes, the *presence* of such a higher-values linkage can push across the line an otherwise debatable case for recognition of some legal holding as constitutionally protected property, it seemingly must follow that the *absence* of such a link can be the reason for such a case falling short of the line. The presence *or absence* of the higher-values link can thus turn out decisive on the 'property' issue. But why should that be so? Why might a regulatory law's adverse effects on the right of a hypothetical someone not now before the court to choose their trade or profession freely *ever* be thought to count in deciding whether 'property' of the present claimant has been invaded? What is thereby achieved that cannot as well be achieved by reserving for the 'is-it-arbitrary' stage any consideration of the bearing of linkage considerations on a final disposition of a claim of a law's unconstitutionality in terms of section 25(1)? And why is the point so important as to cause Froneman J to introduce it *here*, in a case where he himself seems to say that he would have decided the 'property' issue in Shoprite's favor without it? These questions are especially pressing because, as we now proceed to show, there are several objections to this doctrinal

---

[86] *Shoprite Checkers (Pty) Ltd v MEC for Economic Development, Eastern Cape* 2015 (6) SA 125 (CC) para 68.

[87] *Shoprite Checkers (Pty) Ltd v MEC for Economic Development, Eastern Cape* 2015 (6) SA 125 (CC) paras 32 and 48, citing *First National Bank of SA Ltd t/a Wesbank v Commissioner, South African Revenue Service and Another; First National Bank of SA Ltd t/a Wesbank v Minister of Finance* 2002 (4) SA 768 (CC) para 56.

[88] *Shoprite Checkers (Pty) Ltd v MEC for Economic Development, Eastern Cape* 2015 (6) SA 125 (CC) paras 61, 64.

move on Froneman J's part to which his *Shoprite Checkers* judgment does not attend.

4.2 Deviation from the established two-stage approach to bill-of-rights review in South Africa

Injection of the linkage account into the 'is-it-property' issue apparently runs counter to the established 'two-stage' approach of South African constitutional law.[89] The gist of that approach has been to define 'generously' – at what we may call the 'gateway' stage of a bill-of-rights litigation – the scope of a constitutionally designated right, while saving for a dispositive 'justification' stage all questions of adjustment of the extent of the protection to allow for competing concerns. This inclination to presume in favor of the right's application at the gateway has been a topic of critique and contestation,[90] but it has in fact quite plainly controlled the jurisprudence from *S v Makwanyane and Another*[91] onward.[92]

Normally in South African bill-of-rights adjudications, the gateway stage involves the setting of a generous outer scope of a right named in some section of Chapter Two of the Constitution, while the justification stage consists in application of the 'limitation' clause, section 36(1), to see whether a law's limitation of that scope is nevertheless 'reasonable and justifiable' in the terms laid down by that section. It is, however, difficult to see how this can be the procedure with respect to section 25(1). Once given a substantive and context-dependent non-arbitrariness test, a finding of arbitrary deprivation under section 25(1) can leave little – if indeed any – room to save that

[89] AJ van der Walt 'Section 25 vortices' 2016 *TSAR* 412–427, 597–621 602 ff; EJ Marais 'Expanding the contours of the constitutional property concept' 2016 *TSAR* 576–592 583ff.

[90] As generally applied, by S Woolman in 'The amazing, vanishing bill of rights' (2007) 124 *SALJ* 762–794; with specific reference to section 25, by T Roux 'Property' in Woolman S, Roux T & Bishop M (eds) *Constitutional law of South Africa* (2d ed original service Dec 2003) ch 46.

[91] 1995 (3) SA 391 (CC).

[92] *S v Makwanyane and Another* 1995 (3) SA 391 (CC); see I Currie & J de Waal 'Interpretation of the Bill of Rights' in I Currie & J de Waal (eds) *The Bill of Rights handbook* (6 ed 2013) 138–140. For application of the two-stage approach in constitutional property cases involving personal incorporeal rights, see *National Credit Regulator v Opperman and Others* 2013 (2) SA 1 (CC); *Cool Ideas 1186 CC v Hubbard and Another* 2014 (4) SA 474 (CC); *Chevron SA (Pty) Ltd v Wilson* 2015 JDR 1055 (CC).

application of the law under section 36(1).[93] (That could happen only if a legal application found to be substantively arbitrary in context could nevertheless also be found reasonable and justifiable in a society based on human dignity, equality, and freedom.)[94] The result then is that section 25(1)'s non-arbitrary requirement becomes that section's own internal limitation clause. The regular two-stage structure of constitutional appraisal remains in place, only with 'non-arbitrary' effectively substituting for the demand of section 36(1) for 'reasonable and justifiable' laws.[95] The two-stage approach for adjudicating constitutional disputes (ie the gateway and dispositive stages) is therefore still followed, albeit without direct recourse to section 36(1).

Following, then, the 'generous' spirit of the established two-stage approach, it would seem that once a court has found that the wine-selling privilege conferred by Shoprite's grocer's license is asset-like in the respects (as agreed by Froneman J) that it 'is clearly definable and identifiable by persons other than the holder; has value; is capable of being transferred; and is sufficiently permanent',[96] that should suffice to get the claim past the 'property' gate in section 25(1) and so put the state to its burden to justify (as not arbitrary) the adverse alteration of the license entitlement wrought by the challenged legislation. In the full spirit of the usual two-stage approach, it would seem that such a preliminary showing should so suffice without any further demand for higher-values linkage.

We here briefly notice some further, related concerns about Froneman J's proposal for a linkage approach to the is-it-property issue in a section 25(1) litigation. Some commentaries worry about creation of a decisional 'vortex' – a flowing together at the gateway stage of litigation of what are better held apart as the different sets of considerations relevant to deciding (i) a categorical question of whether the claimant has or has not suffered a general sort of injury denoted by a loss of property, and (ii) a follow-on

---

93 *Shoprite Checkers (Pty) Ltd v MEC for Economic Development, Eastern Cape and Others* 2015 (6) SA 125 (CC) para 87; *National Credit Regulator v Opperman and Others* 2013 (2) SA 1 (CC) para 73; *Chevron SA (Pty) Ltd v Wilson* 2015 JDR 1055 (CC) para 31. See also AJ van der Walt 'Section 25 vortices' 2016 *TSAR* 412–427 424–426, 597–621 611–612; T Roux 'Property' in S Woolman, T Roux & M Bishop (eds) *Constitutional law of South Africa* (2 ed 2003 original service Dec 2003) 46–26 to 46–28.

94 See *Shoprite Checkers (Pty) Ltd v MEC for Economic Development, Eastern Cape and Others* 2015 (6) SA 125 (CC) para 87 ('Once the interest is identified and the *FNB* approach to arbitrariness is applied, there can be no further independent infringement that would require further justification under section 36.').

95 Compare AJ van der Walt 'Section 25 vortices' 2016 *TSAR* 412–427 424–426, 597–621 611–612.

96 *Shoprite Checkers (Pty) Ltd v MEC for Economic Development, Eastern Cape* 2015 (6) SA 125 (CC) para 68.

'balancing' decision that takes into account both the gravity of any such loss to the holder and the weight of the state's need to impose it.[97] These same commentaries worry further, and quite plausibly, about a possible resulting blanket exclusion of purely commercial interests, or of juristic-person claimants, from any section 25(1) protection at all.[98]

4.3 *Shifting the gaze: Property old and new*

In the face of these quite reasonable concerns, Froneman J's proposal to weigh a holding's higher-values linkage at the gateway stage of a section 25(1) litigation calls for further explanation. There must be some weighty countervailing reason for it, but what is that reason?

To bring a persuasive answer clearly into view, we must shift the focus from the ostensible new-property setting of the *Shoprite Checkers* case back to the severely troubled old-property heritage of South African law and society. Viewed in the new-property frame, *Shoprite Checkers* represents a class of cases involving business-firm claimants coming to court in quest of protection for various commercially valuable regulatory *status quo ante*. In that class of cases, the apparent general tendency of an injection of linkage considerations at the gateway stage will be toward tightening rather than widening the gates to constitutional review, contrary to the general spirit of the two-stage review conception and with no compensating gain that we can see to overall effectuation of constitutional values and aims (since any considerations of linkage or the lack of it, in the state's favor or against it, can fully do their work at the justification stage).[99]

But now consider a quite different sort of case. A claimant seeks protection against some encroachment, by or under cover of law, not on 'new property' but rather on a land-based possessory position. It is, however, a position of a kind traditionally classified in South African private law as weak, precarious, and temporary – say, a labor tenancy, a customary law interest or a use (or occupation) right.[100] These types of land rights were almost exclusively

---

[97] EJ Marais 'Expanding the contours of the constitutional property concept' 2016 *TSAR* 576–592 586–587; AJ van der Walt 'Section 25 vortices' 2016 *TSAR* 412–427, 597–621 601ff. These writers draw the 'vortex' concern from T Roux 'Property' in S Woolman, T Roux & M Bishop (eds) *Constitutional law of South Africa* (2 ed OS Dec 2003) ch 46.

[98] EJ Marais 'Expanding the contours of the constitutional property concept' 2016 *TSAR* 576–592 586–587; AJ van der Walt 'Section 25 vortices' 2016 *TSAR* 412–427, 597–621 603ff.

[99] EJ Marais 'Expanding the contours of the constitutional property concept' 2016 *TSAR* 576–592 583ff; AJ van der Walt 'Section 25 vortices' 2016 *TSAR* 412–427, 597–621 602ff.

[100] AJ van der Walt 'Dancing with codes – protecting, developing and deconstructing property rights in a constitutional state' (2001) 118 *SALJ* 258–311 276, 287ff.

held by black South Africans and were not of the formal, Roman-Dutch (ie registered ownership and limited real rights) kind. Instead, they derived from customary law and legislation, and were deliberately weakened by apartheid statutes to aid the state's efforts in promoting racial segregation.[101] We are perhaps not yet past a stage where South African lawyers and jurists might still be induced by old-order private-law categories or traces thereof to doubt or question whether these infra-patrimonial positions count as 'property' in South African constitutional-legal lingo so as to get them past the gateway to review set up by section 25(1)'s use of that term. Exclusion of linkage factors from the gateway stage would mean these factors will *not* weigh in positively, as they ought, on the question whether the claimant has constitutionally cognisable 'property' at stake in the dispute. Given the obviousness of the dependency of a person's freedom, security, dignity, privacy, and associations on a due measure of protection for possessory positions of the types we have here in mind, a linkage consideration at the gateway stage seems the perfect antidote against that danger, and one fully in keeping with the Constitution's overall transformative project. The 'property' category is, in Froneman J's phrase, 'extended' so as to 'embrace constitutional entitlements beyond the original ambit of private common-law property'[102] – thus ensuring that the 'negative' protection of section 25(1), no less than the 'positive' guarantees in sections 25(5)–(7), 26–28, contributes positively toward achievement of the Constitution's social-transformative aims.

And so we find ourselves in possession of what looks like a good and sturdy explanation for Froneman J's proposal for taking account of linkage at the section 25(1) gateway. The explanation supposes that Froneman J has had in mind a class of cases quite different from the class that the *Shoprite Checkers* case itself would most naturally seem to represent. (Here we recall André van der Walt's email remark that *Shoprite Checkers* 'might not be the perfect case for' a new holding on the relevance of 'higher' values to the decision of cases brought under section 25(1).) Ultimately propelling Froneman J's opinion, we suggest, is a direction of mind not only to finding the right balance between security for incorporeal holdings based in operations of the regulatory state and the state's needed latitude for regulatory reform (although that is, of course, one important concern for any negative constitutional property clause), but equally toward ensuring a just (and transformative) measure

---

[101] AJ van der Walt 'Dancing with codes – protecting, developing and deconstructing property rights in a constitutional state' (2001) 118 *SALJ* 258–311 276, 287ff.

[102] *Shoprite Checkers (Pty) Ltd v MEC for Economic Development, Eastern Cape* 2015 (6) SA 125 (CC) para 46. Compare section 25(6) of the Constitution.

of security for interests based in habitation and occupancy of spaces and materials of a physical nature – which had, however, been denied the dignity and force of ownership by the categories of pre-constitutional South African private law. When the possessory positions in question are plainly and thickly connected to personal dignity and freedom, those positions are to be counted 'property' protected by section 25(1), regardless of inherited private-law classifications of property.

4.4 *Expansion (not constriction) of protection*

In one of his last published works, André van der Walt pointed to a tension in Froneman J's *Shoprite Checkers* judgment between expansion and constriction of the 'property' gateway in section 25(1).[103] On the one side, the judgment 'lean[s] toward expanding the private-law notion of property . . . to facilitate the protection of a wider range of . . . interests that are important to transformation'. On the other side, though, by its focus on 'the promotion of non-property constitutional rights and objectives', the judgment 'potentially . . . restricts [constitutional protection] to "deserving property" interests that serve the normative constitutional goal of promoting socially situated self-fulfillment'. Or, in other words, that focus could have caused Shoprite, as a merely juristic person, to lose its case at the gateway, before any weighing of state and private interests could take place, which seems wrong within the overall, generous spirit of post-transition South African constitutional law as it has evolved to date.

One proposal in response would be to read the *Shoprite Checkers* judgment of Froneman J as authorising *only* an expansionary, and *not* a constrictive effect of linkage at the gateway stage. That would be in keeping with the established two-stage model of bill-of-rights review. There could be no resulting over-promotion of sheerly proprietary interests at the expense of other constitutional aims and values, nor could there result any undue hindrance of the state's pursuit of important regulatory duties,[104] because all such concerns are covered by the proposal to give linkage its due at the dispositive, is-it-arbitrary stage of the litigation, where Froneman J would normally use a rationality test except insofar as the complaining party herself could invoke those other values on her side of the case. Nor would there then be any 'vortex' effect to worry us. At the gateway 'is-it-property' stage, the

[103] AJ van der Walt 'Section 25 vortices' 2016 *TSAR* 412–427, 597–621 602. See similarly EJ Marais 'Expanding the contours of the constitutional property concept' 2016 *TSAR* 576–592 583ff.

[104] This is indeed the fear of Moseneke DCJ: See *Shoprite Checkers (Pty) Ltd v MEC for Economic Development, Eastern Cape* 2015 (6) SA 125 (CC) para 125.

only effect of the linkage doctrine would be to *open* the gates to claims to section 25(1) protection that they might otherwise be read to have barred, but only for reasons of private-law history antithetical to the Constitution's transformative aims. All the finer-grained work would still be left to the dispositive, 'is-it-arbitrary' stage. There would be no resulting confusion of categorical questions with balancing or qualitative ones.

5 A 'constitutional vision' and a 'modest systemic status' for property: The legacy of Professor AJ van der Walt

Perceptions of property's service to the higher ends of human dignity, equality, and freedom can take either of two warring forms in legal thought. One of these sets up property absolutely as the 'guardian' right in a free and democratic society, on the flat-out uncompromising protection of which all the other rights in such a society must sooner or later depend. The other values property-protection by degrees, according to whether in practice it serves or disserves these higher ends. One stance is abstract and formalistic, the other contextual and pragmatic. The latter is what Froneman J points toward in his *Shoprite Checkers* judgment, the implications of which we discuss in this chapter. The former is what AJ van der Walt condemns in his late, important article 'The modest systemic status of property rights'.[105] There, Van der Walt takes his stance against the absolutist property-as-guardian view. To treat property as the system's special appointed guardian of the higher values – to allow those higher values to 'ride on the back' of property – must inevitably tend, warns Van der Walt, toward an over-inflation of property as a kind of abstract super-right, thus to be given sway more or less automatically over any and all competing claims regardless of context or consequence.[106] Such a view, he maintains, carries the potential to thwart the transformative aims the Constitution seeks to realise, specifically in – though not limited to – the context of land reform.

Denial to property of that sort of reified elevation over the values it supposedly guards is what Van der Walt had in view as a restoration of property to a 'modest' systemic status. 'Restoration' is our word, not his. We choose it because, according to Van der Walt (and not him alone), an abstract-formalist idea of property as a kind of 'mother right' in a free society had gained a strong purchase in pre-constitutional modern South African legal consciousness, and of that purchase more than a remnant still inhabits

[105] AJ van der Walt 'The modest systemic status of property rights' (2014) 1 *J L Prop & Soc'y* 15–106.

[106] AJ van der Walt 'The modest systemic status of property rights' (2014) 1 *J L Prop & Soc'y* 15–106 32–36.

the culture (even if, as Van der Walt also maintains (writing together with Priviledge Dhliwayo), it was far from consistently carried out in case law).[107]

Concern about a deep non-compatibility between old-order ownership conceptions and the social-transformative commitments of the Constitution has long been a signature strain in AJ van der Walt's scholarship, along with a corresponding call for correction in this respect of South African legal discourse.[108] In Van der Walt's body of work, the call for correction finds expression through two characteristic thematisations. One is the theme of the constitutional vision of property.[109] The other is the theme of property's modest systemic status in South African law generally. The two themes are complementary. They can work independently, or side by side, or interactively.

With regard to cases like *Shoprite Checkers*, involving a party's direct invocation of the Constitution's property clause against an act of the state, the typically applicable theme will be that of the constitutional vision for property. An applicant seeks the Constitution's protection against loss to property by force of some law. The theme of the constitutional vision of property says that when you want to claim protection in terms of the Constitution, you must do so on the Constitution's terms, *and those terms do not necessarily track those of pre-constitutional private law*. So maintains Professor van der Walt, and so prescribes Froneman J by his *Shoprite Checkers* judgment.[110]

But what, then, of the countless property-related disputes in which no party thinks to invoke the Constitution and that therefore stand to be judicially resolved in terms of general private law?[111] It is in such cases that the Van der Walt theme of property's modest systemic status in the generality of South African law comes into its own. In terms of this theme, it will not necessarily be the category 'property' that does the main work when adjudicating cases in which a proprietary claim (ie landownership) stands on one side of the dispute. Other claims (such as the rights to life, dignity, expression, equality,

[107] AJ van der Walt & P Dhliwayo 'The notion of absolute and exclusive ownership: A doctrinal analysis' (2017) 134 *SALJ* 34–52 42.

[108] See, amongst some of his last works, AJ van der Walt *Property in the margins* (2009); AJ van der Walt *Constitutional property law* 3 ed (2011); AJ van der Walt *Property and constitution* (2012); AJ van der Walt 'The modest systemic status of property rights' (2014) 1 *J L Prop & Soc'y* 15–106; AJ van der Walt & P Dhliwayo 'The notion of absolute and exclusive ownership: A doctrinal analysis' (2017) 134 *SALJ* 34–52.

[109] See the discussion in section 2 above.

[110] See the discussion in section 2 above.

[111] It is true that courts are enjoined to construe and develop the common law with a view to the due effectuation of constitutional rights and the due promotion of the spirit, purport, and objects of the Bill of Rights: See sections 8(3)(*a*) and 39(2) of the Constitution. Only occasionally, though, in private litigation, does that injunction rise to the surface of the arguments or reasons of the parties and judges.

and freedom of movement) will in appropriate cases provide the starting point for decision.

Daniels v Scribante and Another[112] was not quite such a case, but close enough to let it provide a valedictory for this chapter. The appellant was an occupant on the respondent's land whose occupancy came under the protective coverage of the Extension of Security of Tenure Act.[113] At issue was the appellant's claim, in terms of that legislation, of a right to make certain improvements to the space she occupied – which improvements would enhance the appellant's security of tenure by rendering basically more habitable her home – without the respondent's consent. The court's main judgment, in the appellant's favor, proceeded strictly in terms of statutory interpretation, although of course guided by the Constitution's commitment to security of tenure[114] as a foundation for human dignity, equality, and freedom.

Froneman J, concurring in that judgment, also found the occasion apt for a separate opinion containing strong echoes of Van der Walt's view of a modest systemic status for property. The occasion came from the respondent's apparent assumption that his 'ownership of the farm' must be the 'point of departure' for resolution of the case.[115] Rejecting that view, Froneman J recollected Professor van der Walt's account of the historical contingency of the absolutist ownership conception.[116] He noted the showing by Van der Walt of non-compatibility between 'the absolutisation of ownership . . . and the hierarchy of rights it spawned' and 'the purpose of founding political and economic freedom in South Africa.'[117] He endorsed the view of Sachs J in *Port Elizabeth Municipality v Various Occupiers*[118] that the judge's job is not 'to establish a hierarchical arrangement . . . privileging in an abstract and mechanical way the rights of ownership' but rather is 'to balance out and reconcile the opposed claims in as just a manner as possible taking into account . . . the specific factors relevant in each particular case.'[119] And he

[112] *Daniels v Scribante and Another* 2017 (4) SA 341 (CC).

[113] 62 of 1997.

[114] Section 25(6) of the Constitution.

[115] Paragraph 133. The opinion is notable for other reasons as well, which we do not here explore. As one indication of the intensity of feeling behind it, Froneman J wrote the original of the opinion in Afrikaans. We here refer to the English-language version that Froneman J also supplied and caused to be included in the court's official report of the case.

[116] Paragraph 134, citing AJ van der Walt *Property in the margins* (2009) 29-34.

[117] Paragraph 136.

[118] 2005 (1) SA 217 (CC).

[119] Paragraph 135, citing *Port Elizabeth Municipality v Various Occupiers* 2005 (1) SA 217 (CC) para 23.

ended, as shall we, in a nod of honor to the 'pioneering work' of the departed Professor van der Walt, by allowing 'the last word' on this topic to be his:

> [T]raditional notions of property do not suffice in transformational contexts, where the foundations of the property regime itself are or should be in question because regulatory restrictions, even when imposed in terms of a broadly conceived notion of the public good, simply cannot do all the transformative work that is required. In this perspective it is not sufficient to demonstrate that property is subject to public-purpose restrictions; the point is to identify and explain instances where transformation justifies changes that question the very foundations upon which the current distribution of property rests.[120]

[120] *Daniels v Scribante and Another* 2017 (4) SA 341 (CC) para 136, quoting from AJ van der Walt *Property in the margins* (2009) 16.

Chapter 7

The proprietary consequences of estoppel in light of section 25(1): Testing Van der Walt's hypotheses

Zsa-Zsa Boggenpoel & Clireesh Cloete***

1 Introduction

The late Professor André van der Walt explains that:

> When the South African Research Chair in Property Law (SARCPL) was established in January 2008 as part of the national Department of Science and Technology's South African Research Chairs Initiative (SARChI), its primary research goal was to develop the theoretical foundations for the development of property law in the new constitutional era. Concretely, this required research to establish how the future development of property law (including both traditional, 'private-law' property law and the relatively novel field of constitutional property law) should develop, guided by the Constitution of the Republic of South Africa, 1996 in the democratic, post-1994 South African context.[1]

More specifically, in relation to the interpretation and development of the common law, Van der Walt points out that it is important to view such interpretation and development in a constitutional light. This is the very

* Professor in Private law, Stellenbosch University.

** Doctoral candidate at the South African Research Chair in property law, Stellenbosch University.

[1] AJ van der Walt 'Property in the constitutional democracy' (2017) *Stell LR* 1–23 1.

essence of a single system of law[2] approach to the law generally, and property law more specifically. Van der Walt draws two conclusions (based on two principles) about the development of the common law on the basis of research done on these topics within the SARCPL group. Firstly, if common-law principles authorise *ex lege* or non-consensual creation, loss, transfer or amendment of property rights, this will probably establish a deprivation of property for purposes of section 25(1) of the Constitution. Secondly, if the development of common-law principles of property law causes *ex lege* or non-consensual creation, loss, transfer or amendment of property rights, this will probably establish a *non*-arbitrary deprivation of property for purposes of section 25(1). This principle is subject to the qualification that if the development is subject to the court's discretion, such discretion must be exercised strictly according to the requirements of the common law, and within the limits of what the common law actually authorises. In the end, any deprivation brought about by interpretation or development of the common law will not be arbitrary for purposes of section 25(1) provided that the common-law requirements are properly applied. The proper application of the common-law requirements is necessary especially when they include exercise of a judicial discretion to allow the deprivation and the possibility of a judicial compensation award.

The purpose of this contribution is to test whether Van der Walt's hypotheses relating to the interpretation and development of the common law confirm or bring further nuance to these two principles, or unsettle the principles in any way in the context of the doctrine of estoppel. Section 2 of this chapter, below, sets out the general problem that arises when a holder of property is able to rely on estoppel successfully. The common-law position regarding the consequences of a successful reliance on estoppel seems puzzling in light of recent jurisprudence.[3] At the moment it is not clear whether the successful estoppel holder is simply allowed continued 'hedged' control of the property, or whether ownership passes to such holder, or whether such holder in fact acquires ownership by operation of law. Any one of these proprietary consequences can potentially cause doctrinal and constitutional problems. It does not seem likely that the successful estoppel raiser acquires ownership

---

[2] See AJ van der Walt 'Normative pluralism and anarchy: Reflections on the 2007 term' (2008) 1 *CCR* 77–128; AJ van der Walt *Property and constitution* (2012) 19–24; AJ van der Walt 'The modest systemic approach to property' (2014) 1 *J L Prop & Soc'y* 15–106.

[3] *Oriental Products (Pty) Ltd v Pegma 178 Investments Trading CC and Others* 2011 (2) SA 508 (SCA) paras 23, 31. See also JC Sonnekus *The law of estoppel in South Africa* 3 ed (2012) 331; JC Sonnekus 'Eienaars en ander reghebbendes mag ervaar dat swye nie altyd goud werd is nie' 2013 *TSAR* 326–339 327; ZT Boggenpoel *Property remedies* (2017) ch 2.

by way of derivative acquisition of ownership, as there is no real agreement which allows ownership to pass from the owner to the holder of the property.[4] Section 3 of the chapter will focus specifically on whether development of the common law in this respect is necessary and/or desirable. It should be noted that if development of the common law does take place, to recognise a new form of original acquisition of ownership, which is what is argued most probably happens in this case, the owner may lose her property right, in terms of the doctrine of estoppel.[5] Therefore, besides the doctrinal issues that arise in this context, there may be constitutional property law implications that may need to be addressed. If it is recognised that the owner of the property, by original means, loses ownership by operation of law, the question arises whether such loss of ownership is in line with section 25 of the Constitution. This is considered in more detail in section 4 below.

The consequences of estoppel are analysed with the ultimate aim of testing Van der Walt's hypotheses in the context of the development and interpretation of the common law. In other words, if it is established that the common law authorises the development, the loss of property that occurs should not amount to arbitrary deprivation of property. It will be interesting to see whether Van der Walt's assumptions about the development of the common law and its impact in relation to section 25(1) stand up to scrutiny in the context of the consequences of the doctrine of estoppel.

2 The proprietary consequences of estoppel revisited

The doctrine of estoppel is based on the idea that a person (the representor) makes a representation either by words or conduct to another person (the representee). The representee in good faith acts on the basis of the representation to her detriment because she believes the representation to be true. The Supreme Court of Appeal judgment in *Oakland Nominees (Pty) Ltd v Gelria Mining*[6] confirmed the basic requirements of the defence. These are: firstly, that the owner created a representation that directed the estoppel raiser to believe that the disposer of the property was the owner of the property or that the disposer had the right to dispose of the property. Secondly, that the representation is the result of the owner's culpable conduct.

[4] DL Carey Miller *The acquisition and protection of ownership* (1986) 309; JC Sonnekus *The law of estoppel in South Africa* 3 ed (2012) 350–351; JC Sonnekus 'Eienaars en ander reghebbendes mag ervaar dat swye nie altyd goud werd is nie' 2013 *TSAR* 326–339 334.

[5] CG van der Merwe *Sakereg* 2 ed (1989) 373; JC Sonnekus 'Eienaars en ander reghebbendes mag ervaar dat swye nie altyd goud werd is nie' 2013 *TSAR* 326–339 337; FB Pelser 'Aspekte van eiendomsverkryging deur estoppel' (2005) 38 *De Jure* 153–162 159.

[6] *Oakland Nominees (Pty) Ltd v Gelria Mining* 1976 (1) SA 441 (A).

Thirdly, that the estoppel raiser in good faith relied upon the representation by the owner. The fourth requirement is that the reliance on the owner's representation must have resulted in the estoppel raiser exercising physical control over the property with the *animus domini* to her own detriment. If the requirements of the doctrine of estoppel have been met, the court will find in favour of the estoppel raiser with the result that the owner is unable to reclaim the property with the *rei vindicatio*.[7]

Estoppel operates to prevent (or estop) the representor from denying the factual accuracy of the representation. In this regard, estoppel is viewed as a defence against the owner's *rei vindicatio*,[8] and, consequently, it is not an independent cause of action.[9] The question of what happens after a successful claim based on estoppel has been raised in South African law; more specifically, whether the person who has successfully pleaded estoppel forthwith becomes owner of the thing or simply has hedged possession against the owner's vindicatory power is questionable. In *Barclays Western Bank*

[7] *Oakland Nominees (Pty) Ltd v Gelria Mining & Investment Co (Pty) Ltd* 1976 (1) SA 441 (A) 452. See further CG van der Merwe *Sakereg* 2 ed (1989) 369; JC Sonnekus & JL Neels *Sakereg vonnisbundel* 2 ed (1994) 473; PJ Badenhorst, JM Pienaar & H Mostert *Silberberg and Schoeman's The law of property* 5 ed (2006) 256; CG van der Merwe & A Pope 'Property' in F du Bois *Wille's principles of South African law* 9 ed (2007) 405–729 552; *Standard Bank of SA Ltd v Stama (Pty) Ltd* 1975 (1) SA 730 (A) 743; *Apostoliese Geloofsending van Suid-Afrika (Maitland Gemeente) v Capes* 1978 (4) SA 48 (C) 56; *Oriental Products (Pty) Ltd v Pegma 178 Investments Trading* 2011 (2) SA 508 (SCA) para 27; *Absa Bank Ltd v Knysna Auto Services CC* (266/2015) [2016] ZASCA 93 (1 June 2016) para 16.

[8] CG van der Merwe *Sakereg* 2 ed (1989) 347; PJ Badenhorst, JM Pienaar & H Mostert *Silberberg and Schoeman's The law of property* 5 ed (2006) 242; CG van der Merwe & A Pope 'Property' in F du Bois (ed) *Wille's principles of South African law* 9 ed (2007) 405–729 539; CG van der Merwe 'Things' in WA Joubert & JA Faris (eds) *LAWSA* Vol 27 Part 2 2 ed (2014) para 233; JC Sonnekus 'Bona fide-verkryging vir waarde en estoppel' (1999) 62 *THRHR* 463–469 463; FB Pelser 'Aspekte van eiendomsverkryging deur estoppel' (2005) 38 *De Jure* 153-162 153; *Chetty v Naidoo* 1974 (3) SA 13 (A) 20.

[9] DL Carey Miller *The acquisition and protection of ownership* (1986) 309; CG van der Merwe *Sakereg* 2 ed (1989) 372; JC Sonnekus *The law of estoppel in South Africa* 3 ed (2012) 30–34; *Pandora's Trustee v Beatley & Co* 1935 TPD 358 at 363; *Union Government v National Bank of South Africa Ltd* 1921 AD 121 at 128; *Oriental Products (Pty) Ltd v Pegma 178 Investments Trading CC and Others* 2011 (2) SA 508 (SCA) para 31. Although this is the position taken, there are some scholars that question whether estoppel should only have an evidentiary function. In this regard see JC van der Walt 'Die beskerming van die bona fide besitsverkryger: 'n Vergelyking tussen die Suid-Afrikaanse en Nederlandse reg' in JJ Gauntlett (ed) *JC Noster 'n Feesbundel* (1979) 73–96 96; HJO van Heerden 'Estoppel: 'n Wyse van eiendomsverkryging' (1970) 33 *THRHR* 19–25 20; JW Louw 'Estoppel en die *rei vindicatio*' (1975) 38 *THRHR* 218–238 221–223; PJ Visser 'Estoppel en die vekryging van eiendomsreg in roerende eiendom' (1994) 57 *THRHR* 633-636 636; FB Pelser 'Aspekte van eiendomsverkryging deur estoppel' (2005) 38 *De Jure* 153–162 155–156.

Ltd v Fourie,[10] the person who was successful with the defence of estoppel was unable to claim the thing back from another person (not the owner) or to claim damages for harm caused to the property. The court in *Apostoliese Geloofsending van Suid Afrika (Maitland Gemeente) v Capes*[11] held that, although the owner of the property remains owner after a successful defence of estoppel has been raised, the owner is unable to disturb the defendant's possession of the thing. Both judgments seem to indicate that estoppel simply gives the estoppel raiser hedged control against the owner, rather than a substantive claim to the property, especially against third parties. Accordingly, it seems as though, on the one hand, the traditional position is that a successful estoppel defence against an owner's *rei vindicatio* results in suspension of the owner's entitlement to vindicate the property in the hands of the successful estoppel raiser.[12] This means that the owner is prohibited from claiming back her property from the *bona fide* possessor against whom she unsuccessfully raised her *rei vindicatio*. On the other hand, the successful estoppel raiser is allowed to remain in possession of the property.

Although estoppel essentially serves as a defence against the owner's *rei vindicatio*, a successful claim based on estoppel can potentially give rise to rights. This possibility was raised by the Supreme Court of Appeal in *Oriental Products (Pty) Ltd v Pegma 178 Investments Trading CC and Others*.[13] In this judgment, the third respondent fraudulently transferred immovable property, owned by the appellant, to the second respondent without the appellant's authority. Subsequent to this transfer, the second respondent transferred the property to the first respondent. Two years after the appellant discovered that the deeds registry reflected the first respondent as the registered owner of the immovable property, the appellant instituted proceedings to vindicate the property. The appellant submitted that it is the owner of the property and that the deeds registry should be rectified accordingly. The first respondent

[10] *Barclays Western Bank Ltd v Fourie* 1979 (4) SA 157 (C) 160.

[11] *Apostoliese Geloofsending van Suid-Afrika (Maitland Gemeente) v Capes* 1978 (4) SA 48 (C) 58.

[12] CG van der Merwe *Sakereg* 2 ed (1989) 373; JC Sonnekus & JL Neels *Sakereg vonnisbundel* 2 ed (1994) 473; PJ Badenhorst, JM Pienaar & H Mostert *Silberberg and Schoeman's The law of property* 5 ed (2006) 259; CG van der Merwe & A Pope 'Property' in F du Bois *Wille's principles of South African law* 9 ed (2007) 405–729 554; *Apostoliese Geloofsending van Suid-Afrika (Maitland Gemeente) v Capes* 1978 (4) SA 48 (C) 58; *Absa Bank Ltd v Knysna Auto Services CC* (266/2015) [2016] ZASCA 93 (1 June 2016) para 20.

[13] *Oriental Products (Pty) Ltd v Pegma 178 Investments Trading CC and Others* 2011 (2) SA 508 (SCA) para 20. See further DL Carey Miller *The acquisition and protection of ownership* (1986) 309; CG van der Merwe 'Things' in WA Joubert & JA Faris (eds) *LAWSA* Vol 27 Part 2 2 ed (2014) para 259; HJO van Heerden 'Estoppel: 'n Wyse van eiendomsverkryging' (1970) 33 *THRHR* 19–25 22.

in turn relied on the doctrine of estoppel by representation as a defence against the appellant's claim. The first respondent argued that the appellant had made a negligent misrepresentation by creating the impression that the second respondent had the right to dispose of the property as the registered owner. This misrepresentation was created when the appellant failed to rectify the deeds registry immediately after learning that the second respondent was reflected as the registered owner of the property.[14] In an attempt to refute the first respondent's defence, the appellant argued that estoppel is a defence and not a weapon to claim that transfer of ownership had occurred. Shongwe JA held that the '[t]he logical consequence of upholding the defence of estoppel is that the person in possession of the goods or property, raising estoppel, acquires *an unassailable right to continue possessing* the goods. In my view, it is still a defence entitling the possessor to continue exercising that right.'[15] This finding of the court accords with the contentious suggestion made by some scholars that what the estoppel raiser has after a successful estoppel defence is a recognised right to possess.[16] In other words, the possessor's unlawful possession is presumably transformed into lawful possession by virtue of the court order.

Harms DP went further than Shongwe JA by endorsing the idea that ownership is transferred by derivative means when a plea based on estoppel is allowed. In this regard he reasoned that if the doctrine of estoppel means that ownership *passed* by virtue of estoppel, then so be it.[17] The above dictum of the court by way of the use of derivative terminology such as 'ownership passes by virtue of estoppel' seems to confirm Van der Merwe's observations about the transfer of ownership that occurs when a possessor of property is successful with estoppel. Van der Merwe asserts that a realistic approach to the question of who owns the property after a successful claim based on estoppel is to recognise that the owner forfeits his property and that ownership in fact passes to the acquirer. Van der Merwe goes on to argue

[14] *Oriental Products (Pty) Ltd v Pegma 178 Investments Trading CC and Others* 2011 (2) SA 508 (SCA) para 18.

[15] *Oriental Products (Pty) Ltd v Pegma 178 Investments Trading CC and Others* 2011 (2) SA 508 (SCA) para 20 (emphasis added).

[16] CG van der Merwe *Sakereg* 2 ed (1989) 373; CG van der Merwe 'Things' in WA Joubert & JA Faris (eds) *LAWSA* Vol 27 Part 2 2 ed (2014) para 259; *Apostoliese Geloofsending van Suid-Afrika (Maitland Gemeente) v Capes* 1978 (4) SA 48 (C) 58; *Absa Bank Ltd v Knysna Auto Services CC* (266/2015) [2016] ZASCA 93 (1 June 2016) para 20.

[17] *Oriental Products (Pty) Ltd v Pegma 178 Investments Trading CC and Others* 2011 (2) SA 508 (SCA) para 31.

that where a successful defence of estoppel is raised, this may in fact be a case of derivative acquisition of ownership.[18]

However, Harms DP also pointed out (seemingly in contrast to the above extract) that, if estoppel were allowed in this case, it would mean that estoppel would not be a means of acquiring ownership, but simply a shield or defence aimed at warding off the claim of the owner based on the *rei vindicatio*.[19] This stands in contrast to the judgment of Shongwe JA in *Oriental Products*, in which he recognised that –

> [i]n the context of this case, the appellant [as owner] is entitled to retransfer of the property but for the fact that it cannot assert its right of ownership because of estoppel. Hence, the applicant *loses its ownership* of the property.[20]

The statements of the judges in this decision are conflicting and very confusing. Harms DP's reasoning that 'ownership passed by virtue of estoppel' seemingly points to the recognition that estoppel results in transfer of property by derivative acquisition of ownership. This is in line with Van der Merwe's assertion that successful reliance on estoppel may be an instance of derivative acquisition of ownership. The statement by Shongwe JA in turn hinting that the 'applicant loses its ownership of the property' when the defendant is successful with a claim based on estoppel creates the impression that, at least theoretically, estoppel may result in a new form of original acquisition of ownership. This, in turn, is in line with Sonnekus's view of the consequences of a successful reliance on the defence of estoppel. Sonnekus argues that –

> [i]n the light of the strong emphasis placed on the real agreement in an abstract system of acquisition of ownership in contrast to the rather low-key attention afforded to the real agreement in a causal system, 'ownership by estoppel' can presumably never be classified as a derivative mode of acquisition.[21]

However, Sonnekus points out that the failure by the same court to assert this development in the subsequent case of *Bester NO v Schmidt Bou Ontwikkeling CC*[22] may indicate that the conflict of interest between an owner and a *bona fide* possessor should still be approached with caution and conservatism.[23] He also notes that the *ratio* for the courts' radical new position is not entirely

[18] CG van der Merwe *Sakereg* 2 ed (1989) 373.

[19] *Oriental Products (Pty) Ltd v Pegma 178 Investments Trading CC and Others* 2011 (2) SA 508 (SCA) para 31.

[20] *Oriental Products (Pty) Ltd v Pegma 178 Investments Trading CC and Others* 2011 (2) SA 508 (SCA) para 23.

[21] JC Sonnekus *The law of estoppel in South Africa* 3 ed (2012) 351.

[22] *Bester NO v Schmidt Bou Ontwikkeling CC* 2013 (1) SA 125 (SCA).

[23] JC Sonnekus *The law of estoppel in South Africa* 3 ed (2012) 331.

clear. The lack of clarity and the court's unwillingness to assert the supposed development of the law in the *Bester* case indicate that the consequences of the successful reliance on estoppel remain uncertain in South African law. It is in this respect that Van der Merwe observes that South African law might be ready to accept a new method of acquisition of ownership by way of the doctrine of estoppel. [24] The question arises whether this is possible and desirable, both doctrinally and constitutionally.

As a general rule, a *numerus clausus* of modes of acquisition of ownership exists in South African law. This implies that no new method of acquisition of ownership can be added to the established methods. In other words, for acquisition of ownership to take place, it has to occur in terms of an established mode of acquisition. The fundamental requirements of the recognised modes of acquisition are physical control (*corpus*) and intention (*animus*).[25] Without some form of *corpus* and *animus*, it cannot be said that ownership is acquired. In South African law the *numerus clausus* of modes of acquisition is divided into two distinct categories, namely original and derivative modes of acquisition of ownership. This categorisation is based, first on whether cooperation of the predecessor in title is required for ownership to be acquired by a new owner and, secondly, on whether the acquirer acquires unburdened or burdened title.[26]

Derivative acquisition takes place when cooperation, in the sense of a bilateral agreement between the predecessor (or an agent) and the acquirer, occurs to transfer ownership.[27] The ownership acquired under derivative mode of acquisition derives from the predecessor's ownership. The primary modes of derivative acquisition are delivery when dealing with movable property and registration when dealing with immovable property.[28] With regard to both movable and immovable property, ownership will not pass

---

[24] CG van der Merwe *Sakereg* 2 ed (1989) 215.

[25] CG van der Merwe & A Pope 'Property' in F du Bois (ed) *Wille's principles of South African law* 9 ed (2007) 405–729 488.

[26] CG van der Merwe *Sakereg* 2 ed (1989) 216; CG van der Merwe & A Pope 'Property' in F du Bois (ed) *Wille's principles of South African law* 9 ed (2007) 405–729 488; *Unimark Distributors (Pty) Ltd v Erf 94 Silvertondale (Pty) Ltd* 1999 (2) SA 986 (T) 1000.

[27] DL Carey Miller *The acquisition and protection of ownership* (1986) 117; CG van der Merwe *Sakereg* 2 ed (1989) 298; JC Sonnekus & JL Neels *Sakereg vonnisbundel* 2 ed (1994) 287; PJ Badenhorst, JM Pienaar & H Mostert *Silberberg and Schoeman's The law of property* 5 ed (2006) 137; CG van der Merwe & A Pope 'Property' in F du Bois (ed) *Wille's principles of South African law* 9 ed (2007) 405–729 519.

[28] DL Carey Miller *The acquisition and protection of ownership* (1986) 117–118; CG van der Merwe *Sakereg* 2 ed (1989) 300; CG van der Merwe & A Pope 'Property' in F du Bois (ed) *Wille's principles of South African law* 9 ed (2007) 405–729 519–520.

if the requirements for a valid transfer are not met.[29] The requirements for valid transfer of ownership are (i) that the property is classified as *res in commercio*, (ii) that the transferor has the capacity to transfer ownership, (ii) that the transferee has the capacity to acquire ownership, (iii) that the transferee and the transferor have the intention to transfer and acquire ownership respectively (the real agreement), (iv) the existence of a contractual agreement that gives rise to the transfer, (v) delivery or registration (*traditio*), and (vi) the payment of the purchase price.[30] Once all these requirements have been met, ownership transfers to the acquirer by way of derivative acquisition of ownership.

Original acquisition of ownership, on the other hand, ensues when a unilateral act on the part of the acquirer suffices to establish acquisition of ownership by operation of law.[31] The leading modes of original acquisition are occupation or appropriation, manufacture, prescription, accession, mixing of liquids and fusing of solids, acquisition of ownership in fruits, forfeiture and expropriation. All these forms of original acquisition have their own unique requirements for validity over and above the requirement that is common to them all and that gives them their original character, namely acquisition without the cooperation of a predecessor in title. Acquisition of ownership by original means provides an acquirer with unburdened property.

In light of the above exposition, it does not seem likely that the successful estoppel holder of property acquires ownership by way of derivative acquisition of ownership. There is no real agreement which allows ownership to pass from the owner to the holder of the property. The question whether the common law should be developed to recognise estoppel as an original mode of acquiring ownership will be considered briefly in the section below.

---

[29] DL Carey Miller *The acquisition and protection of ownership* (1986) 118; CG van der Merwe *Sakereg* 2 ed (1989) 301–302; JC Sonnekus & JL Neels *Sakereg vonnisbundel* 2 ed (1994) 390; CG van der Merwe & A Pope 'Property' in F du Bois (ed) *Wille's principles of South African law* 9 ed (2007) 405–729 520–525.

[30] Most property law textbooks list all these requirements for valid transfer of ownership by way of the derivative mode of acquisition. In this regard, see DL Carey Miller *The acquisition and protection of ownership* (1986) 118; CG van der Merwe *Sakereg* 2 ed (1989) 301–302; JC Sonnekus & JL Neels *Sakereg vonnisbundel* 2 ed (1994) 390; CG van der Merwe & A Pope 'Property' in F du Bois (ed) *Wille's principles of South African law* 9 ed (2007) 405–729 520–525.

[31] CG van der Merwe *Sakereg* 2 ed (1989) 216; JC Sonnekus & JL Neels *Sakereg vonnisbundel* 2 ed (1994) 287; PJ Badenhorst, JM Pienaar & H Mostert *Silberberg and Schoeman's The law of property* 5 ed (2006) 137; CG van der Merwe & A Pope 'Property' in F du Bois (ed) *Wille's principles of South African law* 9 ed (2007) 405–729 488.

3 Development of the common law in favour of original acquisition of ownership

3.1 When is development of the common law appropriate?

The need for clear guidelines for the development of the common law in the constitutional era has been highlighted by academic scholars.[32] Section 39(2) of the Constitution requires that the spirit, purport and objects of the Bill of Rights must be promoted whenever the common law is developed and section 8(3) calls for the development of the common law when applying, and in order to give effect to, a right in the Bill of Rights. It is in this context that the court in *Carmichele v Minister of Safety and Security*[33] said that the development of the common law is not divorced from the constitutional project. Rather, the structuring of the process of, and the justification for, the development of the common law must come from constitutional law in accordance with the constitutional normative framework and the Bill of Rights.

Van der Walt proposes a methodology for the development of the common law within the ambit of the Constitution.[34] The methodology consists of three phases. The first phase concerns (i) determining the applicable source of law according to the subsidiarity principles,[35] and (ii) in the event of the common law being the appropriate source of law, establishing the common-

[32] AJ van der Walt 'Development of the common law of servitude' (2013) 130 *SALJ* 722–756 723; DM Davis 'Where is the map to guide common-law development?' (2014) 1 *Stell LR* 3–14 5. See also A Fagan 'The secondary role of the spirit, purport and objects of the Bill of Rights in the common law's development' (2010) 127 *SALJ* 611–627; AJ van der Walt *Property and constitution* (2012) 19–112; DM Davis 'How many positivist legal philosophers can be made to dance on the head of a pin? A reply to Professor Fagan' (2012) 129 *SALJ* 59–72; A Fagan 'A straw man, three red herrings, and a closet rule-worshipper – A rejoinder to Davis JP' (2012) 129 *SALJ* 788–798; DM Davis 'The importance of reading – A rebutter to the jurisprudence of Anton Fagan' (2013) 130 *SALJ* 52–59.

[33] *Carmichele v Minister of Safety and Security* 2001 (4) SA 938 (CC) paras 54–55.

[34] AJ van der Walt 'Development of the common law of servitude' (2013) 130 *SALJ* 722–756 735.

[35] AJ van der Walt 'Development of the common law of servitude' (2013) 130 *SALJ* 722–756 744; *Ex Parte President of the Republic of South Africa: In re Pharmaceutical Manufacturers Association of South Africa* 2000 (2) SA 674 (CC) para 44. For the subsidiarity principles see AJ van der Walt *Property and constitution* (2012) 21. See specifically *Bato Star Fishing (Pty) Ltd v Minister of Environmental Affairs* 2004 (4) SA 490 (CC) para 25; *Minister of Health NO v New Clicks South Africa (Pty) Ltd (Treatment Action Campaign and Another as Amici Curiae)* 2006 (2) SA 311 (CC) para 96; *Chirwa v Transnet Ltd* 2008 (2) SA 24 (CC) para 23, *Fuel Retailers Association of Southern Africa v Director-General: Environmental Management, Department of Agriculture, Conservation and Environment, Mpumalanga Province* 2007 (6) SA 4 (CC) para 37; *Walele v City of Cape Town and Another* 2008 (6) SA 129 (CC) para 15.

law position by way of an accurate and in-depth historical analysis of the relevant common law authorities.[36]

The second phase of the methodology involves the assessment of the acceptability of the common-law position.[37] In the new constitutional dispensation, assessment of the current common-law position is constitutionally required. Accordingly, the first step in this stage requires an examination of the constitutional framework (values underlying the Constitution and non-property constitutional rights) in order to determine whether the common-law position is in line with the Constitution.[38] In the event that the common-law position aligns with the constitutional framework, development is not constitutionally required.[39] The next step is to determine whether development is essential based on policy considerations. If a policy analysis indicates that development is required, the development takes place on the basis of independent policy reasons.[40] However, if the common-law position fails to promote, or in fact infringes, the constitutional framework, development of the common law will be constitutionally required.[41] Moreover, in the event that independent policy reasons indicate that the common-law position is acceptable, while the constitutional framework points out that the position does not align with the Constitution, the constitutional

[36] AJ van der Walt 'Development of the common law of servitude' (2013) 130 *SALJ* 722–756 737. This stage correlates with Davis' proposition that an accurate understanding of the current common-law position is fundamental to determine whether common-law development is in fact necessary. In this regard see DM Davis 'Where is the map to guide common-law development?' (2014) 1 *Stell LR* 3–14 12.

[37] AJ van der Walt 'Development of the common law of servitude' (2013) 130 *SALJ* 722–756 737.

[38] AJ van der Walt 'Development of the common law of servitude' (2013) 130 *SALJ* 722–756 745. This stage of common law development accords with Dworkin's appeal as explained by Davis that the development of a coherent legal system necessitates engagement with the principles embedded in the legal system. In this regard see DM Davis 'Where is the map to guide common-law development?' (2014) 25 *Stell LR* 3–14 11.

[39] AJ van der Walt 'Development of the common law of servitude' (2013) 130 *SALJ* 722–756 748.

[40] AJ van der Walt 'Development of the common law of servitude' (2013) 130 *SALJ* 722–756 742.

[41] *Carmichele v Minister of Safety and Security* 2001 (4) SA 938 (CC) para 54–55. See also AJ van der Walt 'Development of the common law of servitude' (2013) 130 *SALJ* 722–756 745; DM Davis 'Where is the map to guide common-law development?' (2014) 25 *Stell LR* 3–14 13–14.

justification for development trumps the independent policy reasons against development.[42]

Once it has been decided that it is most appropriate to develop the common law and the ways in which development should occur, the third phase of Van der Walt's methodology kicks in. This phase concerns determining whether the proposed developed position passes constitutional muster. In this regard, the developed position is tested against relevant provisions of the Constitution.[43] In the event that the developed common law position fails constitutional scrutiny, the final step is to consider whether the common law should perhaps be developed differently or whether legislation can provide creative ways to avoid infringements or to provide for compensation where infringements nevertheless might occur.[44]

Although the methodology argued for by Van der Walt concerned the development of the common law of servitudes, his methodology can arguably be applied to the development of any common-law principle in the constitutional dispensation. Therefore, the methodology developed by Van der Walt will be applied in this chapter to determine the appropriateness of the development of the common law to recognise the original method of acquiring ownership in favour of a successful estoppel raiser.

3.2 *Traditional common-law position in the context of estoppel*

Under the first phase of the methodology it is clear that when an owner institutes the *rei vindicatio* to claim back possession of her property from a *bona fide* possessor for value no legislative provision provides protection for the *bona fide* possessor. The *bona fide* possessor is able to rely directly on the common law, which in these circumstances is the defence of estoppel by representation.[45]

---

[42] AJ van der Walt 'Development of the common law of servitude' (2013) 130 *SALJ* 722–756 745. The second phase also involves the consideration of the various ways in which development of the common-law position can take place. In this regard see AJ van der Walt 'Development of the common law of servitude' (2013) 130 *SALJ* 722–756 748.

[43] AJ van der Walt 'Development of the common law of servitude' (2013) 130 *SALJ* 722–756 749. This constitutional analysis concerns testing whether the developed common-law position is in line with section 25 of the Constitution.

[44] AJ van der Walt 'Development of the common law of servitude' (2013) 130 *SALJ* 722–756 756.

[45] DL Carey Miller *The acquisition and protection of ownership* (1986) 306; CG van der Merwe *Sakereg* 2 ed (1989) 368; JC Sonnekus & JL Neels *Sakereg vonnisbundel* 2 ed (1994) 472; PJ Badenhorst, JM Pienaar & H Mostert *Silberberg and Schoeman's The law of property* 5 ed (2006) 255; CG van der Merwe & A Pope 'Property' in F du Bois (ed) *Wille's principles of South African law* 9 ed (2007) 405–729 552; CG van der Merwe 'Things' in WA Joubert & JA Faris (eds) *LAWSA* Vol 27 Part 2 2 ed (2014) para 257. For a complete discussion of

During the nineteenth century, the need to protect *bona fide* possessors arose in situations where the owner's actions were the cause of detriment to an innocent acquirer of the owner's property. In these circumstances, fairness required that the innocent victim should be protected rather than the careless owner.[46] At the time, the English doctrine of estoppel by representation lent itself to the protection of innocent acquirers in these circumstances. Accordingly, estoppel by representation was received into the South African legal system to counter the harsh consequences of the *ubi rem meam invenio ibi* principle from which the owner's right to vindicate flows.[47] Subsequent to estoppel's importation, estoppel left behind its English common-law tradition and it has since developed in accordance with the demands of the South African civilian legal tradition.[48]

Essentially, estoppel operates as a defence to protect *bona fide* parties in certain circumstances. It prevents the owner from relying on the true state of affairs to the detriment of a *bona fide* possessor in circumstances where the conduct of the owner culpably led a *bona fide* possessor to believe that the disposer of the property was legally entitled to dispose of such property.[49]

---

the estoppel doctrine in South African law see JC de Wet *Estoppel by representation in die Suid-Afrikaanse reg* (unpublished LLD thesis Stellenbosch University 1939); JC Sonnekus *The law of estoppel in South Africa* 3 ed (2012).

46 JRL Milton 'Ownership' in R Zimmermann & D Visser (eds) *Southern cross: Civil law and common law in South Africa* (1996) 657–699 688.

47 *Ubi rem meam invenio ibi* principle holds that an owner is able to vindicate her property wherever she finds it. See JRL Milton 'Ownership' in R Zimmermann & D Visser (eds) *Southern cross: Civil law and common law in South Africa* (1996) 657–699; Zimmermann 'Good faith and equity' in R Zimmermann & D Visser (eds) *Southern cross: Civil law and common law in South Africa* (1996) 217–260 217.

48 *Trust Bank of Africa Ltd v Eksteen* 1964 (1) SA 74 (N) 82; *Johaadien v Stanley Porter (Paarl) (Pty) Ltd* 1970 (1) SA 394 (A) 406–408. See further JRL Milton 'Ownership' in R Zimmermann & D Visser (eds) *Southern cross: Civil law and common law in South Africa* (1996) 657–699 688; Zimmermann 'Good faith and equity' in R Zimmermann & D Visser (eds) *Southern cross: Civil law and common law in South Africa* (1996) 217–260 223. Estoppel has been developed in South African law in order to provide more protection to the owner in line with the South African legal tradition that jealously protects ownership. South African estoppel as opposed to its English counterpart now requires negligence on the part of the owner. See *Grosvenor Motors (Potchefstroom) Ltd v Douglas* 1956 (3) SA 420 (A) 427; *Johaadien v Stanley Porter (Paarl) (Pty) Ltd* 1970 (1) SA 394 (A) 409; *Oakland Nominees (Pty) Ltd v Gelria Mining & Investment Co (Pty) Ltd* 1976 (1) SA 441 (A) 452; *Oriental Products (Pty) Ltd v Pegma 178 Investments Trading CC and Others* 2011 (2) SA 508 (SCA) para 19.

49 JC van der Walt 'Die beskerming van die bona fide besitsverkryger: 'n Vergelyking tussen die Suid-Afrikaanse en Nederlandse reg' in Gauntlett JJ (ed) *JC Noster: 'n Feesbundel* (1979) 73–96 81–89; CG van der Merwe *Sakereg* 2 ed (1989) 368; JC Sonnekus & JL Neels *Sakereg vonnisbundel* 2 ed (1994) 473; PJ Badenhorst, JM Pienaar & H Mostert *Silberberg and Schoeman's The law of property* 5 ed (2006) 255–256; CG van der Merwe

Therefore, after the requirements of the doctrine of estoppel have been met, the court will find in favour of the estoppel raiser. As a defence, estoppel operates only as a procedural protection mechanism. This limitation on the function of estoppel has been enunciated by various courts in the statement that estoppel can only be used as a shield (defence) and not as a sword (cause of action).[50]

In view of the evidentiary function (or limited defence function) of estoppel, the traditional position in South African law is that estoppel, as a defence, has no substantive effect. In other words, estoppel as a defence against an owner's *rei vindicatio* cannot result in acquisition of ownership. Therefore, the common-law position regarding the consequence of a successful estoppel defence against an owner's *rei vindicatio* is that the owner is merely estopped from relying on her right to vindicate the property. As a result of the owner's suspended right to vindicate, the successful estoppel raiser may remain in possession of the property.

3.3 *The acceptability of the traditional position*

The second phase of Van der Walt's methodology concerns the assessment of the acceptability of the common-law position. The first step in this stage requires an examination of the constitutional framework (for example, the values underlying the Constitution and the non-property constitutional rights that may be affected) in order to determine whether development of the common law position is constitutionally required. The current common-law position holds that the owner cannot claim her property from the *bona fide* possessor. Consequently, the successful estoppel raiser remains in possession of the property. A cursory assessment of the constitutional values and non-property rights indicates that this position does not seem to compromise the constitutional framework. Therefore, the development of the common-law position is arguably not required by the Constitution itself.

However, the remaining question is whether the common-law position is acceptable in view of independent policy considerations. It seems as though the current position has consequences which are arguably problematic for

& A Pope 'Property' in F du Bois (ed) *Wille's principles of South African law* 9 ed (2007) 405–729 552; JW Louw 'Estoppel en die *rei vindicatio*' (1975) 38 *THRHR* 218–238 218.

[50] *Pandora's Trustee v Beatley & Co* 1935 TPD 358 at 363; *Union Government v National Bank of South Africa Ltd* 1921 AD 121 at 128; *Barclays Western Bank Ltd v Fourie* 1979 (4) SA 157 (C) 160; *Oriental Products (Pty) Ltd v Pegma 178 Investments Trading CC and Others* 2011 (2) SA 508 (SCA) para 31. See further JC Sonnekus & JL Neels *Sakereg vonnisbundel* 2 ed (1994) 472.

the owner of the property, the successful estoppel raiser of the property and even third parties who may be affected in terms of dealings with the property.[51]

The successful estoppel raiser will not be entitled to reclaim the property from a subsequent possessor. Once she loses control of the property, she arguably has no *locus standi* to claim back the property.[52] In the same way, she will not have *locus standi* to claim back the property once the property lands up in the hands of the owner.[53] Furthermore, the successful estoppel raiser will most likely not be entitled to claim compensation from a third party in the event that such third party stole or damaged the property.[54] This is because she will be unable to prove ownership of the property and will therefore not meet the requirements in delict to claim damages.[55] Moreover, she will not be entitled to sell, lease, insure or use the property for security purposes. All of these practical consequences transpire due to the insecure interest the estoppel raiser receives once successful with her defence.

The owner's legal position is also not satisfactory. The owner retains ownership; however, she is precluded from vindicating her property from the successful estoppel raiser. As a result, the owner will not be able to sell, lease or pledge the property because she would not be able to deliver such property.[56] This means that her normal ownership entitlements to dispose of and encumber her property are also suspended with her entitlement to

---

[51] CG van der Merwe *Sakereg* 2 ed (1989) 373; PJ Visser 'Estoppel en die vekryging van eiendomsreg in roerende eiendom' (1994) 57 *THRHR* 633–636 635; FB Pelser 'Aspekte van eiendomsverkryging deur estoppel' (2005) 38 *De Jure* 153–162 154; *Barclays Western Bank Ltd v Fourie* 1979 (4) SA 157 (C) 160.

[52] FB Pelser 'Aspekte van eiendomsverkryging deur estoppel' (2005) 38 *De Jure* 153–162 154.

[53] This is because the *rei vindicatio* is only available to the owner of the property. See CG van der Merwe *Sakereg* 2 ed (1989) 373; FB Pelser 'Aspekte van eiendomsverkryging deur estoppel' (2005) 38 *De Jure* 153–162 154; *Barclays Western Bank Ltd v Fourie* 1979 (4) SA 157 (C) 160.

[54] CG van der Merwe *Sakereg* 2 ed (1989) 373; CG van der Merwe & A Pope 'Property' in F du Bois (ed) *Wille's principles of South African law* 9 ed (2007) 405–729 554–555; FB Pelser 'Aspekte van eiendomsverkryging deur estoppel' (2005) 38 *De Jure* 153–162 154.

[55] With regard to the *lex acquilia*, see *Natal Fresh Produce Grower's Association v Agroserve (Pty) Ltd* 1990 (4) SA 749 (N) 758–759; R Midgley 'Delict' in WA Joubert, RJ Rabie & JA Faris (eds) *LAWSA* Vol 8 Part 1 2 ed (2005) para 42. Regarding the *condictio furtiva*, see *Minister van Verdediging v Van Wyk* 1976 (1) SA 397 (T) 398; R Midgley 'Delict' in WA Joubert, RJ Rabie & JA Faris (eds) *LAWSA* Vol 8 Part 1 2 ed (2005) para 34.

[56] CG van der Merwe 'Things' in WA Joubert & JA Faris (eds) *LAWSA* Vol 27 Part 2 2 ed (2014) para 259; FB Pelser 'Aspekte van eiendomsverkryging deur estoppel' (2005) 38 *De Jure* 153–162 154.

vindicate the property. Furthermore, the owner stands to be held liable for (i) any taxes payable on the property in certain circumstances and (ii) in the event of the property being a domestic animal, any damage caused by the animal.[57] What makes the owner's position even more precarious is that her ownership can potentially be lost if the successful estoppel raiser is sequestrated or defaults in paying rent to such an extent that the lessor's tacit hypothec is triggered and her property is attached and sold in execution.[58] These anomalies transpire due to the suspension of the owner's right to vindicate the property from the successful estoppel raiser. The position of subsequent purchasers of the property also seems problematic in the sense that such purchasers may find themselves in situations where they bought property in good faith for value but arguably have no proprietary recourse/ shield of protection against the true owners' rights to vindicate.[59]

Not only does the current legal position create practical anomalies but it also suppresses further economic dealings with the property in that the owner cannot engage in commercial activities with respect to the property. Moreover, the *bona fide* possessor is equally constrained in this regard.[60]

In view of the problematic consequences of the common-law position, scholars have argued for a more realistic approach to be adopted by the South African courts, namely, acquisition of ownership by the successful estoppel raiser. In the event of ownership acquisition being the consequence

---

[57] CG van der Merwe & A Pope 'Property' in F du Bois (ed) *Wille's principles of South African law* 9 ed (2007) 405–729 555; PJ Visser 'Estoppel en die vekryging van eiendomsreg in roerende eiendom' (1994) 57 *THRHR* 633–636 635; FB Pelser 'Aspekte van eiendomsverkryging deur estoppel' (2005) 38 *De Jure* 153–162 154. For the *actio de pauperie*, see *Loriza Brahman v Dippenaar* 2002 (2) SA 477 (SCA) para 13; JR Midgley 'Delict' in WA Joubert, RJ Rabie & JA Faris (eds) *LAWSA* Vol 8 Part 1 2 ed (2005) para 30; MM Loubser & JR Midgley *The law of delict in South Africa* 2 ed (2012) 28–29.

[58] FB Pelser 'Aspekte van eiendomsverkryging deur estoppel' (2005) 38 *De Jure* 153–162 154. For a discussion of the landlord's tacit hypothec over third parties property see NS Siphuma *The lessor's tacit hypothec: A constitutional analysis* (2013) unpublished LLM thesis Stellenbosch University 44–78; AJ van der Walt & NS Siphuma 'Extending the lessor's hypothec to third parties' property' 132 *SALJ* 518–546 523–533; S Viljoen *The law of landlord and tenant* (2016) 335–339.

[59] A subsequent possessor will arguably not be able to satisfy the requirements of estoppel vis-à-vis the true owner. See CG van der Merwe *Sakereg* 2 ed (1989) 373; CG van der Merwe & A Pope 'Property' in F du Bois (ed) *Wille's principles of South African law* 9 ed (2007) 405–729 554; FB Pelser 'Aspekte van eiendomsverkryging deur estoppel' (2005) 38 *De Jure* 153–162 154.

[60] CG van der Merwe *Sakereg* 2 ed (1989) 373; CG van der Merwe & A Pope 'Property' in F du Bois (ed) *Wille's principles of South African law* 9 ed (2007) 405–729 555; CG van der Merwe 'Things' in WA Joubert & JA Faris (eds) *LAWSA* Vol 27 Part 2 2 ed (2014) para 233; FB Pelser 'Aspekte van eiendomsverkryging deur estoppel' (2005) 38 *De Jure* 153–162 154.

of a successful estoppel defence, the above-mentioned doctrinal anomalies will be resolved. It can therefore be argued that independent policy reasons require development of the common law. However, the suitable method of acquisition in the event of development of the common law still seems controversial. As indicated above, some scholars argue for original acquisition of ownership, while others argue that the derivative mode of acquisition is more suitable. The section below sets out and critically analyses the academic divide on the most suitable mode of acquisition of ownership by way of a successful estoppel defence ultimately to show whether the original method of acquisition is preferable to the derivative mode.

3.4 *Is development in favour of original acquisition of ownership preferable in this context?*

Proponents of the derivative mode in the context of acquisition of ownership by way of a successful estoppel defence argue that the original mode is incapable of transferring all the burdens the acquirer's predecessor carried. Accordingly, the only viable method of acquisition is the derivative mode of acquisition where encumbered ownership is in effect transferred from the owner to the successful estoppel raiser by the operation of estoppel.[61] Van der Merwe points out that this would imply that a person who in any event has no entitlement to alienate the property would in terms of the operation of estoppel transfer the property to another person.[62] In this regard, he acknowledges that acquisition by way of estoppel does not fit into the traditional scope of the derivative mode in that it lacks the intention to transfer on the part of the owner. However, he argues that it might be time to recognise a new form of derivative acquisition of ownership in order to accommodate acquisition by way of estoppel.[63]

Interestingly, other proponents of the derivative mode in this context argue that estoppel, by precluding the owner from denying the misrepresentation (the lack of intention to sell the property), accepts the facts of the misrepresentation as the truth for legal purposes. In this way, constructive

[61] CG van der Merwe *Sakereg* 2 ed (1989) 373; FB Pelser 'Aspekte van eiendomsverkryging deur estoppel' (2005) 38 *De Jure* 153–162 159.

[62] CG van der Merwe *Sakereg* 2 ed (1989) 373. The focus does not fall on the act of transfer but rather on the misrepresentation. See HJO van Heerden 'Estoppel: 'n Wyse van eiendomsverkryging' (1970) 33 *THRHR* 19–25 22.

[63] CG van der Merwe *Sakereg* 2 ed (1989) 373.

intention to sell on the part of the owner is established.[64] Pelser submits that the nature of acquisition by way of estoppel concerns a fictional consent that is elevated to the level of truth. Accordingly, it is by nature a two-party transaction where the intention to transfer the property is established by way of a constructed bilaterial agreement.[65]

However, opponents of the derivative mode of acquisition in the context of estoppel point out that the intention to transfer and to receive ownership is fundamental to the derivative mode of acquisition of ownership. They argue that in the estoppel scenario the owner by instituting the *rei vindicatio* against the *bona fide* possessor asserts her intention to remain the owner of the property. Accordingly, acquisition by a successful estoppel defence can never take place in terms of the derivative mode of acquisition. This is simply because there was no intention to transfer the property to the acquirer and therefore no real agreement. Interestingly, Carey Miller submits that even if we accept that a successful estoppel defence establishes constructive consent, this constructive consent is not sufficient for ownership to pass. The owner is required to have actually intended to transfer ownership at the time of delivery or registration.[66]

Furthermore, the *nemo plus iuris* rule renders transfer of ownership to the successful estoppel raiser impossible. The *nemo plus iuris* rule holds that one cannot transfer more rights than one has. The unauthorised seller of the property had no rights to transfer to the successful estoppel raiser; therefore, the successful estoppel raiser cannot acquire ownership in these circumstances in terms of the *nemo plus iuris* rule.[67] In light of the *nemo plus iuris* rule rendering transfer in the estoppel scenario impossible, and the absence of actual intention to transfer the property in terms of the derivative mode of acquisition also rendering transfer impossible, it can be argued that the derivative mode is doctrinally unsuitable for acquisition of ownership by way of a successful estoppel defence.

---

[64] DL Carey Miller *The acquisition and protection of ownership* (1986) 308; PJ Visser 'Estoppel en die vekryging van eiendomsreg in roerende eiendom' (1994) 57 *THRHR* 633–636; FB Pelser 'Aspekte van eiendomsverkryging deur estoppel' (2005) 38 *De Jure* 153–162 159.

[65] FB Pelser 'Aspekte van eiendomsverkryging deur estoppel' (2005) 38 *De Jure* 153–162 159.

[66] DL Carey Miller *The acquisition and protection of ownership* (1986) 308–309.

[67] JC Sonnekus 'Bona fide-verkryging vir waarde en estoppel' (1999) 62 *THRHR* 463–469 465; FB Pelser 'Aspekte van eiendomsverkryging deur estoppel' (2005) 38 *De Jure* 153–162 159. For a contrasting argument see HJO van Heerden 'Estoppel: 'n Wyse van eiendomsverkryging' (1970) 33 *THRHR* 19–25 22.

Original acquisition of ownership may seem more appropriate in these circumstances. Original acquisition of ownership ensues when a unilateral act on the part of the acquirer suffices to establish ownership by operation of law.[68] The requirement that is common to the different forms of original acquisition is acquisition without the cooperation of a predecessor in title.[69] A successful estoppel defence that has as a consequence ownership acquisition in effect takes place by way of operation of law and does not require the consent of the predecessor. Moreover, original acquisition of ownership is not in conflict with the *nemo plus iuris* rule. Accordingly, if the law is developed to recognise acquisition of ownership by way of a successful estoppel defence, the most doctrinally suitable method is the original mode of acquisition.[70] This would mean that the estoppel denier's rights are extinguished and the estoppel raiser obtains new unburdened title.

However, some scholars argue that because original acquisition provides acquirers with new and unburdened ownership, the rights of the owner as well as potential holders of limited real rights may be extinguished if successful estoppel raisers acquire ownership in terms of the original method.[71] This consequence has led Sonnekus to point out that such an approach to acquisition may lead to the violation of the owner's and limited real right holders' constitutional property rights as enshrined in section 25 of the Constitution.[72] This concern triggers the final stage of Van der Walt's methodology for the development of the common law, namely determining whether the developed position would be in line with section 25(1) of the Constitution. The section below considers possible constitutional

---

[68] CG van der Merwe *Sakereg* 2 ed (1989) 216; JC Sonnekus & JL Neels *Sakereg vonnisbundel* 2 ed (1994) 287; PJ Badenhorst, JM Pienaar & H Mostert *Silberberg and Schoeman's The law of property* 5 ed (2006) 137; CG van der Merwe & A Pope 'Property' in F du Bois (ed) *Wille's principles of South African law* 9 ed (2007) 405–729 488.

[69] CG van der Merwe *Sakereg* 2 ed (1989) 217; JC Sonnekus & JL Neels *Sakereg vonnisbundel* 2 ed (1994) 287–388; PJ Badenhorst, JM Pienaar & H Mostert *Silberberg and Schoeman's The law of property* 5 ed (2006) 137–134; CG van der Merwe & A Pope 'Property' in F du Bois (ed) *Wille's principles of South African law* 9 ed (2007) 405–729 488–519; *Unimark Distributors (Pty) Ltd v Erf 94 Silvertondale (Pty) Ltd* 1999 (2) SA 986 (T) 1000.

[70] JC Sonnekus *The law of estoppel in South Africa* 3 ed (2012) 350–351; JC Sonnekus 'Eienaars en ander reghebbendes mag ervaar dat swye nie altyd goud werd is nie' 2013 *TSAR* 326–339 334.

[71] CG van der Merwe *Sakereg* 2 ed (1989) 373; JC Sonnekus 'Eienaars en ander reghebbendes mag ervaar dat swye nie altyd goud werd is nie' 2013 *TSAR* 326–339 337; FB Pelser 'Aspekte van eiendomsverkryging deur estoppel' (2005) 38 *De Jure* 153–162 159.

[72] JC Sonnekus 'Eienaars en ander reghebbendes mag ervaar dat swye nie altyd goud werd is nie' 2013 *TSAR* 326–339 339.

implications that may arise if the common law is developed to recognise original acquisition of ownership by the successful estoppel raiser. More importantly, the section below tests the assertion made by Van der Walt that if it is established that the common law authorises the development, the loss of property will arguably amount to deprivation of property and such deprivation will most likely not be arbitrary.

4 Possible constitutional implications of development of the common law

Section 25(1) of the Constitution prohibits arbitrary deprivation of property. *First National Bank of SA Ltd t/a Wesbank v Commissioner, South African Revenue Service and Another; First National Bank of SA Ltd t/a Wesbank v Minister of Finance*[73] developed a set of questions from which a section 25 analysis should proceed to determine whether section 25 has been infringed in a given case. Firstly, it should be established whether the alleged infringed interest constitutes 'property' for purposes of section 25(1) of the Constitution.[74] In *FNB* the court established that the property concept has to be interpreted generously,[75] when it decided that it would not be wise to ascribe a fixed meaning to constitutional property.[76] The court held that if a court finds that the interest qualifies as property for purposes of section 25, the threshold requirement for a section 25 analysis is met and the court can proceed to the second question.

In the scenario of a successful estoppel defence, the developed common-law position allows for the situation where ownership and limited real rights over

[73] *First National Bank of SA Ltd t/a Wesbank v Commissioner, South African Revenue Service and Another; First National Bank of SA Ltd t/a Wesbank v Minister of Finance* 2002 (4) SA 768 (CC).

[74] *First National Bank of SA Ltd t/a Wesbank v Commissioner, South African Revenue Service and Another; First National Bank of SA Ltd t/a Wesbank v Minister of Finance* 2002 (4) SA 768 (CC) paras 46(a), 51.

[75] See also *Reflect-All 1025 CC and Others v MEC for Public Transport, Roads and Works, Gauteng Provincial Government and Another* 2009 (6) SA 391 (CC) para 32; *Shoprite Checkers (Pty) Ltd v MEC for Economic Development, Eastern Cape and Others* 2015 (6) SA 125 (CC) para 104; IM Rautenbach 'Dealing with the social dimensions of property' 2015 *TSAR* 822–833 825–829; AJ van der Walt 'Property vortices (part 1)' 2016 *TSAR* 412–427 416–419; AJ van der Walt 'Property vortices (part 2)' 2016 *TSAR* 597–621 599–605; EJ Marais 'Expanding the contours of the constitutional property concept' 2016 *TSAR* 576–592; J Swanepoel *Constitutional property law in Central Eastern European jurisdictions: A comparative analysis* (2016) unpublished LLD thesis Stellenbosch University 211–220.

[76] See *First National Bank of SA Ltd t/a Wesbank v Commissioner, South African Revenue Service and Another; First National Bank of SA Ltd t/a Wesbank v Minister of Finance* 2002 (4) SA 768 (CC) para 51; AJ van der Walt *Constitutional property law* 3 ed (2011) 84.

the property are extinguished and ownership in the property is acquired by the successful estoppel raiser by operation of law. Accordingly, the property interests dealt with here are ownership and limited real rights, respectively. Ownership of land is central to the constitutional concept of property although property is not limited to land.[77] In *Ex Parte Optimal Property Solutions CC*[78] the Western Cape High Court furthermore held that limited real rights also constitute property interest for purposes of the property clause. Accordingly, both ownership and limited real rights are property for purposes of section 25 of the Constitution.

The second question that arises is whether a deprivation of the identified property interest has taken place.[79] In *FNB* the court explained that a deprivation refers to any interference with the use, enjoyment or exploitation of private property belonging to a right- or title-holder of that property.[80] The developed common-law position of ownership acquisition by the successful estoppel raiser amounts in the first place to a forced transfer of ownership from the owner to the estoppel raiser and in the second place to the extinction of limited real rights over the property by operation of law. Accordingly, the

[77] See *First National Bank of SA Ltd t/a Wesbank v Commissioner, South African Revenue Service and Another; First National Bank of SA Ltd t/a Wesbank v Minister of Finance* 2002 (4) SA 768 (CC) para 51. See also AJ van der Walt *Constitutional property law* 3 ed (2011) 93.

[78] *Ex Parte Optimal Property Solutions CC* 2003 (2) SA 136 (C) paras 4–6.

[79] *See First National Bank of SA Ltd t/a Wesbank v Commissioner, South African Revenue Service and Another; First National Bank of SA Ltd t/a Wesbank v Minister of Finance* 2002 (4) SA 768 (CC) paras 46, 57.

[80] *See First National Bank of SA Ltd t/a Wesbank v Commissioner, South African Revenue Service and Another; First National Bank of SA Ltd t/a Wesbank v Minister of Finance* 2002 (4) SA 768 (CC) para 57; *Reflect-All 1025 CC and Others v MEC for Public Transport, Roads and Works, Gauteng Provincial Government and Another* 2009 (6) SA 391 (CC) para 35; *Shoprite Checkers (Pty) Ltd v MEC for Economic Development, Eastern Cape and Others* 2015 (6) SA 125 (CC) para 73. See also AJ van der Walt 'Property vortices (part 1)' 2016 *TSAR* 412–427 420. However, the court has been inconsistent in its description or explanation of what a deprivation is. In both *Mkontwana v Nelson Mandela Metropolitan Municipality* 2005 (1) SA 530 (CC) para 32 and *National Credit Regulator v Opperman and Others* 2013 (2) SA 1 (CC) para 66 the Constitutional Court held that '[w]hether there has been a *deprivation* depends on the extent of interference with the use, enjoyment or exploitation of the constitutionally protected property'. See further AJ van der Walt 'Retreating from the FNB arbitrariness test already? *Mkontwana v Nelson Mandela Metropolitan Municipality; Bisset v Buffalo City Municipality; Transfer Rights Action Campaign v MEC for Local Government and Housing, Gauteng*' (2005) 122 *SALJ* 75–89 79–80; K Bezuidenhout *Compensation for excessive but otherwise lawful regulatory state action* (2014) unpublished LLD thesis Stellenbosch University 16–17; AJ van der Walt 'Property vortices (part 2)' 2016 *TSAR* 597–621 605–609.

loss of both ownership and limited real rights constitute deprivations for purposes of section 25 of the Constitution.

However, it is important to understand that deprivations are part of the normal regulation of property interests and will only be invalid if the deprivation is not consistent with section 25(1).[81] Section 25(1) requires that a deprivation should, firstly, be authorised by law of general application and, secondly, should not be arbitrary. A law of general application refers to a law or a rule that is authorised by valid and properly promulgated legislation, regulation, subordinate legislation, municipal by-laws, rules and principles of common law and customary law, rules of court, and international conventions that apply to the citizenry.[82] In other words, the rule or law should be a valid rule and should not apply selectively to only specific individuals or members of groups.[83]

The law of general application regulating the estoppel defence against the owner's *rei vindicatio* is the common law. The court has on numerous occasions held that the common law constitutes a law of general application for purposes of section 25(1).[84] As a cautionary note, it should be remembered that the common law must authorise the deprivation caused by the loss of ownership. If the common law (as developed) does not authorise the compulsory loss of ownership due to estoppel, the deprivation that results may be unlawful on the basis of the requirement that all deprivations must be authorised in terms of law of general application.[85] The question that arises is whether the common law of estoppel indeed authorises the compulsory loss of ownership. Due to the limited evidentiary function of estoppel, traditionally

---

[81] See *First National Bank of SA Ltd t/a Wesbank v Commissioner, South African Revenue Service and Another; First National Bank of SA Ltd t/a Wesbank v Minister of Finance* 2002 (4) SA 768 (CC) para 61; K Bezuidenhout *Compensation for excessive but otherwise lawful regulatory state action* (2014) unpublished LLD thesis Stellenbosch University 14, 20–21.

[82] S Woolman & H Botha 'Limitations' in S Woolman & M Bishop (eds) *Constitutional law of South Africa* 2 ed (RS 6, 2014) 34–1 34–53. See also AJ van der Walt *Constitutional property law* 3 ed (2011) 232–237 for an explanation of the requirements any law or rule must comply with in order to constitute law of general application.

[83] S Woolman & H Botha 'Limitations' in S Woolman & M Bishop (eds) *Constitutional law of South Africa* 2 ed (RS 6, 2014) 34–1 34–50; T Roux 'Property' in S Woolman & M Bishop (eds) *Constitutional law of South Africa* 2 ed (RS 6, 2014) 46–1 46–21; K Bezuidenhout *Compensation for excessive but otherwise lawful regulatory state action* (2014) unpublished LLD thesis Stellenbosch University 21–22.

[84] *Du Plessis and Others v De Klerk and Another* 1996 (3) SA 850 (CC) para 44; *S v Thebus and Another* 2003 (6) SA 505 (CC) paras 64–65. See further S Woolman & H Botha 'Limitations' in S Woolman & M Bishop (eds) *Constitutional law of South Africa* 2 ed (RS 6, 2014) 34–1 34–53.

[85] See ZT Boggenpoel 'The decision to order transfer of encroached-upon land: A constitutional analysis' (2013) 76 *THRHR* 313–326 320.

estoppel merely suspended the owner's *rei vindicatio* against the successful estoppel raiser. However, it is now suggested that the result of a successful estoppel defence should be changed to recognising ownership acquisition by the successful estoppel raiser. This suggestion raises the question whether estoppel indeed authorises a court to order that ownership is lost by operation of law. In light of the limited evidentiary function of estoppel a court may only order that the owner is estopped from asserting her ownership rights. In this regard, estoppel lacks substantive operational effect to have as a consequence compulsory loss of ownership. In other words, the question whether estoppel can have a substantive effect should first be settled in our law before one can argue for compulsory loss of ownership. Only once estoppel is confirmed to have more than an evidentiary function, the substantive function of estoppel can be relied on as providing the court with the power and authority at common law to authorise the compulsory loss of ownership. However, as long as the functionary scope of estoppel remains uncertain, there will be no authority at common law for the deprivation that will be caused by the loss of ownership. Consequently, as the matter stands currently, the deprivation that may be caused by loss of ownership will be unconstitutional due to non-compliance with the law of general application requirement, unless the substantive effect of estoppel is clarified. Once it has been established that the development is unconstitutional due to the absence of authority for the deprivation, the section 25(1) enquiry should come to an end.[86] However, it may nonetheless be valuable to think about what would have to be taken into account during the arbitrariness enquiry if the common law is in fact authoritatively developed in favour of acquisition of ownership. Therefore, this hypothetical exercise will reflect for a moment on a few aspects of the arbitrariness test in the context of estoppel in order to draw conclusions about the proprietary consequences of estoppel in light of section 25(1), specifically if the common law is developed in favour of original acquisition of ownership.

The second leg of section 25(1) requires that the deprivation must not be arbitrary. *FNB* confirmed that a deprivation will not be arbitrary if it is procedurally fair and if sufficient reason(s) can be established for the deprivation on a rationality to proportionality continuum.[87] Van der Walt points out that the arbitrariness test is contextual, and that the level of scrutiny ('the thickness of the test') will vary depending on the specific

[86] AJ van der Walt *Constitutional property law* 3 ed (2011) 218.

[87] *First National Bank of SA Ltd t/a Wesbank v Commissioner, South African Revenue Service and Another; First National Bank of SA Ltd t/a Wesbank v Minister of Finance* 2002 (4) SA 768 (CC) paras 60, 100. See AJ van der Walt *Constitutional property law* 3 ed (2011) 220–223, 237–241.

context of each case.[88] A complexity of relationships will have to be considered by applying the factors listed in *FNB* when determining whether there is sufficient reason. These are the relationship between the means employed and ends sought to be achieved; the relationship between those whose property rights are affected and the objective of the deprivation; the nature of the property and the objective of the deprivation; and the extent of the deprivation. The reason advanced for the deprivation is required to be more compelling in cases where the deprivation affects all the incidents of ownership completely. Moreover, the nature and extent of the deprivation will be instructive as to whether a rationality inquiry or proportionality inquiry should be applied. In this regard, the court is enjoined to decide which test for establishing sufficient reason should be employed with regard to the extent of the deprivation in the particular case, in order ultimately to determine whether a deprivation is arbitrary.

A number of factors will therefore have to be assessed to determine whether the law authorises arbitrary deprivation of property in the event that the requirements of estoppel are complied with, and the developed law allows for acquisition of ownership in favour of the successful estoppel raiser. From a constitutional property law perspective, and more specifically the investigation in the arbitrariness enquiry that requires a close relationship (or nexus) between the means employed and the ends sought to be achieved, it is questionable whether the purpose of estoppel (and the need to obtain clarity in terms of its proprietary consequences) warrants the result of acquisition of ownership.

Firstly, the purpose of the doctrine of estoppel has to be connected to the property and its owner, otherwise the application of estoppel (especially if acquisition of ownership occurs) may be arbitrary. In terms of the purpose of estoppel, it is clear that the need for the protection of *bona fide* possessors arose in situations where the owner's actions caused detriment to an innocent acquirer of the owner's property.[89] In these circumstances, fairness and equity required that the innocent victim should be protected rather than the careless owner. For this purpose, estoppel was imported to counter the inequitable consequences that would have otherwise ensued from the strict application of the *ubi rem meam invenio ibi* principle. It is therefore clear that a nexus does exist between the purpose of the doctrine of estoppel and the property and its owner. However, the proprietary consequences

---

[88] AJ van der Walt *Constitutional property law* 3 ed (2011) 246; AJ van der Walt 'Property vortices (part 1)' 2016 *TSAR* 412–427 423, 425.

[89] JRL Milton 'Ownership' in R Zimmermann & D Visser (eds) *Southern cross: Civil law and common law in South Africa* (1996) 657–699 688.

of the doctrine have caused great uncertainty regarding efficient future dealings with the property, which is why development of the common law is suggested. Development of the common law of estoppel is required for policy reasons. However, such development would mean that the predecessor's rights are extinguished and the estoppel raiser obtains new unburdened title. This invokes investigation into another aspect of the arbitrariness enquiry, namely, the extent of the deprivation.

A more compelling reason is required if the extent of the deprivation is greater and a closer relationship is required between the means and ends in this respect. The development of the common law to allow for acquisition of ownership by the estoppel raiser would cause a complete removal or loss of ownership of property, whereas the current consequence of estoppel seems only to result in the limitation on an entitlement of ownership, namely the right to vindicate the property from the estoppel raiser. However, even the limitation on the right to vindicate has an impact on other entitlements, like the use and enjoyment of the property and the right to encumber it. Furthermore, the extent of the deprivation is severe in that it results in a permanent (and complete) loss of ownership. The deprivation in the context of development of the common law is therefore severe, as the property owner is divested of ownership, as opposed to only one entitlement being restricted (presumably only temporarily).These are all aspects that would have to be taken into account in the arbitrariness analysis, and can have an impact on whether development in this regard is desirable in light of section 25(1).

5 Conclusion

The discussion of literature and case law in this chapter has revealed that the proprietary consequences of a successful estoppel defence are not clear. It is evident that there is uncertainty as to whether South African law has developed to recognise acquisition of ownership by way of a successful estoppel defence. There is also uncertainty as to the appropriate method for acquisition of ownership in the event that ownership acquisition by the successful estoppel raiser can in fact be justified. Furthermore, it is apparent that the traditional proprietary consequences as well as the proposed developed proprietary consequences of a successful estoppel defence against an owner's *rei vindicatio* may have implications in terms of section 25(1) of the Constitution. It is suggested that the consequences of a successful estoppel defence need to be worked out more clearly in order to provide legal certainty in South Africa.

In terms of Van der Walt's principles, as explained in the first part of this chapter, there are indeed some nuances and refining that come out of the enquiry into the proprietary consequences of estoppel. Van der Walt points out that it is important to view common-law interpretation and development in a constitutional light. One research result that comes out quite clearly from the enquiry undertaken in this study is that the principles of constitutional property law should guide the development of property law doctrine. In particular, this chapter shows how suggestions for the development of the common law may seem appropriate in light of independent policy reasons but if not tested against section 25(1) of the Constitution may lead to serious violations of constitutional rights.

Moreover, investigation into the constitutional implications of development of the proprietary consequences of estoppel confirmed some further nuances to the two principles of common-law development asserted by Van der Walt, namely that if it is established that the common law authorises the development, the loss of property will arguably amount to deprivation of property and such deprivation will most likely not be arbitrary. The findings show that if the common law is developed without taking into account the requirements for a constitutionally valid deprivation of property, namely authority and non-arbitrariness, there will most likely be problems with both the authority and the deprivation question in terms of section 25(1) of the Constitution. In other words, the common-law development will probably constitute a deprivation, but the deprivation will not comply with section 25(1) of the Constitution. It also became clear that if the compulsory loss of ownership takes place in favour of a successful estoppel raiser, without development of the nature of estoppel (from evidentiary to substantive) first, the development of the proprietary consequence of estoppel in favour of loss of ownership will be without authority and therefore unlawful. Accordingly, at this stage it seems as though the common law does not actually authorise the development of compulsory loss of ownership by way of estoppel. This finding reaffirms the importance of the qualification of Van der Walt's second principle that the development should accord with what the common law allows a court to do. Accordingly, although it was expected initially that the development of the common law would be desirable in order to eliminate some of the uncertainties, it is not entirely clear whether such development would pass constitutional muster in line with section 25(1).

Furthermore, in the absence of common-law authority for loss of ownership as a result of a successful estoppel defence, a hypothetical arbitrariness inquiry also raised some (red) flags. A tentative analysis of the arbitrariness test proves that it is certainly more difficult to comply with section 25(1) where the owner loses ownership of the property as a result of estoppel, especially when it comes to justifying the purpose and the extent of the deprivation. One can only hope that caution will be exercised when it is ultimately decided whether development of the common-law doctrine of estoppel is necessary (and/or desirable).

Chapter 8

Property, sharing and identity: Applying André van der Walt's theory of property and social justice in Northern Ireland

Lorna Fox O'Mahony[1]

1 Introduction

André van der Walt made a unique contribution to the field of property theory, social justice and constitutional democracy. His published work was staggering in its range and reach, offering an exceptional blend of intellectual rigour, breadth and depth of insight, and a moral courage to challenge accepted understandings. His writings consistently and tirelessly advanced his underlying commitment to justice through a concern for the property problems of real people, and especially for the poorest and most vulnerable members of society – for those in the margins.[2] This work has particular salience for South Africa, where André played a prominent role in steering an intellectual revolution in property theory and property law, as the country began working to address the legacies of its past, and to realise

[1] Essex Law School, UK. Thanks to Gordon Anthony, Jonathan Doak, Robin Hickey, Rory O'Connell, David O'Mahony, Gordon Peake, delegates at the Annual Meeting of the Association of Law, Property and Society at the University of Michigan in May 2017 and the anonymous reviewers for their advice and feedback. All errors and infelicities remain my own.

[2] AJ van der Walt *Property in the margins* (2009).

its constitutional commitment to 'establish a society based on democratic values, social justice and fundamental human rights; ... [and to] improve the quality of life of all citizens and free the potential of each person ...'[3] But the lessons from André van der Walt's legacy reach far beyond South Africa. His sustained focus on bringing property law doctrines and debates into the public sphere, highlighting the relationships between property law, inequality and our collective concerns as a public, was combined with technical rigour in the practical application of his theoretical commitments. His legacy has not only changed our property imaginations but also provides essential tools and frameworks to enable others to navigate the tricky theoretical, doctrinal and methodological steps that follow from accepting – often against the habits and legends of dominant contemporary theories and accounts – that property rights are not absolute but are defined by the demands of living in a democratic society, characterised by dignity and equality.[4]

This essay applies aspects of André van der Walt's work on property theory and social justice to Northern Ireland. Northern Irish land law, like much in the jurisdiction, is a curious hybrid of Irish and English influences, along with a rich heritage that is all its own. While English land law can reasonably claim to have its roots in the slow evolution of the common law, tracing its heritage to the feudal reforms imposed on England by William the Conqueror after 1066,[5] Irish land law has a more complex lineage. The impact of the British-Irish relationship on Irish land law arguably started with the Norman Conquest of Ireland in 1171-2; this was followed by centuries of tension between customary Irish, or *Brehon*, law and the imposed English common law;[6] by the confiscation and resettlements of Irish land by the British Crown in the sixteenth and seventeenth centuries;[7] and by the enactment of 'Penal Laws' that debarred Irish Catholics from owning land in the eighteenth century. In the nineteenth century, following the Act of Union of Great Britain and Ireland, 1800, the land reform campaign assumed central importance in the contested relationship between Britain and Ireland. Throughout the second half of the nineteenth century, debates about land tenure – the 'Irish

[3] Preamble to the South African Constitution, 1996; cited by Yacoob J in *Government of the Republic of South Africa and Others v Grootboom and Others* 2001 (1) SA 46 (CC) para [1] at 53B–C.

[4] AJ van der Walt 'The modest systemic status of property rights' (2014) 1 *J L Prop & Soc'y* 15–106; JW Singer 'Democratic estates: Property law in a free and democratic society' (2009) 94 *Cornell L Rev* 1009–1062; JW Singer 'Property as the law of democracy' (2014) 63 *Duke LJ* 1287.

[5] MJ Dixon *Modern land law* 7 ed (2010) 2.

[6] Mac Niocaill 'The contact of Irish and common law' (1972) 23 *NILQ* 16–23.

[7] VTH Delaney 'Irish and Scottish land resettlement legislation' (1959) 8 *ICLQ* 299.

land question' – were central to Irish politics, and to the escalating political tensions between Britain and Ireland which by the end of the century became subsumed in the campaign for Irish independence from Britain.

The competing tenets of this ideological conflict will be familiar to contemporary property scholars. Britain, at the height of its own industrial and economic revolution, had adopted *laissez-faire* capitalism as the national economic ideology, underpinned by commitments to strong property rights as a matter of natural law, and a 'ruling principle at common law [of] freedom of enterprise'.[8] Meanwhile, in Ireland, where the politics of the 'land question' was cut across with legacies of conquest and colonisation, sectarian divides between landlords and tenants, economic deprivation and the 'Great Hunger' or Famine of 1845–47,[9] the political and economic discourse of the latter half of the nineteenth century was dominated by Irish campaigns averring the failure of the English individualist model of strong property rights, free disposition, exclusivity and consolidation of proprietary rights in the political, economic and cultural contexts of Ireland.[10] In Ireland, the ownership of land had, and retains, a deep and complex salience that is political, economic, social, cultural, ethnographic and symbolic,[11] in ways that are present, but less prominent, in England.[12] The land reform question had a salience that reached across the legal technicalities of doctrine and legislation, through the political impacts of the nineteenth-century 'Irish Land Wars' on the British-Irish relationship.[13] It was a prominent feature of

[8] DO Wagner 'Coke and the rise of economic liberalism' (1953) 6 *Econ Hist Rev* 30, 44.

[9] See P Bull *Land politics and nationalism: A study of the Irish land question* (1996).

[10] Bull argued that the consolidation of *laissez-faire* as the official ideology of the British state created particular problems for Ireland because '...an economic ideology which to the British ruling classes – and especially the increasingly important middle classes – comprised a set of principles with universal application was increasingly seen in Ireland as peculiarly English and as an instrument of domination. This constituted a formula for conflict and disruption, ensuring that the central discourse on economics, especially insofar as it related to problems of land tenure in Ireland, was one in which there was little common ground and which served to accentuate and escalate polarisation.' See P Bull *Land politics and nationalism: A study of the Irish land question* (1996) 8.

[11] G O'Tuathaigh 'Ireland's land questions' in J Davis (ed) *Rural change in Ireland* (1999) 16–31.

[12] The central achievement of the 1925 legislation was to assimilate land with other property, so that it could be as easily transferable as capital.

[13] See for example, P Bull *Land, politics and nationalism: A study of the Irish land question* (1996).

political and economic debates (the 'class struggle') within Ireland itself,[14] and representative of the socio-cultural revival of Ireland's native, pre-Conquest legal heritage.[15] Indeed, the enduring salience of this native legal heritage through the nineteenth century was evidenced by reports that emphasised the persistence of customary land law practices (for example, the 'Ulster Custom', discussed below), notwithstanding British-imposed legislation to the contrary.

Following the Irish War of Independence, the Partition of Ireland led to twenty-six of Ireland's thirty-two countries forming an independent Irish Free State; while the remaining six were retained within the re-constituted United Kingdom of Great Britain and Northern Ireland. The Partition of Ireland was politically contested from the outset; but throughout the twentieth century the role of land tenure, land reform and land law receded from view at the political front line. Even through the violent conflict that erupted from 1968 – which was triggered by a controversial public housing allocation decision,[16] and which highlighted the inequality of property relations (and other socio-economic distributions) between ethno-religious identity communities – the relationships between property ideologies, 'private' property law, and unequal property relations were largely concealed. Through the twentieth century, the imported English common law, successfully fused with elements of Irish custom and practice and adapted to the local needs of the Northern Irish context, was 'de-politicised', concealed, separated from the public realm of the largely civil and political focus of the conflict. And when the violent conflict of the twentieth century gave way to ceasefire and a peace agreement in 1998 (the Belfast/'Good Friday' Agreement), the agreement and its transition mechanisms focused largely on the 'public' work of crafting new power-sharing Northern Irish institutions to facilitate self-governance; with particular emphasis on mechanisms to promote civil and political equality.

The role of property relations, property law, and social justice in the transition to a peaceful, post-conflict society, were acknowledged but less prominent in the peace agreement and the official transitional arrangements

[14] Paul Bew has argued that accounts of the Irish Land Wars as a feature of the larger historical struggle – as 'the militant consensus of a risen people'– are a myth; and that the conflict is better understood as a civil war amongst the Irish themselves, between large and small farmers, and between farmers and agricultural labourers: P Bew, *Land and the national question in Ireland, 1858-82* (1979) 220.

[15] A British Royal Commission was appointed in 1852 to supervise the transcription and translation of the *Brehon laws* (*ancient laws and institutions of Ireland*) published in 6 volumes 1865–1901; subsequently annotated by Professor Binchy as *Corpus Iuris Hibernici* (1979).

[16] See section 4 below, 'Identity'.

that followed. This relative lack of attention to the relationships between property, poverty, social justice and constitutional democracy has been a prominent campaign issue for NGOs, activists, and scholars of this post-conflict transition. Sociologists Hillyard, Rolston and Tomlinson have argued that, while the Northern Irish conflict has been extensively researched, analysed and documented, the role of poverty and social inequality both in the making of this conflict and in progress towards lasting peace and stable constitutional democracy has been relatively neglected.[17] More recently, the correlation between underlying socio-economic inequality in Northern Ireland, the impact of conflict in exacerbating inequality, and the wider project of transitioning towards a more equal, just and prosperous society, have been brought into the foreground[18] in the context of the 'austerity' measures implemented by the UK government since 2010.[19] These policies – which included welfare retrenchment, social security cuts, and cuts to public services that seek to provide people with a path out of poverty – had profound impacts in Northern Ireland, already one of the poorest regions of the UK.[20] Deep-rooted structural inequalities, intersecting with the fragile political context that followed the 1998 peace agreement, raised concerns that 'the pressure of deepening levels of economic inequality and segregation most visible in Northern Ireland's working-class urban districts threatens the transitional compact and human security in unpredictable ways'.[21] In 2016, more than 90 per cent of social housing in Northern Ireland, and 94 per cent in Belfast, was segregated on grounds of religious background.[22] Rooney and Sawine have argued that these segregated, working-class districts, where housing inequality precipitated civic unrest in the 1960s[23] and which experienced the highest levels of conflict-related violence, have been 'left

---

[17] P Hillyard, B Rolston & M Tomlinson *Poverty and conflict in Ireland: An international perspective* (2005).

[18] See also Committee for the Administration of Justice (CAJ), *Equality in Northern Ireland: The rhetoric and the reality* (2006).

[19] For an account of the impact of austerity in the UK, see M O'Hara *Austerity bites* (2014).

[20] M Brewer, A Muriel, D Phillips & L Sibieta *Poverty and inequality in the UK, 2008* (2008).

[21] E Rooney & A Sawine 'The "long grass" of agreements: Promise, theory and practice' (2012) 12 *Int'l Crim L Rev* 519–548 521.

[22] Housing Executive *Community Cohesion Strategy 2015–2020*; I Shuttleworth & C Lloyd *Belfast mapping segregation report* (2009).

[23] See for example Lord Cameron *Disturbances in Northern Ireland, report of the commission appointed by the Governor of Northern Ireland* (1969); D Smith & G Chambers *Inequality in Northern Ireland* (1991).

behind' and have 'failed to benefit substantially from the peace'.[24] These issues are compounded by the political complexities of addressing a patchwork of relative deprivation that cuts across the polarised identity groupings associated with the conflict (mainly-Catholic Nationalist/Republican and mainly-Protestant Unionist/Loyalist) in what remain Northern Ireland's most segregated communities.

While links between property inequality and the wider transitional project have been widely recognised by activists, advocates and academics alike, the issue has not generally been framed as a 'property law' problem; nor has significant attention between given to potential contributions that property law might make in the search for new political or legal solutions that advance social justice and promote more equal property relations in Northern Ireland. In this chapter, I reflect on why the role of property law and property theory in this aspect of the conflict has been relatively neglected, and explore the critical potential of applying Van der Walt's insights to the Northern Ireland case. In doing so, it is important to recognise the complex relationships between law, politics and culture in the processes of post-conflict transformation and social change.[25] Van der Walt's transformative impact on the South African property imagination was framed by the distinctive constitutional context that emerged in South Africa from the mid-1990s. Attempting a literal 'application' of this approach to another context, culture and conflict, with a different configuration of political progress as the backdrop to legal transformation, would underestimate the cultural specificity of legal strategies for social change, as well as the crucial role of particular political transformations in creating the space for legal transformation. Nevertheless, there are important lessons to be learned from Van der Walt's South African scholarship for property scholarship seeking to engage with the challenges of re-imagining property law's role in transformation and social justice in other post-conflict settings.

Kostiner's account of the culture of law in activism outlined three distinct schemes through which the relationships between law and activism are conceptualised: the instrumental (emphasising the need of marginalised people to have concrete resources); the political (the need of marginalised people to be empowered, united, and politically mobilised) and the cultural (the need to transform the taken-for-granted assumptions that are shared by

---

[24] Rooney & Swaine 'The "long grass" of agreements: Promise, theory and practice' (2012) 12 *Int'l Crim L Rev* 519–548 521.

[25] I Kostiner 'Evaluating legality: Toward a cultural approach to the study of law and social change' (2003) 37 *Law & Soc'y Rev* 323–368.

all members of society).[26] This chapter focuses on identifying the untapped progressive potential embedded in the taken-for-granted assumptions of Northern Irish land law. In doing so, it recognises the role of law in social change as a social construct, constantly produced and reproduced by people's actions and conversations, to create 'narratives of law' that are captured in the stories we tell (and those that go untold).[27] Property scholars have emphasised the importance of 'property stories' in shaping our understandings of the discipline, its rules and limits and its critical potential;[28] indeed, in his earlier work, at the dawn of the new dispensation, Van der Walt highlighted the power of property 'legends' in shaping critical understandings of the role of property law in socio-economic and political structures.[29]

In embarking on a preliminary exploration of Northern Ireland's untold property stories, I draw on two prominent tropes of contemporary property scholarship: first, the emerging literature on 'sharing property',[30] which challenges the claim that 'exclusion' (and the right to exclude) is the essence of property, and highlights the progressive potential of non-exclusionary norms in property doctrine; and secondly, the scholarship of property and identity,[31] which focuses on the identities of people who are included or excluded by the property system, paying particular attention to the identities of the people who live in the margins of property. Together, these lenses reveal the distinctive legends of Northern Irish property law, which speak – in a voice that is radically different from either English or South African normative traditions – of an implicit flexibility and pragmatism, a culturally-normalised comfort with hybridity and compromise, as well as an openness to norms of inclusion and sharing, that stands in contrast to absolutist, pandectist or neoliberal property systems like those of pre-transformation South Africa and contemporary England. The legends of these embedded local norms have gone untold in Northern Ireland's property stories, amidst the struggle for recognition across identity conflicts in a context of inadequate housing

[26] I Kostiner 'Evaluating legality: Toward a cultural approach to the study of law and social change' (2003) 37 *Law Soc Rev* 324–368.

[27] P Ewick & SS Sibley *The common place of law: Stories from everyday life* (1998).

[28] C Rose 'Property as storytelling' in *Property and persuasion: Chapters on the history, theory and rhetoric of ownership* (1994); LS Underkuffler 'Teaching property stories' (2005) 55 *J Legal Educ* 152 – 162; G Korngold & A Morriss (eds) *Property stories* 2 ed (2009).

[29] AJ van der Walt 'Marginal notes on powerful(l) legends: Critical perspectives on property theory' (1995) 58 *THRHR* 396–420 397.

[30] R Dyal-Chand 'Sharing the cathedral' (2013) 46 *Conn L Rev* 647–723; AJ van der Walt 'The modest systemic status of property rights' (2014) 1 *J L Prop & Soc'y* 15–106.

[31] AJ van der Walt *Property in the margins* (2009); L Fox O'Mahony 'Property outsiders and the hidden politics of doctrinalism' (2014) 67 *CLP* 409–445.

provision. This chapter opens up a new seam of 'public' property discourse that, drawing on the traditions of pluralism within Northern Ireland's property law, seeks to offer an alternative narrative through which the people of Northern Ireland might 'appear' and talk to each other about their shared public interests.

2 Property law in the public realm

In 1995, just one year after Nelson Mandela was sworn in as the first post-apartheid President and on the eve of the new South African Constitution of 1996, Van der Walt published a paper that claimed the relatively modest aim of 'enter[ing] into an introductory critical discussion of property theory from the fundamentally political perspective that the power structures underlying property relations should be revealed'.[32] The paper offered an intellectual starting point from which to reflect on the claim that it is incumbent on property scholars to pay attention to the powerful (if sometimes hidden) role of property law in socio-economic and political structures.[33] It mapped out the intellectual challenges facing South African property scholarship in engaging with a process of transformation that included social justice-inspired changes to the extant property regime, and explicitly challenged property theorists to re-imagine property law's role in the process of transformation, towards effective constitutional democracy and in pursuit of social justice. In order for property to do this work of advancing justice and equality, Van der Walt urged the property theorist to 'tear herself loose from the comfortable and well-worn old legends of her intellectual childhood, and come to terms with new stories with different morals and unknown endings'.[34]

I was born in Northern Ireland; I attended a segregated school in Dungannon, County Tyrone, in the 1980s and early 1990s, before moving to Belfast to study law and politics at Queen's University in 1993. Although I studied law in Northern Ireland, most of my scholarship has focused on English property law, especially English land law. As an early career researcher, in my first teaching job in Belfast, it was not at all obvious to me what property law scholarship might have to contribute to a legal and political discourse that – in the 1990s and 2000s – was naturally focused on the challenges of transitional justice and post-conflict transformation.

[32] AJ van der Walt 'Marginal notes on powerful(l) legends: Critical perspectives on property theory' (1995) 58 *THRHR* 396–420 397.

[33] AJ van der Walt 'Marginal notes on powerful(l) legends: Critical perspectives on property theory' (1995) 58 *THRHR* 396–420 397.

[34] AJ van der Walt 'Marginal notes on powerful(l) legends: Critical perspectives on property theory' (1995) 58 *THRHR* 396–420 418–9.

While constitutional and human rights scholars were deeply engaged with questions of post-conflict transition, the doctrinal fabric of land law, of tenure and estates, settlements, co-ownership, easements, even landlord and tenant law, was perceived to be categorically distinct from those areas of (public) law – constitutional law, human rights law, criminal justice – in which the conflict and its legacies were prominent in Northern Ireland's legal discourse.[35] I was reminded of this when I first read André's book *Property in the Margins*. He explained the double effect of the categorical and conceptual distinction drawn between politics and law under South African apartheid: Areas designated as 'law' not 'politics' were concealed behind a façade of neutrality; and those designated as 'politics' not 'law' were beyond judicial scrutiny. Reflecting on the property lawyers who implemented the apartheid regime, Andre wrote that:

> For the most part, these lawyers might well be unable to even understand, let alone acknowledge or question, the fact that they have acted upon and favoured one rather than another moral, political and theoretical approach to property.

In the wake of the first phase of post-apartheid land reform, Van der Walt argued for a reappraisal of 'the whole of the private-law tradition in the sharp light of the new, public-law spirit of constitutionalism'.[36] The bold aim of this approach was to locate the concerns of 'private' law within the realm of society's collective concerns as a public – 'resisting the private-law tradition and all the baggage that accompanies it' to forge a new kind of property discourse: 'a discourse that lives in the public sphere where people appear and talk to each other about the things that affect us all as a public (and not merely as competing private interests)'.[37]

In the Northern Ireland of my 'intellectual childhood', the relationships between land law and contemporary political and constitutional debates were not taught or discussed, or perhaps even widely recognised. This can be understood, in part, as the legacy of a property law discourse (across England, Ireland and Northern Ireland, and echoed in the South African tradition) that tended towards positivism, doctrinalism, and the categorical separation of private law (including land law) from the public realm of

[35] See, for example, K McEvoy & G Ellison 'Criminological discourses in Northern Ireland: Conflict and conflict resolution' in K McEvoy & T Newburn (eds) *Criminology, conflict resolution and restorative justice* (2003) 51–88.

[36] AJ van der Walt 'Undoing things with words: the colonisation of the public sphere by private-property discourse' 1998 *Acta Juridica* 235–281 280.

[37] AJ van der Walt 'Undoing things with words: the colonisation of the public sphere by private-property discourse' 1998 *Acta Juridica* 235–281 279.

politics.[38] While accounts of Northern Irish land law often emphasise its historical dimension,[39] this is typically framed in terms of a chronology of legislation and case law, rather than a politically or socially contextualised account. When differences of approach between English, Irish and Northern Irish land law are specifically identified, seminal accounts concentrated on technical differences, sometimes explaining patterns of difference through the historical timeline, but typically eliding the question of underpinning ideological commitments where land law has 'acted upon and favoured one rather than another moral, political and theoretical approach to property'. This chapter argues that such accounts – consistent with what McEvoy described as a 'culture of quietism' amongst Northern Ireland's lawyers, who during the conflict (mostly) performed the role of 'paid technicians' within a wider tradition of legal positivism[40] – are not 'neutral', but run counter to the property challenges surrounding conflict and transition. Van der Walt argued that the 'legend' of property law as 'a neutral and abstract system of logical and coherent concepts and institutions' is not merely a 'fairy tale' but, by its very existence, is apt to distract us from the pressing questions of social justice, which constitute 'the real work of maintaining the democratic legal system...' This chapter sets out to mine below the surface of Northern Ireland's under-told story of property theory and property law, and to reflect on its critical potential to support transition and transformation of the democratic legal system in Northern Ireland.

3 Sharing

While the proposition that the 'essence' of ownership is the right to exclude[41] has dominated many of the stories told about property law since the 1980s,[42] in recent years, progressive scholars have articulated a new story that recognises and promotes property law's inherent norms of 'inclusion' and

---

[38] For a discussion of this phenomenon and its effects in English property discourse, see L Fox O'Mahony 'Property outsiders and the hidden politics of doctrinalism' (2014) 67 *CLP* 409–445.

[39] See, for example, JCW Wylie *Irish land law* 3 ed (1997): 'Land law can only be understood if its essentially historical and evolving nature is always remembered. A knowledge of legal history is often essential for its understanding' para 1.09.

[40] K McEvoy 'What did the lawyers do during the "war"? Neutrality, conflict and the culture of quietism' (2011) 74(3) *Mod L Rev* 350–384 381.

[41] TW Merrill 'Property and the right to exclude' (1998) 77 *Neb L Rev* 730–755; J Penner *The idea of property in law* (1997); TW Merrill & HE Smith 'The morality of property' (2007) 48 *Wm & Mary L Rev* 1849–1895; L Katz 'Exclusion and exclusivity in property law' (2008) 58 *U Toronto LJ* 275–315.

[42] C Rose 'Property as storytelling' in *Property and persuasion: Chapters on the history, theory and rhetoric of ownership* (1994).

'sharing'. This debate is underpinned by the fundamental questions facing property scholarship in an age of identity polarisation: *whether* property law works; *for whom* property law works; and – for those who believe that property law could and should work differently – *how* property law can be made more progressive, more inclusive, and more effective in meeting the demands of maintaining a democratic society in which each person is treated with equal concern and respect.[43] Daniel Kelly's account of property law's power to promote inclusion[44] – through consensually inclusive property forms such as easements, leases, trusts, concurrent estates, and co-ownership arrangements, and through 'involuntary inclusion' (anti-discrimination/ public accommodations provisions) – explores the social and economic benefits of hanging a different sign; instead of 'keep out', saying 'come on in'. The legal power to include has been a powerful enabler of innovation, from the 'sharing economy' – for-profit platforms like Air BnB and Uber, and not-for-profit initiatives like foodbanks and makerspaces – to collaborative uses of new technologies as drivers for economic growth, innovation and micro-entrepreneurialism. Sharing norms promise to facilitate access to property, resources, time and skills for those who are excluded from opportunities under conventional ownership models,[45] in a newly reconstituted normative framework of alternative capitalist enterprise that values co-operation and social and environmental sustainability.[46]

Building on the notion of a 'sharing economy', recent literature developing a theory of 'sharing property' makes the normative case for property pluralism: for our ideas about the meaning of property to reference both *sharing* and *exclusion*; to recognise under-told commitments to sharing within property doctrine and discourse; to identify or develop tools or remedies to apply sharing solutions to property conflicts; and to embed this way of thinking about, talking about, and resolving property conflicts within the frame of property law. Just as the 'sharing economy' movement has opened up an alternative economic space in which to challenge the hegemony of global capitalism and commoditisation, the 'sharing property' movement offers an alternative legal space in which to challenge the hegemony of the exclusion norm. This intellectual project has been framed as: 'a powerful means of

[43] JW Singer 'Democratic estates: Property law in a free and democratic society' (2009) 94 *Cornell L Rev* 1009–1062.

[44] DB Kelly 'The right to include' (2014) 63 *Emory LJ* 857–924.

[45] D Wosskow *Unlocking the sharing economy: An independent review* (2014).

[46] L Gold *The sharing economy: Solidarity networks transforming globalisation* (2004); J Hamari, M Sjöklint & A Ukkonen 'The sharing economy: Why people participate in collaborative consumption' (2016) 67 *J Am Soc Inf Sci Tec* 2047–2059; H Heinrichs 'Sharing economy: A potential new pathway to sustainability' (2013) 22 *GAIA* 228–231.

addressing property inequalities'.[47] Yet, just as the 'sharing economy' movement has come under challenge over the extent to which it actually reduces economic inequalities,[48] analyses of *sharing property* norms must also keep a clear focus on *identity*[49] – on *who benefits* from sharing – if it is to sustain its claim to be a progressive norm.

The framing norms of sharing, exclusion and identity provide a useful lens through which to reflect on the role of property law and property theory in Northern Ireland. While English land law has sustained a more or less steadily increasing commitment to the norm of exclusion since Britain adopted *laissez-faire* capitalism as the national economic philosophy in the mid-nineteenth century,[50] Northern Ireland land law has a distinctively pluralist character. The exclusion norm can be found in some areas of doctrine and practice: for example, Northern Ireland led the way (later followed in England and Wales) in establishing a strictly pro-creditor approach towards the exercise of discretion under section 36 of the Administration of Justice Act, 1970, which governs the court's jurisdiction to delay repossession proceedings in cases involving dwelling houses.[51] Similarly, the fundamental structures of landlord and tenant law established under 'Deasy's Act' (discussed below) signal to the personal, not proprietary, nature of the leasehold relationship.[52] Yet, at the same time, Northern Irish land law has also retained some distinctively inclusive 'sharing' norms. For example, while the English law of co-ownership limits the degree to which the law governing co-ownership of land can accommodate sharing of title through co-ownership (including a bar on the severance of the joint tenancy at law, and a maximum of four joint tenants), Northern Ireland permits severance of the joint tenancy at law, and places no limit on the number of joint tenants.[53] Northern Ireland has implemented a system of land registration, but its approach has balanced

---

[47] R Dyal-Chand 'Sharing the cathedral' (2013) 46 *Conn L Rev* 647–723.

[48] J Schor 'Debating the sharing economy', Great transition initiative (October 2014); available at http://greattransition.org/publication/debating-the-sharing-economy.

[49] E Rosser 'The ambition and transformative potential of progressive property' (2013) 101 *Cal L Rev* 107–171.

[50] L Fox O'Mahony 'Property outsiders and the hidden politics of doctrinalism' (2014) 67 *CLP* 409–445 412.

[51] The strict exclusionary interpretation of s 36 in the Northern Ireland Chancery Division in *National and Provincial Building Society v Lynd* [1996] NI 47 was later adopted by the English Court of Appeal in *National Westminster Building Society v Norgan* [1996] 1 All ER 449; 26 HLR 703 (CA).

[52] Landlord and Tenant Law (Amendment) Act (Ireland), 1860.

[53] This distinctive difference between English and Northern Irish law reflects a feature of the nineteenth-century campaigns: one aim of the imposition of the English capitalist model was to address perceived inefficiencies due to subdivision of land into small units.

the advantages of registration with other goals of the land law system.[54] This offers a stark contrast to the English approach, where the pursuit of a 'tighter' system of registration has been a major driver for the land law reforms focused on protecting legal title holders and purchasers (the 'strong rights' claim[55] of property 'insiders')[56] against 'informal' claims, such as those brought by squatters, or claims to overriding interests (the 'weak right' or 'no right' claims of property 'outsiders').[57]

While the law of adverse possession has been significantly curtailed in England and Wales,[58] in Northern Ireland the traditional principles of limitation – described by the Northern Ireland Law Commission as a good fit for local practices[59] – continue to apply. The Northern Ireland Land Registry's practice of entering the name of the successful adverse possessor as the new owner on the dispossessed owner's title, as if there had been a statutory conveyance,[60] also reflects a 'sharing norm'. Although Northern Ireland's courts accepted that the 'no Parliamentary conveyance' principle was binding on unregistered land (where it has limited effect), rejecting this approach in registered land had significant 'sharing' implications, particularly in leasehold land. In England and Wales, the 'no Parliamentary conveyance' rule meant that a twelve year limitation against the dispossessed lessee barred only her claim against the squatter, without invalidating other rights

---

[54] Title to approximately 50% of properties in Northern Ireland is registered (mainly in rural areas or recent development estates on the periphery of towns), and the remaining properties (in established urban areas) are dealt with by the Registry of Deeds, which provides a system of registration for documents relating to unregistered land. The compulsory first registration programme was not extended to all of Northern Ireland until 2003, compared to 1990 in England and Wales.

[55] AJ van der Walt *Property in the margins* (2009).

[56] L Fox O'Mahony 'Property outsiders and the hidden politics of doctrinalism' (2014) 67 *CLP* 409–445 412.

[57] This approach is typified in the Law Commission reports preceding the Land Registration Act 2002, and in the Act itself: Law Commission *Land registration for the 21st century: A consultative document* (Law Com No 254) (1998); Law Commission *Land registration for the 21st century: A conveyancing revolution* (Law Com No 271) (2001).

[58] For discussion, see M Dixon 'The reform of property law and the Land Registration Act 2002: A risk assessment' (2003) *Conv & Prop Law* 136–156; M Dixon 'Adverse possession and human rights' (2005) *Conv & Prop Law* 345–351; M Dixon 'Adverse possession in three jurisdictions' (2006) *Conv & Prop Law* 179; N Cobb & L Fox 'Living outside the system: The (im)morality of urban squatting after the Land Registration Act 2002' (2007) 27 *LS* 236–260; L Fox O'Mahony & N Cobb 'Taxonomies of Squatting: Unlawful occupation in a new legal order' (2008) 71 *Mod L Rev* 878–911.

[59] See below, notes 63–66 and associated text.

[60] Contrary to the English principle of 'no Parliamentary conveyance', established by the House of Lords in *Fairweather v St Marylebone Property Co Ltd* [1963] AC 510, confirming the decision of the Irish Court of Appeal in *Tichbourne v Weir* (1892) 67 LT 735.

under the lease. This led English courts to conclude that the lessee was entitled to surrender up the lease, enabling the lessor to bring an immediate action on her own title to evict the long-term squatter.[61] The Northern Ireland practice, in contrast, protected the successful squatter who had established twelve years in adverse possession against eviction through this technique.

The Northern Ireland Law Commission's 2011 Report on *Land law*[62] – the first major project carried out by the newly formed Law Commission[63] – reinforced the contrast in property cultures between England and Northern Ireland. With the primary aim of making proposals for the reform and modernisation of land law and conveyancing law, the commission focused on finding 'local solutions':[64] in some areas, assimilating the law of Northern Ireland with that of England and Wales; in others, adopting solutions from Irish law; in a few cases, following the Scottish model; and in still more, producing new solutions *sui generis* designed to fit local practices on the ground. This reflects the pluralist nature of Northern Ireland's land law, and sits in sharp contrast to the exclusionary turn in English land law.[65] The Northern Ireland Law Commission explicitly rejected the English move

[61] For a critique of the exclusionary effects of this decision on squatters of leasehold land, see Wade 'Landlord, tenant and squatter' (1962) 78 *LQR* 541–559. See also H Wallace 'Adverse possession of leaseholds – The case for reform' (1975) 10 *Ir Jur (ns)* 74–80; JCW Wylie 'Adverse possession: An ailing concept?' (1965) 16 *NILQ* 467–490. England later adopted the long-standing Northern Irish practice of entering the successful squatter title-claimant on the registered title of the dispossessed owner rather than creating a new record (*Spectrum Investment Co v Holmes* [1981] 1 WLR 221; *Central London Commercial Estates Ltd v Kato Kagaku Ltd* [1998] 4 All ER 948), but this was followed fairly swiftly by decisive action to significantly curtail the circumstances in which squatters can acquire title in registered land in England in any event (Land Registration Act, 2002, s 75 and Schedule 6).

[62] Northern Ireland Law Commission Consultation Paper: *Land law* (NILC 2, Belfast: Northern Ireland Law Commission, 2009); Northern Ireland Law Commission Supplementary consultation paper, *Land law* (2010); NILC, Report on land law (NILC 8, 2010).

[63] The Northern Ireland Law Commission was created under s 50 of the Justice (Northern Ireland) Act, 2002, implementing recommendations following the Belfast Agreement (or 'Good Friday Agreement') that underpinned the new institutional structures to govern Northern Ireland after the conflict.

[64] Northern Ireland Law Commission, Consultation paper: *Land law* (NILC 2 (2009) para 1.20.

[65] For a detailed discussion, see L Fox O'Mahony 'Property outsiders and the hidden politics of doctrinalism' (2014) 67 *CLP* 409–445 412.

to curtail adverse possession,[66] noting instead the useful role the doctrine continues to play in Northern Ireland. Reflecting on the (anti-squatter) moral arguments which have dominated the recent English approach,[67] the commission took a more balanced approach, noting that '...if ethical considerations are to be brought into play, it is arguable that they should be applied also to the dispossessed paper title owner'.[68] Reflecting on the English exclusionary approach, the commission expressed 'considerable reservations' about reforms that had 'greatly increase[d] the protection of the owner from a failure to keep an eye on the property'. In explicitly resisting England's exclusionary turn against squatters, the commission underlined the distinctiveness of property culture in Northern Ireland, and its enduring preference for normative pluralism over the monist norm of exclusion. These recommendations have not yet been implemented; perhaps their significance as a pillar of a new legal order based on pluralism in property relations, and so also in the socio-economic and political power relations and struggles that are foregrounded in Northern Ireland legal and political discourse, was too well concealed beneath the technicalities of land law. Alternatively, the failure to implement these recommendations might simply be understood as a reflection of the dysfunction of the Assembly and its inability to enact major legislative change.

The historical, technical divergence of English and Northern Irish land law can be traced to the '1925 legislation' – a series of Acts that are widely recognised as the blueprint for English land law's commitment to norms of exclusion, alienability, protection of purchasers, and 'strong property rights'[69] – which did not extend to Northern Ireland. The 1925 legislation came fresh in the wake of the Partition of Ireland – establishing the independent Irish Republic and creating Northern Ireland as a new jurisdiction of the United Kingdom – in 1921. Partition followed half a century of political conflict that

[66] Northern Ireland Law Commission *Supplementary consultation paper, land law* (NILC 3) (2010) para 2.36. Cf Law Commission & HM Land Registry 'Land registration for the twenty-first century: A consultative document' (Law Com 254) (1998); Land Registration Act, 2002, Schedule 6.

[67] L Fox O'Mahony, D O'Mahony & R Hickey (eds) *Moral rhetoric and the criminalisation of squatting: Vulnerable demons?* (2014).

[68] For discussion of these provisions, see L Fox O'Mahony 'Something old, something new, something borrowed: Land law reform in Northern Ireland' (2011) 75 *Conv & Prop Law* 355–378.

[69] In England, the '1925 legislation' was an important landmark which embedded the values associated with free-market economic philosophies – alienability, exclusion, individualism – into the foundations of property law. For discussion of the values embedded through the 1925 legislation, see D Cowan, L Fox O'Mahony & N Cobb *Great debates in land law* 2 ed (2016) ch 3.

had its roots in competing property ideologies: between the English ideology of strong property rights, free disposition, individualism and exclusivity – manifest through the consolidation of the landlord's proprietary rights – and Irish customary practices and beliefs rooted in possession, strong ideological commitment to the social function of land, security of tenure, and tenant-rights based in use and occupation.[70]

In 1845 the Devon Commission,[71] reporting on the 'State of the law and practice in respect of occupation of land in Ireland', recognised that the established practice (particularly in the north-east) of 'Ulster Custom' or 'tenant right', whereby 'a tenant, upon leaving his holding for whatever cause, claimed the privilege of exacting from his successor a sum of money running up to ten or fifteen years' rent';[72] had generated 'a feeling of proprietorship [that] had grown up in the tenants which was wholly anomalous in reference to ordinary [English] notions of property.'[73] While some areas of England practised versions of this custom, the Devon Commission recognised that the Irish practice of 'tenant improvements' went significantly beyond English practices; Irish tenants built dwelling houses and farm buildings and made fences. The beliefs underpinning this 'native' approach were championed by English political economist John Stuart Mill, who argued that Ireland's 'sharing' norm was essential to the effective operation of political economy in Ireland; and that these inclusive property practices delivered the greatest comfort to the greatest number of Irish people. Yet, despite recognising the strength and depth of these norms,[74] the Devon Commission aligned with the British government's economic philosophy of *laissez-faire* capitalism by recommending a policy of consolidation of farms. One nineteenth-century evaluation of the report concluded that '[n]othing more clearly shows the character of [British] thought than the frequent recurrence in the report of the phrase 'the just rights of property', and the repeated refusal, after the presentation of serious evils, to recommend legislative intervention for their removal'.[75] Notwithstanding the strength of local needs and practices, British property culture, characterised by strong property rights and the economic rationality of *laissez-faire* capitalism, demanded that –

[70] P Bull *Land, politics and nationalism: A study of the Irish land question* (1996).

[71] Report from her Majesty's Commissioners of Inquiry into the State of the Law and Practice in Respect of Occupation of Land in Ireland (1845).

[72] WA Dunning 'Irish land legislation since 1845. I' (1892) 7 *Pol Sci Q* 57–79 59.

[73] WA Dunning 'Irish land legislation since 1845. I' (1892) 7 *Pol Sci Q* 57–79 59.

[74] WA Dunning 'Irish land legislation since 1845. I' (1892) 7 *Pol Sci Q* 57–79.

[75] WA Dunning 'Irish land legislation since 1845. I' (1892) 7 *Pol Sci Q* 57–79 62.

> the 'owners' of the land are indeed its owners in absolute terms, with the right to sell or lease as they pleased and at whatever price allowed by the market. Any interference with these 'property rights' was anathema...[76]

Collinson Black argued that the British economic philosophy of: 'treating the non-renewable resource of land as a commodity...lay at the heart of the Irish problem, since it involved violent offence to native perceptions of the occupier's relationship to the land'.[77] This approach was at the core of the enactment of the Landlord and Tenant Law (Amendment) Act (Ireland), 1860 ('Deasy's Act') – the first major piece of Irish land tenure reform legislation enacted by the British government – which expressly declared that the relationship between a landlord and a tenant was based in contract, not property. Deasy's Act only highlighted the incompatibilities of British and Irish property cultures: ' ... declar[ing] that what was coming increasingly to be seen as the [sharing] reality of Irish land tenure was in fact not so... The Act made explicit in law the assumptions of English landed society, restating the absolute rights of ownership vested in the landlord, clarifying the contractual nature of the relationship with the tenant, and strengthening the powers of the landlord in relation to eviction.'

It is perhaps unsurprising that these themes did not feature in my Northern Ireland land law education in the 1990s. For one thing, the ideological conflict over land tenure and competing normative accounts of property rights has only relatively recently come to prominence in revisionist accounts of the emergence of the Irish nationalist proto-state in the late nineteenth century.[78] Even more recently, the emergence of 'property sharing' theory, in conjunction with a renewed focus on property and identity, offers fresh opportunities to 'mine under the coalface' of property law's abstract neutrality,[79] and to re-imagine an inclusive public discourse of Northern Ireland land law in the context of wider normative debates about social justice, political equality and constitutionalism. To this task, Van der Walt's methodological strategies offer a helpful framework for beginning to imagine a role for property stories in Northern Ireland's transition to peace and pluralism. In his essay 'A South African reading of Frank Michelman's theory of social justice', André

[76] P Bull *Land, politics and nationalism: A study of the Irish land question* (1996) 11.

[77] RD Collinson *Black economic thought and the Irish question* 1817–1870 (2015) 28–29.

[78] Margaret O'Callaghan *British high politics and a nationalist Ireland: Criminality, land and the law under Forster and Balfour* (1994); for the period from the 'Easter Rising' in 1916 through the formation of the Irish Free State (now the Republic of Ireland) in 1921, and the Irish Civil War of 1922–23, see F Campbell & T Varley (eds) *Land questions in modern Ireland* (2013).

[79] AJ van der Walt 'Marginal notes on powerful(l) legends: Critical perspectives on property theory' (1995) 58 *THRHR* 396–420 420.

explained why, for those who are interested in pursuing social justice approaches to property problems, a 'multi-stranded theoretical approach' is required, weaving a twisted rope, a 'pluriform' theoretical strategy to address different categories of interests or sets of circumstances.[80] Van der Walt argued that this theoretical strategy should include (at least) a property-rights-based approach (on the basis of something resembling vested or acquired rights); a needs-based approach (to protect the social and economic rights of the poorest and those in positions of marginality or vulnerability); and a 'middle-ground' approach, which balances equality and economic rationality in cases where the claimant has neither vested rights nor extreme need, but where the transformation project, towards constitutional democracy and political equality, requires that weak and insecure claims be strengthened and bolstered to lift them above the threshold of minimum protection, commensurate with the state's obligations.[81]

The outcome of Ireland's nineteenth-century land conflict was a single-strand approach that strengthened vested rights within the individualist model. Gladstone's Land Act, 1870, recognised the native concept of 'Ulster custom' in a diluted form[82] but, while this represented a significant compromise against the English concept of landlords' absolute property rights, it did not satisfy the broader aspirations of Irish tenant farmers, or address the fundamental incompatibility between English and Irish concepts of ownership. Between 1870 and 1909, the British government passed five Land Acts making further concessions. The Irish Land Act, 1881 (enacted in response to further agitation) expanded the space between the concepts of ownership in England and Ireland yet further with the introduction of a concept of 'peasant proprietorship' or 'dual ownership', 'predicated on an assumption of shared responsibility between landlord and tenant and of a co-operative approach to both agricultural and social questions'.[83] With hindsight, one might wonder whether this approach could have paved the way towards a different kind of property system, and a different kind of politics. However, against a backdrop of rising nationalism and anti-landlordism, the Irish campaign refocused on the transfer of sole ownership to tenants through land purchase schemes. It was paradoxical that, when this aim was achieved

---

[80] AJ van der Walt 'A South African reading of Frank Michelman's theory of social justice' in H Botha, A van der Walt & J van der Walt (eds) *Rights and democracy in a transformative constitution* (2004) 163–212 204.

[81] AJ van der Walt 'A South African reading of Frank Michelman's theory of social justice' in H Botha, A van der Walt & J van der Walt (eds) *Rights and democracy in a transformative constitution* (2004) 163–212 208–9.

[82] Diluted from 'peasant proprietorship' to liability to compensate for improvements.

[83] P Bull *Land, politics and nationalism: A study of the Irish land question* (1996) 90.

through leasehold enfranchisement legislation between 1885 and 1903, 'the outcome of the most effective socio-political movement of collective action in modern Irish history [was] the entrenchment of a decidedly individualistic system of farm ownership'.[84]

The replacement of landlordism with a privatised system of owner-occupation applied a property rights solution that satisfied the needs of a sub-population of existing tenants. Van der Walt described this move through which the 'weak rights' of existing tenants were strengthened into full-blown ownership, on the standard exclusionary model of *laissez-faire* property ownership –[85]

> ... confirm[ing] (rather than unsettl[ing]) the traditional hierarchy of rights, according to which the protection of interests depends on their recognition as vested rights in terms of established legal principles. Instead of improving the current unequal division of wealth, this approach actually exacerbates inherent inequalities in the current situation, because it reduces the debate about wealth and poverty in a constitutional democracy to a mechanical process in which everything depends on the classification of recognised and protected versus unrecognised and unprotected interests, inside versus outside the circle of advantage, while more difficult questions about the reasons and motivation for inclusion and exclusion remain unasked and unanswered.[86]

The enfranchisement of native occupiers and the end of English landlordism in Ireland provided a solution for Irish tenants; however, by privileging leasehold enfranchisement at the expense of other land issues, this solution was focused on strengthening the (weak) rights of existing tenants at the expense of people who were even more marginalised than the tenant population, the 'weaker-' or 'no-right' populations outside the property system altogether.

Against this backdrop, Northern Ireland land law's distinctive normative pluralism continues to reflect its complex origins. In the west and south, the tenant farmer population was predominately Catholic,[87] while in the north-east of the island – what became Northern Ireland – enfranchised tenants were predominately Presbyterian. On the one hand, the practice of 'Ulster custom' – what would in contemporary property theory be framed as

[84] Gearóid Ó Tuathaigh 'Irish land questions in the state of the Union' in F Campbell & T Varley (eds) *Land questions in modern Ireland* (2013) 3–24 17.

[85] CA Reich 'The new property' (1964) 73 *Yale LJ* 733–787; CA Reich 'Individual rights and social welfare: The emerging legal issues' (1965) 74 *Yale LJ* 1245–1258.

[86] AJ van der Walt 'A South African reading of Frank Michelman's theory of social justice' in H Botha, A van der Walt & J van der Walt (eds) *Rights and democracy in a transformative constitution* (2004) 163–212 170.

[87] P Bull *Land, politics and nationalism: A study of the Irish land question* (1996) 188.

'sharing' norms and beliefs – had been particularly prominent[88] in the rural north of the island. At the same time, the development of a modern industrial capitalist economy in the urban north-east in the nineteenth century, and other ties to British economic and political ambitions, aligned Belfast's urban industrialised Unionists with the English *laissez-faire* revolution and its property ideology of individualism and exclusion.[89] Almost a century after the creation of Northern Ireland, its land law continues to mediate cultural commitment to the (rural) social function of land and recognition of its (urban) economic power. It combines elements of English and Irish influences, adapted to meet local needs, and mediating between norms of sharing and exclusion. As a first strand in Van der Walt's 'twisted rope', land law's normative pluralism has an important and under-realised contribution to make to public property discourses seeking to anchor collective, public concern for social justice within the project of political equality and constitutional democracy.

4 Identity

Reflecting on the role of property scholarship in fostering a progressive society, Tim Mulvaney[90] proposed that it attend to three criteria: transparency – a 'forthright acknowledgement that property rules are never value-neutral'[91] – with commitment to open conversations about the reasons for preferring one set of rules or standards over the alternatives;[92] humility – acknowledging the 'limited reach of human knowledge and the mutability of our normative positions';[93] and identity – 'contextual concern for the current status, including the social, economic, and political needs, of the groups or individuals involved in particular resource conflicts'.[94] Positivist doctrinal property scholarship's claim to neutrality obviates these criteria, concealing the identity-impacts

[88] Or perhaps was better documented; in Ulster, the avoidance of customary rights was also cut across with Presbyterian tenants' concerns that Catholics seeking tenancies might be willing to forego the protections and accept shorter leases on less favourable terms: A Boserup 'Contradictions and struggles in Northern Ireland' (1972) 9 *Socialist Register* 157–192 161.

[89] '[A]djustment to capitalism was made easier on account of the North's location as hinterland to a thriving industrial centre, thus replicating some of the conditions of the transition to industrial capitalism observable in the British experience'; P Bull *Land, politics and nationalism: A study of the Irish land question* (1996) 188–9. See also Irish Communist Organisation pamphlet *The economics of partition* (1969).

[90] P Bull *Land, politics and nationalism: A study of the Irish land question* (1996) 358.

[91] P Bull *Land, politics and nationalism: A study of the Irish land question* (1996) 358.

[92] P Bull *Land, politics and nationalism: A study of the Irish land question* (1996) 359.

[93] P Bull *Land, politics and nationalism: A study of the Irish land question* (1996) 361.

[94] P Bull *Land, politics and nationalism: A study of the Irish land question* (1996) 366–7.

of property laws and policies, and simultaneously shoring up existing inequalities when it prioritises – through 'face-neutral' doctrine – the claims of propertied 'insiders' (those who have relatively more property power in the form of rights and assets) over those of less- or un-propertied outsiders.[95] The hidden politics of doctrinalism in English law (as in pre-transformation South Africa), with its emphasis on 'strong' property rights and the self-fulfilling power of ownership, conceals its effects on less-propertied parties who compete for ownership or access to resources. Yet, in Northern Ireland, the hidden ideology of land law is more complex and more nuanced: the product of a plurality of influences, it has resisted the ideological-exclusionary turn of English law, and retained a more material, organic and pragmatic tradition. This freedom from the ideological constraints of neoliberal exclusionary norms has fostered the resilience of inclusionary and progressive norms, where these are aligned to the practicalities of land use on the ground. A pluriform theoretical framework for property in Northern Ireland must weave together the positivist doctrinalism and normative pluralism of 'private' land law with the processes that govern access to housing and home for people in the margins. If we accept that a democratic account of property values demands that norms that are valued and enjoyed by owner-insiders should have equivalent normative strength for marginalised-outsiders,[96] the 'surfacing' of Northern Ireland's land law pluralism has implications for other property problems.

An important feature of the twentieth-century property landscape in Northern Ireland (and in the UK more generally in this period) was the emergence of 'housing law and policy' as a new field of public law.[97] In England and Wales, the emergence of housing law as a branch of administrative or public law was widely regarded as a source of succour for the weakest, most vulnerable property subjects – for those in the margins.[98] While the

[95] L Fox O'Mahony 'Property outsiders and the hidden politics of doctrinalism' (2014) 67 *CLP* 409–445, especially 412–418.

[96] Akhil Reed Amar 'Forty acres and a mule: A republican theory of minimal entitlements' (1990) 13 *Harv J L & Pub Pol* 37–43 37.

[97] Although the history of provisions creating public sector powers and responsibilities for housing the working classes dates back to 1851, they began to become effective in 1890, and developed significantly after the First World War. The Housing and Town Planning Act, 1919, set the scene for a new era in the development of public sector housing. For a discussion of the tensions between the public housing function and private property rights, particularly from 1930, see F Frankfurter & W Ivor Jennings 'Courts and administrative law – The experience of English housing legislation' (1936) 49 *Harv L Rev* 426 443–451.

[98] F Frankfurter & W Ivor Jennings 'Courts and administrative law – The experience of English housing legislation' (1936) 49 *Harv L Rev* 426–455 452–453.

exclusionary norms of English (private) land law perfected the protection of strong property rights, the 'public law' of housing provided a counterpoint to the exclusionary norm, based in the social aims of housing legislation.[99] It is paradoxical that while the emergence of public housing law in Britain in the twentieth century tempered English property law's exclusion norm in areas of greatest need, Northern Ireland's pluralist land law norms – which mostly operate in cases of relative privilege, where parties compete over ownership claims – were undermined by the failure of pluralism in public housing, where the more fundamental property problem of access to adequate housing to meet basic needs was at stake. While the role of identity in determining access to housing was a prominent feature of the twentieth-century conflict, the bifurcation of Northern Ireland's property discourse into land law – pluralist norms operating within the 'circle of advantage' of 'private law' – and housing law, focused around weak or no right exclusion, inequality and 'needs' – kept these intersecting strands of property discourse categorically separate.

For most of the twentieth century, the political institutions that governed Northern Ireland were largely controlled by a majoritarian Unionist administration,[100] which at the local level managed the building and allocation of public housing.[101] The context for identity conflict was rooted in the scarcity of adequate housing in the wake of the First World War, exacerbated by the conflict surrounding Partition and still further when Northern Ireland was excluded from the UK's post-1919 housing investment strategies.[102] CEB Brett, former Chair of the Northern Ireland Housing Executive, claimed that: '[t]here was no city in England, Wales or Scotland whose house-building record in the inter-war years, whether in the public or private sector or taking the two together, was worse than that of Belfast.'[103] In addition to an absolute shortfall of housing, overcrowding, and poor quality stock, Brett claimed that

---

[99] In *Johnson v Leicester Corporation* [1934] 1 KB 638 (CA) 648, Maugham LJ stated that the Housing Acts recognised 'the fact that the housing of the working classes was very unsatisfactory and very much smaller in extent than was desirable'. Shifts in housing policy since the 1980s have attenuated the sharing norm within English housing legislation and strengthened the exclusionary rights of landlords within these frameworks.

[100] B O'Leary & J McGarry *The politics of antagonism: Understanding Northern Ireland* (2016) ch 3.

[101] The relationship between access to housing, identity and political equality was direct: before the Electoral Law Act (NI), 1969, and the Housing Executive Act (NI), 1971, votes in local authority elections were restricted to householders and their spouses (maximum two votes per household), so control over access to housing also gave local authorities control over the franchise.

[102] CEB Brett *Housing a divided community* (1986) 21.

[103] CEB Brett *Housing a divided community* (1986) 22.

there were 'glaring disparities between the standards of housing enjoyed respectively by the majority and minority communities'.[104] When serious civil unrest broke out in the late 1960s, one of the primary grievances asserted by the minority Catholic population was a claim of systematic, identity-based discrimination in the allocation of public housing.[105]

The failure of sharing in Northern Ireland's public housing continues to cast a long shadow over the conflict and the now twenty-year-old peace process. Public housing segregation remains acute, with more than 90 per cent of social housing in Northern Ireland, and 94 per cent in Belfast, still segregated on grounds of religious background in 2016.[106] This dual-market has ongoing implications for the effective management of limited housing resources,[107] in a context of housing deprivation and complex intersecting identity inequalities. In 1994, as the conflict began to shift towards a prospect of peace, Boyle and Hadden argued that Northern Ireland faced a choice, between *separation* – strategies to accommodate differences between communities by maintaining separate systems, separate facilities, and residential and social segregation, and *sharing* – structures to enable communities to live together and share resources, to 'encourage cooperation between the two communities and to maintain institutions in which representatives of each can share power and responsibility'.[108] The institutional framework proposed in the Belfast (Good Friday) Agreement, and implemented through the Northern Ireland Act 1998, opted for *sharing*, and paragraph 13 of the Belfast Agreement stated that '[a]n essential aspect of the reconciliation process is the promotion of ... initiatives to facilitate and encourage integrated education and mixed housing'. Section 75(2) of the Northern Ireland Act, 1998, places the Housing Executive under a

---

[104] CEB Brett *Housing a divided community* (1986) 36.

[105] See B Dickson 'The legal response to the 'Troubles' in Northern Ireland' in Patrick John Roche & Brian Barton (eds) *The Northern Ireland question: Myth and reality* 2 ed (2013) 213 *et seq*; D Birrell 'Relative deprivation as a factor in conflict in Northern Ireland' (1972) 20 *Sociol Rev* 317–343. For competing views concerning the nature and extent of housing discrimination, see C Hewitt 'Catholic grievances, Catholic nationalism and violence in Northern Ireland during the civil rights period: A reconsideration' (1981) 32 *Br J Sociol* 362–380; Denis O'Hearn 'Catholic grievances, Catholic nationalism: A comment' (1983) 34 *Br J Sociol* 438–445; C Hewitt 'Discrimination in Northern Ireland: A rejoinder' (1983) 34 *Br J Sociol* 446–451.

[106] Housing Executive, *Community Cohesion Strategy 2015–2020* I Shuttleworth & C Lloyd *Belfast mapping segregation report* (2009).

[107] The Housing Executive's Community Cohesion Strategy 2015–2020 claimed that community division and segregation is a barrier to best use being made of existing housing and land.

[108] K Boyle & T Hadden *Northern Ireland: The choice* (1994) 13.

statutory duty to promote good relations,[109] and the Northern Ireland Housing Executive describes its 2017 'Vision for Housing' as 'one where housing plays its part in creating a peaceful, inclusive, prosperous and fair society'.[110]

Housing segregation, and its relationship with broader poverty and inequality issues, remains a major concern for human rights campaigners.[111] In the 2016 Report of the Special Rapporteur on the Promotion of Truth, Justice, Reparation and Guarantees of Non-recurrence on his mission to the United Kingdom of Great Britain and Northern Ireland,[112] addressing housing segregation and socio-economic inequality and poverty were described as important aspects of an 'enabling context' for non-recurrence.[113] More generally, socially integrative sharing and socio-economic equality have been central to campaigns to promote engagement and participation, across Northern Ireland's identity communities, as 'equal members of a shared, collective political project'.[114] Yet the process of facing up to social and economic inequality has been challenging on several fronts. For one thing, while South Africa's transitional process explicitly prioritised the goal of seeking 'visible and significant social and economic reforms [to] redress some of the direct effects of apartheid inequality and rectify the general maladministration of social and economic privilege, wealth and power'[115] as an 'inevitable and non-negotiable prerequisite for success of the negotiated settlement', Northern Ireland's Peace Agreement focused on civil and political equality and power-sharing institutions over actions to address socio-economic inequalities. It was not until 2006[116] that section

[109] The Northern Ireland Housing Executive (NIHE) has noted that 80 per cent of people questioned in consultation said they would live in 'shared housing' (in ethno-religious mixed areas) if the circumstances were right. Data from Northern Ireland *Life and Times Survey*, quoted in Housing Executive, Community Cohesion Strategy 2015–2020 5. See also C Knox 'Cohesion, sharing, and integration in Northern Ireland' (2011) 29 *Environ & Plan C: Gov't & Pol'y* 548–566 551.

[110] The Community Cohesion strategy set out to advance this vision by addressing the complex housing needs of a divided society, while facilitating and encouraging mixed housing as far as is practicable, desirable and safe.

[111] See, for example, the work of Participation in the Practice of Rights (pprproject.org) on the right to housing.

[112] A/HRC/34/62/Add.1; November 2016, paras 82–85 and 136. Available online at https://documents-dds-ny.un.org/doc/UNDOC/GEN/G16/257/49/PDF/G1625749.pdf?OpenElement.

[113] Paragraphs 82, 136.

[114] Paragraphs 13, 14.

[115] AJ van der Walt *Property in the margins* (2009) 13.

[116] Northern Ireland (St Andrews Agreement) Act 2006.

28E, inserted (by amendment) into the Northern Ireland Act 1998,[117] required the Assembly's Executive Committee to 'adopt a strategy setting out how it proposes to tackle poverty, social exclusion and patterns of deprivation based on objective need'. This coincided with analysis asserting that while Northern Ireland as a whole had experienced unprecedented economic growth following the Peace Agreement, 'the poorest members of our society, both Catholics and Protestants, are relatively worse off than they were ten years ago'.[118]

Calls for action to address poverty and relative deprivation have been cut across by the UK government's policies of welfare retrenchment under 'austerity'.[119] The application of these UK-wide measures to the devolved jurisdiction of Northern Ireland has been particularly contentious, in light of the commitments underpinning the peace agreement. The failure of the Northern Ireland Executive to discharge its legal obligation under section 28E by adopting an anti-poverty strategy gave rise to a successful judicial review in 2016.[120] The court held that the Executive Committee of the Northern Ireland Assembly had failed to act on its legal obligation in terms of section 28E(1) to adopt a strategy; and, further, that the government had not yet adopted a working definition of 'objective need'. Mr Justice Treacy stated (*obiter*) that the intention with section 28E, in adopting the new concept of 'objective need' as the benchmark for tackling poverty, social exclusion and patterns of deprivation, was 'to remove or reduce the scope for discrimination by tying the allocation of resources to neutral criteria that measure deprivation irrespective of community background or other affiliation'.[121]

Since this decision, the Northern Ireland Assembly has been in ongoing crisis, with elections in 2016 and 2017 so far failing to yield stable power-sharing administrations. Although the terms of the Good Friday Agreement included reference to a Bill of Rights for Northern Ireland, and the proposition has been vigorously debated, little progress in this area leaves the framework for transition and transformation in Northern Ireland incomplete.

---

[117] While the Belfast/Good Friday Agreement provided for a 'Targeting Social Need' (TSN) initiative and a range of measures aimed at combating unemployment and eliminating the unemployment differential, the St Andrews Agreement took this a step further by placing the concept of 'objective need' on a statutory basis, and providing for the concept to be the basis of a statutory duty to tackle poverty, social exclusion and patterns of deprivation.

[118] Committee for the Administration of Justice *Equality in Northern Ireland: The rhetoric and the reality*, https://caj.org.uk.

[119] The Welfare Reform Act, 2012, applied wide-ranging welfare cuts in Great Britain.

[120] *In the Matter of an Application by The Committee on the Administration of Justice (CAJ) and Brian Gormally's Application for Judicial Review* [2015] NIQB 59.

[121] Paragraph 51.

Bell and McVeigh have argued that '[e]quality was not an optional extra to the [Good Friday Agreement] – it was the principle on which reconciliation and peacebuilding was to be built'.[122] Yet local political debates have struggled to negotiate the complex realities of sectarian-identity patterns in the distribution of relative deprivation.[123] The Equality Commission has identified a wide range of emerging and persistent housing inequalities, including the impact of identity-segregated housing markets on access to social housing; key inequalities in housing adequacy based on protected identity characteristics; and challenges to housing sustainability, security of tenure and long-term affordability.[124] These property questions remain central to debates about how Northern Ireland can achieve a peaceful, inclusive, prosperous and fair society.

5 Conclusions

Property relations were central to the breakdown of the British-Irish relationship in the nineteenth and early twentieth century; property inequalities were at the heart of the twentieth century conflict in Northern Ireland; and action to address housing segregation, and the legacies of 'separation', remain critical to achieving lasting peace. Yet property law and theory have been curiously absent from debates in the public sphere, where scholarship, advocacy and activism have focused on the strategic deployment of constitutional and human rights norms and standards as the frameworks for transition to a pluralist, post-sectarian legal and political system.[125] This is perhaps not surprising: it is only relatively recently that historians of nineteenth-century Ireland have cast new light on the role of property ideologies in fracturing British-Irish relations; and that property theory, led by the work of André van der Walt, has developed the frameworks and methodologies to reimagine the role of property theory and property law in facing up to the challenges, post-conflict, of establishing a democratic society, characterised by justice, dignity and equality.

The putative separation of land law from 'housing', of 'private' rights from the public realm, of 'neutral', technical law from contested, ideological politics, is not unique to Northern Ireland. But the effects of this disconnection between property norms and concern for social justice and equality *are* distinctive to

---

[122] *Ibid*, p70.

[123] Bell and McVeigh, 64–65.

[124] Equality Commission for Northern Ireland *Key inequalities in housing and communities, draft statement* (2016).

[125] See, for example, the strategies of the Committee for the Administration of Justice (www.caj.org.uk) and Participation in the Practice of Rights (www.pprproject.org).

the Northern Ireland context. While critiques of property and constitutional democracy in other jurisdictions[126] have typically sought to draw from constitutional commitments to social justice and equality to recalibrate pandectist, absolutist or exclusionary norms of private property law, the Northern Irish configuration suggests a reverse strategy; that embedded property norms hold untapped progressive and pluralist potential that, brought into the public realm, could play a significant role in recalibrating problematic public norms.

At the same time, the counter-narrative of Northern Ireland's pluralist property norms problematises the (unqualified) claim that the 'sharing norm' in property law is necessarily 'progressive'. Certainly, in some cases, Northern Ireland's pluralist land law norms reflect underpinning commitments to recognising the social function of land as well as its economic value, eschewing property absolutism and potentially providing routes (for example, through adverse possession) by means of which relatively weaker claims can be bolstered in progressive ways. But its legacies of 'silo-ed sharing', of inclusive norms but limited availability on identity lines, provide an important reminder of the need to cross-check normative commitments to sharing with attention to identity: to ask not only who benefits from these sharing norms, and who is excluded, within the land law frame, but also who qualifies (as a subject of land law), and who is excluded (as a subject of 'housing'). From this perspective, the Northern Ireland case offers a cautionary tale about the complex intersections between sharing and identity, monism and pluralism, across the public (housing) and private (land law) realms that collectively govern the access of each person to housing and home.

Scholarship on post-conflict consensus-building has recognised the powerful impact of tapping in to the 'collective identity' of embedded local norms, values and concepts; of 'existing patterns of belonging, established and enshrined in local traditions and customs'[127] in shaping successful outcomes. In seeking to scale the political and theoretical walls that have been built between different types of claim to housing and home, a 'pluriform' theoretical strategy might usefully consider how the failure of pluralism in public housing – where the more fundamental property problem of access

---

[126] AJ van der Walt 'Undoing things with words: the colonisation of the public sphere by private-property discourse' 1998 *Acta Juridica* 235–281; Singer *op cit*.

[127] A von Bogdandy, S Häußler, F Hanschmann & R Utz 'State-building, nation-building, and constitutional politics in post-conflict situations: Conceptual clarifications and an appraisal of different approaches' (2005) *Max Planck UNYB* 579 587; also T Donais *Peacebuilding and local ownership: Post-conflict consensus building* (2012); OP Richmond 'Becoming liberal, unbecoming liberalism: Liberal-local hybridity via the everyday as a response to the paradoxes of liberal peacebuilding' (2009) 3 *JISB* 324.

to adequate housing to meet basic needs is at stake – might be remedied by the embedded norms of sharing in land law. The conceptual separation between (private) land law and (public) housing is mirrored in the contrast between Northern Ireland's relatively integrated owner-occupied sector, and the stark segregation of public housing; and in the unequal distribution of the 'peace dividend', with benefits accumulating for property 'insiders' at the expense of the poorest – those living in segregated public housing enclaves, who suffered most during the conflict and have benefitted least from the peace.[128] With growing property inequalities fuelling fresh concerns that the failure of social justice might undermine the prevailing political settlement, land law's embedded, pluralist, sharing norms could usefully influence the normative discourse of the public realm, casting new light on the property norms and values that (alongside appeal to human rights standards) could usefully inform legal and political debates. This is particularly relevant for Northern Ireland in its current political context, where the collapse of popular support for moderate nationalist and unionist parties since the peace agreement has coincided with support for political parties becoming even more polarised on sectarian grounds. As political leaders continue to struggle with power-sharing itself, and to achieve cross-party support for policies that advance inclusion and sharing, the scale of the challenges to law and scholarship require us to reach beyond the conventional realm of 'public' law and its transformational tools (constitutional, administrative and human rights law), to seek out new strategies that draw on other legal stories, of successful hybridisation to achieve local solutions, and resistance to exclusionary or identity-driven ideology in favour of pragmatism and compromise solutions. They place a powerful onus on land lawyers to use the tools and methodologies that progressive property theorists have advanced, and which resonate with embedded land law norms, to support the work of constitutional and human rights scholarship in contributing to the realisation of Northern Ireland's commitment to 'sharing' under the peace agreement.

André van der Walt understood the role of property, and property law, in seeding conflict; and, equally, its powerful potential to contribute to transformation in divided societies. In *Property in the margins*, he recognised that –

> [p]roperty interests, the social and economic distribution of property and the social and political power associated with property, occupied a significant position in

---

[128] C Coulter 'Under which constitutional arrangement would you still prefer to be unemployed? Neoliberalism, the peace process, and the politics of class in Northern Ireland' (2014) 37 *Stud Confl Terror* 763.

> the historical development and the social and political processes leading up to and inhabiting the South African transformation...[129]

André urged property theorists to recognise property's power to shape public processes of constitutionalism and democracy and to understand the importance of the choices we make, when we think, talk, and write about property law. For Northern Ireland, the opportunities of thinking, talking and writing differently about property law – in ways that look beyond its doctrinal and technical rules to tap into its pluralist normative commitments – are brought into sharp relief by the pressures that residual, and growing, property inequality places on the transition project. As Northern Ireland faces afresh the challenges of delivering a sustainable peace settlement with effective and inclusive constitutional democracy built on principles of sharing and political equality, its embedded property norms have the potential to contribute, at least in a modest way, to the discourse of a pluralist, progressive and workable balance between exclusion and inclusion, separation and sharing, segregation and integration. André urged us to 'tear [ourselves] loose from the comfortable and well-worn old legends of [our] intellectual childhood'. Applying the lessons of his legacy opens an intriguing and important opportunity for Northern Ireland's land lawyers to move into the public realm, to seek out new solutions, and to contribute to 'new stories with different morals and unknown endings'.[130]

---

[129] AJ van der Walt *Property in the margins* (2009) 9–10.

[130] AJ van der Walt *Property in the margins* (2009) 418–9.

Chapter 9

The closeness of property

*Wian Erlank**

At the beginning of this chapter, it would perhaps be appropriate to offer a brief apology for the way in which I shall be treating the concept of virtual property in this chapter.[1] While I have been doing research in this field for a number of years, it is still regarded as being of a controversial nature by many authors, for a number of reasons,[2] some of which I shall briefly mention here. The biggest debate regarding virtual property probably comes down to the question whether virtual property should be treated in the same way as tangible property. Many authors consider virtual property to be either an aspect of intellectual property (ie conceptualised in terms of licences and contract) or else to comprise purely frivolous artefacts of the online gaming and entertainment industry that have no real value, and certainly no property rights attached to them. However, these debates fall outside the scope of this chapter and have been exhaustively dealt with in other articles by myself and many other authors. I shall therefore assume in this chapter that virtual property found in virtual worlds is capable of being regarded as real-world property in certain instances. I also accept that even if the vesting of property rights is denied or prohibited by some (but not all) virtual world developers in terms of contract, there are instances where private property rights can be acquired to virtual property without the co-operation of (and in contradiction to) the developers and IP rights-holders of virtual worlds. Furthermore, I wish to note that the purpose of this chapter is one of introspection and consideration of the (tentative) development of a new theoretical framework for understanding how property, both real and virtual, as well as virtual worlds can be explained or better understood in terms of André van der Walt's broad view of the interplay between the public and private aspects of property. The intention is not to deal exhaustively and critically with the various theories touched on in this chapter, but rather to

* Associate Professor of Law, North-West University.

[1] This apology is written mainly in response to the feedback from the anonymous peer-reviewers, whose invaluable input and feedback is much appreciated and will continue to inform future research in this field.

[2] For a relatively comprehensive exposition of these debates and the diverging opinions, see in general W Erlank *Property in virtual worlds* (2012).

set the stage for possible future and more in-depth analyses.[3] Finally, while the term 'virtual property' includes other intangible property interests or assets such as eBooks, digital music files, email accounts, asset-backed securities and cryptocurrencies, the focus in this chapter will be on property as contained within virtual worlds.

Now on to the closeness of property. In 2004, an article written by André van der Walt titled 'The public aspect of private property' was published in the journal *Suid Afrikaanse Privaatreg / South African Private Law*.[4] I was unaware at the time of both the article and André's stature. At that stage I was completing my LLM in international trade law and property was the last thing on my mind. I eventually discovered the article when I started writing my doctorate under André's supervision at the (then) newly created South African Research Chair in Property Law.

André is probably best known and remembered for his work on the theoretical[5] and constitutional[6] aspects of property law. He also had a special concern for those who find themselves on the fringes of property (which he dealt with in his seminal work *Property in the margins*.)[7] This is clearly reflected in his article 'The public aspect of private property',[8] in which he deals with the interplay between private and public property and how this interplay creates tension between private rights to one's own property and the public interest. Hidden in the complexity of this article, André discusses (almost in passing) the differing expectations that one can have regarding the ability to exclude others from one's property, being dependent on how far away the property is located from the inner sanctum of one's home. This struck a special chord with me. I shall therefore discuss the theory that

---

[3] Much of the constructive criticism raised by the peer-reviewers has served as valuable points of departure that I plan to address in a future book about the interplay between the social aspects of property in the real and virtual world worlds.

[4] (2004) 19 *SAPR/PL* 676 707.

[5] Articles concerning property theory to which I return time and again include his three-part series on 'a review of property theories and debates in recent literature'. These are AJ van der Walt 'Unity and pluralism in property theory – a review of property theories and debates in recent literature: part 1' (1995) 1 *TSAR* 15–42, AJ van der Walt 'Subject and society in property theory – a review of property theories and debates in recent literature: part 2' (1995) 2 *TSAR* 322–345, and AJ van der Walt 'Rights and reforms in property theory – a review of property theories and debates in recent literature: part 3' (1995) 3 *TSAR* 493–526.

[6] See, for example, apart from all his articles on the matter, AJ van der Walt *Constitutional property clauses: A comparative analysis* (1999) followed by AJ van der Walt *Constitutional property law* (2005), now in its third edition (2011).

[7] AJ van der Walt *Property in the margins* (2009).

[8] AJ van der Walt 'The public aspect of private property' (2004) 19 *SAPR/PL* 676–723.

André set out in this article as I apply it to my own research on new areas of property such as those contained in the field of virtual property.[9]

André starts his article by discussing a couple of property disputes about water (which are however of general application). He notes the following:

> A final observation that emerges from the cases is that water cases are not only difficult and complex because of the interaction of public and private law and the tension between private rights and the public interest – they always involve policy decisions that reflect deeply contested visions of what is private and what is public in the first place, and therefore the problem I am discussing here is more than finding the right balance between individual and collective (or private and public) interests. My point is that the very distinction between private and public is unstable and contested because the orthodox definition of property itself is unstable and contested, and that historical developments have left us with an impoverished and eroded concept that reduces the public to public control and harmonisation of private individual economic interests.[10]

He then touches on the age-old dispute about whether property is a pre-societal or post-societal construct.[11] After careful deliberation he notes that –

> … property cannot be a pre-constitutional, pre-societal human faculty or power that every individual carries with him into the social compact; it has to be a contingent, temporary, partial arrangement developed in the social context – 'in between regimes' – and therefore open for further amendment as demanded by the context, according to the principles of justice and legality that operate in that specific society at a given moment.

He continues by stating:

> In this view, the public inevitably involves aspects of civic or societal life without which individual life is unthinkable; aspects that transcend both purely individual interests in property and the public interest in the narrow sense of protecting and harmonising individual economic interests. This richer view of the public loses its threatening relationship with private individual interests, because it is not primarily concerned with the restriction, limitation or regulation of private use of property but rather with the custody of those 'intangible and fragile bonds'

---

[9] I also apply this to a certain extent in my research about property in (outer) space, especially when discussing when one should allow the allocation of private property rights to objects in space. However, I will not delve into that aspect in this chapter. For more on this see W Erlank 'Rethinking *terra nullius* and property law in space' 2015 (18) 7 *PELJ* 2503–2523 and W Erlank 'Property rights in space: Moving the goal posts so the players don't notice' *PELJ* (2016) 19 1–31.

[10] AJ van der Walt 'The public aspect of private property' (2004) 19 *SAPL* 676–723 697.

[11] AJ van der Walt 'The public aspect of private property' (2004) 19 *SAPL* 676–723 711.

> that characterise social life in a community with concrete common ends and responsibilities. The protection of the public interest in this wider and richer sense may certainly have dramatic effects on private individual rights, and perhaps the losses caused in the process may have to be compensated in all or in some instances, but that is a different question altogether; not because individual interests are subjected to the public interest but because they are enabled by it and enabling of it, protected by and protective of it, secured by and security for it.[12]

The aspects that were even more fascinating for me stem from his discussion based on Alexander[13] as well as Gray and Gray,[14] dealing with the civic view of property where –

> ... the distinction or relationship between public and private in property should not be seen as a direct conflict or a strict dichotomy but rather as two extremes on a continuum ...

This thought led me down the rabbit hole to one of his previous articles called 'Un-doing things with words: The colonisation of the public sphere by private-property discourse'.[15] In a discussion heavily influenced by Arendt,[16] he notes:

> In Arendt's analysis, it is the exterior appearance of property that is important for the public realm – the interior aspect of property relates to the household and has no public significance because it remains hidden. The exterior appearance of property 'as it appears in the realm of the city through the boundaries between one household and another', that was previously an actual space and that used to be associated with the law itself, is a boundary line, a 'kind of no man's land' between the private and the public, sheltering them from each other (but also binding them to each other?).[17]

This interplay between the private right to exclude and the public interest to prevent exclusion forms the basis of his article and he eloquently argues that

---

[12] AJ van der Walt 'The public aspect of private property' (2004) 19 *SAPL* 676–723 721–722; K Gray & SF Gray 'Private property and public property' in J McLean (ed) *Property and the constitution* (1999) 11–39 39.

[13] GS Alexander *Commodity and propriety: Competing visions of property in American legal thought 1776–1970* (1997) 1–2.

[14] AJ van der Walt 'The public aspect of private property' (2004) 19 *SAPR/PL* 676–723 714; K Gray & SF Gray 'Private property and public property' in J McLean (ed) *Property and the constitution* (1999) 11–39.

[15] AJ van der Walt 'Un-doing things with words: The colonisation of the public sphere by private-property discourse' 1998 *Acta Juridica* 235–281.

[16] H Arendt *The human condition* (1958) 64.

[17] AJ van der Walt 'The public aspect of private property' (2004) 19 *SAPL* 676–723 710 fn 131.

instead of taking something away from one's ownership, the public aspect of private property, in fact, supports, underscores and enriches one's private property. André finally concludes his article by providing a clear example of how this is done. He mentions the example of the Great Court at Trinity College, Cambridge:

> Students used to wash at the Trinity College Fountain in the days before en suite facilities were installed in college rooms. The design of the Fountain made special provision for this purpose: each panel in the octagonal base of the Fountain used to include a water tap and a lead-lined basin. Now, of course, students have access to private bathroom facilities in or near their rooms, making it unnecessary to expose the intimate details of their daily lives to relentless public visibility, allowing them to withdraw into privacy for those aspects of our lives that belong to the 'shadowy interior of the household'.[18]

This continuum mentioned earlier led to my current understanding of the continuum between the absolute right to protect one's privacy and ownership interests by excluding everyone else, and the public interest that society at large may have in one's property. For me, this often comes down to a question about the closeness of one's property. How close is the property in terms of physical proximity as well as human flourishing / personality theory?[19] Van der Walt summarises Radin's concept of human flourishing as follows:

> Margaret Jane Radin makes use of the concept of 'human flourishing' to distinguish between property that is closely related to and important for personhood ('personal property'), and property that is not ('fungible property'), and concludes that the protection of property has to reflect the relative importance and function of the two categories. In view of this approach it is possible to say that personal property– such as a house, which is the ultimate guarantee of a person's personhood and privacy– deserves stricter protection because of its importance for human dignity …
>
> It seems, then, that the strong protection of the exclusivity of at least certain categories of private property, such as the family home, can be justified as being

[18] AJ van der Walt 'The public aspect of private property' (2004) 19 *SAPL* 676–723 722.

[19] See MJ Radin 'Property and personhood' (1982) 34 *Stan L Rev* 957–1015. In his article 'The public aspect of private property' (2004) 19 *SAPL* 676–723 689 Van der Walt only mentions Radin with reference to the fact that '… not all property necessarily needs to be available for private rights, so that certain categories of property can justifiably be removed from the sphere of private rights if the public interest should require that'. In this sense, he refers to certain aspects that are regarded as market inalienability and commodification. See MJ Radin 'Market inalienability' (1987) 100 *Harvard L Rev* 1849; MJ Radin *Contested commodities: The trouble with trade in sex, children, body parts, and other things* (1996); AJ van der Walt 'Un-doing things with words: The colonisation of the public sphere by private-property discourse' 1998 *Acta Juridica* 235–281 246, 247.

> in the interests of human flourishing; and that this goal can be in line with (rather than in conflict with) the general or public interest, especially if the protection of the family home is carried through with sensitivity for the position of socially and economically weak families. Here, the exclusivist language of private-property discourse seems to have a positively progressive effect.

If one were to keep using the analogy of withdrawing into privacy for aspects that belong to the shadowy interior of one's household, it can be explained as follows (and here I rely heavily on conversations between André and myself and his other students during our weekly rigorous property theory seminars). We can use the example of one's home, which is especially applicable to property in virtual worlds where this continuum between inclusion and exclusion is actually coded into the game code.[20] One's home (real or virtual) is situated on a piece of property, where the visual outside is clearly in the public eye and therefore part of the public aspect of one's private property. As one moves into the property, further away from the general public areas of the street and the rest of the public neighbourhood, the ability to exclude others from the private aspects of one's home increases. We are happy for anyone to approach the property and ring the bell, and most people, including strangers such as delivery and utility personnel, will be invited in and allowed inside the gate. Beyond that lies the front door, and we carefully choose a smaller selection of people who are invited beyond that into the reception areas of the home; we avert the public gazing eye by means of blinds or curtains. Moving further into the home, the innate ability and wish to exclude others from the most private areas of our homes and property increase, with an even smaller select few invited into the daily living areas such as the kitchen and guest rooms. Finally, we reach the inner sanctum of the home, being one's bedroom, where we are at our most vulnerable and need to feel safe and comfortable, precisely because we can (and do) exclude almost everyone. Perhaps the only more private area will be the en-suite bathroom where one performs ablutions. This shows that as one approaches the most personal areas of property, one's need and ability and right to exclude others can and should be aggressively protected. But as we move away from this, we must (in order to participate in society) increasingly relinquish this reliance on exclusion and in fact include more and more of the public and the public interest into and onto our property. Others may read and understand André's article slightly differently, and take away other aspects that are more important to them. But this article informed my

[20] I will deal with this aspect in more detail later in the chapter.

understanding of the closeness of property, and I am glad that I am able to return to it from time to time.

In my own research, I have found analogies in virtual property when I was investigating how property systems function inside virtual worlds. Of interest was the fact that even though developers can conceivably create any new property system that humans can devise, by means of using computer code to create nearly immutable laws in the virtual worlds, invariably they fall back on familiar and instantly recognisable property systems similar to their products' real-world counterparts. What is of further interest is that because of the way in which these property laws are coded into the virtual worlds, it is necessary to deconstruct their base components systematically (albeit arguably unconsciously) to be able to reconstruct them via a systematic coded system. This illustrates what we have seen above in the example defining the level of protection (or exclusion, if you will) of property, depending on how closely it approaches one's person and centre of privacy.

We now move from the real to the virtual. In a virtual world, there is no meaningful distinction between software and law.[21] What the software does not allow is impossible in (virtual) law as well. This leads to an area of law in virtual worlds where 'there is no room for mediation because any "legal" mediation embodied in the software immediately becomes part of the "natural" world'.[22] This means that a player's property rights can be guaranteed inviolably by the programming. As the 'owner' of a virtual sword, an avatar is guaranteed that the rights that he or she has in the sword will be protected and enforced against any other player by means of the game-code.[23] While the player 'owns' the sword, no other player can interfere with this player's right, or even make use of it. This is generally true, but as in real life, property rights are not totally absolute or exclusive in a virtual world. A player's property rights will be guaranteed only insofar as the software makes allowance for it.[24] For example, a feature of the virtual world of *Ultima Online* is that players are enabled, by the software and game-design, to steal

[21] This is not a universally accepted view, but from the perspective of a player participating in a virtual world, this tends to be true. Of course, as in real world law, there are always exceptions and in this case, it would be the ability to 'hack' the virtual world to circumvent coded rules or laws.

[22] JTL Grimmelmann 'Virtual worlds as comparative law' (2004) 49 *NYL Sch L Rev* 147–184 150; L Lessig 'The law of the horse: What cyberlaw might teach' (1999) 113 *Harv LR* 501–549 522, 531. See in general L Lessig *Code and other laws of cyberspace* (1999).

[23] JTL Grimmelmann 'Virtual worlds as comparative law' (2004) 49 *NYL Sch L Rev* 147–184 150.

[24] This is if the virtual law is derived from the computer code. Players may also create legal norms among themselves that are not designed or enforced by the code-based legal norms.

from one another.[25] In other virtual worlds, the software can render theft physically impossible. Obviously, the programming choice inherent in this difference has significant implications for the protection of property. This aspect of the virtual world legal system starts taking shape before any code is typed to create the virtual world. The rules are created by the game's designers when they plan the basic functions and operation of the virtual world. One example would be when a designer has to make a decision about what happens when a player picks up an item (and also when he or she drops the item).[26] From the designer's viewpoint there are just two options. Either the item becomes part of the things that the avatar carries around on a permanent basis (ie the avatar has permanent possession of the item), or else the avatar only has control over the item as long as he or she carries it around. This duality of choice is then coded into the game and leaves the player with no other options besides the two that the developer envisioned, as set out above.

A more complex example of the creation of such a rule would be when the designers think about how to create and implement a way for players to store items that they have gathered.[27] Essentially, this entails a method of not only acquiring property by means of physical possession, but now allowing ownership of property separate from real-time physical possession. The designer could decide to allow players to have a house and to use it to store items that they have bought or acquired in the game inside the house. In such a case, there have to be practical policies about how this function of the house is going to work. Will an item that is put down by the player inside the house stay inside the house (ie have permanence) or will it disappear? Who will be allowed inside the house? Will only the player be allowed to access the inside of the house, which in effect will safeguard the player's belongings, or will other people have access to the house? If so, what happens when someone else comes into the house? Can the player who uses the house for storage keep other people out? Can such a player prevent people who do in fact come in from taking items that the player has put down in the house? What happens if someone who comes to visit drops

---

[25] JTL Grimmelmann 'Virtual worlds as comparative law' (2004) 49 *NYL Sch L Rev* 147–184 150 fn 11; Lastowka FG & Hunter D 'Virtual crimes' (2004) 49 *NYL Sch L Rev* 293–316 309. Certain virtual worlds even include the class of 'thief' as one of the types of avatar that a player can choose to create.

[26] See the discussion on the acquisition of virtual property in W Erlank 'Acquisition of ownership inside virtual worlds' (2013) 3 *De Jure* 770–782 775.

[27] JTL Grimmelmann 'Virtual worlds as comparative law' (2004) 49 *NYL Sch L Rev* 147–184 150-154.

one of his or her (the visitor's) own items? Does it become the property of the house-owner, or does it stay the property of the original player?

To address these practical issues, the designer makes policy decisions about how the game will handle the problem. As soon as the policies are implemented in the game by programming them into the code, the rules of virtual law are created.[28] Because this is part of the game-code there is usually no way for a player to circumvent these policies. If the code determines that one can only enter one's own house in the game, there is absolutely no way of entering the house of another person and, by inference, it is impossible to steal someone else's items out of their house. Unfortunately, even in the virtual world there is always an exception. The exception here would be that the code could be illegally modified, misused or abused to get access to something that was not intended by the programmers. In essence, the only way to break the laws that are coded into the game is to 'hack' the system.[29] This distinguishes these laws from the laws of nature, which can never be altered, and thus brings them closer to laws in the real world, which can be broken.[30]

The beauty of code as rules is that, even though these design issues and questions tend to lead to ever-increasing complexity, they do not suffer from the cognitive problems associated with the enforcement of such a complex rule-set in the real-life environment. In the real world, an increasingly

---

[28] P Edelmann 'Framing virtual law' 2005 *Proceedings of DiGRA 2005 conference: Changing views – worlds in play* at http://www.digra.org:8080/Plone/dl/db/06278.45351.pdf 1–10 5.

[29] For more information about the different hacking methods see Chun Feng 'Playing with shadows – exposing the black market for online game password theft' 2008 *18th Virus Bulletin Conference;* FG Lastowka & D Hunter 'Virtual crimes' (2004) 49 *NYL Sch L Rev* 293–316 298, 313. This is such an important issue that developers tend to address it in the end user licence agreement (EULA).

[30] Although this is an example of where code as law is similar to real-world law, the analogy is not totally accurate. When a player 'hacks' the code-level law to change one of the unchangeable laws of the game, it is closer to performing real magic in the real world than to just breaking the law. An example is the act of levitation in the real world. The law of gravity determines that a person cannot levitate on earth, but if a magician were to break this unbreakable rule of nature and use magic to levitate himself, he would not merely be making a choice to break a law, but in fact doing the impossible. The same can be said of a player who changes the code-based rules by hacking the system. See in general Ung-cho Yoon U 'South Korea and indirect reliance on IP law: Real money trading in MMORPG items' (2008) 3 *JIPLP* 174–179; FG Lastowka & D Hunter 'Virtual crime' 2004 *SSRN* at http://ssrn.com/abstract=564801; FG Lastowka & D Hunter 'Virtual crimes' (2004) 49 *NYL Sch L Rev* 293–316 298, 313.

complex set of questions creates an increased discretion of enforcement;[31] in the virtual code-based world it stays simple. No matter how complex the rule-set becomes, the outcome is not open to discretion and will always be decided according to a binary and objective test by the computer. Software does not have the discretion of a judge and therefore every software decision embedded in code is always predetermined.[32]

Returning now to some issues already touched upon above, it would perhaps be illuminating to look at the problem of what happens with virtual possessions from the perspective of the differences between ownership and possession. The concept of 'ownership' is a problematic one inside virtual worlds and it is often easier (and probably more correct) to describe players' property rights towards the things that they 'own' in virtual worlds as possessory.[33] The reason for this is that the right of ownership is normally inferred from the fact of possession. Because a player is not enabled by the game's code to possess an item 'belonging' to another player, the mere fact of possession often equates to ownership inside the virtual world.[34] In many virtual worlds, property rights attach to a possessor of an object for as long as

[31] JTL Grimmelmann 'Virtual worlds as comparative law' (2004) 49 *NYL Sch L Rev* 147–184 153; P Edelmann 'Framing virtual law' 2005 *Proceedings of DiGRA 2005 Conference: Changing views – worlds in play* at http://www.digra.org:8080/Plone/dl/db/06278.45351.pdf 1–10 5. See in general Lessig *Code and other laws of cyberspace* (1999).

[32] JTL Grimmelmann 'Virtual worlds as comparative law' (2004) 49 *NYL Sch L Rev* 147–184 at 150–154; P Edelmann 'Framing virtual law' 2005 *Proceedings of DiGRA 2005 Conference: Changing views – worlds in play* at http://www.digra.org:8080/Plone/dl/db/06278.45351.pdf 1–10 5–6. While this generally holds true, with the advance of artificial intelligence (AI) and systems utilising autonomous user agents, it is becoming more and more common that software decisions are in fact not pre-determined. This, however, falls outside the scope of this discussion.

[33] JTL Grimmelmann 'Virtual worlds as comparative law' (2004) 49 *NYL Sch L Rev* 147–184 151.

[34] This is a basic rule of thumb and certain virtual worlds do in fact allow some form of leasing or lending which means that they distinguish between ownership and some holders (or in wider terms, possessors), therefore not always equating possession with ownership. However, one should remember that this rule of possession being equal to ownership is the *de facto* code-based rule with which a virtual world will be programmed. It also forms the foundation of the property systems in virtual worlds that do make a distinction. One should bear in mind that insofar as the system is regulated by the game-code, the distinction between ownership and lease is just a more nuanced implementation of the game-code.

the item is carried around by the avatar.[35] As soon as the avatar drops[36] the object, it constitutes abandonment and the item immediately becomes *res derelicta*.[37] The next person to pick up the item will become the new owner.[38] The example mentioned here is a very simplistic use of the ownership concept in a virtual world and many worlds are far more sophisticated in their approach to the ownership concept as well as in the implementation of it via code. This is due to the pressure on developers to implement more detailed code-based property rules and not only a simple 'possession-is-all' rule.[39]

Returning now to the central tenet of this chapter, the closeness of property, an example of a more complex code-based property system is the one of virtual homeownership.[40] The default rule in virtual worlds is that all players have access to all areas at all times. The next more developed rule is to allow only the owner of a house into her virtual home, which is counterintuitive if a home-owner wishes to invite guests over without giving them access to roam freely around the premises. Since many of the virtual worlds have socialisation at the centre of their existence, the ability to invite others into your personal space and have them interact with you and your possessions is of paramount importance. To solve this dilemma, developers have created

---

[35] This is often referred to as 'equipping' an item. See: Sony 'EverQuest II Manual' *EverQuest II* at http://everquest2.com/manual /EQII_Manual.pdf 1-71 16.

[36] Or 'unequips' the item. In certain instances, an object is 'bound' to the user and can never be transferred to another player; the act of abandonment or 'dropping' results in the item's demise and removal from the virtual world.

[37] One should bear in mind that the fact that a legal system (real or virtual) acknowledges abandonment does not mean that it equates ownership with possession. All legal systems will in some cases equate possession with ownership by means of original acquisition of ownership, while making a distinction for other instances where ownership and possession is split by for example leasing, lending, pawning, and even servitudes. If virtual worlds recognise such instances they are similar to real worlds. However, this is the basic rule that will be coded into a virtual world on which developers can build and create more nuanced systems of complexity to mimic the real world.

[38] JTL Grimmelmann 'Virtual worlds as comparative law' (2004) 49 *NYL Sch L Rev* 147–184 151. For example, Ultima Online's Playguide describes the procedure and consequences of dropping items as follows: 'You can remove items from your inventory and drop them almost anywhere on the screen near your character. If, for some reason, the item can't be dropped in the location you've selected, either an error noise will sound or the item will return to your inventory. A dropped item will stay where it is until it deteriorates naturally or someone picks it up. Dropped items don't tend to stay around for long.' Mythic 'Ultima Online Playguide: Environment Manipulation' (2010) *UO Herald*.

[39] JTL Grimmelmann 'Virtual worlds as comparative law' (2004) 49 *NYL Sch L Rev* 147–184 151.

[40] See also JTL Grimmelmann 'Virtual worlds as comparative law' (2004) 49 *NYL Sch L Rev* 147–184 151.

a nuanced system of levels of exclusionary capacity that they build into the code-based property system. Grimmelmann refers to this (making use of English property law terminology) as a 'virtual fee simple' with a new estate carved out called the 'right to visit'.[41] This so-called 'right to visit' is a perpetual, non-transferable right and is subject to revocation by the owner of the house at any stage, making it a typical precarious right. When applied to civil law, it could be described as a 'virtual ownership right' with a new entitlement (or stick in the bundle of ownership that is carved out for eligible visitors) called the 'right to visit'.[42]

This right to visit has a measurable effect on the ability of both owner and visitor to interact with their own property as well as the property of others. In the example above about ownership being lost by the dropping of an item, the rules of the acquisition of the object in question were clear. However, if one were to integrate that example into the context of a virtual home in a virtual world, a number of problems would arise. One such problem (and a main reason why any player would wish to own a home – virtual or real) would be to have a secure environment where they could store their collected movable virtual items without losing their property rights in it.[43] Apart from this need to store movables, homeowners would also like to have guests over for functions and other social visits. However, what would the consequences be of inviting visitors to a player's house? Would an item dropped by a guest become the property of the homeowner, or would any guest that picks up or uses an item in the house become the new owner of that item? It is clear that in this case the general rule of possession equating to virtual ownership is not satisfactory. In order to solve this problem, the nuanced system of exclusion mentioned above incorporates a number of new options. A homeowner can choose between certain categories of access that he or she wishes to assign to a visitor. Depending on the category that a homeowner assigns to a visitor,

---

[41] JTL Grimmelmann 'Virtual worlds as comparative law' (2004) 49 *NYL Sch L Rev* 147–184 152.

[42] This will only happen in a virtual world since the level of control that is given by the game-code will mean that a licence is worth a lot more than in the real world. In the real world, it is questionable whether a precarious right like this amounts to carving out a stick, since in English law this will probably be a called a revocable licence. However, as applied to the content of virtual worlds this makes for a good analogy.

[43] Even if items are not taken by other players, they are subject to 'decay' as is explained in the Ultima Online Playguide. 'In Ultima Online, items that are placed on the ground (ie not locked down or secured in a house, or placed in your bank box) can decay. This means that after a period of time, the item will disappear from the game. There's no way to retrieve items that have decayed. To keep your items safe from decaying, you need to either lock them down or place them in a secure container in a house that you own, co-own, or are a friend of, or store them away in your bank box.'

that visitor will not only be able to access certain areas of the home, but the visitor's interaction with the items in the home will also be defined. For example, one visitor might have access to enter the house, but not to pick anything up. Another visitor might just have permission to pick items up in the house but not to remove the items, while yet another visitor might be given circumscribed permission to carry off any item in the home.[44]

This sophisticated example does not equate possession with ownership and begins to distinguish between ownership, possession and limited rights of control that could resemble limited real rights or personal rights. In other words, as soon as some complexity is built into the system, the rudimentary virtual world feature of possession equating to ownership falls away, and makes way for a more wholesome level of interaction between participants in the virtual world. It also illustrates the idea discussed by Van der Walt above that the public and the private aspects of property by necessity influence each other. The ability to exclude others from one's virtual home holds no meaning if there are no others, and it adds value when one is able to share the private things, possessions and areas of one's home with others, on one's own terms. It is also clearly illustrated that, as in the real world, the need to exclude and the usefulness of excluding others from one's property diminish not only the further one moves away from the inner sanctum of the home, but also depending on how closely one is related to or trusts a visitor.

While this example illustrates the closeness of property in terms of physical proximity to an absolute centre of protectable excludability, an analogy can also be found in the virtual world in relation to sentimental closeness. However, before I get to that, it is essential that we take another quick look at Radin's personality theory.

Hegel,[45] who is regarded as the father of personality theory,[46] had the view that property should be seen as an extension of one's personality.[47] The essence of his theory, and those based upon it, is that 'property rights are related – either as necessary conditions for, or as connected to – human rights such as liberty, identity and privacy'.[48] Alternatively, personality theory is described by Radin[49] as the idea that property rights are linked to

[44] The level of complexity with regard to rules of access can become extremely high.
[45] GWF Hegel *Hegel's philosophy of right* (1896, Knox TM translation 1967).
[46] MJ Radin 'Property and personhood' (1982) 34 *Stan L Rev* 957–1015 958.
[47] FG Lastowka & D Hunter 'The laws of the virtual worlds' (2004) 92 *Cal L Rev* 1–74 48.
[48] FG Lastowka & D Hunter 'The laws of the virtual worlds' (2004) 92 *Cal L Rev* 1–74 48.
[49] MJ Radin 'Property and personhood' (1982) 34 *Stan L Rev* 957–1015.

personhood and identity.[50] As such, property rights are justified when objects are inseparably bound up with the personality and liberty of their owner.[51]

Boone[52] wrote an article on the application of the personhood theory to virtual property that focuses on the value of Radin's normative argument for the justification of property rights for virtual property. Radin's theory can be summarised as follows.[53] Property or property relations can be either personal or fungible. The first, personal property, are things that have become bound up with the individual. Radin describes these as 'objects that are closely bound up with personhood because they are part of the way we constitute ourselves as continuing personal entities in the world.'[54] If a person were to lose such personal property it would be a much worse loss than its correlative monetary value would indicate.[55] The classic example of this will be recognition of the fact that due to the subjective sentimental value of something for a specific person, there should be a property interest in that thing.[56] Examples of these are things like wedding rings, homes and

---

[50] For purposes of this chapter the terms 'personality theory' and 'personhood theory' are used interchangeably. Radin prefers to use the term 'personhood' in her seminal article 'Property and personhood'. See Boone MS 'Virtual property and personhood' (2008) 24 *Santa Clara Computer & High Tech LJ* 715–747 721 fn 24.

[51] MJ Radin 'Property and personhood' (1982) 34 *Stan L Rev* 957–1015 957; TJ Westbrook 'Owned: Finding a place for virtual world property rights' (2006) 3 *Mich St L Rev* 779–812 798.

[52] MS Boone 'Virtual property and personhood' (2008) 24 *Santa Clara Computer & High Tech LJ* 715–747. Boone analyses the connection between virtual property and personhood extensively and relies mainly on Radin's personhood theory for his arguments. For the purposes of this chapter it is sufficient to rely mainly on Radin's initial work, MJ Radin 'Property and personhood' (1982) 34 *Stan L Rev* 957–1015. However, Boone analyses Radin's development of the theory by also integrating her later works, including her book *Reinterpreting property* (1993) and her article 'Market inalienability' (1987) 100 *Harv L Rev* 1849–1937. Also see, in general, MJ Radin 'Lacking a transformative social theory: A response' (1993) 45 *Stan L Rev* 409–424; MJ Radin 'The Colin Ruagh Thomas O'Fallon memorial lecture on reconsidering personhood' (1995) 74 *Or L Rev* 423–448 and MJ Radin *Contested commodities: The trouble with trade in sex, children, body parts, and other things* (1996).

[53] MS Boone 'Virtual property and personhood' (2008) 24 *Santa Clara Computer & High Tech LJ* 7 15–747 723.

[54] MJ Radin 'Property and personhood' (1982) 34 *Stan L Rev* 957–1015 959.

[55] Boone MS 'Virtual Property and Personhood' (2008) 24 *Santa Clara Computer & High Tech LJ* 715-747 723.

[56] MJ Radin 'Property and personhood' (1982) 34 *Stan L Rev* 957–1015 959–960; see also MS Boone 'Virtual property and personhood' (2008) 24 *Santa Clara Computer & High Tech LJ* 715–747 723.

body parts (now also virtual wedding rings and virtual homes).[57] Even in the absence of any other normative justifications for the existence of property rights in such items, personality theory determines that such property rights should be recognised in order to fulfil the need for self-realisation and other human needs.[58]

Fungible property is the second type. If something is not regarded as 'personal property', according to Radin it would be classified as 'fungible property'. Fungible property could be defined as 'property that is perfectly replaceable'.[59] This is the theoretical opposite of 'personal property'.[60] Radin states that '[t]he opposite of holding an object that has become part of oneself is holding an object that is perfectly replaceable with other goods of equal market value'.[61] The prime example of such fungible property would be money. Other examples are items that are held purely instrumentally, such as a wedding ring held by a jeweller (for the purposes of resale), an automobile held by a motor dealer and an apartment in the hands of a landlord, held for the sole purpose of letting.[62] Even though Radin categorises property as being either one of the two types of property mentioned above, the classification should be seen as a continuum between the two rather than a dichotomy.[63] Since a wedding ring can be either personal or fungible property, it is clear that the nature of the property is not determined by some type of characteristic, but rather by an individual's relationship with the thing.[64] The test for determining whether it is fungible or personal will be connected to the question of 'whether the thing and the rights in it have become bound up

[57] See especially MJ Radin 'Market inalienability' (1987) 100 *Harv L Rev* 1849–1937 1855–1859, in which she discusses the contested issues relating to the commodification of objects such as infants, children, human organs etc.

[58] FG Lastowka & D Hunter 'The laws of the virtual worlds' (2004) 92 *CLR* 1–74 48.

[59] MS Boone 'Virtual property and personhood' (2008) 24 *Santa Clara Computer & High Tech LJ* 715–747 723.

[60] MJ Radin 'Property and personhood' (1982) 34 *Stan L Rev* 957–1015 960.

[61] MJ Radin 'Property and personhood' (1982) 34 *Stan L Rev* 957–1015 959-960.

[62] MJ Radin 'Property and personhood' (1982) 34 *Stan L Rev* 957–1015 960.

[63] MJ Radin 'The Colin Ruagh Thomas O'Fallon Memorial Lecture on reconsidering personhood' (1995) 74 *Or L Rev* 423–448 427; MJ Radin *Reinterpreting property* (1993) 3. See also MS Boone 'Virtual property and personhood' (2008) 24 *Santa Clara Computer & High Tech LJ* 715–747 723.

[64] MS Boone 'Virtual property and personhood' (2008) 24 *Santa Clara Computer & High Tech LJ* 715–747 725.

with the individual.'[65] Or, in terms of the classical subject/object relationships, 'property becomes personal when it becomes more subject and less object, which is other to or outside of the self/subject.'[66] In essence, if this happens, property is said to contribute to the self-constitution[67] of an individual.[68]

How then does this theory affect property on a practical level? The personhood theory has two effects on property rights.[69] Firstly, it appears that personal property is given preferential treatment over fungible property. If something is classified as 'personal' property, that personal property interest should be protected to the detriment of a fungible property interest held by another person. Secondly, an object that has been classified as 'personal' rather than fungible could be regarded in certain instances as being 'market inalienable' and should be maintained in a non-commodified state.[70] The example given to illustrate these two effects concerns a tenant's property right, which can be considered 'personal' and is maintained in preference to the landlord's fungible property interest in the same object.

This continuum between personal and fungible once again brings up the visual imagery of the closeness of property. Apart from the other methods of determining whether something is personal or fungible, one can once again ask how closely something is tied to the personality or flourishing of an individual. How sentimental and closely personal an object is for and to an individual will define the allocation of competing property rights between

---

[65] MS Boone 'Virtual property and personhood' (2008) 24 *Santa Clara Computer & High Tech LJ* 715–747 724. Radin states that '[o]ne may gauge the strength or the significance of someone's relationship with an object by the kind of pain that would be occasioned by its loss. On this view, an object is closely related to one's personhood if its loss causes pain that cannot be relieved by the object's replacement. If so, that particular object is bound up with the holder. For instance, if a wedding ring is stolen from a jeweller, insurance proceeds can reimburse the jeweller, but if a wedding ring is stolen from a loving wearer, the price of the replacement will not restore the status quo – perhaps no amount of money can do so': MJ Radin 'Property and personhood' (1982) 34 *Stan L Rev* 957–1015 959.

[66] MS Boone 'Virtual property and personhood' (2008) 24 *Santa Clara Computer & High Tech LJ* 715–747 724.

[67] 'Constitutive' or 'self-constitution' can be used interchangeably with 'personal' in terms of Radin's theory. Radin notes in the introduction to *Reinterpreting property,* which she wrote after her initial 'Property and personhood' article, that she maybe should rather have referred to 'personal property' as 'constitutive', since 'personal property' already means something else: MJ Radin *Reinterpreting property* (1993) 2.

[68] MJ Radin 'The Colin Ruagh Thomas O'Fallon Memorial Lecture on reconsidering personhood' (1995) 74 *Or L Rev* 423–448 426.

[69] MS Boone 'Virtual property and personhood' (2008) 24 *Santa Clara Computer & High Tech LJ* 715–747 729.

[70] MS Boone 'Virtual property and personhood' (2008) 24 *Santa Clara Computer & High Tech LJ* 715–747 730.

two parties. When applied to the topic of this chapter, it can be argued that the more closely the property is bound up with the individual's flourishing, the more strongly we will protect the individual's property right in that object to the detriment of others. Or, to put it differently, the closer the object is in terms of importance/flourishing/privacy for the individual, the more we will accept and encourage the exclusion of others from the property in question.

This brings us full circle back to André's influence in making me think of the duality, or rather the continuum, between public and private property. It is clear that the two influence each other, and in fact each is a necessary and beneficial requirement for the existence of the other. Whether one wishes to determine how much one can protect one's property by excluding others depending on how closely the property is located either in distance to the inner sanctum of one's home or the inner sanctum of one's own flourishing, it remains clear that the closeness of property is an important factor to take into consideration when thinking about the private/public property continuum. It remains one that I will continue to heavily rely upon in my future academic works.

Chapter 10

Squatting in the Low Countries: On the conflict between ownership and housing

Vincent Sagaert and Koen Swinnen***

1 Introduction

1.1 Ownership as the right to exclude

Property law aims at exclusivity. That is even more valid for ownership than for the other property rights, as it is the most complete and comprehensive property right. The exclusive nature of ownership (and property rights in general) is mainly rooted in the French Revolutionist idea that the exclusivity of ownership would prevent a division of ownership between *dominium utile* and *dominium directum*, which division underlays the feudal regime. The topic of exclusivity is one of the many topics in which the multidimensional nature of André van der Walt's research career is demonstrated. In the early years of his career he conducted extensive historical research into the *duplex dominium*, showing that this was not an invention of the Napoleonic draftsmen, as its foundations can be traced back to Roman law.[1] André continued to analyse this and other principles on a more constitutional level, with a focus on law as an instrument for society and societal developments.

* Full Professor private law University of Leuven, Director Institute for Property Law.

** Assistant Professor private law Erasmus University Rotterdam, Senior Researcher Institute for Property Law.

[1] AJ van der Walt & DG Kleyn '*Duplex dominium*: The history and significance of the concept of divided ownership' in DP Visser (ed) *Essays on the history of law* (1989) 213 et seq.

This multidimensional in-depth scientific expertise in all aspects of property law, history of law, constitutional law, insolvency law and private law marks André van der Walt as a unique legal scholar. Moreover, André has set new standards for property law scholars in both South Africa and Europe, was a source of inspiration for dozens of young researchers and was at the core of an international property law network, facilitated by his loyalty and warm hospitality. It is beyond doubt that his legacy will last for decades to come.

Recent research, again inspired by the work of André van der Walt, rightly points out that the exclusivity principle has several dimensions.[2] The positive dimension of exclusivity covers the impossibility of dividing the ownership power between several persons without re-characterising the ownership right. The negative dimension of the exclusivity principle covers the right to exclude from the parcel third parties to whom the owner has not granted a property right or any other benefit.

This negative dimension of exclusivity has come under attack, because it gives rise to the '*tragedy of the anti-commons*': in excluding others, society can merely benefit from the economic value of a parcel through the single owner, which often results in a suboptimal use of the parcel. This 'right to exclude' is, from a legal-economic point of view, harmful to society. If, for instance, somebody does not use a building she owns, it could be better for society if a third party, who is homeless, were allowed to use it.

This contribution aims at analysing the right to exclude from the angle of the right to respect for one's home, with particular focus on the national legal systems of the authors, Belgian law and Dutch law. Can a Belgian or Dutch owner under all circumstances exclude everybody from using her property? It will emerge from the analysis that although the protection of ownership occupies a central place in both legal systems, over the years the Belgian law of squatting and the Dutch law of squatting have developed along quite different lines.

1.2 Right to ownership versus housing rights

In excluding third parties, one's ownership rights can come into conflict with other fundamental rights. For instance, the negative dimension of exclusivity comes into play when ownership comes into conflict with housing rights.[3]

[2] D Gruyaert *De exclusiviteit van het eigendomsrecht* (2016) 27–32.

[3] For a general overview: JM Milo 'The margin of appreciation doctrine of the European Court of Human Rights: Protection of ownership and the right to a home' in E Reid & D Visser (eds) *Private law and human rights: Bringing rights home in Scotland and South Africa* (2013) 482–496.

Both the protection of ownership and the right to housing (article 23, 3° Belgian Constitution, article 22, section 2 Dutch Constitution) are sealed in the Belgian constitution and the Dutch (and South-African)[4] constitution respectively. Moreover, the right to ownership is protected under article 1 of the First Additional Protocol to the European Convention on Human Rights (ECHR), while the right to respect for one's home – which should not be confused with the right to housing – is laid down in article 8 of the ECHR. According to case law of the European Court for Human Rights, the latter is a question of fact and does not depend on the lawfulness of the occupation under domestic law.[5] Therefore, a squatter himself can argue on the basis of his right to respect for his home. In the same case law, the court has held that –

> the loss of one's home is a most extreme form of interference with the right to respect for the home. Any person at risk of an interference of this magnitude should in principle be able to have the proportionality of the measure determined by an independent tribunal in the light of the relevant principles under Article 8 of the Convention, notwithstanding that, under domestic law, his right of occupation has come to an end.

Squatting cases form the domain par excellence where the right to ownership on the one hand and the right to respect for one's home as well as the right to housing can come into conflict with each other. Squatters are people who use an unoccupied building without the owner's consent or any other legal title. By doing so, squatters violate the owner's rights by occupying the building without any right or title, on the basis of which the owner's right to exclude is triggered. Squatters can have many motives underlying their actions: they can act because they have no alternative housing, they aim to make a principled statement on housing policy, they want to have a '*safe house*' for criminal activities, etc. However, in a conflict with owners, squatters frequently argue on the basis of their right to housing and/or their right to respect for their home in order to justify the occupation of a building which is not in use anyway.

The approach to this conflict differs from legal system to legal system. In some developing countries, it is clear that case law makes a balance between the housing rights and the ownership rights. That is also the case in the Netherlands, where the right of ownership and the right to respect for one's home are balanced against each other, as will be elaborated on below. André

[4] See ss 25–26 of the South-African Constitution, 1996.

[5] ECHR 13 May 2008, no 19009/04 (McCann / United Kingdom) http://www.echr.coe.int §46.

van der Walt has extensively analysed this weighing of property against housing in South African law.[6] In most western European countries, the law tends to protect ownership in a rather absolute manner, although also in these countries some developments are under way. The recent refugee crisis has put the constitutional right to housing in the picture of both legal and political debate again and has also raised major housing issues in so-called developed countries.

2 The position of squatters in Belgian law

2.1 *The traditional Belgian legal perspective on squatting*

Belgian constitutional law protects ownership in article 16 of the Belgian Constitution:

> No one can be deprived of his property except in the case of expropriation for a public purpose, in the cases and manner established by the law and in return for fair compensation paid beforehand.

This provision is to be complemented by article 544 of the Belgian Civil Code, which provides the definition of ownership:

> Ownership is the right to enjoy an asset or dispose of an asset in the most comprehensive manner, to the extent that the asset is not used in a manner contradicting laws and regulations.[7]

Apart from the right of ownership, the Belgian Constitution and the ECHR also protect the inviolability of the home.[8] This right to respect for one's home is not only awarded to the owner of a house, but to all its occupiers. In this sense, a squatter could even protect his privacy on this basis, but not in relation to the lawful possessor of that house.[9]

The right to housing is protected in article 23 of the Belgian constitution:

> Everyone has the right to have a life in respect with human dignity. To this end, the laws, regional decrees and rules referred to in Article 134 guarantee economic, social and cultural rights, taking into account corresponding obligations, and determine the conditions for exercising them. These rights include among others: (…)3° the right to decent housing.

---

[6] AJ van der Walt 'Exclusivity of ownership, security of tenure, and eviction orders: A model to evaluate South African land-reform legislation' 2002 *TSAR* 254–289.

[7] This provision is still identical in the French Civil Code.

[8] Article 15 of the Belgian Constitution; art 8 of the ECHR; art 17 of the International Covenant on Civil and Political Rights.

[9] T Vandromme 'Het kraken van panden bekeken vanuit de grondrechten, het strafrecht en het burgerlijk recht (inclusief het procesrecht)' 2014–15 *RW* 1363–1378 1366.

The right to housing is formulated in terms of an obligation imposed upon public authorities and does – according to its literal interpretation – not grant any direct enforceability against private persons.[10] This limitation clearly corresponds to the intention of the Belgian constitutional legislature when introducing this provision.[11]

The Belgian constitutional legislature does not specify or moderate this constitutional right. The further specification of the right to housing in Belgian law is complicated, as the housing policy has been transferred to the regional entities in the federal Belgian state. So, different rules (can) exist between the Flemish Region, Brussels Region and Walloon Region. The regional entities have a wide range of autonomy in establishing a housing policy, in order to achieve an effective right to housing. This does not only involve the property policy to build social houses, create social rents, etc, but also encompasses tax autonomy (for instance taxes on empty buildings) and (recently) own competence to develop the rules on leases of houses used as main residence.

The right to decent housing is traditionally considered to be an obligation, imposed on the competent authorities, to conduct a policy aimed at improving housing issues. However, recent scholars tend to reinforce the effect of the right to housing by implementing it as an obligation to achieve the result, which would be enforceable against public authorities.[12]

Traditionally, Belgian law takes a very strict viewpoint in the conflict between ownership and housing rights. Squatters are considered to violate ownership rights, and can therefore be evicted. Squatters act extra-judicially and try to award a right to themselves. Such behaviour should, according to the case law, not be rewarded. Squatters can generally not justify an occupation on the ground of the right to housing, as the latter right is not directly enforceable against private owners. Therefore, the right of ownership

---

[10] Court of Appeal Liège 9 January 2015, 2015 *Jurisprudence de Liège, Mons et Bruxelles* 1076; Court of Appeal Brussels 29 January 2001, 2001 *JT* 576. Cf T Vandromme 'Het kraken van panden bekeken vanuit de grondrechten, het strafrecht en het burgerlijk recht (inclusief het procesrecht)' 2014–15 *RW* 1365. Cf Belgian Council of State 24 March 2005 No 142.620. For a national analysis of the right to housing, we would like to refer to N Bernard 'Le droit au logement' in B Kohl (ed) *Actualité en droit du bail* (2014) 349–366; T Vandromme 'Het recht op wonen: een stand van zaken' in B Hubeau & T Vandromme (ed) *Vijftien jaar Vlaamse Wooncode. Sisyphus (on)gelukkig?* (2013) 15–40.

[11] *Parliamentary Works* Senate 1991–92, n° 100–2/4 5 (www.senate.be).

[12] Compare N Bernard & B Hubeau (ed) *Recht op wonen: naar een resultaatsverbintenis?* (2013).

is traditionally thought to prevail over the right to housing.[13] The lack of horizontal effect of the constitutional right to adequate housing underlies this traditional position.[14] The squatters do not have to be relocated by the public authorities before being able to evict them.[15] The fact that a squatter maintains the real estate and does not cause any nuisance does not change anything in the position of most case law.[16] The most favourable case law traditionally only awards a period of a couple of days or – at most – weeks to leave the occupied building and make it empty.[17] The mere fact that the owner of a house does not make effective use of this house does not in itself constitute an abuse of his ownership rights.[18]

Squatters have also tried to use other arguments in order to give weight to their claim. For instance, in a case with regard to university buildings, the squatters argued that the occupation was necessary in order to exercise their right to cultural development. The judge dismissed the squatters from their position: an eviction order was awarded in favour of the university in order to terminate the occupation.[19]

From a procedural point of view, the owner must submit a plea to evict the squatters before courts and tribunals.[20] She can do so in normal proceedings

---

[13] Court of Appeal Liège 9 January 2015, 2015 *Jurisprudence de Liège, Mons et Bruxelles* 1076, note N Bernard; Court Brussels 29 January 2001, 2001 *JT* 576; Justice of the Peace Zomergem 9 November 2012, 2013–14 *RW* 552.

[14] Justice of the Peace Zomergem 9 November 2012, 2013–14 *RW* 552; Justice of the Peace Ghent 26 December 2011, 2012 *TGR* 171; Justice of the Peace Wavre 2 December 2010, 2012 *T Vred* 463, annotation K De Greve; Justice of the Peace Leuven (1) 30 June 1999, 1999–00 *RW* 1033.

[15] Justice of the Peace Brussels 14 November 2006, 2008 *TBBR* 482, annotation A Vandeburie.

[16] Justice of the Peace Ghent 26 December 2011, 2012 *TGR* 171.

[17] Justice of the Peace Brussels 22 December 2006, 2008 *TBBR* 486, comment A Vandeburie.

[18] E Brems 'Geen recht op kraken' (annotation under Justice of the Peace Ghent 5 May 2003) 2003 *Juristenkrant* 13. See however G Smaerts 'De strafbaarheid van het kraken van woningen naar Belgisch recht' 1987 *RW* 2193–2218 2216.

[19] Justice of the Peace Wavre 2 December 2010*T Vred* 2012, 463, annotation K De Greve.

[20] We refer to the case law cited above from the European Court of Human Rights. Similarly: Belgian Constitutional Court 10 July 2008 (No 101/2008) 2008 *Arresten Grondwettelijk Hof* 2008 1605: 'La possibilité de priver de la sorte les locataires de la garantie de l'intervention préalable d'un juge en cas de dissolution du bail par le bailleur pour manquement à leurs obligations n'est pas proportionnée à l'objectif d'assurer la qualité de l'habitat dans les quartiers de logements sociaux et porte atteinte à la sécurité du logement dans le secteur du logement social qui est un élément fondamental de la concrétisation du droit à un logement décent garanti par l'article 23 de la Constitution.'

or, in case of urgency,[21] in summary proceedings.[22] In the latter case, the claimant must demonstrate the urgent nature of her request, and the judge will only render his judgment on the basis of a *prima facie* assessment. Moreover, the owner can initiate proceedings on the basis of a unilateral non-contradictory request, without having to inform the squatters. Such proceedings are, under Belgian law, exceptional, as the right to contradict is absent, but they have often been admitted in squatter cases. The absolute necessity to proceed in this way, which is a prerequisite for such proceedings, is often inferred from the fact that the owner of the building does not know the identity of the squatters, leave alone their domicile. The president of the tribunal must determine on the basis of the specific circumstances at hand in such unilateral proceedings whether these conditions are met. In the case of an affirmative answer, she can grant an order 'to evict everyone who is occupying an identified building'.

This strict viewpoint in the civil-law conflict between the owner and the squatter does not mean, however, that squatting, in traditional Belgian law, is punishable on a criminal level. In itself, the occupation of somebody else's house is not a crime in Belgian law.[23] Only in two instances does Belgian law qualify the actions of squatters as a criminal act.

Firstly, criminal sanctions are possible if these actions result in the violation of domestic privacy ('trespassing'), which necessarily implies that the occupied house was not empty (article 439 Belgian Criminal Code). Trespassing only occurs when the occupied building is used for household purposes or, if it is used for commercial purposes, the building contains confidential documents. Secondly, the actions of squatters also fall under the scope of the Criminal Code if they cause the destruction of the property (or some of its elements). The Belgian *Cour de cassation* has interpreted this criminal provision in an extensive manner.[24]

Could squatters argue that they have become owners on the basis of acquisitive prescription? In others words, are their actions rewarded through the acquisition of ownership after a sufficiently long period of time? In Belgian law, the lawful possession of a movable or immovable good results in acquisitive prescription after thirty years, regardless the good or bad faith

---

[21] The urgency does not follow in itself from the ownership of the building.

[22] These are regulated in arts 1035–1041 of the Belgian Judicial Code (1967).

[23] D Gruyaert *De exclusiviteit van het eigendomsrecht* (2016) No 248; V Sagaert *Belgisch Privaatrecht. Goederenrecht* (2014) No 194.

[24] Court of Cassation 23 June 2004, 2014 *Arresten van het Hof van Cassatie* 1174.

of the possessor.[25] The lawfulness of the possession requires the possession to be peaceful (without violence), unequivocal, continuous and public.[26] The main issue is often the absence of violence. If the squatters have used violence, they will be excluded from the possibility of acquisition.

2.2 Developments in Belgian case law

As we have seen under section 2.1 above, Belgian case law traditionally denies direct effect to the right of housing, in such a way that squatters cannot use this argument in relation to private parties (eg owners). As a result, ownership in traditional Belgian law prevails over the right of housing in case law. This traditional, strict viewpoint in Belgian law has been mitigated over the last years.

First of all, case law adheres to a more nuanced approach of the said conflict between fundamental rights. In some cases, case law tends to take into account the necessity to find a balance between the fundamental rights at stake. For instance, some case law grants entitlement to the squatters if they occupy public buildings for which no use has been specified at the moment of the occupation. In this case, the lack of enforceability of the right to housing against private individuals would not come into play, as the parties involved are public authorities as against squatters. This standpoint has considerable validity if the owner of the building is the public centre for social welfare, which is directly responsible for the adequate housing of people in need.[27] If this centre therefore requests the eviction of a squatter, a balance will have to be sought. Some case law also extends this solution to the unlawful occupation of buildings owned by another public authority than the one that is obliged or has the competence to promote adequate housing policies.[28] However, this case law is restricted to the specific situation in which the building is a public building. It still remains the minority perspective as against that of private individuals.

The balancing of interests is also advanced in legal scholarship. Legal scholars point to international conventions that take priority over the internal

[25] It must be noted that shorter terms of ten or twenty years respectively apply if the possessor is in good faith and has a legal title (art 2265 C civ). As squatters do not meet these requirements, we will not deal further with this provision.

[26] Article 2229 of the Belgian Civil Code.

[27] Tribunal Brussels 29 January 2001, 2001 *JT* 577; Justice of the Peace Charleroi 22 June 2016 (16/A/25) (unpublished).

[28] President Tribunal Liège 28 October 2014, 2015 *Jurisprudence Liège, Mons et Bruxelles* 519.

legal order, and which require these fundamental rights to be observed.[29] Courts must take into account the specific circumstances of each case, such as the alternative housing possibilities for the squatters, specific plans existing with regard to the building by the owners, reasons why the owners are absent, etc.[30]

2.3 *Recent developments in Belgian legislation*

The lenient attitude of the Belgian legislature towards squatting, as far as criminal law is concerned, has recently come under pressure. These legislative initiatives start from the fact that the number of squatter cases, especially in large cities (such as Ghent), is increasing dramatically.[31] Some recent cases of squatters who have prevented the owners from occupying their homes, after their return from holiday, have touched public opinion in Belgium.

An early statutory provision, with limited scope, was introduced in the Act of 12 January 1993, in article 134*bis* of the Act on municipalities. According to this provision, a mayor can, at the request of the president of the public centre for social welfare, notify an owner of the fact that the owner's building has been abandoned for more than six months, and that it will be used for homeless people. Such a notification can only have effect if it is issued within six months, and the owner is entitled to equitable compensation.

More general initiatives have, until recently, been lacking in Belgian law. Pursuant to some prior initiatives by members of parliament, which failed, the federal governmental agreement of 2014 provided that 'the current regulations with regard to squatters will be revised, in order to speed up the eviction'.[32] The legislative attempts have finally been successful through the adoption of the Act of 18 October 2017 'on the unlawful intrusion in, occupation of or residence in somebody else's house', published in the Belgian *Official Gazette* on 6 November 2017. The main motive for the legislative action is to facilitate the obtaining and execution of eviction orders in favour of owners. The new Act broadens the scope of article 439 of the Criminal Code, and thus enlarges the notion of 'trespassing'. The new Act criminalises all forms

[29] Cf D Gruyaert *De exclusiviteit van het eigendomsrecht* (2016) no 249; V Sagaert *Belgisch Privaatrecht. Goederenrecht* (2014) No 202. Also: N Bernard & B Hubeau (eds) *Recht op wonen: naar een resultaatsverbintenis?* (2013) 281.

[30] T Vandromme 'Het kraken van panden bekeken vanuit de grondrechten, het strafrecht en het burgerlijk recht (inclusief het procesrecht)' 2014–15 *RW* 1363–1378 1367–1368.

[31] There is even a private housing association which has opened a website on squatting, including its legal aspects: krakengent.squat.net/.

[32] http://www.premier.be/sites/default/files/articles/Accord_de_Gouvernement_-_Regeerakkoord.pdf 133.

of intrusions in somebody else's house without her consent, by threatening people or using violence against people, by forced entry, climbing or false keys, resulting in the occupation of or residence in another's house without the consent of the owners. The criminalisation is independent of whether the building is in use or not, and the proscribed conduct constitutes trespassing under this new Act.[33] It can be punished with imprisonment of eight days to one year.

Meanwhile, the new Act provides for a procedural framework for the eviction of squatters, which will be included in article 1344*octies* et seq of the Belgian Judicial Code. This procedural framework aims to safeguard the constitutional rights of ownership and housing. It confirms that each title holder can, in a contradictory procedure or, in case of absolute necessity, by unilateral proceedings, sue the squatters in order to obtain an eviction order. If the judge grants an eviction order, it will only be enforceable at the earliest on the eighth day after the notification of the judgment.[34] This term can be longer if the judge holds that for exceptional, compelling reasons, a longer stay is justified. These exceptional circumstances are specified in the Act itself, and apply where the squatters cannot be housed in circumstances that will preserve the family's unity and meet its financial and family needs, especially in wintertime.

It is interesting to see that the sharpening of the eviction possibilities goes hand in hand with the intervention of the Public Social Welfare Centre during these proceedings. The latter must guide the evicted squatters and help them to find a solution to their housing difficulties.

2.4 Conclusion: Volatility in Belgian squatting discussions

It follows from the developments outlined above that Belgian case law tends to be very strict against squatters: they can be evicted, as they unlawfully violate the ownership rights of others. On the face of it, two contradictory developments can be detected in Belgian law in general. On the one hand, there is a prudent tendency in case law and legal scholarship to weigh the conflicting fundamental rights. On the other hand, the Belgian *legislature* very recently amended the Criminal Code in order to make squatting a crime. Closer observation shows, however, that the criminalisation of squatting

[33] 'Proposition de Loi modifiant le Code pénal en ce qui concerne l'occupation d'un immeuble sans l'autorisation du propriétaire of 2 April 2015' 2014–15 *Parlementaire Stukken* Kamer No 1008/1. Compare 'Proposition de Loi incriminant le squat d'immeubles et étendant l'incrimination de la violation de domicile' 2014–15 *Parlementaire Stukken Kamer* No.1016/01.

[34] The notification of the eviction must precede the eviction by at least five days.

is not a stand-alone decree: it goes with a procedural framework for the enforcement of eviction orders which also takes into account the social housing needs of the squatters.

Some Belgian scholars have criticised the criminalisation of squatting from a social housing perspective.[35] That should, however, not blind us to the housing considerations, in civil and procedural law, which also underlie the Act. The policy reasons behind these critical observations continue to override the more legal debate on the adequate standard to apply in case of a conflict between different fundamental rights.

3 The position of squatters in Dutch law

3.1 Introduction

The Dutch law of squatting displays an interesting intertwining of different branches of law. Initially, only civil law and/or criminal law were involved in proceedings aimed at the eviction and/or conviction of squatters. Over the years and pursuant to the case law of the Dutch Supreme Court, human rights law has also made itself felt. Today squatters can only in exceptional situations be evicted without a judge having assessed the proportionality of the eviction vis-à-vis the squatters' right to respect for their home, protected by article 12 of the Dutch Constitution and article 8 of the European Convention on Human Rights.

The Dutch law of squatting has not developed overnight into the complex and heterogeneous body of law it is today, but has done so gradually. Due to the limited scope of this chapter, it is impossible to provide the reader with an exhaustive chronological overview, but some history needs to be told. Particular attention will be paid to the changes brought about by the Anti-Squatting Act of 2009 and to the standards Dutch courts use to decide eviction cases.

3.2 Developments in legislation

3.2.1 The eviction and punishing of squatters before the Anti-Squatting Act

A first way in which the owner of premises occupied by squatters can act against the squatters is by starting a civil eviction procedure. That option already existed before the Anti-Squatting Act and still exists today. At the core of a civil eviction procedure is the protection of ownership. By residing

[35] For instance, T Vandromme 'Het kraken van panden bekeken vanuit de grondrechten, het strafrecht en het burgerlijk recht (inclusief het procesrecht)' 2014–15 *RW* 1363–1378 1366.

in and using the owner's property without the latter's consent (and without any title), squatters violate her right of ownership.

The Dutch Civil Code explicitly allows owners to take action against people who infringe their right of ownership. Article 5:2 of the Civil Code empowers owners to claim restitution of their property from 'everyone who keeps it without a right or title', in this case the squatters. In fact, article 5:2 of the Civil Code is not the only civil law provision that enables the owner to act against squatters. By violating the owner's right of ownership, the actions of the squatters fall within the scope of article 6:162 section 2 of the Civil Code.[36] Under the first section of that article, the damage caused by a tortious act is to be compensated by the person who has committed the tortious act, provided that person can be held accountable for it.

As is the case in Belgian law, a civil eviction procedure can take two forms.[37] Firstly, it can take the form of summary proceedings, provided the owner's claim is urgent (article 254 Section 1 Code of Civil Procedure). The burden of proof of the urgency lies with the owner, which is counterbalanced by the fact that summary proceedings are faster[38] and less costly[39] than normal proceedings. The second form a civil eviction procedure can take is that of a 'normal' civil procedure (on the merits of the case), for which no urgency is required.

The goal of a civil procedure is the clearance of the premises occupied by squatters. That goal can also be achieved by means of a criminal procedure, although such proceedings are primarily aimed at imposing a criminal punishment on the squatters. Before the introduction of the Anti-Squatting Act, squatting was only punishable if the squatted premises had been unoccupied for less than twelve months. That rule, laid down in article 429*sexies* Criminal Code, resulted in squatters keeping track of the use and occupation of buildings and counting down to their vacancy's 'first birthday'.[40] From that birthday on, starting a civil eviction procedure was

---

[36] See eg Tribunal Almelo 15 January 2010, ECLI:NL:RBALM:2010:BK9655, www.rechtspraak.nl; HJ Moné & N Eeken 'Kraken en leegstand: genezen en voorkomen (I)' 2010 *TBR* 128–138 134.

[37] See among others JA de Groot *De civielrechtelijke ontruiming van krakers. Een kritische beschouwing van de voor-en nadelen van de civielrechtelijke ontruimingsprocedure voor de eigenaar van het kraakpand* (2011) 38; HJ Moné & N Eeken 'Kraken en leegstand: genezen en voorkomen (I)' 2010 *TBR* 128–138 135.

[38] See eg HJ Moné & N Eeken 'Kraken en leegstand: genezen en voorkomen (I)' 2010 *TBR* 128–138 135.

[39] See eg JG Brouwer & AE Schilder 'Noot onder Hoge Raad 28 oktober 2011' 2012 *AB Rechtspraak Bestuursrecht* No. 350.

[40] J Ten Hoopen, A. Slob & B. Van der Burg *31560 – No. 3: Memorie van toelichting* (2007–08) www.tweedekamer.nl/kamerstukken 6.

generally the only remedy left for the owner. This often made real estate owners feel powerless, as nothing prevented the squatters from squatting other (nearby) premises after being evicted.[41] In other words, problems were not solved but just moved around and the civil eviction procedure that owners could resort to did not have a deterrent effect. In fact, the same can be said of the risk squatters ran of being convicted by a criminal court, as the maximum term of imprisonment squatters could be sentenced to was 'only' four months. In addition to that, at least according to the drafters of the Anti-Squatting Act, hardly any squatter had been sentenced to imprisonment at the time of the submission of their proposal.[42]

Before the introduction of the Anti-Squatting Act, a clear provision that empowered the authorities to evict people suspected of squatting was lacking. The provisions the authorities usually based evictions on were article 124 of the Judicial Organization Act and article 2 of the Police Act. These provisions entrust the Public Prosecutor and the police with the task of upholding and enforcing public order, but do not explicitly mention the power to evict. This statutory lacuna was often exploited by squatters who argued that a criminal eviction infringed their right to respect for their home and that therefore, in accordance with article 8 section 2 of the ECHR and the ECtHR's jurisprudence, the power to evict must be based on a formal Act that is sufficiently accessible and allows the squatters to foresee interferences with their fundamental right, which requirements according to the squatters were not met by article 124 of the Judicial Organization Act and article 2 of the Police Act. This argument had been approved by some Dutch courts and disapproved of by others before the Supreme Court ruled in 2009 that the public prosecutor and the police do not have the power to evict squatters if the latter are protected by the right to respect for their home.[43]

3.2.2 The eviction and punishing of squatters after the Anti-Squatting Act

With the Anti-Squatting Act, the legislature has not tackled all of the problems we just mentioned. For instance, the rules on the civil eviction procedure (including their flaws) were left untouched, although the draftsmen of the Act were clearly aware of their flaws, as is evidenced by their memorandum in which they explicitly refer to these flaws. In the memorandum, the

[41] J Ten Hoopen, A Slob & B Van der Burg *31560 – No 3: Memorie van toelichting* (2007–08) www.tweedekamer.nl/kamerstukken 7.

[42] J Ten Hoopen, A Slob & B Van der Burg *31560 – No 3: Memorie van toelichting* (2007–08) www.tweedekamer.nl/kamerstukken 9.

[43] Dutch Supreme Court 9 October 2009, ECLI:NL:HR:2009:BJ1254, 2010 *Nederlandse Jurisprudentie* 213.

draftsmen emphasise that thanks to the proposed criminal amendments, a (costly and often slow) civil procedure will no longer be the only remedy the owners of premises occupied by squatters can turn to in order to have their premises cleared.[44]

Unlike the rules on the civil eviction procedure, those on the criminal eviction and prosecution of squatters were fundamentally amended through the Anti-Squatting Act. The problem of insufficient deterrent effect was solved by introducing a new article 138a into the Criminal Code, which makes squatting punishable by imprisonment for up to one year; the maximum penalty was more than doubled. Another major amendment is that the time during which the premises had been unoccupied before squatters moved in is no longer relevant. This change has put an end to the widespread practice among squatters of keeping track of a building's (lack of) occupancy and of waiting for the expiration of a one-year term of vacancy before moving into the building.

The criminal eviction problem was tackled by introducing article 551a into the Code of Criminal Procedure. This provision explicitly empowers the authorities to remove anyone staying in another's building unlawfully if there is a suspicion of squatting. As a result of this provision, squatters can no longer argue that the Public Prosecutor and the police do not have the power to evict them as soon as they are protected by the right to respect for their home.

These changes look like a big step forward for both the authorities and the owners of properties occupied by squatters. The Supreme Court, however, has blown the whistle on the Anti-Squatting Act and in particular on the (draftsmen's) underlying idea that the interests of the squatters on the one hand and the interests of the owner of the occupied premises on the other hand would no longer have to be weighed against each other, as squatting (after the introduction of the Act) would be unlawful in any case.[45] In its decision of 28 October 2011, which will be elaborated on below, the Supreme Court basically ruled that being evicted constitutes a very severe infringement of a person's right to respect for her home and that therefore squatters must be given the opportunity to have the proportionality of the eviction assessed by a court.[46]

---

[44] J Ten Hoopen, A Slob & B Van der Burg *31560 – No 3: Memorie van toelichting* (2007–08) www.tweedekamer.nl/kamerstukken 10.

[45] J Ten Hoopen, A Slob & B Van der Burg *31560 – No 3: Memorie van toelichting* (2007–08) www.tweedekamer.nl/kamerstukken 10.

[46] Dutch Supreme Court 28 October 2011, ECLI:NL:HR:2011:BQ9880, 2013 *Nederlandse Jurisprudentie* 153.

The Anti-Squatting Act was clearly a criminal law answer to the growing problem of squatting. By means of this Act, changes were made to the Criminal Code and the Code of Criminal Procedure but not to the Civil Code and the Code of Civil Procedure. One should not be fooled by appearances, though. It is true that only criminal law provisions were amended, but it is a private law right that benefits from and was (to a large extent) behind these amendments. At multiple places in their memorandum, the drafters stress the importance of respect for and protection of one's right of ownership and even call the enhanced protection of that right one of the main goals of the Act.[47]

3.3 *Developments in Dutch case law*

3.3.1 The Supreme Court's decision of 28 October 2011

The intertwining of private law and criminal law discussed above was taken a step further by the Supreme Court's decision of 28 October 2011. That decision marked the entry of a third branch of law into the Dutch law of squatting, making the latter an even more heterogeneous body of law. As we said above, the Supreme Court ruled that an eviction constitutes a very severe infringement of one's right to respect for one's home and that therefore squatters must be given the opportunity to have the proportionality of the eviction assessed by an independent court.

The litigation that led up to this decision was started by a collective of squatters, although the authorities had yet not started any eviction procedure. There was just a suspicion, or rather fear, on the side of the squatters that such a procedure would soon be started, and they wanted the court to prohibit the authorities from doing so. They argued (among other things) that the violation an eviction would cause to their right to respect for their home, protected by article 8 of the ECHR, would be unjustified in that the eviction was not assessed in advance by an independent court. They added that the protection offered by the possibility to start summary proceedings is insufficient because these proceedings can only lead to a temporary decision, and because it remains to be seen whether it will be possible to start these proceedings within the time allowed.

The squatters' claim was dismissed by the summary proceedings judge and sustained by the appellate court, which grounded its decision on

47 J Ten Hoopen, A Slob & B Van der Burg *31560 – No 3: Memorie van toelichting* (2007–08) www.tweedekamer.nl/kamerstukken 3, 8, 10. See also JM Milo 'The margin of appreciation doctrine of the European Court of Human Rights: Protection of ownership and the right to a home' in E Reid & D Visser (eds) *Private law and human rights. Bringing rights home in Scotland and South Africa* (2013) 482–496 491.

articles 8 and 13 of the ECHR as well as on the European Court of Human Rights' case law. On numerous occasions that court had held that an eviction constitutes the most severe violation of one's right to respect for one's home and that anyone running the risk of suffering such infringement should be able to have the proportionality of the measure evaluated by an independent court.[48] Moreover, it follows from article 13 of the ECHR that these people are entitled to an effective remedy. The appellate court pointed out that under the European Court of Human Rights' jurisprudence a remedy is only an effective remedy if it is capable of preventing a severe inroad upon certain human rights. The appellate court found the possibility to start summary proceedings not to meet that requirement, leading to the conclusion that the criminal eviction of squatters, provided they are protected by article 8 of the ECHR's right to respect for their home, is at odds with the ECHR.

The decision of the appellate court was upheld by the Supreme Court. The state had argued that in squatting cases there is no need for a court to carry out a proportionality test as it follows from article 551a of the Code of Criminal Procedure that the interests of the owner of the squatted premises prevail anyway and that hence an eviction is always proportional.

The Supreme Court was not convinced. It held that although in most cases the owners' interests will indeed outweigh the squatters' interests, it is not impossible that the peculiarities of a specific case may tip the scales in favor of the squatters, which is to be assessed by an independent court. The Supreme Court went on to say that the burden of proof of facts or circumstances that tip the scales in their favor lies with the squatters and that the owner's right to use her premises as she pleases must be the court's starting point when evaluating these facts or circumstances. This addition is interesting, because it reveals that the Supreme Court, despite rejecting the argument put forward by the state, takes the view that in principle (respect for) the owner's right of ownership prevails over the squatters' interests, including their right to respect for their home protected by article 8 of the ECHR. Unlike the state, however, it does not take the view that the aforementioned right always prevails. This is in line with its very own case law about the conflict of fundamental rights, according to which these rights must be weighed against each other taking into account all relevant elements of the case.[49]

[48] The appellate court referred to *McCann/UK* (19009/4) 2008 ECHR 385 and *Zehenter/Austria* (20082/02) 2009 ECHR 1119.

[49] Dutch Supreme Court 18 January 2008, ECLI:NL:HR:2008:BB3210, 2008 *Nederlandse Jurisprudentie* 274; Dutch Supreme Court 6 January 1995, ECLI:NL:HR:1995:ZC1602, 1995 *Nederlandse Jurisprudentie* 422.

This decision has reshuffled the cards. It has restrained the authorities' power to evict people suspected of squatting and strengthened the position of the latter, at least in terms of time (during which the squatters can stay in the occupied premises). Obviously the decision has also changed the owner of the occupied premises' position as it causes criminal eviction procedures to last longer and makes their outcome (more) uncertain.

As to the state's restrained powers, it is worth mentioning that the authorities had already taken action prior to the judgment of the Supreme Court. The Board of Procurators General had drawn up a policy document containing some rules that must be complied with in criminal eviction cases, aimed at providing squatters with the means of defence they are entitled to under articles 8 and 13 of the ECHR. These rules were explicitly approved of by the Supreme Court in its decision of 28 October 2011. The backbone of these rules is the obligation for the authorities, with a few exceptions, to notify squatters in writing (1) of an imminent criminal eviction seven days in advance, as well as (2) of the possibility to start summary proceedings within that period. If the squatters decide to initiate such proceedings, the authorities will have to wait for the court's decision to start the eviction. They will not have to wait, however, for an appellate decision. This was also explicitly approved of by the Supreme Court, which held that the ability to start summary proceedings in one instance constitutes an effective remedy under article 13 of the ECHR.[50]

These rules caused the Supreme Court's decision not to be welcomed with open arms by certain legal practitioners. Only recently one wrote that nowadays the public prosecutor usually refuses to start a criminal eviction procedure, leaving the owner of the occupied premises with no option but to start a (costly) civil eviction procedure.[51] The official evaluation of the Anti-Squatting Act, carried out in 2015 by order of the Ministry of Foreign Affairs and the Ministry of Safety and Justice, seems to give a slightly different picture of the situation. It is mentioned in the evaluation's conclusion that according to the interviewees the number of civil eviction procedures has gone down since the introduction of the Anti-Squatting Act.[52] A footnote added by the writers of the evaluation, however, emphasises that this finding

---

[50] Consideration 3.5.11 of Dutch Supreme Court 28 October 2011, ECLI:NL:HR:1995: ZC1602.

[51] L Opsteen 'Pandeigenaren trekken bij kraak niet langer aan het kortste eind' 2017 *NJB* 474.

[52] S Zeelenberg, E van Kessel, I Giebers & Y Grooten 'Van ontruimen naar inruimen. Evaluatie van de Wet kraken en leegstand', 2015, www.rijksoverheid.nl/documenten/rapporten/2016/02/01/van-ontruimen-naar-inruimen 49.

is solely based on the impressions of the interviewees and that its accuracy was not verified.

3.3.2 The aftermath of the Dutch Supreme Court's decision of 28 October 2011

3.3.2.1 General

It is clear from the above analysis that in order to provide squatters with an effective remedy in criminal eviction cases, a preliminary proportionality test must be carried out. In the vast majority of cases we have seen, which will be discussed below, the application of this test works out badly for the squatters. In other words, the decision of 28 October 2011 has bought squatters some time, but has not resulted in courts and tribunals finding in their favor.

If one has a closer look at how Dutch courts carry out the proportionality test, it does not take long to realise that 'winner elements' that inevitably tip the scale in favor of the owner or, even more unlikely, the squatters, are hard to find, if they exist at all. Of course a lot depends on the arguments put forward by the parties and the specific facts and circumstances they adduce. In the next section, some of the factors Dutch courts and tribunals have or have not taken into account will be analysed.

Before doing that, it is worth mentioning that the proportionality test, which according to the Dutch Supreme Court requires the parties' interests to be weighed against each other, is carried out in both criminal eviction cases and civil eviction cases,[53] although the Supreme Court's judgement of 28 October 2011 was rendered in a criminal eviction case. In our opinion, there are some good grounds for taking the view that the proportionality test should also be carried out in civil eviction cases. First, like the criminal eviction of squatters, their civil eviction is both decided on and carried out by the state. The decision to evict the squatters is made by a court, which is a body of the state, and its execution is taken care of by the police, which is a body of the state as well. Moreover, it is yet another body of the state,

[53] Some examples of civil eviction cases in which the proportionality test (or the need to balance the parties' interests) is explicitly mentioned are: Court of Appeal Arnhem-Leeuwarden 17 June 2013, ECLI:NL:GHARL:2013:CA3417, www.rechtspraak.nl; Tribunal The Hague 15 February 2017, ECLI:NL:RBDHA:2017:2108, 2017 *Nederlandse Jurisprudentie Feitenrechtspraak* 172; www.rechtspraak.nl; Tribunal The Hague 15 January 2016, ECLI:NL:RBDHA:2016:330 and ECLI:NL:RBDHA:2016:333, www.rechtspraak.nl; Tribunal Noord-Nederland 26 February 2016, ECLI:NL:RBNNE:2016:753, www.rechtspraak.nl; Tribunal Zeeland-West-Brabant 11 August 2015, ECLI:NL:RBZWB:2015:5351, www.rechtspraak.nl; Tribunal The Hague 24 April 2014, ECLI:NL:RBDHA:2014:5098, www.rechtspraak.nl.

the legislature, which has created the entire legal framework that allows for squatters to be evicted (by means of a civil procedure) the way they can be evicted today. An even better ground, however, seems to be the Supreme Court's decision of 9 January 1987,[54] in which it held that article 8 of the ECHR also affects the relationship between citizens. In others words, article 8 of the ECHR has horizontal effect.[55]

It could add to the confusion that in summary proceedings the court has to weigh the parties' interests against each other anyway.[56] That weighing of interests must be done in order to assess the (sufficient) urgency of the claim and should not be confused with the weighing of interests against each other we discussed above, although a certain overlap is not unlikely to occur.[57] Whereas in the latter balancing of interests only the owner's right of ownership and its legal protection are taken into account, the former balancing of interests requires special circumstances on the side of the owner (eg the intended sale of the occupied premises is hampered by the fact that they are occupied)[58] to be demonstrated and taken into account.[59]

As a result of some fundamental differences between civil proceedings and criminal proceedings, the proportionality test in civil eviction cases will not be the exact same test as in criminal eviction cases. Criminal procedures are aimed at punishing behavior that society finds inadmissible and blameworthy. Society, represented by the state, is even a full party to these

---

[54] Dutch Supreme Court 9 January 1987, ECLI:NL:HR:1987:AG5500, 1987 *Nederlandse Jurisprudentie* 928.

[55] About the horizontal effect of article 8 of the ECHR, see eg JEA van der Alkema 'Bespiede bijstandsmoeder' 1987 *Nederlandse Jurisprudentie* 928; FH van der Burg 'Noot onder HR 9 January 1987' 1987 *AB Rechtspraak Bestuursrecht* 231. See also Tribunal Noord-Holland 29 June 2017, ECLI:NL:RBNHO:2017:5126, www.rechtspraak.nl.

[56] Dutch Supreme Court 29 November 2002, ECLI:NL:HR:2002:AE4553, 2003 *Nederlandse Jurisprudentie* 78, where the Supreme Court held that the question whether the plaintiff's claim is urgent must be answered by weighing the interests of the parties against each other. See also (among others) Tribunal The Hague 12 August 2016, ECLI:NL:RBDHA:2016:9824, www.rechtspraak.nl; Tribunal Noord-Nederland 26 February 2016, ECLI:NL:RBNNE:2016:753, www.rechtspraak.nl.

[57] In some decisions these two balancing exercises even intertwine. See eg Tribunal Amsterdam 9 March 2017, ECLI:NL:RBAMS:2017:1575, www.rechtspraak.nl.

[58] Tribunal Arnhem 12 December 2012, ECLI:NL:RBARN:2012:BY7922, www.rechtspraak.nl.

[59] Although some courts seem to find the mere fact that there is a (lasting) violation of the owner's right of ownership or that the squatters stay in the owner's premises without his consent to be sufficient. See eg Tribunal Noord-Nederland 26 February 2016, ECLI:NL:RBNNE:2016:753, www.rechtspraak.nl (provided the lasting violation causes damage to the owner); Tribunal The Hague 15 January 2016, ECLI:NL:RBDHA:2016:330, www.rechtspraak.nl; Tribunal The Hague 24 April 2014, ECLI:NL:RBDHA:2014:5098, www.rechtspraak.nl.

procedures. Civil procedures, on the other hand, are aimed at restoring the balance between individuals, without society and the state being parties to them. This is reflected in the interests the court has to take into account when carrying out the proportionality test. In its decision of 28 October 2011 the Supreme Court held that the proportionality test requires the squatters' interest to be balanced against the owner's interests as well as interests of public order and the fact that an eviction would put an end to a criminal action. Obviously these last two factors do not need to be taken into account in civil eviction procedures.

3.3.2.2 Some factors (not) taken into account by the courts

The time during which premises had been unoccupied before they were occupied by squatters is a first factor taken into account by some courts.[60] The longer that time, the better things are for the squatters. Both the Court of Appeal of Arnhem-Leeuwarden and the Tribunal of Noord-Nederland have held that a period of one year is the very minimum.[61] It was ruled that if premises that have been unoccupied for *less* than one year are occupied by squatters, the interests of the latter are generally of lesser importance than the owner's right of ownership, the exclusive character of which was emphasised.

Another factor that features in a couple of decisions is the future of the occupied premises. What will happen to them after the eviction of the squatters? Some courts count the fact that the premises will remain empty or unoccupied (for a long time) as an argument in favor of the squatters.[62] For instance, the Court of Appeal of Amsterdam has rejected a leaseholder's (civil law) eviction claim on the grounds that she had failed to refute the

[60] See eg Court of Appeal Arnhem-Leeuwarden 29 September 2015, ECLI:NL:GHARL:2015:7329, www.rechtspraak.nl; Tribunal Noord-Nederland 26 February 2016, ECLI:NL:RBNNE:2016:753, www.rechtspraak.nl. See also Dutch Supreme Court 28 May 2013, 2014 *Nederlandse Jurisprudentie* 239, where the Supreme Court held that under certain circumstances squatters who have stayed in the occupied premises for only a short time do not have the right to respect for their home (consideration 3.4).

[61] Court of Appeal Arnhem-Leeuwarden 29 September 2015, ECLI:NL:GHARL:2015:7329, www.rechtspraak.nl; Tribunal Noord-Nederland 26 February 2016, ECLI:NL:RBNNE:2016:753, www.rechtspraak.nl. See also Tribunal Limburg 4 December 2013, ECLI:NL:RBLIM:2013:9479, www.rechtspraak.nl, where the court denied squatters who had occupied a building for only eight minutes the right to respect for one's home.

[62] See among other cases Tribunal Midden-Nederland 4 October 2013, ECLI:NL:RBMNE:2013:4752, www.rechtspraak.nl; Tribunal The Hague 14 June 2013, ECLI:NL:RBDHA:2013:9960, www.rechtspraak.nl; Tribunal Noord-Nederland 11 January 2013, ECLI:NL:RBNNE:2013:BY8200, 2013 *NJF* 71; Tribunal Arnhem 12 December 2012, ECLI:NL:RBARN:2012:BY7922, www.rechtspraak.nl.

squatter's argument that the buyer would demolish the premises and erect a new building right after the eviction.[63] Later on in the procedure, however, the long leaseholder admitted that the buyer would wait for the zoning scheme to be modified before starting the realisation of the project. As the zoning scheme was not likely to be modified in the near future, the court found the long leaseholder's argument not convincing. More remarkable, however, was the court's position on the long leaseholder's argument that the contract with the buyer of the premises obliged him to deliver them empty under penalty of a heavy fine. The court ruled that this argument carried insufficient weight vis-à-vis what it called the 'principal rule' that a summary proceedings judge cannot sustain an eviction claim if the eviction is likely to lead to the unjustified vacancy of the premises occupied by squatters.[64] A similar argument about an imminent fine payable to the local authorities was also found not to carry sufficient weight vis-à-vis that rule, making it into an almost absolute rule. In other words, the balancing of interests that the Supreme Court had in mind when it rendered its judgement of 28 October 2011 was anything but present in the Court of Appeal's decision.

Much closer to the aforementioned judgement of the Supreme Court are a fairly recent decision of the Tribunal of Rotterdam[65] and a slightly older one of the Tribunal of Midden-Nederland.[66] In both cases the squatters had started summary proceedings to prevent a criminal eviction. In line with the Supreme Court's decision both courts started off by underlining that it is up to the squatters to produce facts or circumstances that tip the scales in their favor, as the owners' right to use their premises as they please is the starting point. The tribunals then went on to shed some light on which facts or circumstances could tip the scales. According to the Tribunal of Rotterdam, squatters will only be successful if they have (and demonstrate) personal interests in staying in the premises and (in addition) if they manage to demonstrate that the owner lacks any interest in the clearance of the premises as well as that the eviction will lead to the premises being unoccupied for a long time.[67] The court held that the squatters had failed to

[63] Court of Appeal Amsterdam 31 January 2017, ECLI:NL:GHAMS:2017:273, www.rechtspraak.nl.

[64] The Tribunal of Arnhem called this rule the 'starting point' of a summary proceedings court assessment in (civil) eviction cases. Tribunal Arnhem 12 December 2012, ECLI:NL:RBARN:2012:BY7922, www.rechtspraak.nl.

[65] Tribunal Rotterdam 21 June 2016, ECLI:NL:RBROT:2016:5862, www.rechtspraak.nl.

[66] Tribunal Midden-Nederland 4 October 2013, ECLI:NL:RBMNE:2013:4752, www.rechtspraak.nl.

[67] Consideration 4.9. Reference was made to Court of Appeal Leeuwarden 18 December 2012, ECLI:NL:GHLEE:2012:BY7413, www.rechtspraak.nl.

demonstrate the latter, whereas the state had made a reasonable case for the position that the owner of the occupied premises intends to demolish them. The Tribunal of Midden-Nederland dismissed the claim of the squatters on the grounds that they had failed to tip the scales in their favor. It pointed out that the squatters had (among other things) failed to demonstrate particular circumstances, eg that after the eviction the squatted premises would be unoccupied for a long time.

A third factor that is sometimes taken into account is the squatters' inability to find other affordable housing.[68] That inability can be due to several causes, some of which will be touched upon in the following lines. Before doing that, it must be noted that, at least according to the Tribunal of Rotterdam, the mere fact that after the eviction the squatters will be homeless is not a particular circumstance able to tip the scales in their favor.[69]

A first possible cause is a housing shortage in the area the squatted premises are located in, which was recognised by a court as a particular circumstance.[70] This is consistent with the European Court of Human Rights' jurisprudence on the subject matter. The following consideration about the (seriousness of the) interference with the squatters' right to respect for their home features in several decisions of the court: 'If no alternative accommodation is available the interference is more serious than where such accommodation is available.'[71] In other words, this is a factor that the courts must attach particular importance to when balancing the interests. The fact that finding housing on the private housing market is beyond the squatter's ability, on the contrary, was denied the status of particular circumstance (by another court).[72]

Another possible cause of a squatter's inability to find affordable housing is a lack of financial means. In a recent decision, however, the squatter's argument that she earned a very low salary and did not qualify for a supplementary benefit was dismissed. The court found this not to be a

[68] See eg Court of Appeal Arnhem-Leeuwarden 29 September 2015, ECLI:NL:GHARL:2015:7329, www.rechtspraak.nl; Tribunal Noord-Nederland 26 February 2016, ECLI:NL:RBNNE:2016:753, www.rechtspraak.nl; Tribunal Almelo 15 August 2012, ECLI:NL:RBALM:2012:BX4743, www.rechtspraak.nl.

[69] Tribunal Rotterdam 21 June 2016, ECLI:NL:RBROT:2016:5862, www.rechtspraak.nl.

[70] Tribunal Zeeland-West-Brabant 11 August 2015, ECLI:NL:RBZWB:2015:5351, www.rechtspraak.nl. See however Court of Appeal Arnhem-Leeuwarden 17 June 2013, ECLI:NL:GHARL:2013:CA3417, www.rechtspraak.nl.

[71] See eg *Winterstein and others v France* (27013/07) http://hudoc.echr.coe.int (consideration 148); *Chapman v United Kingdom* (27238/95) http://hudoc.echr.coe.int (consideration 103).

[72] Tribunal The Hague 13 January 2017, ECLI:NL:RBDHA:2017:1139, www.rechtspraak.nl.

particular circumstance.[73] The same goes for the fact that the squatter needs the address of the occupied premises to receive a pension,[74] the squatter's ineligibility for public housing[75] and the existence of long waiting lists for rental houses.[76]

Yet another factor worth mentioning is a complete lack of interest in the clearance of the occupied premises on the part of the owner. As discussed above, the Tribunal of Rotterdam and the Court of Appeal of Leeuwarden require such lack of interest (as well as other circumstances) to be demonstrated in order for the scales to be tipped in favor of the squatters.[77] Closely related to this is the question whether the owner of the occupied premises is abusing her power to have the squatters evicted. The Tribunal of Midden-Nederland mentioned this as a ground for dismissal of a (civil) eviction claim.[78] Moreover, it seems that this particular tribunal considered it to be one of only two possible grounds for dismissal of such a claim by a summary proceedings court, a lack of urgency being the other one. In its judgement the tribunal wrote that given the presence of the squatters in the occupied premises without any title, in principle the owner's claim should be allowed, followed by a sentence that starts with '*[t]his is only different if...*'[79]. The tribunal ruled that in the case presented to it there was no abuse of power because the owner had offered alternative housing to the squatters, which was declined by the squatters, and no conclusive evidence of the inadequacy of that offer was produced. The tribunal came to the same conclusion in another case in which the squatters had played the abuse of power card. It based its conclusion (among other things) on the fact that the occupied premises were going to be demolished and replaced by new buildings.[80]

---

[73] Tribunal The Hague 13 January 2017, ECLI:NL:RBDHA:2017:1139, www.rechtspraak.nl. See also Court of Appeal Arnhem-Leeuwarden 17 June 2013, ECLI:NL:GHARL:2013:CA3417, www.rechtspraak.nl.

[74] Tribunal The Hague 14 June 2013, ECLI:NL:RBDHA:2013:9960, www.rechtspraak.nl.

[75] Tribunal Midden-Nederland 4 October 2013, ECLI:NL:RBMNE:2013:4752, www.rechtspraak.nl.

[76] Tribunal The Hague 15 February 2017, ECLI:NL:RBDHA:2017:2108, www.rechtspraak.nl; Tribunal The Hague 13 January 2017, ECLI:NL:RBDHA:2017:1139, www.rechtspraak.nl.

[77] See also Tribunal Noord-Nederland 11 January 2013, ECLI:NL:RBNNE:2013:BY8200, 2013 *Nederlandse Jurisprudentie Feitenrechtspraak* 71 (where the tribunal called the owner's lack of interest an element that might tip the scales in favor of the squatter).

[78] Tribunal Midden-Nederland 8 May 2013, ECLI:NL:RBMNE:2013:BZ9792, www.rechtspraak.nl.

[79] Own translation.

[80] Tribunal Midden-Nederland 4 October 2013, ECLI:NL:RBMNE:2013:4752, www.rechtspraak.nl.

4 Conclusion

Squatting is a subject of the kind that André van der Walt liked the most: at the crossroads of property law, constitutional law, civil procedure law, criminal law and human rights law.

It has emerged from both the Belgian and the Dutch example that legislation/the legislature and case law/the courts are not always and necessarily on the exact same wavelength. In fact, in both countries the legislative developments and the developments in case law even seem to be contradictory. On the one hand, the legislature aims at being more severe on the criminal level by categorising squatting as a crime and making it punishable by more severe penalties. Whereas in Belgium these developments are very recent, in the Netherlands they have at an earlier stage resulted in the adoption of an Act through which the Criminal Code and the Code of Criminal Procedure were substantially amended to the prejudice of squatters.

On the other hand, the case law of both legal systems shows or has shown important developments towards a more 'balanced' approach to squatting cases. This approach is, roughly speaking, one of weighing the owners' right of ownership against the interests of the squatters, in particular the latter's right to respect for their home, taking into account the specific circumstances and peculiarities of each individual case.[81] Also, with regard to these developments, Dutch law is ahead of Belgian law as the number of cases in which the parties' interests are weighed against each other is significantly higher. Today's Dutch law of squatting is a heterogeneous body of law the study of which requires a strongly multi disciplinary approach, which definitely would have aroused André's interest. Belgian law has also, through a very recent legislative amendment, achieved a better balance between the constitutional rights at stake.

[81] Compare, on a more general level: R Dyal-Chand 'Sharing the cathedral' 2013 *Conn L Rev* 689–691.

Chapter 11

Constitutional reasons for developing the common-law security obligation of usufructuaries in terms of the right of access to housing*

*Lizette Grobler*** & *Gerrit Pienaar****

1 Background

One of André van der Walt's main contributions as constitutional property lawyer was to promote the establishment of a unitary property law system where statutory law, common law, customary law and case law all reflect the constitutional values, principles and requirements. This requires the development of established common-law rules and principles to blend in with the constitutional dispensation. In this regard he stated:[1]

> Constitutional analysis has to date received only sparse attention in South African servitude law. It has become clear that constitutional analysis in the context of the development of the common law cannot adopt the oversimplified form of

* This article is based on the unpublished LLD dissertation of L Grobler, *The* salva rei substantia *requirement in personal servitudes* (2015) Stellenbosch University.

** Postdoctoral Research Fellow, South African Research Chair in Property Law, Department of Public Law, Stellenbosch University.

*** Extra-Ordinary Professor at the Faculty of Law, North-West University.

1 AJ van der Walt *Law of servitudes* (2016) 37.

> simply checking whether a particular common-law principle, rule or institution (or some desired development of it) directly conflicts with any constitutional right or principle. For much the same reason, simply offering a constitutional right or principle in support of a preferred interpretation or a particular direction or strategy of development is too facile to be meaningful. ... The starting point for constitutional analysis of this kind has to be the supremacy of the Constitution, combined with the single-system-of-law principle articulated by the Constitutional Court.

In this contribution we endeavour to examine briefly some aspects of the law of servitudes, namely the obligations of the usufructuary and the remedies of the bare owner in pre-constitutional context, and analyse the development of the common-law principles to be incorporated in the constitutional paradigm. The common-law right of the bare owner to evict a usufructuary who neglects her duties will be analysed in terms of the constitutional right to have access to adequate housing in terms of section 26(1) of the Constitution.

2 Definition and nature of usufruct

Usufruct is a personal servitude that grants the usufructuary a limited real right to use the object of another and to draw the fruits thereof, with the obligation to return the object to the bare owner without impairing its substance.[2] Usufruct normally functions as a means to provide the usufructuary with an income derived from the object of the usufruct, as well as the use and enjoyment of the property and fruit during her lifetime, while the object remains the property of another.[3] The object of the usufruct may be a single movable or immovable thing or a collection of things (*universitas rerum*),[4] but in the context of this article the emphasis will fall on a usufruct over immovable property.[5]

[2] L Grobler *The* salva rei substantia *requirement in personal servitudes* (2015) unpublished LLD dissertation Stellenbosch University 45; AJ van der Walt *Law of servitudes* (2016) 57–58; CG van der Merwe *Sakereg* 2 ed (1989) 508; MJ de Waal 'Servitudes' in R Zimmermann & D Visser *Southern cross: Civil law and common law in South Africa* (1996) 785-817 810.

[3] CG van der Merwe *Sakereg* 2 ed (1989) 508 describes this as the social function of usufruct; see also CP Bezuidenhout *Sakeregtelike aspekte van vruggebruik in die Suid-Afrikaanse reg* (1990) unpublished LLD dissertation Stellenbosch University 89.

[4] CG van der Merwe & MJ de Waal 'Servitudes' in WA Joubert & JA Faris (eds) *LAWSA* vol 24 2 ed (2010) para 58; *Antje Komen v Hendrik de Heer* (1908) 29 NLR 237; *Geldenhuys v Commissioner for Inland Revenue* 1947 (3) SA 256 (C).

[5] CG van der Merwe *Sakereg* 2 ed (1989) 509 based on Grotius 2 39 2; Voet 7 1 14 and Van der Linden *Supplementum ad* Voet 7 1 14.

A characteristic of usufruct, relevant to this discussion, is that it has a limited duration. Generally, usufruct spans the lifetime of the usufructuary.[6] However, it may also be granted for a specified period or until the fulfilment of a condition,[7] in which case it would expire with the earlier death of the usufructuary.[8] Accordingly, an assessment of the maintenance of the object until its eventual return to the bare owner is inevitable. In order to facilitate and ensure the return of the property the usufructuary has the obligation to use and return the property *salva rei substantia* (without impairing its substance). To maintain the usufructuary object *salva rei substantia* certain rights are granted to the usufructuary and specific duties are imposed on her.

3 Obligations of the usufructuary

The general principle underlying usufruct is the usufructuary's duty to exercise her entitlements like a rational[9] or sensible person.[10] Alternatively, writers refer to the *civiliter modo* principle,[11] based on reasonable behaviour required of a *bonus paterfamilias*.[12] The general principle is usually discussed in conjunction with the requirement to return the property *salva rei substantia*.[13] The other obligations of the usufructuary flow from this overarching point of departure.

---

[6] Grotius 2 39 1; CG van der Merwe *Sakereg* 2 ed (1989) 520.

[7] *Watson v Fraetas* 1899 16 SC 263; Voet 7 4 11; CG van der Merwe *Sakereg* 2 ed (1989) 520; MM Corbett 'Usufruct, *usus* and *habitatio*' in HR Hahlo (ed) *The law of succession in South Africa* (1980) 378–401 379.

[8] Voet 7 4 11, 12; *Day's Trustees v Registrar of Deeds & Another* 1910 CPD 361; AJ van der Walt *Law of servitudes* (2016) 483–486; L Grobler *The* salva rei substantia *requirement in personal servitudes* (2015) unpublished LLD dissertation Stellenbosch University 49; CG van der Merwe *Sakereg* 2 ed (1989) 520.

[9] CG van der Merwe & MJ de Waal 'Servitudes' in WA Joubert & JA Faris (eds) *LAWSA* vol 24 2 ed (2010) para 593.

[10] CG van der Merwe & A Pope 'Servitudes and other real rights' in F du Bois (ed) *Wille's principles of South African law* 9 ed (2007) 591–629 608.

[11] AJ van der Walt *Law of servitudes* (2016) 475; CG van der Merwe *Sakereg* 2 ed (1989) 466; CP Bezuidenhout *Sakeregtelike aspekte van vruggebruik in die Suid-Afrikaanse reg* (1990) unpublished LLD dissertation Stellenbosch University 108.

[12] CP Bezuidenhout *Sakeregtelike aspekte van vruggebruik in die Suid-Afrikaanse reg* (1990) unpublished LLD dissertation Stellenbosch University 116; CP Joubert 'Die vruggebruiker se verpligting om verbeterings aan te bring' (1958) 21 *THRHR* 256–276 256, 261.

[13] AJ van der Walt *Law of servitudes* (2016) 473–483; L Grobler *The* salva rei substantia *requirement in personal servitudes* (2015) unpublished LLD dissertation Stellenbosch University 53; CG van der Merwe *Sakereg* 2 ed (1989) 516.

3.1 *The* salva rei substantia *requirement*

Within the context of usufruct the *salva rei substantia* requirement[14] can be described as the obligation of the usufructuary to use and enjoy the object of the usufruct without impairment of the essential quality of the object.[15]

One can interpret the *salva rei substantia* requirement in either a flexible or a rigid manner.[16] A rigid interpretation would entail strictly prohibiting the deterioration or impairment of the object of the usufruct, without taking the nature of the object, the context (including the locality and circumstances regarding its enjoyment) or the practice and custom of prudent users of similar property into account.[17] It seems that a rigid approach primarily pertains to the preservation of the physical object, based on a literal interpretation of the *salva rei substantia* requirement. In *Fourie v Munnik*[18] McGregor J points out the negative consequences of a narrow interpretation:

> [F]or while on the one hand there must be no destruction or substantial impairing or undue deterioration of the usufructuary property, one should, conversely, not insist on such counsels of perfection regarding the user as to make the enjoyment something unsubstantial, unproductive or illusory.

A flexible approach normally allows for some physical impairment or interference, provided that the economic destination of the object of the usufruct is not altered. Interference would be justified by contextual factors such as the locality, established practices in the area, the nature of the object of the usufruct and circumstances relevant to its enjoyment.[19] It has been proposed that a flexible approach might also entail accepting economic gain (in the sense that it increases the value of the object of the usufruct) as a valid

---

[14] See in particular CG van der Merwe 'Regsbegrippe en regspolitiek' (1979) 42 *THRHR* 9–20 10. He uses the term 'requirement' ('vereiste').

[15] Case law from the constitutional era recognises this obligation: see *Mkontwana v Nelson Mandela Metropolitan Municipality and Another* 2005 (1) SA 530 (CC) para 55; *Van der Heever NO and Others v Coetzee and Another* 2003 JDR 0863 (T) 11.

[16] The existence of both a flexible and a narrow approach can be deduced from the pronouncements of the judiciary opting for a flexible approach; *eg Fourie v Munnik* 1919 OPD 73 79.

[17] *Brunsdon's Estate v Brunsdon's Estate and Others* 1920 CPD 159 74ff; *Geldenhuys v Commissioner for Inland Revenue* 1947 (3) SA 256 (C) 263–264; *contra Fourie v Munnik* 1919 OPD 73 79, where the locality and the practice of the 'experienced prudent farmer in the same neighbourhood', and 86–87, where the nature of the object of the usufruct and the 'circumstances attending its enjoyment', were taken into account.

[18] *Fourie v Munnik* 1919 OPD 73 87.

[19] *Fourie v Munnik* 1919 OPD 73 79, 87.

and sufficient reason for changing the economic destination of the object of the usufruct.[20]

All these factors contribute to the conclusion that the *civiliter modo* principle differs from the *salva rei substantia* requirement in the sense that the latter affords customised protection that is more extensive than in the case of the *civiliter* principle.

3.2 Specific entitlements of the usufructuary

As a basic premise, the usufructuary has the entitlement to use and control the property to the extent necessary for the cultivation and acquisition of fruits.[21] The question is whether this wide entitlement of use allows the usufructuary some flexibility in relation to the *salva rei substantia* requirement to administer and control the usufructuary property. In *Steyn v Registrar of Deeds*[22] it was noted that the right to possession, administration and control is an essential feature of usufruct. It is, therefore, necessary to determine the scope of these entitlements, particularly of the entitlement with regard to administration and control of the property. In case law these entitlements are sometimes conflated. For example, in *Furnivall v Cornwell's Executors*[23] the right of administration was described as the right to control, along with the right to possess and take custody, of the usufructuary property.[24] In *Steyn v Registrar of Deeds*[25] Watermeyer J decided that the interest involved did not amount to a usufruct as the survivor neither had possession, nor control or administration.[26]

To summarise, the entitlements of administration and control are acknowledged in South African law but the scope of these entitlements is not clear. Therefore, it is not clear how these entitlements might facilitate a flexible approach to the *salva rei substantia* requirement in South African law.

---

[20] R Zimmermann *Das römisch-holländische recht in Südafrika: Einführung in die Grundlagen und* Usus Hodiernus (1983) 175; AJ van der Walt *Law of servitudes* (2016) 476–477; L Grobler *The* salva rei substantia *requirement in personal servitudes* (2015) unpublished LLD dissertation Stellenbosch University 56–57.

[21] *Barnett & Others v Rudman & Another* 1934 AD 203; CG van der Merwe *Sakereg* 2 ed (1989) 510.

[22] *Steyn v Registrar of Deeds* 1933 CPD 109 112.

[23] *Furnivall v Cornwell's Executors* (1895) 12 SC 6.

[24] Another example is *Furnivall v Cornwell's Executors* (1895) 12 SC 6, where the controller of the property also took due care that the premises were repaired and insured.

[25] *Steyn v Registrar of Deeds* 1933 CPD 109 112.

[26] *Steyn v Registrar of Deeds* 1933 CPD 109 112.

3.3 *Duties flowing from the* salva rei substantia *requirement*

3.3.1 The requirement to frame an inventory

The usufructuary is under the obligation to frame an inventory on request of the bare owner.[27] The inventory informs the *dominus* of the scope and nature of the usufructuary object to be returned on termination of the usufruct.[28] The inventory, therefore, plays an instrumental role in establishing whether the usufructuary property was returned *salva rei substantia*.[29]

The importance of this duty flowing from the *salva rei substantia* requirement is emphasised by the sanction for non-compliance with the request to frame an inventory. Where there is an insistence on an inventory, compliance is viewed as a condition that must be satisfied in order for the usufructuary to use and enjoy the property subject to the usufruct.[30] Accordingly, the usufructuary is not entitled to its use and enjoyment until this condition is met.[31] Furthermore, the usufructuary who fails to comply with a court order demanding an inventory (and security) may be ejected.[32] This sanction shows that determining the content and condition of the usufructuary property is significant in assessing whether the usufructuary property is returned *salva rei substantia*. The severity of the remedies available to the bare owner in case of non-compliance seems to point to a strict doctrinal interpretation of the *salva rei substantia* requirement.[33]

---

[27] *Van Rensburg v Mulder* 1998 JDR 0756 (T); *Stain v Hiebner* 1976 (1) SA 34 (C) 36; *Schoeman v Schoeman and Another* 1953 (2) SA 441 (T) 442; Grotius 2 39 20; Voet *Commentarius* 7 9 2, 7 9 7; Groenewegen *ad* Grotius 2 39 2; Van Leeuwen *RHR* 2 9 10, *CF* 1 2 15 6; Schorer *ad* Grotius 2 39 3; Van der Keessel *Praelectiones ad* Grotius 2 39 3; CG van der Merwe *Sakereg* 2 ed (1989) 516.

[28] CP Bezuidenhout *Sakeregtelike aspekte van vruggebruik in die Suid-Afrikaanse reg* (1990) unpublished LLD dissertation Stellenbosch University 109–110.

[29] CP Bezuidenhout *Sakeregtelike aspekte van vruggebruik in die Suid-Afrikaanse reg* (1990) unpublished LLD dissertation Stellenbosch University 110.

[30] MM Corbett 'Usufruct, *usus* and *habitatio*' in HR Hahlo (ed) *The Law of succession in South Africa* (1980) 378–401 391.

[31] MM Corbett 'Usufruct, *usus* and *habitatio*' in HR Hahlo (ed) *The Law of succession in South Africa* (1980) 378–401 392.

[32] *Schoeman v Schoeman* 1953 (2) SA 441 (T). Whether such an order will still be accepted in a constitutional dispensation is questionable. See section 6 below.

[33] CP Bezuidenhout *Sakeregtelike aspekte van vruggebruik in die Suid-Afrikaanse reg* (1990) unpublished LLD dissertation Stellenbosch University 109.

3.3.2 The requirement to provide security

If required by the *dominus*, the usufructuary is obliged to provide security[34] that she will use and enjoy the object of usufruct in a civilised manner (*civiliter modo)*[35] and return the usufructuary object *salva rei substantia*[36] upon termination of the usufruct.[37] Returning the property in the condition in which she received it would satisfy the goal of the bare owner to receive the property in an undamaged condition. Certain exceptions to the *salva rei substantia* rule exist, for example, fair wear and tear through *bona fide* use,[38] which includes the fair wear and tear not ascribed to the usufructuary and devaluation not caused by the usufructuary.

Security may be demanded at the commencement or during the course of the usufruct.[39] In *Van Rensburg v Mulder*[40] Hartzenberg J argues for a nuanced approach in determining the amount of security due. In fact, he argued that judges, who have the discretion to determine whether and to what extent an impecunious usufructuary should provide security, indeed have the discretion to determine a reasonable amount where an unreasonable demand for security is made.[41] *Van Rensburg v Mulder,*[42] therefore, exemplifies a nuanced and reasonable approach to the duty of the usufructuary to provide security. Only a small number of cases favour awarding a discretion to the court to exempt the usufructuary from the duty to provide security when it has been demanded. [43] The unwillingness to depart from the duty to provide security, except where common-law principles allow a margin of discretion,

---

[34] See CG van der Merwe *Sakereg* 2 ed (1989) 517 and CP Bezuidenhout *Sakeregtelike aspekte van vruggebruik in die Suid-Afrikaanse reg* LLD dissertation Stellenbosch University (1990) 111 for the wealth of Roman-Dutch literature and case law in this regard.

[35] CG van der Merwe *Sakereg* 2 ed (1989) 516; CP Bezuidenhout *Sakeregtelike aspekte van vruggebruik in die Suid-Afrikaanse reg* (1990) unpublished LLD dissertation Stellenbosch University 111. The measure of care required to satisfy the *civiliter modo* requirement is the *bonus paterfamilias* standard; see footnote 11 and 12 above.

[36] CP Bezuidenhout *Sakeregtelike aspekte van vruggebruik in die Suid-Afrikaanse reg* (1990) unpublished LLD dissertation Stellenbosch University 111 and CG van der Merwe *Sakereg* 2 ed (1989) 516 state that the usufructuary object must be returned in a 'good condition'.

[37] CG van der Merwe *Sakereg* 2 ed (1989) 516; CP Joubert 'Die vruggebruiker se verpligting om verbeterings aan te bring' (1958) 21 *THRHR* 256–276 256, 257.

[38] *Van Rensburg v Mulder* 1998 JDR 0756 (T) 8.

[39] Voet 7 9 11; CG van der Merwe *Sakereg* 2 ed (1989) 517.

[40] *Van Rensburg v Mulder* 1998 JDR 0756 (T).

[41] *Van Rensburg v Mulder* 1998 JDR 0756 (T) 11.

[42] *Van Rensburg v Mulder* 1998 JDR 0756 (T).

[43] AJ van der Walt *Law of servitudes* (2016) 481–483; L Grobler *The* salva rei substantia *requirement in personal servitudes* (2015) unpublished LLD dissertation Stellenbosch University 79.

might still indicate a strict approach to the *salva rei substantia* requirement in general.

If the usufructuary fails to furnish security, she is not entitled to the fruits of the usufructuary property. [44] The fruits of the usufructuary object are then deemed part and parcel of the capital to which the owner is entitled. The failure to provide security may even result in a court order entitling the owner to repossess the usufructuary property in certain circumstances. [45]

In terms of case law, therefore, it seems that thus far only a small number of cases have awarded discretion to the court to exempt the usufructuary from the duty to provide security. The unwillingness to depart from the duty to provide security, except where common-law principles allow a margin of discretion, may in general indicate a strict approach to the *salva rei substantia* requirement. [46]

3.3.3 The requirement to maintain and repair

The usufructuary has to take responsibility for the ordinary repairs and expenses necessary for normal maintenance of the property.[47] The usufructuary does not have to pay for extraordinary repairs, insurance premiums or the replacement of buildings that have fallen into disrepair due to age or that have been accidently destroyed. Normal deterioration is not for the account of the usufructuary either and she only has to return the property in the state that it is in at the termination of usufruct.[48] Bezuidenhout describes maintenance as work that must be done continually, sometimes daily or otherwise with longer breaks, in order to extend or guarantee the life of the object of the usufruct, especially due to day-to-day wear and tear.[49]

In the case of repairs, the duty to execute moderate repairs is distinguished from the execution of extraordinary repairs. It seems that this distinction is necessary to allocate the liability of the usufructuary in terms of her duty to execute moderate repairs. The duty of the usufructuary with regard to repairs and maintenance should further be distinguished from improvements to the property. According to Joubert, South African academic writing

---

[44] Voet 7 9 1, 2, 3; Schorer *ad* Grotius 2 39 3; *Holl Cons* VI 326 *in fine*; Van der Keessel *Praelectiones* op Grotius 2 39 3; CG van der Merwe *Sakereg* 2 ed (1989) 517.

[45] CG van der Merwe *Sakereg* 2 ed (1989) 517.

[46] *Schoeman v Schoeman & Another* 1953 (2) SA 441 (T); CG van der Merwe *Sakereg* 2 ed (1989) 517.

[47] CG van der Merwe & MJ de Waal 'Servitudes' rev CG van der Merwe in WA Joubert & JA Faris (eds) *LAWSA* vol 24 2 ed (2010) para 594.

[48] Paragraphs 595–597.

[49] CP Bezuidenhout *Sakeregtelike aspekte van vruggebruik in die Suid-Afrikaanse reg* (1990) unpublished LLD dissertation Stellenbosch University 119.

corresponds to Roman-Dutch law, which placed a maintenance duty on the usufructuary, but not a duty to improve the property.[50] The usufructuary had to do ordinary repairs (*modicae refectiones*) which a reasonable person would have done to temporarily (*ad temporaneam rei conservationem spectant*) keep the usufructuary property in a good condition (*sarta tecta*). The measure for determining whether ordinary repairs are necessary is the judgment of a reasonable person. Joubert views the criterium as flexible since it is objective.

4 Remedies and termination

4.1 Introduction

Apart from the duties of the usufructuary, two other aspects of usufruct, namely the remedies available to the bare owner and termination of usufruct, reflect the strict approach to the *salva rei substantia* requirement. The severity with which impairment of the substance of the object of the usufruct is visited is a telling indicator of this approach.

In Roman-Dutch law, the grounds for termination related to the *salva rei substantia* requirement were wider than dereliction of duties by the usufructuary since, under certain circumstances, a fraudulent transfer of land by the usufructuary was also held to terminate the usufruct.[51]

4.2 Remedies

The remedies available to the *dominus,* in case of impairment of the substance of the usufructuary object, and the strictness with which they are enforced to ensure the return of the usufructuary object *salva rei substantia,* may be an indication of a strict approach towards the *salva rei substantia* requirement.

The South African common-law remedies[52] include an interdict, a declaratory order, a delictual claim for damages and the *actio negatoria* in cases where the holder of the servitude exceeds the limits of the servitude and acts outside the right afforded to her.[53] The *actio negatoria* allows the

---

[50] References are to CP Joubert 'Die vruggebruiker se verpligting om verbeterings aan te bring' (1958) 21 *THRHR* 256–276 275–276 unless indicated otherwise.

[51] CP Bezuidenhout *Sakeregtelike aspekte van vruggebruik in die Suid-Afrikaanse reg* (1990) unpublished LLD dissertation Stellenbosch University 79 with reference to A Duyck *Decisien en resoluties van den hove van Holland* (1751) 74, 100.

[52] CG van der Merwe *Sakereg* 2 ed (1989) 543–544; also AJ van der Walt *Law of servitudes* (2016) 264–265.

[53] JC Sonnekus 'Bewoningsreg (*habitatio*) – Aard van die regsobjek en die effek dáárvan op die registrasie van die reg' (2015) 26 *Stell LR* 63–85 63; PJ Badenhorst, JM Pienaar & H Mostert *Silberberg and Schoeman's The law of property* 5 ed (2006) 262 referring to Voet 8 5 5 and *JH Wade v AM Paruk* (1904) 25 NLR 219.

owner to claim a prohibition on further infringement, damages, security against future infringement,[54] removal of any unlawfully erected structures[55] and a declaration of rights.[56]

4.3 Termination

South African legal scholars acknowledge that servitudes may be terminated in a number of ways.[57] The two methods of extinction that are relevant to the *salva rei substantia* requirement are termination by permanent impossibility of exercise or enjoyment (if the object is destroyed or changed substantially) and termination by misuse, including dereliction of the usufructuary's duties discussed at 3.3.1 to 3.3.3 above. However, the latter seems to be disputed.[58]

It seems as though the second measure of termination is heavily qualified. According to Roman-Dutch law, excessive use of the object of usufruct, which exceeds the measure of use as indicated in the agreement that established the usufruct, terminates the usufruct.[59] Some authors argue that the usufructuary may not be deprived of her right of usufruct if she misuses the usufructuary property. Others argue that extreme misuse might terminate the usufruct, for example, misuse when the usufructuary fraudulently sells the usufructuary property or attempts to destroy the substance of the usufructuary property.[60] It seems that the threshold for termination in terms of misuse is very high and accordingly allows a relatively wide discretion as to the use of the property.

---

[54] CG van der Merwe *Sakereg* 2 ed (1989) 543 citing Voet 7 6 1, 8 5 5 and Huber *HR* 2 44 16.

[55] PJ Badenhorst, JM Pienaar & H Mostert *Silberberg and Schoeman's The law of property* 5 ed (2006) 262 citing *D* 8 5 14 pr and Voet 8 5 5.

[56] PJ Badenhorst, JM Pienaar & H Mostert *Silberberg and Schoeman's The law of property* 5 ed (2006) 262 citing Voet 8 5 6.

[57] CG Hall & EA Kellaway *Servitudes* 3 ed (1973) 175–176.

[58] According to CG van der Merwe *Sakereg* 2 ed (1989) 540 and CG Hall & EA Kellaway *Servitudes* 3 ed (1973) 176 a usufructuary may not be deprived of her right of usufruct if she misuses the usufructuary property. The usufructuary can be interdicted and compelled to give security for the return of the object of the usufruct in a proper condition. CP Bezuidenhout *Sakeregtelike aspekte van vruggebruik in die Suid-Afrikaanse reg* (1990) unpublished LLD dissertation Stellenbosch University 141 does not rule out the possibility; also L Grobler *The* salva rei substantia *requirement in personal servitudes* (2015) unpublished LLD dissertation Stellenbosch University 93–97.

[59] CG van der Merwe *Sakereg* 2 ed (1989) 540; CP Bezuidenhout *Sakeregtelike aspekte van vruggebruik in die Suid-Afrikaanse reg* (1990) unpublished LLD dissertation Stellenbosch University 141.

[60] CG van der Merwe *Sakereg* (1989) 540 n 626 cites Voet 7 4 4; Van Leeuwen *CF* 1 2 15 25. Cf Groenewegen *ad* Grotius 2 39 16; Van Leeuwen *RHR* 2 9 14.

5 Eviction in the pre-constitutional era

In the pre-constitutional era, according to the common law of usufruct, eviction orders could be obtained against a usufructuary who did not comply with a court order mandating the framing of inventory or the provision of security.[61]

Particularly in the pre-constitutional era, the rules and procedures in eviction proceedings gave precedence to the right of ownership.[62] The plaintiff, who would be the bare owner, merely had to prove that she was the owner of the property and that the defendant, the usufructuary, was in occupation. The onus was then on the usufructuary to establish a right to continue occupation. If the usufructuary pleaded lawful occupation in terms of usufruct, the bare owner had to answer this plea. If the bare owner conceded the existence of a usufruct, she was burdened with proving lawful termination of the usufructuary's right to occupy the property in terms of the usufruct.

In regard to a usufructuary faced with the threat of eviction in reaction to her failure to provide security mandated by a court order, the pre-constitutional case of *Schoeman v Schoeman*[63] serves as an illustration of the manner in which the courts approached the eviction of a usufructuary prior to the Constitution. In this case Roper J considered whether the bare owner was entitled to an order of ejectment against a non-compliant usufructuary and holder of a servitude of habitation of the usufructuary property.[64] With reference to Voet,[65] he concluded that the applicant was entitled to an order of ejectment if the usufructuary did not comply with an order of court for inventory and security to be supplied within one month from the date of the order.[66] In the particular case, the applicant was the registered owner of immovable property subject to a usufruct, in respect of one-half thereof, in favour of the first respondent.[67] Furthermore, the usufructuary was entitled to reside in a house on one of the plots of land until his death. The second

---

61 *Schoeman v Schoeman and Another* 1953 (2) SA 441 (T); *Stain v Hiebner* 1976 (1) SA 34 (C).

62 I Currie & J de Waal *The Bill of Rights Handbook* 6 ed (2013) 587; L Grobler *The* salva rei substantia *requirement in personal servitudes* (2015) unpublished LLD dissertation Stellenbosch University 307.

63 *Schoeman v Schoeman and Another* 1953 (2) SA 441 (T).

64 *Schoeman v Schoeman and Another* 1953 (2) SA 441 (T) 442.

65 Voet 7 9 2; 7 9 9; 7 9 11.

66 *Schoeman v Schoeman and Another* 1953 (2) SA 441 (T) 442; AJ van der Walt *Law of servitudes* (2016) 480–481; L Grobler *The* salva rei substantia *requirement in personal servitudes* (2015) unpublished LLD dissertation Stellenbosch University 69, 308.

67 *Schoeman v Schoeman and Another* 1953 (2) SA 441 (T) 441.

respondent was in occupation of a portion of the house as lessee of the first respondent and the order also applied to him.[68] The case does not contain details of the personal circumstances of the usufructuary or the lessee.

The conclusion reached in this decision, namely that a bare owner would be entitled to an order of ejectment in an instance where a usufructuary fails to frame an inventory and provide security in response to a court order, was based solely on passages from Voet, without considering the circumstances of the respondents. The crucial question is whether such a finding of the court would pass muster in the constitutional dispensation. Not only the usufructuary but also the lessee was affected, since the limited real right of the landlord (the usufructuary in this case) would be terminated.[69] The rigid application of the inventory and security obligations tied to the *salva rei substantia* requirement resulted in the usufructuary and the lessee being deprived of their right to occupy the premises.

The crisp question is what the outcome of such a matter will be in the present constitutional dispensation, especially in the light the right of the usufructuary and lessee not to be deprived of adequate housing in terms of section 26(3) of the Constitution.[70]

6 Usufruct and the right of access to housing

In the event that the usufructuary's right of access to adequate housing is threatened by the deprivation of a right of usufruct, or where her property right in the form of a usufruct is terminated due to the disfigurement, misuse or substantial change in form or destruction of the usufructuary property, the right of access to housing may be compromised.

Usufruct, like the personal servitude of habitation, has the function of securing 'personal residential or housing interests' in cases involving immovable property.[71] Consequently, these servitudes reveal a public law dimension since they have the potential to trigger constitutional scrutiny where the right of access to adequate housing is impaired. Apart from enhancing economic liberty through its utilitarian purpose of securing housing interests, constitutional liberty is also bolstered by personal

---

[68] *Schoeman v Schoeman and Another* 1953 (2) SA 441 (T) 441–442.

[69] PJ Badenhorst, JM Pienaar & H Mostert *Silberberg and Schoeman's The law of property* 5 ed (2006) 433 and n 51.

[70] Compare AJ van der Walt 'Development of the common law of servitude' (2013) 130 *SALJ* 722–756 743. G Muller *The impact of section 26 of the Constitution on the eviction of squatters in South African law* (2011) unpublished LLD dissertation Stellenbosch University 92 remarks that courts have not considered that 'evictions more often than not lead to homelessness, which undermines the right of access to adequate housing'.

[71] AJ van der Walt 'The continued relevance of servitude' (2013) 3 *Prop L Rev* 3–35 30.

servitudes since the rules governing their creation, amendment and termination help shape a free and democratic society.[72] This civic or democratic function of servitude law implies that the Constitution, as the bulwark of a democratic society, needs to be the point of departure for the examination and, if need be, the development of the law of servitude. Furthermore, such an investigation and development should be guided by constitutional guidelines prioritising the analysis of the impact of the common law on higher democratic constitutional provisions. This would include analysis of the impact of the law of usufruct and particularly the *salva rei substantia* requirement on the operation of the housing clause. Does enforcement of the *salva rei substantia* requirement in certain instances exacerbate the already prevalent housing shortage in South Africa? Usufructuaries faced with the enforcement of the preservation requirement may, like those affected by the enforcement of mortgage bonds, be living in poverty, or experience a decrease in welfare.[73] Whereas other areas of law, such as mortgage law, have already been shaped by developments to deal with homelessness,[74] this is not the case regarding the common law of usufruct. The crucial question is whether development is not required to address possible consequences of enforcement of the preservation requirement that may aggravate homelessness.

The usufructuary's right of access to adequate housing is only threatened in limited circumstances, namely in a case involving the deprivation of a usufruct right due to non-compliance with the security and inventory duties where the usufructuary is 'holding over'.[75] The main question in this part of the

---

[72] AJ van der Walt 'The continued relevance of servitude' (2013) 3 *Prop L Rev* 3–35 31.

[73] Compare R Brits *Mortgage foreclosure under the Constitution: Property, housing and the National Credit Act* (2012) unpublished LLD dissertation Stellenbosch University 60; GF Wright 'Die onvermoënde vruggebruiker' (1995) 58 *THRHR* 86–91 86.

[74] R Brits *Mortgage foreclosure under the Constitution: Property, housing and the National Credit Act* (2012) unpublished LLD dissertation Stellenbosch University 61.

[75] A person is deemed to be 'holding over' if she qualifies as an unlawful occupier. The court in *Ndlovu v Ngcobo; Bekker v Jika* 2003 (1) SA 113 (SCA) included parties who previously were lawful but later became unlawful. In *Schoeman v Schoeman and Another* 1953 (2) SA 441 (T) the court established that a holder of the right of habitation would not 'be entitled to the use and enjoyment of the property' until an inventory and security had been provided at the bare owner's insistence. Roper J relied on Voet, who states that wilful non-compliance with the security requirement will deprive the usufructuary 'of all the benefit of the usufruct' for the period of her noncompliance. Furthermore, the bare owner is entitled to claim the property by means of vindication. For the duration of her non-compliance, the usufructuary therefore does not have the right in law to the usufructuary property. The definition of an unlawful occupier would therefore be applicable to the usufructuary who does not provide security at the insistence of the bare owner and in response to a court order. The court in *Vorster v Van Niekerk, Van Niekerk en Enige Ander Onregmatige Okkupeerders Welke Gevind Mag Word op Eiendom Bekend*

contribution is whether and how the substantive law that governs usufruct should develop in response to the housing clause.[76] More concretely, when and how should the law of usufruct allow for the eviction of a usufructuary? Furthermore, when is it unjustifiable to evict the usufructuary? For example, would it be unjustifiable to evict the usufructuary if less invasive measures exist to protect the bare owner or if the result of the limitation of the right of usufruct is disproportionate?

Section 26(1) of the Constitution[77] states: 'Everyone has the right to have access to adequate housing'. Furthermore, subsection (3) prescribes that '[n]o one may be evicted from their home, or have their home demolished, without an order of court made after considering all the relevant circumstances. No legislation may permit arbitrary evictions'. These provisions of the Bill of Rights protect the right of access to adequate housing and provide for procedural fairness when a party who has access to adequate housing is faced with eviction.

The right of access to adequate housing is categorised as a socio-economic right.[78] Socio-economic rights embody the transformative impetus of the Constitution.[79] As such, they create the opportunity to live a 'life of dignity, freedom and equality'.[80] Liebenberg emphasises that judicial review in terms of these constitutional rights and values functions to create the possibility to disengage the entrenched power and privileged position of those who

---

as *Saffierstraat 6, Jordania* Case no 6723/2008 (OFSPD) decided 2009-02-05, interpreted the facts as an example of 'holding over' where PIE was applicable. *In casu* the first respondent averred that the respondents (the applicant's maternal grandfather and his wife) had acquired a life right (*lewensreg*). Therefore, based on case law expanding the scope of the definition of an unlawful occupier, it would seem plausible that PIE could also be applicable to usufructuaries who are 'holding over'. See L Grobler *The* salva rei substantia *requirement in personal servitudes* (2015) unpublished LLD dissertation Stellenbosch University 319–320.

[76] R Brits *Mortgage foreclosure under the Constitution: Property, housing and the National Credit Act* (2012) unpublished LLD dissertation Stellenbosch University 67.

[77] Section 26(1) of the Constitution of the Republic of South Africa, 1996.

[78] I Currie & J de Waal *The Bill of Rights handbook* 6 ed (2013) 565; R Brits *Mortgage foreclosure under the Constitution: Property, housing and the National Credit Act* (2012) unpublished LLD dissertation Stellenbosch University 62, particularly n 8.

[79] S Liebenberg 'The application of socio-economic rights to private law' 2008 *TSAR* 464–480 464; I Currie & J de Waal *The Bill of Rights Handbook* 6 ed (2013) 564.

[80] I Currie & J de Waal *The Bill of Rights handbook* 6 ed (2013) 564. Socio-economic rights are categorised as second-generation rights. They are predominantly conceptualised as positive rights imposing duties on the government based on the interconnection between human rights and basic social living conditions. They may however entail both positive and negative duties. R Brits *Mortgage foreclosure under the Constitution: Property, housing and the National Credit Act* (2012) unpublished LLD dissertation Stellenbosch University

already have access to socio-economic resources, and works against the 'exclusion and marginalisation of those who currently lack the means to participate meaningfully in the social and economic institutions of society'.[81]

The right of access to adequate housing has the purpose of alleviating homelessness and of preventing its unjustified escalation.[82] In this regard, the first two subsections are aimed at the alleviation of homelessness. The first subsection may also be viewed as preventing existing housing being lost, along with subsection three, which regulates evictions.[83] In the context of eviction of usufructuaries who use the usufructuary property unlawfully, only section 26(1) and (3) would be relevant to the discussion.

According to section 26(1), everyone has the right of access to adequate housing. Although this right imposes the duty on the state to provide access to adequate housing in terms of s 26(2), it does not entail an unqualified obligation. The duty is not only imposed on the state, but is also binding on private parties. This was indicated in *Government of the Republic of South Africa v Grootboom*,[84] where it was held that section 26(1) entails 'at the very least, a negative obligation upon the State and all other entities and persons to desist from preventing or impairing the right of access to adequate housing'.[85] In *Jaftha v Schoeman; Van Rooyen v Stolz*[86] the content of this negative duty was fleshed out. The court decided that 'any measure which permits a person to be deprived of existing access to adequate housing, limits the rights protected in section 26(1)'.[87] As Liebenberg notes, this finding indicates that private law rules which allow parties to be deprived

62 states that socio-economic rights are mainly associated with public law, but not limited to this field. As S Liebenberg 'The application of socio-economic rights to private law' 2008 *TSAR* 464–480 464 and I Currie & J de Waal *The Bill of Rights handbook* 6 ed (2013) 565 note, this is the case since common-law rules (including the law of usufruct) 'structure access to socio-economic resources' in property law.

81 S Liebenberg 'The application of socio-economic rights to private law' 2008 *TSAR* 464–480 465.

82 R Brits *Mortgage foreclosure under the Constitution: Property, housing and the National Credit Act* (2012) unpublished LLD dissertation Stellenbosch University 62.

83 R Brits *Mortgage foreclosure under the Constitution: Property, housing and the National Credit Act* (2012) unpublished LLD dissertation Stellenbosch University 62–63.

84 *Government of the Republic of South Africa v Grootboom* 2001 (1) SA 46 (CC) para 34.

85 S Liebenberg 'The application of socio-economic rights to private law' 2008 *TSAR* 464–480 467.

86 *Jaftha v Schoeman and Others; Van Rooyen v Stoltz and Others* 2005 (2) SA 140 (CC).

87 *Jaftha v Schoeman and Others; Van Rooyen v Stoltz and Others* 2005 (2) SA 140 (CC) para 34.

of existing access to socio-economic rights such as the right of access to adequate housing, are inconsistent with section 26(1).[88]

When a usufruct is terminated as a result of non-compliance with a court order to frame inventory or provide security, a usufructuary may lose her home and her right of access to adequate housing may be threatened or compromised. According to the common law, the bare owner has the right to evict the usufructuary as the latter qualifies as an unlawful occupier after termination of the right of usufruct.

Subsection 26(3) entails procedural and substantive requirements safeguarding parties against arbitrary eviction.[89] In terms of the procedural requirements, academic literature indicates a gradual 'proceduralisation to give "remedial bite" to the right'.[90] Procedural principles, particularly those relating to joinder of municipalities, the obligation to report and meaningful engagement, are used 'to move towards establishing the substantive content of the section 26 housing right'.[91] However, the substantive requirements of the subsection are not developed to the same extent.[92] Brits notes that section 26(1) impacts on the content of section 26 as a whole.[93] The section aims to provide and protect access to adequate housing.[94] Therefore, the judicial oversight and discretion mandated by section 26(3) are aimed at ensuring that all the relevant circumstances are taken into account when the right to access to adequate housing is limited. In the application of the Prevention of Illegal Eviction from and Unlawful Occupation of Land Act 19 of 1998 (PIE), the principal piece of legislation promulgated to give effect to section 26, consideration of the relevant circumstances is of significance.

Upon termination of the usufruct, the owner may evict the usufructuary by means of PIE. It is necessary, on an individualised basis, to determine the relevant circumstances that need to be taken into account in deciding whether the usufructuary should be evicted. Section 26(3) does not provide

[88] S Liebenberg 'The application of socio-economic rights to private law' 2008 *TSAR* 464–480 468.

[89] I Currie & J de Waal *The Bill of Rights handbook* 6 ed (2013) 589.

[90] I Currie & J de Waal *The Bill of Rights handbook* 6 ed (2013) 589.

[91] I Currie & J de Waal *The Bill of Rights handbook* 6 ed (2013) 589.

[92] I Currie & J de Waal *The Bill of Rights handbook* 6 ed (2013) 590; R Brits *Mortgage foreclosure under the Constitution: Property, housing and the National Credit Act* (2012) unpublished LLD dissertation Stellenbosch University 65.

[93] R Brits *Mortgage foreclosure under the Constitution: Property, housing and the National Credit Act* (2012) unpublished LLD dissertation Stellenbosch University 65–66.

[94] R Brits *Mortgage foreclosure under the Constitution: Property, housing and the National Credit Act* (2012) unpublished LLD dissertation Stellenbosch University 66.

guidance as to the content and scope of relevant circumstances.[95] PIE provides 'legislative texture'[96] and refers to certain relevant circumstances although other unspecified circumstances may also be pertinent.[97] Pienaar and Mostert also note that a *numerus clausus* of relevant circumstances does not exist.[98] They do, however, attempt to draw conclusions from case law in this regard.[99] Firstly, the identity of the applicant is significant. In cases where the state is the applicant, more stringent requirements and additional duties are involved.[100] In a usufruct case where a bare owner is an applicant in eviction proceedings, the requirements would therefore probably be less strict. Secondly, the vulnerability, indigence, and exigence of the defendants would also be serious considerations where an eviction order is at issue.[101] In the case of an impecunious usufructuary, the court would have to consider the dire need and vulnerability of the defendant, as was amply illustrated in *Van den Heever NO and Others v Coetzee and Another*.[102] Third, the social responsibility of the owner of the property might be a consideration.[103] If the latter cannot or does not want to use the property at issue for better social objectives, it might count in favour of the defendant. In the context of eviction cases concerning usufructuaries, this might imply that the bare owner set on evicting a usufructuary might have to bring evidence of a worthy use for the property, which would probably not outweigh the usufructuary's need for

95 R Brits & AJ van der Walt 'Application of the housing clause during mortgage foreclosure: A subsidiarity approach to the role of the National Credit Act (Part 1)' 2014 *TSAR* 288–305 291.

96 *Port Elizabeth Municipality v Various Occupiers* 2005 (1) SA 217 (CC) para 24.

97 JM Pienaar & H Mostert 'Uitsettings onder die Suid-Afrikaanse Grondwet: Die verhouding tussen artikel 25(1), artikel 26(3) en die uitsettingswet (deel 2)' 2006 *TSAR* 522–536 527.

98 JM Pienaar & H Mostert 'Uitsettings onder die Suid-Afrikaanse Grondwet: Die verhouding tussen artikel 25(1), artikel 26(3) en die uitsettingswet (deel 2)' 2006 *TSAR* 522–536 527.

99 JM Pienaar & H Mostert 'Uitsettings onder die Suid-Afrikaanse Grondwet: Die verhouding tussen artikel 25(1), artikel 26(3) en die uitsettingswet (deel 2)' 2006 *TSAR* 522–536 533–534 also discuss other considerations not applicable to eviction disputes involving usufructuaries.

100 JM Pienaar & H Mostert 'Uitsettings onder die Suid-Afrikaanse Grondwet: Die verhouding tussen artikel 25(1), artikel 26(3) en die uitsettingswet (deel 2)' (2006) *TSAR* 522–536 528.

101 JM Pienaar & H Mostert 'Uitsettings onder die Suid-Afrikaanse Grondwet: Die verhouding tussen artikel 25(1), artikel 26(3) en die uitsettingswet (deel 2)' (2006) *TSAR* 522–536 531.

102 *Van der Heever NO and Others v Coetzee and Another* 2003 JDR 0863 (T).

103 JM Pienaar & H Mostert 'Uitsettings onder die Suid-Afrikaanse Grondwet: Die verhouding tussen artikel 25(1), artikel 26(3) en die uitsettingswet (deel 2)' (2006) *TSAR* 522–536 533.

housing. Fourth, considerations of equity and fairness are paramount – but need not *per se* imply that the occupier's interests will trump those of the applicant.[104] In the application of this factor, the courts, in instances where owners of private property seek eviction, have started to develop the content of subsection 26(3) by giving meaning to the 'just and equitable' requirement mandated in the legislation enacted to give effect to the housing right, namely PIE.[105] In *City of Johannesburg Metropolitan Municipality v Blue Moonlight Properties 39 (Pty) Ltd,*[106] Van der Westhuizen J established that the court should take an 'open list of factors' into consideration when determining whether the eviction would be just and equitable.[107] These factors could include the duration of the occupation, previous lawfulness and potential homelessness of either of the two litigating parties. In *City of Johannesburg v Changing Tides 74 (Pty) Ltd,*[108] the court held that the right of property owners is not absolute, which would imply that there may be cases where an eviction order in favour of a private landowner would not be just and equitable. Private landowners should even, in cases where it would be just and equitable to grant an eviction order, exercise patience where needed to fulfil the requirements of PIE and to prevent temporary homelessness.[109]

Furthermore, in *Ndlovu v Ngcobo; Bekker and Another v Jika,*[110] the court held that the personal circumstances of occupiers are relevant.[111] As Muller observes, the obligation to consider all relevant circumstances marks a significant shift from the common-law position, where eviction was treated as 'an abstract or absolute remedy for a private landowner without regard for the personal circumstances of the occupiers'.[112]

---

[104] JM Pienaar & H Mostert 'Uitsettings onder die Suid-Afrikaanse Grondwet: Die verhouding tussen artikel 25(1), artikel 26(3) en die uitsettingswet (deel 2)' (2006) *TSAR* 522–536 534.

[105] Prevention of Illegal Eviction from and Unlawful Occupation of Land Act 19 of 1998.

[106] *City of Johannesburg Metropolitan Municipality v Blue Moonlight Properties 39 (Pty) Ltd* 2012 (2) SA 104 (CC) para 39.

[107] *City of Johannesburg Metropolitan Municipality v Blue Moonlight Properties 39 (Pty) Ltd* 2012 (2) SA 104 (CC) para 39; I Currie & J de Waal *The Bill of Rights handbook* 6 ed (2013) 590.

[108] 2012 (6) SA 294 (SCA) n 22.

[109] *City of Johannesburg Metropolitan Municipality v Blue Moonlight Properties 39 (Pty) Ltd* 2012 (2) SA 104 (CC) paras 40, 100; *Occupiers of Skurweplaas 353 JR v PPC Aggregate Quarries (Pty) Ltd and Others* 2011 ZACC 36 paras 11, 13; *City of Johannesburg v Changing Tides 74 (Pty) Ltd* 2012 (6) SA 294 (SCA) para 25.

[110] *Ndlovu v Ngcobo; Bekker and Another v Jika* 2003 (1) SA 113 (SCA).

[111] G Muller *The impact of section 26 of the Constitution on the eviction of squatters in South African law* (2011) unpublished LLD dissertation Stellenbosch University 101.

[112] G Muller *The impact of section 26 of the Constitution on the eviction of squatters in South African law* (2011) unpublished LLD dissertation Stellenbosch University 99.

The factors above may also be considered in disputes where a former usufructuary as an unlawful occupier is faced with eviction. A former usufructuary will be an unlawful occupier when her right of usufruct is terminated while she still occupies the usufructuary property. According to PIE, the court is mandated to consider all relevant factors when deciding whether an unlawful occupier should be evicted. Although *Troskie and Another v Liquidator of RSD Construction CC, Wilbecar Liquidators CC t/a Bureau Trust Gauteng RSD Construction CC and Others*[113] dealt with an unregistered usufruct, it not only gives an indication of relevant factors the court might consider in a usufruct case; it also shows how unlawful occupiers in an eviction case should take responsibility for providing sufficient supporting evidence that the court can take into consideration when determining whether an eviction would be just and equitable.[114] Furthermore, the court also distinguished between unlawful occupiers who may be categorised as poor and vulnerable, those whose 'protection was obviously foremost in the legislature's mind when it enacted PIE',[115] and those who do not belong to this class.[116] Factors considered in the decision include the age of the holder of the personal right, the duration of occupation of the premises, whether the property was used to generate an income and whether another source of income was available. The court also considered whether alternative accommodation was available, the health of the holder of the personal right and the urgency of the party bringing the application for an eviction order.[117] In *Troskie*, the parties were elderly people who had

---

113 *Troskie and Another v Liquidator of RSD Construction CC Wilbecar Liquidators CC t/a Bureau Trust Gauteng RSD Construction CC and Others* (71322/2010) [2015] ZAGPPHC 321.

114 *Troskie and Another v Liquidator of RSD Construction CC Wilbecar Liquidators CC t/a Bureau Trust Gauteng RSD Construction CC and Others* (71322/2010) [2015] ZAGPPHC 321 paras 70–71.

115 Van der Berg AJ in *Troskie and Another v Liquidator of RSD Construction CC Wilbecar Liquidators CC t/a Bureau Trust Gauteng RSD Construction CC and Others* (71322/2010) [2015] ZAGPPHC 321 referred to *Wormald NO v Kambule* 2006 (3) SA 562 (SCA) 571E–F para 20. In paras 25–26 of the latter case it was assumed without deciding that according to customary law the widow 'enjoys a type of personal servitude of *usus* or *habitatio*' of the residence she was permitted to occupy. However, the court found her occupation to be unlawful and had to decide whether her eviction would be just and equitable. She was likened to an affluent tenant holding over and consequently not 'in dire need for accommodation'. Therefore, the court concluded that an eviction would be equitable and fair.

116 *Troskie and Another v Liquidator of RSD Construction CC, Wilbecar Liquidators CC t/a Bureau Trust Gauteng RSD Construction CC and Others* (71322/2010) [2015] ZAGPPHC 321 para 72.

117 Paragraphs 69, 73.

lived on the property for 37 years, and the first applicant had acute heart problems. However, they did not reveal their financial position. Van der Berg AJ ruled that they did not belong to the class of persons PIE was enacted to protect from eviction, presumably because they did not disclose their financial position. Consequently, the eviction order was granted. An open list of factors is taken into account as relevant circumstances to determine whether an eviction would be just and equitable. Although these factors might *prima facie* indicate that an eviction might not be just and equitable, certain factors such as the financial position of the unlawful occupier might weigh more than other indicators of vulnerability.

Section 34 governs the right of access to courts and mandates judicial oversight in the settling of private disputes.[118] Brits views section 26(3) as an embodiment of this constitutional value in eviction law, since it underlines that an eviction may only be effected where a court has taken all the relevant circumstances into account.[119] It therefore combines a procedural with a substantive safeguard. Furthermore, as Van der Walt points out, *Jaftha v Schoeman and Others; Van Rooyen v Stoltz and Others*[120] established that court procedures may not be abused. In particular, those facilitating '"normal" commercial processes may not be abused to exploit or exacerbate the economic and social weakness and marginality of the poor, especially when doing so has a negative impact on state efforts to alleviate homelessness'.[121] It is therefore imperative that eviction proceedings, in what would traditionally be seen as private law disputes, take place within this constitutional framework. Evictions can no longer be based on administrative decisions only, but require the authority of a court order granted after all the relevant circumstances have been taken into account.[122] A relevant subsequent question would be how the courts should approach this inquiry where a potential eviction may infringe the right to adequate housing.

Case law pertaining to an eviction order issued to a usufructuary who fails to provide security at the insistence of the bare owner is scarce, both prior to and during the constitutional dispensation. *Schoeman v Schoeman and*

[118] R Brits *Mortgage foreclosure under the Constitution: Property, housing and the National Credit Act* (2012) unpublished LLD dissertation Stellenbosch University 92.

[119] R Brits *Mortgage foreclosure under the Constitution: Property, housing and the National Credit Act* (2012) unpublished LLD dissertation Stellenbosch University 92.

[120] *Jaftha v Schoeman and Others; Van Rooyen v Stoltz and Others* 2005 (2) SA 140 (CC).

[121] AJ van der Walt 'Property, social justice and citizenship: Property law in post-apartheid South Africa' (2008) 19 *Stell LR* 325–346 331–332; R Brits *Mortgage foreclosure under the Constitution: Property, housing and the National Credit Act* (2012) unpublished LLD dissertation Stellenbosch University 76.

[122] I Currie & J de Waal *The Bill of Rights handbook* 6 ed (2013) 587.

Another[123] typifies the common-law response during the pre-constitutional era. Only one notable case after the enactment of the Constitution, namely *Van der Heever NO and Others v Coetzee and Another*,[124] illustrates the consideration of relevant circumstances pertaining to the usufructuary where an eviction order is demanded. However, this case neither refers to the Constitution nor revises the common law-position on the requirement to provide security, as stated in *Schoeman v Schoeman*, although it highlights the exercise of judicial discretion regarding the enforcement of the security obligation.

In *Van der Heever NO and Others v Coetzee and Another*,[125] the usufructuary was clearly impecunious.[126] The usufructuary only possessed an old vehicle and no other assets. Furthermore, she was dependent on the monthly rental income received from letting the house. Accordingly, the court found that she was not able to provide the security that was demanded of her.[127] In the absence of relevant case law, the court referred to an article by Wright on the impecunious usufructuary.[128] Wright discusses the common-law authorities and concludes that the viewpoint taken by Voet, namely that the judge should exercise discretion where an impecunious usufructuary is involved, is the most equitable.[129] Following this approach would also give effect to the intention of the deceased testator to benefit the usufructuary.[130] Van der Byl AJ also found that equity was an important consideration in this case. The court applied its common-law discretion and relieved the usufructuary of the obligation to provide security.

The approach advocated by Van der Byl AJ not only aligns with the dominant viewpoint of Roman-Dutch writers,[131] but would also be in accordance with section 26(3) of the Constitution, which prescribes consideration of all the relevant circumstances. It therefore seems possible to approach cases where an eviction order is demanded on non-compliance with the security requirement in a way that takes cognisance of the relevant circumstances,

---

[123] *Schoeman v Schoeman and Another* 1953 (2) SA 441 (T).

[124] *Van der Heever NO and Others v Coetzee and Another* 2003 JDR 0863 (T).

[125] *Van der Heever NO and Others v Coetzee and Another* 2003 JDR 0863 (T).

[126] *Van der Heever NO and Others v Coetzee and Another* 2003 JDR 0863 (T) 12.

[127] *Van der Heever NO and Others v Coetzee and Another* 2003 JDR 0863 (T) 13.

[128] *Van der Heever NO and Others v Coetzee and Another* 2003 JDR 0863 (T) 12–13.

[129] *Van der Heever NO and Others v Coetzee and Another* 2003 JDR 0863 (T) 12–13. The viewpoint of Voet is also supported by Van der Linden and is the predominant approach of textbook writers. Van der Keessel however advocates a stricter approach not allowing for a lenient approach towards the impecunious usufructuary.

[130] *Van der Heever NO and Others v Coetzee and Another* 2003 JDR 0863 (T) 13.

[131] See discussion of Voet and Van der Linden in GF Wright 'Die Onvermoënde Vruggebruiker' (1995) 58 *THRHR* 86–91.

although it was clearly mandated by the position of the respondent as an impecunious usufructuary. In the absence of further relevant case law on this point during the constitutional dispensation, it is unclear whether the court would consider the relevant circumstances in every instance.

7 Conclusion

From the discussion above, it is evident that section 26 provides mandatory reasons for the development of the common law regarding the *salva rei substantia* requirement.

Enforcement of the *salva rei substantia* requirement that ends in termination of the usufruct will have to comply with the PIE requirements for eviction when applicable. In some instances, it might require the development of the common law to avoid eviction.

Since it is within the power of the courts to develop the common law, and they are constitutionally mandated to do so, they have no discretion to avoid development. Mandatory development of the common law required by the housing clause will have to be considered before property issues are even addressed.

Chapter 12

The development of the social function of ownership: Exploring the pioneering efforts of Otto von Gierke and Léon Duguit

Lars van Vliet and Agustín Parise***

1 Introduction

It is often necessary to limit the powers given by the right of ownership. Those limitations can have different reasons, can trigger different changes in legislation and court decisions, and can have different effects on rights holders and on society at large. André van der Walt was familiar with many of these required limitations, since a key theme in his research was constitutional property law and the question how the powers of ownership were limited by the new South African Constitution.[1] André van der Walt had a leading role in the South African debate about the limitations to ownership, as did Otto von Gierke in Germany and Léon Duguit in France earlier in time. This chapter will therefore focus on two of André van der Walt's predecessors in the tradition of the social function paradigm for ownership.

This chapter is divided into three sections. In the first section, the emergence of a social function for ownership is presented. In the second section, the early

* Assistant Professor, Maastricht University, Faculty of Law.

** Assistant Professor, Maastricht University, Faculty of Law.

[1] See, for example, *Constitutional property law* 2 ed (2005), 3 ed (2011); *Property in the margins* (2009); and *Property and constitution* (2012).

efforts of Otto von Gierke are described, placing them within the evolving German context. In the third section, the efforts of Léon Duguit are set out, showing how they drew attention extending beyond France. The chapter aims to illustrate the changes that ownership has experienced, starting at the turn of the twentieth century, showing the remarkable resilience of that important area of private law.

2 Social function

From the last decades of the nineteenth century the paradigm of ownership started to move away from a purely liberal paradigm. It was gradually replaced by one that advocated for the social function of property. The social function paradigm spread across the western hemisphere and motivated changes in the interpretation given to ownership by the courts, with corresponding changes in the wording of constitutions and civil codes, and with the development of special legislation curbing the powers contained in the right of ownership. The idea of a social function has been explored by jurists both in continental Europe and within the English-language legal discourse.[2]

2.1 *Origins*[3]

This contribution will focus on the socialisation process of the period 1890–1930, yet this was not the first time that the social aspect received attention in legal systems. Already in Roman law the landowners' powers were very much restricted by law.[4] In crowded cities, but also elsewhere, rules of public law restricted owners' use of their land, for instance by regulating the kind of building materials that could be used (eg forbidding wooden walls and straw roofs because of the danger of fire) and the building lines that should be respected.[5] Moreover, neighbour law developed and restricted the owners of land in the free use of their property.[6] This may be

---

[2] See, for example, TT Ankersent & T Ruppert 'Tierra y libertad: the social function doctrine and land reform in Latin America' (2006) 19 *Tul Envtl LJ* 69–120; NM Davidson 'Sketches for a Hamiltonian vernacular as a social function of property' (2011) 80 *Fordham L Rev* 1053–1070 1069. It should be noted that volume 80 of the *Fordham L Rev* (2011) offered a notable English-language collection of papers on the Social Function paradigm.

[3] Parts of this section were extracted *verbatim* from A Parise *Ownership paradigms in American civil law jurisdictions: Manifestations of the shifts in the legislation of Louisiana, Chile, and Argentina (16th–20th centuries)* (2017).

[4] M Kaser *Das römische Privatrecht* vol 1 (1971) para 31 V.

[5] See, for example, the legislation in Maastricht, The Netherlands: *Recueil der recessen, wegens beyde de genaedige heeren ende princen, alhier geëmaneert in den Jaere 1665 tot Maestricht* (1719), cap V.

[6] See, for example, J-F Fournel *Traité du voisinage* 2 vols 3 ed (1812).

called the classical approach or classical paradigm of ownership. The starting point of this classical approach is the owner's liberty, but the liberalism is mitigated by a certain level of social duties. However, especially in the nineteenth century, in a reaction to the feudal burdens of previous centuries, more emphasis was laid on the liberal aspect of the classical paradigm. The idea was that, after the last remaining burdens of the feudal system had (largely) been cast off, ownership was in principle free of constraints. It led to a new and extreme, reactionary, form of paradigm, referred to as a liberal paradigm.

Private law experienced a socialisation process in the period 1890–1930,[7] since the liberal paradigm had offered few limitations to the right of ownership. Gradual changes started to occur in society regarding the extent of that right, and the social function paradigm started to develop across the western hemisphere. That approach entailed a less 'egoistic' understanding of ownership.[8] The aim of the social function advocates was to mitigate the liberal paradigm of ownership. This led to a rebalancing of the liberal paradigm, finding a balance between liberalism and social duties. Changes had occurred in the social and economic structures of different jurisdictions, with massive migrations into cities and the effects of the Industrial Revolution.[9] Accordingly, the crude individualistic paradigm started to be challenged in reaction to the social problems that were developing across the western hemisphere.[10]

The change was sensed early with the revolutionary events of 1848[11] and with the writings of, among others, Pierre-Joseph Proudhon,[12] Karl Heinrich Marx,[13] and Auguste Comte.[14] In 1851, Comte had already stated

---

[7] J-L Halpérin *Histoire du droit privé français depuis 1804* (1996) 186.

[8] B Areán *Curso de derechos reales: privilegios y derecho de retención* 3 ed (1994) 188.

[9] E Cordero Quinzacara 'De la propiedad a las propiedades. La evolución de la concepción liberal de la propiedad' (2008) 31 *Revista de Derecho de la Pontificia Universidad Católica de Valparaíso* 493–525 503.

[10] G Azcárate (de) *Ensayo sobre la historia del derecho de propiedad y su estado actual en Europa* vol III (1883) 357-453.

[11] G Azcárate (de) *Ensayo sobre la historia del derecho de propiedad y su estado actual en Europa* vol III (1883) 359.

[12] M Peset 'Fundamento ideológico de la propiedad' in S de Dios et al (coord) *Historia de la propiedad en España siglos XV-XX. Encuentro interdisciplinar. Salamanca, 3-6 de junio de 1998* (1999) 441–470 443, 449.

[13] MI Adrogué *El derecho de propiedad en la actualidad. Introducción a sus nuevas expresiones* (1991) 32.

[14] TT Ankersent & T Ruppert 'Tierra y libertad: the social function doctrine and land reform in Latin America' (2006) 19 *Tul Envtl LJ* 69–120 95; J-L Bergel *La propriété* (1994) 18; MI Adrogué *El derecho de propiedad en la actualidad. Introducción a sus nuevas expresiones* (1991) 34.

that ownership had a social function that aimed to shape and administer the goods for subsequent generations.[15] Changes in the understanding of ownership therefore started to develop in academic circles, followed by decisions by courts and by the implementation of changes in the positive laws, both in Europe and in the Americas. The idea of a social function, it should be noted, was not limited to property law, being present to different extents in other areas of the law,[16] including family law, succession,[17] and civil procedure.[18] Those advocating for the adoption of a broad social function paradigm could aim to find in the legal provisions a replication of social reality,[19] where law should be a product of reality.[20] Therefore, the social function could be subject to alteration, according to mutations in the social circumstances of different societies at different times.[21]

Advocates for a change in paradigm soon emerged throughout continental Europe, not limited to socialist scholars and their writings.[22] It is important to stress that the social function paradigm should not be confused with socialism. In fact, emphasising the social function had as its purpose a rebalancing of the liberal paradigm. Spain, being particularly important for the Americas due to historical relations, welcomed the new paradigm of a social service or function.[23] As early as 1883, Gumersindo de Azcárate had highlighted the existence of a social function, because ownership entailed duties linked with personality, such as morals, religion, science,

---

[15] See, for example, A Comte *Système de politique positive, ou traité de sociologie, instituant la religion de l'humanité* vol I (1851) 156. See also J Camps y Arboix (de) *La propiedad de la tierra y su función social* (1953) 200.

[16] See, for example, LM Lloredo Alix 'Rafael Altamira y Adolfo Posada: Dos aportaciones a la socialización del derecho y su proyección en Latinoamérica' (2012) 20 *Rechtsgeschichte* 209–233 214.

[17] P Caroni *Escritos sobre la codificiación* translation by AM Cañada & M Martínez Neira (2012) 340–341; P Caroni *Lecciones de historia de la codificación* edition by AM Cañada & M Martínez Neira (2013) 89–99. The latter work addressed the social function in the law of succession in Switzerland.

[18] RR Verkerk *Fact-finding in civil litigation: A comparative perspective* (2010) 257–277.

[19] A Hernández Gil *La función social de la posesión (ensayo de teorización sociológico-jurídica)* (1969) 74.

[20] Th Keiser *Eigentumsrecht in Nationalsozialismus und Fascismo* (2005) 162.

[21] GA Ruíz B *La función social de la propiedad agrícola en la ley de reforma agraria venezolana de 1960* (1964) 39.

[22] J Castán Tobeñas *La propiedad y sus problemas actuales* 2 ed (1963) 63; V Bolgár 'The magic of property and public welfare' (1960) 2 *Inter-American Law Review* 283–298 288.

[23] See, for example, the claim of the development of an early school of thought in Spain available at I Casso y Romero (de) *El problema de la propiedad de la tierra (discurso leído en la Universidad de Sevilla en el acto de la apertura del curso académico el 1º de octubre de 1923)* (1923) 29–30.

art, and industry.[24] Later, the new paradigm would be especially reflected in the writings of José María de Semprún y Gurrea.[25] German-speaking jurisdictions were represented by, among others, Otto von Gierke, who advocated against the egoism of the previous paradigm,[26] and Anton Menger, who advocated from a more socialist standpoint.[27] In a lecture delivered in Vienna in 1889, Von Gierke argued that 'our [German] private law will be more social, or it will not exist'.[28] France was well represented by Duguit, being the globaliser[29] and paladin of the social function paradigm, and by Henri Hayem, whose 1910 doctoral dissertation[30] was very influential in the writings of the former jurist.[31] All approaches to the new paradigm agreed

---

[24] G Azcárate (de) *Ensayo sobre la historia del derecho de propiedad y su estado actual en Europa* vol III (1883) 268, and generally 267–275.

[25] JM de Semprún y Gurrea built upon the social function of Léon Duguit in his 1933 PhD dissertation (see JM Semprún y Gurrea (de) *Sentido funcional del derecho de propiedad como caso concreto del que corresponde a todo derecho. Con un ensayo de representación matemática* (1933)). That work included several references to the French author (eg at 120–122, 135, 330–331). The Spaniard, however, claimed that the meaning of the social function should be changed to one of rational-logical function (5).

See also S Carretero Sánchez *La propiedad: bases sociológicas del concepto en la sociedad postindustrial* (1994) PhD thesis Universidad Complutense de Madrid 117.

[26] S Carretero Sánchez *La propiedad: bases sociológicas del concepto en la sociedad postindustrial* (1994) PhD thesis Universidad Complutense de Madrid 117; and P Caroni *Lecciones de historia de la codificación* edition by AM Cañada & M Martínez Neira (2013) 95. On the reception of the social function in nineteenth-century Germany, see generally T Repgen *Die soziale Aufgabe des Privatrechts* (2001).

[27] P Lira Urquieta *El código civil y el nuevo derecho* (1944) 172. See, for example, A Menger *Über die sozialen Aufgaben der Rechtswissenschaft. Inaugurationsrede gehalten am 24. Oktober 1895 bei Übernahme des Rektorats der Wiener Universität* 2 ed (1905). That 1905 edition indicated that the work of Anton Menger had been translated into French, Russian, and Spanish. See also E Cordero Quinzacara 'De la propiedad a las propiedades. La evolución de la concepción liberal de la propiedad' (2008) 31 *Revista de Derecho de la Pontificia Universidad Católica de Valparaíso* 493–525 506.

[28] O von Gierke, *Die soziale Aufgabe des Privatrechts, Vortrag gehalten am 5. April 1889 in der juristischen Gesellschaft zu Wien* (1889) 45.

[29] French-speaking jurists were considered the globalisers of the new paradigm. See D Kennedy 'Three globalisations of law and legal thought: 1850–2000' in D Trubek & A Santos (eds) *The new law and economic development: A critical appraisal* (2006) 19–73 37.

[30] H Hayem *Essai sur le droit de propriété et ses limites* (1910). Henri Hayem stated in the introduction to that work that private property was certainly one of the topics that raised the most passion during the nineteenth century and would surely raise even more passion during the twentieth century. He stated that 'there is a social function that consists of being the owner' (324).

[31] MC Mirow 'The social-obligation norm of property: Duguit, Hayem, and others' (2010) 22 *Fla J Int'l L* 191–226 216.

that owners, to some extent, had to share the benefits produced by their goods with other members of society.[32]

Heinrich Ahrens, of German origin though active for a time at the French-speaking Free University of Brussels, deserves special attention.[33] Ahrens studied social problems at an early stage and noted that private property had two elements: one individual and the other social.[34] This precursor of later writers claimed in his work *Cours de droit naturel* (1838), which was widely circulated, that 'property, [being] one of the main objects of the law, also contains a set of conditions for the physical and intellectual development of mankind'.[35] He also excelled in disseminating the ideas of his mentor Karl Christian Friedrich Krause in Spanish-speaking circles.[36] The *Cours* of Ahrens was immediately translated into Spanish,[37] and was adopted as teaching material in several American universities as early as 1843.[38]

The need for change was also present in English-speaking jurisdictions, though not necessarily along the same lines or to the same extent as in continental Europe.[39] In the UK, courts during the late nineteenth century addressed the limitation of landowners' freedom on ethical grounds.[40] At the same time, authors in the UK and US addressed the matter. For example, James Barr Ames, Oliver Wendell Holmes Jr, and Sir Frederic Pollock all discussed the matter in their writings.[41] In addition, Benjamin Nathan Cardozo stated that 'property, like liberty though immune under the

---

[32] A Alessandri Rodríguez et al *Tratado de los derecho reales* 6 ed, vol I (2010) 41.

[33] H Welzel 'Ahrens, Heinrich' in *Neue Deutsche Biographie* vol 1 (1953) 113 113.

[34] R Colina Garea *La función social de la propiedad privada en la constitución española de 1978* (1995) PhD thesis Universidad de La Coruña 289.

[35] H Ahrens *Cours de droit naturel ou de philosophie du droit, fait d'après l'état actuel de cette science en Allemagne* (1838) 57. See also A Levaggi 'Ideas acerca del derecho de propiedad en la Argentina entre 1870 y 1920' (2007) 1.1 *Revista Electrónica del Instituto de Investigaciones 'Ambrosio L. Gioja'* 120–133 125.

[36] A Levaggi *Manual de historia del derecho argentino (castellano-indiano/nacional)* 2 ed, vol I (1996) 248. See generally OC Stoetzer *Karl Christian Friedrich Krause and his influence in the Hispanic world* (1998).

[37] See generally H Ahrens *Curso de derecho natural ó de filosofía del derecho, formado con arreglo al estado de esta ciencia en Alemania* translation by R Navarro Zamorano (1841).

[38] AA Roig *Los krausistas argentinos* (1969) 43.

[39] See, for example, the contemporary comparison between the limitations to ownership in Germany and the US, which touch upon the new paradigm. See generally R Lubens 'The social obligation of property ownership: A comparison of German and US law' (2007) 24 *Ariz J Int'l & Comp L* 389–449.

[40] AWB Simpson 'Land ownership and economic freedom' in HN Scheiber (ed) *The state and freedom of contract* (1998) 13–43 27.

[41] AWB Simpson 'Land ownership and economic freedom' in HN Scheiber (ed) *The state and freedom of contract* (1998) 13–43 28.

Constitution from destruction, is not immune from regulation essential for the common good'.[42] Even citing Duguit, he then indicated that 'men are saying today that property, like every other social institution, has a social function to fulfill'.[43] According to the English-speaking advocates for change, landowners' rights in common-law jurisdictions had to be limited, to some extent, in defence of public interest.[44] A closer example is found in the 1950s, when the literature referred to a property-obligation theory. That theory developed rapidly because of the crowded living conditions that resulted in awareness of the use of property by neighbours.[45]

The new paradigm was also present in the writings of the Roman Catholic Church,[46] which did not deny the existence of both a social and an individual character of ownership.[47] The Church therefore recognised an intrinsic social function of private ownership,[48] since all goods should be oriented towards the sustainability of mankind.[49] Accordingly, the Church dealt with basic tenets of property law, aiming to protect the most vulnerable groups.[50] A social doctrine of the Church was developed, and aimed to humanise property.[51] Origins of that social doctrine can be traced back to the Sermon on the Mount,[52] and to the writings of Saint Basil, Saint Ambrose,[53] Saint Augustine, and Saint Thomas Aquinas.[54] For example, Aquinas stated that the Church recognised that property law was part of natural law. However,

---

42 BN Cardozo *The nature of the judicial process* 13th printing (1946) 87.

43 BN Cardozo *The nature of the judicial process* 13th printing (1946) 87–88.

44 AWB Simpson 'Land ownership and economic freedom' in HN Scheiber (ed) *The state and freedom of contract* (1998) 13–43 27.

45 JJ Cox 'Outdoor advertisements – aesthetics and the "public right"' (1959) 33 *Tulane L Rev* 852–869 868.

46 MI Adrogué *El derecho de propiedad en la actualidad. Introducción a sus nuevas expresiones* (1991) 34.

47 See, for example, the statement of Pope Pius XI in the encyclical *Quadragesimo anno* ('Quadragesimo anno'. The Holy See. http://w2.vatican.va/content/pius-xi/en/encyclicals/documents/hf_p-xi_enc_19310515_quadragesimo-anno.html at § 45.

48 See, for example, the statement of Pope Saint John XXIII in the encyclical *Mater et magistra* ('Mater et magistra'. The Holy See. http://w2.vatican.va/content/john-xxiii/en/encyclicals/documents/hf_j-xxiii_enc_15051961_mater.html at § 119.

49 B Areán *Curso de derechos reales: privilegios y derecho de retención* 3 ed (1994) 188.

50 A Alessandri Rodríguez et al *Tratado de los derecho reales* 6 ed, vol I (2010) 42.

51 MI Adrogué *El derecho de propiedad en la actualidad. Introducción a sus nuevas expresiones* (1991) 34.

52 See Matthew 5–7.

53 J Castán Tobeñas *La propiedad y sus problemas actuales* 2 ed (1963) 76.

54 MI Adrogué *El derecho de propiedad en la actualidad. Introducción a sus nuevas expresiones* (1991) 35. See, for example, the late nineteenth-century lecture by Simon Deploige at the University of Leuven on the theory of Aquinas on property. See S Deploige 'La théorie thomiste de la propriété' (1895) 2 *Revue néo-scolastique* 61–82.

private property only derived from natural law, being deduced directly by use of reason.[55] More recent precedents of the social doctrine of the Church can be found in a selection of nineteenth- and twentieth-century encyclicals.[56] These are important documents, because they tend to define long-term papal policies.[57] The following encyclicals are central components of the social doctrine: *Rerum novarum*[58] (1891), of Pope Leo XIII; *Quadragesimo anno*[59] (1931), of Pope Pius XI; *Mater et magistra*[60] (1961), of Pope Saint John XXIII; and *Populorum progressio*[61] (1967), of Pope Paul VI.[62] In the encyclical *Rerum novarum,* Pope Leo XIII was clear in defending the inviolability of private property and in rejecting socialist ideas.[63] Pope Pius XI later declared in *Quadragesimo anno* that the Church never denied the social and individual aspect of ownership.[64] He also claimed that '[...] certain kinds of property, it is rightly contended, ought to be reserved to the state since they carry with them a dominating power so great that cannot without danger to the

---

[55] A Alessandri Rodríguez et al *Tratado de los derecho reales* vol I 6 ed (2010) 42.

[56] The social doctrine is present in other Church documents, however.

[57] A Alessandri Rodríguez et al *Tratado de los derecho reales* vol I 6 ed (2010) 42.

[58] See generally 'Rerum novarum. Encyclical of Pope Leo XIII on capital and labor'. The Holy See. http://www.vatican.va/holy_father/leo_xiii/encyclicals/documents/hf_l-xiii_enc_15051891_rerum-novarum_en.html.

[59] See generally 'Quadragesimo anno'. The Holy See. http://w2.vatican.va/content/pius-xi/en/encyclicals/documents/hf_p-xi_enc_19310515_quadragesimo-anno.html.

[60] See generally 'Mater et magistra'. The Holy See. http://w2.vatican.va/content/john-xxiii/en/encyclicals/documents/hf_j-xxiii_enc_15051961_mater.html.

[61] See generally 'Populorum progressio. Encyclical of Pope Paul VI on the Development of Peoples'. The Holy See. http://www.vatican.va/holy_father/paul_vi/encyclicals/documents/hf_p-vi_enc_26031967_populorum_en.html.

[62] MI Adrogué *El derecho de propiedad en la actualidad. Introducción a sus nuevas expresiones* (1991) 35; and MJ Calvo San José *La función social de la propiedad y su proyección en el sistema de compensación urbanística* (2000) 43.

[63] For example, the encyclical read at § 15:

> [...] it is clear that the main tenet of socialism, community of goods, must be utterly rejected, since it only injures those whom it would seem meant to benefit, is directly contrary to the natural rights of mankind, and would introduce confusion and disorder into the commonweal. The first and most fundamental principle, therefore, if one would undertake to alleviate the condition of the masses, must be the inviolability of private property [...].

'Rerum novarum. Encyclical of Pope Leo XIII on capital and labor'. The Holy See. http://www.vatican.va/holy _ father/leo _ xiii/encyclicals/documents/hf _ l-xiii _ enc _ 15051891 _ rerum-novarum _ en.html. See also A Castro Mayer (de) et al *Reforma agraria: problema de conciencia* (1963) 70.

[64] J Castán Tobeñas *La propiedad y sus problemas actuales* 2 ed (1963) 27.

general welfare be entrusted to private individuals'.[65] Another important precedent is the *Social Code of Mechelen* (1927). That text took its inspiration and foundations directly from the encyclicals and the interpretations made by the episcopate.[66] That code offered a synthesis of the social doctrine of the Church, and naturally dealt with ownership.[67] The second edition of the Social Code, dated 1933, stated in article 94 that property had a two-fold aspect: one individual and private, and another social and public. [68] The Belgian text was even considered a *vade mecum* for all Catholics interested in social matters,[69] being drafted and disseminated by the Intentional Union of Social Studies of Mechelen.[70] The combination of the encyclicals and the postulates of the Social Code showed that the Church advocated for a right of ownership that predated the creation of the states, a natural right that was also inviolable.[71]

2.2 *Contemporary approaches*[72]

The reception of the social function paradigm was not limited to the first decades of the twentieth century or to the European legal discourse.[73] A series of social and ideological twentieth-century shifts (evidenced, for example, in the First and Second World Wars and the Mexican revolution) also had an impact on the reshaping of ownership.[74]

The paradigm was welcomed in legislation and scholarly writings throughout the century, entering even into the twenty-first century. A diversity of legal provisions reflected a departure from the purely liberal paradigm. For example, at the European level, article 1 of Protocol 1 to the

---

[65] See the encyclical at § 114 'Quadragesimo anno'. The Holy See. http://w2.vatican.va/content/pius-xi/en/encyclicals/documents/hf_p-xi_enc_19310515_quadragesimo-anno.html. See also A Alessandri Rodríguez et al *Tratado de los derecho reales* 6 ed, vol I (2010) 43.

[66] Unión Internacional de Estudios Sociales *Código Social de Malinas* (1949) 13.

[67] Unión Internacional de Estudios Sociales *Código Social de Malinas* (1949) 8.

[68] Unión Internacional de Estudios Sociales *Código Social de Malinas* (1949) 41.

[69] Unión Internacional de Estudios Sociales *Código Social de Malinas* (1949) 14.

[70] Unión Internacional de Estudios Sociales *Código Social de Malinas* (1949) 8.

[71] MJ Calvo San José *La función social de la propiedad y su proyección en el sistema de compensación urbanística* (2000) 45.

[72] Parts of this section were extracted *verbatim* from A Parise *Ownership paradigms in American civil law jurisdictions: Manifestations of the shifts in the legislation of Louisiana, Chile, and Argentina (16th–20th centuries)* (2017).

[73] See also MC Mirow 'The social-obligation norm of property: Duguit, Hayem, and others' (2010) 22 *Fla J Int'l L* 191–226 196.

[74] ST Ramella 'Propiedad en función social en la Constitución de 1949: Una "mentalidad" del Antiguo Régimen representada en el constitucionalismo social de la época' (2007) 35 *Revista de Historia del Derecho* 297–354 320.

Convention for the Protection of Human Rights and Fundamental Freedoms (1953) referred to limitations due to public interest.[75] Similarly, the *American Convention on Human Rights* (1969) addressed interest in a social dimension for property.[76] A diversity of authors, likewise, have made manifest a departure from the traditional liberal paradigm. For example, in the US, contemporary authors refer to the renaissance of a new and social paradigm that departs from the liberal paradigm.[77] Accordingly, Joseph William Singer speaks of a social relations model, which 'reconceptualizes property as a social system composed of entitlements which shape the contours of social relationships',[78] being able to include relations between people 'both at the level of society as a whole (the macro level) and in the context of particular relationships (the micro level).'[79] Other US scholars also speak of a social-obligation theory.[80] For example, Gregory S. Alexander addresses an approach to the social-obligation theory that focuses on human flourishing.[81] He argues that 'an owner is morally obligated to provide to the society of which the individual is a member those benefits that the society reasonably regards as necessary

[75] Article 1 of Protocol 1 to the *Convention for the Protection of Human Rights and Fundamental Freedoms* ('Protocol', in *European Convention on Human Rights*. European Court of Human Rights – Council of Europe 31–37 http://www.echr.coe.int/Documents/Convention_ENG.pdf.

[76] Article 21 of the *American Convention on Human Rights* ('American Convention on Human Rights "Pact of San Jose, Costa Rica" (B–32)'. Department of International Law, Organisation of American States, Washington DC http://www.oas.org/dil/treaties_B-32_American_Convention_on_Human_Rights.htm. See also B Areán *Curso de derechos reales: privilegios y derecho de retención* 3 ed (1994) 189.

[77] MC Mirow 'The social-obligation norm of property: Duguit, Hayem, and others' (2010) 22 *Fla J Int'l L* 191–226 194.

[78] JW Singer 'Property and social relations: From title to entitlement' in GE van Maanen & AJ van der Walt (eds) *Property law on the threshold of the 21st century: Proceedings of an international colloquium 'Property law on the threshold of the 21st century', 28–30 August 1995, Maastricht* (1996) 69–90 78.

[79] JW Singer 'Property and social relations: From title to entitlement' in GE van Maanen & AJ van der Walt (eds) *Property law on the threshold of the 21st century: Proceedings of an international colloquium 'Property law on the threshold of the 21st century', 28–30 August 1995, Maastricht* (1996) 69–90 78.

[80] See generally GS Alexander 'Pluralism and property' (2011) 80 *Fordham L Rev* 1017–1052.

[81] See generally GS Alexander 'The social-obligation norm in American property law' (2009) 94 *Cornell L Rev* 745–819; GS Alexander 'Ownership and obligations: The human flourishing theory of property' (2013) 43 *Hong Kong LJ* 451–462. See also MC Mirow 'The social-obligation norm of property: Duguit, Hayem, and others' (2010) 22 *Fla J Int'l L* 191–226 194.

for human flourishing'.[82] All these notions can be traced back to the social function paradigm that took force during the period 1890–1930.

2.3 *A* Mos africanus australis *by André van der Walt*

André van der Walt advocated through his research for the development of a new theoretical paradigm for property law based on the values of the post-apartheid era, a property law based on the South African Constitution, 1996. He firmly believed from the very beginning that the Constitution would have a far-reaching influence on property law and the concept of ownership. André van der Walt summarised the research goals of his Chair in a 2017 self-evaluation report. In his words:

> The general premise for this specific research aim was that pre-constitutional property law has developed within a theoretical framework that has been informed by liberal, social and neo-liberal economic thinking and that this theoretical framework promoted a set of property rules and principles that are dominated by notions of individualised, exclusionary power.
>
> The second premise was that this set of property rules within this individualistic, exclusionary theoretical framework had a negative effect on the development of property law in that it facilitated and supported the kind of thinking that was relied upon by the apartheid governments to justify large-scale forced removals and the separate development of residential areas that characterised the apartheid era. The apartheid laws have now largely been scrapped; however, the underlying theoretical approach will not automatically cease to influence the development of law in the constitutional era, in fact, it is likely that it will continue to be influential unless it is countered by a different, critical approach that is better attuned to constitutional goals.
>
> The most important part of this second premise was that apartheid-era thinking of property specifically inhibits the suitable development of post-apartheid law because it continues to render eviction simple and easy (by placing emphasis on the right to exclude) and it restricts the possibilities of large-scale transformative government intervention in the property regime.
>
> The third underlying premise was that a new theoretical framework would have to be developed to overcome or at least balance out the effects of individualism, exclusivism and anti-regulatory autonomy in current property law thinking, and that such a theoretical framework would have to be based on constitutional goals such as social and legal transformation and the attainment of greater equality, justice and equitable access to natural resources and property.[83]

---

[82] GS Alexander 'The social-obligation norm in American property law' (2009) 94 *Cornell L Rev* 745–819 774.

[83] Five-year review of the DST/NRF South African Research Chair Self Evaluation Report (9 March 2017) 12.

Van der Walt stressed in this report that property law could no longer be studied by concentrating on the common law only, but that the Constitution, and most notably the property guarantee in article 25, had to be taken into account as well. Despite the apparent division between common law and constitutional law, property law should be seen as an overarching field. This influence of the Constitution on private law is what van der Walt called the 'single system of law' principle.[84]

A balance must be found in transforming property law, and André van der Walt was well aware of that important fact. In South African law that balance encompassed, on the one hand, the protection of existing property rights (the liberal paradigm) and, on the other hand, broadening access to and redistributing property (the social paradigm).[85]

3 A *Mos teutonicus* by Otto von Gierke

During the Middle Ages jurists had developed the idea of split ownership in order to explain the feudal relationships in Roman law terminology. Split ownership distinguishes between *dominium directum*, ownership of the feudal lord, and *dominium utile*, ownership of the vassal.[86] At the start of the nineteenth century it was Anton FJ Thibaut who brought the definitive evidence that the theory of split ownership, still to be found in German law of his time, was based on a wrong interpretation of the Roman sources.[87] In legal theory Thibaut's publication opened the possibility to formulate the classical liberal definition of ownership as a power over an object that was in principle unlimited. In practice, though, it took a lot more time to remove all feudal burdens.[88] It should be noted, however, that the classic definition by Bernhard Windscheid already indicated that ownership had certain limits: 'ownership itself is unlimited, but it tolerates exceptions'.[89] The Pandectists

---

[84] AJ van der Walt *Property and constitution* (2012) 16–17 and ch 2.

[85] AJ van der Walt 'Property theory and the transformation of property law' in E Cooke (ed) *Modern studies in property law* vol III (2005) 361–380.

[86] For more information on *dominium duplex*, see R Feenstra 'Les origines du "dominium utile" chez les glossateurs' in R Feenstra, JHA Lokin & N van der Wal (eds) *Flores legum HJ Scheltema antecessori Groningano oblati* (1971) 49–93; P Grossi 'La proprietà e le proprietà nell'officina dello storico' in P Grossi *Il dominio e le cose: Percezioni medievali e moderne dei diritti reali* (1992) 603–665 637–648. On a current approximation to *dominium duplex*, see D Heirbaut 'Feudal law: The real *ius commune* of property in Europe, or: Should we reintroduce *duplex dominium*?' (2003) 3 *Europ Rev Pvt L* 301–320.

[87] AFJ Thibaut *Ueber dominium directum und utile* in AFJ Thibaut *Versuche über einzelne Theile der Theorie des Rechts* vol 2 2 ed (1817) 67.

[88] See Ph Becker *Süddeutsche Lehenrechtsgesetzgebung im 19. Jahrhundert, Das Lehenwesen und die Mobilisierung des Grundeigentums* (2014).

[89] B Windscheid & Th Kipp *Lehrbuch der Pandekten* vol 1 8 ed (1900) para 167.

of the nineteenth century,[90] such as Windscheid, were well aware of the limits to powers of the owner, especially in cases of land ownership. The term 'unlimited' therefore had a normative meaning and was not meant as a description of legal reality.[91] Windscheid showed in detail how the right of landownership was limited in the general interest.[92]

The nineteenth century pandectist, liberal view on ownership was built on a right of ownership which was at last freed of feudal burdens. To prevent misunderstandings, it should be stressed that this liberal view did not mean that ownership had no limits, but it had fewer limits than the classical ownership paradigm. In the second half of the nineteenth century this liberal view came under attack. The attack came from different sides, but this chapter will concentrate on the attack by Otto von Gierke, one of the most prominent members of the so-called School of Germanic law. He was born in Stettin in 1841 and had read law in Berlin and Heidelberg. This prominent jurist died during the inter-war period, in 1921 in Berlin.[93] The 'Germanic law' movement insisted on a reduction of the influence of Roman law on the then modern nineteenth-century German law and sought a reorientation on what the school regarded as Germanic law developed in the German-speaking areas from the Middle Ages. Two of Von Gierke's most important books about Germanic law are his multi-volume works entitled *Das deutsche Genossenschaftsrecht* (4 vols 1868–1913) and *Deutsches Privatrecht* (3 vols 1895–1917).[94] He was one of the most prominent critics of the drafts of a new civil code for the German Empire, which he regarded as too much influenced by the individualistic ideas of Roman law and of the early nineteenth century. In his 1889 lecture, already mentioned above, he expressed one of his main points of criticism, namely the idea that the draft civil code was not social enough. These efforts are clearly reflected in the title of that lecture, which in translation reads 'The social task of private law'.[95] The following analysis

---

[90] The German academics studying Roman law as applied in practice in the nineteenth century.

[91] K Kroeschell *Die nazionalsozialistische Eigentumslehre* in M Stolleis & D Simon (eds) *Rechtsgeschichte im Nationalsozialismus* (1989) 43, 44.

[92] B Windscheid *Lehrbuch des Pandektenrechts* vol 1 3 ed (1870) para 169. Cf AJ van der Walt & P Dhliwayo 'The notion of absolute and exclusive ownership: A doctrinal analysis' (2017) 134 *SALJ* 34–52.

[93] G Kleinheyer & J Schröder *Deutsche Juristen aus fünf Jahrhunderten* 3 ed (1989) 96–101.

[94] In 2010 a fourth volume was published from Von Gierke's draft texts.

[95] *Die soziale Aufgabe des Privatrechts, Vortrag gehalten am 5. April 1889 in der juristischen Gesellschaft zu Wien*. An English translation has been made by Ewan McGaughey under the title *The social role of private law*, SSRN-id2861875.pdf.

focuses on Von Gierke's views on the right of ownership and leaves aside his remarks on other parts of private law.

3.1 Postulates

In his lecture Von Gierke points to the Roman divide between private law and public law, and stresses that Roman private law first and foremost protected individual interests, whereas public law protected public interests.[96] He said that ultimately this sharp divide is untenable and that a legal system should not forget the common goals of both private law and public law.[97] Von Gierke then added that the legal system should also in the area of private law, 'although it cares foremost for individual interests, strive for the common good, and in public law, although it looks first to the whole, it should be just towards the individual'.[98] He was of the opinion that the individualism of Roman private law was unable to protect against forces undermining society.[99] Von Gierke regarded it as a huge advantage that the underdeveloped Germanic law had never embraced such a distinction between private law and public law, that in Germanic law the two branches of the law were much more a unity than in Roman law.[100] He added '[p] rivate law remained unfree, bound by an admixture of public law: but it was through and through social!'[101]

Von Gierke, however, was well aware of the extreme positions of his time and warned against them: on the one hand, the extreme of stressing individual freedom and, on the other hand, the socialism in which the interests and freedom of individuals were sacrificed, in which private law would be transformed into a body of public administration. In stark words he warned that –

> [b]oth views have to be fought against. The removal of public law from the State, in the sense of natural law individualism, would mean dissolution and death, while turning private law into public law in the sense of socialism would mean bondage

[96] O von Gierke *Die soziale Aufgabe des Privatrechts, Vortrag gehalten am 5. April 1889 in der juristischen Gesellschaft zu Wien* (1889) 5.

[97] O von Gierke *Die soziale Aufgabe des Privatrechts, Vortrag gehalten am 5. April 1889 in der juristischen Gesellschaft zu Wien* (1889) 5, 6.

[98] O von Gierke *Die soziale Aufgabe des Privatrechts, Vortrag gehalten am 5. April 1889 in der juristischen Gesellschaft zu Wien* (1889) 6.

[99] O von Gierke *Die soziale Aufgabe des Privatrechts, Vortrag gehalten am 5. April 1889 in der juristischen Gesellschaft zu Wien* (1889) 7.

[100] O von Gierke *Die soziale Aufgabe des Privatrechts, Vortrag gehalten am 5. April 1889 in der juristischen Gesellschaft zu Wien* (1889) 7.

[101] O von Gierke *Die soziale Aufgabe des Privatrechts, Vortrag gehalten am 5. April 1889 in der juristischen Gesellschaft zu Wien* (1889) 7 and 8.

> and barbarism [...] We cannot break away from the great Germanic idea of the unity of all law without giving up our future. And this idea will in eternity be incompatible with an absolutistic public law, but it will equally in eternity be incompatible with an individualistic private law.[102]

He further claimed that '[s]tated simply: our public law should be blown a scent of natural law freedom and our private law must absorb a drop of socialist oil.'[103] In 1919 he repeated his warning against socialism's curbing of individual freedom in a lecture: 'Our State should be a social State. Social, but not socialistic.'[104]

In Von Gierke's view the 'power over things without any obligation is out of the question' and there should be 'no right without obligation' since 'ownership without obligations has no future'.[105] He criticised the draft civil code for overstressing the individual freedom of owners and their right not to take into account the reasonable interests of third parties. In his view there was a danger that the doctrine of abuse of right would not be able to solve this problem in a sufficient way; and he therefore added that '[i]f needed, the legal order must not shy away from not merely prohibiting the abuse of ownership, but should turn the duty of its just use to a socially necessary extent into a legal duty'.[106]

Von Gierke published, also in 1889, his critical review of the draft civil code for the German Empire (first reading),[107] which described not only the general approach of the drafters but also the various provisions in great detail. It shows why Von Gierke thought that the draft civil code was not social enough.[108] Many pages of the book contain derogatory remarks about

---

[102] O von Gierke *Die soziale Aufgabe des Privatrechts, Vortrag gehalten am 5. April 1889 in der juristischen Gesellschaft zu Wien* (1889) 11–12.

[103] O von Gierke *Die soziale Aufgabe des Privatrechts, Vortrag gehalten am 5. April 1889 in der juristischen Gesellschaft zu Wien* (1889) 13. The translation of this sentence is largely based on McGaughey's translation, but his translation 'ointment' was replaced with 'oil'. The German word can mean both oil and ointment, but it is likely that von Gierke meant oil. Von Gierke's expression of 'socialist oil' became one of his famous expressions, although the expression was first used by Heinrich Brunner. See T Repgen *Die soziale Aufgabe des Privatrechts* (2001) 4.

[104] O von Gierke *Der germanische Staatsgedanke, Vortrag gehalten am 4. Mai 1919* (1919) 27.

[105] O von Gierke *Die soziale Aufgabe des Privatrechts, Vortrag gehalten am 5. April 1889 in der juristischen Gesellschaft zu Wien* (1889) 17–18.

[106] O von Gierke *Die soziale Aufgabe des Privatrechts, Vortrag gehalten am 5. April 1889 in der juristischen Gesellschaft zu Wien* (1889) 19.

[107] O von Gierke *Der Entwurf eines bürgerlichen Gesetzbuchs und das deutsche Recht* (1889).

[108] This chapter focuses on the right of ownership. For that reason the analysis of von Gierke's book will equally be confined to his criticism of the provisions on ownership.

Roman law and the drafters' preference for Roman law. It seems that often his main argument against a certain provision in the draft was the mere fact that the provision was based on Roman law rather than Germanic law.

The most important example can be found in the definition of ownership itself. Von Gierke preferred the view that the definition itself of ownership already contained certain limitations. He pointed to the fact that in the German law of his time ownership of land was certainly not without boundaries. Owners could not in principle do whatever they liked. Therefore, Von Gierke fiercely opposed the traditional liberal view, adopted in the draft, that the right of ownership was in principle without limits, and that the owner's freedom could only be limited by express exceptions. In § 848 the draft read: 'The owner of a thing has the right, to the exclusion of others, to use the thing and dispose of the thing in an arbitrary way, as far as there are no limits set by legislation and by rights of third parties.' In Von Gierke's own words:

> This blunt formulation of the Roman notion of ownership is then immediately moderated by adding 'as far as there are no limits set by legislation and by rights of third parties.' And in §§ 850–867 the draft sets up a number of neighbour law restrictions of landownership. However, since for the rest the text of the draft makes no mention of statutory restrictions of landownership [...] a completely distorted picture is drawn. Fortunately, in reality, already the current German law twists this supposed owner's power of arbitrariness right round in the case of land-ownership! The draft cannot change this.[109]

He criticised the fact that the drafters had explicitly rejected the view of the 1794 Prussian *Allgemeines Landrecht* (ALR), according to which the right of ownership had internal limits already in its very definition, referring to ALR I 8 §§ 27–28, and I 22 § 3.[110] Von Gierke's remark is not really justified, as I 8 §§27 and 28 contain definitions of abuse of right. A few provisions earlier, the ALR provided that the rights of the owner were in principle limitless and were only limited by the rights of third parties and legislation (I 8 § 13 and § 26). This view is no different from the definition of the 1804 French civil code and the draft civil code for the German Empire (first reading).

---

[109] O von Gierke *Der Entwurf eines bürgerlichen Gesetzbuchs und das deutsche Recht* (1889) 103. That current German private law had already become more social was something Von Gierke also showed in his 1889 lecture. But he regretted that the social influence was left to specific legislation and was not adopted in the core of private law. See O von Gierke *Die soziale Aufgabe des Privatrechts, Vortrag gehalten am 5. April 1889 in der juristischen Gesellschaft zu Wien* (1889) 15–16.

[110] O von Gierke *Der Entwurf eines bürgerlichen Gesetzbuchs und das deutsche Recht* (1889) 324.

A second example is to be found in his more detailed treatment of the various property law provisions, where he criticised the drafters' suggestion that the provisions on *bona fide* purchase were largely based on Roman law but contained some exceptions. Von Gierke rightly pointed out that in fact the draft codified something very different: a broadly formulated third party protection, as was already found in the Germanic principle of '*Hand wahre Hand*.' This principle offered third party protection where owners had entrusted their thing to another person, who abused this confidence. In such cases owners had to sue their contractual counterparties, but could not reclaim the thing from a *bona fide* third party.[111] The Germanic principle had been largely discarded by the Roman rule that in these cases the thing could be reclaimed for the *bona fide* third party.[112] Rather than showing his satisfaction that the drafters codified a broad third party protection regime, Von Gierke reproached the Motive (explanatory notes) of referring to Roman law and not making an explicit reference to Germanic law instead. Only after this general reproach did he go into detail, criticising some of the details of the regime.[113]

3 *Impact on the legal discourse*

The claims of Von Gierke received attention in the legal narrative of his time. For example, Gottlieb Planck, one of the most important members of the first and second drafting committee of the German civil code,[114] reacted to the claims, yet was not at all impressed by Von Gierke's attacks. He countered Von Gierke's view that the owner's powers in the case of land ownership, unlike in the case of ownership of movables, had to be further limited. In his words:

> That should certainly be acknowledged, but it does not follow that the provision of § 848 is therefore incorrect. On the contrary, by adding 'as far as there are no limits set by legislation and by rights of third parties' the draft expressly points to the existence of limits. As [Von] Gierke stresses, the amount of limitations is very large; they are partly to be found in the following provisions of the draft, and partly in those matters that are left to state legislation. It would naturally have

[111] JF Runde *Handbuch des heutigen deutschen Privatrechts: nach dem Systeme des Herrn Hofraths Runde* vol 2, edited by WAF Danz (1800) para 199.

[112] JF Runde *Grundsätze des gemeinen deutschen Privatrechts* 2 ed (1795) para 199.

[113] O von Gierke *Der Entwurf eines bürgerlichen Gesetzbuchs und das deutsche Recht* (1889) 337–341.

[114] M Coester 'Gottlieb Planck (1824–1910), Ein Vater des neuen bürgerlichen Rechts' in F Loos (ed) *Rechtswissenschaft in Göttingen, Göttinger Juristen aus 250 Jahren*, Göttinger Universitätsschriften, Serie A Schriften, vol 6 (1987) 299–315.

> been impossible to put all these limitations in the provisions in question, and it was only possible, as was done, to refer to them.[115]

As Murray Raff showed, in the nineteenth century there was continuing recognition of the responsibilities inherent in ownership.[116] Raff pointed to the fact that the influential nineteenth-century author Rudolph von Jhering had already asserted that the owner had no absolute power of disposition, and that such an absolute ownership could not be tolerated by society and was never tolerated.[117]

The idea that ownership had a social function also played a role in the constitutional sphere. The 1919 Weimar Constitution, officially called the Constitution of the German Empire (*Verfassung des Deutschen Reichs*), reflected the large influence of social politics.[118] The drafts even showed clear socialist or communist provisions.[119] The social view on ownership was reflected in the provision about the right of ownership. Article 153 read:

> (I) Ownership is guaranteed by the Constitution. Its content and its borders arise from legislation.
>
> (II) Expropriation can take place only in the general interest and on a statutory basis. It takes place against fair compensation, unless a Reich statute provides otherwise. [...]
>
> (III) Ownership creates obligations. Its use should at the same time be a service to the general interest.

Article 153 (I), providing that the content and the boundaries of the right of ownership were set by legislation, encapsulates an idea that can already be found in Von Gierke's works. It is a clear departure from the liberal view in which the powers of owners are in principle limitless and in which legislation may make exceptions to this freedom. Konrad Beyerle, one of the drafters of the Weimar Constitution, and the drafter of the part on fundamental rights, sent his draft on fundamental rights[120] to several academics, including Otto von Gierke, inviting them to give advice on the draft within 8 days. Von

[115] G Planck 'Zur Kritik des Entwurfs eines bürgerlichen Gesetzbuches' (1889) 75 AcP 327 397. Cited from K Kroeschell 'Die nazionalsozialistische Eigentumslehre' in M Stolleis & D Simon *Rechtsgeschichte im Nationalsozialismus* (1989) 46.

[116] M Raff *Private property and environmental responsibility: A comparative study of German real property law* (2004) 156.

[117] M Raff *Private property and environmental responsibility: A comparative study of German real property law* (2004) 156-157. We are grateful to Murray Raff for drawing our attention to Jhering's views. See R von Jhering *Der Zwang im Recht* vol 1 (1877) 510.

[118] H Hattenhauer *Grundbegriffe des bürgerlichen Rechts* 2 ed (2000) 145.

[119] Such as articles 60 and 61 of Beyerle's draft of 6 May 1919.

[120] It was the draft of 6 May 1919, published in W Pauly *Grundrechtslaboratorium Weimar* (2004) 79–91. See also W Pauly *Grundrechtslaboratorium Weimar* (2004) 43.

Gierke's advice[121] showed that Von Gierke agreed with the first paragraph of article 58 of the draft, which would become the first paragraph of article 153 with minor changes. He recommended the addition of the legal obligations to society created by ownership. In that case paragraph 3 could be removed, which paragraph 'fits as poorly into the fundamental rights as the expression "noblesse oblige"'.[122] However, Von Gierke criticised paragraph 2 of article 58 fiercely, as it allowed expropriation without fair compensation. He wrote: 'Should then a simple Reich statute be able to provide for an expropriation without compensation, a simple confiscation, for the benefit of society?'[123]

He was also squarely against article 60,[124] which in paragraph 3 read: 'The cultivation and exploitation of the land is a duty of the possessor of land as against society. The increase in the value of land which is not the result of labour or financial investment should be made useful for the tasks of society through tax legislation.' Von Gierke's advice was only partly followed. Article 60 was removed altogether, but article 58, which was to become 153, was hardly changed. Von Gierke's advice to remove the second paragraph (expropriation without compensation) was not followed. This aberration in article 153(II) of the Constitution did not return in the post-World War II German Constitution.

As indicated by Hans J Wieling, a responsible legal system should seek the right compromise between the liberal approach of the right of ownership (emphasising the owner's freedom) and the social approach (emphasising the owner's obligations). He noted that '[t]he extreme forms cannot be found in praxis. Even the allegedly so liberal Roman ownership was in reality subject to considerable restrictions'.[125] Wieling further summarised the problem by means of a clarifying historical overview:

> Enlightenment and the French revolution led to liberalism and individualism in the nineteenth century. The traditional bonds lapsed, ownership became the right to absolute power. However, ownership was never, not even during the time of liberalism, an unlimited right.
>
> Limits of ownership have always existed, although to a different degree in different times. At the end of the nineteenth century liberalism was topped with and replaced with socialistic tendencies [footnote referring to Von Gierke's 1889 lecture]. The 1919 Weimar Constitution, it is true, laid down in Art. 153 I a constitutional protection of ownership, but stressed in Art. 153 I the social

[121] The advice was published in W Pauly *Grundrechtslaboratorium Weimar* (2004) 107–113.

[122] W Pauly *Grundrechtslaboratorium Weimar* (2004) 107–113, 111.

[123] W Pauly *Grundrechtslaboratorium Weimar* (2004) 107–113, 111.

[124] W Pauly *Grundrechtslaboratorium Weimar* (2004) 107–113, 111.

[125] HJ Wieling *Sachenrecht* vol 1 2 ed (2006) 264.

> obligations of ownership [...] National Socialism exaggerated these tendencies, in that it raised the general interests to the dominating value, and neglected the interests of the individual. The Constitution in Art. 14 II again emphasises the protection of ownership, but emphasises at the same time in Art. 14 II the social bonds of ownership [...].[126]

Was the urge to socialise the concept of ownership a merely theoretical debate? Certainly not. In practice, land ownership was more and more regulated and restricted, certainly under the influence of socialist politicians in the 1970s, as Karl Kroeschell stressed.[127] Nowadays, in many jurisdictions it is only natural that ownership does not give unlimited powers and that in order to describe the powers of the owner it is vital not to concentrate on private law only but to look to public law and constitutional law at the same time. After all, property law, to use André van der Walt's expression, underlies the 'single system of law' principle.[128] The *exposé* by Wieling refers to a legal norm in German constitutional property law that has long been a central point of reference for André van der Walt and many of his disciples. Article 14 of the German Constitution and the rich literature and case law surrounding it, including its in-depth comparison by André van der Walt[129] and his scholars with South African law, will be of lasting importance to South African law. In his 2012 *Property and constitution,* André van der Walt summarised the influence of the South African Constitution on property law as follows:

> In view of the supremacy of the Constitution and the one-system-of-law principle [...] we cannot simply assume that our pre-1994 understanding of property or the logic of the common law can solve property conflicts adequately, or even that we may legitimately rely on them for that purpose. [...] Judging from comparable foreign law (especially German law), this aspect of the problem [i.e. interpreting property legislation and developing the common law principles and institutions of property in the light of the Constitution] requires the development of a constitutionally driven notion of property that can inform the interpretation of legislation and the development of the common law in a direction that will tend to create a single system of law that promotes the spirit, purport and objects of the Bill of Rights in particular and of the Constitution in general. [...] In the end I argue in favour of a notion of property that takes its cue not from the nature and content of individual property rights, but from an overall system of property that includes all the sources of property law (Constitution, legislation and common

[126] HJ Wieling *Sachenrecht* vol 1 2 ed (2006) 264–265.

[127] K Kroeschell *Die nazionalsozialistische Eigentumslehre* in M Stolleis & D Simon (eds) *Rechtsgeschichte im Nationalsozialismus* (1989) 56–59.

[128] AJ van der Walt *Property and constitution* (2012) 16–17.

[129] See, for example, AJ van der Walt *Property and constitution* (2012) 126–131.

law) and the diverse collection of values, principles, institutions, practices, rights and obligations that emerges from them.[130]

The writings by Von Gierke can be also analysed in light of the National Socialist and fascist movements that took the stage during the twentieth century. These attempts at curbing private ownership made partial use of ideas previously developed by jurists advocating for a more social use of ownership. In Germany, Nazi jurists used Von Gierke's idea that in Germanic law ownership had internal limitations.[131] Unlike Von Gierke, who recognised the importance of limitations set by the law, Nazi jurists wanted to curb the individual freedom given by the right of ownership by reference to the vague notion of the well-being of the nation, thus abandoning clear limitations set by legislation. In fact, this vagueness was meant to create uncertainty and anxiety.[132] Also in fascist Italy, during the process of drafting the new civil code, a new anti-liberal definition of ownership was drafted in 1937. Article 18 of the draft Book on property law read: 'Ownership is the right to exclusive use and disposition of the thing in conformity with the social function of this right. Moreover, the owner should observe the limits set by legislation and regulations and rights of third parties in the same thing.'[133] The drafting committee pointed out that the reference to the social function was intended to implement a fascist principle that ownership is a right and obligation at the same time.[134] However, this definition encountered fierce opposition from Italian academics and was rejected.[135] The definition ultimately adopted in the 1942 civil code was hardly different from the liberal definition of the 1865 code, which in turn was based on the example of the French civil code.[136]

A final note is needed on the aberrations in totalitarian systems. The idea that ownership, and private law as a whole, had a social function was abused by the two extreme forms of socialism which the twentieth century experienced: international socialism, or communism, and National Socialism, which for this purpose includes fascism. To an unprecedented extent the freedom of private individuals was curbed by the fundamental legal norm that private ownership and other private law rights had to be used in a way that served the well-being of the nation or people of the nation, where the

---

130 AJ van der Walt *Property and constitution* (2012) 16–17.

131 Th Keiser *Eigentumsrecht in Nationalsozialismus und Fascismo* (2005) 140–141.

132 M Stolleis *Gemeinwohlformeln im nationalsozialistischen Recht* (1974) 114–118, 114.

133 The translation is based on the text as found in Th Keiser *Eigentumsrecht in Nationalsozialismus und Fascismo* (2005) 148.

134 Th Keiser *Eigentumsrecht in Nationalsozialismus und Fascismo* (2005) 148.

135 Th Keiser *Eigentumsrecht in Nationalsozialismus und Fascismo* (2005) 181–183, who mentions, among others, the name of Antonio Cicu.

136 Th Keiser *Eigentumsrecht in Nationalsozialismus und Fascismo* (2005) 184.

definition of well-being was set by a dictatorship to serve its own horrible goals. Although both National Socialist and fascist jurists developed their views by criticising the early nineteenth-century liberal paradigm,[137] just like German jurists at the end of the nineteenth century had done, in fact, the reference by these dictatorships to the social function of ownership and private law had nothing to do with the social function advocated at the end of the nineteenth century as a reaction to the liberal paradigm. It was used as a mere guise to justify a dictatorship's goal of suppressing individual freedom or even unjustly depriving individuals of their rights.

Various German academics specialising in Roman law tried to defend the importance of Roman law against the Nazis, who despised Roman law as a foreign legal system incompatible with Germanic law. Nazi jurists criticised the Roman concept of ownership for being highly individualistic. This prompted authors like Ernst Schönbauer,[138] Fritz Schulz, and Max Kaser to show that in reality Roman law ownership was limited by many legal norms aimed at protecting society's interests against the owner's individual interests.[139]

4 A *Mos gallicus* by Léon Duguit[140]

Léon Duguit was the paladin of the social function paradigm,[141] claiming early that the liberal paradigm was extinct.[142] Born in France in 1859 and deceased in 1928, Duguit held teaching positions at several universities in France, and also taught in Bucharest, Cairo, Coimbra, and New York.[143] He

[137] Th Keiser *Eigentumsrecht in Nationalsozialismus und Fascismo* (2005) ch III.

[138] Ernst Schönbauer was a member of the NSDAP, the Nazi party.

[139] M Stolleis *The law under the swastika* (1998) 53 ff and M Kaser *Römisches Recht als Gemeinschaftsordnung* (1939).

[140] Parts of this section were extracted *verbatim* from A Parise *Ownership paradigms in American civil law jurisdictions: Manifestations of the shifts in the legislation of Louisiana, Chile, and Argentina (16th-20th centuries)* (2017).

[141] On the life and work of Léon Duguit, see generally the commemorative volume in F Melleray (dir) *Autour de Léon Duguit: Colloque commémoratif du 150e anniversaire de la naissance du doyen Léon Duguit. Bordeaux, 29-30 mai 2009* (2011); J Calvo González & JL Monereo Pérez 'Léon Duguit (1859–1928): jurista de una sociedad en transformación' (2005) 4 *Revista de Derecho Constitucional Europeo* 483–547.

On the general tenets of Léon Duguit, see L Claro Solar *Explicaciones de derecho civil chileno y comparado* vol III:VI:I (1979) 409–412; M Réglade 'Théorie générale du droit dans l'œuvre de L. Duguit' (1932) 1–2 *Archives de Philosophie du droit et de Sociologie juridique* 21–67.

[142] L Duguit *Les transformations générales du droit privé depuis le Code Napoléon* (1912) 155.

[143] MC Mirow 'The social-obligation norm of property: Duguit, Hayem, and others' (2010) 22 *Fla J Int'l L* 191–226 197–198.

was very much influenced by the writings of Comte,[144] while he further found grounding for his works in the sociological postulates of Émile Durkheim,[145] with whom he was acquainted.[146] Some of Duguit's writings were available also in the Americas, being translated, for example, into Spanish by Carlos González Posada[147] and into English by Harold Joseph Laski.[148]

4.1 Postulates

Duguit claimed that ownership *entailed* a social function, or, indeed, that ownership *was* a social function.[149] A status of isolation was considered a fiction,[150] and he therefore argued that the holder of a thing should fulfil a social function, and if the holder fulfilled the mission, the activities of the holder would be protected by law. However, if the holder did not fulfil the mission, the state could intervene and ensure that the holder used the thing according to its purpose and to the benefit of all members of society.[151] Duguit popularised the term 'social function' (*fonction sociale*) used in 1905,[152] at a lecture in the *Congrès National de la Propriété Bâtie*.[153] On that occasion he referred to a social mission,[154] role,[155] and function.[156] A few years later, in

[144] MJ Calvo San José *La función social de la propiedad y su proyección en el sistema de compensación urbanística* (2000) 43.

[145] J-L Halpérin *Histoire du droit des biens* (2008) 220.

[146] MC Mirow 'The social-obligation norm of property: Duguit, Hayem, and others' (2010) 22 *Fla J Int'l L* 191–226 198.

[147] L Duguit *Las transformaciones generales del derecho privado desde el Código de Napoleón* translation by CG Posada (1912).

[148] MC Mirow 'The social-obligation norm of property: Duguit, Hayem, and others' (2010) 22 *Fla J Int'l L* 191–226 196.

[149] B Areán *Curso de derechos reales: privilegios y derecho de retención* 3 ed (1994) 189; GA Ruíz B *La función social de la propiedad agrícola en la ley de reforma agraria venezolana de 1960* (1964) 43.

[150] D Bonilla 'Liberalism and property in Colombia: Property as a right and property as a social function' (2011) 80 *Fordham L Rev* 1135–1170 1155.

[151] L Duguit *Les transformations générales du droit privé depuis le Code Napoléon* (1912) 21, cited also by A Alessandri Rodríguez et al *Tratado de los derecho reales* vol I 6 ed (2010) 41.

[152] J-L Halpérin *Histoire du droit privé français depuis 1804* (1996) 197.

[153] E Cordero Quinzacara 'De la propiedad a las propiedades. La evolución de la concepción liberal de la propiedad' (2008) 31 *Revista de Derecho de la Pontificia Universidad Católica de Valparaíso* 493–525 509.

[154] L Duguit *Congrès national de la propriété bâtie de France. Séance d'ouverture, 13 Juin 1905. Discours* (1905) 9.

[155] L Duguit *Congrès national de la propriété bâtie de France. Séance d'ouverture, 13 Juin 1905. Discours* (1905) 16.

[156] L Duguit *Congrès national de la propriété bâtie de France. Séance d'ouverture, 13 Juin 1905. Discours* (1905) 20–21.

August and September 1911, he delivered a series of six lectures[157] at the University of Buenos Aires (Argentina),[158] where he advocated for the social function in private law,[159] upon reflecting on the changes experienced in private law since the adoption of the *Code Napoléon*. Those lectures resulted from early efforts to establish cultural links between Argentina and Europe.[160] Duguit then transcribed the Buenos Aires Lectures, and published them in Paris in 1912, making them available to French readers.[161] A second edition was published in 1920, also in Paris,[162] showing the significant impact and circulation of the first edition. During the following decade, in the period 1920–1921, Duguit delivered a series of lectures at Columbia University (US) on freedom and sovereignty.[163] On that occasion, he emphasised that there was a conception of freedom in terms of which freedom was a duty and not a right.[164] At Columbia he strongly argued that humans were social beings by nature.[165]

Duguit contended that property should be directed towards the collective interest.[166] He made it clear to readers of his lectures, however, that he was against class conflict or class struggle.[167] In the second Buenos Aires lecture,

---

157 On the content of the six lectures, see also MC Mirow 'The social-obligation norm of property: Duguit, Hayem, and others' (2010) 22 *Fla J Int'l L* 191–226 203–209.

158 L Duguit *Les transformations générales du droit privé depuis le Code Napoléon* (1912) I; MC Mirow 'The social-obligation norm of property: Duguit, Hayem, and others' (2010) 22 *Fla J Int'l L* 191–226 198.

159 For a study on the impact of the postulates of Léon Duguit on private law, see generally G Morin 'L'œuvre de Duguit et le droit privé' (1932) 1–2 *Archives de Philosophie du droit et de Sociologie juridique* 153–162.

160 See 'León Duguit: a 100 años de sus conferencias en la Facultad'. *Derecho al Día X:187.* December 1, 2011. Universidad de Buenos Aires. http://www.derecho.uba.ar/derechoaldia/tapa/leon-duguit-a-100-anos-de-sus-conferencias-en-la-facultad/+4162. For additional information on the gestation and development of the conferences, see A Levaggi 'Catedráticos europeos en la Facultad de Derecho alrededor del Centenario' in T Ortiz (coord) *El Bicentenario de la Revolución de Mayo* (2010) 191–208 205–208.

161 MC Mirow 'The social-obligation norm of property: Duguit, Hayem, and others' (2010) 22 *Fla J Int'l L* 191–226 199.

162 L Duguit *Les transformations générales du droit privé depuis le Code Napoléon* 2 rev ed (1920). See also MC Mirow 'The social-obligation norm of property: Duguit, Hayem, and others' (2010) 22 *Fla J Int'l L* 191–226 199.

163 L Duguit *Souveraineté et liberté. Leçons faites à l'Université Columbia (New-York) 1920–1921* (1922).

164 L Duguit *Souveraineté et liberté. Leçons faites à l'Université Columbia (New-York) 1920–1921* (1922) 141.

165 L Duguit *Souveraineté et liberté. Leçons faites à l'Université Columbia (New-York) 1920–1921* (1922) 142.

166 M Mariani de Vidal *Derechos reales* vol I 7 ed (2004) 270.

167 L Duguit *Les transformations générales du droit privé depuis le Code Napoléon* (1912) 161.

he stated that men and society did not have rights, yet 'every individual ha[d] a certain function to fulfil in society, a certain task to undertake'.[168] In the sixth lecture, dealing mainly with the social function of property, he indicated that ownership was subject to socialisation, implying two things: 'that individual ownership [was] no longer an individual right, and was transform[ed] into a social function; and second, that there [was] an increase in the number of cases of wealth allocated to collectivities, that [should] be subject to juridical protection'.[169] Duguit also stated that owners could use things as long as they fulfilled a social function. They had to undertake three duties:[170] (i) to enjoy things when satisfying individual or collective needs;[171] (ii) not to leave things unutilised;[172] and (iii) to allow the use of things when aiming to fulfil social interests.[173] The author addressed the existence of subjective rights, and argued that 'ownership [was] therefore not the subjective right of the owner, it [was] the social function of the holder of the wealth'.[174] Duguit even indicated correctly that the liberal paradigm was present in article 17 of the Argentine Constitution of 1853.[175] Readers were warned, however, that in the early twentieth century, Latin American jurisdictions were on the threshold of the social function paradigm.[176]

---

168 L Duguit *Les transformations générales du droit privé depuis le Code Napoléon* (1912) 24.

169 L Duguit *Les transformations générales du droit privé depuis le Code Napoléon* (1912) 148–149.

170 L Duguit *Les transformations générales du droit privé depuis le Code Napoléon* (1912) 165–166, cited also by A Alessandri Rodríguez et al *Tratado de los derecho reales* vol I 6 ed (2010) 41–42. See also RM Salvat *Tratado de derecho civil argentino: derechos reales* vol II 5 ed (1962) 17.

171 L Duguit *Les transformations générales du droit privé depuis le Code Napoléon* (1912) 165–166.

172 L Duguit *Les transformations générales du droit privé depuis le Code Napoléon* (1912) 166–167.

173 L Duguit *Les transformations générales du droit privé depuis le Code Napoléon* (1912) 168–169.

174 English text extracted from MC Mirow 'The social-obligation norm of property: Duguit, Hayem, and others' (2010) 22 *Fla J Int'l L* 191–226 207. See the French text in L Duguit *Les transformations générales du droit privé depuis le Code Napoléon* (1912) 158.

175 L Duguit *Les transformations générales du droit privé depuis le Code Napoléon* (1912) 152.

176 L Duguit *Les transformations générales du droit privé depuis le Code Napoléon* (1912) 150.

4.2 Impact on the legal discourse

The ideas and writings of Duguit triggered debate and further studies.[177] He could have been considered an iconoclast, someone breaking with the symbols of the past.[178] Duguit was criticised because property should *have* a social function and not *be* a social function.[179] Scholars, many being trained in the civil law,[180] claimed that the subjective right of holders should be acknowledged and not denied.[181] Accordingly, Duguit's views were not received favourably by some scholars, because they implied a rejection of the subjective right of ownership, suggesting that the owner was simply a functionary.[182] However, his ideas did generate awareness of the need for ownership to serve both collective and individual needs.[183] In France, his ideas could not overcome the movements that supported the pre-eminence of private property,[184] yet they continued circulating during the inter-war period, as demonstrated by the work of Georges Renard and Louis Trotabas.[185] Duguit continued to be a subject of study in France after his death, as a 1933 PhD dissertation recognised when focusing on his social doctrine.[186] In Spain, scholars valued Duguit's work,[187] yet some with reservations due to the socialist tinge they might have acquired, as indicated by Emilio Miñana

---

[177] On the different degrees of acceptance and rejection of the ideas of Léon Duguit, see the detailed study in N Hakim 'Duguit et les privatistes' in F Melleray (dir) *Autour de Léon Duguit: Colloque commémoratif du 150e anniversaire de la naissance du doyen Léon Duguit. Bordeaux, 29-30 mai 2009* (2011) 81–114.

[178] N Hakim 'Duguit et les privatistes' in F Melleray (dir) *Autour de Léon Duguit: Colloque commémoratif du 150e anniversaire de la naissance du doyen Léon Duguit. Bordeaux, 29–30 mai 2009* (2011) 81–114 101.

[179] A Alessandri Rodríguez et al *Tratado de los derecho reales* 6 ed, vol I (2010) 42; J Castán Tobeñas *La propiedad y sus problemas actuales* 2 ed (1963) 79.

[180] J-L Halpérin *Histoire du droit privé français depuis 1804* (1996) 187.

[181] A Alessandri Rodríguez et al *Tratado de los derecho reales* vol I 6 ed (2010) 42.

[182] MJ Calvo San José *La función social de la propiedad y su proyección en el sistema de compensación urbanística* (2000) 42.

[183] MJ Calvo San José *La función social de la propiedad y su proyección en el sistema de compensación urbanística* (2000) 42.

[184] J-L Halpérin *Histoire du droit des biens* (2008) 221.

[185] G Renard & L Trotabas *La fonction sociale de la propriété privée* (1930). See also J-L Halpérin *Histoire du droit privé français depuis 1804* (1996) 197.

[186] See generally MP Markovitch *La doctrine sociale de Duguit – ses idées sur le syndicalisme et la représentation professionnelle. Thèse pour le doctorat présentée et soutenue le 6 Décembre 1933* (1933).

[187] See generally TR Fernandez 'Duguit lu: l'Espagne' in F Melleray (dir) *Autour de Léon Duguit: Colloque commémoratif du 150e anniversaire de la naissance du doyen Léon Duguit. Bordeaux, 29–30 mai 2009* (2011) 255–275.

y Villagrasa in a 1917 lecture.[188] His ideas even reached the English-language legal discourse,[189] being discussed, for example, in Australia and in the UK by William Jethro Brown.[190] They were discussed early in US literature, as demonstrated by a 1917 note published in the *Harvard Law Review*[191] and in writings by Roscoe Pound.[192] Duguit's ideas, moreover, had some influence in the drafting of the civil code in Russia after the Bolshevik Revolution and in the allotment of vacated lands after the First World War.[193] With time, the perception and reception of Duguit's ideas altered. In the 1930s, scholars considered his ideas also from the perspective of social doctrine, enlarging their audience and degree of acceptance.[194]

The postulates of Duguit were welcomed in the Americas, especially after his Buenos Aires lectures.[195] Those lectures were translated into Spanish[196]

---

[188] Emilio Miñana y Villagrasa spoke of a '[...] brand-new concept of ownership, that because of its socialist tinge, may be repugnant to some [...].' E Miñana y Villagrasa *Conferencia del señor D. Emilio Miñana y Villagrasa. Pronunciada en la sesión pública de 27 de marzo de 1917. Tema: Bases para la transformación del régimen de la propiedad territorial* (1917) 19.

[189] See generally C Harlow 'The influence of Léon Duguit on Anglo-American legal thought' in F Melleray (dir) *Autour de Léon Duguit: Colloque commémoratif du 150e anniversaire de la naissance du doyen Léon Duguit. Bordeaux, 29–30 mai 2009* (2011) 227–254.

[190] C Harlow 'The influence of Léon Duguit on Anglo-American legal thought' in F Melleray (dir) *Autour de Léon Duguit: Colloque commémoratif du 150e anniversaire de la naissance du doyen Léon Duguit. Bordeaux, 29–30 mai 2009* (2011) 227–254 232–234.

[191] See HJ Laski 'A Note on M. Duguit' (1917) 31 *Harv L Rev* 186–192. See also MC Mirow 'The social-obligation norm of property: Duguit, Hayem, and others' (2010) 22 *Fla J Int'l L* 191–226 196; and C Harlow 'The influence of Léon Duguit on Anglo-American legal thought' in F Melleray (dir) *Autour de Léon Duguit: Colloque commémoratif du 150e anniversaire de la naissance du doyen Léon Duguit. Bordeaux, 29–30 mai 2009* (2011) 227–254 235.

[192] Roscoe Pound referred to the Buenos Aires Lectures of Léon Duguit in one of the lectures that he delivered at Cambridge (UK) in 1922, and that were published in the US. See R Pound *Interpretations of legal history* (1923) 86–87.

[193] J-L Halpérin *Histoire du droit des biens* (2008) 221.

[194] E Cordero Quinzacara 'De la propiedad a las propiedades. La evolución de la concepción liberal de la propiedad' (2008) 31 *Revista de Derecho de la Pontificia Universidad Católica de Valparaíso* 493–525 511.

[195] Th Keiser 'Social conceptions of property and labour – private law in the aftermath of the Mexican revolution and European legal science' (2012) 20 *Rechtsgeschichte* 258–273 269.

[196] See L Duguit *Las transformaciones generales del derecho privado desde el Código de Napoleón* translation by CG Posada (1912).

and English,[197] giving them a readership in the Americas. The lectures circulated in France, Spain and the US, and in Latin American jurisdictions.[198] In Mexico, for example, Duguit's writings were often advanced in support of a local decision, as a way to illustrate how a potential change in Mexico had already been welcomed in the legal discourse of other jurisdictions.[199] In Colombia, in the 1930s, Duguit's writings were known to members of the judicial, legislative, and executive branches.[200] His ideas also reached Chile, since even President Alessandri Palma used the words of Duguit, when he claimed that 'the concept of property as a subjective right disappears, to be replaced by the concept of property as a social function'.[201] According to the records of the 1925 Constitutional Reform Commission, Alessandri Palma on that occasion used Duguit's words to 'somehow dissipate the fears that some experience when property law is addressed'.[202] The ideas likewise reached Argentina at the time of constitutional reform. For example, Arturo Sampay, one of the members of the 1949 Constitutional Convention, stated that 'private property – even when preserving its individual character – assumes a double function: personal and social'.[203] His words called to mind the postulates of Duguit and of the social doctrine, and he even mentioned Aquinas.[204] Another

---

[197] An English translation of the six lectures was published as ch 3 of vol XI of *The continental legal history series*. See generally L Duguit 'Changes of principle in the field of liberty, contract, liability, and property' in JH Wigmore et al (eds) *The progress of continental law in the nineteenth century* vol XI *The continental legal history series* (1918) 65–146.

[198] MC Mirow 'The social-obligation norm of property: Duguit, Hayem, and others' (2010) 22 *Fla J Int'l L* 191–226 199.

[199] Th Keiser 'Social conceptions of property and labour – private law in the aftermath of the Mexican revolution and European legal science' (2012) 20 *Rechtsgeschichte* 258–273 269.

[200] D Bonilla 'Liberalism and property in Colombia: Property as a right and property as a social function' (2011) 80 *Fordham L Rev* 1135–1170 1154; KL Karst & KS Rosenn *Law and development in Latin America: a case book* (1975) 286–287.

[201] MC Mirow 'Origins of the social function of property in Chile' (2011) 80 *Fordham L Rev* 1183–1217 1183, 1200-1202.

[202] Ministerio del Interior *Actas oficiales de las sesiones celebradas por la comisión y sub-comisiones encargadas del estudio del Proyecto de Nueva Constitución Política de la República* (1925) 114. See also MC Mirow 'Origins of the social function of property in Chile' (2011) 80 *Fordham L Rev* 1183–1217 1201.

[203] *Diario de sesiones de la Convención Nacional Constituyente. año 1949. 24 de enero – 16 de marzo* vol I (1949) 278. See also ST Ramella 'Propiedad en función social en la Constitución de 1949: Una "mentalidad" del Antiguo Régimen representada en el constitucionalismo social de la época' (2007) 35 *Revista de Historia del Derecho* 297–354 305.

[204] *Diario de sesiones de la Convención Nacional Constituyente. año 1949. 24 de enero – 16 de marzo* vol I (1949) 278.

member of the convention, Rodolfo G Valenzuela, claimed that 'it must be said, together with Duguit, that the state loses its Napoleonic conception, and adopts another that is broader, more flexible, more protective, and more humane'.[205] It is therefore evident that the ideas formulated in France by Duguit soon spread across the Atlantic, paving the way for a change in the paradigm of ownership.

5 Closing remarks

Limitations to the owner's powers started to be perceived clearly around the turn of the twentieth century. Since then, efforts to limit those powers have emerged in different places at different times, and these efforts can be understood as different ways that share common traits. This chapter briefly addressed earlier developments in German and French law limiting the owner's powers and similar more recent developments in South African law. These developments all share some characteristics that may be called a universal method or *Mos universalis* of balancing the owner's freedom and the social function of ownership. Accordingly, this chapter first discussed the emergence of a social function for ownership since the 1890s. Its origins and current approaches were initially addressed, and were followed by a reference to the ideas advocated by André van der Walt in South Africa. This chapter then focused on the ideas of the German author Otto von Gierke. The main postulates of this influential author were presented, together with some indications of the impact his ideas had in the legal discourse mainly until the first half of the twentieth century. This chapter finally addressed the efforts by the French author Léon Duguit and how his thoughts were received on both sides of the Atlantic. Duguit has rightly been regarded as the paladin of the social function paradigm. These two authors, although very influential at the time, were not the only ones advocating for the social function of ownership. At the time, there was a lively discussion about the social function in which many authors in many jurisdictions participated. These authors operated within different contexts and triggered different changes. Yet, they are all links in a chain of change.

The ideas presented by these advocates for change took some time to percolate into the fabric of society, but in many other instances they summarised and highlighted changes in legislation that had already been

[205] *Diario de sesiones de la Convención Nacional Constituyente. año 1949. 24 de enero - 16 de marzo* vol I (1949) 315. See also ST Ramella 'Propiedad en función social en la Constitución de 1949: Una "mentalidad" del Antiguo Régimen representada en el constitucionalismo social de la época' (2007) 35 *Revista de Historia del Derecho* 297–354 309.

made. The social function paradigm of ownership not only led to lively debates on the limits of the owner's powers, but eventually these ideas even led to changes in legislation. These ideas, and their adoption by legislators and courts, are needed when aiming for change. André van der Walt knew that ideas must be followed by efforts that will bring about real change. He devoted his life to writing in support of that belief. Like Von Gierke and Duguit, and many other jurists, he has sowed the seeds for change, not only in his native South Africa, but also in other jurisdictions where his ideas are being read. He has therefore joined those who have excelled in showing the remarkable resilience of property law.

Chapter 13

Property in law

Priviledge Dhliwayo & Rashmi Dyal-Chand***

Page

Contents

1 Introduction: From social context to systemic role

Our theoretical starting point for this exploration is the following observation. One apparent trajectory in Professor Van der Walt's scholarship about property theory begins with a deep exploration of the social context surrounding the development of property law in post-apartheid South Africa and ends with the conclusion that property ultimately serves a modest systemic role in law. Stated differently, once we really understand the great extent to which social context affects decision-making about property rights, we can recognise that, far from being absolute or superior among legal rights, property has – and *should* have – a more modest status.

Although we could choose from many of Professor Van der Walt's works to demonstrate this trajectory, we have chosen two of his best-known works, published five years apart. The first is his extraordinary book, *Property in the margins*.[1] In it, Professor Van der Walt thoroughly examines the right of a property owner to evict non-owners from her property. He analyses this right in a range of legal and social contexts, including landlord-tenant relationships, situations concerning unlawful occupiers such as squatters, and circumstances involving servitudes, public lands and

* MERC Fellow, Department of Public Law, South African Research Chair in Property Law, Stellenbosch University.
** Professor of Law and Research Director, Northeastern University.

[1] AJ van der Walt *Property in the margins* (2009).

building encroachments. Even as facts, doctrine and context are at the core of his analysis, Professor Van der Walt's main conclusions are deeply and broadly theoretical. Ultimately, he argues, these particular kinds of property disputes teach us a great deal about property as a legal concept. While many theoretical claims have been made about the absolute nature of property rights, we cannot rely on abstract notions about property if we wish to understand and utilise its full potential – especially in a society that is undergoing substantial political and social change. Specifically, if a society, including its legal decision-makers, views property only from the perspective of the property owner, it cannot fully implement the legal reforms necessary to reflect the arc of change and progress (and indeed, transformation) in the society.

Professor Van der Walt identifies this tendency in favor of the owner's 'rights paradigm' as a particular propensity of lawyers. And he is sympathetic to this tendency, in part because lawyers, and the legal system, are guardians of stability. But as Professor Van der Walt argues, stability can all too often turn into an instinctual resistance to change:

> As lawyers, we ... accept, often ... unreflectively, that property is a central organizing concept in law and legal theory. Because of these assumptions, we are unwilling or slow to adopt or accept legal developments that do not reflect and correspond with the central position of property in society and in legal thinking and, to the extent that such developments might be necessary or beneficial for social change, we tend to resist or inhibit change.[2]

To correct this one-sided perspective on property, Professor Van der Walt urges us to think from the perspective of people marginalised from property ownership (or even participation). Rather than beginning with, and adjudicating from, the perspective of a landowner wishing to exclude someone from travelling across her property for the purpose of honouring a religious or cultural tradition, he urges us to consider the perspective of the non-property-owner seeking to honour that tradition. Rather than favouring the landlord in a property relationship with a tenant, he urges us to consider the needs and rights of the tenant. Rather than protecting the political rights of the property owner seeking to exclude a demonstrator from her property, he urges us to consider the political rights of the demonstrator. Professor Van der Walt recognises that doing so is both difficult and at times paradoxical:

[2] AJ van der Walt *Property in the margins* (2009) 231.

> Marginality thinking has its own logic in that it forces one to look for the paradox and the contradiction rather than for broad theory and grand narrative, for diversity rather than uniformity, for dissent rather than consensus, for conflict and chaos rather than consent and order. In other words, it directs our attention to faultlines and disputes or historical breakdowns rather than concentrating on or searching for the golden thread of continuity.[3]

But engaging in 'marginality thinking' can restore a vital balance in the law. The result, he argues, is a systemic reprioritisation:

> Thinking and arguing about property in a way that takes the persons in [marginalised] positions and their interests and circumstances seriously means, at the very least, that we have to try and think away the power and the centrality of rights, entitlements and privileges and to imagine a legal order not dominated by the hierarchies built on the distinction between their presence or absence.[4]

It is appropriate to pause here to note the difficulty of following Professor Van der Walt's directive to 'think away' the power and centrality of property's hierarchies.[5] They are all around us, serving as a backdrop for much of our systemic thinking in law. The bundled view of property ownership is one example, but it is only the proverbial tip of the iceberg. Principles such as the *numerus clausus* bolster it. So does the ubiquity of injunctive relief in property law. Even more reformist theories such as Legal Realism and Progressive Property are grounded fundamentally in some of property's hierarchies. Consider Legal Realism's implicit prioritisation of rights in the property 'bundle'.[6] Consider also Progressive Property's argument that property ownership can be an important mechanism for representing and protecting marginalised people, so long as this mechanism can be made more inclusive.

By contrast, especially to exclusion theories about property hierarchies,[7] Professor Van der Walt's marginality thinking requires us to ask even more demanding – indeed at times existential – questions about property's role. Thinking about the concept of property access, for example, of what value

[3] AJ van der Walt *Property in the margins* (2009) 245.

[4] AJ van der Walt *Property in the margins* (2009) 241–242.

[5] Indeed, Professor Van der Walt's work is also instrumental in reminding us that hierarchies exist in property law.

[6] The conceptualisation of property as a 'bundle of rights', which has no fixed core or constituent element, is typically attributed to W Hohfeld and AM Honoré. See JE Penner 'The "bundle of rights" picture of property' (1996) 43 *UCLA L Rev* 711–820 712. The bundle approach does not define property as a single right, but rather as a bundle of rights, including the rights to use, transfer and exclude.

[7] And even at times by contrast to more progressive theories.

is access to property owned by others? How are marginalised individuals served by such access? By requiring owners to share access, how are we valuing ownership? What if we assumed no ownership in some situations? In such cases, what values would access serve?

Though these questions may seem theoretical, we believe that Professor Van der Walt asked them for the most practical of reasons. It seems to us that he profoundly believed in their transformative potential for those who are marginalised. Moreover, he appeared to believe that it was imperative for legal scholars in particular to ask such questions and attempt to answer them for the benefit of a society seeking legal and social progress.

And indeed if we consider some of the last scholarly pieces he produced in his life, that is exactly what Professor Van der Walt appears to have been doing in his own writing. In 2014, he gave a keynote address at the annual meeting of the Association for Law, Property and Society in Vancouver. He published a version of that speech in that Association's journal. In the article, he reflects on what he describes as the 'modest systemic role of property':

> Protecting property rights is a legitimate objective of the legal order, but relative to the primary norms that prescribe how we want to live in society it is a systemically modest one. In at least some instances … that status will show up and should be reflected in the way property conflicts are adjudicated.
>
> … If property rights are protected in the space left over once the fundamental democratic conditions have been secured, that will not only affect the instances in which property rights will enjoy protection but also our methodology in determining and analyzing their protection. Instead of featuring front and centre in the solution of every conflict that involves property rights, either by providing primary, *super*-constitutional protection for a landowner whose established rights are affected, or by lending primary, constitutional support to the beneficiaries of competing non-property rights, my conclusion in this article is that the protection of property rights often only features after the fact, once the primary constitutional goals of securing fundamental democratic objectives have been achieved.'[8]

Professor Van der Walt's normative conclusion about property's systemic role is clear. It deserves its modest place in the law. Rather than having a status above the law, or beyond the reach of the law, property ownership is *one* consideration among a number of legal considerations. This is especially true when constitutional rights are at issue. But as Professor Van der Walt began to explore in articles such as 'Sharing servitudes', it is also true when considering and balancing the rights and relationships of individuals over

[8] AJ van der Walt 'The modest systemic status of property rights' (2014) 1 *J L Prop & Soc'y* 15–106 102–103.

property in circumstances where such rights are governed by statutory and other laws that are hierarchically inferior to constitutional law.[9] Thus, in his article on sharing and servitudes, Professor Van der Walt traced the development of sharing as a core property norm by analyzing disputes over servitudes in South African courts.

As a doctrinal matter, Professor Van der Walt provides clear descriptions for judges and scholars of the actual devices judges use in resolving disputes over property. He pulls away the curtain and reveals to us the much greater level of balancing, and the much deeper consideration of social context, than some property law scholars acknowledge is occurring in the everyday (and critical!) work of property adjudication. In so doing, he further legitimises the consideration of social context. His message to us is that such consideration is essential, and it is normatively appropriate. Moreover, such a consideration can and at times should lead to a conclusion that property rights are not as central as they may at first seem.

At the same time, the theoretical trajectory in this line of scholarship, beginning with *Property in the margins* and ending with his work on property's modest systemic role, is of great importance for property thinkers. As a theoretical matter, Professor Van der Walt has opened up new and productive space for property thinkers to re-conceptualise property's role. In our own scholarship on property law, we have been inspired by this trajectory to re-evaluate the nature of absolute ownership and the right of exclusion. We have also begun to consider the role and value of property sharing as a social and legal norm. In the following sections, we demonstrate the value of this trajectory in Professor Van der Walt's scholarship by analysing its relevance in both the South African and American contexts. We begin, in section 2, by using Professor Van der Walt's 'marginality thinking' to analyse a range of theoretical perspectives on absolute ownership and exclusion. In section 3, we continue this analysis by considering the implications of Professor Van der Walt's lessons on social context and the systemic status of property in the South African legal context. Finally, in section 4, we consider these implications in the American legal context.

2 A reflection on absolute ownership and exclusivity: A theoretical perspective

2.1 Introduction

Arguments in favour of the idea that ownership is absolute, that the right to exclude is central to ownership, and that limitations of either are exceptional,

[9] AJ van der Walt 'Sharing servitudes' (2015) 4 *EPLJ* 162–222.

are often bundled with an appeal to certain property theories.[10] The main question is whether the idea of absolute ownership implies that the right to exclude is either absolute as well or central to ownership. The assumption is that support from the theories in question would strengthen the claims in favour of exclusivity. But if we reconsider these theories using a perspective 'in the margins', we can see that these theories do not always provide the necessary support for exclusion arguments.

2.2 *The strong version of absoluteness*

2.2.1 Moral property theories

Our discussion commences with what Professor Van der Walt[11] refers to as moral property theories.[12] Moral property theories can be divided into labour (Locke) and first-occupation (Hegel) theories.[13] These theories are often said to offer historical support for the claims of the exclusion theory in justifying not only the acquisition and protection of property in general, but also its exclusivity, autonomy and absoluteness.[14] This means that interferences with property should at least be limited to the minimum to allow the owner to exercise her rights freely and to protect the owner's rights and values. Professor Van der Walt's observations about property's modest systemic

---

[10] JB Baron 'The contested commitments of property' (2010) 16 *Hastings LJ* 917–968 reviews this scholarly debate with reference to two theoretical approaches to property, which she describes as information theory and progressive theory. The information (exclusion) theorist group is led by Thomas Merrill and Henry Smith, while the progressive scholars are led by Gregory Alexander, Eduardo Peñalver, Joseph Singer and Laura Underkuffler. Both groups have made powerful and seemingly irreconcilable claims about the function and normative value of exclusion rules in property law. For further discussion of the debate see JA Lovett 'Progressive property in action: The Land Reform (Scotland) Act 2003' (2011) 89 *Neb L Rev* 739–818; E Rosser 'An ambition and transformative potential of progressive property' (2013) 101 *Cal L Rev* 107–172; AJ van der Walt 'The modest systemic status of property rights' (2014) 1 *J L Prop & Soc'y* 15–106; P Dhliwayo *A constitutional analysis of access rights that limit landowners' right to exclude* (2015) unpublished LLD dissertation University of Stellenbosch ch 2.

[11] AJ van der Walt 'Property rights, land rights and environmental rights' in DH van Wyk, J Dugard, B de Villers & D Davis (eds) *Rights and constitutionalism: The new South African legal order* (1994) 455–501.

[12] The discussion is limited to an analysis of the theories of private property propounded by Hegel and Locke as justifications for the institution of private property.

[13] AJ van der Walt 'Property rights, land rights and environmental rights' in DH van Wyk, J Dugard, B de Villers & D Davis (eds) *Rights and constitutionalism: The new South African legal order* (1994) 455–501 455–456.

[14] AJ van der Walt 'Property rights, land rights and environmental rights' in DH van Wyk, J Dugard, B de Villers & D Davis D (eds) *Rights and constitutionalism: The new South African legal order* (1994) 455–501 455–456.

status, however, inspire us to ask the important question whether the moral- and value-based arguments for property indeed support an absolute or a relative but strong right to exclude.

Some natural rights theorists argue that all rights are derived from a conception of property as 'self-ownership'.[15] Locke is regarded as the first to make the case for private property as a natural right of the individual and it remains the standard justification for private property.[16] Natural rights were held to be natural because of their historical or moral precedence over legal rights. Locke employed the idea of there being a 'state of nature' in which man's natural rights are governed by natural law.[17] Consequently, governments were legitimate insofar as they protected natural rights and illegitimate if they violated them.[18]

Locke's theory provides an effort to define the limits of sovereign power. In terms of Locke's theory the existence of individual property rights is justified on the basis of the labour argument, specifically in order to protect

---

[15] A Ryan *Property* (1987) 61. R Barnes *Property rights and natural resources* (2009) 30 argues that property as a natural right approach starts from the proposition that individuals have certain essential rights that derive from their independence and dignity as individuals, as expressed in terms of rights over self. Such rights arise without the operation of law.

[16] EF Paul *Property rights and eminent domain* (1987) 198; R Barnes *Property rights and natural resources* (2009) 30; GS Alexander & EM Peñalver *An introduction to property theory* (2012) 38–41; H Howe 'Lockean natural rights and the stewardship model of property' (2013) 3 *Prop L Rev* 36–50 38. J Locke *Two treatises of government* (reproduced in P Laslett *Two treatises of government: A critical edition with an introduction and apparatus criticus* (1963)) para 27 states:

> Though the Earth, and all inferior Creatures be common to all Men, yet every Man has a Property in his own Person. This no Body has any Right to but himself. The Labour of his Body and the Work of his Hands, we may say, are properly his. Whatsoever then he removes out of the State that Nature hath provided, and left it in, he hath mixed his Labour with, and joined to it something that is his own, and thereby makes it his Property. It being by him removed from the common state nature placed it in, it hath by his labour something annexed to it, that excludes the common right of other men. For this Labour being the unquestionable Property of the Labourer, no Man but he can have a right to what that is once joined to, at least where there is enough, and as good left in common for others.

In this chapter, we do not intend to discuss Locke but rather the claim in secondary literature that his theory supports a strong exclusion thesis. Therefore, we refer to the secondary literature.

[17] H Howe 'Lockean natural rights and the stewardship model of property' (2013) 3 *Prop L Rev* 36–50 38.

[18] A Ryan *Property* (1987) 62.

those rights against interference by the sovereign.[19] The US Constitution has a classic example of a property clause that reflects this understanding of Locke's theory, providing constitutional protection for life, liberty and property as the parameters of personal freedom and individuality.[20] In this form, the property clause is part of a specific perception of the social function of property relationships, namely that private property forms a guaranteed enclave of individual freedom within which the individual is shielded from the threats posed by society.[21]

The right to exclude has been identified as the most important among the rights established within the state of nature.[22] An exclusive property right is derived from the 'mixing-labour' argument for property.[23] The labour argument suggests that when people mix labour with something from the commons, it is by their labour that they acquire something (property), which excludes the common rights of others.[24] As a result, they acquire claim-rights to the property's exclusive possession, use and control, and correlative duties are imposed on all others not to interfere with the property that they acquired through their labour.[25] In this regard, the right to exclude others becomes important as emphasis is placed on the individual. From this perspective, Locke is said to have viewed ownership as an exclusive and unlimited right because it is based on individual labour.

---

[19] ET Freyfogle *Bounded people, boundless lands: Envisioning a new land ethic* (1998) 94–95 states that Locke's interpretation of the Bible acknowledges that God originally gave earth to humankind as collective property, yet any individual could seize a piece of land from the common stock and make it his own simply by mixing labour with it. This seems to suggest that before labour was added, the land had no value, and once labour was applied, the tilled land gained value and became private property. On this basis, one gained the right to exclude non-owners from his tilled land.

[20] AJ van der Walt 'Property rights, land rights and environmental rights' in DH van Wyk, J Dugard, B de Villers & D Davis (eds) *Rights and constitutionalism: The new South African legal order* (1994) 455–501 461.

[21] AJ van der Walt 'Property rights, land rights and environmental rights' in DH van Wyk, J Dugard, B de Villers & D Davis (eds) *Rights and constitutionalism: The new South African legal order* (1994) 455–501 462.

[22] GS Alexander & EM Peñalver *An introduction to property theory* (2012) 146; H Howe 'Lockean natural rights and the stewardship model of property' (2013) 3 *Property LR* 36–50 38.

[23] A Mossoff 'What is property? Putting the pieces back together' (2003) 45 *Ariz L Rev* 371–444 387–389.

[24] H Howe 'Lockean natural rights and the stewardship model of property' (2013) 3 *Prop L Rev* 36–50 38; WNR Lucy & FR Barker 'Justifying property and justifying access' (1993) 6 *Can J L & Jurisprudence* 287–318 299–300.

[25] WNR Lucy & FR Barker 'Justifying property and justifying access' (1993) 6 *Can J L & Jurisprudence* 287–318 297.

Locke's labour theory creates the impression that owners should be able to exclude others from the fruits of their labour. The labour argument adds the essential element of exclusion to property rights.[26] It is labour that transforms the inclusive claim-rights in the state of nature into exclusive property rights, which is one of the primary rights civil society is formed to protect.[27] To this extent, Locke's labour theory strengthens the rights of the individual in that, once an individual acquires property, he has the right to exclude others from his property.[28] Locke's labour theory justifying private property is also important for promoting personal autonomy in that it creates a sense of personal freedom and individuality. Therefore, allowing the landowner to exclude non-owners from private property ensures that the owner can establish a sphere of personal autonomy and exercise his unique power of personal autonomy.[29]

In the same vein, Hegel's idea of property is said to present the right to exclude as necessary and essential to property.[30] His first occupation theory entails that a thing belongs to the person who happens to be the first in time to take the thing into her possession.[31] Property is an abstract and indeterminate concept, which emanates from an individual's will;[32] a person has a right to put her will into any and every thing, thereby making it hers with the absolute right of appropriation that a person has over all things.[33] Hegel identifies three essential phases of property, namely possession, use

[26] A Mossoff 'What is property? Putting the pieces back together' (2003) 45 *Ariz L Rev* 371–444 388. WNR Lucy & FR Barker 'Justifying property and justifying access' (1993) 6 *Can J L & Jurisprudence* 287–318 297 state that an individual acquires private property through her labour and in so doing, she unilaterally deprives all others of the resource she acquires.

[27] A Mossoff 'What is property? Putting the pieces back together' (2003) 45 *Ariz L Rev* 371–444 389.

[28] GS Alexander & EM Peñalver *An introduction to property theory* (2012) 146.

[29] AJ van der Walt 'Tradition on trial: A critical analysis of the civil-law tradition in South African property law' (1995) 2 *SAJHR* 169–206 179.

[30] GWF Hegel *Hegel's philosophy of right* (1952 translated with notes by TM Knox 1967). We do not intend to undertake an extensive analysis of Hegel, rather we analyse the secondary literature that points to or denies the contention that Hegel's first occupation theory provides a strong justification for exclusion.

[31] GWF Hegel *Hegel's philosophy of right* (1952 translated with notes by TM Knox 1967) 45.

[32] WE Conklin *Hegel's law: The legitimacy of a modern legal order* (2008) 119–120.

[33] GWF Hegel *Hegel's philosophy of right* (1952 translated with notes by TM Knox 1967) 41. See also L Fox O'Mahony & JA Sweeney 'The idea of home in law: Displacement and dispossession' in L Fox O'Mahony & JA Sweeney (eds) *The idea of home in law: Displacement and dispossession* (2011) 1–11 2.

and alienation.[34] Each of these phases requires that an individual be entitled to exclude others, at least to some degree.[35] Let us take for example a sign on private property saying 'No trespassers'. According to Hegel, this sign indicates that an owner has put her will into the thing, which symbolises that she is the sole owner and that non-owners should recognise her ownership of the thing.[36] The sign can also be a means of keeping non-owners out of the private property. This provides an individual owner with the exclusionary powers that enable her to exclude others from the property interest and this also suggests that the owner has complete ownership of the property.[37]

The moral property theories seem to support the strong view of absoluteness. Ryan observes that Hegel's view of property is that the human will is essentially individual and property therefore essentially private[38] in the sense of excluding others from the property.[39] Another person can use the property but only if the owner decides to alienate her property, thereby disembodying her will.[40] But for Hegel, possession, use and alienation are simultaneously individualistic and relational. Hegel does recognise a right to exclude, but because of the relational character embodied in his property theory, the right to exclude is not absolute; nonetheless, it is essential in depicting the nature and extent of private ownership.[41] At least from one reading of Locke's and Hegel's property theories, the right to exclude others is justified, on a moral basis, because it promotes personhood and personal autonomy. The result is that any limitation of the owner's right to exclude is exceptional and immoral except if the limitation is in accordance with the owner's will. Although these property theories play an important role in the understanding of property, they should not be interpreted as an unqualified endorsement of an absolute right to exclude.

---

[34] GWF Hegel *Hegel's philosophy of right* (1952 translated with notes by TM Knox 1967) 46.

[35] GS Alexander & EM Peñalver *An introduction to property theory* (2012) 143.

[36] GWF Hegel *Hegel's philosophy of right* (1952) (translated with notes by TM Knox 1967) 49. See also D Knowles *Routledge philosophy guidebook to Hegel and the philosophy of right* (2002) 131.

[37] WE Conklin *Hegel's law: The legitimacy of a modern legal order* (2008) 123.

[38] A Ryan *Property* (1987) 60.

[39] WE Conklin *Hegel's law: The legitimacy of a modern legal order* (2008) 123.

[40] GWF Hegel *Hegel's philosophy of right* (1952 translated with notes by TM Knox 1967) 52.

[41] GS Alexander & EM Peñalver *An introduction to property theory* (2012) 143.

2.2.2 Contemporary exclusion theory

A strong-absolute version of ownership and the right to exclude is integral to a set of more recent exclusion theories. Generally, within the private property system, ownership of a given resource is assessed on the basis of who can exclude others from interfering with the resource without the consent of the owner.[42] Merrill argues that by virtue of simply excluding others, a landowner is free to determine the use of her property.[43] The right of a property owner to exclude others is not just one of the most essential sticks in the bundle that is seen as comprising property, but is in fact the '*sine quo non*' of property. He puts it as follows:

> Give someone the right to exclude others from a valued resource ... and you give them property. Deny someone the exclusion right and they do not have property.[44]

The conception of property is grounded in exclusion because, while property owners enjoy various legal rights, the right to exclude is both necessary and sufficient for identifying the existence of property.[45]

Exclusion theorists argue that the right to exclude is at the centre of the property system because it consolidates a large number of powers in one property owner, which sends a simple message to non-owners to keep off.[46] Merrill proposes a model of ownership that emphasises the owner's right to exclude non-owners from the property as the central defining feature of ownership.[47] This model is referred to as the 'boundary' or 'exclusion-based' approach because it focuses on the owner's power to decide who may cross the boundaries of the property. In an exclusion-based (or boundary) approach, ownership is the product of a norm that protects the boundaries around an object so as to exclude the whole world except the owner.[48] It follows that the

---

42 WNR Lucy & FR Barker 'Justifying property and justifying access' (1993) 6 *Can J L & Jurisprudence* 287–318 293.

43 TW Merrill 'Property and the right to exclude' (1998) 77 *Neb L Rev* 730–755 741.

44 TW Merrill 'Property and the right to exclude' (1998) 77 *Neb L Rev* 730–755 730.

45 TW Merrill 'Property and the right to exclude' (1998) 77 *Neb L Rev* 730–755 731. See also H Dagan *Property: Values and institutions* (2011) 38–39.

46 JB Baron 'The contested commitments of property' (2010) 16 *Hastings LJ* 917–968 936–940, citing HE Smith 'Exclusion and property rules in the law of nuisance' (2004) 90 *Virginia LR* 965–1049 984; HE Smith 'Property and property rules' (2004) 79 *NY Univ Law Rev* 1719–1798 1754. See also AJ van der Walt 'The modest systemic status of property rights' (2014) 1 *J L Prop & Soc'y* 15–106 23.

47 TW Merrill 'Property and the right to exclude' (1998) 77 *Neb L Rev* 730–755.

48 L Katz 'Exclusion and exclusivity in property law' (2008) 58 *UTLJ* 275–315 281. See also ER Claeys 'Property 101: Is property a thing or a bundle?' (2009) 32 *Seattle U L Rev* 617–650 638, who states that Merrill and Smith construe exclusion to refer to boundaries and the incidents of control and use protected by boundaries.

owner controls access to the attributes of the resource within the boundaries, which are his by virtue of the exclusion of others. The essential feature of the exclusion-based approach is the power to determine who can enter and who must keep out. In effect, ownership has a gatekeeping function in that property law constructs not a wall but rather a gate, which an owner may open or shut according to her preferences. This metaphor is a reminder that property creates power relationships among people.[49]

Exclusion theorists value property's stability over change. Merrill and Smith argue that property institutions employ boundaries, which economise on information costs by delegating most decision-making about the exercise of rights to owners.[50] Furthermore, they argue, by establishing boundaries and by granting owners the broad power to control access to property within those boundaries, the institution of private property rewards people who successfully gather information about the most productive use for the thing they own.[51] Interestingly, the economic argument for individual ownership is sometimes made with reference to the tragedy of the commons,[52] in that, by protecting the right to exclude, social costs or negative externalities are reduced. Even though negative externalities are reduced, the possibility for non-owners to negotiate access when transaction costs are low indicates a qualified but strong version of the right to exclude.

It is one thing to say that the right to exclude is the most essential or core right of property and quite another to say the right to exclude is absolute. None of the justificatory grounds embodied in moral property theories or in the more recent exclusion theory indicates that a landowner has an absolute right to exclude. These theories appear to support a strong but qualified right to exclude. The justifications support exclusionary practices to some extent, but they also allow for access rights, and sometimes they even require or recognize non-owners' access rights.[53]

---

[49] B Ziff *Principles of property law* 5 ed (2010) 6–7.

[50] TW Merrill & HE Smith 'What happened to property in law and economics?' (2001) 111 *Yale LJ* 357–398 389.

[51] TW Merrill & HE Smith 'What happened to property in law and economics?' (2001) 111 *Yale LJ* 357–398 389. See also GS Alexander & EM Peñalver *An introduction to property theory* (2012) 136.

[52] B Ziff *Principles of property law* 5 ed (2010) 14. See also H Demsetz 'Toward a theory of property rights ll: The competition between private and collective ownership' in F Parisi & CK Rowley (eds) *The origins of law and economics: Essays by the founding fathers* (2005) 241–262; G Hardin 'The tragedy of the commons' (1968) 162 *Science* 1243–1248.

[53] H Dagan 'The public dimension of private property' (2013) 24 *King's LJ* 260–288 284.

2.3 *The qualified view of absoluteness*

2.3.1 Exclusive-use theories

There are some interesting variations on the idea that the right to exclude is the defining feature of property. Exclusive use theorists such as Katz, Mossoff and Claeys embrace the idea that some kind of unifying and robust exclusion right exists at the core of property ownership. However, their arguments differ descriptively from the exclusion theorists' arguments on the ground that exclusion is not always about physical exclusion, creating boundaries or a simple keep-off message.[54] Rather, exclusion is an exclusive right to use,[55] or to determine the use, of the property,[56] or an exclusive right of agenda-setting.[57] A landowner has the power to control and make decisions regarding the use of her property but cannot exclude non-owners. Exclusive-use decision-making can be limited by law (regulation) in specific instances, depending on the nature of the property and the identity of the owner. Exclusive-use theory creates the potential for mutual accommodation with regard to the property, whereas exclusion theory merely states a particular outcome, a simple keep-off rule. The exclusive use theorists' conception of property suggests that property is a social concept, that is, it plays a role in structuring social relations, which is more or less what the progressive property theorists argue as well.

2.3.2 Progressive property and exclusivity

Progressive property theorists attempt to ground the system of property on values rather than on transaction costs and externalities of information.[58] These theorists focus on the role that property and property law play in a free and democratic society, and often remark that property rights can be limited

[54] In this regard see JA Lovett 'Progressive property in action: The land reform (Scotland) Act 2003' (2011) 89 *Neb L Rev* 739–818 751; A Mossoff 'What is property? Putting the pieces back together' (2003) 45 *Ariz L Rev* 371–444 375; L Katz 'Exclusion and exclusivity in property law' (2008) 58 *U Toronto LJ* 275–315 275; ER Claeys 'Property 101: Is property a thing or a bundle?' (2009) 32 *Seattle U L Rev* 617–650 631; H Dagan *Property: Values and institutions* (2011) 39–40.

[55] A Mossoff 'What is property? Putting the pieces back together' (2003) 45 *Ariz L Rev* 371–444.

[56] ER Claeys 'Property 101: Is property a thing or a bundle?' (2009) 32 *Seattle U L Rev* 617–650.

[57] L Katz 'Exclusion and exclusivity in property law' (2008) 58 *U Toronto LJ* 275–315.

[58] JB Baron 'The contested commitments of property' (2010) 16 *Hastings LJ* 917–968 924.

to further the interests of society or to enforce human values.[59] This implies that property is often subject to limitations and obligations to secure these interests and values. Singer, Peñalver, Alexander, Underkuffler and Purdy propose a democratic model of property, which recognises that property serves plural values and that the law should reflect those multiple values.[60]

The view that property serves human values seeks to justify limiting the right to exclude and to strengthen arguments about the social-obligation norm.[61] Since property serves human values and concerns social relations, landowners have obligations in addition to rights. Alexander has advanced arguments for the social-obligation norm, in light of the commitment to human flourishing.[62] An analysis of the social-obligation norm paves the way to look at further theoretical justifications that highlight the relative nature of the right to exclude and justifications for limiting the right to exclude, such as virtue ethics;[63] human flourishing;[64] democratic governance;[65] and public policy.[66]

---

[59] Perhaps such scholarly remarks are informed by the US Supreme Court decision in *State of New Jersey v Shack* 58 NJ 297 (1971). As R Dyal-Chand 'Pragmatism and postcolonialism: Protecting non-owners in property law' (2014) 63 *Am U L Rev* 1683–1748 1689 puts it: 'It is no small wonder that *State v Shack* has achieved iconic status in property law, and particularly among property scholars who identify (or are identified) as progressives.' See also E Rosser 'An ambition and transformative potential of progressive property' (2013) 101 *Cal L Rev* 107–172 125, who gives an indication that the *Shack* decision has a bearing on the arguments propounded by the progressive theorists.

[60] JW Singer 'Democratic estates: Property law in a free and democratic society' (2009) 94 *Cornell L Rev* 1009–1062 1046–1047, 1054. See also GS Alexander & EM Peñalver 'Properties of community' (2009) 10 *Theoretical Inquiries in Law* 127–160; GS Alexander 'Pluralism and property' (2011) 80 *Fordham L Rev* 1017–1052; LS Underkuffler *The idea of property: Its meaning and power* (2003); J Purdy 'A freedom-promoting approach to property: A renewed tradition for new debates' (2005) 72 *U Chi L Rev* 1237–1298.

[61] Also known as the social function norm of property.

[62] GS Alexander 'The social-obligation norm in American property law' (2009) 94 *Cornell L Rev* 745–819.

[63] EM Peñalver 'Land virtues' (2009) 94 *Cornell L Rev* 821–888.

[64] GS Alexander & EM Peñalver 'Properties of community' (2009) 10 *Theoretical Inquiries in Law* 127–160; GS Alexander 'Pluralism and property' (2011) 80 *Fordham L Rev* 1017–1052; GS Alexander 'Governance property' (2012) 160 *U Pa L Rev* 1853–1887; GS Alexander 'Property's ends: The publicness of private law values' (2014) 99 *Iowa L Rev* 1257–1296. See also ET Freyfogle 'Private ownership and human flourishing: An exploratory overview' (2013) 24 *Stell LR* 430–454.

[65] JW Singer 'Democratic estates: Property law in a free and democratic society' (2009) 94 *Cornell L Rev* 1009–1062; JW Singer 'Property law as the infrastructure of democracy' (2014) 63 *Duke LJ* 1287–1335; JW Singer 'The rule of reason in property law' (2013) 46 *UC Davis L Rev* 1369–1434.

[66] JW Singer *Introduction to property* 2 ed (2005) 39.

The idea of the social-obligation norm signifies that property rights should have their share of social responsibility.[67] Mirow points out that the notion of the social-obligation norm contrasts with the idea of absolute ownership and that it has been used to justify limitations on the use of property by its owner, such as in cases of expropriation and the redistribution of property through land reform programmes.[68] Mirow concludes that the social-obligation theory is important because property rights are defined and enshrined in constitutions and civil codes.[69] An analysis of the social obligation theory of ownership assists in determining the justification for limiting the right to exclude; the nature of the concept of ownership;[70] and the appropriate way to reconcile and balance the landowners' with non-owners' interests in land so as to promote human flourishing. The arguments advanced by the progressive property theorists provide valuable justifications or the basis for justificatory arguments for limiting a landowner's right to exclude by granting non-owners access rights to her property.

3 Absolute ownership and exclusivity in South African law

These theoretical considerations do not support a strong view of the right to exclude. Firstly, moral property theories do not provide theoretical support for such a strong notion of absolute ownership and exclusion that requires a moral justification whenever any limitation is imposed on the right to exclude. This is because moral property theorists such as Locke and Hegel do not discuss the issue of absoluteness directly and the different readings of both theories (labour and first occupation) make it controversial to support a strong, absolute view of the right to exclude. Secondly, modern property theory does not provide support for the strong notion of absolute ownership and exclusion either. Proponents of a strong exclusion theory tend to view property through the lens of the right to exclude. Exclusion theorists therefore treat limitations on ownership as exceptional, arguing that as a point of departure, the right to exclude should be upheld and protected. However, even when exclusion theorists see the right to exclude as the most important, core, or essential property entitlement, that

[67] MC Mirow 'The social-obligation norm of property: Duguit, Hayem and others' (2010) 22 *Fla J Int'l L* 191–226 192. See also GS Alexander 'Pluralism and property' (2011) 80 *Fordham L Rev* 1017–1052 1022–1023. See also C Crawford 'The social function of property and the human capacity to flourish' (2011) 80 *Fordham L Rev* 1089–1134, who argues that the social function of property can be understood as a notion that aims to secure the goal of human flourishing for all citizens within any state.

[68] MC Mirow 'The social-obligation norm of property: Duguit, Hayem and others' (2010) 22 *Fla J Int'l L* 191–226 192.

[69] MC Mirow 'The social-obligation norm of property: Duguit, Hayem and others' (2010) 22 *Fla J Int'l L* 191–226 226.

[70] GS Alexander 'Pluralism and property' (2011) 80 *Fordham L Rev* 1017–1052 1023.

does not mean that it is unlimited. The right to exclude can be limited, even if the limitations are viewed as exceptional. The only outcome of this view is that any limitation must be proved specifically; requires special justification; and might require compensation. In fact, modern exclusion theorists describe the right to exclude as relative and accept limitations for pragmatic reasons such as efficiency. Thirdly, there are theoretical views that support a limited or qualified right to exclude. Exclusive use and progressive property theorists agree that a landowner is presumed to have a right that is free of limitations, but add that there is always a possibility that limitations could be imposed, and these limitations are not seen as exceptional in the sense that they are almost impossible. Some theories accept that limitations on the right to exclude are not only possible but normal and relatively common. Progressive property theorists take into account the fundamental human values and interests of non-owners, and they do not simply prioritise the protection of the right to exclude. Limitations on the right to exclude are therefore accepted readily, sometimes even without compensation.

Exclusion, exclusive use and progressive property theorists acknowledge the existence of limitations on property and on the right of exclusion in particular, but they have different views on the nature of the limitations. The exclusion theorists view limitations as exceptions to the absolute-exclusion rule, while the exclusive use and progressive property theorists view limitations as inherent elements of the property system. On the whole it cannot be said that property theory offers strong or unanimous support for an approach that treats the right to exclude as an absolute entitlement, even when it is regarded as a core or essential property right.

Of interest to this discussion and in line with Professor Van der Walt's thinking (specifically in the South African context as well as the legal and constitutional system), these theories to a greater or lesser extent show that the enforcement of property rights, the right to exclude in particular, stops where there is a need for both non-owners and other landowners to have access rights to be on or to pass over the landowner's land. In this context, although access rights are limitations, they are not described as exceptions. This means that sometimes not the access rights but the exclusion of non-owners must be justified.

The notion of property as an absolute right to exclude is problematic because it does not take into account the social context. In the South African context, the right to exclude is in fact subject to a wide range of limitations,[71]

[71] The right to exclude is limited extensively, both at common law and by statutory control measures or constitutional provisions, allowing non-owners to have access to land for various purposes.

often for overriding, non-property reasons that are justified by the broader constitutional scheme, which makes it difficult to conceive the right as absolute and the limitations as exceptional.

It is perhaps appropriate to reflect briefly on the South African case of *Victoria and Alfred Waterfront (Pty) Ltd and Another v Police Commissioner, Western Cape and Others (Legal Resources Centre as Amicus Curiae)*,[72] in which the court confirmed that the right to exclude can be limited in instances where the right to life and freedom of movement depends on reasonable access to land.[73] The case involved access to a quasi-public place for a purpose, namely begging, that was not the purpose the owner had in mind when he opened his property to the public. The court ruled against the landowners, stating that:

> The issue of begging frequently raises a direct tension between the right to life and property rights. In that event, the property rights must give way to some extent. The rights to life and dignity are the most important of all human rights. By committing ourselves to a society founded on the recognition of human rights we are required to value those rights above all others.[74]

Exclusion of non-owners in this case would amount to a violation of the constitutional right to life, which may be negatively affected if non-owners are prohibited from begging (which is regarded as a source of their livelihood). The court held that the right to life encompasses more than 'mere animal existence', since it includes the right to a livelihood.

The decision shows that the right to exclude is not prioritised abstractly and that exclusion of non-owners is not always a preferred outcome. The landowner's right to exclude is limited when it concerns a quasi-public space or even private property (with restricted access), if access to the land is reasonably necessary to secure important non-property constitutional rights. Upholding the right to exclude absolutely and abstractly may in practice derogate from fundamental human rights. Thus the court refused to grant a blanket prohibition against entry on the premises, among other reasons, so as to protect the respondents' right to life, dignity and freedom of movement. As Professor Van der Walt argues, the right to exclude is directly and justifiably limited by constitutional provisions to ensure that

---

[72] 2004 (4) SA 444 (C).

[73] The court had to consider whether prohibition from entering the premises would offend against the entrenched constitutional provisions guaranteeing the right to life (section 11) and the right of freedom of movement (section 21(1), (3)) of the Constitution of the Republic of South Africa, 1996.

[74] *Victoria and Alfred Waterfront (Pty) Ltd and Another v Police Commissioner, Western Cape and Others (Legal Resources Centre as Amicus Curiae)* 2004 (4) SA 444 (C) 448–451.

non-property constitutional rights are secured when the exercise of those rights depend on access to land.[75]

The focus of the limitation and justification debate should therefore move to legislation and common law that regulate the exercise of ownership. The theoretical perspectives on the limitation of the right to exclude point towards a notion of ownership that functions within a legal system, which includes property and of which limitations are an inherent part. Furthermore, theoretical views show that justification for limitations has a specific meaning. In particular, justification does not require normative grounds for the existence of every limitation, because ownership and the right to exclude are not regarded as pre-social, pre-legal or pre-constitutional rights. The limitations are not imposed on pre-law rights; the right to exclude is limited within the legal system, and therefore the normative question whether to limit it is decided (during the constitution- or statute-writing process) before a particular dispute arises. Therefore, one can assume that property rights are in principle limited and contextual. From a constitutional perspective, limitations are from the beginning part of the system within which property functions. Consequently, justification refers to justifying the authority and reasons for and effect of a specific limitation imposed on the right to exclude, instead of justifying the very existence of a limitation.

4 Absolute ownership, exclusivity and sharing in US property law

As we have discussed, even while he provides rich and cross-cutting lessons in property theory for scholars around the world to develop, Professor Van der Walt grounds much of his analysis in South African law. Consequently, those who are familiar with his scholarship can recognise the range of examples in South African constitutional, statutory and common law in which property ownership is balanced with other core rights.[76] While Professor Van der Walt pushes for deeper and more explicit norms protecting such balances, those examples provide the descriptive foundation for his theoretical moves. Indeed, Professor Van der Walt has been the preeminent authority on constitutional

---

[75] AJ van der Walt 'The modest systemic status of property rights' (2014) 1 *J L Prop & Soc'y* 15–106 55.

[76] In decisions such as *Port Elizabeth Municipality v Various Occupiers* 2005 (1) SA 217 (CC); *President of the Republic of South Africa and Another v Modderklip Boerdery (Pty) Ltd and Others* 2005 (5) SA 3 (CC); *Victoria and Alfred Waterfront (Pty) Ltd and Another v Police Commissioner, Western Cape and Others (Legal Resources Centre as* Amicus Curiae*)* 2004 (4) SA 444 (C); *Kidson v Jimspeed Enterprises CC* 2009 (5) SA 246 (GNP); *Daniels v Scribante and Another* 2017 (4) SA 341 (CC) the landowners' rights have not been allowed to trump the constitutional rights of non-owners, such as the right to equality, human dignity and the right to have access to adequate housing.

property in South Africa, for which there is really no analog in American law. The very existence of this doctrinal area evidences the balance between property and other rights contemplated in post-apartheid South African law.

In the US, one might be tempted to conclude that there is less fodder for exploring Professor Van der Walt's claims about the importance of social context and about property's modest systemic role. After all, some of the thickest versions of exclusion theory mine American common law for support. Yet in our own work, we have discovered that there is ample space within American property law for exploring the theoretical implications of Professor Van der Walt's normative claims.

For instance, as in South African law, there are recurring situations in American property law where the right to exclude, rather than the right of access, must be justified. One key example lies in cases protecting the right of access to public accommodations. All American jurisdictions protect such access on grounds of what Singer calls the antidiscrimination principle.[77] The source for such protection includes both federal constitutional and statutory law. An iconic case exemplifying this balance between property and other rights is *Heart of Atlanta Motel, Inc. v United States*, where the Supreme Court of the United States stated:

> It is doubtful if in the long run appellant will suffer economic loss as a result of the [Civil Rights Act of 1964]. Experience is to the contrary where discrimination is completely obliterated as to all public accommodations. But whether this be true or not is of no consequence since this Court has specifically held that the fact that a 'member of the class which is regulated may suffer economic losses not shared by others ... has never been a barrier' to such legislation ... Likewise in a long line of cases this Court has rejected the claim that the prohibition of racial discrimination in public accommodations interferes with personal liberty. ... Neither do we find any merit in the claim that the Act is a taking of property without just compensation.[78]

Some jurisdictions, such as the State of New Jersey, go even further, protecting the right of access even when there is no claimed issue of discrimination. Thus, in the case of *Uston v Resorts International Hotel, Inc*,[79] the Supreme Court of New Jersey overruled earlier cases protecting the right of owners of public accommodations to arbitrarily exclude patrons, holding instead that a casino did not have the right to exclude a patron simply on the grounds

---

[77] JW Singer 'No right to exclude: Public accommodations and private property' (1996) 90 *Nw U L Rev* 1283–1497; JW Singer 'Property and equality: Public accommodations and the Constitution in South Africa and the United States' (1997) 12 *SA Public Law* 53–86.

[78] 379 US 241 (1964).

[79] 445 A.2d 370 (N.J. 1982).

that he was 'counting cards' in the game of Blackjack, thereby increasing his odds of winning. The New Jersey Supreme Court's jurisprudence on cases such as *Uston*, in which the right of access is balanced against the owner's right to exclude, epitomises the relevance of social context in achieving an appropriate balance. For example, as first-year law students studying the *Uston* case learn, the court's references to cases such as *State v Schmid*[80] and *State v Shack*[81] in its opinion have far less doctrinal value than what we might describe as contextual value. *Schmid* was a case in which the New Jersey Supreme Court upheld the right of individuals to distribute literature on a private university campus. *Shack* was a case in which that same court upheld the right of migrant workers housed on their employer's property to receive visitors at their housing. These cases provide a rich social context as a backdrop for the decision about whether the card-counting individual in *Uston* ought to have a continuing right of access to the casino, notwithstanding the financial loss to the casino. The exclusion of racial and other minorities, on grounds that were legally difficult to claim as race-based, was also central to the court's analysis.

Cases like *Uston* can and should be understood through the lens of non-owners. Just as Professor Van der Walt has done in describing the value of access from the perspective of those who are 'in the margins', such cases ought to be read and valued as cases that teach us about the relevance of social context in decision-making about property. As Underkuffler has cogently stated, in analysing speech and property rights:

> If we persist in the simplistic idea that property is – and should be – an invariably powerful right; if we refuse to acknowledge the interconnected and distributive qualities of property rights and property systems – we will simply encourage false beliefs of entitlement, and mask the critical social choices that property necessarily and inevitably involves.[82]

These examples, in which access has been privileged over exclusion, and also in which core civil and political rights have been privileged over ownership, have been a source of inspiration for American property scholars to explore the theoretical place of property *in* American law. In this chapter, we have provided examples from progressive property scholars, exclusive use theorists, and others in which property's role has been understood within specific social contexts. The work of these scholars also lays a foundation for exploring a more modest systemic role for property in American law.

---

[80] 423 A.2d 615 (N.J. 1980).

[81] 277 A.2d 369 (N.J. 1971).

[82] LS Underkuffler 'When should rights "trump"? An examination of speech and property' (2000) 52 *Maine L Rev* 311–322 322.

One additional area of theoretical development that Professor Van der Walt's scholarship has influenced is the recent scholarship on sharing as a foundational norm in property law. Indeed, there remains much room for scholars of property sharing to explore more deeply the implications of social context and property's systemic role as they develop the theoretical concept of property sharing. One of the core assumptions underlying the concept of property sharing is the idea that property ownership involves not only rights but also social obligations. Alexander and Peñalver have developed this assumption extensively, using the Aristotelian notion of 'virtue' to argue (among many other things) that property owners have obligations to share property in certain circumstances.[83]

In our own work, we have explored the possibility that sharing could, to a meaningful extent, replace exclusion as a starting point in resolving a range of common property disputes. In exploring this concept in American law, it has been proposed that an 'interest-outcome' model for resolving disputes, which begins with an exploration of interests among both non-owners and owners in a dispute, should be followed.[84] The model next proposes consideration of appropriate remedies, or outcomes, that could balance the legitimate interests of all the parties involved in the dispute. Finally, as a third step, the model proposes consideration of property and other entitlements. The interest-outcome model explicitly calls for consideration of social context as part of the first level of inquiry, that of determining each party's interests. This is one respect in which Professor Van der Walt's theoretical development of the importance of social context in property law has been deeply relevant and productive. Rather than relying on predetermined understandings of the entitlements associated with property ownership and other social and legal categories, the inquiry into 'interest' explores the particular, socially embedded *needs* and values of individual parties. In so doing, this inquiry takes a lesson developed 'in the margins' of property law and applies that lesson to common, 'everyday' disputes.

Toward the end of his brilliantly productive scholarly life, Professor Van der Walt developed the theory underlying the interest-outcome model considerably further. In his article 'Sharing servitudes', he 'consider[ed] the light that an explicitly stated interest-outcome approach and the idea of sharing remedies can shed on established principles of servitude law' in South African jurisprudence.[85] After exploring courts' analysis of sharing in

[83] GS Alexander 'The social-obligation norm in American property law' (2009) 94 *Cornell L Rev* 745–819; EM Peñalver 'Land virtues' (2009) 94 *Cornell L Rev* 821–888.

[84] R Dyal-Chand 'Sharing the cathedral' (2013) 46 *Conn L Rev* 647–723.

[85] AJ van der Walt 'Sharing servitudes' (2015) 4 *EPLJ* 162–222 168.

a range of cases involving both private law and constitutional law, Professor Van der Walt concluded:

> The South African examples from constitutional law are more interesting. Firstly, these examples show that sharing remedies do not have to be inspired by fairness considerations relating to conflicting private interests in the use of property; they can also emerge from the promotion of non-property constitutional rights and goals such as equality, dignity or access to housing. Secondly, in these cases the demand to share property can sometimes favour beneficiaries who have no legal right to use the property. Thirdly, while compensation seems to be an important feature of sharing remedies generally, is not a necessary element of sharing in the constitutional context. Finally, sharing does not have to take the form of creating or recognising a competing property right in favour of the beneficiary – in some instances it is sufficient to limit the exclusion right of the property owner in such a way that the beneficiary is allowed to use the property for a specified purpose and possibly for a limited time. To that extent, these outcomes do represent remedial innovations that involve sharing.[86]

With these conclusions, Professor Van der Walt took the next logical step in the theoretical trajectory that we have described in his scholarship: moving beyond considerations of social context, he also considered the implications for property's systemic role that might result from upholding sharing as a foundational norm in property law.

In so doing, Professor Van der Walt shone a light on a path that we hope American property law scholars can continue to follow. Clearly, as he himself recognised, it is not possible to make direct comparisons between the analysis of sharing in South African constitutional law and the analysis of sharing in American property law. In contrast to South African constitutional cases, where the protection of sharing is 'inspired by a strong and clearly defined constitutional obligation, such as protecting human dignity or preventing homelessness',[87] there are no such clearly defined constitutional obligations in American property law. But this absence makes the questions Professor Van der Walt raises about property's systemic role all the more pressing. In the absence of a set of constitutional mandates such as those contained in section 25 of South Africa's Constitution,[88] what is the justification for limiting the right of exclusion? What authority or authorities define property's systemic role? At bottom, what are the implications in American law of sharing as a foundational norm?

---

[86] AJ van der Walt 'Sharing servitudes' (2015) 4 *EPLJ* 162–222 219.

[87] AJ van der Walt 'Sharing servitudes' (2015) 4 *EPLJ* 162–222 220.

[88] The Constitution of the Republic of South Africa, 1996.

These questions are deeply relevant to the ongoing exploration of sharing in American property law. And they are relevant to a broader set of considerations as well. They go to the very heart of the continuing debate in property scholarship about the value and attributes of property ownership. As is generally true of Professor Van der Walt's scholarship, they engage deeply with questions of property theory as well as practice.

Chapter 14

The impact of recent EU conflicts of law regulations on land registration

A theoretical and practical perspective

Sjef van Erp & Katja Zimmermann***

Page

Contents

1 Land registration law as part of a 'single system' of European property law?

One of the most impressive aspects of André van der Walt's scholarly achievements is how he combined a thorough knowledge and a rigorous analysis of existing law and legal technique with a strong desire to change existing unjust legal conditions in South African society. By following that path, fundamental change became an integral part of how he perceived the fabric of the law. As a result André van der Walt rethought existing law in an amazingly creative way to achieve peaceful changes in an atmosphere of mutual understanding and respect. In his view, South African society demanded 'a fundamental shift from abstract, rights-based to contextual,

* Full professor of civil law and European private law at Maastricht University, Member of the Executive Committee of the European Law Institute, Vienna.

** Junior PhD researcher at Maastricht University and academic researcher at the Netherlands Cadastre, Land Registry and Mapping Agency.

non-hierarchical thinking about property rights'.[1] Consequently, property law needed a rethinking in two areas:[2]

> Two areas of property law probably deserve the most urgent attention in the next decade. One is (...) ways to avoid constructive-expropriation interpretations of regulatory laws aimed at reform of property law, possibly by placing more emphasis on provision for compensation payments for otherwise lawful, non-expropriatory state action that happens to have excessively unfair results for one or a small number of property owners or users. The second is the development of the common law of property. This implies reconsidering all the well-known areas, institutions and rules of common law property to determine whether, where and how they may need to be developed or reformed, either through the introduction of new legislation; the amendment of existing legislation; or the judicial development of traditional interpretations, understandings and applications of the relevant common-law principles.

By doing so he aimed to start an evolution towards revolutionary change, balancing the legal status of those who are at the margins of society against those who have vested interests.[3] His starting point of legal thinking was the famous decision by the South African Constitutional Court in *Pharmaceutical Manufacturers Association of South Africa and Another: In re Ex Parte President of the Republic of South Africa and Others* that the whole of law must be seen as one single system (within which constitutional law has the hierarchically highest authority) and should be interpreted in such a way that it fulfilled the aspirations and requirements of the constitution.[4] In the words of the court (Chaskalson P):

> [44] There are not two systems of law, each dealing with the same subject matter, each having similar requirements, each operating in its own field with its own highest court. There is only one system of law. It is shaped by the Constitution which is the supreme law, and all law, including the common law, derives its force from the Constitution and is subject to constitutional control.

---

[1] AJ van der Walt *Constitutional property law* 3 ed (2011) 521.

[2] AJ van der Walt *Constitutional property law* 3 ed (2011) 521, 528.

[3] AJ van der Walt *Property in the margins* (2009). Several years ago André van der Walt, after Sjef van Erp had delivered the first annual South African Research Chair in Property Law (SARCPL) lecture in August 2013, gave him a book by M Ramphele *Laying ghosts to rest: Dilemmas of the transformation in South Africa* (2008). We cannot find any clearer statement of André van der Walt's hope and vision for South Africa than is expressed in the title of that book. For the text of the first annual SARCPL lecture entitled 'Fluidity of ownership and the tragedy of hierarchy' see (2015) 4 *EPLJ* 56-80.

[4] *Pharmaceutical Manufacturers Association of South Africa and Another: In re Ex Parte President of the Republic of South Africa and Others* 2000 (2) SA 674 (CC).

An example of the balancing test which André van der Walt had in mind can be found in the case of *Port Elizabeth Municipality v Various Occupiers*.[5] At the heart of the case was a conflict between those who claimed that their right of ownership was at stake and those who claimed that they were entitled to live somewhere, in other words, a conflict between two basic human rights (right of ownership and right to housing). The Constitutional Court (Sachs J) stated the balancing test as follows:

> [23] In sum, the Constitution imposes new obligations on the courts concerning rights relating to property not previously recognised by the common law. It counterposes to the normal ownership rights of possession, use and occupation, a new and equally relevant right not arbitrarily to be deprived of a home. The expectations that ordinarily go with title could clash head-on with the genuine despair of people in dire need of accommodation. The judicial function in these circumstances is not to establish a hierarchical arrangement between the different interests involved, privileging in an abstract and mechanical way the rights of ownership over the right not to be dispossessed of a home, or vice versa. Rather it is to balance out and reconcile the opposed claims in as just a manner as possible taking account of all the interests involved and the specific factors relevant in each particular case.

What if such a 'single system' approach, and the contextual non-hierarchical balancing method, were to be applied in a European context as a starting point for an examination of the relationship between national law and the law of the European Union? Before this question can be answered a preliminary question must be asked: Is not this a very specific approach to solve problems of political transition, characteristic of the situation in South Africa which is still experiencing considerable societal problems after apartheid? The Court of Justice of the European Union (CJEU) has made it abundantly clear that the European framework treaties (Treaty on European Union and Treaty on the Functioning of the European Union) have created an autonomous legal order, which has precedence over the national legal orders.[6] The CJEU has also made it very clear that this might go as far as a duty resting on national courts to apply *moto proprio* or *ex officio* certain parts of EU law (such as, recently, consumer law).[7] In that sense it could be argued that private law in Europe is part of an all-encompassing European Union law and that national private law *stricto sensu* no longer exists, but that all private law is now

[5] *Port Elizabeth Municipality v Various Occupiers* 2005 (1) SA 217 (CC).

[6] Cf *Van Gend en Loos v Nederlandse administratie der belastingen* (Case C-26/62) Court of Justice of the European Communities 5 February 1963 (ECLI:EU:C:1963:1).

[7] Cf *Océano Grupo Editorial and Salvat Editores* (Joined Cases C-240/98 to C-244/9) Court of Justice of the European Communities 27 June 2000 (ECLI:EU:C:2000:346).

European private law. Within that framework national private law and EU law could be seen as one single system. However, this is not the same type of single system as in South Africa. In the European Union there is no need for a drastic change in societal relations because of a revolutionary break with an unjust past. The role of the framework treaties is, therefore, different from the impact of the new South African Constitution. The European treaties aim, first of all, to create an internal market and, following from that, closer cooperation also in other areas; in the words of article 1 of the Treaty on European Union (TEU), 'an ever closer union among the peoples of Europe'. Because of these historical and societal differences it cannot be argued that the 'single system' approach as developed in South African law can be applied directly to the situation in Europe. However, analysing national and EU law as constituent parts of one whole system of law might still prove to be useful as an exercise in legal thinking, if we reformulate that approach as an analytic tool to examine the impact of EU law on national law. Still, even purely seen as a tool or technique, the words of André van der Walt ring true that the practical consequence might be a need to fundamentally reconsider those areas of property law which are closely connected with European integration, either because of positive integration (resulting from directives and regulations) or negative integration (resulting from the impact on national law of the four freedoms upon which the European internal market is built: freedom of goods, persons, services and capital). It can, of course, be debated whether this legal-technical analysis should be conducted bottom-up (national law will then be the starting point; EU law will be applied as part of the national legal system) or top-down (European Union law will then be seen as the overall framework, national law almost as a 'gap filler'), but one thing appears to be clear from a practitioner's viewpoint: in legal practice, everywhere in Europe, the bottom-up approach seems to prevail. Taking that latter approach as our starting point, we will focus on recent developments in the areas of cross-border succession, matrimonial regimes, and property consequences of registered partnerships, by offering, first of all, an overview of recent EU legislation in those areas and the impact of that legislation on the national property law systems, particularly land registration.[8] The

[8] Regulation (EU) No 650/2012 of the European Parliament and of the Council of 4 July 2012 on jurisdiction, applicable law, recognition and enforcement of decisions and acceptance and enforcement of authentic instruments in matters of succession and on the creation of a European Certificate of Succession, OJ 2012, L 201/107; Council Regulation (EU) 2016/1103 of 24 June 2016 implementing enhanced cooperation in the area of jurisdiction, applicable law and the recognition and enforcement of decisions in matters

Succession Regulation already entered into force on 17 August 2015; the other two regulations will soon follow and enter into force on 29 January 2019. After having discussed various practical problems which surfaced almost immediately after the Succession Regulation had entered into force, we will ask ourselves the more fundamental question of how far the influence of EU law will reach in this area and whether old, well-established, conflict of laws mechanisms such as, in particular, public policy can be used to reach a result which, at the level of member states, is seen as acceptable. How far does the reach of public policy go to protect national land registration law from the influence of EU law, to preserve internal (national) coherence? The final, more general, question to be answered will be, what may take precedence: the preservation of national law or the *effet utile* of EU law? Before we attend to these questions, one last remark might be appropriate: even the most thoroughly prepared piece of legislation cannot complete its baptism of fire before it is used in practice. The reason for that is clear: it is simply impossible to map out all scenarios that can cause problems for governmental institutions, practitioners, and citizens. It is only when the actors are working with the legislation that it can be put to the acid test. As a matter of course, this also holds true for the EU Succession Regulation and the even newer EU Regulations on Matrimonial Property Regimes and on the Property Consequences of Registered Partnerships. Much has been written on the uniform private international law rules that are at the heart of these regulations, but contributions that discuss practical implications and challenges that the regulations may pose for land registrars could so far not be found. The aim of this article is also to contribute to the closing of this gap and to encourage other practitioners to follow by sharing their experiences with these regulations.

2 The European succession regulation: Introducing a uniform European Certificate of Succession

On 17 August 2015 the much awaited European Succession Regulation entered into force.[9] The aim of this regulation is to clear the way for an

---

of matrimonial property regimes, OJ 2016, L 183/1; and Council Regulation (EU) 2016/1104 of 24 June 2016, implementing enhanced cooperation in the area of jurisdiction, applicable law and the recognition and enforcement of decisions in matters relating to the property consequences of registered partnerships, OJ 2016, L 183/30.

[9] Regulation (EU) No 650/2012 of the European Parliament and of the Council of 4 July 2012 on jurisdiction, applicable law, recognition and enforcement of decisions and acceptance and enforcement of authentic instruments in matters of succession and on the creation of a European Certificate of Succession, OJ 2012, L 201/107. The Regulation does not apply to Denmark, Ireland and the United Kingdom.

efficient solution of cross-border succession cases by establishing a uniform set of private international law rules to govern succession and by providing a standardised European Certificate of Succession (hereafter: the Certificate). The regulation is based on establishing a parallelism between applicable law and competent court (both based on the last habitual residence of the deceased) and application of one legal system to the whole of the estate.[10] In other words: succession to immovable property will no longer be governed by the *lex rei sitae*, as was the case in some member states. It is possible to make a choice of law, but limited to a person's nationality at the time of making the choice or at the time of death.[11] During the period that this regulation was discussed in the various European institutions it became quickly apparent that, although the regulation's only aim was to unify the rules on private international law, such unification could also have an impact on the substantive property law systems of the European Union. Recognition of foreign law might result in friction at a national level if the particular rules of foreign law differed from the rules of the state in which these rules had to be incorporated. For this reason the regulation does not apply to 'the nature of rights *in rem*' and 'any recording in a register of rights in immovable or movable property, including the legal requirements for such recording, and the effects of recording or failing to record such rights in a register'.[12] The latter exception implies that, although the *lex rei sitae* could no longer govern succession to immovable property, it re-entered through the back door, as the law governing land registries (the so-called *lex registrationis*, which often coincides with the *lex rei sitae*) was exempt from the impact of the regulation. In addition, the regulation contains a provision on how to adapt a foreign right *in rem* in the receiving system (which at the same time includes criteria to refuse such adaptation) and contains a provision on when the receiving system may refuse to accept the foreign solution on the basis of its public policy ('*ordre public*'). Article 31 on adaptation provides the following:

> Where a person invokes a right *in rem* to which he is entitled under the law applicable to the succession and the law of the Member State in which the right is invoked does not know the right *in rem* in question, that right shall, if necessary and to the extent possible, be adapted to the closest equivalent right *in rem* under the law of that State, taking into account the aims and the interests pursued by the specific right in rem and the effects attached to it.

[10] Article 21(1) Succession Regulation. Only in exceptional circumstances will the law of the closest connection be applied: see art 21(2) of the Succession Regulation.

[11] Article 22 of the Succession Regulation.

[12] Article 1(2)(k) and (l) of the Succession Regulation.

In other words, adaptation is the positive side to recognition problems: the national legal system accommodates (in fact: accepts non-essential changes) in its property law to make recognition possible. Article 35 on the impact of public policy, however, shows the negative side of recognition problems:

> The application of a provision of the law of any State specified by this Regulation may be refused only if such application is manifestly incompatible with the public policy (*ordre public*) of the forum.

But even with regard to public policy the approach, although at first sight clearly of a negative nature, still is more positive than it might seem, as only in cases where the foreign solution is 'manifestly incompatible' with the law of the receiving state the latter may refuse recognition. Legal scholarship in this area has shown that the public policy under discussion here is not the same as public policy at a national level, which, in most cases, is aimed at limiting the autonomy of private parties to shape their legal relations.[13] The public policy as applied in foreign legal recognition cases is of a different nature. In a case which has connections with more than one legal system, a certain friction of differing rules will always be seen. Unless a legal system is the carbon copy of another legal system, rules will differ and even in situations of legal transplants, the formal (black-letter) rules may be the same, but the application and interpretation will show divergence. Public policy at a private international law level is therefore, by its very nature, more restricted than national public policy. This is even more so if recognition of a foreign solution happens within an overall public international law framework in which states to a lesser or greater degree cooperate and states even, as is the case with the European Union, may have transferred parts of their sovereignty to a higher authority.[14] Within the European Union, the member states share a common cultural, political and economic heritage, from which it can be deduced that differences in legal solutions are not a matter of principle, but of divergence within a certain bandwidth. This

[13] Cf for a brief overview G Cuniberti *Conflict of laws: A comparative approach, text and cases* (2017) 131ff.

[14] For an elaborate study see: J Föhlisch, Der gemeineuropäische ordre public (Frankfurt a/M: Lang, 1997) and T Corthaut, *EU ordre public* (2012). Cf. also HP Meidanis 'Public policy and ordre public in the private international law of the EU: traditional positions and modern trends' *European L Rev* 2005 95ff. and T Hoško 'Public policy as an exception to the movement within the internal market and the European judicial area: A comparison' 2014 *Croatian Yearbook of European Law and Policy* 189ff.

makes adaptation easier and invoking public policy less likely.[15] If, however, the law of a third country applies, this might be different. What also matters is whether the foreign solution violates fundamental human rights or basic principles of fair legal proceedings. These are generally seen as so essential that violation of these rights and principles is seen as sufficient justification for invoking the public policy exception. Sometimes the public policy exception may be cloaked as an exclusion based on 'reasonableness and fairness', based upon justified expectations. The parties could not have expected that the applicable law would be so fundamentally different from the law with which they are familiar. As such, this 'reasonableness and fairness' exclusion could even be used against application of the forum's own law. These latter cases, however, are exceptional.[16] So far, probably this all sounds quite familiar. What is, however, different from more traditional private international law instruments is that the Succession Regulation, building upon the basic elements described above, also introduces a document which has to be issued by a competent authority, which proves who is entitled to the estate and which has to be recognised in all participating EU member states: the European Certificate of Succession. The reasons for introducing such a document are, in essence, very simple: heirs need proof that they are entitled to the estate, such proof is required in all participating member states, there is consensus as to the basic elements which such a document should contain, and therefore sufficient common ground exists to introduce a compulsory uniform model. In the words of article 69(2) of the Succession Regulation:

> The Certificate shall be presumed to accurately demonstrate elements which have been established under the law applicable to the succession or under any other law applicable to specific elements. The person mentioned in the Certificate as the heir, legatee, executor of the will or administrator of the estate shall be presumed to have the status mentioned in the Certificate and/or to hold the rights or the

[15] See E Pataut 'The public-policy exception and the Proposal for a Regulation of the European Parliament and of the Council on jurisdiction, applicable law, recognition and enforcement of decisions and authentic instruments in matters of succession and the creation of a European Certificate of Succession' (COM(2009)154), a Note written for the Legal Affairs Committee of the European Parliament (Brussels: European Parliament, 2010) and B Hess *et al* Regulation (EC) n 650/2012 of July 2012 on jurisdiction, applicable law, recognition and enforcement of authentic instruments in matters of succession and on the creation of a European Certificate of Succession, a Note written for the Legal Affairs Committee of the European Parliament (Brussels: European Parliament, 2012) 18/9.

[16] Cf a recent Dutch case in which application of certain rules of Dutch matrimonial property law was refused as the Dutch default rules (total community of property) were from a comparative perspective highly exceptional and came as a complete surprise: Hoge Raad 17 February 2017 ECLI:NL:HR:2017:276.

powers stated in the Certificate, with no conditions and/or restrictions being attached to those rights or powers other than those stated in the Certificate.

This looks clear enough, but if you have ever seen the standard forms which together constitute the Certificate, you will not have failed to notice its complexity.[17] This is due to the fact that the standard forms are quite elaborate. The Certificate alone makes seven pages. In addition, depending on the circumstances of the succession case, it will also be necessary to fill in one or more of its annexures. It seems that this complexity is a necessary byproduct of European harmonisation; in the end, this one standard form must do justice to the entirety of the diverging national laws. But the Succession Regulation also knows a deeper level of complexity, which does not reveal itself at first sight. A number of examples will be given below to illustrate this deeper level. Yet it is to be stressed that these are merely illustrations and it is not intended to provide a conclusive overview of all layers of complexity that may exist in this legal instrument.

2.1 Personal information

In addition to the mandatory information about the deceased, their heirs, and the person who applied for the issuance of the Certificate, the Certificate provides the option of filling in more personal information about either party, such as their personal phone numbers and their email addresses. If the issuing authority decides to fill in this information voluntarily, any person who consults the Certificate through the land registry will be able to see and potentially use this information. Why would an issuing authority fill in this information? Essentially, there are two scenarios. First, it is possible that the provision of any of these voluntary pieces of information is a requirement for registration of the Certificate in one of the member states. In the end, the registration requirements are excluded from the scope of the Succession Regulation. Therefore, member states may apply their own national registration requirements when deciding whether to register a Certificate. Second, it might well be that the issuing authority (frequently a civil law notary)[18] fills in the information despite the fact that it is strictly speaking unnecessary for the Certificate to be registered. This situation could occur for

[17] Commission Implementing Regulation (EU) No 1329/2014 of 9 December 2014, establishing the forms referred to in Regulation (EU) No 650/2012 of the European Parliament and of the Council on jurisdiction, applicable law, recognition and enforcement of decisions and acceptance and enforcement of authentic instruments in matters of succession and on the creation of a European Certificate of Succession, OJ L 359, 16.12.2014 30–84.

[18] Cf arts 64 and 3(2) of the Succession Regulation.

two reasons. On the one hand, the issuing authority may be used to providing this information when drafting a national succession certificate. On the other hand, the issuing authority may be driven by a desire to draft a Certificate that is as complete as possible in order to be on the safe side and to facilitate the situation of the applicant. In the end, if they fail to provide information that is required for registration in a different member state, the applicant will have to take additional measures to get the Certificate registered. The second scenario, in which the issuing authority provides more personal information than is strictly necessary, contains a hidden trap. This is because member states apply different criteria to determine which persons may be granted access to the land registry. The result is a scale that extends from total disclosure of all land registry information to any person consulting the land registry to very restricted access to the information. It is quite possible that the issuing authority, when drafting the Certificate, does not realise that the foreign member state in which the Certificate is used applies a more open approach towards publicity of land registry content than what they are used to in their home member state, with the result that an issuing authority in that member state would likely decide against including surplus personal information. To prevent this situation, the issuing authority would have to gather information about the foreign requirements for registration of a Certificate, and the publicity of land registry information in that foreign member state, before drawing up the Certificate. From a practical viewpoint, it can be quite challenging to find out about all registration requirements in a foreign country. What would be beneficial is the setting up of a database in which practitioners can easily find useful information about registration requirements in the different member states.[19] For the time being, assistance could be sought through the European Land Registration Network, which makes it possible to send a cooperation request to the ELRN contact person of one of the connected land registries.

2.2 *The existence of a cross-border element*

Can a Certificate be used in purely national succession cases or is it restricted to those cases that have a cross-border element? The answer can be found in article 62(1) of the Succession Regulation, which states:

> This Regulation creates a European Certificate of Succession (hereinafter referred to as 'the Certificate') which shall be issued for use in another Member State and shall produce the effects listed in Article 69.

[19] The database that can be found on the website http://www.buyingmyhome.eu/ could serve as an inspiration in this respect.

The Certificate is thus intended for cross-border succession cases. This can also be found in article 63 (1) of the Succession Regulation, which reads:

> The Certificate is for use by heirs, legatees having direct rights in the succession and executors of wills or administrators of the estate who, in another Member State, need to invoke their status or to exercise respectively their rights as heirs or legatees and/or their powers as executors of wills or administrators of the estate.

When departing from the position of the land registrar, two questions arise. To begin with, should the land registry actively control the existence of a cross-border element? The presumption of correctness with regard to the Certificate, which is laid down in article 69 of the Succession Regulation, seems to oppose to such an active control. But even if the land registrar wanted to control whether such a cross-border element exists, would she at all be able to do so? The answer is that it depends on the individual case. For example, if the Certificate states that the deceased had Dutch nationality, that his last residual residence was in the Netherlands and that the applicable law is Dutch law, it seems at first sight that this is a purely national succession case. The Certificate does not prescribe an exhaustive description of the succession estate. Instead, Annex IV of Form V on the 'status and rights of the heir(s)' asks the issuing authority to specify the heir's 'share of the estate'.[20] The possibility to determine whether a cross-border element is present in a given succession case thus depends on the preciseness of the information provided by the issuing authority in this regard. In other cases, the existence of a cross-border element is more evident. This is for example the case if the Certificate is issued to deal with the succession of a Dutch person who had his last habitual residence in Germany and whose succession is governed by German law.

2.3 *On 'forms' and 'extracts'*

Article 67(1) of the Succession Regulation states that the issuing authority must use the standard form when drawing up a Certificate. According to article 1(5) of Implementing Regulation (EU) No 1329/2014, this standard form is form V as contained in its annex 5.[21] This definition may seem pretty clear, yet differing interpretations cannot be ruled out. To begin with, is the

[20] Form V, Annex IV, point 8.

[21] Commission Implementing Regulation (EU) No 1329/2014 of 9 December 2014 establishing the Forms referred to in Regulation (EU) No 650/2012 of the European Parliament and of the Council on jurisdiction, applicable law, recognition and enforcement of decisions and acceptance and enforcement of authentic instruments in matters of succession and on the creation of a European Certificate of Succession, OJ L 359, 16.12.2014 30–84.

use of this standard form always required? In *Alpha Bank Cyprus Ltd v Dau Si Senh and Others*, the CJEU ruled on the question whether the use of the standard forms provided by Regulation No 1393/2007 is mandatory.[22] The court came to the following conclusion:

> In the light of all the foregoing considerations, the answer to the three questions referred is that Regulation No 1393/2007 must be interpreted as meaning that:
>
> – the receiving agency is required, in all circumstances and without it having a margin of discretion in that regard, to inform the addressee of a document of his right to refuse to accept that document, by using systematically for that purpose the standard form set out in Annex II to that regulation ...[23]

As noted above, the Certificate is quite extensive and for one reason or another, the parties involved might not want all the information supplied in it to be available to third parties, which would be the case if it was registered in the land registry. Would it thus be possible to offer an extract of the Certificate that is drawn up by the relevant authority for registration? To avoid Babylonian confusion, we must be aware that two different notions of the word 'extract' are used in the context of the Succession Regulation. Its first notion refers to the issuing authority that draws up the Certificate by filling in the standard form with the information that is necessary for its purpose. In some situations, the parties concerned might find it desirable that some information contained in this original Certificate (for example their personal email address) does not find its way into the land registry, where it could be accessed by third parties. To this end, they could approach the issuing authority with the question whether it would instead be possible to offer an extract of this original Certificate (thus a copy of the Certificate that excludes certain information) for registration. May this request be honored? Article 70(1) and paragraph 72 of the Succession Regulation state that the issuing authority is to 'issue one or more certified copies of the Certificate to the applicant and to any other person demonstrating a legitimate interest'. A legal basis for the possibility of providing the applicant with an extract of the Certificate cannot be found in the Succession Regulation. For this reason, the possibility to submit an extract from the Certificate for registration must be ruled out.

---

[22] Case C-519/13 *Alpha Bank Cyprus Ltd v Dau Si Senh and Others* ECLI:EU:C:2015:603, paras 25–26. Regulation (EC) No 1393/2007 of the European Parliament and of the Council of 13 November 2007 on the service in the Member States of judicial and extrajudicial documents in civil or commercial matters (service of documents), and repealing Council, Regulation (EC) No 1348/2000, OJ 2007, L 324/79.

[23] Case C-519/13 *Alpha Bank Cyprus Ltd v Dau Si Senh and Others* ECLI:EU:C:2015:603 paras 77–78.

On the other hand, it is possible for the issuing authority to draw up a partial Certificate, which is sometimes also referred to as 'extract'. What is the difference between an extract as described above and a partial Certificate? A partial Certificate is essentially a certificate that does not contain all information that can be supplied in the standard form. This is possible on the ground of article 68 of the Succession Regulation, which states that 'the Certificate shall contain the following information, to the extent required for the purpose for which it is issued: …' In other words, the issuing authorities are under no obligation to fill in the entire standard form when they draw up the Certificate, but must only provide the information that is necessary to serve the purpose for which it is requested. The partial Certificate thus relates to the drawing up of the original Certificate itself while the extract relates to the production of a narrowed copy of the original Certificate.

2.4 Translations

In the Netherlands, documents that are registered in the land registry must be drawn up in Dutch.[24] Article 41 *Kadasterwet* states the following:

1. Ter inschrijving van een feit dat is opgenomen in een stuk gesteld in een vreemde of de Friese taal, wordt naast dat ter inschrijving aangeboden stuk een letterlijke vertaling in het Nederlands ter inschrijving aangeboden, vervaardigd en voor overeenstemmend verklaard door een voor die taal als bevoegd toegelaten beëdigd vertaler, of, indien het een in te schrijven notariële akte in de Friese taal betreft, door de notaris voor wie de akte is verleden.
2. Het bepaalde in het eerste lid lijdt uitzondering ingeval met betrekking tot luchtvaartuigen een proces-verbaal van inbeslagneming, opgemaakt in het buitenland door een deurwaarder of door een andere volgens de daar geldende wet daartoe bevoegde persoon en gesteld in een vreemde taal, aan de bewaarder wordt toegezonden of bij deze wordt ingeleverd. Alsdan wordt door de zorg van de bewaarder zo spoedig mogelijk een vertaling van een zodanig proces-verbaal vervaardigd door een in Nederland toegelaten beëdigd vertaler.
3. De vertalingen worden ingeschreven in plaats van de in de vreemde of Friese taal gestelde stukken, die onder de bewaarder blijven berusten.

The underlying rationale is that third parties who consult these documents through the land registry must be able to read them. A similar condition exists in German law.[25] §184 *Gerichtsverfassungsgesetz* states:

Die Gerichtssprache ist deutsch. Das Recht der Sorben, in den Heimatkreisen der sorbischen Bevölkerung vor Gericht sorbisch zu sprechen, ist gewährleistet.

[24] Article 41 of the Kadasterwet.

[25] §184 of the Gerichtsverfassungsgesetz.

If a Certificate is offered for registration that is drawn up in a foreign language, may the land registrar then demand an official translation of the (entire) Certificate? As a point of departure, we must remind ourselves that the Certificate is a standard form which is available in all official languages of the EU. In theory, one could thus argue that the land registrar, who is confronted with a Certificate drawn up in a foreign language, may only demand a translation of the free text, but not of the standard form as such. This is because he could read the foreign standard form by simply putting the official standard form in his own language next to it. In practice, however, this argument puts a high burden on the land registrar. A major problem is the absence of dynamic forms with the aid of which the Certificate could be drawn up digitally; thus the issuing authorities either print the Certificate and fill in the paper version which they submit for registration or they have made their own digital forms. The land registrar is thus required to check whether the Certificate has been fully incorporated by the issuing authority, to make sure that all mandatory information is filled in. In most cases, this should not be an issue, but if this happens not to be the case, the registrar is confronted with a difficult task. An easy comparison is not possible when the standard form is not translated. But even if the form is drawn up in a language that the registrar understands, but was digitalised by the issuing authority, it is impossible for him to judge in a glance whether the standard form is completely followed, as the issuing authority may not have used the same front size or letter type or may have added much free text, with the result that eg page 4 of the Certificate does not correspond to page 4 of the standard form. Would dynamic forms change this argumentation? That would only be the case if the registrar could rely on the fact that the Certificate that claims to be drawn up with the help of such a dynamic form was indeed drawn up by the dynamic form and that it is not possible for a party to adapt its format. Another whole level of complexity is added when the Certificate is drawn up in a different alphabet. This can also happen within the EU. Think of a Certificate drawn up in Greece in the Greek alphabet or in Bulgaria in Cyrillic. A land registrar, who is 'only' familiar with the Latin alphabet, will not only have problems to decipher the free text but also relatively simple information, such as names. An example might clarify the problems:

Bulgarian Alphabet:	Проф. Андр ван дер Уолт
Greek Alphabet:	Προφ. Ανδρε ϝαν δερ Ωαλτ

Above you see the exact same name in Bulgarian and Greek, and from the context of this commemorative collection of essays you might have been able to decipher it, but imagine having to decipher an entire Certificate plus annexes in a foreign alphabet. Against this background it seems defendable that the land registrar may demand a full translation in this case.

2.5 *The value of the asterisk ('*')*

In the Certificate, some information fields are marked with an asterisk ('*'). This means that this information must be filled in. One could thus conclude that the provision of all information that is not marked with an asterisk is merely optional. The question that then arises is whether a land registrar can demand that certain pieces of optional information must be filled in before the Certificate can be registered. To this end, recital 18 of the Succession Regulation states:

> In order to avoid duplication of documents, the registration authorities should accept such documents drawn up in another Member State by the competent authorities whose circulation is provided for by this Regulation. In particular, the European Certificate of Succession issued under this Regulation should constitute a valid document for the recording of succession property in a register of a Member State. This should not preclude the authorities involved in the registration from asking the person applying for registration to provide such additional information, or to present such additional documents, as are required under the law of the Member State in which the register is kept, for instance information or documents relating to the payment of revenue. The competent authority may indicate to the person applying for registration how the missing information or documents can be provided.

Read in conjunction with article 1(2)(l) and article 68 of the Succession Regulation, it follows that the registration requirements are excluded from the scope of the regulation and are thus set by the national law of the member state in which the Certificate is to be registered. Against this background it seems defensible to argue that the asterisk merely indicates the bare minimum information that must be given in all member states in order to allow for the registration of a Certificate. If we follow this line of argumentation we can conclude that the land registrar must be able to demand the provision of all information necessary to meet the national registration requirements, even if a particular piece of information is marked as optional information in the standard form.

3 The European regulations on matrimonial property regimes and on the property consequences of registered partnerships

The Succession Regulation explicitly states that it does not apply to questions relating to matrimonial property regimes or the property consequences of relationships which the applicable law considers as comparable to marriage.[26]

---

[26] Article 1(2)(d) of the Succession Regulation.

These matters are dealt with in two different regulations: the Matrimonial Property Regulation and the Registered Partnerships Property Regulation.[27] The Matrimonial Property Regulation assumes that the spouses have made a choice for the applicable law (either based on habitual residence or on nationality); if not, the regulation has a multi-level conflict of laws rule (again based on habitual residence or nationality and the 'closest connection' as relevant factors).[28] With regard to registered partners, the Registered Partners Property Regulation again assumes that the partners have made a choice (with habitual residence, nationality and the law of the state under whose law the registered partnership was created as the only possible connecting factors); if not, the law of the state where the partnership was registered applies.[29] Both regulations have the same exceptions to the scope of application as can be found in the Succession Regulation with regard the nature of rights *in rem* and any recording in a register of rights in immovable or movable property, including the legal requirements for such recording, and the effects of recording or failing to record such rights in a register.[30] Both regulations also mirror the Succession Regulation in their provisions on adaptation and public policy.[31]

Although the Matrimonial Property Regulation and the Registered Partnerships Property Regulation, unlike the Succession Regulation, do not introduce a uniform European document comparable to the European Certificate of Succession, both regulations indirectly end up in a standardised document, as form V belonging to the Succession Regulation (which contains the standard European Certificate of Succession) has an obligatory Annex

[27] Council Regulation (EU) 2016/1103 of 24 June 2016 implementing enhanced cooperation in the area of jurisdiction, applicable law and the recognition and enforcement of decisions in matters of matrimonial property regimes, OJ 2016, L 183/1 and Council Regulation (EU) 2016/1104 of 24 June 2016 implementing enhanced cooperation in the area of jurisdiction, applicable law and the recognition and enforcement of decisions in matters of the property consequences of registered partnerships, OJ 2016, L 183/30. These regulations are the result, as can be read in their official title, of so-called 'enhanced cooperation' (see art 20 TEU and arts 326–334 TFEU), which means that not all member states are bound, but only a certain number. The member states which take part in these regulations are Belgium, Bulgaria, Cyprus, the Czech Republic, Germany, Greece, Spain, France, Croatia, Italy, Luxembourg, Malta, the Netherlands, Austria, Portugal, Slovenia, Finland and Sweden. For all of the non-participating states their national laws on these topics remain effective.

[28] Articles 22, 26 of the Matrimonial Property Regulation.

[29] Articles 22, 26 of the Registered Partnership Property Regulation.

[30] Article 1 (2)(g), (h) of the Matrimonial Property Regulation and Registered Partnership Property Regulation.

[31] Articles 29, 31 of the Matrimonial Property Regulation and Registered Partnership Regulation.

III, in which information must be given on the 'matrimonial property regime or other equivalent property regime of the deceased'.[32] This annex is based on article 68 of the Succession Regulation, which enumerates the information which the Certificate 'shall contain'. Under paragraph (h) it is stated:

> Information concerning a marriage contract entered into by the deceased or, if applicable, a contract entered into by the deceased in the context of a relationship deemed by the law applicable to such a relationship to have comparable effects to marriage, and information concerning the matrimonial property regime or equivalent property regime.

This, of course, makes perfect sense, because the Certificate must give information on the assets which are part of the deceased's estate and this can only be stated if, first of all, it has become clear which assets are part of the deceased's estate resulting from any matrimonial property regime, either by default or as the outcome of a contractual arrangement.

In practice, the question might arise whether a European Certificate of Succession without the information in Annex III can be registered. This will depend upon the statutory role which the land registrar in a given national system of land registration may have. In those systems where land registrars are passive, such as in the Netherlands, the registrar will probably have to accept the Certificate as it is presented, with or without Annex III. In member states where the registrar plays an active role in the process of land registration, such as in Germany, this might be different. A question which may arise here, for the time being still more theoretical than practical, is whether land registrars can invoke the exception of article 1(2)(l) of the Succession Regulation, thus arguing that their role is a matter of the *lex registrationis*; or whether general principles of European Union law, particularly the duty to implement and enforce European law so that it has full effect ('*effet utile*'), still compel registrars from a more passive system of oversight to take a more active stance.

4 Not a limited public policy exception, but '*effet utile*' as the final expression of a single system of European land registration law?

Unifying private international law in the area of succession, matrimonial property and property consequences of registered partnerships has proven

[32] Commission Implementing Regulation (EU) No 1329/2014 of 9 December 2014 establishing the Forms referred to in Regulation (EU) No 650/2012 of the European Parliament and of the Council on jurisdiction, applicable law, recognition and enforcement of decisions and acceptance and enforcement of authentic instruments in matters of succession and on the creation of a European Certificate of Succession, OJ L 359, 16.12.2014 30–84, 75–6.

to be more complicated in land registration practice than might have been expected. Although the nature of rights *in rem* and the law relating to land registration has been excluded from the scope of the regulations discussed above, it again becomes clear that certainly in the area of property law the creation of watertight compartments between the law of succession, property law and land registration law has proven to be extremely complicated. Foreign applicable law will always need some form of adaptation in the receiving system, but any receiving system will have its own limits as to what it finds acceptable. An outright refusal to apply the outcome of foreign law in a particular case on the basis of public policy is used to demarcate the outer limits of acceptability. Although the public policy exception has, within the framework of the European Union, been severely curtailed and is only possible (and justifiable) if there is a 'manifest' violation of a member state's basic principles underlying that state's political, socio-economic and cultural order, particularly fundamental human rights and principles of fair legal proceedings, still, also within the European legal order, this exception survives. The Court of Justice of the European Communities plainly realised the imminent danger to the proper functioning of the autonomous European legal order which could emanate from an unfettered use of the public exception. Already in a case from 1974 (*Van Duyn v Home Office*, a case on freedom of establishment) the court stated that public policy should be used sparingly.[33] This is true particularly at a European level, where it is has to be applied in an atmosphere of mutual trust and confidence between member states and their institutions (including the judiciary), in light of the four freedoms underlying the European internal market.[34] In the words of the court:[35]

> It should be emphasized that the concept of public policy in the context of the Community and where, in particular, it is used as a justification for derogating from the fundamental principle of freedom of movement for workers, must be interpreted strictly, so that its scope cannot be determined unilaterally by each Member State without being subject to control by the institutions of the

---

[33] C-41/74 *Yvonne van Duyn v Home Office* ECLI:EU:C:1974:133.

[34] Cf art 4(3) of the Treaty on European Union: 'Pursuant to the principle of sincere cooperation, the Union and the Member States shall, in full mutual respect, assist each other in carrying out tasks which flow from the Treaties.

The Member States shall take any appropriate measure, general or particular, to ensure fulfilment of the obligations arising out of the Treaties or resulting from the acts of the institutions of the Union.

The Member States shall facilitate the achievement of the Union's tasks and refrain from any measure which could jeopardise the attainment of the Union's objectives.'

[35] *Van Duyn v Home Office* para 18.

> Community. Nevertheless, the particular circumstances justifying recourse to the concept of public policy may vary from one country to another and from one period to another, and it is therefore necessary in this matter to allow the competent national authorities an area of discretion within the limits imposed by the Treaty.

Or, as the court stated in another case (*Adoui and Cornlaille v Belgium*, also a freedom of establishment case):[36]

> It should be noted in that regard that reliance by a national authority upon the concept of public policy presupposes (...) the existence of 'a genuine and sufficiently serious threat affecting one of the fundamental interests of society'. Although Community law does not impose upon the Member States a uniform scale of values as regards the assessment of conduct which may be considered as contrary to public policy, it should nevertheless be stated that conduct may not be considered as being of a sufficiently serious nature to justify restrictions on the admission to or residence within the territory of a Member State of a national of another Member State in a case where the former Member State does not adopt, with respect to the same conduct on the part of its own nationals, repressive measures or other genuine and effective measures intended to combat such conduct.

From the perspective of a single system of law, unifying national and European private law, this can be no surprise, but it does create tensions within and among member states, which might feel that part of the sovereignty which they ceded to the European Union is, against their will, being extended by a European judiciary. The nature of the European Union is that it is based on the principle of conferral: the EU only has the powers which are given to it by the member states, all other sovereign powers remaining with these member states.[37] Particularly in the area of property law, which directly touches upon the distribution of wealth in a society, member states retain their own traditional approaches, and it is this area of the law that proves to be far more self-preservative than private law areas such as contract and tort law. It is against this political background that the exceptions in the Succession Regulation, Matrimonial Property Regulation and the Registered Partnerships Property Regulation regarding the nature of rights *in rem* and land registration law should be understood.

---

[36] Joined cases C-115 and 116/81 *Rezgula Adoui and Cornuaille v Belgium* ECLI:EU:C:1982:183 para 8.

[37] Cf art 5(1), (2) Treaty on European Union: '1. The limits of Union competences are governed by the principle of conferral. The use of Union competences is governed by the principles of subsidiarity and proportionality. 2. Under the principle of conferral, the Union shall act only within the limits of the competences conferred upon it by the Member States in the Treaties to attain the objectives set out therein. Competences not conferred upon the Union in the Treaties remain with the Member States.'

The tension between, on the one hand, the duty to accommodate a foreign legal solution flowing from the principle of sincere cooperation and, on the other hand, the desire to retain existing property law, has already surfaced, very soon after the enactment of the Succession Regulation, in three cases which have reached the CJ EU for a preliminary ruling. One of these cases directly concerns the question how far the exceptions to the scope of application of the nature of the rights *in rem* and the law of land registration extend. The facts of that case are as follows. Mrs Kubicka, together with her husband and minor children living in Germany, wanted to use the possibility which the regulation offers to choose the law of her nationality (Polish law) as the applicable law to her succession, instead of German law as the – most likely – law of her last habitual residence. The reason for doing so was that under Polish law a legacy immediately upon the death of the testator, without any further formalities, confers ownership of the bequeathed object upon the legatee. In this case the object was her part in the co-ownership of the matrimonial home. Under German law, however, such a legacy only entitles the legatee to transfer of the object, which means that in the case of an immovable a notarial deed of transfer has to be registered before the legacy becomes effective. It is an old distinction between competing theories of acquisition of a legacy: is it a *legatum per vindicationem* (Polish law) or a *legatum per damnationem* (German law)? The Polish notary, who had been asked to draw up the last will, however refused to do so, arguing that German law would not recognise the desired effect of the legacy. Mrs Kubicka then initiated court proceedings, appealing against the decision by the notary. The court referred the case to the CJ EU for a preliminary ruling. At the moment of writing this contribution only the opinion of the Advocate-General Bot is available; the court took time for consideration.[38] The Advocate-General concluded:[39]

> Elle doit aussi être appréciée en corrélation avec le mécanisme d'adaptation, prévu à l'article 31 de ce règlement, lorsque les droits acquis ne sont pas connus de la loi applicable au lieu de leur enregistrement, ce qui manifeste l'impossibilité d'exclure un droit et la volonté forte du législateur de l'Union de donner un effet utile au choix de la loi successorale.

The Advocate-General states that it is the clear intention of the legislator, given the mechanism of adaptation as can be found in article 31 of the regulation, to provide an effective enforcement ('*effet utile*') of the applicable

[38] Case C-218/16 Kubicka, Opinion by Advocate-General M Yves Bot, ECLI:EU:C:2017:387. No English translation was available at the moment that we wrote this contribution.

[39] ECLI:EU:C:2017:387 para 72.

law.[40] It is, as yet, uncertain if the CJ EU will follow this approach, but it does seem that this effective enforcement approach might appear to create a counterbalance against too restrictive an interpretation of the exemption of land registration law from the ambit of the regulation. Such a counterbalance in fact prevents an undisclosed re-introduction of public policy. Although not openly invoking this doctrine against a particular outcome of a foreign rule (explicitly only allowed if this goes manifestly against the public policy of the forum), a broad interpretation of the exception would strengthen the compartmentalisation of succession law, property law and land registration law, thus severely limiting the unifying effect of the regulation, to protect national interests. In fact, it would imply a resurrection of the de-unifying conflict of laws *lex rei sitae* rule, because the property effects of the applicable law with regard to immovable property would be ineffective and replaced by local law.[41] It would, to put it differently, mean a re-introduction of the *lex rei sitae* for all registered property by arguing that the *lex registrationis* prevents the application of the *lex successionis*, even though the regulation considers the *lex successonis* as the law applicable to the whole of the estate wherever assets are located.[42] The choice to apply one law to the whole of a person's assets, upon which principle the Succession Regulation, the Matrimonial Property Regulation and the Registered Partnerships Property Regulation are built, would in one blow have been made meaningless, by simply invoking an ingeniously crafted exception aimed at conserving the *status quo ante* with regard to national interests, which traditionally are shielded by the *lex rei sitae* rule. European Union law would have been made ineffective, would lose *effet utile*, a principle aimed at making the European internal market operative as a place where European citizens can fully use the rights and freedoms which the European framework treaties want to realise. In that sense, also, national and European Union law are to function as a 'single system of law', which demands, in André van der Walt's inspiring words, a 'fundamental shift from abstract, rights-based to contextual, non-hierarchical thinking about property rights'. When it comes to giving full effect to European Union law, hierarchical, and thus compartmentalised, thinking about what should be considered succession law, being different from property law and again

[40] Cf on *effet utile* D Chalmers, G Davies & G Monti *European Union law* (2010) 1015 ff; U Šadl 'The role of *effet utile* in preserving the continuity and authority of European Union law: Evidence from the citation web of the pre-accession case law of the Court of Justice of the EU' (2015) 8 *Eur J Legal Stud* 18 ff.

[41] See S van Erp 'Lex rei sitae. The territorial side of classical property law' in Chr Godt (ed) *Regulatory property rights: The transforming notion of property in transnational business regulation* (2017) 61ff.

[42] Article 21(1) of the Succession Regulation.

being different from land registration law, will result in undoing the aimed unification of European conflicts of law rules in the areas of succession, matrimonial property and property effects of registered partnerships. It will result in a re-nationalisation of conflict of laws, at the end of the day to the detriment of European citizens. The explicit decision was taken to overcome national differences in the areas of cross-border succession and the property consequences of marriages and registered partnerships. Land registrars, notaries and courts have no other option but to faithfully implement this in an atmosphere of sincere cooperation, giving *effet utile* to the choices made, leaving aside vested thought patterns and interests. The (in this case, European Union) context cannot be ignored, as André van der Walt taught us.

5 Final remarks

In the discussion above we began by saying that one of the most impressive aspects of André van der Walt's scholarly achievements is combining thorough knowledge with a rigorous analysis of existing law and legal technique, aimed at creating a legal framework for change in post-apartheid South African society. What we intended to show was how, by analysing land registration practice regarding the new EU Succession Regulation and a recent case to be decided by the CJEU, a possible perspective could be traced on how European private international law might be developed. It was attempted in order to avoid embarking upon an analysis based on a-priori assumptions resulting in legal-ideological theories as to how the European Union should develop, unrelated to actual land registration practice and day-to-day problems of European citizens. For André van der Walt, people's prospering in their daily lives mattered and a rigorous analysis of legal practice was a means to that end. Let us never forget that message.

Post Scriptum

After we finished writing this chapter, but shortly before the final publication date, the CJEU decided the *Kubicka* case[43]. The decision was in line with what was argued above. The court's decision can be summarised as follows. It was ruled that, if under the regulation a property right had validly come into existence, such a property right could not be denied effect merely on the basis of land registration rules. These rules were exempted from the regulation, because how land administration is organised was a matter left to the member states. However, demanding a German notarial deed before

[43] Case C-218/16 *Aleksandra Kubicka v Przemysława Bac, acting in her capacity as notary* [2017] ECR I not yet published.

registration was unrelated to land administration as such. Consequently, a vindication legacy that resulted in an immediate transfer of ownership upon the death of the testator, which in accordance with the regulation had been validly created under Polish law, must be recognised as such in Germany, if registration of ownership is asked on the basis of a European Certificate of Succession. Because ownership under Polish law was not substantially different from ownership under German law, the circumstance that German law demanded a notarial deed before ownership resulting from a legacy could pass was irrelevant. The transfer requirement was not an essential ownership condition making German ownership fundamentally different from Polish law, and consequently the mechanism of adaptation was moot. Furthermore, the transfer requirement could not qualify as a purely administrative registration requirement, and could thus not be used to refuse registration in the German land register. The aim and purpose of the regulation was to create as far as possible one legal regime for the passing of succession wherever the assets were located and the *lex rei sitae* rule was pre-empted, except as to land administration as such, to give this regime full effect ('*effet utile*').

Chapter 15

Application of single system of law and subsidiarity: Constitutional damages as effective relief within the eviction paradigm

Juanita M Pienaar & Tina Kotzé***

Page

Contents

1 Introduction

André van der Walt's contribution to property law generally, and constitutional property law in particular, is immense, leaving a global footprint. In this regard his research, coupled with the research embarked on and produced by the Research Chair in Property Law under his guidance, has been especially direction-giving in advancing the 'single system of law'[1] concept and corresponding subsidiarity rules.[2] He explains that endorsing

* Professor of Private Law, Stellenbosch University.

** Doctoral candidate, Stellenbosch University.

[1] *Pharmaceutical Manufacturers Association of South Africa: In re Ex Parte President of South Africa* 2000 (2) SA 674 (CC) para 44: 'There is only one system of law. It is shaped by the Constitution which is the supreme law and all law, including the common law, derives its force from the Constitution and is subject to constitutional control.' AJ van der Walt *Property and constitution* (2012) 20; E van der Sijde *Reconsidering the relationship between property and regulation: A systemic constitutional approach* (2015) unpublished LLD thesis Stellenbosch University 181, 184.

[2] AJ van der Walt 'Property law in the constitutional democracy' (2017) 28 *Stell LR* 8–25.

the notion of a single system of law, tied to subsidiarity rules, illuminates the unifying systemic relationship between the Constitution, legislation, common law and customary law and prevents the parallel development of different systems of law within one jurisdiction.[1]

There are many reasons why such a notion and its reach ought to be advanced, including the promotion of legal certainly, the pursuit of justice and equity and eliminating the possibility of applicants shopping around for the most advantageous avenue to follow.[2] The notion and its principles level the playing field and ultimately promote and, to some extent, guarantee the effective operation of law within a constitutional paradigm.

Embedded in the single system of law and subsidiarity rules is the methodological dimension. In other words: which angle ought to be employed so as to approach the legal quagmire most effectively, in light of the overall considerations of justice and constitutionality. Not only would the specific angle employed be instrumental in attempting to solve the dilemma at issue, but the angle would also guide the specific steps to be followed and have an impact on the ultimate outcome.[3] Within these broad parameters André van der Walt developed specific methodological steps when conflicting fundamental rights met head-on: be it property and property rights or, as is often encountered, property and non-property rights, including fundamental rights involving dignity and equality.[4]

Proceeding from the first point, that subsidiarity entails employing legislative measures to seek a solution where specific legislation was enacted to deal with the matter, the common law cannot, in these instances, be the first port of call. Where a property right and a non-property right are thus in conflict and legislation was enacted to deal with the latter specifically, the first step is to ensure the safe-guarding of the non-property constitutional right in accordance with relevant legislation. These kinds of disputes are thus not solved by weighing up or balancing the conflicting rights as such.

---

[1] AJ van der Walt 'Property law in the constitutional democracy' (2017) 28 *Stell LR* 10–11.

[2] See also AJ van der Walt 'Normative pluralism and anarchy: Reflections on the 2007 term' (2008) 1 *CCR* 77–128. He underlines the necessity to promote constitutional reform goals while simultaneously respecting democratic legislative interventions, thereby also reflecting reformist or stabilising policies – 125.

[3] ZT Boggenpoel 'Can the journey affect the destination? A single system of law approach to property remedies' (2016) 32 *SAJHR* 71–86.

[4] AJ van der Walt 'Property law in the constitutional democracy' (2017) 28 *Stell LR* 8–25 13.

Essentially, the property element does not dominate the inquiry purely on the basis that it is constitutionally protected.[5]

The temptation may always be there to prioritise some rights over others. It is especially within the domain of housing interests and eviction that the temptation is great to prioritise some rights, from the outset, and risk the development of parallel systems of law.[6] That is the case because, very often, property rights – enshrined in section 25 of the Constitution, the property clause – and non-property rights *per se* – invariably embodying human dignity – clash in a very real, confrontational manner. In this arena of housing concerns, dignity informs the right to access to housing, the right not to be arbitrarily evicted from one's home[7] and tenure security, recently highlighted specifically in the Constitutional Court judgment of *Daniels v Scribante*.[8] By employing the single-system-of-law approach, coupled with the subsidiarity rules, unlawful occupation of land and eviction have been integrated into constitutional law at an overarching level. Effectively this has prevented the development of separate, parallel systems of law in this arena.

But what do the single system of law principle and subsidiarity rules mean in cases where an eviction application was lodged and an eviction order was granted successfully, but the eviction order was, for whatever reason, not executed or has been delayed for an unreasonable period of time? To what extent does the single system of law concept guide and assist in these instances, where the conflicting rights remain, despite the methodology alluded to above having been employed? In such a case, the relevance and applicability of the single system of law and subsidiarity principles remain to be explored in a further context, namely in sculpting specific effective relief. Therefore, our contribution is not aimed at revisiting the single system of law concept or re-evaluating the subsidiarity rule and its parameters grounded by Van der Walt, and commented on by other authors,[9] but aims to explore the relevance of these concepts and rules in a specific instance, namely where an eviction order was granted, but not executed, generally; and constitutional damages as effective relief, specifically.

---

5 AJ van der Walt 'Property law in the constitutional democracy' (2017) 28 *Stell LR* 8–25 13.

6 AJ van der Walt 'Property law in the constitutional democracy' (2017) 28 *Stell LR* 8–25 14.

7 AJ van der Walt 'Property law in the constitutional democracy' (2017) 28 *Stell LR* 8–25 15.

8 *Daniels v Scribante* 2017 (4) SA 341 (CC).

9 See eg KE Klare 'Legal subsidiarity and constitutional rights: a reply to AJ van der Walt' (2008) 1 *CCR* 129–154.

In order to explore the theme effectively, some contextualisation is required. This is provided with reference to the methodology suggested by Van der Walt above and elaborated on by Justice Albie Sachs in the well-known case of *Port Elizabeth Municipality v Various Occupiers,*[10] followed by a description of the kind of scenario that forms the focus of our contribution, given the various phases of eviction litigation. Having illustrated the need for effective relief in light of conflicting rights, we thereafter elaborate on the concept of constitutional damages and how it has been approached in case law. By unpacking *President of the Republic of South Africa v Modderklip Boerdery (Pty) Ltd,*[11] in light of the single system of law concept and subsidiarity rules, we reflect on methodology, the desired outcome, and question whether effective relief was achieved, finally.

2 Contextualisation

2.1 Juxtaposition of rights and interests

Land ownership holds certain entitlements for the owner, including the 'usual entitlements' of use, enjoyment and protection of property.[12] Where occupation of land occurs without the owner's consent, be it specific or tacit, or in the absence of a right to occupy, unlawful occupation ensues.[13] In this scenario the landowner's section 25 rights are juxtaposed to the non-property rights of the unlawful occupier, embodying access to housing, which also resonates with the right to dignity.

As was elucidated in *Port Elizabeth Municipality v Various Occupiers,*[14] a delicate balancing act is necessary that serves and 'optimises' both interests, instead of (automatically) ranking one right higher than the other.[15] The Act promulgated to give effect to these rights is the Prevention of Illegal Eviction from and Unlawful Occupation of Land Act 19 of 1998 (hereafter PIE).[16] During the early days of delineating the scope and application of PIE,

---

[10] *Port Elizabeth Municipality v Various Occupiers* 2005 (1) SA 217 (CC).

[11] *President of the Republic of South Africa v Modderklip Boerdery (Pty) Ltd* 2005 (5) SA 3 (CC).

[12] Compare H Mostert & A Pope (eds) *The principles of the law of property* (2010) 92–93; AJ van der Walt & GJ Pienaar *Introduction to the law of property* 7 ed (2016) 47–48; PJ Badenhorst, JM Pienaar & H Mostert *Silberberg and Schoeman's The law of property* 5 ed (2006) 92–93; CG van der Merwe *Sakereg* 2 ed (1989) 173.

[13] Section 1 of the Prevention of Illegal Eviction from and Unlawful Occupation of Land Act 19 of 1998.

[14] *Port Elizabeth Municipality v Various Occupiers* 2005 (1) SA 217 (CC).

[15] AJ van der Walt *Property and constitution* (2012) 21.

[16] AJ van der Walt *Property and constitution* (2012) 22; JM Pienaar *Land reform* (2013) 481–482, 701–784.

the 2003 Supreme Court of Appeal judgment in *Ndlovu v Ngcobo and Bekker v Jika*[17] already highlighted that the right to property was not stronger or weaker than any other right, whether it was a real right, a personal right, contractual, delictual or a constitutional right.[18] In this context it could not (in principle) be elevated to a status higher or stronger than any other right.[19] While the 'status' or 'place' of the right to property was commented on, the process or methodology as to how the various rights were to be approached in litigation and adjudication was not dealt with in the Supreme Court of Appeal judgment. Justice Albie Sachs in the *Port Elizabeth Municipality* case suggested that, in dealing with these interests, an equitable balance needed to be achieved between the security interests in upholding established rights (section 25) and the justice interest in promoting more equitable access to, and secure tenure of, land and housing (section 26), without upholding (an old) or establishing (a new) hierarchy between them. As André van der Walt explained:

> Instead of a binary opposition between two conflicting goals, upholding existing rights and promoting equitable access are presented as two interlinked processes that form part of one single legal and constitutional goal.[20]

As both interests are constitutionally protected, they ought to be promoted equally and simultaneously, as part of a single system of law.[21] The key to guiding the endeavour and achieving an intertwined single track, rather than parallel legal tracks, is encapsulated in section 39(2) of the Constitution, which enjoins all courts, tribunals and fora to promote the spirit, purport and objects of the Bill of Rights when interpreting legislation and when developing the common law or customary law.

Given the methodology suggested by Van der Walt and the directions crafted by Justice Albie Sachs, PIE is the starting point, as it is the relevant legislative measure promulgated to deal with these instances specifically. In this regard the balancing act starts with neither the Constitution itself, nor the common law. Interpreting PIE and applying it in particular factual situations is thus imperative. In this light it becomes clear that PIE provides more than a procedural right only to unlawful occupiers.[22] As Justice Sachs highlights in *Port Elizabeth Municipality,* the mere establishment of unlawfulness on

---

17 *Ndlovu v Ngcobo and Bekker v Jika* 2003 (1) SA 113 (SCA).
18 *Ndlovu v Ngcobo and Bekker v Jika* 2003 (1) SA 113 (SCA) 106I.
19 *Ndlovu v Ngcobo and Bekker v Jika* 2003 (1) SA 113 (SCA) 107A.
20 AJ van der Walt *Property and constitution* (2012) 22.
21 AJ van der Walt *Property and constitution* (2012) 22.
22 AJ van der Walt *Property and constitution* (2012) 161.

the part of the occupiers does not trigger an automatic eviction. Instead, each case has to be considered in light of its own particular circumstances.[23]

Accordingly, ownership on the one hand and unlawful occupation on the other do not automatically amount to the granting of an eviction order.[24] Once the formalities and procedural requirements have been met, the court still has to determine whether the granting of an eviction order would be just and equitable. While section 26(3) of the Constitution is broad in its reference to 'all relevant circumstances', PIE lists various factors and considerations specifically, including the relevance of the period of unlawful occupation – either less than or longer than six months;[25] and the rights and needs of the elderly, children, disabled persons and households headed by women.[26] Despite these particular considerations, courts have to devise their own measures to ensure that all relevant circumstances are before them, including the interests of vulnerable persons.[27] Integral to the interpretation and application of PIE is its historical backdrop and the extant constitutional framework.[28]

Whereas the methodology suggested by Van der Walt and the directions crafted by Justice Albie Sachs operate in deliberating the matter, the question emerges whether the same methodology is equally useful and relevant in all eviction litigation phases. It is within this context that the various stages of litigation in situations of unlawful occupation and eviction emerge, highlighting the specific focus of this contribution.

2.2 Phases in eviction litigation

Where immovable property utilised for residential purposes is concerned, the eviction process can broadly be subdivided into three phases: the procedural, adjudicatory and execution phases.[29] While all of these phases combined encapsulate eviction litigation, our focus is on the last phase, the execution phase, where an eviction order was not executed or where execution was delayed for an unreasonably long period. The adjudicatory phase follows the procedural phase and embodies the substantive determination by the

---

[23] *Port Elizabeth Municipality v Various Occupiers* 2005 (1) SA 217 (CC) para 31.

[24] AJ van der Walt *Property and constitution* (2012) 159.

[25] Which impacts on whether the availability of suitable alternative accommodation has to be considered.

[26] Section 4(7) of Prevention of Illegal Eviction from and Unlawful Occupation of Land Act 19 of 1998.

[27] AJ van der Walt *Property and constitution* (2012) 160.

[28] *Port Elizabeth Municipality v Various Occupiers* 2005 (1) SA 217 (CC) paras 8–23.

[29] T Kotzé *Effective relief regarding residential property following a failure to execute an eviction order* (unpublished LLM thesis, Stellenbosch University, 2016) 2.

courts,[30] aligned with the single system of law concept and subsidiarity rules. The execution phase follows when an eviction order was granted by the court. In line with PIE, just and equitable dates, depending on the facts and circumstances of the matter, are also set for eviction[31] and for the execution of the eviction order.[32] Where the land or property is vacated voluntarily on the date set, the eviction process is complete. When the land or property is not vacated as required, the eviction order is executed on the further date, as set out in the eviction order, invariably with the assistance of the South African Police Services or other state agents or officials, and involves the removal of unlawful occupiers from the property in question.[33]

Failure by the state to execute eviction orders has become more prominent and therefore, increasingly, contentious.[34] Various factors influence non-execution, including the reluctance of state officials to adhere to the rule of law and respect court orders,[35] deficiencies in the court's approach,[36] a lack of transparency and consultation; absence of inter-governmental cooperation and coordination where more than one sphere of government

---

[30] *Port Elizabeth Municipality v Various Occupiers* 2005 (1) SA 217 (CC) para 33. See eg *Pitje v Shibambo* 2016 (4) BCLR 460 (CC); *City of Johannesburg v Changing Tides 74 (Pty) Ltd* 2012 (6) SA 294 (SCA); S Liebenberg *Socio-economic rights: Adjudication under a transformative Constitution* (2010) 268–316, 349–351.

[31] Section 4(8)(a) of Prevention of Illegal Eviction from and Unlawful Occupation of Land Act 19 of 1998; JM Pienaar *Land reform* (2013) 725–727.

[32] Section 4(8)(b) of Prevention of Illegal Eviction from and Unlawful Occupation of Land Act 19 of 1998; JM Pienaar *Land reform* (2013) 725–727.

[33] Section 205(3) of the Constitution, read with s 14 of the South African Police Service Act 68 of 1995.

[34] C Mbazira 'You are the "weakest link" in realising socio-economics rights: Goodbye: Strategies for effective implementation of court orders in South Africa' (2008) Socio-economic Rights Project, Community Law Centre, University of the Western Cape vi; C Mbazira 'Non-implementation of court orders in socio-economic rights litigation in South Africa: Is the cancer here to stay?' (2008) 9 *ESR Review* 2–8. See eg *Residents of Joe Slovo Community, Western Cape v Thubelisha Homes* 2011 (7) BCLR (CC); *Pheko v Ekurhuleni Metropolitan Municipality (No 2)* 2015 (6) BCLR 711 (CC).

[35] C Mbazira 'You are the "weakest link" in realising socio-economics rights: Goodbye: Strategies for effective implementation of court orders in South Africa' (2008) Socio-economic Rights Project, Community Law Centre, University of the Western Cape vi.

[36] C Mbazira 'You are the "weakest link" in realising socio-economics rights: Goodbye: Strategies for effective implementation of court orders in South Africa' (2008) Socio-economic Rights Project, Community Law Centre, University of the Western Cape vi.

is involved; and, generally, incapacity to carry out socio-economic reform.[37] Incapacity, in terms of providing adequate housing, has made timely delivery of quality housing very difficult.[38] In these instances the landowner is left without a remedy to protect property effectively,[39] whereas the unlawful occupier's position, with regard to the acquisition of land[40] and adequate housing,[41] remains in limbo.[42] It is in this context that the need for effective relief emerges.

2.3 *The need for effective relief*

Aligned with the well-known principle *ubi jus, ibi remedium* is the duty of courts to find or forge[43] remedies where there is a proven rights violation.[44]

---

[37] C Mbazira 'You are the "weakest link" in realising socio-economics rights: Goodbye: Strategies for effective implementation of court orders in South Africa' Socio-economic Rights Project, Community Law Centre, University of the Western Cape (2008) vi. See in general J van Wyk 'The role of local government in evictions' (2011) 14 *PELJ* 50–83; JM Pienaar & H Mostert 'Uitsettings onder die Suid-Afrikaanse grondwet: die verhouding tussen artikel 25(1), artikel 26(3) en die Uitsettingswet (slot)' 2006 *TSAR* 522–536.

[38] C Mbazira 'You are the "weakest link" in realising socio-economics rights: Goodbye: Strategies for effective implementation of court orders in South Africa' (2008) Socio-economic Rights Project, Community Law Centre, University of the Western Cape vi.

[39] Section 25(1) of the Constitution; AJ van der Walt *Constitutional property law* 3 ed (2011) 17–18; T Roux 'Property' in S Woolman & M Bishop (eds) *Constitutional law of South Africa* 2 ed (Original Service, Dec 2003) ch 41 1–37.

[40] Section 25(6) of the Constitution; JM Pienaar *Land reform* (2014) 378–509; JM Pienaar & J Brickhill 'Land' in S Woolman & M Bishop (eds) *Constitutional law of South Africa* (Original Service March 2007) ch 48 25–52; J van Wyk 'The relationship (or not) between the rights of access to land and housing: de-linking land from its components' (2005) 16 *Stell LR* 466–487.

[41] Section 26(1) of the Constitution; *Government of the Republic of South Africa v Grootboom* 2001 (1) SA 46 (CC); S Liebenberg *Socio-economic rights: Adjudication under a transformative Constitution* (2010) 344–351; G Muller *The impact of section 26 on the eviction of squatters in South Africa* (2011) unpublished LLD thesis Stellenbosch University 75–82; K McLean 'Housing' in S Woolman & M Bishop (eds) *Constitutional law of South Africa* (Original Service, Jul 2006) ch 55 8–14.

[42] M Kruger 'Arbitrary deprivation of property: An argument for the payment of compensation by the state in certain cases of unlawful occupation' (2014) 131 *SALJ* 328–330; G Muller & S Liebenberg 'Developing the law of joinder in the context of evictions of people from their homes' (2013) 59 *SAJHR* 554 555; S Wilson 'Breaking the tie: Evictions from private land, homelessness and a new normality' (2009) 126 *SALJ* 270–290; JM Pienaar & H Mostert 'Uitsettings onder die Suid-Afrikaanse grondwet: Die verhouding tussen artikel 25(1), artikel 26(3) en die Uitsettingswet (slot)' 2006 *TSAR* 522–536.

[43] M Bishop 'Remedies' in S Woolman & M Bishop (eds) *Constitutional law of South Africa* 2 ed (Revision Service Jun 2014) ch 9 6.

[44] C Mbazira 'You are the "weakest link" in realising socio-economics rights: Goodbye: Strategies for effective implementation of court orders in South Africa' (2008) Socio-economic Rights Project, Community Law Centre, University of the Western Cape 5.

South African courts are mandated to grant appropriate and effective relief where constitutional rights have been infringed.[45] The state has a corresponding obligation to ensure the effectiveness of the order granted by the court.[46] Absent an effective remedy, it is not only the right itself which is rendered trivial but also the values underlying the Constitution, which may also give rise to further constitutional breaches. The court will be in breach of its constitutional duty to grant litigants appropriate and effective relief,[47] while the state will be in breach of its obligation to 'respect, protect, promote and fulfil the rights in the Bill of Rights',[48] as well as its constitutional duty to provide measures to ensure the effectiveness of an order granted by the court.[49] Inevitably, this has an impact on the right of access to courts,[50] and also violates the rule of law,[51] one of the founding values of the South African constitutional dispensation.

The role of the courts is to determine *what* would constitute appropriate and effective relief in a particular case,[52] and it is the state's role to ensure

---

45 Sections 38 and 172(1)(b) of the Constitution; *President of the Republic of South Africa v Modderklip Boerdery (Pty) Ltd* 2005 (5) SA 3 (CC) paras 18, 33. See also *Fose v Minister of Safety and Security* 1997 (3) SA 786 (CC) para 69; M Bishop 'Remedies' in S Woolman & M Bishop (eds) *Constitutional Law of South Africa* 2 ed (Revision Service Jun 2014) ch 9 65–78; C Mbazira 'You are the "weakest link" in realising socio-economics rights: Goodbye: Strategies for effective implementation of court orders in South Africa' (2008) Socio-economic Rights Project, Community Law Centre, University of the Western Cape; S Liebenberg *Socio-economic rights: Adjudication under a transformative Constitution* (2010) 377–461.

46 Sections 34 and 165(4) of the Constitution; *Modderklip Boerdery (Edms) Bpk v President van die Republiek van Suid-Afrika* 2003 (1) All SA 465 (T) para 43.

47 Sections 38, 164, 165, 172, 173 of the Constitution; *Fose v Minister of Safety and Security* 1997 (3) SA 786 (CC) para 69; M Bishop 'Remedies' in S Woolman & M Bishop (eds) *Constitutional law of South Africa* 2 ed (Revision Service Jun 2014) ch 9 65–78; C Mbazira 'You are the "weakest link" in realising socio-economics rights: Goodbye: Strategies for effective implementation of court orders in South Africa' (2008) Socio-economic Rights Project, Community Law Centre, University of the Western Cape 5; S Liebenberg *Socio-economic rights: Adjudication under a transformative Constitution* (2010) 377–461.

48 Section 7(2) of the Constitution; S Liebenberg *Socio-economic rights: Adjudication under a transformative Constitution* (2010) 82–87, 344–347; S Viljoen 'The systemic violation of section 26(1): An appeal for structural relief by the judiciary' (2015) 30 *SAPL* 44–46.

49 Sections 34 and 165(4) of the Constitution; *Modderklip Boerdery (Edms) Bpk v President van die Republiek van Suid-Afrika* 2003 (1) All SA 465 (T) para 43.

50 A Pillay 'South Africa: Access to land and housing' (2007) 5 *IJCL* 544–545.

51 Section 1(c) of the Constitution.

52 *Fose v Minister of Safety* 1997 (3) SA 786 (CC) para 18.

that the relief granted is realised in practice. Given these considerations, the question arises as to what constitutes *effective* relief.[53]

In the eviction context, effective relief is essentially two-dimensional: on the one hand, effective relief has to encompass the rights of the relevant parties, namely the landowner's right to be protected against arbitrary deprivation of property[54] and the unlawful occupier's right to have access to land[55] and adequate housing,[56] and her right not to be arbitrarily evicted from her home without a court order.[57] On the other hand, effective relief requires the state to act in accordance with its mandate to 'respect, protect, promote and fulfil the rights'[58] of the relevant parties. Following the guidelines set out by Sachs J in the *Port Elizabeth Municipality* case alluded to above, courts may grant eviction orders where all the procedural and substantive requirements have

[53] M Bishop 'Remedies' in S Woolman & M Bishop (eds) *Constitutional law of South Africa* 2 ed (Revision Service Jun 2014) ch 9 65–78; *Fose v Minister of Safety and Security* 1997 (3) SA 786 (CC) para 69; C Mbazira 'You are the "weakest link" in realising socio-economics rights: Goodbye: Strategies for effective implementation of court orders in South Africa' (2008) Socio-economic Rights Project, Community Law Centre, University of the Western Cape 5.

[54] Section 25(1) of the Constitution; *First National Bank of South Africa Ltd t/a Wesbank v Commissioner, South African Revenue Service; First National Bank of South Africa Ltd t/a Wesbank v Minister of Finance* 2002 (4) SA 768 (CC); AJ van der Walt *Constitutional property law* 3 ed (2011) 190–333; T Roux 'Property' in S Woolman & M Bishop (eds) *Constitutional law of South Africa* 2 ed (Original Service Dec 2003) ch 41 17–28; J Strydom & S Viljoen (Maass) 'Unlawful occupation of inner-city buildings: A constitutional analysis of the rights and obligations involved' (2014) 17 *PELJ* 12071261 1220–1223, 1231–1235; M Kruger 'Arbitrary deprivation of property: an argument for the payment of compensation by the state in certain cases of unlawful occupation' (2014) 131 *SALJ* 336–341.

[55] Section 25(6) of the Constitution; JM Pienaar *Land reform* (2013) 378–509; JM Pienaar & J Brickhill 'Land' in S Woolman & M Bishop (eds) *Constitutional law of South Africa* (Original Service Mar 2007) ch 48 25–52; J van Wyk 'The relationship (or not) between the rights of access to land and housing: De-linking land from its components' (2005) 16 *Stell LR* 466–487.

[56] Section 26(1) of the Constitution; *Government of the Republic of South Africa v Grootboom* 2001 (1) SA 46 (CC); S Liebenberg *Socio-economic rights: Adjudication under a transformative Constitution* (2010) 344–351; G Muller *The impact of section 26 on the eviction of squatters in South Africa* (2011) unpublished LLD thesis Stellenbosch University 75–82; K McLean 'Housing' in S Woolman & M Bishop (eds) *Constitutional law of South Africa* (Original Service Jul 2006) ch 55 8–14.

[57] Section 26(3) of the Constitution; G Muller *The impact of section 26 on the eviction of squatters in South Africa* (2011) unpublished LLD thesis Stellenbosch University 93–99; S Liebenberg *Socio-economic rights: Adjudication under a transformative Constitution* (2010) 344–347.

[58] Section 7(2) of the Constitution; S Liebenberg *Socio-economic rights: Adjudication under a transformative Constitution* (2010) 82–87.

been met and the granting of the eviction order was just and equitable.[59] Ideally, an effective remedy here would be an *executable* eviction order granted in terms of PIE, meaning that alternative accommodation is *immediately* available.[60] Such a remedy not only realises the respective rights and interests of the landowner and the unlawful occupier, but also ensures that the rule of law is upheld.

However, while the concept of effective relief may be determined in principle, there may be certain inevitable limits on achieving it.[61] In this context courts have accepted that there will be particular cases where 'other considerations will justify affording relief that is less perfect [for all the affected parties]'.[62] Firstly, conflicting rights and interests may be of such a nature that the rights in question cannot all be satisfied.[63] The obtainment of an eviction order in terms of PIE will be in the primary interest of the

---

[59] J Strydom & S Viljoen (Maass) 'Unlawful occupation of inner-city buildings: A constitutional analysis of the rights and obligations involved' (2014) 17 *PELJ* 1207–1261.

[60] Section 25(1) and ss 25(6) and 26(1) and (3) of the Constitution; J Strydom & S Viljoen (Maass) 'Unlawful occupation of inner-city buildings: A constitutional analysis of the rights and obligations involved' (2014) 17 *PELJ* 1207–1261; M Swart 'Left out in the cold? Crafting constitutional remedies for the poorest of the poor' (2005) 21 *SAJHR* 217-240. See generally AJ van der Walt *Constitutional property law* 3 ed (2011) 17–18; T Roux 'Property' in S Woolman & M Bishop (eds) *Constitutional law of South Africa* 2 ed (Original Service Dec 2003) ch 41 1–37; JM Pienaar *Land reform* (2013) 378–509; JM Pienaar & J Brickhill 'Land' in S Woolman & M Bishop (eds) *Constitutional law of South Africa* (Original Service Mar 2007) ch 48 25–52; S Liebenberg *Socio-economic rights: Adjudication under a transformative Constitution* (2010) 344–351; G Muller *The impact of section 26 on the eviction of squatters in South Africa* (2011) unpublished LLD thesis Stellenbosch University 75–82; and K McLean 'Housing' in S Woolman & M Bishop (eds) *Constitutional law of South Africa* (Original Service Jul 2006) ch 55 8–14.

[61] M Bishop 'Remedies' in S Woolman & M Bishop (eds) *Constitutional law of South Africa* 2 ed (Revision Service Jun 2014) ch 9 71.

[62] M Bishop 'Remedies' in S Woolman & M Bishop (eds) *Constitutional law of South Africa* 2 ed (Revision Service Jun 2014) ch 9 60–61; *Port Elizabeth Municipality v Various Occupiers* 2005 (1) SA 217 (CC) para 23; S Wilson 'Breaking the tie: Evictions from private land, homelessness and a new normality' (2009) 126 *SALJ* 270; M Kruger 'Arbitrary deprivation of property: an argument for the payment of compensation by the state in certain cases of unlawful occupation' (2014) 131 *SALJ* 328.

[63] M Bishop 'Remedies' in S Woolman & M Bishop (eds) *Constitutional law of South Africa* 2 ed (Revision Service Jun 2014) ch 9 71; J Strydom & S Viljoen (Maass) 'Unlawful occupation of inner-city buildings: A constitutional analysis of the rights and obligations involved' (2014) 17 *PELJ* 1207–1261 1211.

landowner, enabling continued use and enjoyment of the property.[64] However, the landowner's rights may be restricted temporarily to allow the state to provide alternative accommodation.[65] Justice Sachs emphasised in *Port Elizabeth Municipality* that the rights of landowners should be understood against the social and historical background of forced evictions and the consequent need for developing secure property rights for those who were either denied access to land or deprived of such rights during apartheid.[66]

Depending on the circumstances, a temporary restriction on the rights of the landowner may amount to an indefinite deprivation of rights, which may be regarded as an arbitrary deprivation of property.[67] On the other hand, the Constitution affords everyone, including unlawful occupiers, a right of access to adequate housing.[68] Realising the right of access to housing is

---

[64] G Muller *The impact of section 26 on the eviction of squatters in South Africa* (2011) unpublished LLD thesis Stellenbosch University 17, 22; S Liebenberg *Socio-economic rights: Adjudication under a transformative Constitution* (2010) 266–316, 349–351. The approach to evictions and the remedies available for eviction in the pre- and post-constitutional era differ dramatically – see eg CT Cloete *A critical analysis of the approach of the court in the application of eviction remedies in the pre- and post-constitutional context* (2016) unpublished LLM thesis Stellenbosch University; P Dhliwayo *A constitutional analysis of access rights that limit landowners' right to exclude* (2015) unpublished LLD thesis Stellenbosch University 102; P Dhliwayo & AJ van der Walt 'The notion of absolute and exclusive ownership: A doctrinal analysis' (2016) 134 *SALJ* 34–52 40.

[65] *City of Johannesburg v Rand Properties (Pty) Ltd* 2007 (6) SA 417 (SCA) para 30; J Strydom & S Viljoen (Maass) 'Unlawful occupation of inner-city buildings: A constitutional analysis of the rights and obligations involved' (2014) 17 *PELJ* 1211–1261.

[66] *Port Elizabeth Municipality v Various Occupiers* 2005 (1) SA 217 (CC) para 15. See G Muller *The impact of section 26 on the eviction of squatters in South Africa* (2011) unpublished LLD thesis Stellenbosch University 33–53 for an overview of the urban and land tenure measures that deprived people of their land during apartheid.

[67] J Strydom & S Viljoen (Maass) 'Unlawful occupation of inner-city buildings: A constitutional analysis of the rights and obligations involved' (2014) 17 *PELJ* 1207–1261 1211, 1220, 1222–1223, 1231–1235; *Blue Moonlight Properties 39 (Pty) Ltd v Occupiers of Saratoga Avenue* 2009 (1) SA 470 (W) paras 34, 35, 39–40; K Bezuidenhout *Compensation for excessive but otherwise lawful regulatory state action* (2015) unpublished LLD thesis Stellenbosch University 249–250. See also M Kruger 'Arbitrary deprivation of property: an argument for the payment of compensation by the state in certain cases of unlawful occupation' (2014) 131 *SALJ* 336–341, who discusses whether an unreasonable delay in the execution of an eviction order amounts to an arbitrary deprivation of property.

[68] Section 26(1) of the Constitution. See in general *Government of the Republic of South Africa v Grootboom* 2001 (1) SA 46 (CC); S Liebenberg *Socio-economic rights: Adjudication under a transformative Constitution* (2010) 344–351; G Muller *The impact of section 26 on the eviction of squatters in South Africa* (2011) unpublished LLD thesis Stellenbosch University; K McLean 'Housing' in S Woolman & M Bishop (eds) *Constitutional law of*

intrinsically linked to the provision of access to land,[69] legally secure tenure[70] (also resonating with dignity) and the right to be protected against arbitrary evictions.[71] While the application of PIE may enable access to land and housing on an interim basis, as guided by the circumstances,[72] the position of unlawful occupiers continues to be vulnerable, as relief is only interim.[73] Although courts are often unable to provide secure land and housing rights, there is a duty on the state to address insecure tenure progressively.[74] Accordingly, realising the primary interests of the landowner and the unlawful occupiers will inevitably necessitate state involvement.[75] The progressive realisation of these rights requires the state to enact reasonable legislation and other measures to achieve these objectives.[76] This process

---

South Africa (Original Service Jul 2006) ch 55 8–14; S Wilson 'Breaking the tie: Evictions from private land, homelessness and a new normality' (2009) 126 *SALJ* 270–290; JM Pienaar & H Mostert 'Uitsettings onder die Suid-Afrikaanse grondwet: Die verhouding tussen artikel 25(1), artikel 26(3) en die Uitsettingswet (slot)' 2006 *TSAR* 522–536.

[69] Section 25(5) of the Constitution; JM Pienaar 'Land reform and housing: Reaching for the rafters or struggling with foundations?' (2015) 30 *SAPL* 1-25 8; J van Wyk 'The relationship (or not) between the rights of access to land and housing: De-linking land from its components' (2005) 16 *Stell LR* 466–487.

[70] Section 25(6) of the Constitution; Pienaar *Land reform* 378–509; JM Pienaar & J Brickhill 'Land' in S Woolman & M Bishop (eds) *Constitutional law of South Africa* (Original Service Mar 2007) ch 48 25–52.

[71] Section 26(3) of the Constitution, read with ss 4(6) and 6(1) of the Prevention of Illegal Eviction from and Unlawful Occupation of Land Act 19 of 1998. See G Muller *The impact of section 26 on the eviction of squatters in South Africa* (2011) unpublished LLD thesis Stellenbosch University 93–99; S Liebenberg *Socio-economic rights: Adjudication under a transformative Constitution* (2010) 344–347; JM Pienaar 'Land reform and housing: Reaching for the rafters or struggling with foundations?' (2015) 30 *SAPL* 1–25 20.

[72] JM Pienaar 'Land reform and housing: Reaching for the rafters or struggling with foundations?' (2015) 30 *SAPL* 1–25 20.

[73] S Viljoen 'The systemic violation of section 26(1): An appeal for structural relief by the judiciary' (2015) 30 *SAPL* 42–70 47, 64; J van Wyk 'The relationship (or not) between the rights of access to land and housing: De-linking land from its components' (2005) 16 *Stell LR* 466–487.

[74] S Viljoen 'The systemic violation of section 26(1): An appeal for structural relief by the judiciary' (2015) 30 *SAPL* 42–70 47.

[75] S Viljoen 'The systemic violation of section 26(1): An appeal for structural relief by the judiciary' (2015) 30 *SAPL* 42–70 44.

[76] JM Pienaar 'Land reform and housing: Reaching for the rafters or struggling with foundations?' (2015) 30 *SAPL* 1–25 8–9; S Viljoen 'The systemic violation of section 26(1): An appeal for structural relief by the judiciary' (2015) 30 *SAPL* 42–70 44; J Strydom & S Viljoen (Maass) 'Unlawful occupation of inner-city buildings: A constitutional analysis of the rights and obligations involved' (2014) 17 *PELJ* 1207–1261 1216–1218. See eg the Housing Act 107 of 1997; the Rental Housing Act 50 of 1999; the Home Loan and Mortgage Disclosure Act 63 of 2000 and the Housing Consumer Protection Measures Act 95 of 1998.

may necessitate a reasonable degree of patience from the landowner.[77] Where alternative accommodation is readily available, the need to occupy the owner's land unlawfully will diminish.

Secondly, it may be practically impossible for an effective remedy to be executed,[78] as in the *Modderklip* case scenario,[79] discussed in more detail below.[80] More often, problems with execution, irrespective of the reasons, obstruct *immediate* effective relief only. Although some commentators contend that only immediate relief constitutes effective relief,[81] we endorse the notion that effective relief constitutes appropriate relief that can be executed within a *reasonable* time.[82] In the absence of a precise definition of what constitutes a reasonable time, we suggest the eviction process as a whole be considered in light of the particular relevant circumstances. In this regard various factors become relevant, including the complexity of the case;[83] the conduct of the landowner in instituting eviction proceedings;[84] the conduct of the relevant state officials and departments;[85] and the consequences of an

---

[77] *City of Johannesburg Metropolitan Municipality v Blue Moonlight Properties 39 (Pty) Ltd* 2012 (2) SA 104 (CC) para 100.

[78] M Bishop 'Remedies' in S Woolman & M Bishop (eds) *Constitutional law of South Africa* 2 ed (Revision Service Jun 2014) ch 9 72.

[79] A Christmas 'The Modderklip cases: Evictions and the right of access to adequate housing: case review' (2003) 6 *ESR Review* 4–7.

[80] See section 4 below.

[81] M Swart 'Left out in the cold? Crafting constitutional remedies for the poorest of the poor' (2005) 21 *SAJHR* 217-240 argues that 'the emphasis in developing new effective remedies must be on immediacy. An effective remedy will be a remedy which is capable of immediate implementation'. See also M Bishop 'Remedies' in S Woolman & M Bishop (eds) *Constitutional law of South Africa* 2 ed (Revision Service Jun 2014) ch 9 65–78.

[82] G Budlender 'Access to courts' (2004) 121 *SALJ* 339–358 354; M Bishop 'Remedies' in S Woolman & M Bishop (eds) *Constitutional law of South Africa* 2 ed (Revision Service Jun 2014) ch 9 60–78 acknowledges that *immediate* relief will constitute the ideal but is not necessarily attainable, thereby employing 'other considerations … affording relief that is less than perfect'; *Hoffmann v South African Airways* 2001 (1) SA 1 (CC) para 45; *Fose v Minister of Safety and Security* 1997 (3) SA 786 (CC) para 69; C Mbazira 'You are the "weakest link" in realising socio-economics rights: Goodbye: Strategies for effective implementation of court orders in South Africa' (2008) Socio-economic Rights Project, Community Law Centre, University of the Western Cape 5.

[83] Council of Europe/European Court of Human Rights 'Guide on Article 6: The right to a fair trial' (2013) 52.

[84] For example, where a landowner's conduct amounts to a negligent or unreasonable delay – see *Mkontwana v Nelson Mandela Metropolitan Municipality* 2005 (1) SA 530 (CC); Council of Europe/European Court of Human Rights 'Guide on Article 6: The right to a fair trial' (2013) 52–53.

[85] Council of Europe/European Court of Human Rights 'Guide on Article 6: The right to a fair trial' (2013) 53.

excessive delay in the proceedings as a whole.[86] Although 'reasonable time' seems rather vague and may create some uncertainty, the time period has to be flexible in light of the variables mentioned here. What is 'reasonable' is therefore case-specific and context-sensitive. In this light, an eviction order that cannot be executed within a reasonable time does not constitute effective relief.

3 Constitutional damages

3.1 Introduction

In light of the above, it is clear that the single system of law principle and subsidiarity rules are integral to the adjudicatory phase of the eviction process in order to determine whether the granting of an eviction order is indeed just and equitable, given the rights, interests and circumstances of the particular case. Where an eviction order is granted, it will only constitute effective relief for parties involved if the eviction order is executed within a reasonable time. As explained, this may require some degree of patience from landowners. Where an eviction order so granted cannot be executed within a reasonable time, the situation remains unresolved and effective relief remains elusive. Arguably, various options emerge in the pursuit for effective relief in these instances, including employing a structural interdict,[87] granting contempt of court orders[88] and awarding constitutional damages.

It is within this context that we turn to constitutional damages as a potential remedy, which may provide 'effective relief' within the eviction paradigm. In this light we explore the concept of damages, its various dimensions and how it has been approached and applied in South African case law. We thereafter reflect on the *Modderklip* case scenario specifically and reconsider its approach and decision in light of the Van der Walt methodology, ultimately aimed at achieving effective relief.

[86] Council of Europe/European Court of Human Rights 'Guide on Article 6: The right to a fair trial' (2013) 54–55.

[87] In theory, a structural interdict appears to be the ideal solution where there has been a failure to execute an eviction order. However, case law has illustrated that it may not always be an ideal solution, often because of a lack of willingness on the part of the parties to engage meaningfully and in good faith with each other and/or due to inattentiveness, incompetence or intransigence on the part of the state in general or at different levels of government. See for a detailed analysis T Kotzé *Effective relief regarding residential property following a failure to execute an eviction order* (unpublished LLM thesis, Stellenbosch University, 2016) ch 2.

[88] T Kotzé *Effective relief regarding residential property following a failure to execute an eviction order* (unpublished LLM thesis, Stellenbosch University, 2016) ch 4.

3.2 Dimensions and conceptions

Constitutional damages can be regarded as a remedy available for the violation of constitutional rights,[89] generally encompassing two broad categories: indirect constitutional damages and direct constitutional damages.[90] The former constitute damages that are awarded in terms of a statute or the common law that gives effect to a constitutional right,[91] whereas direct constitutional damages flow directly from the Constitution.[92] Whether indirect or direct constitutional damages are applicable has to be determined in accordance with the single system of law concept and subsidiarity rules, set out above. Accordingly, where a litigant seeks to vindicate the infringement of a constitutionally protected right, that person must first rely on legislation enacted to protect that right and may not rely on the common law first or on the constitutional provision directly.[93] Absent applicable legislation, courts should thereafter rely on the common law before making a direct appeal on constitutional provisions.[94] Only where the common law is 'unconstitutional or incapable of serving the relevant constitutional goals',[95] and cannot be developed, should reliance be placed directly on the Constitution.

3.2.1 Indirect constitutional damages

Indirect constitutional damages are monetary damages that are awarded in terms of the common law or a statute that gives effect to a constitutional right.[96] In this regard, Bishop views every award of delictual damages where the right asserted is also a constitutional right as a constitutional remedy, because the indirect constitutional remedy serves to cure the violation of

[89] M Bishop 'Remedies' in S Woolman & M Bishop (eds) *Constitutional law of South Africa* 2 ed (Revision Service Jun 2014) ch 9 150; M Loubser, R Midgley, A Mukheibir, L Niesing & D Permunal *The law of delict in South Africa* 2 ed (2012) 33–35.

[90] M Bishop 'Remedies' in S Woolman & M Bishop (eds) *Constitutional law of South Africa* 2 ed (Revision Service Jun 2014) ch 9 151; M Loubser, R Midgley, A Mukheibir, L Niesing & D Permunal *The law of delict in South Africa* 2 ed (2012) 33–35.

[91] M Bishop 'Remedies' in S Woolman & M Bishop (eds) *Constitutional law of South Africa* 2 ed (Revision Service Jun 2014) ch 9 151.

[92] M Bishop 'Remedies' in S Woolman & M Bishop (eds) *Constitutional law of South Africa* 2 ed (Revision Service Jun 2014) ch 9 151.

[93] AJ van der Walt *Property and constitution* (2012) 36.

[94] AJ van der Walt *Property and constitution* (2012) 81–82.

[95] AJ van der Walt *Property and constitution* (2012) 82; M Bishop 'Remedies' in S Woolman & M Bishop (eds) *Constitutional law of South Africa* 2 ed (Revision Service Jun 2014) ch 9 157.

[96] M Bishop 'Remedies' in S Woolman & M Bishop (eds) *Constitutional law of South Africa* 2 ed (Revision Service Jun 2014) ch 9 151.

the constitutional right.[97] The Constitutional Court first enunciated this proposition in *Fose v Minister of Safety and Security* ('*Fose*')[98] when it held that there will be many cases where the common law will be broad enough to provide all the relief that would be appropriate for breach of constitutional rights.[99] *In casu* the claim for constitutional damages was adjunct to a claim for delictual damages arising out of alleged assault and torture of the plaintiff by members of the police force.[100] The cause of action was based on the infringement of the plaintiff's constitutional right to dignity and the right not to be unlawfully tortured.[101] The court per Ackermann J held that delictual damages constituted an adequate vindication of the plaintiff's right and an additional claim for constitutional damages was thus refused.[102] Direct constitutional damages will thus be inappropriate where the existing law provides a remedy that fully vindicates the constitutional right.[103] In such cases there is no need to rely on the Constitution to create a new self-

---

[97] M Bishop 'Remedies' in S Woolman & M Bishop (eds) *Constitutional law of South Africa* 2 ed (Revision Service Jun 2014) ch 9 151; M Loubser, R Midgley, A Mukheibir, L Niesing & D Permunal *The law of delict in South Africa* 2 ed (2012) 33: 'This is possible where there is an overlap between a fundamental [constitutional] right and a private-law (subjective) right that the law of delict recognises...One can easily find a delictual counterpart for the following fundamental rights: human dignity (section 10), life (section 11), freedom and security of the person (section 12), privacy (section 14)...and *property (section 25)*...[However] some fundamental rights simply do not lend themselves to actions in delict....[A] person is unlikely to have an action in delict if, for example, that person's *right to housing (section 26)*...is infringed' (emphasis added).

[98] *Fose v Minister of Safety and Security* 1997 (3) SA 786 (CC); S Liebenberg *Socio-economic rights: Adjudication under a transformative Constitution* (2010) 438.

[99] *Fose v Minister of Safety and Security* 1997 (3) SA 786 (CC) para 58. Nugent JA in *MEC Department of Welfare, Eastern Cape v Kate* 2006 (4) SA 478 (SCA) para 30 expressed the view that the common law of delict is capable of being extended to encompass state liability for the breach of constitutional obligations. In *Law Society of South Africa v Minister of Transport* 2011 (1) SA 400 (CC) para 74 Moseneke DCJ stated 'it seems that in an appropriate case a private-law delictual remedy may serve to protect and enforce a constitutionally entrenched fundamental right. Thus a claimant seeking appropriate relief to which it is entitled, may properly resort to a common-law remedy in order to vindicate a constitutional right.'

[100] S Liebenberg *Socio-economic rights: Adjudication under a transformative constitution* (2010) 438.

[101] *Fose v Minister of Safety and Security* 1997 (3) SA 786 (CC) para 1; S Liebenberg *Socio-economic rights: Adjudication under a transformative constitution* (2010) 438.

[102] *Fose v Minister of Safety and Security* 1997 (3) SA 786 (CC) para 67.

[103] *Fose v Minister of Safety and Security* 1997 (3) SA 786 (CC) para 67; M Bishop 'Remedies' in S Woolman & M Bishop (eds) *Constitutional law of South Africa* 2 ed (Revision Service Jun 2014) ch 9 152; M Loubser, R Midgley, A Mukheibir, L Niesing & D Permunal *The law of delict in South Africa* 2 ed (2012) 33.

standing remedy.[104] This is in line with the single system of law notion and subsidiarity rules.

In subsequent judgments, the law of delict was developed to recognise claims based on constitutional values and rights.[105] While courts in this regard have in the past developed the common law to provide remedies for those who have suffered physical injury as a result of state negligence or abuse,[106] it has been less sympathetic to those persons who have incurred (only) financial loss as a result of state negligence.[107] Accordingly, courts may be less inclined to award delictual damages to a landowner suffering financial loss where land is occupied unlawfully and an eviction order cannot be executed.

3.2.2 Direct constitutional damages

Despite the court's cautious approach to award constitutional damages in *Fose*, the court nevertheless affirmed that there was no reason in principle why appropriate relief could not include an award of direct constitutional damages, where necessary.[108] Accordingly, where neither the common law nor statute provides for adequate and effective relief to remedy the infringement of a constitutional right, a landowner may rely on a claim for

---

[104] M Bishop 'Remedies' in S Woolman & M Bishop (eds) *Constitutional law of South Africa* 2 ed (Revision Service Jun 2014) ch 9 152; AJ van der Walt *Property and constitution* (2012) 36, 40–43, 81–91.

[105] S Liebenberg *Socio-economic rights: Adjudication under a transformative constitution* (2010) 439. *Carmichele v Minister of Safety and Security* 2001 (4) SA 938 (CC); *Minister of Safety and Security v Van Duivenboden* 2002 (6) SA 431 (SCA); *Van Eeden v Minister of Safety and Security* 2003 (1) SA 389 (SCA); *Zealand v Minister for Justice and Constitutional Development* 2008 (4) SA 458 (CC).

[106] See *Van Eeden v Minister of Safety and Security* 2003 (1) SA 389 (SCA) para 19: 'An important consideration in favour of recognising delictual liability for damages on the part of the State in circumstances such as the present is that there is no other practical and effective remedy available to a victim of violent crime. Conventional remedies such as review and mandamus or interdict do not afford the victim of the crime any relief at all. The only *effective* remedy is a private law delictual action for damages.' *Minister of Safety and Security v Van Duivenboden* 2002 (6) SA 431 (SCA) para 22: 'There is no effective way to hold the state to account in the present case other than by way of an action for damages.'

[107] M Bishop 'Remedies' in S Woolman & M Bishop (eds) *Constitutional law of South Africa* 2 ed (Revision Service Jun 2014) ch 9 154. See *Olitzki Property Holdings v State Tender Board* 2001 (3) SA 1247 (SCA); *Premier of the Province of the Western Cape v Fair Cape Property Developers (Pty) Ltd* 2003 (6) SA 13 (SCA); *Steenkamp v Provincial Tender Board of the Eastern Cape* 2007 (3) 121 (CC), where courts refused to develop common-law administrative principles to provide for compensation where the constitutional right to administrative justice had been infringed.

[108] *Fose v Minister of Safety and Security* 1997 (3) SA 786 (CC) para 60.

direct constitutional damages.[109] In the context of direct constitutional damages, three types have been recognised notionally:[110] damages to compensate for loss;[111] punitive damages in addition to damages already claimed;[112] and nominal or symbolic damages.[113] How South African courts have approached constitutional damages in an eviction paradigm is explored below with reference to the *Modderklip* case scenario.

4 Forging effective relief: Reflecting on the *Modderklip* case scenario

4.1 Background

To date, the Constitutional Court has only awarded direct constitutional damages in one, very unusual case as a remedy in the context of eviction, in *President of the Republic of South Africa v Modderklip Boerdery (Pty) Ltd.*[114] The facts were briefly the following: in the 1990s, due to overcrowding in the area, spontaneous occupation occurred on land later known as the Chris Hani informal settlement. After being evicted from Chris Hani, about 400 persons moved onto a portion of the Modder East farm, which settlement soon grew to 18 000 persons.[115] The landowner applied for and obtained an eviction order.[116] On the date set for eviction, the unlawful occupants

---

[109] *MEC, Department of Welfare, Eastern Cape v Kate* 2006 (4) SA 478 (SCA); RJ de Beer & S Vettori 'The enforcement of socio-economic rights' (2007) 3 *PELJ* 2–26.

[110] M Bishop 'Remedies' in S Woolman & M Bishop (eds) *Constitutional law of South Africa* 2 ed (Revision Service Jun 2014) ch 9 157.

[111] *President of the Republic of South Africa v Modderklip Boerdery (Pty) Ltd* 2005 (5) SA 3 (CC); A Christmas 'The *Modderklip* case: the state's obligations in evictions instituted by private landowners: case review' (2005) 4 *ESR Review* 6–10; AJ van der Walt 'The state's duty to protect property owners v the state's duty to provide housing: Thoughts on the *Modderklip* case' (2005) 21 *SAJHR* 144–161.

[112] For punitive damages see M Bishop 'Remedies' in S Woolman & M Bishop (eds) *Constitutional law of South Africa* 2 ed (Revision Service Jun 2014) ch 9 160–161. See *Fose v Minister of Safety and Security* 1997 (3) SA 786 (CC) paras 65, 71, where the court rejected an award for punitive constitutional damages, and the twelve points of criticism against the use of punitive constitutional damages. See also AK Funnah & O Sibanda 'Towards a selective awarding of punitive damages awards in South Africa? A comment on *Fose v Minister of Safety and Security*' (2008) 48 *Codicillus* 36–49.

[113] For nominal or symbolic damages, see M Bishop 'Remedies' in S Woolman & M Bishop (eds) *Constitutional Law of South Africa* 2 ed (Revision Service Jun 2014) ch 9 162.

[114] *President of the Republic of South Africa v Modderklip Boerdery (Pty) Ltd* 2005 (5) SA 3 (CC).

[115] *Modder East Squatters v Modderklip Boerdery (Pty) Ltd, President of the Republic of South Africa v Modderklip Boerdery* 2004 (3) All SA 169 (SCA) para 2; K Tissington 'Demolishing development at Gabon informal settlement: Public interest litigation beyond Modderklip?' (2011) 27 *SAJHR* 192–205 193.

[116] *Modderklip Boerdery (Pty) Ltd v Modder East Squatters* 2001 (4) SA 385 (W).

refused to vacate the land as ordered. In the meantime the number of unlawful occupiers had continued to grow,[117] to the extent that the execution necessitated the assistance of private contractors.[118] The sheriff informed the landowner that a deposit of R1.8 million (later increased to R2.2 million) was required to facilitate the eviction.[119] As that amount exceeded the value of the land, the landowner was not prepared to incur the expense.[120]

The landowner subsequently instituted further proceedings and was successful in the High Court on the basis that the failure to execute the eviction order resulted in an infringement of the landowner's right to property.[121] The court also held that the state had not complied with its constitutional responsibility to provide access to adequate housing,[122] and consequently issued a structural interdict requiring the state to indicate which steps it proposed to take to execute the eviction order.[123] On appeal by the state, the Supreme Court of Appeal confirmed the High Court order, emphasising that the owner's property rights had been infringed and that the state had breached its section 26(1) and (2) obligations.[124] The court emphasised that it had a duty to mould appropriate orders that would provide effective relief

---

117 *Modder East Squatters v Modderklip Boerdery (Pty) Ltd, President of the Republic of South Africa v Modderklip Boerdery* 2004 (3) All SA 169 (SCA) para 3.

118 *Modder East Squatters v Modderklip Boerdery (Pty) Ltd, President of the Republic of South Africa v Modderklip Boerdery* 2004 (3) All SA 169 (SCA) para 4.

119 *Modder East Squatters v Modderklip Boerdery (Pty) Ltd, President of the Republic of South Africa v Modderklip Boerdery* 2004 (3) All SA 169 (SCA) paras 4, 7; K Tissington 'Demolishing development at Gabon informal settlement: Public interest litigation beyond Modderklip?' (2011) 27 *SAJHR* 192–205 193.

120 *Modder East Squatters v Modderklip Boerdery (Pty) Ltd, President of the Republic of South Africa v Modderklip Boerdery* 2004 (3) All SA 169 (SCA) para 4.

121 *Modderklip Boerdery (Edms) Bpk v President van die Republiek van Suid-Afrika* 2003 (1) All SA 465 (T). See also A Christmas 'The Modderklip cases: Evictions and the right of access to adequate housing: case review' (2003) 6 *ESR Review* 4–7.

122 Section 26(1) and (2) read with s 25(5) of the Constitution, 1996; *Modderklip Boerdery (Edms) Bpk v President van die Republiek van Suid-Afrika* 2003 (1) All SA 465 (T) paras 46, 52; JM Pienaar *Land reform* (2013) 772; J van Wyk 'The relationship (or not) between the rights of access to land and housing: De-linking land from its components' (2005) 16 *Stell LR* 466–487.

123 *Modderklip Boerdery (Edms) Bpk v President van die Republiek van Suid-Afrika* 2003 (1) All SA 465 (T).

124 *Modder East Squatters v Modderklip Boerdery (Pty) Ltd, President of the Republic of South Africa v Modderklip Boerdery* 2004 (3) All SA 169 (SCA) para 52; JM Pienaar *Land reform* (2013) 772; AJ van der Walt 'The state's duty to protect property owners v the state's duty to provide housing: Thoughts on the *Modderklip* case' (2005) 21 *SAJHR* 144–161.

to those affected by a constitutional breach.[125] The payment of constitutional damages was ordered to compensate the landowner for what he had lost and what the state had gained by not having to provide alternative land for settlement.[126]

The state once again appealed to the Constitutional Court and averred that the landowner's right to property and the occupier's rights to have access to adequate housing had not been breached.[127] The Constitutional Court held that it was unnecessary to decide that issue,[128] and instead decided that the basis for constitutional damages rested upon an infringement of section 34 of the Constitution and the rule of law.[129]

As a point of departure, the Constitutional Court relied on section 1(c) of the Constitution which enshrined the supremacy of the Constitution and the rule of law.[130] The obligation of the state to provide the necessary mechanisms for citizens to resolve disputes that arose between them flowed from the rule of law.[131] This obligation had its corollary in the right of every person to have access to the courts.[132] Furthermore, the state 'holds the key'[133] to executing the eviction order. Not only was the state obligated to provide necessary mechanisms for citizens to resolve their disputes, it was also obliged to take reasonable steps, where possible, to ensure that large-scale disruptions in the social fabric did not occur in the wake of the execution of court orders.[134] Failure to take such reasonable steps would undermine the rule of law.[135]

---

[125] *Modder East Squatters v Modderklip Boerdery (Pty) Ltd, President of the Republic of South Africa v Modderklip Boerdery* 2004 (3) All SA 169 (SCA) para 44, citing *Fose v Minister of Safety and Security* 1997 (3) SA 786 (CC) para 94 and *Minister of Health v Treatment Action Campaign (No 2)* 2002 (5) SA 721 (CC) para 102.

[126] *Modder East Squatters v Modderklip Boerdery (Pty) Ltd, President of the Republic of South Africa v Modderklip Boerdery* 2004 (3) All SA 169 (SCA) para 52.

[127] *President of the Republic of South Africa v Modderklip Boerdery (Pty) Ltd* 2005 (5) SA 3 (CC) para 22.

[128] *President of the Republic of South Africa v Modderklip Boerdery (Pty) Ltd* 2005 (5) SA 3 (CC) para 26.

[129] *President of the Republic of South Africa v Modderklip Boerdery (Pty) Ltd* 2005 (5) SA 3 (CC) paras 48, 51 read with para 68.

[130] Section 1(c) of the Constitution.

[131] *President of the Republic of South Africa v Modderklip Boerdery (Pty) Ltd* 2005 (5) SA 3 (CC) para 39.

[132] *President of the Republic of South Africa v Modderklip Boerdery (Pty) Ltd* 2005 (5) SA 3 (CC) paras 24, 41.

[133] *President of the Republic of South Africa v Modderklip Boerdery (Pty) Ltd* 2005 (5) SA 3 (CC) para 42.

[134] *President of the Republic of South Africa v Modderklip Boerdery (Pty) Ltd* 2005 (5) SA 3 (CC) para 43.

[135] *President of the Republic of South Africa v Modderklip Boerdery (Pty) Ltd* 2005 (5) SA 3 (CC) para 43.

Accordingly, the landowner's position, as a victim of unlawful occupation of its property on a large scale, was aggravated by the failure to execute the eviction order within a reasonable time.[136] This meant that the landowner, and others similarly placed, would not be able to rely on the state and its organs to protect them from invasions of their property.[137] It was imperative that court orders be executed in a manner that prevented social upheaval,[138] as the purpose of the rule of law would otherwise be subverted.[139]

The extraordinary nature of the *Modderklip* case[140] was highlighted and it was underlined that the mechanisms that would normally be employed to execute eviction orders could not be relied on here.[141] That being said, the court found that it was unreasonable of the state to stand by and do nothing in circumstances where it was impossible for the landowner to effect the eviction.[142] Effective relief was still required,[143] either by the state expropriating the property or by the state providing other land.[144] Either one of these options available to the state would have alleviated the burden on the landowner to provide the unlawful occupiers with accommodation.[145] Consequently, the state's failure to act resulted in a breach of the landowner's constitutional right to an effective remedy as required by the rule of law and entrenched in section 34 of the Constitution.[146]

---

136 *President of the Republic of South Africa v Modderklip Boerdery (Pty) Ltd* 2005 (5) SA 3 (CC) para 44.

137 *President of the Republic of South Africa v Modderklip Boerdery (Pty) Ltd* 2005 (5) SA 3 (CC) para 45.

138 *President of the Republic of South Africa v Modderklip Boerdery (Pty) Ltd* 2005 (5) SA 3 (CC) para 46.

139 *President of the Republic of South Africa v Modderklip Boerdery (Pty) Ltd* 2005 (5) SA 3 (CC) para 46.

140 *Modderklip Boerdery (Pty) Ltd v Modder East Squatters* 2001 (4) SA 385 (W); *Modderklip Boerdery (Pty) Ltd v Modder East Squatters* 2003 6 BCLR 638 (T); *Modder East Squatters v Modderklip Boerdery (Pty) Ltd, President of the Republic of South Africa v Modderklip Boerdery* 2004 (3) All SA 169 (SCA); *President of the Republic of South Africa v Modderklip Boerdery (Pty) Ltd* 2005 (5) SA 3 (CC). See JM Pienaar *Land Reform* (2013) 772.

141 *President of the Republic of South Africa v Modderklip Boerdery (Pty) Ltd* 2005 (5) SA 3 (CC) para 47.

142 *President of the Republic of South Africa v Modderklip Boerdery (Pty) Ltd* 2005 (5) SA 3 (CC) para 48.

143 *President of the Republic of South Africa v Modderklip Boerdery (Pty) Ltd* 2005 (5) SA 3 (CC) para 51.

144 *President of the Republic of South Africa v Modderklip Boerdery (Pty) Ltd* 2005 (5) SA 3 (CC) para 51.

145 *President of the Republic of South Africa v Modderklip Boerdery (Pty) Ltd* 2005 (5) SA 3 (CC) para 51.

146 *President of the Republic of South Africa v Modderklip Boerdery (Pty) Ltd* 2005 (5) SA 3 (CC) para 51.

The Constitutional Court also held that '[a]ppropriate relief must necessarily be effective'.[147] With reference to *Fose* and constitutional damages that court considered the advantages of granting constitutional damages, given the extraordinary circumstances.[148] Firstly, it compensated the landowner for the unlawful occupation and deprivation of his property. The landowner was effectively deprived of his right to use and enjoy his property on a permanent or indefinite basis. Therefore, the severity and extent of the deprivation justified the award of constitutional damages. Secondly, it ensured accommodation for the unlawful occupiers until suitable alternatives were found. Lastly, it relieved the state of the urgent task of having to find such alternatives.[149] Constitutional damages constituted the most effective and expeditious way of vindicating the rights of both the landowner and the unlawful occupiers in these circumstances.

4.2 *Approach and methodology*

It is notable that the Constitutional Court opted not to deal with the question whether section 25(1) had horizontal application and whether section 25(1) rights were in fact breached. A head-on confrontation between property rights and non-property rights was thereby avoided. Instead, falling back on the facts of this particular case,[150] the court emphasised the rule of law, and the state's obligation to provide the necessary mechanisms for citizens to resolve disputes that arose between them, as the point of departure. This necessarily included the right to have access to courts, encapsulated in section 34 of the Constitution.[151] Integral to the resolution of disputes was also the legislative framework, as well as the courts and mechanisms to facilitate the execution of court orders.[152] In this particular instance the efforts of the landowner were frustrated by the ineffectiveness of the mechanisms provided by the state to resolve matters.[153] Furthermore, land invasions, and

---

147 *President of the Republic of South Africa v Modderklip Boerdery (Pty) Ltd* 2005 (5) SA 3 (CC) para 58.

148 *President of the Republic of South Africa v Modderklip Boerdery (Pty) Ltd* 2005 (5) SA 3 (CC) para 58.

149 *President of the Republic of South Africa v Modderklip Boerdery (Pty) Ltd* 2005 (5) SA 3 (CC) para 59.

150 These included the large number of unlawful occupiers, the unavailability of alternative accommodation and the failure of the state to act.

151 *President of the Republic of South Africa v Modderklip Boerdery (Pty) Ltd* 2005 (5) SA 3 (CC) para 39.

152 *President of the Republic of South Africa v Modderklip Boerdery (Pty) Ltd* 2005 (5) SA 3 (CC) para 41.

153 *President of the Republic of South Africa v Modderklip Boerdery (Pty) Ltd* 2005 (5) SA 3 (CC) para 44.

everything connected with them, could have a serious impact on stability and public peace.[154] Execution of orders contributes to stability and prevents further disruptions. In this light the state failed to act reasonably in relation to section 34, as it stood by and did nothing. The state's duty progressively to realise the right to housing was furthermore highlighted.[155]

It is noteworthy that, on the issue of appropriate relief, the court from the outset focused on an award of compensation.[156] It thereafter listed a number of factors to be taken into account in the determination of appropriate relief, including that the occupiers had settled into a community where they built homes for themselves; that their investment had to be weighed against the financial waste that their eviction would represent, and that the cost of avoiding such a waste would be minimal.[157] To these factors the court also added the consideration of the general tone and purpose of relevant legislation.[158] With reference to PIE and section 26(3) specifically, as well as to some development in case law, including *Fose*,[159] the court concluded that 'we are concerned with compensation'.[160] The court reiterated that, in the Supreme Court of Appeal's deliberation about the type of compensation to be awarded to Modderklip Boerdery, that court also considered the advantages of this type of relief, compared to other forms of relief.[161] In this regard, the following part of the judgment is pivotal:

> The question however remains *whether, and under what circumstances,* compensation ought to be awarded as the Supreme Court of Appeal has done [emphasis added].[162]

---

[154] *President of the Republic of South Africa v Modderklip Boerdery (Pty) Ltd* 2005 (5) SA 3 (CC) para 45.

[155] *President of the Republic of South Africa v Modderklip Boerdery (Pty) Ltd* 2005 (5) SA 3 (CC) para 50.

[156] *President of the Republic of South Africa v Modderklip Boerdery (Pty) Ltd* 2005 (5) SA 3 (CC) para 53.

[157] *President of the Republic of South Africa v Modderklip Boerdery (Pty) Ltd* 2005 (5) SA 3 (CC) para 54.

[158] *President of the Republic of South Africa v Modderklip Boerdery (Pty) Ltd* 2005 (5) SA 3 (CC) para 55.

[159] *President of the Republic of South Africa v Modderklip Boerdery (Pty) Ltd* 2005 (5) SA 3 (CC) para 57.

[160] *President of the Republic of South Africa v Modderklip Boerdery (Pty) Ltd* 2005 (5) SA 3 (CC) para 57.

[161] *President of the Republic of South Africa v Modderklip Boerdery (Pty) Ltd* 2005 (5) SA 3 (CC) para 59.

[162] *President of the Republic of South Africa v Modderklip Boerdery (Pty) Ltd* 2005 (5) SA 3 (CC) para 61.

The Constitutional Court then proceeded to deal with expropriation as a possible remedy, referred to the separation of powers and concluded that 'in all the circumstances the award of compensation made by the Supreme Court of Appeal was the most appropriate remedy for this case'.[163] To that end the Constitutional Court confirmed the relief previously granted, notwithstanding that the judgment was based on a different basis from that of the Supreme Court of Appeal.[164]

4.3 Single system of law and subsidiarity?

When the Constitutional Court judgment is considered in light of the single system of law principle and subsidiarity rules, it becomes abundantly clear that the court neither considered and applied these concepts, nor set out a clear methodology. In this regard, two questions follow: how did the court reach their conclusion and what would have been the end result had the single system of law principle and subsidiarity rules been applied? Phrased differently: would the Constitutional Court still have reached the same result had the Van der Walt methodology been applied here?

It is notable that the judgment departs from the viewpoint that in principle only two remedies could potentially provide effective relief: compensation (damages) or expropriation. Even though the court specifically states that the question remains 'whether and in which circumstances' compensation ought to be awarded, the court in effect refrains from answering these questions. Instead, it seems as if the court reached its findings by only taking into account the following: (a) the extraordinary facts of the case; (b) the factors affecting the occupiers as a settled community, which discouraged relocation; and (c) setting up two possible remedies against one another: the one having a list of advantages for all parties involved, whereas the other invited unwelcome questions about the separation of powers principle. There is no indication or elaboration as to how these two potential remedies were identified in the first place. What was the particular approach followed? What methodology was employed? We submit that, in this context, irrespective of whether the adjudication phase had already been dispensed with, and despite the discarding of section 25 as the point of departure, the execution phase in the pursuit of effective relief also necessitated the application of the single system of law principle and subsidiarity rules. Arguably, given our submission, the methodology ought to have been the following:

---

[163] *President of the Republic of South Africa v Modderklip Boerdery (Pty) Ltd* 2005 (5) SA 3 (CC) para 65.

[164] *President of the Republic of South Africa v Modderklip Boerdery (Pty) Ltd* 2005 (5) SA 3 (CC) para 66.

PIE is the starting point, as it is the legislative measure drafted to deal with the constitutional rights in question. That remains the case in both scenarios: where the constitutional right at stake is a section 25 right (the Supreme Court of Appeal judgment), as well as where the constitutional right is embodied in section 34, endorsed in the Constitutional Court judgment. Section 34 resonates in PIE in that procedural requirements and corresponding duties and responsibilities are set out in the eviction context. PIE provides for the protection of immovable property in principle by setting out various application procedures under sections 4,[165] 5[166] and 6,[167] and, simultaneously, facilitates access to court and the rule of law. However, PIE does not provide for compensatory mechanisms. If PIE provided for a compensatory remedy or equalisation measure[168] to address instances where there is a disproportionate and continued violation of the landowner's rights, for example, where the execution of the eviction order is suspended for an unreasonably long period, then those provisions would have been applicable and could arguably have constituted effective relief. As PIE does not have such provisions, the amendment of PIE may be considered in this context.

Returning to the single system of law concept and subsidiarity rules, in the absence of relevant legislative measures to deal with the matter at hand, the next step ought to have been to consider the common law, encapsulating a claim for damages arising out of delict.[169] Interestingly, while the Constitutional Court in *Modderklip* did not consider the common law, it nevertheless stated that '[i]t could even be open to Modderklip to bring a separate delictual action against the State.'[170] It must, however, be borne in mind that, even if the facts showed that the landowner was affected detrimentally, that in itself would not necessarily have resulted in a successful delictual claim.[171] Also pertinent was whether the actions, or more accurately, inaction, of the state in failing to execute the eviction order constituted a wrongful act in relation to the landowner and the unlawful

---

[165] Section 4 provides for 'normal' eviction applications by an owner or person in charge of land.

[166] Section 5 provides for urgent eviction proceedings.

[167] Section 6 provides for the state to institute eviction proceedings.

[168] T Kotzé *Effective relief regarding residential property following a failure to execute an eviction order* (unpublished LLM thesis, Stellenbosch University, 2016) 141–145.

[169] Section 25(1) of the Constitution; M Loubser, R Midgley, A Mukheibir, L Niesing & D Permunal *The* law *of delict in South Africa* 2 ed (2012) 3–35, 39; AJ van der Walt *Constitutional property law* 3 ed (2011) 17–18; T Roux 'Property' in S Woolman & M Bishop (eds) *Constitutional law of South Africa* 2 ed (Revision Service 12, 2003) ch 41 1-37.

[170] *President of the Republic of South Africa v Modderklip Boerdery (Pty) Ltd* 2005 (5) SA 3 (CC) para 60.

[171] *Minister of Police v Mboweni* 2014 (6) SA 256 (SCA) para 18.

occupiers. This would have required the court to decide whether the state had a legal duty to protect the constitutional rights of the parties involved. Not every breach of a constitutional duty is equivalent to unlawfulness in the delictual sense and therefore not every breach of a constitutional obligation would constitute unlawful conduct.[172] While acknowledging the possibility of a common-law delictual claim, the Constitutional Court did not elaborate on this and did not consider the possibility of developing the common law in this context.[173] This could have been an option, given the advances already made in compensation for physical harm alluded to above. In principle, nothing prevented the Constitutional Court from developing the common law in this context, where loss was suffered due to the unreasonable delay in the execution of the eviction order. In any event, on the notion of a single system of law and subsidiarity rules, this option should at least have been considered before proceeding to direct constitutional damages. Phrased differently: in accordance with the Van der Walt methodology, direct constitutional damages would only have been considered if neither the relevant statute nor the common law provided for effective relief to remedy a constitutional right infringement.

4.4 Another result?

Theoretically two options were available to the Constitutional Court before automatically resorting to constitutional damages, namely a possible amendment of PIE to provide for a compensation mechanism or the development of the common law of delict for relevance in the eviction paradigm. As legislative amendment is the domain of the legislative and not the prerogative of the judicial branch of government, deference would have been acceptable here. It is also possible that the development of the common law of delict may have resulted in an award of damages identical or similar to what was achieved in the Constitutional Court judgment. In this regard the question remains as to why one would insist on applying the Van der Walt methodology in both the adjudicatory and execution phases, as is called for

[172] *Steenkamp NO v Provincial Tender Board, Eastern Cape* 2007 (3) BCLR 300 (CC) paras 37–40: whether a legal duty to prevent loss occurring exists, calls for a value judgment embracing all the relevant facts and involving what is reasonable and, in the view of the court, consistent with the common convictions of society. However, where there is a legal duty, not every breach of a constitutional or statutory duty is wrongful in the delictual sense for that reason alone. In addition, it must be reasonable to compensate the plaintiff, ie where the state acted in bad faith or under corrupt circumstances or completely outside the legitimate scope of the empowering provision.

[173] Section 39(2) of the Constitution.

in our contribution. Linked with this question is the further consideration of whether constitutional damages do in fact constitute effective relief.

4.5 Considerations of clarity, certainty and direction-giving

As explained, the Constitutional Court did not set out the methodology it employed to reach its decision that constitutional damages had to be awarded. Inevitably, practicalities and convenience, coupled with factual considerations of large numbers of persons who had settled, peacefully, combined with the separation of powers element, also guided the court's final conclusion. While the end result may be the same – some form of damages or compensation – irrespective of whether the Van der Walt methodology was employed or whether there was direct reliance on the Constitution from the outset, the difficulty lies in the absence of guidance and clear methodology. Clarity and certainty have thus fallen by the wayside. It is rather ironic that, despite the court's own acknowledgment that it had to determine *whether and in which instances* constitutional damages could be awarded, it had failed to do exactly that. What the Constitutional Court effectively did was to choose one remedy above another, essentially based on its advantages in this particular case.

It thus remains unclear (a) whether courts would apply the same or different methodologies in the adjudicatory and execution phases respectively; and (b) when constitutional damages could be resorted to in principle. Inevitably the risk is there that, in the absence of clear methodology, parallel avenues and tracks of law may develop. That is the case because, in principle, it is quite possible that one methodology may be employed in the adjudicatory phase whereas another methodology may be employed in the next phase, namely in the execution phase. Given the prevalence of unlawful occupation of land and eviction and in light of increasing difficulties in executing orders within a reasonable time, more – instead of less – clarity and guidance are needed.

5 Effective relief?

To determine whether constitutional damages provided effective relief, it is necessary to ascertain whether the rights of the respective parties were realised, given the *Fose* context. The landowner was compensated by the state for having to bear the ongoing and indefinite burden of accommodating unlawful occupiers on his property.[174] On the other hand, the order allowing the occupiers to remain on the land until alternative land was made available

[174] *President of the Republic of South Africa v Modderklip Boerdery (Pty) Ltd* 2005 (5) SA 3 (CC) para 48.

protected their housing interests.[175] Effectively, the order also ensured the fulfilment of the state's constitutional obligations.[176] Viljoen remarks that the advantage of this order was that the court circumvented 'the eviction and allocation of land issue, which solved the immediate access to land problem...'[177] Accordingly, the rights of the respective parties were realised *prima facie.*

However, upon further evaluation, it would appear as if the Constitutional Court sanctioned the continued unlawful occupation of land which, according to Viljoen, most likely amounted to an arbitrary deprivation of property.[178] The state's constitutional obligation to provide access to adequate housing was furthermore ignored, as no positive duty was placed on the state to provide services or devise legally secure tenure for the unlawful occupiers.[179]

Other factors that also have an impact on whether constitutional damages constitute effective relief, more broadly, but still within the focus of our contribution, are whether the payment of constitutional damages is sustainable, given budgetary implications and economic constraints;[180] whether expropriation is perhaps not a better option in light of communities

---

[175] *President of the Republic of South Africa v Modderklip Boerdery (Pty) Ltd* 2005 (5) SA 3 (CC) para 68.

[176] *President of the Republic of South Africa v Modderklip Boerdery (Pty) Ltd* 2005 (5) SA 3 (CC) para 59. Other options that may also constitute effective relief, but that are not explored here in detail, include a structural interdict and contempt of court orders – see T Kotzé *Effective relief regarding residential property following a failure to execute an eviction order* (2016) unpublished LLM thesis Stellenbosch University 2–3.

[177] S Viljoen "The systemic violation of section 26(1): An appeal for structural relief by the judiciary" (2015) 30 *SAPL* 42–70 46; JM Pienaar 'Land reform and housing: Reaching for the rafters or struggling with foundations?' (2015) 30 *SAPL* 1–25 7–8. See also *First National Bank of South Africa Ltd t/a Wesbank v Commissioner South African Revenue Service; First National Bank of South Africa Ltd t/a Wesbank v Minister of Finance* 2002 (4) SA 768 (CC); AJ van der Walt *Constitutional property law* 3 ed (2011) 190–333; T Roux 'Property' in S Woolman & M Bishop (eds) *Constitutional law of South Africa* 2 ed (Original Service, Dec 2003) ch 41 17–28; J Strydom & S Viljoen (Maass) 'Unlawful occupation of inner-city buildings: A constitutional analysis of the rights and obligations involved' (2014) 17 *PELJ* 1207–1261 1231–1235

[178] S Viljoen 'The systemic violation of section 26(1): An appeal for structural relief by the judiciary' (2015) 30 *SAPL* 42–70 46.

[179] S Viljoen 'The systemic violation of section 26(1): An appeal for structural relief by the judiciary' (2015) 30 *SAPL* 42–70 46–47; JM Pienaar 'Land reform and housing: Reaching for the rafters or struggling with foundations?' (2015) 30 *SAPL* 7–8.

[180] D Brand 'Judicial deference and democracy in socio-economic rights cases in South Africa' (2011) 22 *Stell LR* 614–638 616.

having settled and stabilised over time;[181] and whether this kind of monetary grant sufficiently addresses the landowner's loss, also in the long term.

In light of monetary considerations, it may also be beneficial to consider whether German equalisation measures, known as *Ausgleich*, would have constituted a more suitable and effective remedy.[182] While comparable, equalisation measures and constitutional damages are not identical. *Ausgleich* can be regarded as a payment of money to lessen the disproportionate burden imposed on ownership rights by legislation.[183] This prevents an otherwise legitimate and lawful regulation of property from being excessive, unconstitutional or invalid.[184] Equalisation payments are thus awarded in terms of specific authorising legislation,[185] whereas constitutional damages are awarded in terms of the common law or by relying on the Constitution, as explained.[186] Although constitutional damages or *Ausgleich* may provide a 'quick' solution, neither option ensures long-term resolution for the parties involved.

6 Conclusion

The single system of law concept and subsidiarity principles dictate that the vindication of constitutional rights and interests must first be approached in line with legislation specifically enacted to protect the rights in question, before relying on the common law or the Constitution.[187] As PIE does not provide for a compensatory mechanism in instances where an eviction order cannot be executed, PIE does not provide effective relief in this context. The next step is to consider the common law before relying directly on the Constitution. As explained, it is unlikely that a court will award delictual damages to a landowner suffering financial loss due to the inability to

---

[181] *Fischer v Persons Listed on Annexure X* (unreported, referred to as [2017] ZAWCHC 99, 30 August 2017).

[182] AJ van der Walt *Constitutional property law* 3 ed (2011) 366–367, 277–280; J Strydom *A hundred years of demolition orders: A constitutional analysis* (2012) unpublished LLD thesis Stellenbosch University 350.

[183] AJ van der Walt *Constitutional property law* 3 ed (2011) 366–367; J Strydom *A hundred years of demolition orders: A constitutional analysis* (2012) unpublished LLD thesis Stellenbosch University 350–351.

[184] AJ van der Walt *Constitutional property law* 3 ed (2011) 277–280; J Strydom *A hundred years of demolition orders: A constitutional analysis* (2012) unpublished LLD thesis Stellenbosch University 329.

[185] AJ van der Walt *Constitutional property law* 3 ed (2011) 277–280, 367; J Strydom *A hundred years of demolition orders: A constitutional analysis* (2012) unpublished LLD thesis Stellenbosch University 329, 350–351.

[186] See section 3 above.

[187] AJ van der Walt *Constitutional property law* 3 ed (2011) 23–24, 35.

execute an eviction order within a reasonable time.[188] While the element of wrongfulness may cause difficulties in succeeding with a claim for delictual damages, the development of the common law of delict could have been a further viable option. In the absence of a compensatory mechanism in PIE and the unlikelihood of a court awarding delictual damages for the failure by the state to execute an eviction order, a landowner may claim direct constitutional damages.

Thus far, the courts have used their own discretion to determine whether constitutional damages will be appropriate, which discretion is not necessarily guided by the single system of law concept and subsidiarity rules. Apart from issues linked to methodology, there is also a risk that constitutional damages may not be effective relief for all parties involved. While the landowner was compensated for what he had lost in *Modderklip*, and while the unlawful occupiers were permitted to remain on the property, their occupation and tenure remained unlawful and insecure.[189] While our focus has been on constitutional damages specifically, it is possible that relief found in other jurisdictions, for example *Ausgleich*, or equalisation measures,[190] may also sufficiently answer the call for justice.

In the absence of clear guidelines in case law and the paucity of methodology-related judgments within the eviction domain specifically, the development of a general framework for direct constitutional damages[191] may also go some way towards providing clarity with regard to when direct constitutional damages would be appropriate and effective relief. Presently, and in future, given the prevalence of eviction-related concerns and difficulties connected to the execution of eviction orders within a reasonable time, coupled with

---

[188] M Bishop 'Remedies' in S Woolman & M Bishop (eds) *Constitutional law of South Africa* 2 ed (Revision Service Jun 2014) ch 9 154. See *Olitzki Property Holdings v State Tender Board* 2001 (3) SA 1247 (SCA); *Premier of the Province of the Western Cape v Fair Cape Property Developers (Pty) Ltd* 2003 (6) SA 13 (SCA); *Steenkamp v Provincial Tender Board of the Eastern Cape* 2007 (3) BCLR 300 (CC).

[189] S Viljoen 'The systemic violation of section 26(1): An appeal for structural relief by the judiciary' (2015) 30 *SAPL* 42–70 46–47; JM Pienaar 'Land reform and housing: Reaching for the rafters or struggling with foundations?' (2015) 30 *SAPL* 1–25 7–8; J van Wyk 'The relationship (or not) between the rights of access to land and housing: De-linking land from its components' (2005) 16 *Stell LR* 466–487.

[190] AJ van der Walt *Constitutional property law* 3 ed (2011) 366–367, 277–280; J Strydom *A hundred years of demolition orders: A constitutional analysis* (2012) unpublished LLD thesis Stellenbosch University 350.

[191] See S Barns 'Constitutional damages: A call for the development of a framework in South Africa' 2013 *Responsa Meridiana* 1–22 and T Kotzé *Effective relief regarding residential property following a failure to execute an eviction order* (unpublished LLM thesis, Stellenbosch University, 2016) 116-123; 191-192.

the methodology lacunae in judgments, the Van der Walt methodlogy as the embodiment of the single system of law principle and subsidiarity rules remain pertinent in providing guidance and legal certainty and ultimately forging tools necessary to promote and instil our constitutional reform goals.

Chapter 16

Ubi remedium, ibi ius: Trespass and the right to exclude

*Emma JL Waring**

Contents

A South African, a Dutchman, an American and a Brit enjoyed a lunch together... This is not the beginning of a wry joke about the foibles of different nationalities, but rather describes a golden afternoon unexpectedly spent in the company of André van der Walt, Joe Singer and Sjef van Erp as a very junior property scholar soaking up their discussions about property and the world. The afternoon encapsulated so much that was typical of the generosity of André, both in his scholarship and his personal characteristics. His immense

* Lecturer, University of York. The author would like to thank the editors, particularly Gustav Muller and Bradley Slade, for their help with this chapter; and attendees at the Society of Legal Scholars Property Law meeting in York for their comments on an embryonic version of this chapter. All errors and omissions are the author's alone.

contribution both to the regeneration and development of South African constitutional and property law, and property teaching, cannot be overstated. However, his legacy extends even further than this already immense achievement, to the continuing impact of his jurisprudence on global property debates. André's work on paper is only half of an extremely noteworthy story, though. For me, and for so many others, André's most special gift was his unobtrusive encouragement, support and mentorship throughout and after my doctoral work. He delighted in facilitating and nurturing connections between property lawyers from wide and varying legal backgrounds. André's outward-looking intellectual stance and personal attributes placed him firmly at the centre of a vibrant inclusive network of open-looking property theorists. It is no exaggeration to say that André's jurisprudence, and the intellectual networks he fostered, have shaped my academic life and will continue to do so for years to come.

* * *

In his 2014 article 'The modest systemic status of property rights'[1] André van der Walt examined ongoing debates about 'property's core', which had, in the words of Baron, 'helped keep exclusion at the front and center of property theory'.[2] In his 2014 article, Van der Walt examined cases involving the clash between an owner's right to exclude and third parties seeking to exercise rights of free movement, free speech, or rights of assembly (over quasi-public land or private land with restricted public access). He argued that property rights were subordinate to these other rights, and that there were sound and important systemic reasons why non-property rights should 'often, if not always, be secured before property'.[3] Further, he observed that the cases demonstrated the 'surprisingly modest purpose that protection of property rights in fact plays, judged against the systemic significance of the exceptions and qualifications'.[4]

Normatively, Van der Walt addressed what he saw as misguided concerns that these findings might undermine what he considered to be the fatally flawed view of property as the guardian of other rights, or guardian of personhood. He argued that bills of rights could protect social rights more directly and explicitly than property protection could, and cautioned that

1 AJ van der Walt 'The modest systemic status of property rights' (2014) 1 *J L Prop & Soc'y* 15–106.

2 JB Baron 'The contested commitments of property' (2010) 61 *Hastings LJ* 917–968 920.

3 AJ van der Walt 'The modest systemic status of property rights' (2014) 1 *J L Prop & Soc'y* 15–106 30.

4 AJ van der Walt 'The modest systemic status of property rights' (2014) 1 *J L Prop & Soc'y* 15–106 27.

the 'pursuit of property objectives might actually frustrate the pursuit of ... personhood- or human-flourishing securing objectives'.[5] Agreeing with Joe Singer's work,[6] Van der Walt concluded that property rights 'can only exist, and can only be protected, in the space allowed by the unavoidable limitations imposed by our primary choice for a society characterised by a certain kind of democracy ... a democracy that is characterised by and founded upon fundamental notions of life, dignity and equality'.[7] Van der Walt ended by reiterating the importance of protecting property rights, but emphasised that while their protection 'is a legitimate objective of the legal order ... relative to the primary norms that prescribe how we want to live in society it is a systemically modest one' that is reflected in the adjudication of property conflicts involving rights of life, speech, freedom, dignity and equality.[8] Van der Walt's conclusion chimes with the Grays' argument that 'it has always been one of the fundamental features of a civilised society' that 'exclusory claims of property stop where the infringement of more basic human freedoms begins'.[9]

This chapter builds on Van der Walt's work by considering the right to exclude from a different perspective. Rather than analysing what happens when the right to exclude clashes with fundamental freedoms, this chapter looks instead at the right to exclude *in ordinary daily life* and considers its application on this plane. Even exclusion theorists positing the right to exclude as the *sine qua non* of property might struggle to justify the right to exclude trumping fundamental rights to life or freedom, for example. While it is conceptually valuable to consider the right to exclude in high-stakes situations, it represents an almost insoluble problem of ranking and balancing competing constitutional values. Therefore, an attempt is made

---

[5] AJ van der Walt 'The modest systemic status of property rights' (2014) 1 *J L Prop & Soc'y* 15–106 42. The arguments draw on the work of other property theorists, particularly J Nedelsky 'Should property be constitutionalised? A relational and comparative approach' in GE van Maanen & AJ van der Walt (eds) *Property on the threshold of the 21st century* (1996) 417–432; CM Rose 'Book review: *The guardian of every other right: A constitutional history of property rights* by James W Ely (1992)' (1993) 10 *Const Commentary* 236–246.

[6] JW Singer 'Property as the law of democracy' (2014) 63 *Duke LJ* 1287–1335; JW Singer 'Democratic estates: property law in a free and democratic society' (2009) 94 *Cornell L Rev* 1009–1062.

[7] AJ van der Walt 'The modest systemic status of property rights' (2014) 1 *J L Prop & Soc'y* 15–106 99.

[8] AJ van der Walt 'The modest systemic status of property rights' (2014) 1 *J L Prop & Soc'y* 15–106 102.

[9] KJ Gray & SF Gray 'Civil rights, civil wrongs and quasi-public space' (1999) 1 *EHRLR* 46–102 62.

to step behind the constitutional significance, or otherwise, of the right to exclude by considering its application in more mundane circumstances.

To this end, a novel approach is taken when considering the right to exclude by describing its *operation*, rather than normatively arguing for a particular *role*. This is not to suggest that fact and theory should be divorced, or that one should take precedence over the other, but rather is an attempt to shine further light on the right to exclude. The operation of the right to exclude in English law is considered from the angle of its remedial protection under the tort of trespass. This is, perhaps, an unexpected perspective in a property article given the often impermeable-seeming subject divide between property and tort in English law,[10] but it allows for a more nuanced appreciation of the right to exclude.

In this chapter, Part I takes the principle *ubi remedium, ibi ius* – where there is a remedy, there is a right – as the starting point in considering the contours of remedial protection afforded to the right to exclude, and alludes briefly to the right to exclude in English law. Parts II, III and IV consider three relevant trespass strands: the legal rules, remedies and exceptions. As a result of considering these three strands Part V argues that behind the traditional English rhetoric, trespass is not a monolithic remedy but instead highly contextual in its availability and application. This conclusion in itself will not be startling to tort or property lawyers, but in the heat of exclusion debates the implications of the contours of trespass for the right to exclude are apt to be overlooked. Reasons of space do not permit an exploration in this chapter of the implications of these findings for progressive property or property exclusion theories.[11]

This chapter does not take a normative stance in arguing that the right to exclude *should* or *should not* be contoured in a way that mirrors its protection under trespass rules, but rather sets out to establish how the remedial rules are tethered to the right to exclude in the first place. Nonetheless, the conclusion that the availability and application of trespass is affected by not

[10] English property textbooks rarely include detailed discussion of remedies such as trespass, which is normally covered in tort textbooks. KJ Gray & SF Gray *Elements of land law* 5 ed (2009) is a notable exception.

[11] GS Alexander, EM Peñalver, JW Singer & LS Underkuffler 'A statement of progressive property' (2009) 94 *Cornell L Rev* 743–744; JA Lovett 'Progressive property in action: The Land Reform (Scotland) Act 2003' (2011) 89 *Neb L Rev* 739–818; ET Freyfogle 'Private ownership and human flourishing: An exploratory overview' (2013) 24 *Stell LR* 430–454; R Dyal-Chand 'Sharing the cathedral' (2013) 46 *Conn L Rev* 647–723; JW Singer 'Property as the law of democracy' (2014) 63 *Duke LJ* 1287–1335. Cf TW Merrill 'Property and the right to exclude' (1998) 77 *Neb L Rev* 730; JE Penner *The idea of property in law* (2000); JE Penner 'The "bundle of rights" picture of property' (1996) 43 *UCLA L Rev* 711–820.

only the nature of the landowner or possessor, but also the nature of the land itself, argues that the concomitant right to exclude should currently be viewed more accurately as a contextually contoured right – even in mundane cases, not just where fundamental freedoms are at stake.

PART I

I *Ubi remedium, ibi ius*

In the event that I argue before a court that the orbit of the International Space Station 250 miles away in space is infringing my property rights over the Moon some 250,000 miles away in space and claim a remedy, I will be laughed out of court. Not just because the infringement seems unlikely given the distances involved, but more importantly because I have no state-or-government-sanctioned recognition of 'my' property rights over the Moon. State failure to recognise property rights, and the unavailability of a remedy or potential for enforcement, leave me with a problem. No matter how vigorously I protest that I have a 'property right' over the Moon, the substantive content and value of that claimed property right appears non-existent because it is unacknowledged and unprotected by the rest of society. If, however, extraordinarily, a court acknowledged that I could have a remedy for the International Space Station's actions, I would suddenly have an immensely significant property right. The availability of a legal remedy is central to the existence of a legal right. While this is a basic point, it is one that can sometimes be forgotten too quickly. The availability of a meaningful remedy is not a neutral issue but one fraught with significance given that the recognition and enforcement of property rights has a momentous, and sometimes unjust, effect in drawing a fundamental divide between those inside and outside property's boundaries.[12]

The choice to frame the axiomatic principle under discussion in this chapter as the *ubi remedium, ibi ius* principle – 'where there is a remedy, there is a right', rather than the more normal *ubi ius, ibi remedium* – 'where there is right, there is a remedy' is deliberate. This formulation is used mainly for historical reasons relating to the development of English land law, but partly because in what might appear to be a chicken-and-egg scenario, actually the remedy is the most significant issue. A law that proclaims that I have a right is good, but a remedy that gives me something if my legal right is breached is even better in practice.

[12] KJ Gray 'Property in thin air' (1991) 50 *Camb LJ* 252–307 269ff discusses the deep significance of excludability.

Traditionally, the development of the substantive law of real property in England has been wholly influenced, from its earliest days, by the legal remedies provided for the recovery of land and the vindication of property rights.[13] The medieval writ of right, writs of entry, the action of ejectment, and tort of trespass all shaped the fundamental content of real property rights.[14] Without an appropriate writ there was no right to claim. The existence of a remedy, in land law in particular, was critical. In *Ashby v White*, a case brought against a returning officer who refused to admit a man's vote, Chief Justice Holt asserted that:

> If the plaintiff has a right, he must of necessity have a means to vindicate and maintain it, and a remedy if he is injured in the exercise or enjoyment of it; and indeed it is a vain thing to imagine a right without a remedy; for want of a right and want of remedy are reciprocal.[15]

The ineluctable link between a meaningful legal right and a strong remedy was also noted in the well-known American property case of *Jacque v Steenberg Homes*, which involved a trespass claim, where Bablitch J rightly asserted that 'a right is hollow if the legal system provides insufficient means to protect it'.[16]

2 'Keep-off' or 'come if you want' messages

We would expect a strong, clear and unequivocal right to exclude to be mirrored by an equally strong, clear and unequivocal remedy. The 'keep-off' message in theory should be grounded by and reflected in the remedy provided in practice. Likewise, a more muted and ambiguous right to exclude would be echoed by an equally muted and ambiguous remedy. Here, the 'come if you want' approach to exclusion would be mirrored by a muted and ambiguous remedy. In fact, the remedial approach does not have to be as binary as a choice between a clear 'keep-off' remedy and an ambiguous weaker 'come if you want' remedy. It is perfectly possible (and perhaps desirable) for a remedy to contain hybrid protection with clear keep-off approaches for some incursions, and a more ambiguous 'come if you want' approach for others.

The possibility of hybrid property rights protection can sometimes be overlooked in the heat of debates about the right to exclude, because the right itself carries so much totemic proprietary significance. Rather than starting

---

[13] C Harpum, S Bridge & M Dixon *Megarry & Wade: The law of real property* 8 ed (2012) 93.

[14] AWB Simpson *A history of the land law* 2 ed (1986).

[15] *Ashby v White* 92 ER 126 (1703) 136 (Holt CJ).

[16] *Jacque v Steenberg Homes Inc,* 563 NW2d 154 (Wis 1997) para 9 (Bablitch J).

the theoretical discussion by asking what we want the right to exclude to represent or do, this chapter looks instead at how the right to exclude is protected and incursions remedied.

Whether the remedy (and thus the right) are clear or equivocal or a hybrid can provide great depth to our property debates about the right to exclude. This added perspective will help to provide a platform for further work and debate about whether to retain, reject or reform the right to exclude, depending on the theoretical standpoint taken towards the significance of the right. This chapter does not take a stance on whether remedies protecting the right to exclude should normatively be clear, equivocal or hybrid, but rather looks instead at delineating the contours of the remedy as it stands. Only then can we identify the landmarks and direction of travel based on a map of the right to exclude in action as mirrored in its remedial protection.

3 The right to exclude

Exclusion and its concomitant remedy of trespass have played a significant constitutional and property-related role in English law for hundreds of years. One of the best known and most influential of such cases is that of *Entick v Carrington*.

3.1 *Entick v Carrington*

John Entick was a British author who was employed in 1762 as a writer by a weekly opposition newspaper, *The Monitor, or, The British Freeholder.*[17] Entick's 'gross and scandalous reflections and invectives'[18] in several editions of the newspaper attacked both the government of the day and notable establishment figures such as Lord Bute, a favourite of King George III. Following a government crackdown on such opposition publications, the Earl of Halifax issued a general warrant, pursuant to which Nathan Carrington and three other King's messengers entered John Entick's house, searched it, broke locks and chests, and seized his papers. Entick did not take this physical invasion of his house sitting down, and instead responded by suing Carrington and the other messengers for trespass to both his house and his goods. Before Lord Camden, Carrington argued that no trespass had been committed because the messengers' acts had been justified by the terms of the warrant. Despite sternly warning that all governments must 'set their faces against libels', Lord Camden ruled unequivocally in Entick's favour.

[17] J Humphreys 'Entick, John (c 1703–1773)' rev Penelope Wilson *Oxford Dictionary of National Biography* (2004) http://www.oxforddnb.com/view/article/8824.

[18] (1765) 19 St Tr 1030 1030.

Lord Camden's ruling was not only significant at the time, but its rhetoric has also resonated through the centuries, taking on a perhaps unforeseen importance, particularly in American constitutional law relating to search and seizure under the Fourth Amendment.[19] Even today, the notion that public officers must show express legal authority for any interference with a citizen's person or property is still constitutionally and practically significant. However, for property lawyers and students, the most spine-tingling phrases in Lord Camden's ruling are those stating that –

> ... [b]y the laws of England, every invasion of private property, be it ever so minute, is a trespass. No man can set his foot upon my ground without my licence, but he is liable to an action, though the damage be nothing.

It is perhaps no surprise that the exclusionary focus of Lord Camden's comments are echoed in Blackstone's *Commentaries*, which were also published for the first time in 1765 the same year that *Entick v Carrington* was handed down. Blackstone's *Commentaries* reinforce the ideas that property rights should be impregnable and affirm the centrality of the right to exclude. The common-law concept of property described by Blackstone, however mythical it may in fact have been,[20] has had great appeal in later centuries. Property in this conception is 'essentially assertive, oppositional and exclusory ... [A] solid, reassuringly three-dimensional concept, resonating with its own unmistakeable message for the world at large'.[21]

3.2 The appeal of exclusion

Following the eighteenth-century development of liberal conceptions of property, the right to exclude has continued to be viewed as a touchstone or hallmark of property by theorists from all sides. Despite the development of the 'bundle of rights' theory of property by legal realists, with its emphasis on viewing property as contextual and relational, the right to exclude has retained its centrality perhaps because it is the only stick in the property bundle that all theorists could agree upon.[22] It has been argued that exclusion is so significant because otherwise property rights would 'simply dissolve into the primeval chaos of the commons' with everything 'constantly up for grabs and in which the process of trading with assets is neither meaningful

[19] See *Boyd v United States* 116 US 616 (1886) 626 describing *Entick v Carrington* as a 'monument' of English freedom.

[20] CM Rose 'Canons of property talk, or, Blackstone's Anxiety' (1998) 108 *Yale LJ* 601–632.

[21] KJ Gray & SF Gray 'Private property and public propriety' in J McLean (ed) *Property and the constitution* (1999) 12.

[22] FS Cohen 'Dialogue on private property' (1954) *Rutgers U L Rev* 357–387 374.

nor necessary'.[23] For those property theorists and philosophers who reject the 'bundle of rights' approach to property, exclusion is wholly central to concepts of property.[24]

Notions of exclusion remain so seductively attractive because they appeal to a deep-seated ancient, and perhaps inherent, lay sense of territoriality. This sense of territoriality, with its ideas of constant vigilance and the need for defence, is however unhelpful and paradoxically signifies a weak form of property.[25] Despite this, the right to exclude has often been viewed in English law as a defensive bulwark against overweening power and trespass has helped to reinforce this message.[26] Not only does the right to exclude enable property to be put to particular uses, or not used, according to the wishes and whims of the owner or possessor.[27] It also enables individuals to insulate themselves (to some degree) from government interference and invasions of privacy. Famously, in the ancient words of *Semayne's Case*, it has been said that 'the house of every one is to him as his castle and fortress, as well for his defence against injury and violence, as for his repose'[28] and William Pitt, the Earl of Chatham, during a Parliamentary debate in 1763 declared that:

> The poorest man may in his cottage bid defiance to all the forces of the Crown. It may be frail – its roof may shake – the wind may blow through it – the storm may enter – the rain may enter – but the King of England cannot enter! – all his force dares not cross the threshold of the ruined tenement![29]

Being able to point to something as 'mine' rather than 'ours' or 'yours' also serves to provide external signals about interests, status, social stability and wealth. It is no surprise that the expansion of the franchise and voting rights have traditionally always been tied so closely to property requirements.

3.3 *John Trenberth Ltd v National Westminster Bank Ltd*

Given some of the roles played by the right to exclude, it would be expected that trespass, as the remedy protecting this right, would also serve multiple

---

[23] KJ Gray & SF Gray *Elements of land law* 5 ed (2009) 99.

[24] TW Merrill 'Property and the right to exclude' (1998) 77 *Neb L Rev* 730–755; JE Penner *The idea of property in law* (2000) 71; JE Penner 'The "bundle of rights" picture of property' 43 *UCLA L Rev* (1996) 711–820 754.

[25] CM Rose 'Property and expropriation: themes and variations in American law' (2000) 1 *Utah L Rev* 1–38 3.

[26] See Part IV discussing police powers.

[27] KJ Gray & SF Gray *Elements of land law* 5 ed (2009) 103.

[28] *Semayne's Case* 77 ER 194 (1604) 195.

[29] W Pitt, speech, March 1763, in Lord Brougham *Historical sketches of statesmen who flourished in the time of George III*, first series (1839) London vol 1, 41–42.

roles. In *John Trenberth Ltd v National Westminster Bank Ltd*[30] the English court considered a difficult trespass case. It involved two adjoining properties, one of which was a bank in a dangerous state of repair. Unfortunately, the bank's dilapidated state could not be remedied without gaining access from the neighbouring property. Having entered into unsuccessful negotiations with its neighbour to gain permission to enter its neighbour's land, the bank found itself in 'an impossible position'. The bank's dilemma was exacerbated by a statutory duty to remedy the dangerous state of its building due to its location abutting a public highway.

There was, as the court described it, 'on the one hand the Scylla of the dangerous building and there was on the other hand the Charybdis of trespassing upon the plaintiffs' land, and they chose ... to go ahead and trespass'.[31] Walton J noted that the trespass had been wholly deliberate and stated that 'if flagrant invasion of another's rights of property of that nature is not sufficient to call forth the interposition of a court of equity, I do not know what invasion could be said to do so'. In dismissing the bank's call for damages as a remedy rather than an injunction against the trespass, Walton J upheld the rights of the aggrieved owner asserting that 'the fact that any damage would be trifling is the very reason why an injunction should be granted'. He added that people should not trespass and then say 'And I am entitled to go on doing it because I am really doing you no tangible harm, and five-pence will amply compensate you for that harm.'[32]

The decision made by Walton J to uphold an owner's right to exclude, and to protect this with property rule rather than liability rule protection, reflects the potential strength of the remedy even in a case demonstrating an unedifying level of dog-in-the-manger behaviour from the neighbour. In *Trenberth* a seemingly strong trespass remedy backs up the right to exclude. Trespass is designed to serve both individual and societal needs – as a deterrent to would-be trespassers and as recognition of individual rights. A strong remedy in such a situation also reduces the attractiveness of messy and contentious 'self-help' remedies. This paradigm case suggests a clear bright-line approach to trespass, which can efficiently warn third parties to stay away from and 'keep off' the land.[33]

---

30 *John Trenberth Ltd v National Westminster Bank Ltd* (1980) 39 P&CR 104.

31 *John Trenberth Ltd v National Westminster Bank Ltd* (1980) 39 P&CR 104 106.

32 *John Trenberth Ltd v National Westminster Bank Ltd* (1980) 39 P&CR 104.

33 TW Merrill & HE Smith 'What happened to property in law and economics?' (2001) 111 *Yale LJ* 357–398 389; TW Merrill & HE Smith 'Making Coasean property more Coasean' (2011) 54 *J L & Econ* S77–S104 S90.

PART II

This part briefly analyses the first of the three trespass strands under consideration – the legal rules outlining the doctrine. Part III will consider the remedies available in a trespass claim, while Part IV will turn to the exceptions that prevent a successful trespass claim.

4 Trespass rules

As noted above, the traditional vindication of the right to exclude is the availability in English law of a tort action in trespass. Even today, trespass occurs whenever anyone is unlawfully present on land possessed by another, and this is a claim *per se* without any need for damage to be proved. The courts have consistently held that 'if the defendant place a part of his foot on the plaintiff's land unlawfully, it is in law as much a trespass as if he had walked half a mile on it'.[34] It is enough that someone is unlawfully present on the claimant's land since this is deemed to be an injury to the claimant's possessory right.

The defendant's unlawful 'presence' might be wholly minimal and will include intentionally walking over the land; taking possession of it unlawfully; remaining on the land once a formerly lawful authority to remain has expired (as with a tenant holding over at the end of a lease); using the land for an unlawful purpose (for example, holding a public protest on the highway without permission); fixing something unlawfully on the land; drilling under land;[35] or invading airspace at a low height over the land by erecting a notice or a crane swinging over the land.[36] Under English law a claim for trespass can be brought even where no actual damage has occurred, as for example in *Anchor Brewhouse Developments Ltd v Berkley House Ltd.*[37] Here, the jib of the defendants' tower crane swung over the claimant's land, which was held to be an actionable trespass over its airspace and an injunction was granted. It is also possible for trespass to be committed by animals where their owner intended the animals to enter the land or failed to prevent their entry.[38]

[34] *Ellis v The Loftus Iron Company* LR 10 CP 10 (1874–75) 12.

[35] *Bocardo SA v Star Energy UK Onshore Ltd* [2011] 1 AC 380.

[36] *Woollerton & Wilson Ltd v Richard Costain Ltd* [1970] 1 WLR 411. It is not a trespass for an airplane to fly at normal heights above land, see *Bernstein v Skyviews & General Ltd* [1978] QB 479.

[37] *Anchor Brewhouse Developments Ltd v Berkley House (Docklands Developments) Ltd* (1987) 284 EG 625.

[38] *League Against Cruel Sports Ltd v Scott* [1986] 1 QB 240. The court held that the negligent failure to control fox-hounds when hunting meant that they committed trespass when they inevitably entered land owned by the League Against Cruel Sports.

Trespass relates to 'land' and the courts construe this to include any trespass to real and corporeal property (such as the soil itself, including limited airspace above and the ground below, buildings, trees and so on). However, trespass is not possible against an incorporeal right such as an easement or fishing right, for example, even though these rights are included within the normal land law statutory definition of land.[39] Nor is it a trespass where the land is affected by another's acts but the land itself is not intruded upon directly. For example, it will not be a trespass where land is affected by a third party creating unpleasant noise or smells, although this might be the basis for a claim in nuisance.

A further signalling feature of the strength of the remedy is that trespass need not be brought by the *owner* of land (something that would be impossible to prove in unregistered land), but merely by a *possessor*. There are compelling historic reasons for this given the link between physical possession of land and seisin in English land law, where possession was legally significant in generating and defending title to land.[40] Any interference with settled possession was historically to be discouraged and the 'presumption of title in a mere possessor … illustrates one of the many instances where uncertainties in evidence are resolved against a wrongdoer'.[41] Possession cannot be used as a sufficient basis for a trespass claim against an owner by a possessor, however. It is for this reason that a squatter holding land under adverse possession doctrines will be able to bring a trespass claim against other third parties, but not against the paper or registered owner.

Even today in the registered land world, possession of land, or deemed possession of land, is sufficient to bring a claim in trespass. The remedy has also been extended to claimants who are not in exclusive possession

[39] Section 205(i)(ix) of the Law of Property Act 1925.

[40] The courts have stretched the law in this area further by holding that a claimant with a personal right under a contractual licence to occupy and control land (but who is not in factual possession), may nonetheless bring an action for possession against a trespassory possessor. See, for example, the decision of the Court of Appeal in *Manchester Airport Plc v Dutton* [2000] QB 133, approved *obiter* by Lord Neuberger MR in *Mayor of London v Hall* [2011] 1 WLR 504. Lord Neuberger MR observed in *Hall* at [27] that 'the modern law relating to possession claims should not be shackled by the arcane and archaic rules relating to ejectment, and… [instead] it should develop and adapt to accommodate a claim by anyone entitled to use and control, effectively amounting to possession, of the land in question…'.

[41] DM Fox 'Relativity of title at law and in equity' (2006) 65 *CLJ* 330–369 339.

of the land, as long as they have exclusive occupation.[42] The corollary of the significance of possession rather than ownership is that a landowner will *not* be able to bring a trespass claim if someone else was lawfully in possession of the land at the time the trespass took place, but if the land is vacant, the owner will retain the right to sue for trespass. The focus on possession may appear surprising, but emphasises the clear and strong nature of the right to exclude – the possession of land is so significant that intrusions can be defended by a wide group of possible claimants, not only by an owner.

As a strict liability tort, the law does not require an intention to *trespass* but merely the intention to *enter* the land, so it is no defence for trespassers who intended to enter land to argue that they mistakenly thought they were on their own land, rather than the possessor's.[43] This harsh crystalline rule was applied in an ancient case where the trespasser mowed grass on his neighbour's land, mistakenly believing it to be his own land. The plea of mistake as a defence to the claim in trespass failed on the grounds that the trespasser had intended to mow the grass, even if he was mistaken about the boundaries. This was sufficient intention to make out the trespass claim. If, however, the trespasser was involuntarily trespassing, the law will excuse this, as in the ancient case of *Smith v Stone*,[44] where the defendant was held not to be liable for trespass where he had been deliberately carried and thrown onto the claimant's land.

Trespass appears to be a strong remedy in that it is available to possessors, in the absence of damage or harm to land, and requires only minimal intention. The law has not created significant hurdles to a claimant bringing a claim in trespass and this sends a clear, unequivocal and strong 'keep off' message to third parties.

PART III

The right to exclude appears to be generously and well protected. However, this view is only part of the story. A trespass claim may be nominally available in myriad circumstances, but in reality its enforcement and the penalties it carries with it are also meaningful. To this end, this Part outlines the potential remedies available in English law once a claim in trespass has been made out, and argues that they provide strong recognition of the right

[42] *National Provincial Bank Ltd v Ainsworth* [1965] AC 1175, 1232 where the deserted wife who had only a personal interest in the matrimonial home was still said *obiter* by Lord Upjohn to have been entitled to bring proceedings against trespassers on the basis of her exclusive occupation.

[43] *Basely v Clarkson* Court of Common Pleas (1682) 3 Lev 37.

[44] *Smith v Stone* (1647) Sty 65.

to exclude. Part IV will outline various situations where trespass cannot be successfully claimed.

5 Remedies – self-help

Clearly when trespassers enter someone else's land, the owners or possessors are entitled to use reasonable force to evict or exclude them. A burglar who enters a building runs the risk that the owner or possessor of the building will challenge his entry and eject him. Likewise, a neighbour's tree branches overhanging a boundary fence can be lopped (although the cut branches remain the neighbour's property and ought to be offered back to her, even if this act may provoke her anger).

The right to exclude trespassers does not give rise to an unfettered right of removal. In *Revill v Newbery*[45] the 76-year-old owner of a shed had been in the habit of sleeping there at night to protect his property from vandals and thieves. When he was awoken by the noise created by two thieves trying to break open the shed, the owner fired his shotgun through a hole in the door and shot the thieves, wounding one of them. The Court of Appeal looked at relevant case law and occupiers' liability legislation before noting that 'an occupier cannot treat a burglar as an outlaw.'[46] Millett LJ stated that while historically, the common law had allowed reasonable force, 'society and … social perceptions' had altered to such an extent that the 'use of excessive force against him is an actionable wrong'.[47]

Unsurprisingly, the right to exclude does not nowadays trump protection of life, although the question of what is 'reasonable in the circumstances' allows for some discretion. It is also worth noting that it is a criminal offence under section 6 of the Criminal Law Act, 1977, if a landowner, possessor or someone on their behalf uses, or threatens to use, violence against people or property to gain entry to a residential property, if there is someone at the property who opposes the entry. Even though it is therefore legally possible to use self-help remedies to evict trespassers, it is sensible first to obtain a court order authorising this.[48] Once a trespasser has been asked to leave by a displaced residential occupier, and fails to leave, the trespasser will however have committed an offence under section 7 of the Criminal Law Act 1977 by remaining.

---

[45] *Revill v Newbery* [1996] QB 567.

[46] *Revill v Newbery* [1996] QB 567, 577.

[47] *Revill v Newbery* [1996] QB 567, 580.

[48] The Civil Procedure Rules (CPR) 55 provide both an accelerated and a standard procedure for obtaining possession of residential property.

6 Damages

Most trespass claims will give rise to monetary damages, but there are a variety of different methods for calculating the sums that should be paid by the trespasser.

6.1 Compensatory damages

Such damages are compensatory, allowing the claimant to recover money for the loss that she has suffered as a result of the trespass. As with other torts, the aim is for the claimant to be put back in the position that she was in before the trespass occurred. Loss might have been suffered due to some compensable damage to the land that has reduced its value in some way, or the trespass might have caused a loss of utility that can be compensated.

6.2 Remedies – nominal damages

The majority of trespass cases result in an award of nominal damages and it could be questioned whether this provides a sufficiently meaningful remedy. It is argued that such awards still send a clear, unequivocal and strong 'keep off' message to trespassing third parties. This is all the more so when it is remembered that costs are normally awarded in favour of the successful party. Even where 'only' judgment is given with nominal damages, the successful claimant will be at a significant advantage in having her costs paid by the trespasser.

6.3 Restitutionary damages

Occasionally, the court will use a different restitutionary approach to damages for trespass.[49] This approach applies where for some reason the normal approach to damages will not suffice; for example, where the claimant has suffered no loss, but where the trespasser has received a significant benefit from using the land. Courts tend to present these cases as justified on the basis of the loss of a hypothetical licence agreement,[50] or the loss of a compulsory acquisition payment. While it used to be thought that such payments were available where the trespasser had directly benefitted from the trespass, this head of damages has also been extended to cases where the trespasser was not the sole or even main trespasser.[51]

---

[49] *Attorney General v Blake* [2001] AC 268, 277-287.

[50] *Stadium Capital Holdings (No 2) v St Marylebone Property Company Plc* [2010] EWCA Civ 952.

[51] *Field Common Ltd v Elmbridge Borough Council* [2008] EWHC 2079 (Ch).

A restitutionary basis is not always generous, though. In *Bocardo v Star Energy*[52] Star Energy had been granted a statutory licence to search for, bore for and obtain petroleum. In order to extract the maximum amount of petroleum from an underground reservoir, Star Energy drilled diagonally from an external point with pipes running under Bocardo's land at a depth of more than 800 feet. Star Energy, however, had not sought a licence from Bocardo, which claimed damages for trespass. The Supreme Court eventually awarded a hypothetical licence fee of £1000 which was termed 'generous' albeit far less generous than the first instance judge who awarded Bocardo nine per cent of the value of the oil extracted through the trespassory pipeline – this amounted to £621,180 plus interest.

6.4 *Mesne profits*

Mesne profits may be charged when a trespasser has used the claimant's land and the claimant will be entitled to 'such sum as should reasonably be paid for the use'[53] of the land. In the Privy Council case of *Horsford v Bird*, where a boundary wall had been built over the claimant's land, expropriating it, the Privy Council not only awarded damages reflecting the value of the land to the claimant, but also allowed mesne profits to be recovered reflecting the fact that the land had been used on an on-going basis.[54] Similarly, in the *Inverugie Investments Ltd v Hackett* the claimants had been wrongfully ejected from 30 apartments in a hotel complex. The Privy Council agreed with the Bahamian Court of Appeal that the trespassers should be liable in damages for the use of each occupied apartment at the going rate for 365 days a year, despite the fact that the apartments had an occupancy rate of no more than 40 per cent.[55]

6.5 *Exemplary damages*

Occasionally, the court can award exemplary damages for trespass, if expressly pleaded, where: (i) the trespasser's behaviour has been an abuse of executive power; or (ii) the trespasser has acted in a calculated and deliberately trespassory manner to maximise profits. Lord Devlin in the House of Lords' case of *Rookes v Barnard* described exemplary damages being justified where the defendant cynically calculated that the 'money to be made out of his wrongdoing will probably exceed the damages at risk';

[52] *Bocardo SA v Star Energy UK Onshore Ltd* [2011] 1 AC 380.

[53] *Swordheath Properties Ltd v Tabet* [1979] 1 WLR 285.

[54] *Horsford v Bird* [2006] UKPC 3.

[55] *Inverugie Investments Ltd v Hackett* [1995] 1 WLR 713.

here the court could award exemplary damages 'whenever it is necessary to teach a wrongdoer that tort does not pay'.[56]

Even in such circumstances, the award of exemplary damages needs to be principled and proportionate. In the High Court case of *Ramzan v Brookwide Ltd*[57] the court awarded exemplary damages of £60,000 against a property owner who had deliberately subsumed part of a neighbouring property into his own premises, also cutting off a fire escape. The Court of Appeal found that exemplary damages were justified in the case, but reduced them to £20,000 stating that they should be principled and proportionate and that such damages did not need to be substantial, since the 'fact of making the award would largely be in itself sufficient'.[58]

7 Injunction

Where a trespass is threatened or continuing, damages may be an inadequate remedy and an injunction may be sought instead. Under the courts' equitable jurisdiction, the grant of an injunction is a discretionary remedy unlike common-law damages. In *Jaggard v Sawyer*[59] the Court of Appeal approved the rule laid down by A L Smith LJ in *Shelfer v City of London Electric Lighting*[60] that an injunction *might* properly be refused by the court where: (i) the injury to the claimant's legal right is small; (ii) the damage is capable of being estimated in money; (iii) the damage can be adequately compensated by a small monetary payment; and (iv) it would be oppressive to the defendant to grant an injunction.

In the Supreme Court in *Coventry v Lawrence*, a nuisance case, Lord Neuberger accepted that the 'prima facie position is that an injunction should be granted, so the legal burden is on the defendant to show why it should not.'[61] He continued by 'cautiously' approving the observations of Lord Macnaghten in *Colls v Home and Colonial Stores Ltd* that an injunction would be necessary if compensation could not remedy the injury, or the defendant had acted in a 'high-handed manner'.[62] In considering A L Smith LJ's four tests from *Shelfer*, Lord Neuberger clarified the law by stating that they should not be applied as a 'fetter' on the court's discretion. He added that in the absence of other circumstances it would normally be 'right to refuse an injunction' if the four tests were satisfied, and that even if the tests had all

56 *Rookes v Barnard* [1964] AC 1129, 1227.
57 *Ramzan v Brookwide Ltd* [2010] EWHC 2453 (Ch).
58 *Ramzan v Brookwide Ltd* [2011] EWCA Civ 985.
59 *Jaggard v Sawyer* [1995] 1 WLR 269.
60 *Shelfer v City of London Electric Lighting* [1895] 1 Ch 287, 322–323.
61 *Coventry (t/a RDC Promotions) v Lawrence* [2014] AC 822 855.
62 *Colls v Home and Colonial Stores Ltd* [1904] AC 179 193.

been met it did not mean that an injunction should be granted.[63] Injunctions are therefore available and their pre-eminent status as the go-to proprietary remedy has remained undented in recent years.

Despite this, the courts are alive to the fact that, especially in urban spaces, threatening a would-be trespasser with an injunction may be part of a carefully calculated financial negotiation rather than necessarily motivated by a pure interest in the protection of the right to exclude. This is particularly the case with over-sail licences in cities so that although Lord Macnaghten in *Colls* agreed that 'a man ought not to be compelled to part with his property against his will', the courts needed to be 'very careful not to allow an action … to be used as means of extorting money'.[64]

8 Criminal trespass

It is also possible for a trespass, in certain situations, to be classified as a criminal offence, not merely a civil wrong. For example, the offence of aggravated trespass[65] under section 68 Criminal Justice and Public Order Act, 1994 (CJPOA 1994), can be committed where someone trespasses on land (or in a building)[66] *and* does anything with the intention of intimidating any one who is engaging in or about to engage in lawful activity on land, or has the intention to obstruct or disrupt that lawful activity. It is worth noting that according to government charging guidelines, aggravated trespass can be committed when trespassing occurs coupled with some other (non-criminal) additional activity, which might include 'playing a musical instrument or taking a photograph' so long as this additional act is accompanied by the relevant intention to intimidate, obstruct or disrupt lawful activity.[67] Other criminal forms of trespass include trespassory assemblies under the Public Order Act, 1986, as amended,[68] and squatting in residential buildings under section 144 of the Legal Aid, Sentencing and Punishment of Offenders Act, 2012 (LASPOA 2012). Under the LASPOA 2012 provision, someone who is living in a residential building as a trespasser and who entered it as a trespasser, and who knows or ought to know that she is a trespasser, is committing a criminal offence and can be fined or imprisoned for no more than six months.

[63] *Coventry (t/a RDC Promotions) v Lawrence* [2014] AC 822 856.

[64] *Colls v Home and Colonial Stores Ltd* [1904] AC 179 193.

[65] Section 68(1) of the Criminal Justice and Public Order Act, 1994 (as amended by section 59 of the Anti-social Behaviour Act, 2003).

[66] *DPP v Chivers* [2010] EWHC 1814 (Admin).

[67] http://www.cps.gov.uk/legal/s_to_u/trespass_and_nuisance_on_land/#a06.

[68] Sections 14A and 14B of the Public Order Act, 1986.

The range of remedies available to a successful claimant in trespass provides the right to exclude with meaningful protection. While an injunction provides strong property protection, the availability of liability protection via damages is significant, as is the possibility of criminal charges in specific instances of trespass.

PART IV

Having considered the first two strands of trespass – the rules and the remedies – this section outlines the circumstances in which trespass claims cannot succeed. In *Entick v Carrington* Lord Camden declared when a trespass would occur, but referred to three circumstances in which an otherwise trespassory act would be acceptable: licensed, empowered by law or excused. It is particularly important to look behind the rhetoric of exclusion to consider the circumstances in which the remedy of trespass cannot operate to vindicate and protect claims to exclusory property rights.

9 Licence

Self-evidently, a claim for trespass cannot be maintained if the 'trespasser' is on the land with the on-going permission of the possessor. Once the permission or licence has been withdrawn, the licensee has a reasonable period in which to leave the land or risk a claim in trespass being made against her. Historically, in tort, once a licence has been withdrawn, trespass could be claimed even if the withdrawal of the licence was a breach of contract.[69] The Victorian high-water mark of this stringent approach, as taken in *Wood v Leadbitter*,[70] has been significantly relaxed.[71] In *Errington v Errington and Woods* Denning LJ observed that at 'common law a licence was always revocable at will, notwithstanding a contract to the contrary... the rule has, however, been altered owing to the interposition of equity... and since 1948 it has been clear that... a licensor will not be permitted to eject a licensee in breach of a contract to allow him to remain.'[72] As a result of the fusion of the administration of courts of law and equity under the Judicature Acts of 1873 and 1875, and the 'infusion of equity' into the common law relating to the revocability of contractual licences, Denning LJ was right to say that

---

[69] *Wood v Leadbitter* (1845) 13 M&W 838, where a ticket-holder for horse races at Doncaster was forcibly ejected by an employee after being asked to leave the course. While the ticket-holder had been wrongly asked to leave, in breach of contract, this was held by the court to be irrelevant in an action in tort for trespass.

[70] *Wood v Leadbitter* (1845) 13 M&W 838.

[71] *Hurst v Picture Theatres* [1915] 1 KB 1; *Winter Garden Theatre (London) Ltd v Millennium Productions Ltd* [1948] AC 173.

[72] *Errington v Errington and Woods* [1952] 1 KB 290 298–299.

'contractual licences have a force and validity of their own and cannot be revoked in breach of the contract'.[73] To this extent, a trespass claim cannot be maintained by a licensor against a licensee who has validly entered land under a contract and continues to observe its terms. Instead the court will be prepared to grant an injunction 'against the licensor to prevent... [the licensee] being turned out'.[74]

9.1 Statutory licence

Many utility companies, such as gas and electricity providers, have rights of entry. There are hundreds of existing statutory powers of entry, some requiring a warrant and many hundreds not requiring this before a variety of office holders have a right to enter land. Following the enactment of section 42 of the Protection of Freedoms Act, 2012, the British government published reports in 2014 from 17 government departments including the Ministry of Justice, Northern Ireland Office, Food Standards Agency, the Home Office and Revenue and Customs.[75] The reports reviewed all statutory powers of entry, which amounted to 1,237 such powers. The government stated that it intends to reduce these powers of entry to 912 and to provide safeguards for 231 existing (and to be retained) rights of entry.[76]

The sheer breadth of the 1,237 statutory rights of entry existing in 2014 is almost overwhelming. They cover not only the expected rights of entry required to ensure that public safety and hygiene standards are adhered to in schools, hospitals, care homes, prisons, ports, airports and so on, but also provide powers to deal with public crises of health, flooding, fires, energy, water and security. The many rights of entry include ones entitling office holders (sometimes with, and sometimes without a warrant) to enter premises in connection with: the inspection of premises carrying out acupuncture, tattooing, ear-piercing and electrolysis;[77] gambling establishments;[78] caravan sites;[79] high hedges;[80] listed buildings;[81] money laundering and terrorist financing;[82] family disputes where a child must be given up to the court;[83]

---

73 *Errington v Errington and Woods* [1952] 1 KB 290 299.

74 *Verrall v Great Yarmouth Borough Council* [1981] QB 202 216.

75 https://www.gov.uk/government/collections/reviews-of-all-powers-of-entry.

76 https://www.gov.uk/guidance/powers-of-entry.

77 Section 17 Local Government (Misc Provisions) Act, 1982.

78 Section 306(1) Gambling Act, 2005.

79 Section 26 Caravan Sites and Control of Development Act, 1960.

80 Section 74 Anti-social Behaviour Act, 2003.

81 Section 88A Planning (Listed Buildings and Conservation Areas) Act, 1990.

82 Paragraphs 20–21, Schedule 7, Counter-Terrorism Act, 2008.

83 Section 34 Family Law Act, 1986.

indecent displays;[84] official secrets;[85] aircraft inspections;[86] food safety;[87] noisy equipment;[88] entry to silence audible intruder alarms;[89] control of public health and infectious diseases;[90] vehicles used for fly-tipping;[91] emergency flood protection works;[92] and many hundreds of other powers of entry.

As noted above, the Earl of Chatham famously described how the poorest man could 'in his cottage bid defiance to all the forces of the Crown...'[93] Nevertheless, it would be truer today to say that given the significant volume and reach of existing statutory powers of entry, the right to exclude has suffered death by a thousand cuts. Each right of entry taken individually seems justifiable as serving a public purpose or need that makes sense in a complex urban democracy. However, *en masse* they have whittled away the right to exclude in so many circumstances that it appears to be more a concept that is 'full of sound and fury, Signifying nothing'.[94] Owners today are likely to find that they have increasingly few grounds to stand on when resisting rights of entry.

10 Empowered by law – neighbouring property

In addition to the hundreds of governmental rights of entry, legislation has also provided rights of entry for private individuals against other private individuals. One of the best known such rights is that contained in the Party Wall Act, 1996 (PWA 1996), which provides a statutory framework enabling neighbours sharing a boundary to carry out building works that involve building or demolishing a party wall or structure, to carry out repairs to a party wall or structure, and to excavate a site up to six metres from neighbouring buildings. The PWA 1996 was explicitly enacted to deal with situations where necessary building repairs to properties were being held up or prevented by intransigent neighbours,[95] and also to ensure that works causing damage to an adjoining owner's buildings or interrupting her enjoyment of the party wall or structure could be better policed.

84 Section 2 Indecent Displays (Controls) Act, 1981.

85 Sections 9(1)–(2) Official Secrets Act, 1911.

86 Section 20 Aviation Security Act, 1982.

87 Section 32 Food Safety Act, 1990.

88 Sections 10(2) and 10(4) Noise Act, 1996.

89 Sections 77–78 Clean Neighborhoods and Environment Act, 2005.

90 Numerous, see for example arts 6 and 10 of the Rabies (Control) Order, 1974.

91 Section 34B Environmental Protection Act, 1990.

92 Section 54 London County Council (General Powers) Act, 1957.

93 W Pitt, speech, March 1763, in Lord Brougham *Historical sketches of statesmen who flourished in the time of George III*, first series (1839) vol 1, 41–42.

94 W Shakespeare, *Macbeth*, Act 5, Scene 5, Nelson Thornes 1992, 54.

95 *Heathcote v Doal* [2017] EWHC B8 (TCC).

Similarly, the Access to Neighbouring Land Act, 1992 (ANLA 1992), allows landowners to enter their neighbour's land, without permission, to carry out reasonably necessary works required for the preservation of their own land. ANLA 1992 was specifically enacted to deal with situations involving 'dog in the manger' neighbours such as those in the *Trenberth* case referred to earlier in this chapter.[96] In proposing the terms of ANLA 1992, the Law Commission stated that the case in favour of reform was based on the argument that 'the absence of any general right to access of neighbouring land means that properties throughout the country are liable to deteriorate for want of repair and maintenance – with consequential financial loss to their owners and some detriment to the public'.[97] While noting that there were strong counter-arguments in favour of protecting an occupier's right to 'exclude unwelcome entrants',[98] the Law Commission concluded that sometimes the erosion of a right of exclusion could be justified since the 'private interest of landowners, does on occasion have to give way to other interests'.[99] In acknowledging that limitations on the right to exclude should be restricted both in 'nature and scope',[100] the Law Commission suggested a statutory scheme, which has been codified in ANLA 1992.

Under this statute, a landowner who needs to carry out works that are 'reasonably necessary' for the preservation of the owner's land and that 'cannot be carried out, or would be substantially more difficult to carry out, without entry'[101] upon neighbouring land can apply to the court for an access order.[102] The court must not make an access order though where this would be unreasonable due to the level of interference or disturbance caused to the neighbour's use or enjoyment of her land, nor can the court make an order where the neighbour would suffer hardship.[103] The statute also limits the type of acceptable works to those that are reasonably necessary 'for the preservation of land' under section 4 ANLA 1992, which includes repair and maintenance of buildings, clearing drains, pipes and sewers and horticultural maintenance. It is possible under ANLA 1992 for improvements, alterations

[96] *John Trenberth Ltd v National Westminster Bank Ltd* (1980) 39 P&CR 104. See 3.3 above.

[97] Law Commission *Rights of access to neighbouring land*, Law Com No 151, 1985, 7[3.8].

[98] Law Commission *Rights of access to neighbouring land*, Law Com No 151, 1985,10, [3.18].

[99] Law Commission *Rights of access to neighbouring land*, Law Com No 151, 1985,10, [3.19].

[100] Law Commission *Rights of access to neighbouring land*, Law Com No 151, 1985,12, [3.28].

[101] Sections 1(2)(a)–(b) ANLA 1992.

[102] Section 1 ANLA 1992.

[103] Section 1(3) ANLA 1992.

and demolition on the applicant's land to be authorised, where these are incidental to reasonably necessary preservation activities, where the court considers this 'fair and reasonable in all the circumstances of the case'.[104]

The grant of an access order may require the applicant to pay a sum of money to the neighbour 'as appears to the court to be fair and reasonable having regard to all the circumstances'.[105] This can be ordered by the court, but not in relation to residential land. This exception is significant. It might have been expected that the law would zealously guard residential property against otherwise trespassory incursions, but paradoxically ANLA 1992 provides most protection (in financial terms) to non-residential land. As such the legislation makes a revealing policy choice in favouring the public interest in preserving well-maintained housing stock, rather than financially recognising the importance of incursions, however limited in scope, on a residential landowner's right to exclude. It is arguable that an element of paternalism is at play here, which favours residential neighbours co-existing relatively peacefully and agreeing informally to limited incursions, rather than being encouraged by the potential for financial compensation under ANLA 1992 to engage in rent-seeking 'unneighbourly' behaviour. Traditional trespass rules, as demonstrated in the *Trenberth* case,[106] positively reinforce a landowner's expansive right to exclude others, including neighbours.

II Empowered by law – right to roam

The right to exclude has also been significantly limited, not just in a neighbour context, but also in favour of the recreational public at large. Under the Countryside and Rights of Way Act, 2000 (CROW 2000), members of the general public are entitled to enter specified land. Under CROW 2000 there is a public right of access to 'access land',[107] which comprises open country (including mountain, moor, heath and down), registered common land, and other dedicated land. A variety of land is excepted and listed in Schedule 1 to CROW 2000, including land that has been ploughed in the previous 12 months, land covered by buildings, land within 20 metres of a dwelling, land used as a park or garden, mineral workings, railways, golf courses, racecourse, aerodromes and so on. The rights of access are restricted such that they normally refer solely to a right of access by foot. Horse riding, cycling, camping and the use of vehicles are not allowed under CROW 2000 unless the landowner specifically permits these activities. Additionally,

---

104 Section 1(5) ANLA 1992.

105 Section 2(5) ANLA 1992.

106 *John Trenberth Ltd v National Westminster Bank Ltd* (1980) 39 P&CR 104.

107 Section 1(1) CROW 2000.

landowners can exclude or restrict access to their land for up to 28 days a year, and can ban dogs being taken onto their land when it is the lambing season, or to protect grouse. Similar, albeit more far-reaching legislation, has been introduced in Scotland under the Land Reform (Scotland) Act, 2003.[108]

CROW 2000 sought to establish a fair balance between landowners and the public interest without the need for compensation. Intriguingly, it has been convincingly argued in recent empirical work that the introduction of minimal limits on the landowner's right to exclude had a visible effect in decreasing property prices in areas with a high percentage of access land when compared to areas with lower percentages of access land.[109] The findings of this research do not mean that a successful regulatory takings type argument could be raised. English courts have traditionally been reluctant to engage with this type of argument, especially where the potential regulatory taking has occurred under the aegis of a statutory scheme authorised by Parliament.[110] In the Privy Council case of *Grape Bay Ltd v Attorney General of Bermuda* Lord Hoffmann stated that the 'give and take of civil society frequently requires that the exercise of private rights should be restricted in the general public interest' and that payment was not required in such circumstances.[111]

The rights secured in CROW 2000 were further expanded by the Marine and Coastal Access Act 2009 (MCAA 2009), which enhanced public access to the English coastline for recreational purposes and created a long-distance walking route around the entire coastline. For landowners in rural or coastal areas whose land has been classified as 'access land' their right to exclude has been significantly curtailed and their ability to claim trespass reduced to virtually nil.

12 Empowered by law – police powers

The courts, and Parliament, have consistently recognised that that it is 'a serious matter for a citizen to have his house entered against his will and by force by police officers'.[112] Section 17 of the Police and Criminal Evidence

---

[108] JA Lovett 'Progressive property in action: the Land Reform (Scotland) Act 2003' (2011) 89 *Neb L Rev* 739–818.

[109] J Klick & G Parchomovsky 'The value of the right to exclude: an empirical assessment' (2017) 165 *U Pa L Rev* 917–966 961.

[110] See JL Anderson 'Countryside access and environmental protection: An American view of Britain's right to roam' (2007) 9 *Envtl L Rev* 241–259; JL Anderson 'Britain's right to roam: Redefining the landowner's bundle of sticks' (2006–2007) 19 *Geo Int'l Envtl L Rev* 375–436.

[111] *Grape Bay v Attorney General of Bermuda* [2000] 1 WLR 574, 583.

[112] *Syed v DPP* [2010] EWHC 81 (Admin) para 12.

Act, 1984 (PACE 1984), governs police entry onto private property and provides that a police constable may enter and search any premises (without a warrant) for the purpose of arresting a person for an indictable offence;[113] arresting a person for an offence of threatening behaviour or intending to cause someone to fear or to provoke violence under section 4 of the Public Order Act, 1986; and saving life or limb or preventing serious damage to property.[114] All other general, common-law powers to enter premises without a warrant were abolished by section 17 PACE 1984, except for the general power to prevent a breach of the peace.[115]

Police officers are entitled to obtain access to premises to search for evidence of an indictable offence if they have obtained a warrant from a magistrate under section 8 of PACE 1984. Such warrants can be either a 'specific premises warrant'[116] or an 'all premises warrant'[117] which allows them to search any premises occupied or controlled by the person named on the warrant. Where the terms of the warrant are not complied with, or it has been improperly authorised, the warrant will be unlawful and will amount to a civil trespass, and possibly a criminal trespass as well. In *R (Faisaltex) v Chief Constable of Lancashire* the court stated that although the requirements for a warrant under section 8 of PACE 1984 'may seem numerous and onerous ... that is only to be expected when a police officer is seeking authority to enter a person's home ... without that person's consent and to search for and seize items present there. It has rightly been described as a draconian power.'[118]

13 Empowered by law – common callings and quasi-public spaces

For centuries, people carrying on a business as an innkeeper, carrier or ferryman have been viewed as having quasi-public roles, and were regulated by the common law obliging them to 'serve all comers without discrimination and to charge only reasonable prices for their goods or services'.[119] In *R v Ivens*, where a traveller had been unreasonably refused entry to an inn late at night on a Sunday, Coleridge J observed that an innkeeper 'is not to select

---

[113] Section 17(b) PACE 1984.

[114] Section 17(e) PACE 1984. *Syed v DPP* [2010] EWHC 81 (Admin) confirmed that 'saving life and limb' refers to an apprehension of serious bodily injury.

[115] *R (Laporte) v Chief Constable of Gloucestershire* [2007] 2 AC 105, where a constable must reasonably apprehend that a breach of the peace is occurring in his or her presence, or is about to occur or, having occurred, may be renewed.

[116] Section 8(1A)(a) PACE 1984.

[117] Section 8(1A)(b) PACE 1984.

[118] *R (Faisaltex) v Chief Constable of Lancashire* [2009] 1 WLR 1687, 1697.

[119] M Taggart *The province of administrative law* (1997) 6.

his guests. He has no right to say to one, you shall come into my inn, and to another you shall not, as every one coming and conducting himself in a proper manner has a right to be received' unless they are 'drunk or behaved in an indecent or improper manner'.[120]

Before the introduction of anti-discrimination legislation, the doctrine of common callings was successful in vindicating the claim of the well-known West Indian cricketer Learie Constantine to stay in a London hotel with his family (he later became the first man of African descent to be made a life peer in the House of Lords in 1969 for his work in politics and racial equality).[121] The traditional common law in this area has also obviously been supplemented and enhanced significantly by anti-discrimination legislation.[122] As a result of this wide range of legislation quasi-public spaces, even including Bed & Breakfast accommodation, cannot discriminatorily exclude people from their premises.[123] Perhaps surprisingly, given the common law's robust approach to common callings, more modern quasi-public commercial spaces such as shopping centres have not received the same level of access rights. It is legally possible for such places to exclude people from entering or overstaying their welcome, as in the case of *CIN Properties Ltd v Rawlins*,[124] even where other rights such as free speech are pleaded.[125]

14 Excused by the law – necessity

It has long been accepted that trespass to land can be defended where the entry was necessary, as long as the defendant did not negligently create or contribute to the necessity.[126] The circumstances in which necessity will be available as a defence to trespass are limited however to those where the

[120] *R v Ivens* 173 ER 94 (1835) 96-97.

[121] *Constantine v Imperial Hotels* [1944] KB 693. See J Wilson 'Crossing boundaries' (2014) issue 7617 *NLJ* 22.

[122] Sex Discrimination Act 1975; Race Relations Act 1976; Disability Discrimination Act 1995; Employment Equality (Religion or Belief) Regulations 2003; Employment Equality (Sexual Orientation) Regulations 2003; Employment Equality (Age) Regulations 2006; Equality Act 2006; Equality Act (Sexual Orientation) Regulations 2007; Equality Act 2010.

[123] *Hall v Bull* [2013] UKSC 73, [2013] 1 WLR 3741.

[124] *CIN Properties Ltd v Rawlins* [1995] 2 EGLR 130. See KJ Gray & SF Gray 'Civil rights, civil wrongs and quasi-public space' (1999) 1 *EHRLR* 46–102.

[125] *Appleby v United Kingdom* (2003) 37 EHRR 38.

[126] *Rigby v Chief Constable of Northamptonshire* [1985] 1 WLR 1242. The case involved the police burning down the claimant's shop with a canister of CS gas, whilst attempting to flush out a dangerous psychopath who had broken into the shop. The court held that while the defence of necessity to trespass was unavailable where the defendant negligently created or contributed to the necessity, it was available to the police here because they had not been negligent on the facts.

defendant was facing immediate and obvious danger such that a reasonable person would conclude that there was no other alternative. The English courts have held that this defence would not, for example, apply to homeless families in dire need of accommodation who occupied empty publicly owned houses. As Lord Denning MR remarked in *Southwark London Borough Council v Williams*:[127]

> There is authority for saying that in case of great and imminent danger, in order to preserve life, the law will permit of an encroachment on private property ... The doctrine so enunciated must, however, be carefully circumscribed. Else necessity would open the door to many an excuse.[128]

15 Excused by the law – limitation periods

A further scenario where trespass can occur and yet a remedy will not be forthcoming is where time has elapsed. In general, all actions of trespass to land must be brought within six years after the cause of the action arises, under section 2 of the Limitation Act 1980. Additionally, not only will a trespass claim be unavailable, but if sufficient time passes it is possible, although relatively difficult now in registered land, for title to land itself to be barred as in adverse possession,[129] or a title generated by prescription.

PART V

Trespass rules are bright line rules sending a strong, clear and unequivocal 'keep-off' message. The unwarranted intrusion onto land, even if this is *de minimis* and lacking an intention to trespass, is still actionable *per se.* Additionally, the survey of remedies in Part III demonstrated a clear commitment on the part of the courts to upholding trespass claims. Even nominal damages have significant implications for costs, making them more than merely declaratory, and the Supreme Court has recently reaffirmed the *prima facie* appropriateness of injunctive relief in land-related tort claims such as nuisance, and by extension, trespass. Thus, trespass appears to offer strong protection for the right to exclude. However, having considered the third strand outlined in this chapter in Part IV – that of exceptions to trespass – a paradox becomes instantly obvious. Trespass is a meaningful and substantive remedy in some areas, while also being much attenuated (if not neutered) in other areas.

---

[127] *Southwark London Borough Council v Williams* [1971] Ch 734.

[128] *Southwark London Borough Council v Williams* [1971] Ch 734 744.

[129] Schedule 6, Land Registration Act 2002. The situation is significantly different in unregistered land, where the mere passage of sufficient time (12 years under section 15 of the Limitation Act, 1980) is enough to bar the paper owner's title to land.

Where the domestic sphere is involved, trespass protection remains high and the right to exclude is carefully justified by the police when exercising powers of entry, by courts in issuing warrants and by government departments in overseeing their rights of entry. This jealous protection of the right to exclude intuitively accords with territorial imperatives and mirrors the fundamental protection of the home and family life contained in article 8 of the European Convention on Human Rights, which was incorporated into domestic law under the Human Rights Act, 1998. Nonetheless, there are reasons to be cautious about glibly assuming that the home remains the impregnable 'castle' and 'fortress' of *Semayne's case*.[130] The vast array of statutory rights of entry allows for a variety of officials (sometimes without a warrant) to enter residential property, if it is for a statutory reason. The statutory framework is wide-ranging, as noted in Part IV, and allows entry on to residential premises for diverse reasons including surveying a disputed high hedge,[131] or switching off a continuously ringing burglar alarm.[132] In these statutory circumstances no remedy of trespass can be successfully sought. Additionally, even if a homeowner does not fit any of the statutory rights of entry, she is always liable to find that her neighbour may have a right to enter her land to shore up a party wall, or for repairing access.[133]

Elsewhere the gleaming shield of trespass looks even more ragged around the edges, if not rather moth-eaten. Although it is a traditional limitation, it is still true that those operating common callings or quasi-public services in some instances will not be able to exclude people. The law here is inconsistent with shopping centres and smaller shops being able to exclude individuals, but the overall tendency is towards non-discriminatory access and has been for hundreds of years. Those who occupy rural and coastal land, which is more likely to be subject to statutory rights to roam, are also significantly limited in their ability to exercise their right to exclude third parties from their land. The various limitations outlined in Part IV demonstrate a contextual and nuanced application of trespass law. Despite the traditional rhetoric, trespass does not in reality provide a wholly clear-cut 'keep-off' message. Instead, trespass is contextual and contoured: its availability and application depends on a series of variables including not only the type of *land*, but also the attributes of the *possessor* – whether the possessor is a residential occupier, a farmer with livestock, a neighbour, or an innkeeper, for example.

---

130 *Semayne's Case* 77 ER 194 (1604) 195.

131 Section 74 Anti-social Behaviour Act 2003.

132 Sections 77–78 Clean Neighborhoods and Environment Act 2005.

133 Party Wall Act 1996; Access to Neighbouring Land Act 1992.

Returning to the *ubi remedium, ibi ius* axiom discussed at the outset of this chapter, the contours of the trespassory remedy necessarily have an impact on its concomitant right, the right to exclude. Trespass requires a 'careful calibration' of the right to exclude across a 'spectrum of spaces'.[134] It is important to recognise explicitly that it is legally impossible in English law to vindicate a right to exclude in circumstances that fit the exceptions in Part IV, whether this is because of a licence, legal empowerment or legal excuse.

This chapter does not, for reasons of space, enter into the normative implications of this finding, but clearly trespass raises significant questions when considering the right to exclude and the relative systemic role it plays, and further work will need to be carried out to explore this in detail. For now, it is sufficient to conclude, first, that focusing on the remedial contours of the tort of trespass enriches debates about the right to exclude; and second, that trespass is highly contextual, varying in its protection depending on not only the type of land but also the possessor. Finally, examining trespass surprisingly reveals that the right to exclude is subordinated in practice not only to fundamental freedoms, but also to a wide variety of interests operating in a democratic society, including public health, leisure and recreation, governmental efficiency, and smooth neighbourly relations. The implications of these incursions on the right to exclude have yet to be explored fully, but it is argued that trespass helps to shine a valuable light when mapping the contours and considering the direction of travel to take in relation to the right to exclude.

[134] A Grear '*Porter v Commissioner of Police for the Metropolis*' in R Hunter, C McGlynn & E Rackley (eds) *Feminist judgments from theory to practice* (2010) 174 178.

Chapter 17

Fault-lines in the settler colony: On the margins of settled law

*Brenna Bhandar**

Page

Contents

1 Introduction

It is with the demarcation of borders, with the partitioning of land and its parcelization, that the colonial order of things displaces, reconfigures, and obscures what was there before. The pasturing and partitioning of land by European colonists brought into being topographical fault-lines, displacing some people in order to settle others in their place. In a gross mimicry of the geological process by which the displacement of matter in the earth's deeper layers by other matter creates irremedial fissures in its surface, the cutting into the soil and the appropriation of land creates a new *nomos*, in the words of Carl Schmitt, an order of land, law, and ultimately, sovereignty.

The colonial order of things imposes a way of seeing the land, the law and its inhabitants, and is rendered in juridical terms that produce racial subjects in conjunction with specific concepts of ownership and land use. This order of things is spatial and material; it structures the way individuals and communities inhabit, use, move through and work in the urban city-scape, the home, rural areas, the factory, etc.... and it is written into the land itself. The rationales and justifications for appropriation render it both discursive and ideological and this order of things is cast with the force of law. In South Africa, the settler colonial order was transformed and intensified by apartheid laws that concretised a racial hierarchy defined, in part, through

* Senior Lecturer, SOAS School of Law.

the right to ownership. That is, the settler colonial order that had produced whiteness as coincidental to the legal position of the rightful owner, and the black subject as one who was by definition without the capacity to be a true owner of land, laid the foundation for an apartheid system that systematically disenfranchised and dispossessed the black South African population.

While the complexities of both settler colonial and apartheid racial legal orders created contradictions and ambiguities, the overall spirit of the *nomos* of colonial and apartheid social and political forms was rather Manichean in nature.

One of the most challenging and fundamental questions in the transition from apartheid to a constitutional liberal democracy was (and remains) the extent to which legal transformation can support and produce a new post-apartheid political order. Schmitt, who lamented the 'odium of colonialism' heralded by the demise of formal European rule, did not believe that decolonisation could produce a new *nomos*. The sheer brutality of WWII and the American intervention on European soil, along with decolonisation, signalled the end of the nomos of the *jus publicae European*. The specificity of an order founded on colonial land appropriation was not capable of being replicated. As Peter Hallward has observed, however, the *Nomos of the Earth* is 'not a prophetic text'[1] in the sense that the structural, ideological and indeed phenomenological dimensions of European colonial projects (and the modes of accumulation they established) persist well into the present.

The friend/enemy distinction that Schmitt believed had disintegrated with WWII and the enmity lines of old continue to structure relations of power in the racial order of South Africa as elsewhere.[2] We are not just dealing with the 'legacies' of apartheid or colonialism in a straightforward way, as if the formal end of apartheid was marked by a wholesale transformation of a racial system of exploitation and oppression. As Joel M Modiri succinctly puts it:

> The legacy of this oppression, of course, continues to persist in post-apartheid South Africa with wealth, education, and power being largely divided along the lines of race. To engage with the vicissitudes of race in post-1994 South Africa, one must also consider the implications of *life under law after apartheid* [emphasis in original] – particularly the reproduction and maintenance of white supremacy and white privilege as well as the systemic exclusion of black people through direct and indirect forms of racial marginalisation.[3]

---

[1] P Hallward 'Beyond Salvage' (2005) 104(2) *SAQ* 237–244 241.

[2] See A Mbembe 'The Society of Enmity' (Nov/Dec 2016) *Rad Phil.*

[3] JM Modiri 'The colour of law, power and knowledge: Introducing critical race theory in (post-) apartheid South Africa' (2012) 28 *SAJHR* 405–436 406.

Modiri's observation of the persistence of white supremacy in the post-apartheid era of liberal constitutionalism begs two questions. The first is whether the transformative constitutionalism that characterised the political transition in South Africa had or has the capacity to alter fundamentally the racial and economic order that was entrenched during the apartheid years. Some have argued that the nature of the compromise embedded in the transition to democracy, namely, the embrace of a neoliberal economic system that effectively privileged the white minority and a growing (if small) black elite, at the expense of the majority of the black population, foreclosed the possibility of realising a truly just political and economic order in the post-apartheid era.[4] Despite the constitutional commitments to the redistribution of land and resources and the recognition of equality before the law, it is clear, as Modiri's observation attests to, that South Africa remains mired in forms of inequality entrenched during apartheid. This first question is thus a complex one about the very nature of constitutions, the constituting of political power and citizenship, and the fundamental (if often obscure) relationship between constitutional democracy and political economy.

The second question, perhaps more precise and definitely more pertinent to my concerns in this chapter, is the extent to which a profound constitutional transformation could break with or rupture an existing order of private law that was at the foundation of the most oppressive aspects of life under law during apartheid. The question then, is not whether a new *nomos* can emerge (or has emerged) with the fall of apartheid, but whether constitutional reform has the potential to break radically with a history of private law doctrine and conventions that were closely allied with the racial subjugation characteristic of settler colonialism and apartheid. As AJ van der Walt noted:

> [I]n a nutshell, the apartheid land rights regime was based on the relative strength and security of white land rights, as opposed to the relative weakness and insecurity of black land rights. this division of strong and weak rights may look like a purely political creation, but in fact it was founded on a well-known and highly valued legal institution, namely the traditional civil-law hierarchy of real rights. The apartheid land-rights regime exploited the power relations implicit in this hierarchy to ensure the political domination and the legal security that entrenched white privilege, and ironically this hierarchy of power was upheld not

---

[4] See, for instance, GE Schneider 'Neoliberalism and economic justice in South Africa: Revisiting the debate on economic apartheid' (2003) 61(1) *Rev Soc Econ* 23–50; P Carmody 'Between globalisation and (post)apartheid: The political economy of restructuring in South Africa' (2002) 28(2) *J South Afr Stud* 255–275.

> only because of racial-political choice, but also because of legal-dogmatical choice in favour of the retention of traditional, common-law institutions.[5]

In his massive *oeuvre* of work, Van der Walt confronted the very profound and complex nexus between the structure of property law as it developed in the Roman-Dutch legal tradition and the racial, capitalist order of a settler colonial, apartheid state. Colonial modes of land appropriation and apartheid era property law created a matrix of dispossession rooted in an entire legal apparatus (legislation, judicial determinations, state agencies and government policies), private corporate and individual interests, and an economic system based on an ideology of possessive individualism. The complicated relationship between the private law domain of property law and the public sphere of government legislation and policy was reflected in the spatial order of apartheid[6] that incorporated a broad range of agents, actors and things. The state could take on the position of a private property owner; the emblematic right to exclude became more than a right of an individual private owner and extended, at times, to the entire public sphere.[7] The Constitution could become the locus of 'super-values' used to legally justify the morally and politically unjustifiable actions of private individual actors.[8]

Van der Walt thus posed the crucial question as to whether transformative constitutional law and property theory could effectively destabilise a public/private divide that entrenched the privileges and powers attached to a hierarchical model of ownership. He recognised the role of the state and the judiciary in protecting the social dimensions of property as they relate most particularly to housing rights and shelter, along with pressing questions of redistribution of land, prescriptive rights to land that had been used and improved by agricultural labourers,[9] and the legitimacy of provisions for the expropriation of land by the state. He consistently revealed the essence of the legal form of private property as being inherently political in its constitution and thus, capable of being interpreted, constructed and lived very differently.

---

5 AJ van der Walt 'Property rights and land policy: Some remarks on land reform in South Africa' background article for paper presented by the Lincoln Institute for Land Policy, Cambridge MA, 6 April 1998 3–4.

6 For an elaboration of Van der Walt's spatial theory of property law, see, for instance, 'Dancing with codes – Protecting, developing and deconstructing property rights in a constitutional state' (2001) 118 *SALJ* 258–311.

7 See AJ van der Walt 'Enclosed property and public streets' (2006) 21 *SAPL* 3–24.

8 AJ van der Walt 'Rendition/eviction? A post-apartheid reflection' in (2005) 15 *Law & Critique* 321–344 331.

9 See AJ van der Walt 'Property, social justice and citizenship: Property law in post-apartheid South Africa' (2008) 19 *Stell LR* 325–346.

Writing in the aftermath of the transition from apartheid to a liberal democratic constitutional order, to which the reform of property law was pivotal, Van der Walt sought to examine what justice demands of property law:

> [C]ertain justice-driven qualifications of and amendments to the property regime are so fundamental that they cannot be accommodated within or explained in terms of the current doctrine – they require a rethink of the system, a reconsideration of the language, the concepts, the rhetoric and the logic in terms of which we explain and justify choices for or against individual security and systemic stability in the property regime.'[10]

Van der Walt explicitly distinguished his work from the body of property theory that examines the limits of property within assumed political, economic and social structures of stability.[11] He created a distinctive body of theory through detailed doctrinal analyses of the most important innovations in land law, a thorough consideration of law's capacity to transform the political sphere alongside its profound limits, and an abiding commitment to social and racial justice.[12]

Van der Walt consistently excavated the fault-line that exists between the worldview and experiences of those in power and those who had been rendered vulnerable to subjugation through histories of dispossession and ownership. In doing so, he attempted to address how and whether the abyssal divide between, on the one hand, the juridical discourse and legal reality of dominant ownership paradigms, and on the other, struggles for self-determination and freedom that fundamentally challenge the ownership paradigm, could be bridged. In attempting to render visible the deep divide between the effects of a racial regime of ownership[13] on subjects deemed to be legitimate owners, whose rights were to be protected and secured by the state, and those who were rendered vulnerable to repeated dispossession, Van der Walt argued that in order for genuine political transformation to

---

[10] AJ van der Walt *Property in the margins* (2009) 15.

[11] AJ van der Walt *Property in the margins* (2009) 14.

[12] However, what marked André out as exceptional was not only the calibre of his work as a scholar, but also his unfailing support for younger scholars and students, which was characterised by an acute sense of how institutional and systemic forms of discrimination permeated the academy and knowledge production itself. His generosity on all counts was a rare thing, perhaps one consequence of his deep and perspicacious view of what true social transformation requires of us as individuals, and collectively too.

[13] For a full elaboration of the concept of racial regimes of ownership, see B Bhandar *Colonial lives of property: Law, land and racial regimes of ownership* (2018). In this book, I explore how modern property law emerges in conjunction with the production of racial subjects.

occur, the perspectives and political imaginaries of those without property, those in the margins, must replace the lexicon of rights embedded at the core of much property doctrine.[14] Van der Walt's project was to distinguish between the reform of property law that reinforces the *status quo* and 'the larger, system-threatening changes and qualifications that are sometimes required in a transformational setting...'[15] He concludes that genuine political transformation requires perspectives from the margins – those of the evicted, property-less, impoverished – to either complement or indeed replace the lexicon of traditional rights that are the focal point of much property doctrine. Van der Walt's understanding of what constitutes a view from the margins is not just about the experience and perspective of the disenfranchised; it is also about positioning oneself as a legal theorist on the margins of settled law, 'a place where one is precariously placed in such a way as to be constantly looking into the abyss of problems that cannot be solved by 'normal' legal science.'[16] This has particular salience in the settler colonial context, where indigenous concepts of ownership and use were submerged beneath a foreign, European legal system. 'Provincialising' European (Dutch and Roman to be more specific) legal concepts of property ownership in the context of indigenous and multiracial South Africa has immense potential for transforming existing relations of power. The idea of placing indigenous systems of law, forms of knowledge, and histories at the centre of one's legal analysis is consonant with many radical political traditions of thought in South Africa,[17] as well as critical indigenous theory emanating from struggles to decolonise other jurisdictions.[18] Arguing for a reversal of perspective in how we understand property law itself draws our attention to the faultline that exists between the worldview and experiences of those with property and those who have been systematically deprived of the security of ownership. Beginning then, as AJ van der Walt sought to do, 'on the margins' of settled law, we can pose the question whether actual transformative changes to property law can go any distance in dismantling

---

14 AJ van der Walt *Property in the margins* (2009).

15 AJ van der Walt *Property in the margins* (2009) 15.

16 AJ van der Walt *Property in the margins* (2009) 22.

17 See for example of the work of MB Ramose 'Philosophy and Africa's struggle for economic independence' (2006) 25 *Politeia* 3–17; 'In Memoriam: Sovereignty and the "new" South Africa' (2007) 16 *Griffith L Rev* 310–329; and see T Madlingozi 'On settler colonialism and post-conquest "constitutionness": The decolonising constitutional vision of African nationalists of Azania/South Africa' draft paper, on file with author.

18 See for example the work of I Watson *Aboriginal peoples, colonialism and international law: Raw law* (2015); G Coulthard *Red skin, white masks: Rejecting the colonial politics of recognition* (2015).

racial regimes of ownership. South Africa, a paradigmatic instance of a settler political order founded on a racial regime of ownership, witnessed radical changes to the law of property in the constitutional transition to democracy in the aftermath of apartheid. Did these legal changes rupture the juridical formation that bound forced evictions and displacement to the radical devaluing of black life? Van der Walt critically evaluated reforms to property law in relation to eviction, which played a massive role in the oppression of black South Africans during apartheid.

Did changes to property laws governing eviction, and their interpretation by South African courts, 'challenge the hegemony of the rights paradigm, or... [were they] simply accommodated within the rights paradigm as 'normal' regulatory restrictions on the exercise of rights?'[19] This is a crucial question, and not just in the South African context, as many of the much touted limitations on the perceived 'absolute right' of owners in non-transformative settings, where political stability is assumed (such as North America), often amount to nothing more than regulatory restrictions,[20] which, while not unimportant, are part of the law of property that ensures the smooth functioning of the *status quo*. Van der Walt focused on the potential for legislative changes to land law to alter the logic and orientation of the common law of eviction, which, with its strong emphasis on the rights of the owner, was ripe for abuse under apartheid's racial regime of ownership.

In the remainder of this chapter, I want to explore Van der Walt's engagement with the transformative potential of post-apartheid laws relating to eviction; setting the scene with a brief discussion of forced removals during the apartheid era and the impact that mass evictions had on black South Africans. The legislative changes relating to the rights of 'unlawful occupiers' (defined below) vis-à-vis privately or state-owned land 'represent a major shift, not only in approach but also in [the] terminology, language, metaphor and logic'

[19] AJ van der Walt *Property in the margins* (2009) 43. This question could also be posed to other anti-eviction movements, such as the *Plataforma de Afectados por la Hipoteca* (the PAH) in Spain, who have in some places halted evictions, taken over empty residential buildings to provide homes for the evicted, and started to negotiate with banks on how to formalise the rights of those in occupancy of residential buildings where they currently have no formal tenancy rights.

[20] Examples, enumerated by Blomley among others, include 'nuisance law (empowering the state to access private property in the interests of public aesthetics and hygiene, for example); the law of adverse possession (placing a time limit on the owners' right to exclude); the doctrine of public or private necessity (requiring an owner to allow others onto their property in moments of extreme need); the law of airplane over-flights... and the right to roam (allowing recreational access to certain wilderness areas)'. See N Blomley 'The territory of property' (2015) *Progress in Human Geography* 1–17 6.

of eviction law.[21] However, while the High Court in South Africa has rendered judgments that reflect a transformative change in accounting for the social, economic and personal needs of the unlawful occupier, Van der Walt notes that this does not mean that 'unlawful occupiers are now favoured above landowners and that landownership is undervalued or denied protection because of the history of apartheid'.[22]

2 Forced removals and eviction

Eviction law in the post-apartheid era can only be assessed if we take stock, however briefly, of the harm and injustices it attempts to remedy. The history of forced removals and evictions in South Africa is long and complex, incorporating varying modes of colonial and apartheid governance from the late nineteenth century onwards. Contrary to what some may think, the removal and eviction of black South Africans from their land and homes begins far before the rise of the Nationalist Party to power in 1948 and the explicit apartheid policies of racial segregation. Decades prior to the formation of the Union of South Africa both the Dutch and British colonial powers introduced legislation to spatially segregate the population based on race and indigeneity.[23] While the motivations behind the creation of the multitude of laws aimed at transforming the landscape of ownership and labour relations along racial and gendered lines differed according from the (sometimes conflicting) labour requirements of the agricultural and industrial sectors,[24] they also had much in common: the destruction of black ownership and tenure of agricultural land; the removal of black populations from urban areas; the prohibition of black ownership except on reserve lands (which, like reserves in Canada, amounted to a very small fraction of native territory); and consequently, the criminalisation of vast swathes of the indigenous population as 'illegal trespassers' throughout much of the territory of which they had been dispossessed. Millions of black Africans were forcibly displaced in South Africa during the twentieth century,[25] and the cost and legacies of this colonial and apartheid social engineering cannot easily be reckoned with.

Some of the techniques used in both the Dutch and British colonies to dispossess black South Africans are common to other settler-colonial

[21] AJ van der Walt *Property in the margins* (2009) 161.

[22] AJ van der Walt *Property in the margins* (2009) 159.

[23] L Platzky & C Walker *The surplus people project* (1985) 80–83.

[24] L Platzky & C Walker *The surplus people project* (1985) 83.

[25] G Marcus 'Section 5 of the Black Administration Act: The case of the Bakwena ba Mogopa' in C Murray & C O'Regan (eds) *No place to rest: Forced removals and the law in South Africa* (1990) 13–27 13.

jurisdictions. For instance, in the late nineteenth-century Dutch colonies of the Transvaal and the Orange Free State, Africans were not allowed to purchase land freely and very few held titles to their land. In the Transvaal, the black population 'could only acquire individual title to land under a complicated and restricting system of trusteeship – the land had to be held in trust for them, by the Commission for Native Affairs'.[26] In the South African colonies, as elsewhere, land title was used as a means to dispossess the indigenous population of their ownership. Another example can be drawn from the Glen Grey Act of 1894, which augmented the reserve policy begun earlier by Sir Grey in the Cape. This Act, developed by none other than Cecil Rhodes, imposed a limited form of self-government on the reserves in the Glen Grey district, and introduced individual land tenure in the form of small garden plots.[27] Rural black communities objected to the Act on the basis that communal tenure was understood as their primary means of access to the use and ownership of land. This Act marked the beginnings of the imposition of a colonial native governance structure within the reserve, and the prohibition of indigenous forms of land use. Furthermore, the Act's importance also lay in the fact that it provided the groundwork for the apartheid policies of segregation that would follow in the mid-twentieth century, which reflected the continued objective of creating cheap migrant labour forces for industry while maintaining exclusively white possession of urban spaces.

Specific legislation that was passed after the Union of South Africa came into being in 1910, which would have a profound effect on the formation of racial regimes of ownership in South Africa, included the *Native Land Act* of 1913, the *Native Administration Act* of 1927, and the *Development Trust and Land Act* of 1936. The *Native Land Act* of 1913 made reserves the only lawful place where black Africans could legally acquire land. Those black sharecroppers and tenant farmers who had been renting land from white owners were to 'be slowly phased out over time.'[28] The total amount of land allocated to reserves at that point in time was approximately 7%, and its occupants could not use the land to farm commercially, but could only grow food for subsistence purposes. Unsurveyed land and land held in freehold by black owners were both omitted from the official schedules that identified

---

[26] L Platzky & C Walker *The surplus people project* (1985) 74. This is not dissimilar to the use of land titling and systems of registration in other settler colonies, such as South Australia and British Columbia. See B Bhandar 'Title by registration: Instituting modern property law and creating racial value in the settler colony' (2015) 42(2) *JOLS* 253–282.

[27] L Platzky & C Walker *The surplus people project* (1985) 81.

[28] L Platzky & C Walker *The surplus people project* (1985) 83–84; C Bundy 'Land, law and power: Forced removals in historical context' in C Murray & C O'Regan (eds) *No place to rest: Forced removals and the law in South Africa* (1990) 3–13 6.

reserve land; the latter, termed 'black spots', would be dealt with through subsequent pieces of legislation that aimed to isolate the already small pockets of black land ownership to the point of unsustainability.

The *Native Administration Act* of 1927 (later renamed as the *Black Administration Act* 38 of 1927) provided for the forced removal of 'any tribe or portion thereof or any Native from any place to any other place within the Union' in the general public interest.[29] Where tribes objected to their removal, the order would require a resolution approving the removal by both Houses of Parliament. This particular section was repeatedly amended until the removal order did not even require prior notice to be given to those who were to be evicted.[30] The *Development Trust and Land Act* 1936 included an attempt to augment the total amount of reserve land to 13% of all the territory of South Africa, but even this nominal amount would not be realised for many decades to come.[31] Significantly, this Act made the state 'the registered owner of almost all of the reserves – title was not to be vested in the people who lived there, except in a few exceptional cases'.[32] The dispossession of black communities who had long-settled state land but whose rights were not recognised, and whose lands were not incorporated into existing reserves, led to the classification of black communities living on state land as illegal squatters, a designation that would have catastrophic effects on the ability of black communities to secure homes.[33]

The laws described above built the foundation for the racial segregation, disenfranchisement and dispossession of black South Africans that were the hallmarks of apartheid. The 1950s saw the continuation of mass forced removals under the auspices of the *Group Areas Act* of 1950, with the continued objective of depriving black communities of ownership and occupation rights. The *Prevention of Illegal Squatting Act* of 1951 was a primary means of controlling squatters in urban areas, and determining where and how they would live.[34] What is evident from the complex legal

---

[29] Section 5(1)(b) of the Native Administration Act 1927, as quoted in G Marcus 'Section 5 of the Black Administration Act: The case of the Bakwena ba Mogopa' in C Murray & C O'Regan (eds) *No place to rest: Forced removals and the law in South Africa* (1990) 18.

[30] G Marcus 'Section 5 of the Black Administration Act: The case of the Bakwena ba Mogopa' in C Murray & C O'Regan (eds) *No place to rest: Forced removals and the law in South Africa* (1990) 19.

[31] L Platzky & C Walker *The surplus people project* (1985) 92.

[32] L Platzky & C Walker *The surplus people project* (1985) 89.

[33] L Platzky & C Walker *The surplus people project* (1985) 90; AJ van der Walt 'Squatting and the right to shelter' 1992 *TSAR* 40–55.

[34] M Sutcliffe, A Todes & N Walker 'State urbanisation strategies since 1986' in C Murray & C O'Regan (eds) *No place to rest: Forced removals and the law in South Africa* (1990) 86–106 98.

framework constructed over centuries of colonial and then apartheid rule, is that while the architecture of the regime of forced removals and eviction was thoroughly legal in nature, backed by the force of police power and militarised violence, its effects on the social fabric of South Africa were wide-ranging and profound, transcending the domain of the law and its effects. While law was a central mode of structuring and realising the radical engineering of ownership and racial dispossession in South Africa, the legal imaginary, in this case as in others, remains too constrained in its conceptualisation of justice and political-social transformation to go beyond a meaningful if basic balancing of interests.

3 Eviction and post-apartheid legal transformation

Eviction, as opposed to removal, takes us squarely into the juridical realm of ownership and property relations. Eviction is incidental to the ownership right, the logical corollary of the right to exclude others from your property, and the right to possess your property exclusively. As such, the right to evict is engaged 'whenever someone else occupies the property against the owner's will or without her permission'.[35] With an ownership model constructed according to a hierarchy of rights, with private ownership occupying its apex, the right to evict, as Van der Walt observes, remains relatively undisturbed by 'even quite dramatic restrictions imposed by legislative regulation of the landlord-tenant relationship.' He also argues that 'the landowner's right to evict is seldom curtailed purely with reference to the general socio-economic context or the personal or economic circumstances of the tenant. It can therefore be said that eviction is still largely based on the hierarchical power of the landowner's superior right to possession, even when that right has been restricted quite severely for public policy considerations related to the regulation of the rental housing market.'[36]

A distinction is made between lawful and unlawful occupiers, the former being those tenants who had a legal right to reside in a property, but whose tenure has come to an end for one reason or another (end of lease, cancellation of tenancy, breach of contractual term, etc). An unlawful occupier, which I will focus on below, is that person (or community) who never had a legally recognised right to reside in or occupy property owned privately by an individual or owned by the state. I focus on the position of the unlawful occupier, because in South Africa, as in many other settler colonial sites, rendering indigenous and racialised populations as 'illegal' or unlawful, often on the basis of their ways of living or relating to land, has been used

35 AJ van der Walt *Property in the margins* (2009) 54.

36 AJ van der Walt *Property in the margins* (2009) 56.

as a primary means of dispossession. Unlawful occupiers are defined by van der Walt as 'persons who occupy land without any legally recognised right, permission or licence'; a definition which, as the forced removals of black communities under apartheid amply demonstrated, 'is very much a matter of political choice'.[37]

In response to the wide-scale forced removals and evictions under apartheid, legislation was passed for the express purpose of protecting the rights of unlawful occupiers.[38] Specifically, the Prevention of Illegal Eviction from and Unlawful Occupation of Land Act 19 of 1998 (PIE) was enacted to give effect to the constitutionally enshrined right to not be evicted from one's home or to be subject to house demolition without a court order.[39] PIE was enacted to prohibit unlawful evictions and to repeal a key piece of apartheid legislation, the *Prevention of Illegal Squatting Act*, Act 52 of 1951 (PISA), and several other related legislative amendments and Acts. In the judgment of *Port Elizabeth Municipality v Various Occupiers* 2005 (1) SA 217 (CC), Justice Sachs gives a compelling interpretation of PIE. Justice Sachs also sums up succinctly the effects of PISA on black communities:

> PISA was an integral part of a cluster of statutes that gave a legal/administrative imprimatur to the usurpation and forced removal of black people from land and compelled them to live in racially designated locations. For all black people, and for Africans in particular, dispossession was nine-tenths of the law. Residential segregation was the cornerstone of the apartheid policy. This policy was aimed at creating separate 'countries' for Africans within South Africa. Africans were precluded from owning and occupying land outside the areas reserved for them by these statutes. The Native Urban Areas Consolidation Act 25 of 1945 was premised on the notion of Africans living in rural reserves and coming to the towns only as migrant workers on temporary sojourn. Through a combination of spatial apartheid, permit systems and the creation of criminal offences the Act strictly controlled the limited rights that Africans had to reside in urban areas. People living outside of what were defined as native locations were regarded as squatters and, under PISA, were expelled from the land on which they lived.[40]

---

[37] AJ van der Walt *Property in the margins* (2009) 74.

[38] Van der Walt puts the constitutional and legislative changes in South Africa into a comparative perspective with the political squatting movements of the 1970s and 1980s in the Netherlands, Germany, and England, and also makes brief reference to the civil rights activism in the US, in order to evaluate some of the political successes gained in housing and tenancy laws in the Netherlands and Germany, and the end of legalised racial segregation in the US: AJ van der Walt *Property in the margins* (2009) 146.

[39] Section 26(3) of the Constitution of the Republic of South Africa, 1996; see Van der Walt *Property in the margins* (2009) 147.

[40] *Port Elizabeth Municipality v Various Occupiers* 2005 (1) SA 217 (CC) para 9.

Briefly, the facts of the case involved 9 families (about 68 people, including 23 children) who faced eviction at the hands of the Municipality of Port Elizabeth, located in the Eastern Cape province. The occupiers had settled on undeveloped, privately-owned land after they had been evicted from a different place. They made it clear that they were willing to leave the land if given reasonable notice and provided with a suitable alternative upon which to construct their dwellings.[41] They had rejected the offer of being moved to a township by the name of Walmer on the basis that it was 'crime-ridden and unsavoury' and that moreover, they would not enjoy any sort of security of tenure there, rendering them vulnerable to further eviction.[42]

The municipality alleged that the occupiers would be 'queue-jumping' if they were granted alternative accommodation after illegally occupying private land, as they would be disrupting the municipality's housing programme and 'forcing the municipality to grant them preferential treatment'.[43] Ultimately, the Constitutional Court found in favour of the occupiers; they held that neither the municipality nor the owners of the land needed to evict the occupiers and that it would not be 'just and equitable' in all of the circumstances to evict this group of occupiers.[44]

The court reached this decision by considering PIE and section 25 of the Constitution, the constitutional property guarantee, as part of a 'constitutional matrix' that does not simply seek to restore common-law property rights in the absence of explicitly racist statutes, but seeks actively to restore 'secure property rights for those denied access to or deprived of them in the past'.[45] The court interpreted section 25 in light of societal considerations and also the economic, social and personal conditions of those facing eviction. Combined with the constitutional protection for the right to adequate housing (found in section 26 of the Constitution), the public and social nature of property rights was given new meaning. As Justice Sachs noted, 'the Constitution imposes new obligations on the courts concerning rights relating to property not previously recognised by the common law. It counterposes to the normal ownership rights of possession, use and occupation, a new and equally relevant right not arbitrarily to be deprived of a home.'[46]

The court upsets the common-law paradigm of ownership in which an owner's right to evict is typically paramount where a person is in unlawful

[41] *Port Elizabeth Municipality v Various Occupiers* 2005 (1) SA 217 (CC) para 2.

[42] *Port Elizabeth Municipality v Various Occupiers* 2005 (1) SA 217 (CC) para 2.

[43] *Port Elizabeth Municipality v Various Occupiers* 2005 (1) SA 217 (CC) para 3.

[44] *Port Elizabeth Municipality v Various Occupiers* 2005 (1) SA 217 (CC) para 59.

[45] *Port Elizabeth Municipality v Various Occupiers* 2005 (1) SA 217 (CC) para 15.

[46] *Port Elizabeth Municipality v Various Occupiers* 2005 (1) SA 217 (CC) para 23.

occupation of the owner's property. Bringing to bear 'substantive justice and equality considerations'[47] on the adjudication of a contest between property and housing rights, Van der Walt argues that the significance of this judgment (and others that followed) is the explicit acknowledgment of the political nature of property relations.[48] The interpretation of PIE and sections 25 and 26 of the Constitution in light of the legacies of apartheid significantly altered the ownership paradigm; 'through land reform, eviction law has become sensitive to social, economic and political marginality, weakness and vulnerability'. However, as Van der Walt goes on to note, 'the rights paradigm still exercises a stabilising effect that can inhibit reforms of the property regime'.[49]

While dramatic constitutional reforms in post-apartheid South Africa certainly provide recognition of the importance of shelter and housing, and protection for some of the most vulnerable communities, it remains situated within a legal framework that seeks to find a balance between the rights of private property owners and illegal occupiers. In other words, even these highly progressive legal reforms did not, and perhaps could not, create conditions in which the right to housing, the right to shelter, is paramount when in conflict with the rights of a property owner. Does the recognition of the right to not be arbitrarily deprived of one's home subvert the regime of ownership and dispossession that took hold from the late nineteenth century onwards? Does this legal recognition and the potential protection it affords disrupt the economic and political legacies of two different colonial powers, who constructed a legal regime based on private property ownership and white possessive nationalism?[50] Does the focus on substantive equality unravel the legal subjectivities of the settler and native, owner, tenant, squatter and landless, that were thoroughly saturated with normative, symbolic and cultural ideals of civilisational and racial superiority and inferiority?

Here, yet another faultline emerges, between the social value derived from specific types of use of property, and the economic (exchange) value attached to property within a capitalist market. AJ van der Walt acknowledged the existing capacity of post-apartheid courts to protect the rights of the vulnerable communities; and it is clear that deep structural change which would bring about social and racial justice requires a fundamental re-think

47 AJ van der Walt *Property in the margins* (2009) 158.

48 AJ van der Walt *Property in the margins* (2009) 158-159.

49 AJ van der Walt *Property in the margins* (2009) 161.

50 On the figure of the 'white possessive', see A Moreton-Robinson *The white possessive: Property, power and indigenous sovereignty* (2015).

of a property paradigm that ultimately and all too often privileges ownership over use. There is an urgent need to grasp other ways of relating to land, for those obscured and repressed through the imposition of the cadastral survey and imperial modes of mapping, through systems of title registration, through the rendering of entire communities as illegal squatters based on their ways of living; ways of relating to land that are not premised on the exploitation of its resources and the often-unbridled destruction of the environment for corporate profit. Indigenous scholars and activists have explained how indigenous ontologies incorporate an embodied and conceptual relationship to the land, animals and plants[51] that reflects ways of being quite alien to capitalist, commoditised visions of land.

4 Concluding thoughts: Property on the margins

Contemporary struggles over property in urban areas and rural land often revolve around the concept of use. If people can use empty residential buildings for shelter, particularly when there are severe housing shortages in many major cities, it is arguable that their interests in property ought to prevail over that of a genuinely absentee owner (ie not an owner who is absent due to war, colonial occupation, or being otherwise exiled). Various housing activists base their struggle for social housing on the idea that the social uses of property (residential housing stock in particular) should have greater weight in defining property interests than its function as an instrument of financial investment and expropriation. In the face of a massive number of foreclosures and evictions in Spain in the aftermath of the 2008 financial crisis, for instance, the *Plataformas Afectados por la Hipoteca* (*PAH*) has sought to reinvigorate the provisions in the Spanish Constitution that explicitly protect the right to housing,[52] and to challenge the primacy of the ideology of ownership itself. It is this latter political challenge that has the potential to redefine what security means, and for whom. Security of one's

---

[51] L Simpson 'Land as pedagogy: Nishnaabeg intelligence and rebellious transformation' (2014) 3(3) *Decolonisation: Indigeneity, education & society*, available online at http://decolonization.org/index.php/des/article/view/22170.

[52] One aspect of the PAH's political campaign is to reassert the right to housing that is enshrined in art 47 of the Spanish Constitution. Article 47 provides that 'all Spaniards have the right to enjoy decent and adequate housing…' The article places a positive duty on the government to make this right effective and to 'prevent speculation'. Article 33 is also of relevance, which stipulates that private property must be limited by the social function of property. Despite these constitutional guarantees, mortgage laws, the deregulation of credit and lending, and the unrestrained bolstering of real estate development at any cost hollowed out the substance of art 47. See A Colau & A Alemany *Mortgaged Lives* (2014) 38–44.

right to a viable home and life, not of one's property as an asset. Ownership not defined on the basis of possession or formal registered interests, but rooted in types of use that are fundamentally relational.

Could placing the interests and perspectives of the marginalised at the centre of legal analysis transform the ownership paradigm itself? Could privileging the social uses of property over the rights of owners, effectively redistribute the security and social power usually attached to ownership? If the right to housing and shelter were rendered paramount, rather than placed in opposition to the rights of the private owner, how would this alter the value of private property ownership and the ideology of possessive individualism? Could using things in a way that is disaffiliated from the typical hallmarks of individual possession (exclusivity, the right to sell, rent, etc) *alienate* property ownership from its current form so much as to make it unrecognisable as a property right?

In a reflection of the expansive and complex nature of the life worlds of property that AJ van der Walt sought to analyse and to envision differently, he relied on and drew from a vast and varied number of resources, contexts, histories, and source materials. It is fitting, then, in reflecting on what it means to place property on the margins, and to 'reconsider the language, the concepts, the rhetoric and the logic in terms of which we explain' the property paradigm, to resort to a literary critic's observations of how new meaning can be given to concepts and practices that are so naturalised as to be taken for granted. In writing about the literary device of *estrangement,* evident in the work of Tolstoi among others, Russian literary theorist Viktor Shklovsky illuminates how artists effectively move beyond the mere recognition of a thing, to creating a new perspective and understanding, a new vision as it were, of the object. By creating an image in which the object is *estranged* from the usual way of perceiving it, we are able to 'perceive the object in a special way'.[53] This new vision of the object presents a radical opportunity for reconceptualising a thing, an object, a practice, a relation, a custom, that we are otherwise so habituated to that we can do little more than acknowledge its presence in our field of perception.

Estrangement, as a literary device, seems to require, in the first instance, not calling the thing by its name. Tolstoi, writes Shklovsky, 'does not call a thing by its name, that is, he describes it as if it were perceived for the first time, while an incident is described as if it were happening for the first time.'[54] It is significant that one of the primary examples Shklovsky draws from the work of Tolstoi is the estrangement of the institution of property.

[53] V Shklovsky *Theory of Prose* (2015) 10.

[54] V Shklovsky *Theory of Prose* (2015) 6.

The power of property is rendered visible through the observations of the owned, not the owner (in this case, a horse). He takes note of the strange and seemingly arbitrary, if tacit, agreement among people to exclude all others from using the word 'mine' in relation to something they have already laid claim to, and the absurd power of the word 'mine' that trumps the real, daily lived practices of using that thing claimed as belonging to another. The animal sums up its observations about what distinguishes horses from humans on the basis that 'the human species is guided, above all, by *words,* while ours is guided by *deeds*'.[55]

Perhaps another way of understanding what it means to put the perspectives of those on the margins at the centre of our understanding of property's violence, and indeed, of situating ourselves on the margins of legal analysis, is to *estrange* and *alienate* the meaning of property from its form as we currently know it. It seems one way to begin this process of estrangement is to replace the static and abstract lexicon of ownership with a vision, an image, a sense of how land and the built environment can provide shelter and homes, places for survival and subsistence, and spaces for free movement. This strategy of estrangement requires bold and imaginative thought and action, certainly a challenge inspired by AJ van der Walt's far-reaching *oeuvre* and legacy.

[55] V Shklovsky *Theory of Prose* (2015) 7.

Chapter 18

Regulation at the edge of the property concept: Judicial treatment of intangible interests

Mikhalien du Bois & Richard M Shay***

Page

Contents

1 Introduction: Police power regulation of intangible property

Intellectual property law scholars' research often deals with categories of intangible property that are ubiquitously recognised by private law and exclusively regulated by statute, such as patents, copyright, trade marks and designs, which constitute the least controversial kind of intangible property, intellectual property. The rights granted over these property objects are established in accordance with a comprehensive and exhaustive statutory regime based on independent but interrelated principles and objectives, and confer property rights over specified legal objects in accordance with the respective statutory regimes. However, there are instances of sincere disagreement about the legal objects at the centre of a dispute and whether these objects are protected as property for constitutional purposes.[1] Such

* Associate Professor, Department of Mercantile Law, University of South Africa.
** Senior Lecturer, Department of Mercantile Law, University of South Africa.
[1] In terms of s 25 of the Constitution of the Republic of South Africa, 1996 (the Constitution).

disputes are further complicated when the alleged intellectual property interest vests in accordance with common law instead of legislation, like trade secrets and unregistered trade marks. Further, in comparison with these relatively clearly defined interests, there has been a notable increase in disputes arising before our courts that involve even more peripheral property interests. We shall investigate the judicial treatment of these forms of property that are located at the edge of the property concept.

André van der Walt's 1999 paper 'Police-power regulation of intangible property and the constitutional property clause'[2] forms the basis for the sections dealing with intangible property in his book *Constitutional property clauses*.[3] It also forms the starting point for the legal scholarship around intangible property law (and intellectual property law in particular) and its treatment under the constitutional property clause. This paper and the principles identified there warrant a revisit to acknowledge André's contribution to intangible property law scholarship in the constitutional realm.

André's paper considers a number of these intangible property interests by reference to a wealth of foreign cases and provides useful guidelines for the treatment of these interests in constitutional property cases. He refers only to intangible property with some form of commercial interest or value, such as business enterprises in general; the goodwill of a business concern; shares in a company; debts; a business interest in a commercial licence, permit or quota; and intellectual property interests in the conventional sense, as well as commercial information protected as trade secrets. His paper only addresses regulation of the use, enjoyment and exploitation of commercial enterprises and property interests that are aimed at the promotion of the public interest, and only those instances that practically destroy the property rights at issue. Naturally this prompts questions about the limitation's nature and validity; in other words, whether it is a regulation or an expropriation, and whether the limitation's effects are so harsh that it may be deemed constitutionally invalid:

> The main reasons for selecting a topic defined by these rather narrow criteria [of intangible property having commercial value that is practically destroyed by

[2] AJ van der Walt 'Police-power regulation of intangible property and the constitutional property clause: A comparative analysis of case law' in P Jackson & DC Wilde (eds) *Property law: Current issues and debates* (1999) 208–280. In the context of constitutional law, the police power principle refers to the state's competence 'to regulate the use and enjoyment of property to protect public health and safety': AJ van der Walt *Constitutional property law* 3 ed (2011) 195.

[3] AJ van der Walt *Constitutional property clauses: A comparative analysis* (1998).

> state regulation] are that it epitomises some of the most intriguing difficulties that confront a student of constitutional property law, and that the case law on this topic is so interesting and confusing that it deserves special attention anyway.[4]
>
> The purpose of this paper is to suggest an avenue for avoiding at least some of the confusions in this field, by introducing a number of distinctions that highlight the dangers of using decisions in one area as authority for cases in another.[5]

Our contribution seeks to revisit André's thesis that the topic of intangible property interests with commercial value being destroyed by the state's exercise of its police power is both interesting and confusing by canvassing case law from the intervening two decades. Our analysis confirms that André's careful, nuanced treatment of diverse intangible property interests was well justified, as successive Constitutional Court judgments have shown exactly how difficult and confusing these cases can be.

When considering the proprietary status of a right, the requirement is usually that the property interest should be established and vested according to the applicable statutory prescriptions before it may be recognised and protected under the constitutional property clause.[6] The general rule is that an intellectual property right will be recognised and protected under the property clause provided these requirements are met and a property right has vested.[7] This rule is derived from the case law of foreign jurisdictions and distilled by André to apply to the South African context,[8] and it provides

[4] AJ van der Walt 'Police-power regulation of intangible property and the constitutional property clause: A comparative analysis of case law' in P Jackson & DC Wilde (eds) *Property law: Current issues and debates* (1999) 208–280 210.

[5] AJ van der Walt 'Police-power regulation of intangible property and the constitutional property clause: A comparative analysis of case law' in P Jackson & DC Wilde (eds) *Property law: Current issues and debates* (1999) 208–280 208.

[6] AJ van der Walt 'Police-power regulation of intangible property and the constitutional property clause: A comparative analysis of case law' in P Jackson & DC Wilde (eds) *Property law: Current issues and debates* (1999) 208–280 253.

[7] Property rights vest automatically once a copyright work meets various requirements in terms of the Copyright Act 98 of 1978 and upon registration of trade marks, patents and designs (regulated by the Trade Marks Act 194 of 1993, the Patents Act 59 of 1978 and the Designs Act 195 of 1993 respectively).

[8] AJ van der Walt *Constitutional property law* 3 ed (2011) 143–150. See AJ van der Walt 'Police-power regulation of intangible property and the constitutional property clause: A comparative analysis of case law' in P Jackson & DC Wilde (eds) *Property law: Current issues and debates* (1999) 208–280 fn 170: 'German case law offers a useful series of decisions that concern all the major immaterial property rights. Compare *BVerfGE 31, 229* [1971] (copyright and confidential information); *BVerfGE 36, 281* [1974] (patents); *BVerfGE 51, 193* [1979] (trade marks).' See also *In Re: Certification of the Constitution of the Republic of South Africa, 1996* 1996 (4) SA 744 (CC) para 75, where the Constitutional Court decided that s 25 can protect intellectual property rights. See further T Roux & D Davis 'Property' in

an invaluable starting point for intellectual property scholars venturing into the field of constitutional property law.[9]

Similarly, the more controversial categories of commercial interests (for example, state-issued licences, debts and common-law claims) receive private law protection via legislation or common law, but not always as property. They share the kind of characteristics with property and intellectual property that render constitutional protection against arbitrary regulation necessary, but these interests should not necessarily be treated similarly in constitutional law.[10]

> [U]nless the characteristics and unique features of different cases in the field of regulation of intangible property are distinguished and accounted for quite carefully, decisions and the reasoning behind them will suffer from unnecessary inconsistency and lack of clarity. This means not only that injustice is done to the individual rights in question, but also that there is insufficient attention for the social, economic and political importance and implications of control and regulation of (intangible) property rights.[11]

2 Intellectual property

On the regulation of immaterial property rights (more commonly referred to as intellectual property rights), the paper states:

> [R]egulatory regimes that impose (or introduce new) police power limitations on the use and exercise of immaterial property rights may and often will cause losses (complete loss of the right or loss in value) for the property holder without thereby necessarily being invalid or attracting compensation claims. The rule seems to be that all property rights are subject to the potentially detrimental effect of police

---

H Cheadle, D Davis & N Haysom (eds) *South African constitutional law: The Bill of Rights* 2 ed (2008) 20–1/20–28 20–17; AJ van der Walt *Constitutional property law* 3 ed (2011) 124–126, 145. However, compare *Lebowa Mineral Trust Beneficiaries Forum v President of the Republic of South Africa and Others* 2002 (1) BCLR 23 (T) 29G–H and criticism of the court's approach: AJ van der Walt 'Resisting orthodoxy – again: Thoughts on the development of post-apartheid South African law' (2002) 17 *SAPL* 258–279 260–265. See further OH Dean 'The case for the recognition of intellectual property in the Bill of Rights' (1997) 60 *THRHR* 105–119 106, 110.

9 M du Bois 'Intellectual property as a constitutional property right: The South African approach' (2012) 24 *SA Merc LJ* 177–193; OH Dean 'Deprivation of trade marks through State interference in their usage' (2013) 35 *EIPR* 576–589; AJ van der Walt & RM Shay 'Constitutional analysis of intellectual property' (2014) 17 *PELJ* 51–85; S Zietsman 'Expropriation or deprivation: The effect of proposed tobacco plain packaging legislation in South Africa on intellectual property rights (2016) 4 *IPLJ* 47–63.

10 AJ van der Walt *Constitutional property law* 3 ed (2011) 151.

11 AJ van der Walt 'Police-power regulation of intangible property and the constitutional property clause: A comparative analysis of case law' in P Jackson & DC Wilde (eds) *Property law: Current issues and debates* (1999) 208–280 216.

power regulation, but property created by or protected in terms of a statutory regime (including immaterial property) may be even more susceptible to these effects than other property rights.'[12]

Intellectual property's susceptibility to regulation can be seen in Australian law, where the High Court of Australia found plain packaging regulations that restricted the permissible branding on tobacco products (implemented to promote health) constitutionally valid despite its harsh effect on the use and exploitation of trade marks (accepted as 'property' for purposes of the constitutional guarantee, section 51(xxxi) of the Australian Commonwealth Constitution, 1900).[13]

In South African law, *Laugh It Off v South African Breweries*[14] (*Laugh It Off*) was the first dispute dealing with intellectual property (trade mark rights) to reach the Constitutional Court; however, there was no regulatory change (such as an amendment to the prevailing statutory regime) at the centre of the dispute. The Supreme Court of Appeal judgment in *Laugh It Off* gave explicit property recognition to trade mark rights, but confirmed that

[12] AJ van der Walt 'Police-power regulation of intangible property and the constitutional property clause: A comparative analysis of case law' in P Jackson & DC Wilde (eds) *Property law: Current issues and debates* (1999) 208–280 256–257.

[13] See *JT International SA v Commonwealth of Australia; British American Tobacco Australasia Limited & Ors v The Commonwealth of Australia* [2012] HCA 43 on the constitutionality of the Australian Tobacco Plain Packaging Act 148 of 2011 and comments on the decision: LTC Harms 'Plain packaging and its impact on trademark law' (2013) 46 *De Jure* 387–400; OH Dean 'Deprivation of trade marks through State interference in their usage' (2013) 35 *EIPR* 576–589; M du Bois 'Trade marks for tobacco products as constitutional property: Australian plain packaging legislation' (2013) 25 *SA Merc LJ* 197–222; S Zietsman 'Expropriation or deprivation: The effect of proposed tobacco plain packaging legislation in South Africa on intellectual property rights (2016) 4 *IPLJ* 47–63. In South Africa, there are also plain packaging regulations restricting trade mark rights in respect of infant formula milk, ostensibly in the interest of promoting the rights to health and life: see the Regulations published in GN 991 *GG* 35941 under the Foodstuffs, Cosmetics and Disinfectants Act 54 of 1972, which intend to promote breastfeeding, which is thought to decrease infant mortality rates. This regulation might attract a constitutional property challenge. See further L Mills 'The regulations relating to foodstuffs for infants and young children (R 991): A formula for the promotion of breastfeeding or censorship of commercial speech?' (2017) 17 *PELJ* 252–295.

[14] *Laugh it Off Promotions CC v South African Breweries International (Finance) BV t/a Sabmark International (Freedom of Expression Institute as Amicus Curiae)* 2006 (1) SA 144 (CC).

intellectual property rights are not immune to constitutional challenge.[15] On appeal to the Constitutional Court, the majority agreed with the Supreme Court of Appeal that 'like other property intellectual property does not enjoy special status under the Constitution' that privileges it against competing values.[16] The right to freedom of expression[17] was weighed up against a trade mark right (and the constitutional right not to be arbitrarily deprived of property, implicitly);[18] it was sufficient to balance the respective rights to find that there was no conflict between the rights, rendering inapplicable the constitutional property methodology propounded in *First National Bank of SA v Commissioner, South African Revenue Service*[19] (*FNB*). This recognises intellectual property as property for purposes of the constitutional property clause and confirms that it may also be regulated or otherwise limited by other constitutional rights, 'like other property'.

Moseneke J's majority decision stated that section 34(1)(c) of the Trade Marks Act 194 of 1993 'must be construed in the light of the Constitution and applied in a manner that does not unduly trample upon freedom of expression', which necessitated the weighing up of the unauthorised user's constitutional safeguard of free expression (exercised in the form of parody) against the trade mark owner's right to intellectual property and freedoms of trade, occupation or profession.[20] This decision viewed the value attaching to the goodwill generated by the trade mark as the commercial interests (property) affected by the expression making use of the trade mark in a detrimental way;[21] what Sachs J called 'marketability' in his concurring minority decision.[22] Instead of deciding whether section 34(1)(c) constituted

---

[15] '[I]n spite of some judicial resistance in certain quarters, trademarks are property, albeit intangible or incorporeal. The fact that property is intangible does not make it of a lower order. Our law has always recognised incorporeals as a class of things in spite of theoretical objections thereto': *Laugh it Off Promotions CC v South African Breweries International (Finance) BV t/a/ Sabmark International* 2005 (2) SA 46 (SCA) paras 10–11 per Harms JA, citing *Ladbroke (Football) Ltd v William Hill (Football) Ltd* [1964] 1 WLR 273 (HL) 291; *MV Snow Delta: Serva Ship Ltd v Discount Tonnage Ltd* 2000 (4) SA 746 (SCA) para 9.

[16] *Laugh it Off Promotions CC v South African Breweries International (Finance) BV t/a Sabmark International (Freedom of Expression Institute as Amicus Curiae)* 2006 (1) SA 144 (CC) para 17 per Moseneke J.

[17] Section 16 of the Constitution.

[18] Section 25 of the Constitution.

[19] 2002 (4) SA 768 (CC).

[20] Paragraph 18 per Moseneke J.

[21] Paragraphs 37–41 per Moseneke J.

[22] Paragraph 102 per Sachs J. While the trade mark owner is not required to prove actual losses, it has to adduce evidence to prove the likelihood of economic prejudice, and cannot make bald assertions when the effect is to stifle otherwise permissible expression.

an unconstitutional limitation on freedom of expression, the decision opted to construe the provision in such a fashion that did not limit freedom of expression (unduly):[23] 'In an open democracy valuable expressive acts in public ought not to be lightly trampled upon by *marginal detriment* or *harm unrelated to the commercial value* that vests in the mark itself.'[24] (emphasis added)

While the Constitutional Court in *Laugh It Off* did not explicitly state that trade mark rights are property, Sachs J's concurring minority judgment held that the right to freedom of expression and the competing property right of the trade mark owner must be balanced proportionately in a context-specific and fact-sensitive way, and that it is not an issue of the limitation of a right, but rather giving each its proper scope. It must be viewed from the vantage point of 'an independent observer who is sensitive to both the free speech values of the Constitution and the *property protection objectives of trademark law* [emphasis added]' to determine whether 'the harm done by the parody to the property interests of the trademark owner outweighs the free speech interests involved'.[25]

In *Phumelela Gaming and Leisure (Ltd) v Gründlingh and Others*[26] (*Phumelela*), the court briefly considered the status of goodwill as property for constitutional purposes of the section 25(1) guarantee in a challenge to the constitutionality of certain provisions in the National Gambling Act 7 of 2004, according to which licences may be conferred by a state authority on proprietors of bookmaking businesses. The applicant in the court a quo operated a 'totaliser' scheme in relation to horse races and sought to prevent various bookmakers from taking 'exotic bets', which, it alleged, were not fixed-odds bets (as bookmakers, opposed to totalisers, were accustomed to devising), meaning that the respondents were not licensed to engage in this commercial activity in terms of the National Gambling Act. The applicant averred that the respondents had engaged in unlawful competition, which constituted a delict against it and an infringement of its property rights.

[23] Paragraph 48 per Moseneke J.

[24] Paragraph 56 per Moseneke J.

[25] Paragraphs 82 and 83. Incidentally, this case provides support for an argument that André developed towards the end of his research career, namely that as a normative and an empirical matter, property seems to occupy a 'systemically modest status' in relation to other constitutional rights, and that conflicts between property rights and competing constitutional rights tend to be resolved with the protection of the non–property right as the priority, leaving property to be protected 'in whatever space remains after the primary objective has been secured', in this case, the full and proper protection of freedom of expression: AJ van der Walt 'The modest systemic status of property rights' (2014) 1 *J L Prop & Soc'y* 15–106.

[26] 2007 (6) SA 350 (CC).

The Supreme Court of Appeal accepted that a particular business model could be protected as property, stating that the applicant had 'developed a business system of such reliability and sophistication that it has earned the trust of the betting public, a trust that is manifested by a readiness to do business with [the respondent]. The resulting income potential is part of its goodwill and as such a valuable asset.'[27] However, the Supreme Court of Appeal found that the respondents' actions were not unlawful, as they were compatible with the gambling community's business ethics and the public *boni mores* as indicated in the history of legislative development and contemporaneous gambling practices.[28] On appeal to the Constitutional Court, the applicant (Phumelela) argued that the Supreme Court of Appeal had failed to develop the common law of unlawful competition in line with section 39(2) of the Constitution[29] and that this interpretation of the common law caused a deprivation of its constitutional property, in breach of section 25(1), as it resulted in the unlawful appropriation of its intellectual property. Langa CJ, in his unanimous decision, refrained from considering the spirit, purport and objects of the Bill of Rights narrowly in relation only to section 25, and instead framed the challenge as a conflict between the appellant's constitutional property rights and the opposing section 22 right to freedom of trade.[30] In weighing up the competing interests, the court held that the latter right was 'consistent with a competitive regime in matters of trade and the recognition of the protection of competition as being in the public welfare';[31] indeed, '[t]he consequence of the right to freedom of trade is competition'.[32]

Although never explicitly stated, the Constitutional Court seemed to accept Phumelela's goodwill (as a species of intellectual property) as property for

[27] *Gründlingh and Others v Phumelela Gaming and Leisure (Ltd)* 2005 (6) SA 502 (SCA) para 33 (majority judgment of Farlam and Conradie JJA para 33, agreeing on this issue with the minority decision of Comrie AJA). The constitutional property issue was first aired in the Constitutional Court and was not raised in the court a quo or the SCA, but the CC agreed with the reasoning and conclusion of the SCA.

[28] This finding was upheld by the Constitutional Court: *Phumelela Gaming and Leisure (Ltd) v Gründlingh and Others* 2007 (6) SA 350 (CC) para 39.

[29] Section 39 of the Constitution states: 'When interpreting any legislation, and when developing the common law or customary law, every court, tribunal or forum must promote the spirit, purport and objects of the Bill of Rights.'

[30] *Phumelela Gaming and Leisure (Ltd) v Gründlingh and Others* 2007 (6) SA 350 (CC) para 35. Section 22 of the Constitution states: 'Every citizen has the right to choose their trade, occupation or profession freely. The practice of a trade, occupation or profession may be regulated by law.'

[31] Paragraph 36.

[32] Paragraph 33.

purposes of section 25,[33] but it did not undertake an analysis in line with the section 25 methodology devised in *FNB*, preferring a balancing of the two provisions to resolve the averred conflict.[34] After concluding that the Supreme Court of Appeal had taken proper account of the spirit, purport and objects of the Bill of Rights – which include both the competition principle as espoused in section 22 and the constitutional property clause, which, it stressed, does not provide absolute protection to property owners 'in a manner that ignores other rights and values'[35] – the court found that the Supreme Court of Appeal's development of the common law of unlawful competition (particularly the competition principle, as determined by the community's legal convictions) did not constitute an arbitrary deprivation of property in terms of section 25(1).[36]

It may seem that André's scholarship has been overlooked in the only cases involving intellectual property interests to reach the Constitutional Court, but this can be explained by the approach taken by the court in both cases. The issues were not framed as section 25(1) disputes because neither case concerned a regulatory amendment to legislation that constituted a deprivation of property rights; rather, two competing constitutional rights were set against each other in an exercise of interpretation and balancing, finding the proper scope of each and weight to assign to each. Hence it was appropriate for the court not to embark on the section 25(1) analysis and not to consult constitutional property law scholarship.

---

[33] Subsequently in *Law Society of South Africa and Others v Minister for Transport and Another* 2011 (1) SA 400 (CC) para 81, the Constitutional Court described the decision in *Phumelela* as '[accepting] that loss of goodwill is protected as property by section 25 of the Constitution'. See also IM Rautenbach 'Overview of the Constitutional Court decisions on the Bill of Rights – 2006' 2007 *TSAR* 391–409 402; AJ van der Walt *Constitutional property law* 3 ed (2011) 154–155; AJ van der Walt 'Constitutional property law' 2012 *ASSAL* 182–199 184.

[34] This is consistent with the approach taken by the Constitutional Court in *Laugh it Off Promotions CC v South African Breweries International (Finance) BV t/a Sabmark International (Freedom of Expression Institute as Amicus Curiae)* 2006 (1) SA 144 (CC), where the court employed a simple balancing exercise in terms of s 36, and found it unnecessary to invoke the s 25 methodology laid out in *FNB*.

[35] *Phumelela Gaming and Leisure (Ltd) v Gründlingh and Others* 2007 (6) SA 350 (CC) para 38.

[36] Paragraph 42. AJ van der Walt 'Police-power regulation of intangible property and the constitutional property clause: A comparative analysis of case law' in P Jackson & DC Wilde (eds) *Property law: Current issues and debates* (1999) 208–280 fn 112 discusses the Northern Irish case of *Ulster Transport Authority v James Brown & Sons, Ltd* (1) [1953] NI 79 (CA), which concerned taxi operators. The property in question entailed business goodwill, and the regulation in question took over part of a business. Such a deprivation can render a regulation unconstitutional for not providing compensation.

3 Debts and claims

Most jurisdictions recognise debts and claims that sound in money as constitutional property.[37] On state debts,[38] André argues that acquisition cannot be characterised simply by reference to that which one party loses and another acquires;[39] it requires a wider interpretation than that used for tangible property. With the cancellation of a state debt, the state acquires the savings by not having to satisfy the debt;[40] for this reason, a statutory cancellation of state debt constitutes a compulsory acquisition of property.[41]

While the case dealt with civil claims and not state debts, a somewhat comparable situation arose in *Law Society of South Africa and Others v Minister for Transport and Another*,[42] where the Constitutional Court considered the status of incorporeal interests as constitutional property, this time in the form of a delictual claim for loss of earning capacity or support. The appellants in *Law Society* challenged the constitutional validity of certain amendments to the Road Accident Fund Act 56 of 1996[43] on the basis that they offended rights in sections 12 (security of person), 25(1) (property), 27 (access to healthcare) and 38 (adequate remedy) of the Constitution. The contentious amendments comprised two legislative provisions: sections 21 (abolishing the common-law right to claim compensation not payable under the Act from a private party or their employer) and 17(4)(c) (limiting the RAF's liability for claims of loss of income, or a dependant's claim for loss of

---

[37] AJ van der Walt *Constitutional property law* 3 ed (2011) 151 and cases cited in fnn 249 and 250.

[38] AJ van der Walt 'Police-power regulation of intangible property and the constitutional property clause: A comparative analysis of case law' in P Jackson & DC Wilde (eds) *Property law: Current issues and debates* (1999) 208–280 216–228.

[39] *Agri South Africa v Minister for Minerals and Energy* 2013 (4) SA 1 (CC) dealt with a regulatory change of mineral rights and not debts, and it was not decided as an arbitrary deprivation issue (para 53) but as an acquisition issue, finding that the state must acquire something akin to the rights that were lost (paras 58–59 per Mogoeng CJ for the majority). See also AJ van der Walt 'Constitutional property law' (2014) *ASSAL* 195–215 201–202 for criticism of this approach; EJ Marais 'When does state interference with property (now) amount to expropriation? An analysis of the *Agri SA* court's state acquisition requirement (part 1)' 2015 18 *PELJ* 2982–3031; EJ Marais 'When does state interference with property (now) amount to expropriation? An analysis of the *Agri SA* court's state acquisition requirement (part 2)' (2015) 18 *PELJ* 3032–3069.

[40] *Peverill v Health Insurance Commission* (1991) 104 ALR 449 (FC) 454ff per Burchett J.

[41] AJ van der Walt 'Police-power regulation of intangible property and the constitutional property clause: A comparative analysis of case law' in P Jackson & DC Wilde (eds) *Property law: Current issues and debates* (1999) 208–280 221.

[42] 2011 (1) SA 400 (CC).

[43] Amended by the Road Accident Fund Amendment Act 19 of 2005, which took effect in August 2008.

support). The court had to determine whether the common-law right to claim compensation from a wrongdoer constituted property, and, if so, whether its extinguishment (cancellation) constituted an arbitrary deprivation.[44]

The appellants argued, on the authority of the Constitutional Court's recognition of goodwill as constitutional property in *Phumelela*,[45] that it was a natural extension to protect a person's earning capacity as property because 'goodwill is to a legal [juristic] person what earning capacity is to a natural person'.[46] The court accepted that, on a plain text reading of section 25(4)(b) of the Constitution, incorporeal property enjoys constitutional property protection, but 'the definition of property for purposes of constitutional protection should not be too wide to make legislative regulation impracticable and not too narrow to render the protection of property of little worth'.[47] Unfortunately, the court then found it unnecessary to determine whether a person's earning capacity was property, because, even on the assumption that it was, the alleged deprivation was not arbitrary.[48] The court thus skipped over the property question and the determination of whether there was a substantial interference with the property that constituted a deprivation, and held that, having already found the legislative scheme to be rationally connected to a legitimate public purpose ('to make the Fund financially viable and sustainable and to render the compensation regime more transparent, predictable and equitable'), the deprivation (if any) was not arbitrary.[49]

The court's reluctance to engage in the property question is, to some degree, understandable, but the reasoning in respect of the arbitrariness inquiry is

---

[44] It was not argued that the amendment constituted a compulsory acquisition, as André suggested may be the case with state debts, because the common-law claim right was against private persons and not against the state and thus the extinguishment of the claim right did not have the effect of relieving the state of a monetary debt.

[45] *Phumelela Gaming and Leisure (Ltd) v Gründlingh and Others* 2007 (6) SA 350 (CC), discussed in section 2 above.

[46] *Law Society of South Africa and Others v Minister for Transport and Another* 2011 (1) SA 400 (CC) para 81.

[47] Paragraph 83.

[48] In the High Court judgment in *Khumalo v Cycle Lab (Pty) Ltd* (31871/2008) [2011] ZAGPJHC 56, the court was reluctant to treat a claim for patrimonial loss arising from the unauthorised use of a celebrity's 'likeness' or image as a proprietary claim distinct from the intellectual property that may exist in this respect in terms of the Trade Marks Act 194 of 1993, stating at para 42: 'It is important to note that the claim for patrimonial loss rests upon the infringement of her personality right to identity and not upon any immaterial property right that the plaintiff holds. ... The immaterial or intellectual property rights held by the plaintiff exist independently of the plaintiff's personality rights and are capable of separate enforcement.'

[49] *Law Society of South Africa and Others v Minister for Transport and Another* 2011 (1) SA 400 (CC) para 86.

open to question. The conclusion that the deprivation (which was assumed) of the property (also assumed) was not arbitrary was entirely based on the preceding conclusion that the amendments to the legislative scheme were rationally connected to legitimate government purposes and therefore did not unjustifiably limit the section 12 right to security of the person, including the right to bodily integrity and freedom from violence from public and private sources. However, it is an unsubstantiated leap then to conclude that the same finding must necessarily hold in respect of section 25, at least not without the benefit of having established the extent of the deprivation (as per the second step of the *FNB* methodology, which the court acknowledged but did not engage in) to determine whether a rationality-type arbitrariness inquiry would suffice, or whether a proportionality-type justification would be required. The court could have considered the constitutional property challenge on its own merits here, which would have provided greater clarity on the arbitrariness question.

Staying with common-law civil claims, the Constitutional Court in *National Credit Regulator v Opperman*[50] (*Opperman*) found that the right to restitution of money paid based on unjustified enrichment constitutes constitutional property. The court had to decide whether section 89(5)(c) of the National Credit Act 34 of 2005 effected an arbitrary deprivation by prohibiting an unregistered credit provider from reclaiming any of the money lent by means of unjustified enrichment since the credit agreement was invalid.[51] The court cited André as authority for the statement that 'the recognition of the right to restitution of money paid, based on unjustified enrichment, as property under section 25(1) is logical and realistic'.[52] The court emphasised that it 'had not [in previous cases] specifically found that personal rights emanating from contract, delict, or enrichment are indeed *property* [original emphasis] under section 25.' However, it noted that it had –

> accepted a trade mark to be property, albeit incorporeal, deserving protection under section 25. Intellectual property, even though incorporeal, is of course different from an enrichment claim. The right to claim restitution on the basis of enrichment is a personal right ... But reliance has been placed on the link to

[50] *National Credit Regulator v Opperman and Others* 2013 (2) SA 1 (CC).

[51] Paragraphs 9–10 per Van der Westhuizen J for the majority.

[52] AJ van der Walt *Constitutional property law* 3 ed (2011) 115–116, 141–142, cited at para 63.

ownership in evaluating whether there is a deprivation or whether section 25 comes into play.[53]

The decision also noted that the court had previously assumed without finding that a claim for loss of earning capacity or support can be protected as property.[54] Therefore, the court found it logical to recognise the right to restitution of money paid based on unjustified enrichment as property under section 25(1): 'Intangible property has become important in modern-day society and *property* [original emphasis] should not be so narrowly interpreted as to diminish the worth of the protection given by section 25.'[55] The court required persuasive reasons for the regulation because it extinguished the credit provider's right to restitution, and found that the means chosen were disproportionate to the purpose because there were less invasive means available, not because the purpose of the regulation was invalid. In the final result, section 89(5)(c) of the National Credit Act was found to effect an arbitrary deprivation and it was held that consumers' interests could be protected without this result.[56] This decision is therefore the first to uphold an incorporeal property right against unjustified regulation.

In *Cool Ideas 1186 CC v Hubbard*[57] (*Cool Ideas*), the issues were comparable to those in *Opperman* in that the purpose of the legislation in issue (the Housing Consumers Protection Measures Act 95 of 1998) was to protect housing consumers against unscrupulous builders (comparable to the purpose of the National Credit Act to protect vulnerable consumers and abate the inequality between credit providers and credit consumers). Also similarly, the property in issue was a claim right.[58] However, here the similarities end, as the court dealt with the arbitrariness question very differently.

The court had to decide on the interpretation of section 10(1)(b) of the Housing Consumers Protection Act (which mandates that a home builder cannot receive payment if it is not registered as a home builder with the relevant authority), and whether the provision effects an arbitrary deprivation of property by abolishing the common-law claim based on unjustified

[53] Paragraph 61 per Van der Westhuizen J, citing *Laugh It Off Promotions CC v SAB International (Finance) BV t/a Sabmark International (Freedom of Expression Institute as* Amicus Curiae*)* 2006 (1) SA 144 (CC); *Phumelela Gaming and Leisure Ltd v Gründlingh and Others* 2007 (6) SA 350 (CC).

[54] Paragraph 62 per Van der Westhuizen, citing *Law Society of South Africa and Others v Minister for Transport and Another* 2011 (1) SA 400 (CC).

[55] Paragraph 63 per Van der Westhuizen, citing AJ van der Walt *Constitutional property law* 3 ed (2011) 115–116, 141–142.

[56] Paragraphs 68, 70–71 per Van der Westhuizen.

[57] *Cool Ideas 1186 CC v Hubbard and Another* 2014 (4) SA 474 (CC).

[58] See AJ van der Walt 'Section 25 vortices: Part 2' 2016 *TSAR* 597–621 600–601.

enrichment that home builders would otherwise have against errant clients. The interpretational difficulty arose in whether the provision required that a home builder must be registered when the contract to build a house is concluded, or whether it is acceptable for the home builder to register later, as long as it is done before payment is sought.[59] The appellant was not registered at the time the contract was concluded, but subcontracted the building work to a company that was registered.

The court found that the objectives of the Act are to regulate the building industry by protecting the housing consumer and maintaining minimum standards for home builders, which, according to Majiedt J, require upfront registration else the protection of the consumer is not achieved.[60] While the right to restitution of money paid based on unjustified enrichment constitutes property for purposes of section 25(1) of the Constitution (as decided in *Opperman*),[61] and there had been a deprivation of the appellant's property as they could not enforce an enrichment claim against their clients, the court held that it was not arbitrary.[62]

The court reasoned that since the deprivation extinguished a right, the reason for the deprivation would have to be compelling and proportionality between the means and end would be required, but since the purpose of the legislation had been established as an important government purpose, it was satisfied that a *rational* connection existed between the legislative provision and its purpose (thereby capitulating from its averred proportionality-type analysis). The court found that depriving a builder of payment for a (perfectly sound) home was proportionate to the important government purpose of protecting consumers (who wish to avoid payment for their home), and thus not arbitrary.[63] The underlying (illegal) building contract remained valid and enforceable by Mrs Hubbard even though Cool Ideas was not entitled to payment due to its failure to register as required by section 10(1)(b).[64]

If the court had continued with the proportionality analysis (checking whether the means of the regulation is proportionate to the purpose as in *Opperman*)[65] instead of switching to rationality (that an important purpose is being served by regulating the building industry, albeit not necessarily in a way that gave adequate protection to property rights), the outcome

---

[59] *Cool Ideas 1186 CC v Hubbard and Another* 2014 (4) SA 474 (CC) paras 23, 27 of the majority decision per Majiedt J.

[60] Paragraphs 30, 34 per Majiedt J.

[61] *National Credit Regulator v Opperman and Others* 2013 (2) SA 1 (CC) para 63.

[62] *Cool Ideas 1186 CC v Hubbard and Another* 2014 (4) SA 474 (CC) para 38 per Majiedt J.

[63] Paragraph 41 – 44 per Majiedt J.

[64] Paragraph 47 per Majiedt J.

[65] *National Credit Regulator v Opperman and Others* 2013 (2) SA 1 (CC) para 63.

might have been more equitable on the facts of the case. This is the step that was missed in *Law Society*, which, had it been properly reasoned, may have required a different magnitude of justification to render the deprivation lawful, which, in turn, may have led to a different outcome in the property challenge before the court.

Jafta J's concurring judgment held the contract invalid, otherwise the provision would amount to an unintended injustice.[66]

Froneman J's dissenting judgment held that fairness may require that Cool Ideas' rights be enforceable, as the important government purpose in question could be equally well-served by an interpretation that does not deprive builders of their property in claim rights.[67] This judgment finds a much more acceptable solution than the majority decision, which results in a very low standard of review to test whether the end justifies the means, disregarding the extent of the deprivation (and, according to the minority judgment, where the purpose of the legislation can be achieved by less invasive means, thus interpreting the legislation in such a fashion as to avoid the (arbitrary) deprivation permitted by the majority decision).[68]

In *Chevron SA (Pty) Limited v Wilson t/a Wilson's Transport and Others*,[69] Madlanga J's unanimous judgment confirmed an order of the High Court[70] that section 89(5)(b) of the National Credit Act 34 of 2005 permitted an arbitrary deprivation and was inconsistent with section 25(1) of the Constitution, but could be read so as to avoid arbitrariness.[71] The regulation would render credit agreements void where the credit provider is not registered as such and mandates the credit provider to refund the credit consumer in full without any provision for judicial discretion. The court confirmed that money in hand is a constitutionally protectable property interest[72] and that the deprivation is substantial[73] (even more so than in *Opperman*). On arbitrariness,[74] the court found the purpose of the legislation (protecting consumers) valid for

66 Paragraphs 66, 96, 98, 102, 103 per Jafta J's separate concurring judgment.

67 Paragraphs 127–128 per Froneman J's dissenting minority judgment.

68 André expressed his agreement with the minority judgment in AJ van der Walt 'Constitutional property law' 2014 *ASSAL* 195–215 196–199.

69 2015 (10) BCLR 1158 (CC).

70 *Chevron SA (Pty) Ltd v Dennis Edwin Wilson t/a Wilson's Transport and Others* [2014] ZAWCHC 121.

71 *Chevron SA (Pty) Limited v Wilson t/a Wilson's Transport and Others* 2015 (10) BCLR 1158 (CC) paras 1–12.

72 Paragraph 16.

73 Paragraphs 17–19.

74 *Chevron SA (Pty) Limited v Wilson t/a Wilson's Transport and Others* 2015 (10) BCLR 1158 (CC) paras 20–24.

providing 'sufficient reason' for the deprivation.[75] While the outcome of the case cannot be faulted (procedural fairness dictates that courts should have a discretion to decide on a just and equitable outcome, which rendered the legislative provision unconstitutional),[76] the arbitrariness question was glossed over once again.[77] The court noted that a creditor's reliance on an unjustified enrichment claim does not ameliorate the deprivation,[78] but then proceeded to a section 36 limitation analysis, finding that the purpose of the legislation is not in balance with the arbitrary deprivation it effected.

Generally, the court has displayed a willingness to accept common-law monetary claims as property, although sometimes only because nothing turns on this question (such as in *Law Society*). There has been some deviation in the way the court treats the property analysis once property is found to exist, but the court has mostly been faithful to the *FNB* methodology – at least in form. However, it has emerged from these intangible constitutional property cases that the government purposes that could be regarded as sufficiently important to withstand section 25 scrutiny are founded on diverse public purposes, ranging from consumer protection in numerous industries to transparency and equitability in compensation schemes. It may be noted that André's call for proper contextualisation and differentiation has not been heeded in all cases of this type, to the detriment of the integrity of constitutional property jurisprudence.

4 Licences, permits and quotas

The next category of intangible property interests pertains to where 'a certain commercial branch or activity is subjected to (generally uncontroversial) regulation in the form of licences, permits or quotas, and the aggrieved party objects to the refusal, cancellation or amendment of a licence, permit or quota that is essential for the continued existence of her enterprise'.[79] The regulation often has the effect of causing a particular business to close down, or sometimes it merely disrupts the preferred business strategy of a particular business.

Licences, permits and quotas may be protected as constitutional property if they display certain characteristics that may be analogised to property,

[75] Paragraphs 20–21.

[76] Paragraphs 22–24.

[77] See AJ van der Walt 'Section 25 vortices: Part 2' 2016 *TSAR* 597–621 607.

[78] *Chevron SA (Pty) Limited v Wilson t/a Wilson's Transport and Others* 2015 (10) BCLR 1158 (CC) paras 25–30.

[79] AJ van der Walt 'Police-power regulation of intangible property and the constitutional property clause: A comparative analysis of case law' in P Jackson & DC Wilde (eds) *Property law: Current issues and debates* (1999) 208–280 248 (see also 249–253).

namely that they have acquired commercial value and have vested according to the relevant statutory or regulatory requirements. Despite this, they are still subject to administrative regulation, amendment and cancellation.[80] Foreign law has awarded some of these interests limited constitutional protection.[81]

Shoprite Checkers (Pty) Ltd v Member of the Executive Council for Economic Development, Environmental Affairs and Tourism: Eastern Cape[82] (*Shoprite*) dealt with the regulation (and, according to at least some of the decisions, complete destruction) of intangible commercial property in the form of licences.[83] The court had to decide whether grocers' wine licences constituted property; whether the amending legislation deprived the holders of such property; and whether the purpose of the legislation was important enough to avoid arbitrariness.[84] This case concerned the role that the kind of property in question and its purpose should play in a constitutional property investigation,[85] and the appropriate application of the arbitrariness test.

---

[80] AJ van der Walt *Constitutional property law* 3 ed (2011) 157–162. See also M Kellerman *The constitutional property clause and immaterial property interests* (unpublished LLD thesis, University of Stellenbosch (2010) 95–96; *S v Lawrence; S v Negal; S v Solberg* 1997 (4) SA 1176 (CC), where the Constitutional Court upheld a regulation that prohibits the sale of alcohol on Sundays. The attack against this law was based on the right to engage in economic activity (s 26) and the right to freedom of religion (s 14) of the Constitution of the Republic of South Africa, 1993. The court held that the prohibition was neither unreasonable nor an infringement of freedom of religion, but a legitimate exercise of the state's police power.

[81] For example, in *Tre Traktörer AB v Sweden* [1989] ECHR Ser A Vol 159, the European Court recognised an alcohol licence as property, but decided that the limiting regulation was proportionate.

[82] *Shoprite Checkers (Pty) Ltd v Member of the Executive Council for Economic Development, Environmental Affairs and Tourism: Eastern Cape* 2015 (6) SA 125 (CC).

[83] Paragraphs 1, 6 per Froneman J. The Eastern Cape Liquor Act 10 of 2003 introduced a new regulatory framework for the sale of liquor in 2003. It permitted the continued sale of wine with food in grocery stores for a period of ten years after the commencement of the Act. After five years from the date of commencement of the Act, the holder could apply for registration to sell all kinds of liquor on separate premises.

[84] Paragraph 5 per Froneman J. The three separate judgments differed on whether the grocer's wine licences constituted property, whether there was a deprivation and whether such deprivation was arbitrary.

[85] Paragraph 4 per Froneman J. The decisions considered why property should be protected and the purpose that it should serve, and asserted that the level of constitutional protection should depend on the kind of constitutional interest involved and the core purpose of that type of property interest.

Both the court of first instance[86] and the Constitutional Court[87] in *Shoprite* quoted André's work and heeded André's warning that different categories of intangible property should be treated differently in constitutional property law, and that one category should not be used as precedent for another.[88]

What is most apparent in this case is the separate Constitutional Court decisions' lack of consensus as to the exact property interest that was taken away by the regulation and how this affected the outcome of each decision.[89] The outcome of each of the three decisions appears to be directly contingent on the particular conception of the interest that was lost through the regulation, precisely but differently conceived and defined in each decision. The main judgment, per Froneman J, viewed the liquor licences as property entitlements that permit otherwise unlawful business activities,

[86] *Shoprite Checkers (Pty) Ltd v MEC for Economic Development, Environmental Affairs and Tourism: Eastern Cape and Others* 2015 (1) BCLR 102 (ECG) paras 55–57 quoted AJ van der Walt *Constitutional property law* 2 ed (2005) 100: '[L]icences, permits and quotas [are regarded] as constitutional property only if they have commercial value and once they have been vested and acquired according to the relevant (statutory or regulatory) requirements'; and referred to cases discussed in AJ van der Walt 'Police-power regulation of intangible property and the constitutional property clause: A comparative analysis of case law' in P Jackson & DC Wilde (eds) *Property law: Current issues and debates* (1999) 208–280.

[87] *Shoprite Checkers (Pty) Ltd v Member of the Executive Council for Economic Development, Environmental Affairs and Tourism: Eastern Cape* 2015 (6) SA 125 (CC) para 103 quoted AJ van der Walt 3 ed (2011) 189: '[E]xisting and new property interests are recognised and protected when and in so far as it is necessary to establish and uphold an equitable balance between individual property interests and the public interest, with due regard for the historical context within which property holdings were established and the constitutional context within which they are now protected'; and referred to cases discussed in AJ van der Walt 'Police-power regulation of intangible property and the constitutional property clause: A comparative analysis of case law' in P Jackson & DC Wilde (eds) *Property law: Current issues and debates* (1999) 208–280.

[88] AJ van der Walt 'Police-power regulation of intangible property and the constitutional property clause: A comparative analysis of case law' in P Jackson & DC Wilde (eds) *Property law: Current issues and debates* (1999) 208–280 208.

[89] In the High Court decision, *Shoprite Checkers (Pty) Ltd v MEC for Economic Development, Environmental Affairs and Tourism: Eastern Cape and Others* 2015 (1) BCLR 102 (ECG) para 43, the court of first instance held that s 25 protection extends to incorporeal personal rights (citing *Law Society of South Africa v Minister of Transport* 2011 (1) SA 400 (CC) para 83; *National Credit Regulator v Opperman and Others* 2013 (2) SA 1 (CC); *Agri SA v Minster for Minerals and Energy* 2013 (4) SA 1 (CC) and stated at para 47: 'It seems only logical to me that a licence granted by the state to a person (or corporation, for that matter) to trade in a certain commodity – which endures for as long as the recipient conducts itself in accordance with the conditions attaching thereto, and which entitles the recipient to invest substantial sums on the understanding that the relevant administrative functionary is by law precluded from arbitrarily revoking the licence – must be worthy of the protection accorded by s 25 of the Constitution.'

its continuance dependent on state powers of regulatory amendment, suspension and cancellation.[90] The classification of the interest in the licence as a property interest was done on the basis that such interest is 'clearly definable and identifiable by persons other than the holder; has value; is capable of being transferred; and is sufficiently permanent'.[91] Additionally, the majority judgment held that the correlation between a liquor licence and the right of a natural person (which the appellant was not) to choose their trade or vocation in terms of section 22 of the Constitution (which, in turn, supports the values of human dignity and self-fulfilment) strongly supported classifying the incorporeal interest in the licence as property.[92]

The loss of the legal entitlement was viewed as not excessive, as there was the option to convert the rights, but still constituted a deprivation of the property.[93] In other words, the option to apply for a liquor licence to sell all kinds of liquor on separate premises (which option already existed) was viewed as sufficient substitution for the wine licence that allowed grocery stores to sell wine on the same premises, negating any requirement for monetary compensation (whether for 'regulatory taking', which does not appear to have been received into South African law, or expropriation).[94] The regulation of the property entitlement was judged as not being arbitrary on the rationality standard.

The concurring judgment of Moseneke DCJ found it unnecessary to characterise the grocer's wine licences as property, because the same outcome could be reached in terms of administrative law by simply testing the

---

[90] *Shoprite Checkers (Pty) Ltd v Member of the Executive Council for Economic Development, Environmental Affairs and Tourism: Eastern Cape* 2015 (6) SA 125 (CC) paras 5, 58 per Froneman J. The Irish case of *State (Pheasantry Ltd) v Donnelly* [1982] ILRM 512 dealt with the forfeiture of a liquor licence and the court held that the licence was a privilege granted by statute and as such subject to change by statute. Consequently, the court was not prepared to grant constitutional property protection to the rights. Only once own effort and investment becomes apparent can there be the possibility of constitutional protection. This is similar to the approach of the German Federal Constitutional Court. No protection is provided to interests that are granted by the state and that can be amended or terminated unilaterally by administrative action.

[91] *Shoprite Checkers (Pty) Ltd v Member of the Executive Council for Economic Development, Environmental Affairs and Tourism: Eastern Cape* 2015 (6) SA 125 (CC) para 68 per Froneman J. However, Froneman J was quick to point out that whether the interest has significant commercial value is not determinative to its protection as property.

[92] Paragraphs 61–68 per Froneman J.

[93] Paragraphs 74–76 per Froneman J.

[94] On the issue of licences and regulatory takings, see AJ van der Walt 'Police-power regulation of intangible property and the constitutional property clause: A comparative analysis of case law' in P Jackson & DC Wilde (eds) *Property law: Current issues and debates* (1999) 208–280 230–231.

legislative provisions for rationality.[95] Whether this does in fact provide the same outcome is debatable, since proportionality might have been required on the facts given that the entitlement was completely extinguished by the amendment. The decision warned against characterising each and every commercial interest as property.

Both Froneman J and Moseneke DCJ pointed to the characteristic of licences issued in terms of a regulatory regime as permitting activity that would otherwise be unlawful.[96] In addition to the empowerment to trade lawfully in a given industry, such a licence creates artificial scarcity and hence value to the holder, in much the same way that copyright and patent law does, although in these cases the rights granted render otherwise lawful conduct unlawful. This may point to part of the reason why the dissenting minority decision of Madlanga J viewed the licences as property, and that which had been taken away as the right to sell wine together with groceries on the same premises. In other words, toting another existing right (to sell wine together with other liquors on separate premises) as a substitute for the lost right (selling wine inside a grocery store) was, according to the minority, simply wrong and the legislation should therefore have been found constitutionally invalid.[97]

The concurring decision of Moseneke DCJ indicates that the court likely would be reluctant to accept the appellant's preferred business strategy as a property interest worthy of protection.[98] This may seem to be at odds with the reasoning of the Supreme Court of Appeal in *Phumelela*,[99] where a business system was found to constitute property by virtue of the public trust that had been cultivated in that system to the extent that 'the resulting income potential is part of [the respondent's] goodwill and as such a valuable asset'.[100] However, it is crucial to regard these cases as not comparable, in

---

[95] *Shoprite Checkers (Pty) Ltd v Member of the Executive Council for Economic Development, Environmental Affairs and Tourism: Eastern Cape* 2015 (6) SA 125 (CC) para 94 per Moseneke DCJ.

[96] Paragraph 58 per Froneman J and paras 119, 122 per Moseneke DCJ.

[97] Paragraphs 151, 169 per Madlanga J. On the question of arbitrariness, Madlanga J held (para 135) that simply doing a rationality test does not allow for application of the sliding scale, which may necessitate proportionality for the arbitrariness enquiry (based on the nature of the property).

[98] Paragraph 102 per Moseneke DCJ.

[99] *Gründlingh and Others v Phumelela Gaming and Leisure (Ltd)* 2005 (6) SA 502 (SCA).

[100] Paragraph 33 (majority judgment of Farlam and Conradie JJA, agreeing on this issue with the minority decision of Comrie AJA).

line with the caveat that André issues to take due cognisance of contextual differences.[101]

On arbitrariness, Froneman J held that 'the lighter standard may be applicable if the nature of the right to property is not strong and the deprivation not too heavy'[102] and that the question necessitates analysing '[t]he complexity of relationships between means (deprivation) and ends (purpose of the law); between the purpose of the law and the person holding property; and between the purpose of the law and the nature of the property and extent of the deprivation'.[103] If the property in question is 'closely connected to fundamental rights and constitutional values', this would necessitate proportionality, but on the facts this was not the case, hence rationality sufficed.[104] This echoes the *FNB* approach and presents a welcome nod to the proper contextualisation of the constitutional property issue that both *FNB* and André's paper advocate.[105]

More recently, in *South African Diamond Producers Organisation v Minister of Minerals and Energy NO and Others*[106] (*Diamond Producers*), the Constitutional Court exercised its power in terms of section 172(2)(a) of the Constitution to set aside an order of constitutional invalidity of a statutory provision made by the High Court (similar to *Chevron*) for breach of sections 22 and 25 of the Bill of Rights.[107] The impugned provision was section 20A of the Diamonds Act 56 of 1986, which amended the existing statutory regime to prohibit explicitly the involvement of unlicensed persons in the diamond trade, effectively closing a 'loophole' (as the Minister of Minerals and Energy saw it) that led to a commercial practice of considerable value to the appellant.

This practice involved unlicensed international experts assisting licensed buyers and sellers to determine the proper market value of unpolished

[101] The differences between the two cases are far more striking than the similarities, and it is safe to say that the Constitutional Court may yet in a different case accept a business system or 'preferred business strategy' as property if it warrants being treated as such.

[102] *Shoprite Checkers (Pty) Ltd v Member of the Executive Council for Economic Development, Environmental Affairs and Tourism: Eastern Cape* 2015 (6) SA 125 (CC) para 77 per Froneman J.

[103] Paragraph 79 per Froneman J.

[104] Paragraphs 80, 83 per Froneman J.

[105] Moseneke DCJ (para 94) found it needless to characterise the grocers' wine licences as property, because the same outcome could be reached by simply testing the legislative provisions for rationality in line with administrative law.

[106] 2017 (6) SA 331 (CC).

[107] High Court decision reported as *South African Diamond Producers Organisation v Minister of Minerals and Energy NO* [2016] ZAGPPHC 817 (6 September 2016).

diamonds. The appellant argued that the abolition of this practice breaches its right to conduct business in a manner it deems fit (its preferred business model) in terms of section 22 of the Constitution (which the Constitutional Court did not accept), and that it arbitrarily deprives it of its right to alienate property by restricting, in breach of section 25(1), its right to receive full market value for the unpolished diamonds. The High Court found the deprivation 'irrational, arbitrary and disproportional'.[108]

In the Constitutional Court, the appellant claimed loss of value in the tangible diamonds that the amendment caused, as well as that the abolition of diamond exchange certificates (which, it alleged, constituted property) in favour of a new regime of trading house licences (under section 26(f) of the Act) constituted an arbitrary deprivation.[109]

The court considered the two property objects (ownership of the diamonds, and the rights bestowed by the licence) separately, and posited that once it has been established that the two respective objects comprise property interests, the preferable approach to determining arbitrary deprivation is to consider whether what has been taken away (comprising a reduction in value due to the price-fixing mechanism being regulated, and a preferred business model) 'constitutes a right or interest worthy of protection, and is substantial enough that its removal constitutes "deprivation"'.[110]

On the issue of the tangible property, the court centred its analysis of whether a deprivation had occurred on the extent of the intrusion into the owner's use and enjoyment of its property, and whether this intrusion 'has

---

[108] *South African Diamond Producers Organisation v Minister of Minerals and Energy NO and Others* 2017 (6) SA 331 (CC) paras 48–49.

[109] Paragraph 20. This is somewhat reminiscent of *Agri South Africa v Minister for Minerals and Energy* 2013 (4) SA 1 (CC), where the Constitutional Court was faced with a challenge to the MPRDA, the promulgation of which amended the licensing regime so that holders of mining licences had to reapply for a different licence on different terms, which the appellant was not able to do due to it being in liquidation at the time of the transition between the two regimes and which, it alleged, was an uncompensated expropriation.

[110] Paragraph 38. The description of a deprivation as 'a substantial interference or limitation that goes beyond the normal restrictions on property use or enjoyment' was adopted from *Mkontwana v Nelson Mandela Metropolitan Municipality* 2005 (1) SA 530 (CC) para 32; this was developed by the same Court in *Offit Enterprises (Pty) Ltd and Another v Coega Development Corporation (Pty) Limited and Others* 2011 (1) SA 293 (CC) 189 para 41, where it stated that 'direct or physical interference is not necessary, [but] the impact must be of sufficient magnitude to warrant constitutional engagement'.

a legally relevant impact on the rights of the affected party'.[111] The court decided that obtaining the highest value for property was not protected under the right to alienate,[112] which confirms that the constitutional property right does not protect value as such: 'A property holder does not generally have a legally protectable interest either in obtaining a specific value for his goods, or in valuing his goods according to a particular method.'[113]

With regard to the appellant's contention that its licences to operate tender houses were subjected to an arbitrary deprivation, the court assumed that the licences were indeed property interests capable of constitutional protection, but that there had been no deprivation of this property. This conclusion was reached on the basis that the business practice of receiving assistance from unlicensed experts was not an entitlement that flowed from the appellant's licence, and hence the amendment did not interfere with any property entitlement granted by the licence; rather, it constituted a preferred business practice, which the Constitutional Court seemed reluctant to protect in terms of the property clause.[114] Similarly, the court found that section 20A did not abolish diamond exchange certificates, and the attack on the provision was misguided in this sense, although it did not dismiss the possibility that this argument could be made in relation to other provisions of the same Act.[115]

Moseneke DCJ's concurring decision in *Shoprite* illustrates an avoidance of the property question that echoes the approach followed in judgments like *Law Society* before it and *Diamond Producers* subsequently. The majority judgment in Shoprite shows a more robust engagement with the property question in respect of the intangible property interest and demonstrates a willingness to explore the constitutional values underlying and supporting property rights.

---

[111] Paragraph 48, consulting *City of Tshwane Metropolitan Municipality v Link Africa (Pty) Ltd and Others* 2015 (6) SA 440 (CC) para 167: Whether a statutory deprivation has occurred 'depends on the extent of the intrusion in the property or limitation of its use and enjoyment. There must be interference with property that is significant enough to "have a legally relevant impact on the rights of the affected party before deprivation of property under s 25 is established"' (quoting the main judgment of Froneman J in *Shoprite* para 73).

[112] Paragraphs 50–51.

[113] Paragraph 53.

[114] Paragraph 61: 'It cannot be that, every time a government decision or regulation makes a particular business strategy unlawful, persons who preferred to conduct their business in accordance with that strategy have been deprived of property.' See also *Shoprite Checkers (Pty) Ltd v Member of the Executive Council for Economic Development, Environmental Affairs and Tourism: Eastern Cape* 2015 (6) SA 125 (CC) para 94 per Moseneke DCJ.

[115] Paragraphs 56–62.

5 Regulatory creation of state monopolies and interference with the management of a business enterprise

The regulatory creation of state monopolies[116] can involve the loss of a business, loss of goodwill, and loss of future profits:

> The implication seems to be that a regulation should be regarded as a compulsory acquisition (and compensated) when its effect is not merely to control (which may include closing down) private enterprises, but actually to take over their business for the benefit of the state (through the creation of a state monopoly).[117]

We are not aware of any South African case law that has considered such state acquisition of private enterprises as a constitutional property matter. However, where a regulation interferes with a private commercial enterprise in such a way that it threatens its existence but with no concomitant state monopoly or competition, the interference can still be significant enough to warrant constitutional consideration. For example, with the restriction of shareholders' rights,[118] the purpose of the regulation can still justify the deprivation but the proportionality test is important in determining this.[119]

The court in *Diamond Producers* was reluctant to consider the intangible property in a preferred business strategy and side-stepped the issue by stating that this interest did not stem from a licensing entitlement. However, one should be wary of reading too much into the way the court dealt with the property interests that were brought before it, and the same court may still

---

[116] AJ van der Walt 'Police-power regulation of intangible property and the constitutional property clause: A comparative analysis of case law' in P Jackson & DC Wilde (eds) *Property law: Current issues and debates* (1999) 208–280 228–235 and foreign cases cited there.

[117] AJ van der Walt 'Police-power regulation of intangible property and the constitutional property clause: A comparative analysis of case law' in P Jackson & DC Wilde (eds) *Property law: Current issues and debates* (1999) 208–280 231.

[118] South African law accepted shares as incorporeal moveable property in *Cooper v Boyes NO and Another* 1994 (4) SA 521 (C), which makes its recognition and protection as constitutional property somewhat easier, since the point of departure is that interests protected as property in private law would also be protected as property in constitutional law. German constitutional law recognises and protects shares as constitutional property even though they are not protected as property in private law. Shares serve the same purpose as property rights in private law, namely to secure a sphere of personal liberty for the individual to achieve independence in the patrimonial field, and this makes shares suitable for inclusion under the constitutional property concept. See AJ van der Walt *Constitutional property law* 3 ed (2011) 154 fn 257.

[119] AJ van der Walt 'Police-power regulation of intangible property and the constitutional property clause: A comparative analysis of case law' in P Jackson & DC Wilde (eds) *Property law: Current issues and debates* (1999) 20–280 235–248 and foreign cases discussed there.

on a different day get to consider whether an investment-backed expectation that arises in a (heavily or lightly) regulated environment may be treated as a property interest.[120] *Phumulela* indicates that if a regulation affects a preferred business strategy that has commercial value to a business owner, for example because the business strategy forms part of the business's goodwill, the business strategy may be accepted as property. If *Diamond Producers* had been argued differently, the court might have considered the business strategy in question as constituting something akin to goodwill with measurable commercial value, which could have led to the property question being decided differently on this aspect.

6 Conclusions

The conclusions in André's paper include some general guidelines on how to deal with intangible property regulation and propose the notion that the property concept is wide and flexible:

> [T]he inclusion or exclusion of a certain right or interest from the protection of a constitutional property clause is a matter of context. ... What is and is not property for purposes of the constitutional property guarantee is a judgment call, which means that we have to decide the matter, every time anew, with full recognition of the facts and the surrounding circumstances of each case.[121]

Following *Laugh It Off*, courts have been comfortable accepting that traditional forms of intellectual property benefit from the protection of section 25.[122] Money in hand and common-law claim rights have been included as

---

[120] In American law (see *Lloyd v Tanner* 407 US 551 (1972)), this may include investment-backed expectations: see AJ van der Walt 'Police-power regulation of intangible property and the constitutional property clause: A comparative analysis of case law' in P Jackson & DC Wilde (eds) *Property law: Current issues and debates* (1999) 208–280 247.

[121] AJ van der Walt 'Police-power regulation of intangible property and the constitutional property clause: A comparative analysis of case law' in P Jackson & DC Wilde (eds) *Property law: Current issues and debates* (1999) 208-280 257–258.

[122] *Laugh it Off Promotions CC v South African Breweries International (Finance) BV t/a Sabmark International (Freedom of Expression Institute as Amicus Curiae)* 2006 (1) SA 144 (CC) 743 (trade mark rights and goodwill – implicit); *Phumelela Gaming and Leisure (Ltd) v Gründlingh and Others* 2007 (6) SA 350 (CC) (goodwill – included); *National Soccer League T/A Premier Soccer League v Gidani (Pty) Ltd* [2014] 2 All SA 461 (GJ) (copyright – included); *Moneyweb (Pty) Limited v Media 24 Limited and Another* 2016 (4) SA 591 (GJ) (copyright – included).

constitutional property.[123] Licences can be included in the constitutional property concept, and indeed the property question received more attention in *Shoprite* than in any of the other cases.[124] Where a preferred business model is prohibited in terms of a regulation, there appears to be some reluctance in providing constitutional property protection.[125]

No court has considered an intellectual property interest as the centre of the enquiry yet where the *FNB* methodology can be employed. Rather, every judicial consideration of intellectual property as a constitutional property right has proceeded by resorting to a balancing of the respective constitutional rights and values involved, invariably concluding that there was no genuine conflict. When considering other constitutional rights and legitimate government purposes, the regulation of such property may constitute permissible internal limitations without amounting to a constitutional property challenge as such. However, once a genuine conflict has been established, the section 25(1) methodology may become applicable to determine the justifiability of the limitation of the property interest.

Due to the nature of the challenge, the *Laugh It Off* decision did not consider the possible arbitrary deprivation in allowing freedom of expression in the form of parody to curtail trade mark rights, but instead used a balancing approach to ensure that trade mark rights would not limit freedom of expression objectives unduly and found that the relevant provision of the Trade Marks Act was capable of being interpreted to save it from hampering these objectives, while simultaneously not impinging on section 25.

Phumelela similarly utilised the balancing approach, also bypassing the question whether the deprivation of goodwill was arbitrary, opting to balance the right to goodwill with the right to freedom of trade (which should not be

---

[123] *Law Society of South Africa and Others v Minister for Transport and Another* 2011 (1) SA 400 (CC) (a delictual claim for loss of earning capacity – assumed but undecided); *National Credit Regulator v Opperman and Others* 2013 (2) SA 1 (CC) (unjustified enrichment claim – included); *Cool Ideas 1186 CC v Hubbard and Another* 2014 (4) SA 474 (CC) (unjustified enrichment claim – included); *Chevron SA (Pty) Limited v Wilson t/a Wilson's Transport and Others* 2015 (10) BCLR 1158 (CC) (money in hand – included).

[124] *South African Diamond Producers Organisation v Minister of Minerals and Energy NO and Others* 2017 (6) SA 331 (CC) (licences – inclusion assumed, but unnecessary to decide on the facts); *Shoprite Checkers (Pty) Ltd v Member of the Executive Council for Economic Development, Environmental Affairs and Tourism: Eastern Cape* 2015 (6) SA 125 (CC) (licences – included per Froneman J and Madlanga J, but excluded per Moseneke DCJ).

[125] *South African Diamond Producers Organisation v Minister of Minerals and Energy NO and Others* 2017 (6) SA 331 (CC) (a preferred business model – excluded); *Shoprite Checkers (Pty) Ltd v Member of the Executive Council for Economic Development, Environmental Affairs and Tourism: Eastern Cape* 2015 (6) SA 125 (CC) (a preferred business model – excluded per Moseneke DCJ; included per Madlanga J).

limited by developing the law of unlawful competition to prohibit lawful and healthy competition).

In *Phumelela* the conflict was seen as the interference with the appellant's way of conducting business that resulted in an enduring loss of profit and thus formed part of its goodwill. The issue in *Diamond Producers* was instead approached on the basis of the right to alienate the tangible property (diamonds) and licensing entitlements, rather than the loss of earnings from the reduced market value that resulted from the preferred business strategy being rendered unlawful.[126] This case is set apart from *Phumelela* by the fact that both constitutional provisions (sections 22 and 25) were invoked to challenge the constitutionality of the amending legislation, whereas the court was confronted with a conflict between the two provisions in *Phumelela*. Additionally, the appellants did not argue that their goodwill in the form of income potential derived from the previously-lawful business system was infringed by the amendment, as it may have been entitled to do after *Phumelela*. It is still open to question whether the court would have accepted this as property or deferred to the legislature (whereas the challenge in *Phumelela* was concerned with an order of the Supreme Court of Appeal).

Diamond Producers did not reach the arbitrariness question, having decided that there was no property entitlement flowing from the licence in question that was interfered with, and that there was no substantial interference with the right to alienate the tangible property (diamonds).

The rationality/proportionality spectrum will only come into the question once it has been established that there is property; but, as seen in *Law Society*, if the property question is glossed over, rationality may be shoe-horned in as a sufficient justification for the deprivation without even having considered the extent of the deprivation, which, in turn, determines the requisite level of scrutiny.

In *Law Society*, the court assumed that there was a property interest and that there was a deprivation of this property, and further assumed that a rational connection between the regulation and the deprivation negated arbitrariness because it had found the legislative scheme to be rational in relation to the section 12 challenge. In *Opperman*, by contrast, the

[126] The respondent in *Diamond Producers* did seek to frame the dispute accordingly, arguing that 'the alleged loss of income complained of by the appellant, in other words the earning of a lesser profit due to not being assisted by knowledgeable non-licensees, does not constitute an arbitrary and disproportional [sic] deprivation of rights under ss 22 and 25(1) of the Constitution ... [because] no "property" was deprived of in that regard': para 45 of the High Court judgment. This contention was also advanced in the Constitutional Court, where it found support.

court recognised that the extinguishment of a property right necessitates compelling reasons for the regulation of the property, and found that the purpose and the effect were not proportionate. In other words, the court did a comprehensive arbitrariness analysis in this case. In *Cool Ideas*, the court also stated that the extinguishment of a property right required that there must be proportionality between the legislation's purpose and the effect on the property, but then proceeded to evaluate the regulation on a rationality basis, without providing any reasons for this about-turn. The *Cool Ideas* reasoning is thus more similar to the leap made in *Law Society*.

Chevron dealt with the arbitrariness question in a very superficial way, deciding the case on procedural fairness instead. *Shoprite*, on the other hand, decided the arbitrariness question in detail, examining a complexity of relationships before concluding that rationality is sufficient.

It may be remarked how few cases involving intellectual property have been decided by the Constitutional Court, but so far it seems that André's scholarship has not been used to contextualise potential deprivations of intellectual property interest holders' constitutional property rights; however, this is presumably due to the court framing the allegation of deprivation as a balancing exercise. Again, this is possibly due to the extremely infrequent revision that intellectual property statutes have experienced, which largely negates the possibility of regulatory action occurring at all – indeed, *Laugh It Off* involved the interpretation of pre-constitutional legislation in view of a right in the Bill of Rights, and *Phumelela* involved an alleged deprivation brought about by the judicial development of the common law. This leaves little room for constitutional property investigations, as the issue turns on proper interpretation exclusively.

André's legacy in the sphere of constitutional property law is evident in the Constitutional Court's approach to determining the property status of intangible interests, specifically in *Opperman* and *Shoprite*. His revolutionary contributions to the field have shaped many minds and realities and we trust that courts will follow in the footsteps of *Opperman* and *Shoprite* in learning from his insights; his scholarship may still find traction in forthcoming cases featuring interests at the edge of the property concept and shape the future of intangible property.

Chapter 19

Reflections on the single system of law principle with reference to the regulation of property and the right to just administrative action

Geo Quinot & Elsabé van der Sijde***

Contents

1 The single system of law principle and constitutional methodology

André van der Walt viewed what has come to be called the 'single system of law' principle as part of 'the development algorithm of post-apartheid South African law'.[1] He argued that the Constitutional Court is developing 'a set of guidelines' to determine which source of law applies to a dispute and how a dispute must be conceptualised within the constitutional framework as a way of dealing explicitly with the tensions that are inherent in the transformative objective of the Constitution of the Republic of South Africa, 1996.[2] These are first and foremost questions of adjudicative methodology and as a matter of logic must be addressed *prior* to reliance on any particular set of substantive legal rules or field of law. It also follows that these questions must be dealt

* Professor, Department of Public Law, Stellenbosch University.

** Research Fellow, Department of Public Law, Stellenbosch University.

[1] AJ van der Walt *Property and constitution* (2012) 23–24.

[2] AJ van der Walt *Property and constitution* (2012) 23–24, 49–58; AJ van der Walt 'Normative pluralism and anarchy: Reflections on the 2007 term' (2008) 1 *CCR* 77–128.

with in the very first stage of adjudication, prior even to asking questions of application. In this contribution we reflect on the developing set of guidelines informing the methodological questions flowing from the single system of law principle.

This contribution is still very much a work in progress. We certainly do not claim to have the answers; in fact, we are still largely grappling to formulate the issue. However, as we endeavour to show in this chapter, we are convinced that there remain significant unanswered questions here despite the ostensible acceptance in South African constitutional adjudication of the single system of law principle. We think that these questions largely raise issues of methodology in constitutional adjudication and show up often, although not exclusively, when the right to administrative justice in section 33 of the Constitution[3] interacts with other rights and their respective regulatory frameworks. In this contribution we use the interaction between the right to administrative justice and property rights under section 25 of the Constitution to explore the more general question. Our choice of this particular interaction is informed by the fact that André van der Walt himself focused heavily on these fields in exploring the methodological questions at issue in this context and we thus take our cue from his work on adjudicative methodology under our Constitution.[4]

We also follow Van der Walt's thinking in one other significant way: like Van der Walt, we acknowledge that some problems do not have quick fixes or easy answers, and are best approached tentatively. Van der Walt himself on many occasions invoked Cilliers's statement that '[i]f something is really complex, it cannot be adequately described by means of a simple theory',[5] or 'complex problems rarely have simple solutions'. In his seminal article, 'Normative pluralism and anarchy: Reflections on the 2007 term',[6] which

---

[3] We refer to the 'right to just administrative action' when only referring to what is contained in section 33 of the Constitution and to 'the right to administrative justice' when referring to the normative dimension of what is contained in section 33.

[4] See AJ van der Walt 'Sosiale geregtigheid, prosedurele billikheid, en eiendom: Alternatiewe perspektiewe op grondwetlike waarborge' (2002) 13 *Stell LR* 59–82, 206–229; AJ van der Walt 'Normative pluralism and anarchy: Reflections on the 2007 term' (2008) 1 *CCR* 77–128; AJ van der Walt *Constitutional property law* 3 ed (2011) 12–79; AJ van der Walt 'Procedurally arbitrary deprivation of property' (2012) 23 *Stell LR* 88–94; AJ van der Walt *Property and constitution* (2012) 35–48; AJ van der Walt 'Property law in the constitutional democracy' (2017) 28 *Stell LR* 8–25.

[5] P Cilliers *Complexity and postmodernism: Understanding complex systems* (1998) ix.

[6] AJ van der Walt 'Normative pluralism and anarchy: Reflections on the 2007 term' (2008) 1 *CCR* 77–128.

inaugurated the *Constitutional Court Review*[7] and in which he introduced most clearly his methodological arguments around the single system of law principle, Van der Walt described his contribution as 'indulging a 30-year obsession'.[8] We will therefore not be so arrogant as to suggest that in this single contribution we can do more than simply sketch the methodological issues at stake here and suggest (tentatively and modestly) contours of future work that can help us better understand 'the development algorithm of post-apartheid South African law'.[9]

Our point of departure is the supremacy of the Constitution, an important implication of which is the 'single system of law principle'.[10] This principle was first expressed by Chaskalson P in the *Pharmaceutical Manufacturers Association* case,[11] where the court held:

> There is only one system of law. It is shaped by the Constitution which is the supreme law and all law, including the common law, derives its force from the Constitution and is subject to constitutional control.

At the core of the principle of a single system of law lies the prohibition against creating (or allowing) parallel systems of law, either in an attempt to shield certain areas from the influence of the Constitution, or alternatively when different sources of law are potentially applicable and different litigation 'routes' are created for litigants to obtain some advantage, or because it is unclear to a court what the appropriate source of law is. Parallel systems may emerge from the relationship between sources of law (the Constitution *vis-à-vis* legislation, the Constitution or legislation *vis-à-vis* the common law) or through the relationship between different areas of law (such as property law and administrative law).[12]

---

[7] Along with the other lead essay by Frank Michelman: FI Michelman 'On the uses of interpretive charity: Some notes on application, avoidance, equality and objective unconstitutionality from the 2007 term of the Constitutional Court of South Africa' (2008) 1 *CCR* 1–61.

[8] AJ van der Walt 'Normative pluralism and anarchy: Reflections on the 2007 term' (2008) 1 *CCR* 77–128.

[9] AJ van der Walt *Property and constitution* (2012) 23.

[10] See AJ van der Walt *Property and constitution* (2012) 23–24; AJ van der Walt 'Normative pluralism and anarchy: Reflections on the 2007 term' (2008) 1 *CCR* 77–128; E Marais & PJH Maree 'At the intersection between expropriation law and administrative law: Two critical views on the Constitutional Court's *Arun* judgment' (2016) 19 *PELJ* 1-54.

[11] *Pharmaceutical Manufacturers Association of South Africa and Another: In re Ex Parte President of the Republic of South Africa and Others* 2000 (2) SA 674 (CC) para 44.

[12] E van der Sijde *Reconsidering the relationship between property and regulation: A systemic constitutional approach* (2015) unpublished LLD thesis Stellenbosch University 182.

In this contribution we reflect on the developing set of guidelines informing the methodological questions flowing from the single system of law principle. Van der Walt argued that the right to just administrative action in section 33 and the property clause in section 25 of the Constitution represent very different approaches to the constitutional transformation of our law. While the section 33 right, upon which post-constitutional administrative law is premised, amounts to 'wholesale replacing of apartheid law with a fundamentally new set of rules, indicating normative unity in reform', the provisions of section 25 'look less like wholesale, unidirectional transformations and more like contradictory products of difficult and inchoate compromises'.[13] However, even in these 'patchwork compromises' an approach premised on the purpose of the single system of law principle in pursuit of 'transformation by, under, and according to law' provides a way out of what may seem like a contradiction.[14] This way out is not 'to deny or resolve the tension [within these compromises], but to explore it in the context of the equally contingent and contradictory justice goals of constitutional transformation itself.'[15] The interaction between the administrative justice and property rights in the Constitution thus provides an ideal site to test fundamental questions of adjudicative methodology under our Constitution.[16] However, these questions also emerge in a number of other areas such as the interaction between the right to just administrative action and socio-economic rights and between the right to just administrative action and labour law respectively, as well as within administrative law and the interaction between administrative justice premised on section 33 and the Promotion of Administrative Justice Act 3 of 2000 ('PAJA') on the one hand and the broader constitutional notion of legality on the other.[17]

[13] AJ van der Walt 'Normative pluralism and anarchy: Reflections on the 2007 term' (2008) 1 *CCR* 77–128 86.

[14] AJ van der Walt 'Normative pluralism and anarchy: Reflections on the 2007 term' (2008) 1 *CCR* 77–128 87.

[15] AJ van der Walt 'Normative pluralism and anarchy: Reflections on the 2007 term' (2008) 1 *CCR* 77–128 87.

[16] AJ van der Walt 'Normative pluralism and anarchy: Reflections on the 2007 term' (2008) 1 *CCR* 77–128; AJ van der Walt 'Procedurally arbitrary deprivation of property' (2012) 23 *Stell LR* 88–94.

[17] This latter instance of the problems we are engaging with in this contribution has become even more acute following the judgment in *State Information Technology Agency SOC Limited v Gijima Holdings (Pty) Limited* [2017] ZACC 40, where the Constitutional Court held that an organ of state cannot rely on section 33 or PAJA to challenge the validity of its own administrative action, but that it must rely on the constitutional principle of legality.

Within a complex system, such as the legal system, there are many sub-components and interdependencies between sub-systems.[18] It is to be expected that there would be some areas of overlap in any legal system, but for a system to be efficient and sustainable and to develop holistically, the areas of overlap should be justifiable, and not the result of careless development. There are distinct risks in the unprincipled development of parallel sub-systems, which in our view raises the need for an appropriate methodology to manage interaction between sub-systems. Broadly speaking and without going into the detail here, a systemic constitutional approach is accordingly called for in which the subsidiarity principles, premised in the first instance on the single system of law principle, form the methodological building blocks.[19]

In the rest of this contribution we highlight the issues stemming from an underdeveloped constitutional methodology as we see them by using the analytical framework of overlap and non-overlap cases. Before doing so, however, we briefly set out the current understanding of the subsidiarity principles.

2 The single system of law principle and the subsidiarity principles

Constitutional supremacy and the single system of law principle necessarily have an impact on how the various sources of law are dealt with in South African law.[20] A set of principles, called subsidiarity principles, can thus be extrapolated from the single system of law principle as first principle. These subsidiarity principles constitute the 'set of guidelines' Van der Walt referred to and serve to determine which source of law applies to a dispute and, more generally, how the dispute is to be conceptualised.[21] Elaboration of these guidelines is necessary to ensure that the source of law that is most likely

[18] E van der Sijde *Reconsidering the relationship between property and regulation: A systemic constitutional approach* (2015) unpublished LLD thesis Stellenbosch University 252–261.

[19] For a detailed discussion on what a systemic constitutional approach would entail in the context of the regulation of the use of property, see E van der Sijde *Reconsidering the relationship between property and regulation: A systemic constitutional approach* (2015) unpublished LLD thesis Stellenbosch University 288–296.

[20] AJ van der Walt *Property and constitution* (2012) 23, 26. The Constitution recognises the common law, legislation, customary law and international law as possible sources of law.

[21] AJ van der Walt *Property and constitution* (2012) 23–24; AJ van der Walt 'Normative pluralism and anarchy: Reflections on the 2007 term' (2008) 1 *CCR* 77–128.

to promote the spirit, purport and object of the Bill of Rights is selected.[22] Stated differently, subsidiarity principles provide guidance when dealing with more than one potentially applicable source of law and ensure selection of the source that will contribute to the development of a single system of law that exhibits the desired characteristics envisioned by the Constitution.[23] While the focus here is specifically on the sources of law used to adjudicate a particular dispute, it must be appreciated that the question is a broader one than simply a technical issue of sources. What is really at stake here is the conceptualisation of the dispute. What type of dispute is it or should or may it be and how should it be dealt with in terms of the single system of law? At an even broader level, the question is one of determining how we should go about incorporating the Constitution's transformative objectives into the law. In our view this is *the* question in constitutional adjudication in South Africa and one that requires urgent attention.[24] Rather than responding to this question on an ad hoc, casuistic basis as cases present particular instances of rules in need of development under the Constitution, we agree with a number of authors that have called for a coherent framework to guide this process.[25]

---

[22] AJ van der Walt *Property and constitution* (2012) 35. Also see L du Plessis '"Subsidiarity": What's in the name for constitutional interpretation and adjudication?' (2006) 17 *Stell LR* 207–231 209 for an explanation of the different kinds of subsidiarity (institutional subsidiarity and strategic subsidiarity) which impact on adjudicative subsidiarity.

[23] AJ van der Walt *Property and constitution* (2012) 35; AJ van der Walt 'Tradition on trial: A critical analysis of the civil-law tradition in South African property law' (1995) *SAJHR* 169–206 203–205.

[24] See DM Davis 'Where is the map to guide common-law development?' (2014) 25 *Stell LR* 3–14 14.

[25] See AJ van der Walt 'Normative pluralism and anarchy: Reflections on the 2007 term' (2008) 1 *CCR* 77–128 90, who speaks of a 'direction-giving approach', and AJ van der Walt *Property and constitution* (2012) 23, where he speaks of a 'central guideline'; 37, where he states that 'the subsidiarity principles … indicate … a methodological discipline to avoid arbitrary resort to established and comfortable ways of thinking'; and 107, where he notes the dangers of 'arbitrary choices as far as the sources of law are concerned, mostly in the form of ignoring or underplaying either the constitutional text of legislation enacted to give effect to it and restricting adjudication to common-law or traditional legal thinking, unaffected by transformative complications'; DM Davis 'Where is the map to guide common-law development?' (2014) 25 *Stell LR* 3–14 14, who calls for 'the development of a guiding framework which would assist in the coherent development of the law'; ZT Boggenpoel 'Can the journey affect the destination? A single system of law approach to property remedies' (2016) 32 *SAJHR* 71–86 80–81, who criticises 'incoherent and confusing jurisprudence' that results from the 'random, ad-hoc manner' in which choices are at times made between different remedies and states that 'this incoherency is simply unacceptable'.

Before turning to the set of subsidiarity principles that have emerged from South African constitutional jurisprudence, it is important to note what subsidiarity in this context is not. Klare has criticised reliance on subsidiarity within the South African context, pointing to its historical baggage and uncritical reliance on 'timeworn and reified conceptions' of the separation of powers.[26] In response, Van der Walt has dealt extensively with this criticism and in the process pointed out that the notion of subsidiarity as used in the present context is a specific one rather than the general notion of subsidiarity.[27] There is no need to repeat Van der Walt's arguments, which we find persuasive, in response to the criticism and in support of the view that the specific form of subsidiarity at issue here is not only useful, but indeed necessary.[28] The only two points that are important to highlight here are, firstly, that we are not talking about subsidiarity in a general sense, but in the very specific sense as developed under the South African Constitution and, secondly, to note the role of the single system of law principle as the basis for the South African subsidiarity principles. Du Plessis, when introducing the very notion of subsidiarity in South African constitutional analysis, emphasised that it is largely due to the single system of law principle, as expressed in the *Pharmaceutical Manufacturers Association* case,[29] that subsidiarity cannot 'justify interpretive and/or adjudicative preference for a non- (or not strictly) constitutional option inconsistent with the Constitution' and that it cannot be relied on to 'enervate the precedence of the Constitution as supreme law'.[30] The single system of law principle is thus a key element of subsidiarity as understood in South Africa to 'promote normative pluralism and constitutional change without succumbing to either normative anarchy or reactionary formalism'.[31] Subsidiarity as understood here is thus not a mechanism for constitutional avoidance, far from it.

The first subsidiarity principle states that if a litigant avers the infringement of a constitutional right and legislation has been specifically enacted to give effect to that right, the litigant must base her claim on the legislation and

[26] KE Klare 'Legal subsidiarity and constitutional rights: A reply to AJ van der Walt' (2008) 1 *CCR* 129–154 135.

[27] AJ van der Walt *Property and constitution* (2012) 98.

[28] AJ van der Walt *Property and constitution* (2012) 97–110.

[29] *Pharmaceutical Manufacturers Association of South Africa and Another: In re Ex Parte President of the Republic of South Africa and Others* 2000 (2) SA 674 (CC) para 44.

[30] L du Plessis '"Subsidiarity": What's in the name for constitutional interpretation and adjudication?' (2006) 17 *Stell LR* 207–231 216.

[31] AJ van der Walt 'Normative pluralism and anarchy: Reflections on the 2007 term' (2008) 1 *CCR* 77–128 100.

cannot rely on the constitutional provision directly.[32] In terms of the second subsidiarity principle, a litigant may not choose to rely on the common law where legislation has been specifically enacted to protect the right in question.[33]

This seems relatively clear and uncomplicated. However, each principle is subject to a proviso. The first principle does not apply if the litigant wishes to challenge the specifically enacted legislation for being 'unconstitutional or inadequate in protecting the right', which means that in this case a litigant may rely on the constitutional provision directly.[34] An inferred proviso to the second principle is that a litigant may rely on the common law if the legislation was not intended to cover a particular aspect of the law, or if it was intended to cover an entire field, but in fact does not cover a particular aspect of the common law. However, the common law can only be applied insofar as the common law does not conflict with the constitutional provision or negate the aims and objectives of the relevant legislative scheme.[35]

The subsidiarity principles as set out above can be applied within a single area of law. Administrative law provides a good example. Section 33 of the Constitution guarantees a right to just administrative action. That right is given content in PAJA, which is legislation intended to cover the field of administrative justice.[36] Within this context, a litigant cannot found a cause of action directly on section 33, but must do so on PAJA. Only if the litigant wishes to challenge the provisions of PAJA (or other legislation) for constitutionality, may she rely directly on section 33 as a cause of action. The litigant can equally not found a cause of action on the common-law administrative law, but must do so on PAJA. Only when PAJA does not cover

---

32 AJ van der Walt *Property and constitution* (2012) 36. This principle is derived from *South African National Defence Union v Minister of Defence* 2007 (5) SA 400 (CC) paras 51–52; *Minister of Health NO v New Clicks South Africa (Pty) Ltd (Treatment Action Campaign and Another as Amici Curiae)* 2006 (2) SA 311 (CC) paras 93–96.

33 AJ van der Walt *Property and constitution* (2012) 36 refers to several important Constitutional Court decisions where these principles were formulated, including *Bato Star Fishing (Pty) Ltd v Minister of Environmental Affairs* 2004 (4) SA 490 (CC) para 25 and *Minister of Health NO v New Clicks South Africa (Pty) Ltd (Treatment Action Campaign and Another as Amici Curiae)* 2006 (2) SA 311 (CC) para 96.

34 AJ van der Walt *Property and constitution* (2012) 36 formulates this proviso with reference to the judgments in *South African National Defence Union v Minister of Defence* 2007 (5) SA 400 (CC) para 52; *Minister of Health NO v New Clicks South Africa (Pty) Ltd (Treatment Action Campaign and Another as Amici Curiae)* 2006 (2) SA 311 (CC) para 437; *Sidumo and Another v Rustenburg Platinum Mines Ltd and Others* 2008 (2) SA 24 (CC) para 249; *Engelbrecht v Road Accident Fund* 2007 (6) SA 96 (CC) para 15.

35 AJ van der Walt *Property and constitution* (2012) 36.

36 C Hoexter *Administrative law in South Africa* 2 ed (2012) 118.

a particular aspect of administrative law, such as the rules pertaining to legitimate expectations, for example,[37] may the litigant rely on the common law.

A further area of application for the subsidiarity principles is when more than one area of law is at issue across different sources of law.[38] Subsidiarity principles should be employed where multiple fields of law are applicable to the same facts. Within this context the subsidiarity framework, premised on the single system of law principle, should guide us in deciding which area of law to rely on when dealing with property regulation disputes. This framework should indicate either exclusively or in what order the different areas of law must be relied on. It is within this particular context that we perceive the subsidiarity framework to be in need of further development.

A further complicating factor, exemplified by the judgment in *State Information Technology Agency SOC Limited v Gijima Holdings (Pty) Limited*,[39] is that different litigants may not have access to the same routes to judicially challenge the same public action essentially on the same substantive arguments. The central question in *Gijima* was on what basis an organ of state may seek to have its own administrative action reviewed by a court. The Supreme Court of Appeal divided on whether an organ of state is obliged to rely on PAJA in seeking such review or whether it may rely on the constitutional principle of legality.[40] The Constitutional Court held, unanimously, that organs of state may not rely on section 33 or PAJA in such cases, but must bring such challenges in terms of legality.[41] It is important to note that the substance of the challenge was not at issue in the case. On whatever basis the review was meant to be considered, the substance of the argument was that the organ of state's conduct fell foul of section 271 of the Constitution. The issue was thus purely how this challenge had to be conceptualised. The outcome of this judgment creates the further difficulty from the perspective of the single system of law principle that the identity of the litigant alone determines how the relevant public action is to be tested against the Constitution. If the challenge is brought by a private litigant it

[37] See *Walele v City of Cape Town* 2008 (6) SA 129 (CC) para 37.

[38] We use 'area of law' in this contribution to refer to different divisions of substantive law, eg administrative law, property law, constitutional law and so forth. In contrast, we use 'source of law' to refer to the recognised sources of South African law, such as legislation, the common law and case law.

[39] [2017] ZACC 40.

[40] *State Information Technology Agency SOC Ltd v Gijima Holdings (Pty) Ltd* 2017 (2) SA 63 (SCA).

[41] *State Information Technology Agency SOC Ltd v Gijima Holdings (Pty) Ltd* 2018 (2) SA 23 (CC) para 37.

will follow one route whereas if the challenge is brought by the organ of state itself it will follow a different route. It is not clear how this differentiation is to be managed within the subsidiarity framework.

3 Sketching the landscape: Regulation in overlap and non-overlap cases

Quinot and Liebenberg have formulated the analytical framework of overlap and non-overlap cases as a means to engage with regulatory questions under the Constitution where more than one area of law is at stake.[42] They were specifically interested in reasonableness as a constitutional notion that features in two constitutional contexts, namely as a standard of review in socio-economic rights and in administrative justice jurisprudence. We think that this framework can be usefully employed in the current context as well.

'Overlap' cases are instances where both property law and administrative law are applicable, in other words, cases involving review of administrative action that has an impact on property,[43] while 'non-overlap' cases refer specifically to cases where the matter falls within the ambit of either property law or administrative law, but not both.

When applied to the regulation of the use of property in the constitutional setting, the framework of overlap and non-overlap cases illustrates a problem that has thus far remained largely unanalysed within a property context. It is an accepted part of organised modern life that the use, exploitation or enjoyment of property is regulated.[44] These regulatory processes (such as those contained in planning law) limit property rights and therefore require regulation or control.[45] The idea of 'regulation of regulation' aptly describes the situation in the property law context, where the imposition of limitations (in the form of regulation) is regulated to ensure adherence to constitutional and statutory requirements. This 'secondary regulatory function' can be fulfilled by the principles of either constitutional property law or administrative law, but it is not always clear which regulatory system applies to a specific case.

---

[42] G Quinot & S Liebenberg 'Narrowing the band: Reasonableness review in administrative justice and socio-economic rights jurisprudence in South Africa' (2011) 22 *Stell LR* 639–663.

[43] The overlap between sections 25 and 33 occurs in various areas of law, including for instance expropriation law, planning law and environmental law.

[44] See E van der Sijde *Reconsidering the relationship between property and regulation: A systemic constitutional approach* (2015) unpublished LLD thesis Stellenbosch University 2–4.

[45] Administrative law is sometimes described as 'the regulation of regulation'. See for example CR Farina 'Administrative law as regulation: The paradox of attempting to control and to inspire the use of public power' (2004) 19 *SAPL* 489–512 490.

The problem is that the use of property is sometimes regulated by administrative action, but not always. Regulatory limitations can also be imposed directly on property by operation of law (with no administrative action) through the common law, legislation or the Constitution, or by acts of the judiciary or the executive. This means that not all instances of regulation can be challenged or reviewed in the same way, or on the same basis. That is, the regulation of the regulation is likely to differ between different contexts. It is therefore necessary to determine when a regulation dispute will be adjudicated in terms of PAJA, and when a litigant can (or should) rely directly on section 25 of the Constitution.[46]

In South African constitutional law, this secondary regulatory function (regulation of regulation) can be carried out within the regulatory framework provided for by section 25 of the Constitution, or alternatively, within the framework created by section 33 of the Constitution together with PAJA. In a systemic constitutional approach premised on the single system of law principle, it must be accepted that each of these systems fulfils some distinct purpose, in a way that does not allow for the creation of parallel systems.[47] Given the subsidiarity principles, the regulation of regulation should primarily be an issue of administrative law, unless the source or authority of the primary regulation (the regulation of the use of property) excludes that option. In such a case, the next option is direct reliance on constitutional principles, which include but are not limited to the constitutional property principles of section 25. However, in such a case the indirect application of administrative law emerges.

Traditionally, property law and administrative law have a strained relationship, because of each area of law's perceived function in terms of the common law. From a liberal (and absolutist) perspective,[48] administrative law should preferably be largely absent from the sphere of property law insofar as it represents an intrusion of the public sphere on the private sphere. However, property and administrative justice are both fundamental rights in

---

[46] E van der Sijde *Reconsidering the relationship between property and regulation: A systemic constitutional approach* (2015) unpublished LLD thesis Stellenbosch University 190.

[47] E van der Sijde *Reconsidering the relationship between property and regulation: A systemic constitutional approach* (2015) unpublished LLD thesis Stellenbosch University 205–210. Also see AJ van der Walt 'The modest systemic status of property rights' (2014) 1 *J L Prop & Soc'y* 15–106 71–84, where he discusses 'property versus privileged statutory non-property rights' to explain the relationship between the protection of property rights of owners and statutory rights of non-owners.

[48] See E van der Sijde *Reconsidering the relationship between property and regulation: A systemic constitutional approach* (2015) unpublished LLD thesis Stellenbosch University 12–19.

the Bill of Rights and therefore it is necessary to reconceive the relationship between private property and the administration. In so doing, administrative law should adopt a more facilitative role in the context of the regulation of the use of property to further the transformational ideals of the Constitution. This is particularly important in a systemic constitutional approach because regulation is a systemic device that can promote a variety of constitutional objectives. The principles of administrative law can, and arguably should, assist with this task.

3.1 Overlap cases

In overlap cases (cases where administrative action has an impact on property) the subsidiarity principles indicate that the applicable regulatory framework is that of PAJA. Property law principles will have some role to play in these cases, but the interaction between the regulatory systems is usually not problematic, since administrative law almost always works with a 'substantive regulatory program'.[49] The nature of administrative law is to regulate 'the process by which regulation occurs'[50] and the substance of the regulation traditionally has little bearing on that function, which, as we shall note later, may again be a particular problem for non-overlap cases.

However, in the context of the regulation of the use of property, property-law principles flowing from the Constitution can influence the normative content of the administrative-law review, although section 25(1) does not function as the constitutional framework of control over the regulation itself. This means that both sections 25 and 33 of the Constitution can be applicable to a dispute where regulation is brought about by administrative action, but PAJA is the framework that fulfils the secondary regulatory function.

Where PAJA is applicable, litigants should not be permitted to sidestep its provisions and rely directly on section 25 (to obtain some advantage or because of practical difficulties with basing their cause of action on PAJA) since this can have unintended systemic consequences. This point can be illustrated with reference to *Arun Property Development (Pty) Ltd v City of Cape Town.*[51]

---

[49] *Walele v City of Cape Town* 2008 (6) SA 129 (CC) is an example of this interaction. Also see CR Farina 'Administrative law as regulation: The paradox of attempting to control and to inspire the use of public power' (2004) 19 *SAPL* 489–512 490.

[50] CR Farina 'Administrative law as regulation: The paradox of attempting to control and to inspire the use of public power' (2004) 19 *SAPL* 489–512 490.

[51] 2015 (2) SA 584 (CC) (*Arun*). See also the extensive discussion of the judgment in E Marais & PJH Maree 'At the intersection between expropriation law and administrative law: Two critical views on the Constitutional Court's *Arun* judgment' (2016) 19 *PELJ* 1–54.

In *Arun* a property developer purchased property with the intention of developing a township. Approval for the required rezoning and subdivision depended on whether the development was in line with the existing land use planning framework, including the structure plan.[52] In terms of the applicable structure plan, provision had to be made for certain primary roads over the property. Arun adhered to the requirements of the planning regime when drawing up its application and approval was subsequently granted for the development, including confirmation of the rezoning of portions of the land to public streets, and conditions pertaining to the design of the road infrastructure.[53] However, Arun was aggrieved by the extent of land that formed part of the road infrastructure and that went beyond what was strictly necessary for the development itself. Arun thus sought compensation from the city for what it considered to be an expropriation in respect of this excess land. This dispute can be conceptualised in a number of different ways – it can be viewed as a deprivation of property under section 25(1) or an expropriation under section 25(2) or as an unjust administrative action under section 33.

The Constitutional Court briefly considered the possibility of adjudicating *Arun* with reference to the provisions of PAJA, but concluded that the developer would face 'a legion of obstacles' with administrative judicial review, and opted to rely on the framework of section 25(2) instead. These obstacles included the 180-day time bar in PAJA, difficulty with finding a decision to impugn and the possible review grounds in PAJA. The court also referred to the question of whether *Arun* was obliged first to seek review or to exhaust other possible remedies before seeking compensation.[54] It is questionable whether the court's reasoning regarding the practical

---

[52] *Arun Property Development (Pty) Ltd v City of Cape Town* 2015 (2) SA 584 (CC) para 7.

[53] *Arun Property Development (Pty) Ltd v City of Cape Town* [2012] ZAWCHC 399 (31 October 2012) para 5. Section 42(2) of the Land Use Planning Ordinance 15 of 1985 (C) makes provision for local authorities to impose conditions on developers when granting approval. Arun applied for approval on three occasions for three phases of the development, and each approval was subject to conditions. The High Court specifically emphasised that it was not made a condition of the approval that the road portions had to be ceded without compensation.

[54] *Arun Property Development (Pty) Ltd v City of Cape Town* 2015 (2) SA 584 (CC) paras 11–12, 24–28, 66. Arun applied for variation of some of the conditions, but did not challenge (in the form of appeal or review) the decisions to impose the conditions or make the approval subject to compliance with the said conditions relating to road designs. The City contended that compensation was not an appropriate remedy because Arun did not exhaust all other remedies – they did not attempt to amend the structure plan, nor did they challenge the lawfulness of the plan or the conditions by means of the mechanism provided for in the legislation.

difficulties with bringing a case for judicial review is convincing, especially given its previous statement in *MEC for Health, Eastern Cape and Another v Kirland Investments (Pty) Ltd* [55] that practical difficulties with PAJA do not justify side-stepping its provisions. The confusion that *Arun* left in its wake regarding the existence of a doctrine of constructive expropriation and the status of *ex lege* expropriation[56] shows that it might have been preferable if the court had faced the practical difficulties of applying PAJA head-on.[57] Because of Arun's interest in claiming compensation for the *ex lege* transfer of excess land, they framed their case as an expropriation challenge with reference to section 25(2) of the Constitution. The single system of law principle, together with the subsidiarity principles, indicates that this preference should not necessarily be allowed. Systemically, there are good reasons for limiting litigants' choice of cause of action to avoid the (unjustifiable) creation of parallel paths of litigation.[58]

Another example that highlights the importance of engaging with the area of overlap between property regulation and administrative justice is *Shoprite Checkers (Pty) Ltd v Member of the Executive Council for Economic Development, Environmental Affairs and Tourism, Eastern Cape and Others.*[59] In the *Shoprite* case an existing regulatory regime was amended by the Eastern Cape Liquor Act,[60] with the consequence that certain categories of rights under the previous regime were abolished. What was challenged was 'a legislative change to the regulatory framework for the sale of liquor, not its administrative enforcement'.[61] However, the role of administrative law was potentially relevant in a different context, as appears from Moseneke DCJ's judgment. Moseneke DCJ points out that not all interests need protection as

[55] 2014 (3) SA 481 (CC) para 83, where the court refers specifically to the 180-day time bar in PAJA.

[56] E Marais & PJH Maree 'At the intersection between expropriation law and administrative law: Two critical views on the Constitutional Court's *Arun* judgment' (2016) 19 *PELJ* 1–54 15–16, 21.

[57] As Marais and Maree persuasively argue, the 'Court could simply have held that the attempted expropriation is *ultra vires* the authorising provision and of no effect', which it could have done on a simple application of administrative law grounds of review. E Marais & PJH Maree 'At the intersection between expropriation law and administrative law: Two critical views on the Constitutional Court's *Arun* judgment' (2016) 19 *PELJ* 1–54 21.

[58] AJ van der Walt 'The modest systemic status of property rights' (2014) 1 *J L Prop & Soc'y* 15–106 71–84; AJ van der Walt 'Property law in the constitutional democracy' (2017) 28 *Stell LR* 8–25 9–13.

[59] 2015 (6) SA 125 (CC).

[60] 10 of 2003.

[61] *Shoprite Checkers (Pty) Ltd v Member of the Executive Council for Economic Development, Environmental Affairs and Tourism, Eastern Cape and Others* 2015 (6) SA 125 (CC) para 30.

'property' for purposes of section 25(1) of the Constitution, because of South Africa's expansive Bill of Rights, especially the expansive administrative justice protections.[62] Here we see the interplay between constitutional property law and administrative justice, not to determine the appropriate regulatory framework to review the regulation of the use of property, but as an antecedent question to determine whether an interest ought to be recognised as property at all. What the *Shoprite Checkers* case thus clearly illustrates is that the need for a coherent guideline to steer the courts in deciding how a dispute must be properly conceptualised under the Constitution emerges at the very first stage of adjudication.

A further, and perhaps to date the clearest, example of the methodological gap is found in *City of Tshwane Metropolitan Municipality v Link Africa (Pty) Ltd and Others.*[63] In this matter, relief was sought in part for what the City deemed an arbitrary deprivation of property and a breach of the principle of legality.[64] There was also a claim for judicial review, based on administrative law grounds. The matter, briefly summarised, stemmed from provisions of the Electronic Communications Act 36 of 2005 which empowered the Independent Communications Authority of South Africa to award licences to qualifying persons. Licensees are awarded wide powers to construct or maintain an electronic communications network or facility on the land of another person (the land owned by the Tshwane Metropolitan Municipality).[65] Link Africa wished to exercise its rights per its duly obtained licence and enter onto the property without notice, while the Tshwane Metropolitan Municipality claimed that in so doing Link Africa was arbitrarily depriving it of its property.

The approach of the minority judgment was to consider the constitutional challenge based on section 25(1) of the Constitution, and thereafter to consider whether PAJA was applicable to the matter.[66] The majority judgment also starts with the question of constitutional validity, and in its interpretation of the relevant statutory provisions relies on the approach prescribed by the common law of servitudes, to render the provisions constitutionally

[62] *Shoprite Checkers (Pty) Ltd v Member of the Executive Council for Economic Development, Environmental Affairs and Tourism, Eastern Cape and Others* 2015 (6) SA 125 (CC) para 115.

[63] 2015 (6) SA 440 (CC).

[64] *City of Tshwane Metropolitan Municipality v Link Africa (Pty) Ltd and Others* 2015 (6) SA 440 (CC) paras 17–19.

[65] *City of Tshwane Metropolitan Municipality v Link Africa (Pty) Ltd and Others* 2015 (6) SA 440 (CC) paras 1–3, 42.

[66] *City of Tshwane Metropolitan Municipality v Link Africa (Pty) Ltd and Others* 2015 (6) SA 440 (CC) paras 65–78.

compliant.[67] The majority judgment therefore avoids the question of whether PAJA is applicable to the matter.[68] The illustration of the problem lies not in evaluating whether the majority judgment was correct in relying on the common law to interpret the relevant provisions of the Electronic Communications Act in line with the Constitution, but in highlighting the importance of having a well-developed methodology that will guide the *a priori* decision-making of where convoluted regulatory disputes *should start*. The areas of overlap in regulatory disputes are vast, and in an increasingly regulatory-minded society, unlikely to disappear. The challenge is then not to minimise the area of overlap, but to refine the constitutional method.

Ultimately, the area of overlap should not be seen in a negative light. We should rather pursue a 'constructive alliance' between provisions in the Constitution in which the courts must engage with the possible overlaps, and consciously and meticulously develop the law to create a coherent system that reflects the 'desired characteristics' envisioned by the Constitution.[69] However, case law shows that the overlap is not always readily identifiable, and that litigants may want to frame their case in such a way that it is adjudicated as a non-overlap case so as to give them a choice between two causes of action.[70] In a constitutional legal system, litigants should not be allowed to side-step applicable national legislation. Allowing litigants the unrestricted freedom to vindicate their rights in the way that suits them best can result in outcomes that are unstructured, unprincipled and inconsistent, with judgments that are difficult to make sense of doctrinally. There is thus a need for a distinct adjudicative methodology in terms of which overlap can be addressed in a principled manner.

3.2 Non-overlap cases

In non-overlap, non-administrative action cases (where the use of property is regulated *ex lege* by the common law, legislation or the Constitution, or through acts of the executive) PAJA is of course not applicable and a different regulatory system should 'regulate the regulation'. The most obvious option

---

[67] *City of Tshwane Metropolitan Municipality v Link Africa (Pty) Ltd and Others* 2015 (6) SA 440 (CC) paras 100–155.

[68] *City of Tshwane Metropolitan Municipality v Link Africa (Pty) Ltd and Others* 2015 (6) SA 440 (CC) para 159.

[69] G Quinot 'An administrative law perspective on "bad building" evictions in the Johannesburg inner city' (2007) 8 *ESR Review* 25–28 28. See AJ van der Walt *Property and constitution* (2012) 26–34 for a discussion of the 'desired characteristics' of the property law system in particular.

[70] *Arun Property Development (Pty) Ltd v City of Cape Town* 2015 (2) SA 584 (CC) para 66.

is the regulatory framework of section 25 of the Constitution, and with reference to acts of the executive, the principle of legality.[71] However, the complicating factor in these typical non-overlap cases is that the principles of administrative law are often still applied indirectly, despite the lack of administrative action.[72]

A striking example of this approach is seen in the development of the notion of 'procedural non-arbitrariness', a subcomponent of the non-arbitrariness requirement for lawful deprivations as per section 25(1) of the Constitution.[73] This notion was accepted in case law which made it clear that procedural fairness in the context of section 25(1) corresponds closely (if not exactly) with what administrative law jurisprudence considers to constitute procedural fairness.[74] In fact, the emphasis on the flexibility of the concept and the importance of determining fairness in a particular context echoes the content of sections 3 and 4 of PAJA.[75] Van der Walt suggested that

---

[71] The role and relevance of the principle of legality is discussed in some detail in E van der Sijde *Reconsidering the relationship between property and regulation: A systemic constitutional approach* (2015) unpublished LLD thesis Stellenbosch University 210–220.

[72] See for example *Mkontwana v Nelson Mandela Metropolitan Municipality and Another; Bissett and Others v Buffalo City Municipality and Others; Transfer Rights Action Campaign and Others v MEC, Local Government and Housing, Gauteng, and Others (KwaZulu-Natal Law Society and Msunduzi Municipality as Amici Curiae)* 2005 (1) SA 530 (CC) paras 65–67; *Reflect-All 1025 CC and Others v MEC for Public Transport, Roads and Works, Gauteng Provincial Government and Another* 2009 (6) SA 391 (CC) paras 39–47. Also see C Hoexter *Administrative law in South Africa* 2 ed (2012) 255.

[73] Procedural fairness is not explicitly required by section 25(1) of the Constitution, but the reference to arbitrariness was judicially interpreted to include both a substantive and a procedural component. See *First National Bank of SA Ltd t/a Wesbank v Commissioner, South African Revenue Service and Another; First National Bank of SA Ltd t/a Wesbank v Minister of Finance* 2002 (4) SA 768 (CC) para 100.

[74] *Mkontwana v Nelson Mandela Metropolitan Municipality and Another; Bissett and Others v Buffalo City Municipality and Others; Transfer Rights Action Campaign and Others v MEC, Local Government and Housing, Gauteng, and Others (KwaZulu-Natal Law Society and Msunduzi Municipality as Amici Curiae)* 2005 (1) SA 530 (CC) para 65 merely states that the Constitutional Court has indicated 'in contexts other than section 25(1)' that procedural fairness is a flexible concept that must be evaluated with reference to the circumstances of each case. *Reflect-All 1025 CC and Others v MEC for Public Transport, Roads and Works, Gauteng Provincial Government and Another* 2009 (6) SA 391 (CC) para 40 accepts the *Mkontwana* dictum. Also see AJ van der Walt "Procedurally arbitrary deprivation of property" (2012) 23 *Stell LR* 88–94 89; K Iles 'Property' in I Currie & J de Waal (eds) *The Bill of Rights handbook* 6 ed (2013) 530–562 541.

[75] See *Reflect-All 1025 CC and Others v MEC for Public Transport, Roads and Works, Gauteng Provincial Government and Another* 2009 (6) SA 391 (CC) paras 15, 40–47, where the court considers the procedural fairness of the deprivation in question. The applicants referred to section 3 of PAJA as a baseline for the requirement of procedural fairness but the court did not expressly engage with this argument, having decided that the

the *Mkontwana* decision can be seen as an indication that the procedural fairness of a deprivation will be evaluated on a similar basis to the test for procedural fairness in the context of just administrative action.[76]

The difficulty is of course what the impact of largely distinct regulatory frameworks between overlap and non-overlap cases will be on the coherence of property law. Allowing property law to develop along different paths in overlap and non-overlap cases may undermine the single system of law principle. A methodological mechanism will thus have to be found to avoid such divergent development.[77]

Divergent development is undesirable on a normative level, since the single system principle assumes the shared constitutional underpinnings of the entire system. Property rights should not be better protected when a regulatory measure is reviewed on one basis (such as administrative law) as opposed to another without it being justifiable with reference to the role that property plays in our new democratic society, and the transformation ideals and objectives of section 25 itself.

One of the main challenges in non-overlap cases is thus to maintain normative coherence across the entire constitutional system when concepts and standards of review are applied in different contexts. The single system

---

publication of lists of roads and designs by the MEC did not constitute administrative action and that PAJA did not apply to the matter. The court then referred to *Masetlha v President of the Republic of South Africa and Another* 2008 (1) SA 566 (CC) as further authority for its contextual approach and held that, under the circumstances, the deprivation was not procedurally arbitrary. The court found that in the particular context, the initial consultations were adequate and it would not be practical or in the public interest to revisit the numerous designs published in terms of the authorising legislation since the consultations took place. Although this is a reasonable conclusion and the court was correct in its finding that the requirements of procedural fairness will depend on the circumstances, it is interesting to note that the authority relied on (the *Masetlha* decision) dealt with procedural fairness requirements under the principle of legality. Moreover, the section of the *Masetlha* judgment that was quoted in *Reflect-All* as authority for its approach stemmed from the minority judgment in *Masetlha*, where Ngcobo J specifically dissented from the majority's view that the principle of legality did not include a procedural fairness component. The quoted section is therefore probably *obiter*, although it still carries weight as an *obiter* statement by the Constitutional Court. The court's use of authority in *Reflect-All* shows that questions regarding the role, content and function of procedural fairness are closely related, despite originating in different fields of law, and that the overarching concern is that the notion of procedural fairness should be informed by constitutional norms and values.

[76] AJ van der Walt 'Procedurally arbitrary deprivation of property' (2012) 23 *Stell LR* 88–94 89.

[77] A step in this direction is taken by Viljoen in the context of expropriation law in S Viljoen 'Substantive adjudication of the decision to expropriate property' (2017) 28 *Stell LR* 444–465.

of law principle should imply that concepts must hold the same normative implications across different contexts, even though the exact impact of such concepts may differ between contexts, depending for example on the variability inherent to the particular concept. Thus, the single system of law principle should not tolerate a scenario where reasonableness or procedural fairness, for example, could hold particular normative implications for regulation in one context and completely different implications in another. If we thus say that reasonableness or procedural fairness are constitutional requirements in the regulation of property it should carry the same implications in all instances of the regulation of property, regardless of whether the instance is one of overlap or non-overlap. However, the single system of law principle also implies that the system would not tolerate purposeless duplication. It is in the non-overlap context where these two implications of the principle come to a head and where the real danger for parallel developments emerge, namely that reasonableness, for example, may hold certain normative implications for the regulation of property in overlap cases based on the application of reasonableness as an administrative-justice requirement, but completely different implications in non-overlap cases based on the application of reasonableness or arbitrariness as section 25 requirements. The same argument can be made for procedural fairness as an administrative justice requirement, as a subcomponent of the non-arbitrariness requirement for lawful deprivations as per section 25(1) under the label of 'procedural non-arbitrariness', or as a section 26 requirement under the label of 'meaningful engagement'.[78]

To be clear, we are not suggesting that the application of these concepts should have the very same effect or entail the very same requirements in assessing the constitutionality of the regulation of property between overlap and non-overlap cases respectively. On the contrary, the need to avoid purposeless duplication within the system suggests that the actual requirements imposed by these concepts would be different between overlap and non-overlap cases, but that difference would be by design. In other words, the difference in what the application of the same norms would require between these contexts should be justifiable in terms of the coherent framework within which the norms exist. For example, the nature of participation in decision-making could be very different as a matter of administrative justice where those affected by regulatory action in overlap

[78] See S van der Berg 'Meaningful engagement: Proceduralising socio-economic rights further or infusing administrative law with substance?' (2013) 29 *SAJHR* 376–398 for a conceptualisation of meaningful engagement under both socio-economic rights and the right to just administrative action around the normative commitment to participation.

cases are entitled to procedural fairness in terms of section 33, compared to the entitlement to participate in decision-making in non-overlap cases based on section 25. The nature of this difference may be justifiable on the basis of the difference in the nature of the regulatory action, administrative action in overlap cases and, for example, legislative action in non-overlap cases. Or the difference, in the context of judicial review, may be justifiable on the basis of who is seeking to review the action, following the reasoning in *Gijima*.[79] While a private party should be able to attack a regulatory action for a failure to adhere to procedural fairness as a matter of administrative justice, it seems justifiable, when the cause of action is premised on legality, to deny an organ of state the same opportunity to challenge its own action based on its own failure to adhere to procedural fairness. The normative requirement of participation, however, should be constant.

We do not delve further into non-overlap cases, as these cases are usually less complex from a methodological point of view. This contribution specifically deals with the development of a constitutional methodology where the single system of law principle is implicated, and therefore non-overlap cases do not, for the most part, present the biggest challenge to creating or adopting a specific methodology.

4 (Preliminary) conclusion

In our view the preceding analysis shows a missing piece of the puzzle of constitutional adjudication, or a missing link. There is a need for a distinct stage or process within constitutional adjudication where the matter at hand can be conceptualised in terms of the system of the Constitution. What is primarily required is an accepted methodology. We think that the single system of law principle can be the basis for that methodology, but much more work is needed to further develop what are currently fairly disconnected notions and principles, that can broadly be described as subsidiarity principles, into a coherent methodology. As we have also endeavoured to show, there are particular aspects of this puzzle that are not adequately addressed by the existing methodological tools.

The preferred methodology in our view should involve substantive reasoning to provide justification for particular choices between different tensions with reference to the objectives of the constitutional system as a whole. In this view, the protection of individual entitlements is but one aspect of the system, and regulation is understood as a mechanism through which a variety of democratic values, such as liberty, dignity and participation,

[79] *State Information Technology Agency SOC Ltd v Gijima Holdings (Pty) Ltd* 2018 (2) SA 23 (CC).

are promoted, while avoiding the unjust concentration of power, haphazard developments and uncertainty regarding the influence of the Constitution on existing property rights.[80] If the courts are consistent in their methodology, it could have the positive effect of aligning the content of constitutional notions such as legality, procedural fairness, meaningful engagement, reasonableness and non-arbitrariness on a normative level. Moreover, it would avoid the creation of parallel routes of development.

We do not think that the answer lies in narrow conceptualism and formalism, which have been adopted in attempts at resolving these issues in other areas. The best example is the approach to similar tensions in the public employment context. Following years of uncertainty as to whether public employment disputes, especially dismissals, should be adjudicated in terms of labour law, contract law and/or administrative law,[81] the Constitutional Court held in *Gcaba v Minister for Safety and Security*[82] that '[g]enerally, employment and labour relationship issues do not amount to administrative action within the meaning of the PAJA.' Despite professing to arrive at this conclusion in terms of policy considerations, which would suggest substantive reasoning, the court in fact adopted a fairly narrow conceptual approach in terms of which administrative law is simply defined out of the equation by stating that the public-employment decision before it raised 'a quintessential labour-related issue'.[83] As Hoexter has succinctly noted in respect of this judgment, the 'categorical or essentialist idea fostered by such an approach is that something is *either* a labour matter *or* an administrative-law matter, but not both'. What is furthermore significant for our purposes is that the court does not explain what methodology it is adopting in reaching its conclusion. The same criticism may be levelled at the Constitutional Court's more recent treatment of review in terms of legality versus PAJA where an organ of state seeks to have its own action set aside.[84] The court again seems to follow a fairly narrow, formal approach in its reasoning to arrive at the conclusion that organs of state may not rely on PAJA under these circumstances.

In developing the methodology that we consider still largely absent from South African constitutional adjudication to implement a subsidiarity

---

[80] JW Singer *Entitlement: The paradoxes of property* (2000) 142–144, 208.

[81] See C Hoexter *Administrative law in South Africa* 2 ed (2012) 210–218; BE Loots *Public employment and the relationship between labour and administrative law* (2011) unpublished LLD thesis Stellenbosch University.

[82] 2010 (1) SA 238 (CC) para 64.

[83] *Gcaba v Minister for Safety and Security* 2010 (1) SA 238 (CC) para 66.

[84] *State Information Technology Agency SOC Ltd v Gijima Holdings (Pty) Ltd* 2018 (2) SA 23 (CC).

framework in a meaningful way, lessons can perhaps be learned from the field of private international law. In that field the unique issue of characterisation has generated considerable scholarship,[85] which may be of use in the current context at a theoretical level. The problem of characterisation in private international law lies in the difficulty of establishing, as a preliminary question, under which area of law the particular potentially applicable rule(s) of law (or norms) must be categorised in order to establish which specific conflict of law rule should apply to identify the applicable legal system.[86] While it is beyond the scope of this contribution to explore this line of enquiry in any detail, it is worthwhile to note that the leading 'solutions' to the problem all entail the recognition of judicial discretion based on a set of principles to guide the discretion as opposed to mechanical, formalistic approaches.[87] In our view, the methodological discipline that has developed within private international law and the theoretical insights regarding the role of characterisation as an essential preliminary question may yield fruitful insights for present purposes.

Our tentative steps towards formulating a more comprehensive approach to the 'methodological gap' we have identified amount to little more than a 'bird's-eye' view of the central issue, with a strong focus on synthesis, in addition to analysis. Waring has stated that this type of 'bird's eye' approach to certain legal problems has merit, especially when the method is used in studies that are broad in scope and aim to give a first broad overview and assessment of the problem, while providing the foundation for further analytical research (where a doctrinal methodology would feature more prominently).[88]

As we continue to build on these tentative steps, we hope to put forward some more concrete suggestions about what the type of methodology that we have in mind should look like, where exactly it should fit into the existing framework of adjudication and what the principles are that should inform such methodology. Along this route, we also hope to continue André van der Walt's reflection on the 'development algorithm of post-apartheid South African law'.[89]

---

[85] CF Forsyth *Private international law* 4 ed (2003) 68 describes the academic literature on this issue as 'immense'.

[86] CF Forsyth *Private international law* 4 ed (2003) 68–81.

[87] CF Forsyth *Private international law* 4 ed (2003) 73, 77–78.

[88] E Waring *Aspects of property: The impact of private takings* (2009) unpublished PhD thesis University of Cambridge 14.

[89] AJ van der Walt *Property and constitution* (2012) 23.

Chapter 20

A supervening lack of utility and the judicial shift toward ex *post* controls in South African servitude law: A critical analysis of *Pickard v Stein* 2015 (1) SA 439 (GJ)

*Warren Freedman**

Page

Contents

1 Introduction

South African property law draws a distinction between two categories of real rights, namely ownership and limited real rights. Unlike ownership, which is the only real right a person may acquire in property that belongs to her, limited real rights are rights that a person may acquire in property that belongs to someone else. It is for this reason that ownership is often referred to as the most complete real right. Apart from its complete nature, ownership is also distinguished from limited real rights on the ground that it confers a much wider range of entitlements on its holder than limited real rights do.

* Professor, School of Law, University of KwaZulu-Natal. It remains for me to expressly acknowledge the humanity, generosity and kindness of spirit André van der Walt always showed towards me, and to express my appreciation for his contribution to my own development as a legal scholar.

As their name suggests, limited real rights confer only limited entitlements on their holders.[1]

Although South African property law accepts that a person may acquire a limited real right in property that belongs to someone else, it also recognises that these rights are burdensome especially when they take the form of servitudes.[2] This is because servitudes are enforceable against the successive owners of the servient land by the successive owners of the dominant land; they are perpetual in nature, at least in the case of praedial servitudes;[3] and they continue to exist even though they have become inefficient or

---

[1] A real right may be defined as a legally supported claim to a thing (see PJ Badenhorst, J Pienaar & H Mostert *Silberberg and Schoeman's The law of property* 5 ed (2006) 47; CG van der Merwe & A Pope 'Property' in F du Bois (ed) *Wille's principles of South African law* 9 ed (2007) 431; H Mostert & A Pope (eds) *Principles of property law in South Africa* (2010) 42.

[2] A servitude may be defined as a limited real right that imposes a burden on the movable or immovable property of a person in terms of which her right of ownership is diminished and confers a benefit on another person (the holder of the servitude) in terms of which the holder is entitled to use and enjoy the owner's property in a specific manner or to prevent the owner from using and enjoying her property in a specific manner (see PJ Badenhorst, J Pienaar & H Mostert *Silberberg and Schoeman's The law of property* 5 ed (2006) 321; CG van der Merwe & A Pope 'Property' in F du Bois (ed) *Wille's principles of South African law* 9 ed (2007) 592; H Mostert & A Pope (eds) *Principles of property law in South Africa* (2010) 236).

[3] South African property law draws a distinction between two categories of servitudes, namely: praedial servitudes and personal servitudes. A praedial servitude relates to at least two pieces of land. It is constituted in favour of one piece of land (the dominant tenement) over another piece of land (the servient tenement). A praedial servitude offers a benefit for the dominant tenement and imposes a burden on the servient tenement. The benefit created by the praedial servitude runs with the dominant land and cannot be detached. This means that a praedial servitude will be transferred automatically to the successors-in-title of the owner of the dominant servitude. A praedial servitude is usually perpetual in duration, although it is possible to register a praedial servitude for a limited period. A personal servitude is always constituted in favour of a particular individual on whom it confers a right to use and enjoy another person's movable or immovable property. A personal servitude is enforceable against the owner of the property which is burdened with it, whoever she might be. Unlike a praedial servitude, a personal servitude is inseparably attached to the holder of the servitude. This means that is it not transferrable to another person. In addition, a personal servitude is not perpetual in duration. This is because it is limited to the lifetime of the holder or to a shorter period of time (see PJ Badenhorst, J Pienaar & H Mostert *Silberberg and Schoeman's The law of property* 5 ed (2006) 321–322; CG van der Merwe & A Pope 'Property' in F du Bois (ed) *Wille's principles of South African law* 9 ed (2007) 593, 604; H Mostert & A Pope (eds) *Principles of property law in South Africa* (2010) 237–240).

obsolete or otherwise undesirable as a result of a change in the surrounding circumstances or a change in the surrounding conditions.[4]

Given their burdensome nature, it follows that an unlimited freedom to create servitudes could result in a proliferation of such rights and that a this would inevitably threaten not only the economically efficient use of land, but also the unitary (undivided) character of ownership. In order to protect the economically efficient use of land and the unitary character of ownership, Van der Walt points out, South African property law has developed a number of legal principles and rules aimed at controlling, not only the creation, but also the continued existence of servitudes. He refers to these principles and rules as anti-fragmentation strategies.[5]

These anti-fragmentation strategies, Van der Walt points out further, may be divided into two categories, namely *ex ante* strategies and *ex post* strategies. *Ex ante* strategies are aimed at controlling the creation of servitudes in the first place. This goal is usually accomplished by imposing restrictions on the kinds of servitudes that can be created or by imposing restrictions on the content of servitudes. *Ex post* strategies are aimed at controlling servitudes after they have been created. This goal is usually accomplished by allowing servitudes to be modified or terminated through a judicial process after they have come into existence.[6]

An important side effect of these anti-fragmentation strategies, Van der Walt goes on to point out, is that they give rise to a conflict between an owner's freedom to dispose of her property by creating servitudes, which is the embodiment of individual autonomy, on the one hand, and the

[4] AJ van der Walt 'The continued relevance of servitude' (2013) 3 *Prop L Rev* 3–35 3 and AJ van der Walt *The law of servitudes* (2016) 258, 415. Changes in the surrounding circumstances and conditions encompass situations where changes in the objective physical conditions of the area in which the servitude is exercised as well as changes in the economic, political, social and technological context either render the servitude itself redundant or bring about the inefficient use of the servient land. In addition, changes in the surrounding circumstances and conditions may also encompass situations where the servitude still serves its purpose, but complicates or inhibits an owner's subjective plans to develop or improve her land (see S van Staden *Ancilliary rights in servitude law* (2015) unpublished LLD thesis Stellenbosch University 16).

[5] AJ van der Walt 'The continued relevance of servitude' (2013) 3 *Prop L Rev* 3–35 3 and AJ van der Walt *The law of servitudes* (2016) 19.

[6] AJ van der Walt 'The continued relevance of servitude' (2013) 3 *Prop L Rev* 3–35 4 and AJ van der Walt *The law of servitudes* (2016) 27. See also S French 'The American Restatement of Servitudes: Reforming doctrine by shifting from ex ante to ex post controls on the risks posed by servitudes' in S van Erp & B Akkermans (eds) *Towards a unified system of land burdens?* (2006) 109–116 110; K Reid 'Modernising land burdens: The new law in Scotland' in S van Erp & B Akkermans (eds) *Towards a unified system of land burdens?* (2006) 63–108 72.

preservation of a single, unitary and absolute concept of ownership, which is the embodiment of legal certainty and security of title, on the other hand. One of the key challenges that characterises the law of servitudes, therefore, is to find an appropriate balance between the protection of an owner's individual autonomy, which requires a more flexible approach to the creation and control of servitudes, and the promotion of legal certainty and security of tenure, which requires a more rigid approach.[7]

Like most other comparative foreign jurisdictions,[8] South Africa has traditionally favoured *ex ante* controls on the creation of servitudes and thus strictly limits the kinds of servitudes that can be created.[9] Although it suffers from a lack of flexibility, a beneficial consequence of this rigid approach is that it promotes a secure and stable system of property rights.[10]

One of the most significant of the *ex ante* controls recognised in South African property law is the subtraction from the *dominium* test which the courts have developed to identify limited real rights in land.[11] This test is aimed at preventing a proliferation of limited real rights (including servitudes) and provides that a right will qualify as a limited real right only if its correlative

[7] AJ van der Walt 'The continued relevance of servitude' (2013) 3 *Prop L Rev* 3–35 11 and AJ van der Walt *The law of servitudes* (2016) 27. See also S French 'The American Restatement of Servitudes: Reforming doctrine by shifting from ex ante to ex post controls on the risks posed by servitudes' in S van Erp & B Akkermans (eds) *Towards a unified system of land burdens?* (2006) 109–116 110; K Reid 'Modernising land burdens: The new law in Scotland' in S van Erp & B Akkermans (eds) *Towards a unified system of land burdens?* (2006) 63–108 72.

[8] Among these comparative foreign jurisdictions are the Netherlands, England, Scotland and Louisiana. For a detailed discussion of the approach adopted in these jurisdictions, see S van Staden *Ancilliary rights in servitude law* (2015) unpublished LLD thesis Stellenbosch University 65.

[9] S van Staden *Ancilliary rights in servitude law* (2015) unpublished LLD thesis Stellenbosch University 60.

[10] AJ van der Walt 'The continued relevance of servitudes' (2013) 3 *Prop L Rev* 3–35 9 and AJ van der Walt *The law of servitudes* (2016) 26.

[11] Section 63(1) of the Deeds Registries Act 47 of 1937 provides in this respect that '[n]o deed, or condition in a deed purporting to create or embodying any personal rights, and no condition which does not restrict the exercise of the right of ownership in respect of immovable property, shall be capable of registration: Provided that a deed containing such a condition as aforesaid may be registered if, in the opinion of the registrar, such condition is complementary or otherwise ancillary to a registrable condition or right contained or conferred in such deed'.

obligation restricts the manner in which current and successive landowners may exercise their entitlements.[12]

Apart from the subtraction from the *dominium* test, there are a number of other significant *ex ante* controls that are aimed more specifically at preventing a proliferation of servitudes and especially praedial servitudes. Among these are the requirements of praediality, utility (*utilitas*), vicinity (*vicinitas*), perpetuity (*perpetua causa*) and passivity (*servitus in faciendo consistere nequit*). These requirements are aimed at ensuring that the benefit a praedial servitude confers on the dominant land outweighs the burden it imposes on the servient land for both the current and successive owners.[13]

More recently, however, there has been a shift of emphasis away from preventative *ex ante* controls towards corrective *ex post* controls in South African property law. This shift in emphasis, which appears to have begun with the judgment in *Linvestment CC v Hammersley,*[14] has recently been confirmed by the judgment in *Pickard v Stein.*[15] While this shift has the potential to undermine the security and stability of property rights, it introduces an element of flexibility into the regulation of praedial servitudes and thus allows the law to address the problems that inefficient, obsolete or otherwise undesirable servitudes give rise to in a more effective manner, especially in a rapidly changing world.[16]

The purpose of this contribution is to examine critically the judgment in *Pickard v Stein*. This judgment is interesting not only because it confirms a change in emphasis towards *ex post* controls on praedial servitudes, but also because it addresses the controversial question of whether a supervening lack of utility is a ground for extinguishing a praedial servitude. Before turning to consider the judgment in *Pickard v Stein*, however, it will be helpful to set out and briefly discuss the requirements governing the establishment of praedial servitudes and especially the requirement of utility.

---

[12] See *Ex parte Geldenhuys* 1926 OPD 125 162. See also *Capex Ltd v Denel (Pty) Ltd* 2001 (3) SA 569 (SCA); *National Stadium South Africa (Pty) Ltd v Firstrand Bank Ltd* 2011 (2) SA 157 (SCA); *Willow Waters Home Owners Association (Pty) Ltd v Koka NO* 2015 (5) SA 304 (SCA).

[13] Apart from praediality, vicinity, utility, perpetuity and passivity, there are a number of other principles that regulate the creation of praedial servitudes. Among these are the principles that there can be no servitude over an existing servitude, that no one can have a servitude over her own property and that servitudes are indivisible (see S van Staden *Ancilliary rights in servitude law* (2015) unpublished LLD thesis Stellenbosch University 32).

[14] *Linvestment CC v Hammersley* 2008 (3) SA 283 (SCA).

[15] *Pickard v Stein* 2015 (1) SA 439 (GJ).

[16] AJ van der Walt 'The continued relevance of servitudes' (2013) 3 *Prop L Rev* 3–35 15, 16.

2 The requirements for a valid praedial servitude

As pointed out above, in order to protect ownership from becoming unduly encumbered and thus fragmented as a result of the uncontrolled proliferation of servitudes, South African property law provides, inter alia, that praedial servitudes may be validly established only if they satisfy certain strict requirements.

Unfortunately, it is not entirely clear what the requirements are for establishing a valid praedial servitude in South African property law. This is because academic commentators have tended to identify a variety of different requirements. Despite these differences, however, there are some common requirements the majority of commentators have accepted as essential or necessary for the creation of a valid praedial servitude. These are praediality, utility (*utilitas*), vicinity (*vicinitas*), perpetuity (*perpetua causa*) and passivity.[17]

The requirement of praediality provides that there must be a dominant and a servient tenement and that the tenements must belong to different persons, while the requirement of utility provides that the servient tenement must confer a benefit on the dominant tenement. For their part, the vicinity requirement provides that the two tenements must be located adjacent or sufficiently close to each other so that the servient tenement can enhance the utility of the dominant tenement, while the perpetuity requirement provides that the benefit conferred upon the dominant tenement by the servient tenement must be derived from a permanent attribute or feature of that tenement. Finally, the requirement of passivity provides that a positive obligation may not be imposed on the owner of the servient tenement.[18]

Out of all of these requirements, the requirement of utility is arguably the most prominent. As explained above, this requirement provides that the servient tenement must confer a benefit on the dominant tenement. Or, to

---

[17] MJ de Waal 'Die vereistes vir die vestiging van grondserwitute: 'n Herformulering' (1990) 1 *Stell LR* 171-185 176. See also CG van der Merwe & MJ de Waal 'Servitudes' in *LAWSA Vol 24* 2 ed (2010) para 546; MJ de Waal 'Servitudes' in R Zimmermann & D Visser (eds) *Southern Cross: Civil law and common law in South Africa* (1996) 785, 789–803; MJ de Waal *Die Vereistes vir die vestiging van grondserwitute in die Suid-Afrikaanse reg* (1989) unpublished LLD thesis Stellenbosch University 27.

[18] MJ de Waal 'Die vereistes vir die vestiging van grondserwitute: 'n Herformulering' (1990) 1 *Stell LR* 171-185 176. See also CG van der Merwe & MJ de Waal 'Servitudes' in *LAWSA Vol 24* 2 ed (2010) paras 547-550; MJ de Waal 'Servitudes' in R Zimmermann & D Visser (eds) *Southern Cross: Civil law and common law in South Africa* (1996) 785 798–803; MJ de Waal *Die vereistes vir die vestiging van grondserwitute in die Suid-Afrikaanse reg* (1989) unpublished LLD thesis Stellenbosch University 30–297. The common law recognises two exceptions to the principle of passivity, namely the servitude of building higher (*servitus altius tollendi*), which imposes a positive obligation on the servient owner

put it another way, it must confer a benefit on the owner of the dominant land in her capacity as owner and not in her personal capacity. A praedial servitude, therefore, cannot be established for the sole benefit of the current owner. Instead, it must be for the benefit of all successive owners.

Given that the requirements of vicinity and perpetuity are aimed largely at ensuring that the servient tenement is capable of conferring an advantage or benefit on the dominant tenement, it is frequently argued that these two requirements should not be classified as separate conditions for the establishment of a valid praedial servitude. Instead, they should rather be classified as elements of the requirement of utility. An important consequence of this approach, De Waal argues, is that there are in fact only three requirements for the establishment of a valid praedial servitude, namely praediality, utility and passivity.[19]

The requirement of utility, however, gives rise to a number of complex questions. One of these is whether this requirement must simply be present when the servitude is created or whether it is a continuing requirement. Or to put it another way, one of the difficult question this requirement gives rise to is whether a supervening lack of utility is a ground for extinguishing a praedial servitude. This question was initially considered in *De Kock v Hänel*[20] and more recently in the judgment which is the focus of this contribution, namely *Pickard v Stein*.[21] Each judgment will be discussed in turn.

3 *De Kock v Hänel*

3 1 The facts

The applicant (De Kock) and the respondent (Hänel) owned neighbouring properties in Cape Town. These properties were known as Erf 4814 and Erf 10231 respectively. A reciprocal praedial servitude of way was registered in both title deeds against Erf 4814 and in favour of Erf 10231 and vice versa. In terms of this servitude the owner of Erf 10231 was entitled, inter alia, to use

---

to construct a building of a certain height, and the servitude of wall support (*servitus oneris ferendi*), which imposes a positive obligation on the servient owner to keep an adjoining wall in a state of good repair (see H Mostert & A Pope (eds) *Principles of property law in South Africa* (2010) 241).

[19] MJ de Waal 'Die vereistes vir die vestiging van grondserwitute: 'n Herformulering' (1990) 1 *Stell LR* 171-185 176. See also CG van der Merwe & MJ de Waal 'Servitudes' in *LAWSA Vol 24* 2 ed (2010) para 549; MJ de Waal 'Servitudes' in R Zimmermann & D Visser (eds) *Southern Cross: Civil law and common law in South Africa* (1996) 785 795–799; MJ de Waal *Die vereistes vir die vestiging van grondserwitute in die Suid-Afrikaanse reg* (1989) unpublished LLD thesis Stellenbosch University 298.

[20] *De Kock v Hänel* 1999 (1) SA 994 (C).

[21] *Pickard v Stein* 2015 (1) SA 439 (GJ).

an existing road on Erf 4814. The road was indicated by a line drawn on a diagram attached to the certificate of consolidated title.

After De Kock (the owner of Erf 4814) and Hänel (the owner of Erf 10231) acquired ownership of their respective properties, a dispute arose between them as to the existence and proper use of the servitude. As a part of this dispute, De Kock argued that Hänel was using the servitude wrongfully to cross Erf 4814 in order to gain access to a public road known as Tamarisk lane. Hänel's conduct was wrongful, De Kock argued further, because the purpose of the servitude was to allow the various parties to gain access to a vineyard that existed at the time the servitude was created. It was not to gain access to Tamarisk lane, which did not exist at the time.

Following an unsuccessful attempt to resolve the dispute amicably, De Kock applied to the High Court in Cape Town for an order declaring that the servitude of way had been extinguished. De Kock based his application on a number of grounds. One of these was that the servitude had been extinguished because the vineyard no longer existed and, consequently, that the servitude no longer offered a permanent benefit to Hänel's property; in other words, that the servitude had been extinguished as a result of a supervening lack of utility.[22]

3 2 The judgment

The Court (per Davis AJ) dismissed the application. In arriving at this decision Davis AJ began by pointing out that insofar as the question of utility was concerned, he had to decide two issues: first, whether the fact that a servitude no longer offers a permanent benefit to the dominant tenement does extinguish a servitude; and second, if so, what the test is for determining whether a servitude still offers a permanent benefit to the dominant tenement.

Insofar as the first issue was concerned, Davis AJ started by pointing out that in support of his argument De Kock referred to *Maasdorp's Institutes of Cape Law*, where the authors explicitly stated that when a servitude no longer provides a permanent benefit to the dominant tenement, the servitude itself will be extinguished.[23]

---

[22] A more detailed discussion of the facts of this case can be found in RRM Paisley & CG van der Merwe 'From here to eternity: Does a servitude road last forever?' (2000) 11 *Stell LR* 452-479 452.

[23] See CG Hall *Maasdorp's Institutes of Cape Law* 6 ed (1936) 200–201, where the authors stated that '[c]onsequently when the utility of the servitude has permanently ceased the servitude will itself become extinguished'.

In support of this proposition, Davis AJ pointed out further, the authors of *Maasdorp's Institutes of Cape Law* relied on two specific sources of authority, namely a statement in fragment 34.22.4 of the *Digest* and an example by Voet in section 8.5.4 of his *Commentarius ad Pandectas*.[24]

Unfortunately, Davis AJ held, neither of these sources actually provided support for Maasdorp's and therefore De Kock's argument. In fact, other titles in the *Digest* appear to suggest the direct opposite.[25] In addition, none of the modern textbooks refer to a supervening lack of utility as a ground for extinguishing a praedial servitude.[26]

Despite finding that there was no authority to support De Kock's argument, Davis AJ held further, he was nevertheless prepared to assume that a supervening lack of utility does extinguish a praedial servitude. Given this assumption, it was necessary to turn to the second issue:

> It is possible, as Mr *Sholto-Douglas* urged, that by implication, there is a continuing requirement of *utilitas*; that is, if the requirement does not continue the servitude terminates, as its use has ended. None of the authorities provide for such a ground, but I shall proceed on the assumption that there is merit in this proposition.[27]

Insofar as the second issue was concerned, Davis AJ started by pointing out that Hänel claimed that his property was located on an extremely steep bank; that the only way in which he could access the bottom of his property from a public road was by using Tamarisk lane together with the servitude road; and that De Kock was aware of this when he took occupation of his property.

Given that Hänel claimed that the servitude did provide a benefit to the dominant tenement and that this claim was reasonable, Davis AJ pointed out further, he was prepared to find that the servitude did still offer a permanent benefit to the dominant tenement and, consequently, that it had not been

---

24 *De Kock v Hänel* 1999 (1) SA 994 (C) 998H–I.

25 *De Kock v Hänel* 1999 (1) SA 994 (C) 998J–999A. In support of this argument, Davis AJ referred to Digest 8.3.13, where Javolenus stated that '[a] servitude can be acquired for a particular type of estate, for example, a vineyard, because in this case the right attaches to the soil rather than to the surface. For this reason, the servitude remains in force, even if the vineyard is removed.'

26 *De Kock v Hänel* 1999 (1) SA 994 (C) 999B–D. In support of this argument, Davis AJ referred to the chapter on servitudes in *Wille's principles of South African law* (see CG van der Merwe 'Property' in D Hutchinson, B van Heerden, D Visser & CG van der Merwe (eds) *Wille's principles of South African law* 8 ed (1991) 326–327) and to the title on servitudes in *LAWSA* (see CG van der Merwe & MJ de Waal 'Servitudes' *LAWSA vol 25* para 100). In neither of these works is a supervening lack of utility expressly identified as a ground for the termination of a praedial servitude.

27 *De Kock v Hänel* 1999 (1) SA 994 (C) 999E.

extinguished. The test for determining whether a servitude still offers a permanent benefit to the dominant tenement, therefore, is whether there is a reasonable claim for such utility by the dominant owner and whether this test has been satisfied:

> ... There might be some scope for debate as to whether the test for the existence of utility be objective or subjective. However, in the light of the discussion by the authorities and given that the dominant tenement holder claims the existence of utility, I consider that it is justified to conclude that there is *utilitas* when there is a reasonable claim for such *utilitas* by the dominant tenement holder.[28]

4 *Pickard v Stein*

4 1 The facts

The applicant (Pickard) and the first respondent (Stein) owned neighbouring properties in Johannesburg. A praedial servitude of light was registered in both title deeds against Pickard's property and in favour of Stein's property. In terms of this servitude the owner of the servient tenement was prohibited from erecting any structure or planting any vegetation exceeding 0.91 metres in height or erecting a fence (except a diamond wire mesh fence) exceeding 1.22 metres in height in the servitude area.

Some time after he acquired ownership of the servient property, Pickard subdivided it into two new portions and the servient area fell into one of the new portions. Pickard then sold this portion to the second respondent (Beira) who intended to build a house on it. Unfortunately, Pickard failed to inform Beira of the existence of the servitude at the time of the sale. When this oversight was subsequently brought to his attention, however, Pickard agreed to take all necessary steps to cancel the servitude, including paying for the legal costs.

In order to secure the cancellation of the servitude, Pickard organised a meeting between himself, Stein, Stein's husband and Beira. At this meeting Pickard and Beira drew Stein and her husband's attention to the servitude of light which they appeared to be unaware of. In addition, Pickard and Beira assured Stein and her husband that Beira had no intention of building a double

[28] *De Kock v Hänel* 1999 (1) SA 994 (C) 999J. The test adopted by Davis AJ in order to determine whether a praedial servitude still provides utility has been criticised on the grounds that it focuses on the dominant owner rather than the dominant tenement. As Van der Merwe and Pienaar point out, the crucial question is not whether the current owner is obtaining some benefit from the praedial servitude but rather whether the land itself is deriving a benefit from the praedial servitude (see CG van der Merwe & J Pienaar 'The law of property' 1999 *ASSAL* 304).

story house on the plot and referred them to the plans and computerised sketches of the envisaged house.

After this meeting Stein's husband was taken to the plot and shown the layout of the foundations. During this inspection and acting on his wife's behalf, Stein's husband asked Beira to remove the dense vegetation that was growing on the servitude area and to erect a solid brick wall on the top of the existing boundary wall. Beira agreed to do so at his own expense.

After Beira removed the vegetation and extended the boundary wall, he was asked by Stein's husband to extend it yet again. Shortly after doing so, however, Stein's husband informed Beira that they took exception to the fact that his house encroached onto the servitude area and, consequently, that Stein was no longer prepared to agree to the cancellation of the servitude.

Following several unsuccessful attempts to resolve this conflict, Pickard applied to the High Court for an order declaring that the praedial servitude of light had been extinguished. Pickard based his application on two grounds: first, that the servitude no longer provided a permanent benefit to Stein's property; in other words, that it had been extinguished as a result of a supervening lack of utility; and second, that the servitude had been abandoned.

4 2 The judgment

The court (per Dodson AJ) rejected Pickard's first argument. In arriving at this conclusion, Dodson AJ began by pointing out that there is no doubt that one of the requirements for creating a valid praedial servitude is that it must provide a distinct benefit to the dominant tenement.[29] Unfortunately, he pointed out further, it is not so clear whether the corollary of this principle, namely that a supervening lack of utility extinguishes a praedial servitude, also forms a part of South African law.[30]

One of the reasons why it is not clear whether the corollary applies in South African law is because even though this issue was raised in *De Kock v Hänel* supra, Davis AJ was not prepared to accept that the corollary does apply. Instead, he was only willing to assume that it does.[31] His reluctance to make a definitive ruling on the grounds that there is no authority for such a rule, however, Dodson AJ pointed out further, appeared to be mistaken. This is because there are at least two relevant sources, namely a statement by Pomponius in fragment 8.1.15 of the *Digest* and the example given by Voet in section 8.5.4 of his *Commentarius* ad Pandectas.

[29] *Pickard v Stein* 2015 (1) SA 439 (GJ) para 34.

[30] *Pickard v Stein* 2015 (1) SA 439 (GJ) para 35.

[31] *Pickard v Stein* 2015 (1) SA 439 (GJ) paras 36–37.

In the *Digest* Pomponius states at 8.1.15:

> Whenever a servitude is found not to be for the benefit of an individual or an estate, then it is of no effect in that no neighbour has any interest in it, as, for example, a servitude preventing you from walking across or occupying your own land.[32]

And, in his *Commentarius* ad Pandectas Voet states at 8.5.4:

> [A declaratory action on servitudes] however fails if . . . when the owner of a more remote tenement owes a servitude of not building higher, while an intermediate tenement is free, such owner has built up higher after the owner of the intermediate free tenement has already built up higher in his own right. The very owner of the servient tenement cannot appear in that way to have done anything contrary to the servitude established, inasmuch as the servitude has already been lawfully obstructed by the intermediate owner.[33]

Despite the existence of these two sources, Dodson AJ observed, it was unnecessary to finally determine whether there is authority for the argument that the corollary applies in our law. This is because the applicant also argued that in light of the judgment in *Linvestment CC v Hammersley*[34] the courts have a broad discretion to cancel a servitude whenever it operates prejudicially on one of the parties.[35]

In *Linvestment CC v Hammersley*, the appellant's property was subject to a defined praedial servitude of way in favour of the respondent's property. After the respondent refused to consent to the relocation of the servitude, the appellant applied for an order declaring that it had the right to unilaterally relocate such a servitude where the circumstances had changed and the relocation would not prejudice the dominant owner. Although a servient owner's right to unilaterally relocate a defined praedial servitude of way had been rejected by the Supreme Court of Appeal in its much earlier judgment in *Gardens Estate Ltd v Lewis*,[36] the court nevertheless found in favour of the appellant and granted the order.[37]

In arriving at this decision, the Supreme Court of Appeal held that the decision in *Gardens Estate Ltd v Lewis* should be overruled on the grounds, inter alia, that it was in the interests of justice to develop the common law and adopt a more flexible approach to the relocation of servitudes.

[32] P Mommsen, T Krueger & A Watson (eds) *The Digest of Justinian* Vol 1 (1985) 251.

[33] P Gane *The Selective Voet, being the commentary on the pandects by Johannes Voet and the supplement to that work by Johannes van der Linden* Vol 2 (1955–1958) 510.

[34] *Linvestment CC v Hammersley* 2008 (3) SA 283 (SCA).

[35] *Pickard v Stein* 2015 (1) SA 439 (GJ) para 43.

[36] *Gardens Estate Ltd v Lewis* 1920 AD 144.

[37] *Pickard v Stein* 2015 (1) SA 439 (GJ) paras 41–42. See also *Linvestment CC v Hammersley* 2008 (3) SA 283 (SCA) para 35.

Servitudes, the court held further, 'are by their nature often the creation of preceding generations devised in another time to serve ends which must now be satisfied in a different environment'. Given these facts, it is difficult to understand why a dominant owner should be entitled to resist the relocation of a defined servitude of way when there is no prejudice to him or her. Provided it is properly regulated, the court concluded, there is no reason why flexibility should 'set an unhealthy precedent or encourage abuse'.[38]

Unfortunately, Dodson AJ observed further, the applicant's interpretation of this judgment went too far. It did not confer a broad power on the courts to cancel a servitude whenever it operates prejudicially on one of the parties. Instead, it simply confers the power on the courts to incrementally develop the common law. Applying section 173 of the Constitution and taking into account the interests of justice, Dodson AJ then held, the common law should be incrementally developed to include the principle that a praedial servitude is extinguished if the discrete benefit the servient tenement conferred on the dominant tenement is extinguished as a result of a change in the circumstances:

> As I understood his argument, Mr *Bekker* relied on [the judgment in *Linvestment CC v Hammersley*] as conferring a broad power on the court to cancel a servitude where it was shown to operate prejudicially on one of the parties. I agree with Mr *Katzew*, who appeared on behalf of Stein, that the decision cannot be taken that far. What is does justify, though, is for the courts to take the more limited, incremental step of developing the common law (to the extent that it is necessary) so as to acknowledge the corollary of the principle to which I have referred. Applying s 173 and taking into account the interests of justice, I have come to the view that if the utility that a praedial servitude previously provided to the dominant tenement has permanently ceased, the servitude itself will become extinguished.[39]

After developing the common law to include a supervening lack of utility as a ground for extinguishing a praedial servitude, Dodson AJ turned to apply this developed principle to the facts of the cases. In this respect, Pickard argued that the servitude no longer offered a benefit to the dominant tenement because the orchards it had originally been created to serve no longer existed. Instead, they had been replaced by urban tenements which required high walls to keep out criminals and ensure privacy, not flimsy fences aimed at preserving light.[40]

---

[38] *Pickard v Stein* 2015 (1) SA 439 (GJ) para 42. See also *Linvestment CC v Hammersley* 2008 (3) SA 283 (SCA) para 31.

[39] *Pickard v Stein* 2015 (1) SA 439 (GJ) paras 43–44.

[40] *Pickard v Stein* 2015 (1) SA 439 (GJ) para 45.

The problem with this view of life in Johannesburg, Dodson AJ held, is that it was not based on empirical evidence and he was not prepared to take judicial notice of it. While it was true that that many of the inhabitants of Johannesburg have chosen 'to sacrifice open views and light for the security of high boundary walls', it could not be said, 'that the preference or need for security and privacy had become so pervasive that the servitude of light had for these reasons permanently lost its utility'. The argument, therefore, had to be dismissed.[41]

After dismissing the argument based on a supervening lack of utility, Dodson AJ turned to consider Pickard's second argument, namely that the servitude had been abandoned. Insofar as this argument was concerned, Dodson AJ found that the evidence clearly showed that the solid brick wall which had been erected by Beira on top of the existing boundary wall had dramatically reduced the flow of light onto Stein's property[42] and, consequently, that it 'necessarily and naturally' obstructed the servitude in all its components.[43] Given these facts, it followed that Stein had abandoned the servitude when she gave Pickard and Beira the right to build the solid brick wall.[44]

5 Comment

5.1 Introduction

Despite being unable to find 'either on the evidence presented or on the basis of judicial notice that the preference or need for security and privacy [in Johannesburg] had become so pervasive that the servitude of light had for these reasons permanently lost its utility', the judgment in *Pickard v Stein* provides clear authority for the principle that utility is not only a constitutive requirement of a praedial servitude, but also a continuing one in the sense that the servitude would be terminated if utility was no longer present.[45]

An important consequence of this judgment is that the principles governing a supervening lack of utility have been brought into line with those governing a supervening lack of praediality resulting from the merger of the dominant

[41] *Pickard v Stein* 2015 (1) SA 439 (GJ) para 46.

[42] *Pickard v Stein* 2015 (1) SA 439 (GJ) para 63.

[43] *Pickard v Stein* 2015 (1) SA 439 (GJ) para 65.

[44] *Pickard v Stein* 2015 (1) SA 439 (GJ) para 72.

[45] Despite stating that there is 'clearly no authority whether a supervening lack of *utilitas* terminates [a] servitude', the court in *Lodetti v Rykov* [2015] ZAKZDNC 39 (15 March 2015), like the court in *De Kock v Hänel*, was nevertheless prepared to assume that such authority does exist. In arriving at this decision, however, the court appears to have overlooked the judgment in *Pickard v Stein*.

and servient tenements.[46] Perhaps even more significantly, they have also been brought into line with the principles governing a supervening lack of vicinity and perpetuity. As Van der Merwe and Pienaar have pointed out in this respect, a supervening lack of vicinity and/or perpetuity has always served as a ground upon which a praedial servitude may be extinguished.[47]

5.2 *Flexible ex post controls*

Apart from confirming that a supervening lack of utility serves as a ground upon which a praedial servitude may be terminated, the judgment in *Pickard v Stein* also reflects a change in emphasis towards more flexible *ex post* controls on praedial servitudes in South African property law. This change emulates a similar shift towards *ex post* controls in comparative foreign jurisdictions such as the Netherlands, England, Scotland and Louisiana.[48] Out of all of these comparative jurisdictions, perhaps the most dramatic shift in emphasis took place in Scotland following the enactment of the Title Conditions (Scotland) Act in 2003.[49]

---

[46] PJ Badenhorst 'Extinction of a praedial servitude of light' (2015) 5 *Prop L Rev* 49-57 55.

[47] CG van der Merwe & JM Pienaar 'The law of property' 1999 *ASSAL* 303. Van der Walt points out in this respect that the role of the perpetuity requirement in modern South African law is to acknowledge the continuing role of the utility requirement. If utility is simply a constitutive and not also a continuing requirement, then it is difficult to understand how the purpose of the perpetuity requirement could be fulfilled (see AJ van der Walt *The law of servitudes* (2016) 164).

[48] S van Staden *Ancillary rights in servitude law* (2015) unpublished LLD thesis Stellenbosch 65.

[49] The Title Conditions (Scotland) Act 2003 distinguishes between affirmative real burdens, negative real burdens and servitudes. Affirmative real burdens impose an obligation on the burdened owner to do something on her own property. Negative real burdens impose an obligation on the burdened owner not to do something on her own property. Servitudes impose on obligation on the burdened owner to allow the benefited owner to use the burdened property in some limited manner. Prior to the coming into operation of the Title Conditions (Scotland) Act 2003, real burdens could be created only by registering them, while servitudes did not have to be registered. Rigid *ex ante* controls that prevented the creation of new kinds of servitudes or positive servitudes could also be avoided simply by creating a real burden rather than a servitude. Following the coming into operation of the Act both real burdens and servitudes have to be registered and the two categories are distinguished from one another by providing that real burdens can impose positive or negative burdens on the servient owner, while servitudes confer a limited use right on the benefited owner. It is important to note, however, that while servitudes can still be acquired by acquisitive prescription, real burdens cannot (see K Reid 'Modernising land burdens: The new law in Scotland' in S van Erp & B Akkermans (eds) *Towards a unified system of land burdens?* (2006) 63 69–71).

Besides conferring the freedom on parties to create new and previously unknown kinds of servitudes (with the exception of servitudes acquired by prescription),[50] this Act also creates new *ex post* controls to review and terminate inefficient, obsolete or otherwise undesirable real burdens and servitudes. One of these controls is the power to judicially review and, if appropriate, vary or discharge a real burden or servitude. Section 90(1) provides in this respect that a burdened owner may apply to the Lands Tribunal for an order discharging or varying a real burden or servitude, and that the Lands Tribunal must grant such an order if it is reasonable to do so after taking into account a variety of factors.[51]

Another *ex post* control created by the Title Conditions (Scotland) Act is a presumptive time limit. Section 20 of the Act provides in this respect that all real burdens are presumptively discharged after 100 years.[52] In order to protect the benefited owner, however, the discharge does not take placed automatically. Instead, the burdened owner must give notice to the benefited

---

[50] Section 76 of the Title Conditions (Scotland) Act.

[51] Section 98 of the Title Conditions (Scotland) Act. The factors which must be taken into account are set out in section 100. Section 100 provides in this respect that the factors mentioned in section 98 are:

(a) any change in circumstances since the title condition was created (including, without prejudice to that generality, any change in the character of the benefited property, of the burdened property or of the neighbourhood of the properties);
(b) the extent to which the condition: (i) confers benefit on the benefited property; or (ii) where there is no benefited property, confers benefit on the public;
(c) the extent to which the condition impedes enjoyment of the burdened property;
(d) if the condition is an obligation to do something, how: (i) practicable; or (ii) costly, it is to comply with the condition;
(e) the length of time which has elapsed since the condition was created;
(f) the purpose of the title condition;
(g) whether in relation to the burdened property there is the consent, or deemed consent, of a planning authority, or the consent of some other regulatory authority, for a use which the condition prevents;
(h) whether the owner of the burdened property is willing to pay compensation;
(i) if the application is under section 90(1)(b)(ii) of the Act, the purpose for which the land is being acquired by the person proposing to register the conveyance; and
(j) any other factor which the Lands Tribunal considers to be material.

[52] Section 20(1) of the Title Conditions (Scotland) Act.

owner,[53] who may then apply to the Lands Tribunal for an order renewing the real burden.[54] The factors which the Lands Tribunal must take into account before deciding to grant such an order are the same as those which it must take into account before varying or discharging a real burden or servitude.[55]

Even though the judgment in *Pickard v Stein* reflects a change in emphasis towards flexible *ex post* controls and, therefore, emulates a similar shift in comparable foreign jurisdictions such as Scotland, a significant difference between the approaches followed in South Africa and Scotland is that the shift towards flexible *ex post* controls in Scotland was driven by the legislature and not the judiciary. The judicial development of flexible *ex post* controls has been criticised by academic commentators on a number of grounds. Among these are that it takes place in an incremental and piecemeal fashion, that it increases information costs for third parties and that it may introduce an element of uncertainty into the law.[56]

The potential for the judicial development of flexible *ex post* controls to introduce an element of uncertainty into the law is exacerbated when the courts do not base their judgments on policy grounds, but rather on vague notions such as the interests of justice, as occurred in *Pickard v Stein.* In arriving at his decision, Dodson AJ suggested that both Roman and Roman-Dutch law provide authority for the rule that a supervening lack of utility terminates a praedial servitude, but did not make a firm finding in this respect. Instead, he based his decision primarily on the grounds that it was in the interests of justice to adopt such a rule without explaining why this was the case.

Dodson AJ's failure to base his judgment on policy grounds is somewhat surprising given that there do appear to be strong policy grounds for developing the common law in the manner in which he did. Among these are the implied intention of the parties and the elimination of bilateral monopolies.

The first ground entails that if the parties who created the servitude had thought about the issue, they would have realised that circumstances might change in such a way that the servitude would lose its utility. Instead of trying to imagine the changes that might take place and incurring the expense of creating a mechanism to deal with future changes (an ultimately impossible task given that humans do not have perfect foresight), they left

[53] Section 21(1) of the Title Conditions (Scotland) Act.

[54] Section 90(1) of the Title Conditions (Scotland) Act.

[55] Section 100 of the Title Conditions (Scotland) Act.

[56] AJ van der Walt 'The continued relevance of servitudes' (2013) 3 *Prop L Rev* 3–35 22.

the matter open in the belief that the law would provide a solution. The law, therefore, should do so.[57]

The second ground is that if a dominant owner was entitled to enforce a servitude after it has lost its utility not only would the value of the servient tenement be reduced, but the law would be turned into an instrument of extortion. This is because the dominant owner could then demand an unreasonably high price to terminate the servitude even though the servitude has no other value and interferes with the ability of the servient owner to use her property. The law should not allow this sort of bilateral monopoly.[58]

Both of these grounds have also been used by the authors of the *Restatement (Third) of Property Law: Servitudes* to justify the United States doctrine of changed conditions.[59] This doctrine provides that when conditions have changed to such an extent since the creation of a servitude that it is no longer possible to accomplish the original purpose for which the servitude was created, a court may terminate the servitude.[60]

Despite the fact that the courts have traditionally used the doctrine of changed conditions to terminate servitudes in the US, the *Third Restatement* suggests that instead of taking such a drastic step the courts should consider modifying the servitude, provided this would allow the servitude to continue serving the purpose for which it was designed to an extent that is worthwhile and, provided further, that any such modification does not increase the burden on the servient tenement.[61]

In addition, the *Third Restatement* suggests that when a servitude is modified or terminated, a court should consider awarding compensation to the dominant owners for any damage they will suffer as a result of the

---

[57] See S Sterk 'Foresight and the law of servitudes' (1988) 73 *Cornell L Rev* 956–970.

[58] See JA Lovett 'A bend in the road: Easement relocation and pliability in the new *Restatement (Third) of Property: Servitudes*' (2005) 38 *Conn L Rev* 1–77.

[59] Section 7.10(a) of the American Law Institute *Restatement (Third) of Property Law: Servitudes* (2000).

[60] Section 7.10(a) of the American Law Institute *Restatement (Third) of Property Law: Servitudes* (2000). When it comes to the application of this doctrine, however, the United States courts have traditionally adopted a very cautious approach and held that they will terminate a servitude only when it is clear that the continued existence of that servitude will serve no useful purpose and will create unnecessary harm to the owner of the servient tenement (see section 7.10(c) of the American Law Institute *Restatement (Third) of Property Law: Servitudes* (2000) and JA Lovett 'Meditations on *Strathclyde:* Controlling private land use restrictions at the crossroads of legal systems' (2008) 36 *Syracuse J Int'l L & Com* 1-42).

[61] Section 7.10(a) of the American Law Institute *Restatement (Third) of Property Law: Servitudes* (2000).

modification or termination.[62] Apart from the United States, the idea of awarding compensation in order to resolve property disputes has gained popularity in other jurisdictions as well. This is because it allows the inconvenience or harm caused by the *ex post* variation or termination of servitudes to be balanced out.[63]

5.3 The constitutional context

Apart from the criticisms set out above, Dodson AJ's decision to base his judgment primarily on the vague notion of the interests of justice may also be criticised on the grounds that it ignores the constitutional context within which the development of the common law must now take place and, perhaps even more importantly, overlooks the insightful and pioneering work Van der Walt has done in this respect.

In an article entitled 'Development of the common law of servitudes', Van der Walt argues that the development of the common law must be based on constitutional rather than common-law considerations. This means that it is no longer sufficient to simply check whether the development of a particular common-law principle or rule directly conflicts with a random constitutional right.[64] Instead, the development of the common law has to take place within an analytical framework created by the supremacy of the Constitution and the single-system-of-law principle.[65]

---

[62] Section 7.10(a) American Law Institute *Restatement (Third) of Property Law: Servitudes* (2000). The *Third Restatement* thus defines the doctrine of changed conditions as follows:

(1) When a change has taken place since the creation of a servitude that makes it impossible as a practical matter to accomplish the purpose for which the servitude was created, a court may modify the servitude to permit the purpose to be accomplished. If modification is not practicable, or would not be effective, a court may terminate the servitude. Compensation for resulting harm to the beneficiaries may be awarded as a condition of modifying or terminating the servitude.

(2) If the purpose of a servitude can be accomplished, but because of changed conditions the servient estate is no longer suitable for uses permitted by the servitude, a court may modify the servitude to permit other uses under conditions designed to preserve the benefits of the original servitude.

(3) The rules stated in section 7.11 govern modification or termination of conservation servitudes held by public bodies and conservation organisations, which are not subject to this section

[63] AJ van der Walt *The law of servitudes* (2016) 389.

[64] AJ van der Walt 'Development of the common law of servitudes' (2013) 130 *SALJ* 722–756 736; AJ van der Walt *The law of servitudes* (2016) 19.

[65] AJ van der Walt 'Development of the common law of servitudes' (2013) 130 *SALJ* 722–756 738; AJ van der Walt *The law of servitudes* (2016) 37–38.

When it comes to developing the common law within this analytical framework, the first step that must be taken is to identify which legal source applies to the dispute in question. In a series of decisions, the Constitutional Court has set out and applied two principles in terms of which the applicable legal source must be identified. Van der Walt refers to these as the first subsidiarity principle and the second subsidiarity principle.[66]

The first subsidiarity principle provides that where a person alleges that a constitutional right has been infringed, he or she must 'rely on legislation specifically enacted to protect that right and may not rely on the constitutional provision directly when bringing action to protect the right'. Only when there is no such legislation may a person rely directly on the constitutional provision.[67]

The second subsidiarity principles provides that where a person alleges that a constitutional right has been infringed, he or she must 'rely on legislation specifically enacted to protect that right and may not rely on the common law directly when bringing an action to protect the right'. Only where there is no such legislation, may a person rely directly on the common law.[68]

Given that servitudes are governed primarily by the common law and not by legislation, it follows that in most servitude cases the common law will be the applicable legal source.

Once the common law has been identified as the applicable source of law, the second step in the constitutional analysis is to accurately determine what the common law actually is. At this stage the question is not whether the common law is fair and just or whether the common law is in need of development. Instead, it is simply to analyse the common law authorities in order to establish the common law positon. Once the common law position has been established, or once it is clear that the common law position is

[66] AJ van der Walt 'Development of the common law of servitudes' (2013) 130 *SALJ* 722–756 739-40; AJ van der Walt *The law of servitudes* (2016) 39–40.

[67] AJ van der Walt 'Development of the common law of servitudes' (2013) 130 *SALJ* 722–756 739; AJ van der Walt *The law of servitudes* (2016) 39–40. See also *South African National Defence Union v Minister of Defence* 2007 (5) SA 400 (CC) paras 51–52; *MEC for Education: KwaZulu-Natal v Pillay* 2008 (1) SA 474 (CC) paras 39–40; *Chirwa v Transnet Ltd* 2008 (2) SA 24 (CC) paras 59, 69.

[68] AJ van der Walt 'Development of the common law of servitudes' (2013) 130 *SALJ* 722–756 740; AJ van der Walt *The law of servitudes* (2016) 39–40. See also *Bato Star Fishing (Pty) Ltd v Minister of Environmental Affairs* 2004 (4) SA 490 (CC) para 25; *Minister of Health NO v New Clicks South Africa (Pty) Ltd* 2006 (2) SA 311 (CC) para 96; *Chirwa v Transnet Ltd* 2008 (2) SA 24 (CC) para 23; *Fuel Retailers Association of Southern Africa v Director-General: Environmental Management, Department of Agriculture, Conservation and Environment, Mpumalanga Province* 2007 (6) SA 4 (CC) para 37; *Walele v City of Cape Town* 2008 (6) SA 129 (CC) para 15.

uncertain or inconclusive, the third step is to determine whether the common law position directly or indirectly conflicts with the Constitution.[69]

Given that the purpose of property is to secure, not only the economic interests of its holders, but also 'higher order non-property constitutional or democratic rights and values such as human dignity, equality and freedom', the first question that must be asked at this stage of the analysis is whether the common law conflicts with any non-property constitutional rights, such as the rights to human dignity and equality. If it does, the common law must be developed to give effect to that constitutional right. In other words, the starting point for developing the common law here will be the Constitution. If it does not, then the common law does not have to be developed to give effect to a constitutional right, but may be developed to give effect to comparative, economic, historical and/or other policy considerations. In other words, the starting point for developing the common law here will not be the Constitution, but rather policy considerations.[70]

The decision to develop the common law, however, has a number of consequences. One of these is usually a forced 'establishment, exercise, transfer or termination of a property right', which will inevitably involve a forced transfer of property entitlements. The forced transfer of property entitlements constitutes a deprivation of property and leads to the second question at this stage of the constitutional analysis, namely whether the decision to develop the common law conflicts with the right to property guaranteed in section 25 of the Constitution. In order to answer this question, the courts will essentially have to decide whether the forced transfer is arbitrary in the sense there is an insufficient reason for it.[71]

Although the judgment in *Pickard v Stein* came to the conclusion that the servitude of light in question had not lost its utility and, therefore, had not been extinguished, the court nevertheless did develop the common law. Given that this development recognised a new ground in terms of which a praedial servitude can be extinguished, the court's decision to develop the common law should ideally have taken place in accordance with the constitutional analysis identified by Van der Walt.

---

[69] AJ van der Walt 'Development of the common law of servitudes' (2013) 130 *SALJ* 722–756 741; AJ van der Walt *The law of servitudes* (2016) 41.

[70] AJ van der Walt 'Development of the common law of servitudes' (2013) 130 *SALJ* 722–756 742, 745; AJ van der Walt *The law of servitudes* (2016) 41–46.

[71] AJ van der Walt 'Development of the common law of servitudes' (2013) 130 *SALJ* 722–756 743, 750; AJ van der Walt *The law of servitudes* (2016) 45.

If the court in *Pickard v Stein* had done so, then the first issue it should have addressed was the appropriate source of law. Given that there is no legislation governing the termination of servitudes due to a supervening lack of utility, the court would undoubtedly have found, not only that the common law is the appropriate source, but also that none of the common-law sources definitively recognises a supervening lack of utility as a ground upon which a praedial servitude may be extinguished.

Having found that none of the common-law sources definitively recognises a supervening lack of utility as a ground upon which a praedial servitude may be extinguished, the court should have gone on to determine whether the failure to do so conflicts with any non-property constitutional rights such as human dignity and equality. In this respect, there does not appear to be any such right that requires a praedial servitude to be extinguished on the grounds of a supervening lack of utility. The common law, therefore, does not have to be developed in order to give effect to the Constitution.

Although there is no constitutional provision that directly requires the development of the common law, there is no constitutional provision that prohibits it either. In the absence of any constitutional requirement or prohibition, the court in *Pickford v Stein* was free to rely on doctrinal, economic, historical or policy considerations in order to determine whether the case was strong enough to justify the development of the common law. The policy considerations that could be used to justify the development of the common law include the parties failure to anticipate changed circumstances and the deleterious effects of bilateral monopolies.

An important consequence of developing the common law, however, is that the court would now be faced with a common-law rule that results in a forced transfer of entitlements from the dominant owner to the servient owner, whose land is no longer burdened by the servitude. The court would then have to determine whether this deprivation was arbitrary or not. In this respect, it may be argued that the deprivation was not arbitrary. This is because the purpose of the forced transfer (it supplements the lack of foresight on the part of the parties, it enhances the utility and value of the servient property and it addresses the problem of bilateral monopolies) outweighs the infringement of the right to property (the termination of a servitude that provides no benefit to the dominant tenement).

6 Conclusion

Although the constitutional analysis set out above yields exactly the same conclusion as the one in the judgment of *Pickard v Stein*, it illustrates the nuanced, pioneering and progressive arguments that were the hallmark of André van der Walt's vast body of work. It consequently reflects in a small way his enormous contribution to the development of a constitutionally compliant system of property law in South Africa and the great loss that his untimely death has caused both to the study and practice of property law in our country.

List of Postgraduate Students Supervised by AJ van der Walt

DOCTORAL STUDENTS

1991 **Jeannie van Wyk**
Restrictive conditions as urban land-use planning instruments

1994 **Wilhelmus Jacobus Nel**
Prospekteerregte in die Suid-Afrikaanse Mineraal- en Mynreg (with Dr MO Dale as co-promotor)

1995 **Rena van den Bergh**
Die omskrywing en funksies van die fisiese beheerelement in die sakereg

1997 **Irma J Kroeze**
Between conceptualism and constitutionalism: Private-law and constitutional perspectives on property (with Prof. GE van Maanen as co-supervisor)

1998 **Johannes Erasmus**
The interaction between property rights and land reform in the new constitutional order in South Africa

2001 **Rian Cloete**
Onstoflike sake in die nuwe Suid-Afrikaanse reg

2005 **Gerhard du Toit**
The significance of postmodern theories of interpretation for contractual interpretation: A critical analysis (with Prof. GF Lubbe as co-promoter

2007 **Geo Quinot**
The judicial regulation of state commercial activity (with Prof. GF Lubbe as cosupervisor)

2009 **Danie Brand**
Courts, socio-economic rights and transformative politics

Wilhelmina J du Plessis
Compensation for expropriation under the Constitution

2010 **Mikhalien Kellerman**
The constitutional property clause and immaterial property interests

Sue-Mari Maass
Tenure security in urban rental housing

Zsa-Zsa Temmers
Building encroachments and compulsory transfer of ownership

2011 **Ernst Jacobus Marais**
Acquisitive prescription in view of the property clause

Gustav Muller
The impact of section 26 of the Constitution on the eviction of squatters in South African law (with Prof. S Liebenberg as co-promotor)

2012 **Reghard Brits**
Mortgage foreclosure under the Constitution: Property, housing and the National Credit Act (with Prof. GF Lubbe as co-promotor)

Wian Erlank
Property in Virtual Worlds

Carolina Augusta Koch
The right to a view: Common law, legislation and the Constitution

Bradley Virgill Slade
The justification of expropriation for economic development

Janke Strydom
A hundred years of demolition orders: A constitutional analysis

2014 **Karen Bezuidenhout**
Compensation for excessive but otherwise lawful regulatory state action (with Prof. ZT Boggenpoel as co-promotor)

2015 **Priviledge Dhliwayo**
A constitutional analysis of access rights that limit landowners' right to exclude

Lizette Grobler
The salva rei substantia requirement in personal servitudes

Jan-Harm Swanepoel
Constitutional property law in Central Eastern European jurisdictions: A comparative analysis (with Prof. ZT Boggenpoel as co-promotor)

Elsabe van der Sijde
Reconsidering the relationship between property and regulation: A systemic constitutional approach (with Prof. G Quinot as co-promotor)

Sonja van Staden
Ancillary rights in servitude law

MASTERS STUDENTS

1995 **Henrietté Engelbrecht**
Die begrip 'regte in eiendom' in artikel 28(1) van die Grondwet van die Republiek van Suid-Afrika 200 van 1993

2000 **Elana Hopkins**
Grounds for review of administrative action: The interaction between the Constitution, the Act and the Common Law

2009 **Kudakwashe Boyd**
Lateral and subjacent support

Phephelaphi Dube
Reconsidering historically based land claims
Xolisa Human Nginase
The meaning of 'public purpose' and 'public interest' in section 25 of the final Constitution

2010 **Gino Frantz**
Repealing the Subdivision of Agricultural Land Act: A constitutional analysis
Leigh-Ann Kiewitz
Relocation of a specified servitude of right of way
Alton Ulrich Samuels
The history, development and future of public nuisance in light of the Constitution
Bradley Virgill Slade
International law in the interpretation of sections 25 and 26 of the Constitution (with Mrs A Rudman as co-supervisor)
Zerlinda van der Merwe
Constitutionality of the rules governing sectional title schemes (with Prof. GJ Pienaar as co-supervisor)

2012 **Priviledge Dhliwayo**
Tenure security in relation to farmland (with Prof. JM Pienaar as co-supervisor)
Richard Michael Shay
Users' entitlements under the fair dealing exceptions to copyright (with Prof OH Dean as co-supervisor)

2013 **Tshilidzi Norman Raphulu**
The right of way of necessity: A constitutional analysis
Nzumbululo Silas Siphuma
The lessor's tacit hypothec: A constitutional analysis

2014 **Nhlanhla Lucky Sono**
Development of the law regarding inaedificatio: A constitutional analysis (with Dr ZT Boggenpoel as co-supervisor)

List of publications by AJ van der Walt

Books

— *Constitutional property clauses* (1999) Kenwyn: Juta & Co.
— *Property in the margins* (2009) Oxford and Portland: Hart Publishing
— *The law of neighbours* (2010) Claremont: Juta & Co.
— and Faure M (eds) *Globalization and private law: The way forward* (2010) Cheltenham and Northampton: Edward Elgar
— *Constitutional property law* 3rd edition (2011) Claremont: Juta & Co.[1]
— *Property and constitution* (2012) Pretoria: Pretoria University Law Press
— and Pienaar GJ *Introduction to the law of property* 7th ed (2016)[2]
— en Pienaar GJ *Inleiding tot die sakereg* 7de uit (2016)[3]
— *Property law casebook for students* 8th ed (2016)[4]
— *The law of servitudes* (2016) Claremont: Juta & Co.

Book chapters and journal articles

— 'The *bona fide* occupier of land' (1983) 100 *SALJ* 257–265
— 'Three cases on the *mandament van spolie*' (1983) 100 *SALJ* 689–699
— 'Naidoo v Moodley 1982 4 SA 82 (T) – *mandament van spolie* (1983) 46 *THRHR* 237–240
— 'Nog eens *Naidoo v Moodley* – 'n repliek' (1984) 47 *THRHR* 429–439
— '*Curatoren of Pioneer Lodge No 1 v Champion* 1879 OFS 51 – mandament van spolie – *spoliatus ante omnia restituendus est – nemo sibi ius dicere potest*' (1984) 47 *THRHR* 359–363
— '*Refrigerated Transport (Edms) Bpk v Mainline Carriers (Edms) Bpk* 1983 3 SA 121 (A) – aquiliese aksie van die huurder van 'n saak wat homself aanspreeklik gestel het vir skade aan die saak (1984) 47 *THRHR* 109–112
— '*Bank van die Oranje-Vrystaat v Rossouw* 1983-09-19 KPA Saak A 60/83 ongerapporteer' (1984) 47 *THRHR* 154–170

---

[1] The 2nd edition of this book was published in 2005 and the first edition was published in 1997 as *The constitutional property clause: A comparative analysis of section 25 of the South African constitution of 1996*.

[2] Earlier editions of this book was published as follows: 6th edition (2009), 5th edition (2006), 4th edition (2002), 3rd edition (1999), 2nd edition (1997) and first edition (1996).

[3] Earlier editions of this book was published as follows: 6de uit (2009), 5de uit (2006), 4de uit (2002), 3de uit (1999), 2de uit (1997) and 1ste uit (1996).

[4] Earlier editions of this book was published as follows: 7th edition (2009), 6th edition (2006), 5th edition (2002), 4th edition (1999), 3rd edition (1997), 2nd edition (1995) and first edition (1992).

— 'Artikel 10 van die Wet op Menslike Weefsel 65 van 1983 in 'n juridiese, etiese en filosofiese perspektief' 1984 *TSAR* 154–170

— 'Defences in spoliation proceedings' (1985) 102 *SALJ* 172–180

— 'Toepassing van die mandament van spolie op onroerende sake – *AM Cassim v The Community Development Board and Another* saak no 10765/84 1984-06-12' 1986 *TSAR* 223–232

— 'Relatiewe Saaklike Regte?' 1986 *TSAR* 173–179

— '*Dominium*, *possessio* en *detentio* in Antonius Gomezius se kommentaar op die *leges Tauri* (1986) 49 *THRHR* 425–433

— '*Quarrying Enterprises (Pvt) Ltd v John Viol (Pvt) Ltd* 1985 3 SA 575 (ZHC) – verbeteringe – *mala fide* besitter – retensiereg' (1986) 49 *THRHR* 90–95

— 'Bartolus se omskrywing van *dominium* en die interpretasies daarvan sedert die vyftiende eeu' (1986) 49 *THRHR* 305–321

— 'The effect of environmental conservation measures on the concept of landownership' (1987) 104 *SALJ* 469–479

— 'Saaklike regte en persoonlike serwitute – *Cowley v Hahn* 1987 1 SA 440 (OK)' (1987) 50 *THRHR* 343–352

— 'Possibilities for the conservation of the built-up environment in current South African statutory law' (1986) 19 *CILSA* 209–229

— 'Onteiening van die reg op laterale en onderstut – *EVKOM v JJ Fourie* 1986-12-22 saak no 19674 86 (T) (ongerapporteer)' (1987) 50 *THRHR* 462–474

— 'Die beskerming van besit en houerskap in die Suid-Afrikaanse Reg' (1987) 50 *THRHR* 139–153

— 'Gedagtes oor die herkoms en ontwikkeling van die Suid-Afrikaanse eiendomsbegrip' (1988) 21 *De Jure* 16–35

— 'Gedagtes oor die herkoms en ontwikkeling van die Suid-Afrikaanse eiendomsbegrip' (1988) 21 *De Jure* 306–325

— 'Die funksies en omskrywing van besit (deel 1)' (1988) 51 *THRHR* 276–296

— 'Die funksies en omskrywing van besit (deel 2)' (1988) 51 *THRHR* 508–514

— 'The need for conservation of the built-up environment' (1988) 53 *Koers* 73–105

— 'Die mandament van spolie en *quasi*-besit – *Bon Quelle (Edms) Bpk v Munisipaliteit van Otavi* 1989 1 SA 508 (A)' (1989) 52 *THRHR* 444–453

— 'Uitsettingsbevele en die huurder se vergoedingseis vir verbeteringe aan die huursaak – *Syfrets Participation Bond Managers Ltd v Estate and Co-op Wine Distributors* 1989 1 SA 106 (W)' (1989) 52 *THRHR* 590–599

— '*Vrystaat Lewendehawe Kooperasie Bpk v De Klerk en Zinman* 1989 1 SA 632 (O)' (1989) 22 *De Jure* 352–356

— and Kleyn DG '*Duplex dominium*: The history and significance of the concept of divided ownership' in Visser DP (ed) *Essays on the history of law* (1989) Wetton: Juta & Co., 213–260

— 'Towards the development of post-*apartheid* land law: An exploratory survey' (1990) 23 *De Jure* 1–45
— 'The doctrine of subjective rights: A critical reappraisal from the fringes of property law' (1990) 53 *THRHR* 316–329
— 'Die *condictio furtiva* en die besitsaksie' (1990) 53 *THRHR* 238–250
— 'Developments that may change the institution of private ownership so as to meet the needs of a non-racial society in South Africa' (1990) 1 *Stell LR* 26–48
— 'Land law without the land acts – Predicaments and possibilities' (1991) 54 *THRHR* 738–752
— 'De onrechtmatige bezetting van leegstaande woningen en het eigendomsbegrip' (1991) 17 *Recht en Kritiek* 329–359
— 'Introduction' in Van der Walt AJ (ed) *Land reform and the future of landownership in South Africa* (1991) Wetton: Juta & Co., 1–7
— 'The future of common law landownership' in Van der Walt AJ (ed) *Land reform and the future of landownership in South Africa* (1991) Wetton: Juta & Co., 21–35
— 'The South African law of ownership: A historical and philosophical perspective (1992) 25 *De Jure* 446–457
— 'Squatting and the right to shelter' 1992 *TSAR* 40–55
— 'Roman-Dutch land and environmental land-use control' (1992) 7 *SAPL* 1–11
— 'Personal rights and limited real rights: An historical overview and analysis of contemporary problems related to the registrability of rights' (1992) 55 *THRHR* 170–203
— 'Informal housing and the environment: Land rights in transition' (1992) 7 *SAPL* 201–214
— 'The fragmentation of land rights' (1992) 8 *SAJHR* 431–450
— 'Der Eigentumsbegriff' in Feenstra R and Zimmerman R (eds) *Das Römisch-Holländische Recht* (Berlin: Duncker & Humblot, 1992) 485-520
— 'The impact of a bill of rights on property law' (1993) 8 *SAPL* 296–319
— 'Reflections on the teaching of property law in future' (1993) 4 *Stell LR* 88–99
— 'Ownership and personal freedom: Subjectivism in Bernhard Windscheid's theory of ownership' (1993) 56 *THRHR* 569–589
— 'Comparative notes on the constitutional protection of property rights' (1993) 19 *Recht en Kritiek* 39–71
— 'The future of private ownership of land' (1994) 34 *Codicillus* 4–18
— 'Notes on the interpretation of the property clause in the new constitution' (1994) 57 *THRHR* 181–203

— 'Kritiese vrae oor die leerstuk van subjektiewe regte in die Suid-Afrikaanse regsleer' (1994) 27 *De Jure* 43–60

— 'Property right, land rights, and environmental rights' in Van Wyk D, Dugard J, De Villiers B and Davis DM (eds) *Rights and constitutionalism – The New South African Legal Order* (1995) Oxford: Clarendon Press, 455–501

— 'Unity and pluralism in property theory – A review of property theories and debates in recent literature: Part I' 1995 *TSAR* 15–42

— 'Tradition on trial: A critical analysis of the civil-law tradition in South African property law' (1995) 10 *SAJHR* 169–206

— 'Subject and society in property theory – A review of property theories and debates in recent literature: Part II' 1995 *TSAR* 322–345

— 'Marginal notes on powerful(l) legends: Critical perspectives on property theory' (1995) 58 *THRHR* 396–420

— 'Towards a theory of rights in property: Exploratory observations on the paradigm of post-apartheid property law' (1995) 10 *SAPL* 298–345

— 'Rights and reforms in property theory – A review of property theories and debates in recent literature: Part III' 1995 *TSAR* 493–526

— 'Land reform in South Africa since 1990 – An overview (1995) 10 *SAPL* 1–30

— 'The limits of constitutional property' (1997) 12 *SAPL* 275–330

— 'Squatting, spoliation orders and the new constitutional order – *Rikhotso v Northcliff Ceramics (Pty) Ltd* 1997 1 SA 526 (W) (1997) 60 *THRHR* 522–529

— and Botha H 'Coming to grips with the new constitutional order: Critical comments on *Harksen v Lane NO*' (1998) 13 *SAPL* 17–41

— 'Un-doing things with words: The colonisation of the public sphere by private-property discourse' 1998 *Acta Juridica* 235–281

— ''Double' property guarantees: A structural and comparative analysis' (1998) 14 *SAJHR* 560–586

— 'Roman law, fundamental rights, and land reform in South Africa (1998) 61 *THRHR* 400–422

— 'Compensation for excessive or unfair regulation: A comparative overview of constitutional practice relating to regulatory takings' (1999) 14 *SAPL* 273–331

— 'Property rights and hierarchies of power: A critical evaluation of land-reform policy in South Africa' (1999) 64 *Koers* 259–294

— 'Modernity, normality, and meaning: The struggle between progress and stability and the politics of interpretation – Part I' (2000) 11 *Stell LR* 21–49

— 'Modernity, normality, and meaning: The struggle between progress and stability and the politics of interpretation – Part II' (2000) 11 *Stell LR* 226–243

— 'Civil forfeiture of instrumentalities and proceeds of crime and the constitutional property clause' (2000) 16 *SAJHR* 1–45
— 'Tentative urgency: Sensitivity for the paradoxes of stability and change in social transformation decisions of the Constitutional Court' (2001) 16 *SAPL*1–27
— 'Dancing with codes – protecting, developing and deconstructing property rights in a constitutional state' (2001) 128 *SALJ* 258–311
— 'Closure and openness on difference and democracy – A response to Justice Johan Froneman' (2001) 12 *Stell LR* 28–39
— 'The promotion of administrative justice Act benchbook by Currie & Klaaren' (2001) 12 *Stell LR* 519–522
— 'Negating Grotius – The constitutional validity of statutory security rights in favour of the state: *First National Bank of SA t/a Wesbank v Commissioner of the South African Revenue Service* 2001 (7) BCLR 715 (C)' (2001) 17 *SAJHR* 86–113
— 'Sosiale geregtigheid, prosedurele billikheid, en eiendom: Alternatiewe perspektiewe op grondwetlike waarborge (Deel een)' (2002) 13 *Stell LR* 59–82
— 'Resisting orthodoxy – again: Thoughts on the development of post-apartheid South African Law' (2002) 17 *SAPL* 258–279
— 'Property rights v religious rights: *Bührmann v Nkosi*' (2002) 13 *Stell LR* 394–414
— 'Moving towards recognition of constructive expropriation? *Steinberg v South Peninsula Municipality* 2001 4 SA 1243 (SCA)' (2002) 65 *THRHR* 459–473
— 'Exclusivity of ownership, security of tenure and eviction orders: A critical evaluation of recent case law' (2002) 18 *SAJHR* 372–420
— 'Exclusivity of ownership, security of tenure, and eviction orders: A model to evaluate South African land-reform legislation' 2002 *TSAR* 254–289
— 'Living with new neighbours: Landownership, land reform and the property clause' (2002) 119 *SALJ* 816–840
— and Sutherland PJ 'Dispossession of incorporeals or rights – Is the *mandament van spolie* the appropriate remedy?' (2003) 15 *SA Merc LJ* 95–109
— 'The public aspect of private property' (2004) 19 *SAPL* 676–723
— 'The property clause in the new federal constitution of the Swiss confederation' (2004) 15 *Stell LR* 326–332
— 'Striving for the better interpretation – A critical reflection on the constitutional court's *Harksen* and *FNB* decisions on the property clause' (2004) 121 *SALJ* 854–878

— 'An overview of developments in constitutional property law since the introduction of the property clause in 1993' (2004) 19 *SAPL* 46–89

— and Sandham LA 'Social aspects of sustainable rural development – A case study in Lepelfontein' (2004) 86 *South African Geographical Journal* 68–75

— 'A South African reading of Frank Michelman's theory of social justice' (2004) 19 *SAPL* 253–307 (also published in Botha H, Van der Walt AJ, Van der Walt J (eds) *Rights and Democracy in a Transformative Constitution* (2003) Stellenbosch: SUNMedia, 168–212)

— 'Rendition/eviction – A post-apartheid reflection' (2004) 15 *Law and Critique* 321–344

— 'Transformative constitutionalism and the development of South African property law (part 1)' 2005 *TSAR* 655–689

— 'The state's duty to protect property owners v the state's duty to provide housing: Thoughts on the *Modderklip* case' (2005) 21 *SAJHR* 144–161

— 'The state's duty to pay 'just and equitable' compensation for expropriation: Reflections on the *Du Toit* case' (2005) 122 *SALJ* 765–778

— 'Retreating from the *FNB* arbitrariness test already? *Mkontwana v Nelson Mandela Metropolitan Municipality; Bissett v Buffalo City Municipality; Transfer Rights Action Campaign v MEC for Local Government and Housing, Gauteng*' (2005) 122 *SALJ* 75–89

— 'Ownership and eviction: Constitutional rights in private law' (2005) 9 *Edinburgh LR* 32–64

— 'Property theory and the transformation of property law' in Cooke E (ed) *Modern Studies in Property Law* 3 ed (2005) Oxford and Portland, Oregon: Hart Publishing, 361–380

— 'Transformative constitutionalism and the development of South African property law (part 2)' 2006 *TSAR* 1–31

— 'Reconciling the state's duties to promote land reform and to pay 'just and equitable' compensation for expropriation (2006) 123 *SALJ* 23–40

— 'Legal history, legal culture and transformation in a constitutional democracy' (2006) 12 *Fundamina* 1–47

— 'Enclosed property and public streets' (2006) 21 *SAPL* 3–24

— 'Constitutional property law' 2007 *ASSAL* 241–268

— 'Developing the law on unlawful squatting and spoliation' (2008) 125 *SALJ* 24–36

— 'Normative pluralism and anarchy: Reflections on the 2007 term' (2008) 1 *CCR* 77–128

— 'Property, social justice and citizenship: Property law in post-apartheid South Africa (2008) 19 *Stell LR* 325–346

— 'Replacing property rules with liability rules: Encroachment by building' (2008) 125 *SALJ* 592–628
— 'Constitutional property law' 2008 *ASSAL* 231–264
— 'The protection of private property under the Irish Constitution: A comparative and theoretical perspective' in Carloan E and Doyle O (eds) *The Irish Constitution: Governance and values* (2008) London: Thomson Round Hall 398–411
— 'Regulation of building under the constitution' (2009) 42 *De Jure* 32–47
— 'Constitutional property law' 2009 *ASSAL* 218–258
— 'Sport and nuisance law' (2009) 127 *SALJ* 274–303
— 'Property and refusal' in Van Marle K (ed) *Refusal, transition and post-apartheid law* (2009) Stellenbosch: Sun Media 39–56
— 'The soft vengeance of a freedom fighter on the constitutional court' (2010) 25 *SAPL* 1–24
— 'Constitutional property law' 2010 *ASSAL* 251–294
— 'Property and marginality' in Alexander GS and Penalver EM (eds) *Property and community* (2010) New York: Oxford University Press 81–105
— and Faure M 'Introduction' in Faure M and Van der Walt AJ (eds) *Globalization and private law: The way forward* (2010) Cheltenham and Northampton: Edward Elgar 21–35
— and Faure M 'Comparative and conclusing remarks' in Faure M and Van der Walt AJ (eds) *Globalization and private law: The way forward* (2010) Cheltenham and Northampton: Edward Elgar 548–561
— 'Constitutional property law' 2011 *ASSAL* 245–292
— and Maass SM 'The case in favour of substantive tenure reform in the landlord-tenant framework: *The Occupiers, Shulana Court, 11 Hendon Road, Yeoville, Johannesburg v Steel; City of Johannesburg Metropolitan Municipality v Blue Moonlight*' (2011) 128 *SALJ* 436–451
— 'Common law, expropriation and human rights in the intersection between expropriation and eviction law' in Fox-O'Mahony L and Sweeney JA (eds) *The Idea of Home in Law: Displacement and Dispossession* (2011) Surrey: Ashgate 55–100
— 'The give-and-take spirit of neighbour law' in Mostert H and De Waal MJ (eds) *Essays in honour of CG van der Merwe* (2011) Durban: LexisNexis Butterworths 57–74
— and Brits R 'The purpose of judicial oversight over the sale in execution of mortgaged property: *Gundwana v Steko Development* 2011 3 SA 608 (CC); *Nedbank Ltd v Fraser and Four Other Cases* 2011 4 SA 363 (GSJ)' (2012) 75 *THRHR* 322–329

— and Slade BV 'Public purpose and changing circumstances: *Harvey v Umhlatuze Municipality and Others* 2011 (1) SA 601 (KZP)' (2012) 129 *SALJ* 219–235
— 'Constitutional property law' 2012 *ASSAL* 182–199
— 'Procedurally arbitrary deprivation of property' (2012) 23 *Stell LR* 88–94
— and Maass SM 'The enforceability of tenants' rights (part 1)' 2012 *TSAR* 35–52
— and Maass SM 'The enforceability of tenants' rights (part 2)' 2012 *TSAR* 228–246
— and Marais EJ 'Eiendomsverlies deur verkrygende verjaring: Onteiening sonder vergoeding – of nie?' (2012) 9 *LitNet Akademies*
— and Marais EJ 'The constitutionality of acquisitive prescription: A section 25(1) analysis' 2012 *TSAR* 714–736
— and Kellerman M 'The importance of the commons in the context of intellectual property' (2013) 24 *Stell LR* 31–54
— and Marais EJ 'The constitutionality of adverse possession under the European Convention 1950: *JA Pye (Oxford) Ltd v United Kingdom* (2008) 46 EHRR 45 (GC)' (2013) 76 *THRHR* 261–269
— 'Constitutional property law' 2013 *ASSAL* 216–230
— and Brits R 'Application of the housing clause during mortgage foreclosure: A subsidiarity approach to the role of the National Credit Act (Part 1)' 2014 *TSAR* 288–305
— and Brits R 'Application of the housing clause during mortgage foreclosure: A subsidiarity approach to the role of the National Credit Act (Part 2)' 2014 *TSAR* 508–519
— and Raphulu TN 'The right of way of necessity: A constitutional analysis' (2014) 77 *THRHR* 468–484
— and Shay RM 'Constitutional analysis of intellectual property' (2014) 17 *PELJ* 54–87
— 'Constitutional Property Law' 2014 *ASSAL* 195–215
— 'The modest systemic status of property rights' (2014) 1 *Journal for Law, Property and Society* 15–106
— 'Property law on the edge of the legal order' in De Groot G-R (ed) *Kritiek op recht: Liber amicus vir GE van Maanen* (2014) Wolters: Kluwer 459–474
— 'Constitutional property law' 2015 *ASSAL* 189–233
— and Viljoen S 'The constitutional mandate for social welfare: Systemic differences and links between property, land rights and housing rights' (2015) 18 *PELJ* 1035–1090
— and Siphuma NS 'Extending the lessor's hypothec to third parties' property' (2015) 132 *SALJ* 518–546
— 'Sharing servitudes' (2015) 4 *European Property Law Journal* 162–222

— and Kriek CA 'The right to a view reconsidered' 2015 *TSAR* 482–515

— 'The civil law tradition in constitutional perspective' in Milo JM, Smits JM and Lokin JHA (eds) *Tradition, Codification and Unification* (2015) Cambridge, Antwerp and Portland: Intersentia, 29–44

— 'Legal research and legal education 20 years after the advent of democracy' in De Ville J (ed) *Memory and meaning: Lourens du Plessis and the haunting of justice* (2015) LexisNexis: Pietermaritzburg 203-218

— 'Constitutional property law' 2016 *ASSAL* 195–215

— 'Section 25 vortices (part 1)' 2016 *TSAR* 412–427

— 'Section 25 vortices (part 2)' 2016 *TSAR* 597–621

— and Kriek CA 'Alternative strategies to protect the existing view from a property' 2016 *TSAR* 20–44

— and Sono NL 'The law regarding *inaedificatio*: A constitutional analysis' (2016) 79 *THRHR* 195–212

— and Van Staden S ''Progressive' judicial interpretation of servitudes and ancillary servitude entitlements – *Jersey Lane Properties (Pty) Ltd t/a Fairlawn Boutique Hotel & Spa v Hodgson* (A5030/11) [2012] ZAGPJHC 86 (7 May 2012)' (2016) 79 *THRHR* 671–678

— and Dhliwayo P 'The notion of absolute and exclusive ownership: A doctrinal analysis' (2017) 134 *SALJ* 34–52

— 'Novel servitudes' 2017 *TSAR* 408–420

Juta's Quarterly Review

– 'Constitutional Property Law' May 2006–2014

– 'Property Law' May 2006–2011

Abbreviations

Am U L Rev	American University Law Review
Ariz J Int'l & Comp L	Arizona Journal of International & Comparative Law
Ariz L Rev	Arizona Law Review
ASSAL	Annual Survey of South African Law
BC L Rev	Boston College Law Review
Br J Sociol	British Journal of Sociology
Cal L Rev	California Law Review
Camb LJ	Cambridge Law Journal
Can J L & Jurisprudence	Canadian Journal of Law and Jurisprudence
CCR	Constitutional Court Review
CLP	Current Legal Problems
Colum L Rev	Columbia Law Review
Const Commentary	Constitutional Commentary
Conv & Prop Law	Conveyancer and Property Lawyer
Cornell L Rev	Cornell Law Review
Denv L Rev	Denver University Law Review
Dublin ULJ	Dublin University Law Journal
Duke LJ	Duke Law Journal
Econ Hist Rev	Economic History Review
EHRLR	European Human Rights Law Review
EIPR	European Intellectual Property Review
Emory LJ	Emory Law Journal
Environ & Plan C: Gov't & Pol'y	Environment and Planning C: Government and Policy
Envtl L Rev	Environmental Law Review
EPLJ	European Property LJ
ERPL	European Review of Private Law (their abbr)
ESR Review	Economic and Social Rights (in South Africa)
Fla J Int'l L	Florida Journal of International Law
Fla St U L Rev	Florida State University Law Review
Fordham L Rev	Fordham Law Review
GAIA	Ecological Perspectives for Science and Society
Geo Int'l Envtl L Rev	Georgetown Environmental Law Review
Griffith L Rev	Griffith Law Review
Harv J L & Pub Pol'y	Harvard Journal of Law & Public Policy
Harv L Rev	Harvard Law Review
Hastings LJ	Hastings Law Journal

Hong Kong LJ	Hong Kong Law Journal
ICLQ	International and Comparative Law Quarterly
IJCL	Indian Journal of Constitutional Law
Int Insolv Rev	International Insolvency Review
Int'l Crim L Rev	International Criminal Law Review
IPLJ	Intellectual Property Law Journal
Ir Jur (ns)	Irish Jurist (new series)
J Am Inst Planners	Journal of the American Institute of Planners
J Am Soc Inf Sci Tec	Journal of the American Association for Information Science and Technology
J L Prop & Soc'y	Journal of Law, Property, and Society
J Legal Educ	Journal of Legal Education
J Legal Stud	Journal of Legal Studies
J South Afr Stud	Journal of Southern African Studies
JIPLP	Journal of Intellectual Property Law and Practice
JISB	Journal of Intervention and State Building
JJS	Journal for Juridical Science
JOLS	Journal of Law and Society
JT	Journal des Tribunaux
J Urb L	Journal of Urban Law
Eur J Legal Stud	European Journal of Legal Studies
Law & Critique	Law and Critique
Law & Soc'y Rev	Law and Society Review
Law Soc Inq	Law and Social Inquiry
LQR	Law Quarterly Review
LS	Legal Studies
Mich L Rev	Michigan Law Review
Mich St L Rev	Michigan State Law Review
MLJ	Malawi Law Journal
Mod L Rev	Modern Law Review
Neb L Rev	Nebraska Law Review
NILQ	Northern Ireland Legal Quarterly
NJB	Nederlands Juristen Blad
NLJ	New Law Journal
Nw U L Rev	Northwestern University L aw Review
NYL Sch L Rev	New York Law School Law review
NYU Envtl LJ	New York University Law Journal
NYU L Rev	New York University Law Review
Or L Rev	Oregon Law Review
PELJ	Potchefstroom Electronic Law Journal

Pol Sci Q	Political Science Quarterly
Prop L Rev	Property Law Review
Rad Phil	Radical Philosophy
Rev Soc Econ	Review of Social Economy
Rutgers Race & L Rev	Rutgers Race & L Rev
Rutgers U L Rev	Rutgers University Law Review
RW	Rechtskundig Weekblad
SA Merc LJ	South African Mercantile Law Journal
SAJHR	South African Journal on Human Rights
SALJ	South African Law Journal
Santa Clara Computer & High Tech LJ	Santa Clara Computer and High Technology Law Journal
SAPL	South African Public Law
SAQ	South Atlantic Quarterly
Seattle U L Rev	Seattle University Law Review
Sociol Rev	Sociological Review
Stan L Rev	Stanford Law Review
Stell LR	Stellenbosch Law Review
Stud Confl Terror	Studies in conflict and terrorism
Syracuse J Int'l L & Com	Syracuse Journal of International Law and Commerce
T Vred	Tijdschrift van de Vrederechters
TBBR	Tijdschrift voor Belgisch Burgerlijk Recht
TBR	Tijdschrift voor Bouwrecht
Tex A&M L Rev	Texas A&M Law Review
TGR	Tijdschrift voor Gentse Rechtspraak
THRHR	Tydskrif vir Hedendaagse Romeins-Hollandse Reg
TSAR	Tydskrif vir die Suid-Afrikaans Reg / Journal of South African Law
Tul Envtl LJ	Tulane Environmental Law Journal
Tulane L Rev	Tulane Law Review
U Chi L Rev	University of Chicago Law Review
U Pa L Rev	University of Pennsylvania Law Review
U Toronto LJ	University of Toronto Law Journal
UC Davis L Rev	University of California Davis Law Review
UCLA L Rev	University of California Los Angeles Law Review
Wm & Mary L Rev	William and Mary Law Review
Yale LJ	Yale Law Journal

Table of Cases

South Africa

Belgian

England, Wales and UK

European Court of Human Rights

Ireland

Netherlands

New Jersey

United States

Table of Legislation

DRAFT LEGISLATION

FOREIGN LEGISLATION

Argentina

Australia

Belgium

England

France

Germany

Great Britain

Holland

PROVINCIAL LEGISLATION

CONVENTIONS AND TREATIES

REGULATIONS

RULES

Index

B

C

D

E

F

J

K

L

O

T

U

V

W

Z

www.ingramcontent.com/pod-product-compliance
Lightning Source LLC
LaVergne TN
LVHW060012210926
848481LV00013B/3692
* 9 7 8 1 4 8 5 1 2 8 9 1 5 *